41: *Afro-American Poets Since 1955*, edited by Trudier Harris and Thadious M. D̶ ̶ ̶(̶1̶9̶8̶5̶)̶

42: *American Writers for Children Before 1900*, edited by Glenn E. Estes (1985)

43: *American Newspaper Journalists, 1690-1872*, edited by Perry J. Ashley (1986)

44: *American Screenwriters*, Second Series, edited by Randall Clark, Robert E. Morsberger, and Stephen O. Lesser (1986)

45: *American Poets, 1880-1945*, First Series, edited by Peter Quartermain (1986)

46: *American Literary Publishing Houses, 1900-1980: Trade and Paperback*, edited by Peter Dzwonkoski (1986)

47: *American Historians, 1866-1912*, edited by Clyde N. Wilson (1986)

48: *American Poets, 1880-1945*, Second Series, edited by Peter Quartermain (1986)

49: *American Literary Publishing Houses, 1638-1899*, 2 parts, edited by Peter Dzwonkoski (1986)

50: *Afro-American Writers Before the Harlem Renaissance*, edited by Trudier Harris (1986)

51: *Afro-American Writers from the Harlem Renaissance to 1940*, edited by Trudier Harris (1987)

52: *American Writers for Children Since 1960: Fiction*, edited by Glenn E. Estes (1986)

53: *Canadian Writers Since 1960*, First Series, edited by W. H. New (1986)

54: *American Poets, 1880-1945*, Third Series, 2 parts, edited by Peter Quartermain (1987)

55: *Victorian Prose Writers Before 1867*, edited by William B. Thesing (1987)

56: *German Fiction Writers, 1914-1945*, edited by James Hardin (1987)

57: *Victorian Prose Writers After 1867*, edited by William B. Thesing (1987)

58: *Jacobean and Caroline Dramatists*, edited by Fredson Bowers (1987)

59: *American Literary Critics and Scholars, 1800-1850*, edited by John W. Rathbun and Monica M. Grecu (1987)

60: *Canadian Writers Since 1960*, Second Series, edited by W. H. New (1987)

61: *American Writers for Children Since 1960: Poets, Illustrators, and Nonfiction Authors*, edited by Glenn E. Estes (1987)

62: *Elizabethan Dramatists*, edited by Fredson Bowers (1987)

63: *Modern American Critics, 1920-1955*, edited by Gregory S. Jay (1988)

64: *American Literary Critics and Scholars, 1850-1880*, edited by John W. Rathbun and Monica M. Grecu (1988)

65: *French Novelists, 1900-1930*, edited by Catharine Savage Brosman (1988)

66: *German Fiction Writers, 1885-1913*, 2 parts, edited by James Hardin (1988)

67: *Modern American Critics Since 1955*, edited by Gregory S. Jay (1988)

68: *Canadian Writers, 1920-1959*, First Series, edited by W. H. New (1988)

69: *Contemporary German Fiction Writers*, First Series, edited by Wolfgang D. Elfe and James Hardin (1988)

70: *British Mystery Writers, 1860-1919*, edited by Bernard Benstock and Thomas F. Staley (1988)

71: *American Literary Critics and Scholars, 1880-1900*, edited by John W. Rathbun and Monica M. Grecu (1988)

72: *French Novelists, 1930-1960*, edited by Catharine Savage Brosman (1988)

73: *American Magazine Journalists, 1741-1850*, edited by Sam G. Riley (1988)

74: *American Short-Story Writers Before 1880*, edited by Bobby Ellen Kimbel, with the assistance of William E. Grant (1988)

75: *Contemporary German Fiction Writers*, Second Series, edited by Wolfgang D. Elfe and James Hardin (1988)

76: *Afro-American Writers, 1940-1955*, edited by Trudier Harris (1988)

77: *British Mystery Writers, 1920-1939*, edited by Bernard Benstock and Thomas F. Staley (1988)

78: *American Short-Story Writers, 1880-1910*, edited by Bobby Ellen Kimbel, with the assistance of William E. Grant (1988)

79: *American Magazine Journalists, 1850-1900*, edited by Sam G. Riley (1988)

(Continued on back endsheets)

Dictionary of Literary Biography® • Volume One Hundred Eighteen

Twentieth-Century German Dramatists, 1889-1918

Dictionary of Literary Biography® • Volume One Hundred Eighteen

Twentieth-Century German Dramatists, 1889-1918

4837

Edited by
Wolfgang D. Elfe
University of South Carolina

and

James Hardin
University of South Carolina

A Bruccoli Clark Layman Book
Gale Research Inc.
Detroit, London

Printed in the United States of America

Published simultaneously in the United Kingdom
by Gale Research International Limited
(An affiliated company of Gale Research Inc.)

The paper used in this publication meets the minimum requirements
of American National Standard for Information Sciences—Permanence
Paper for Printed Library Materials, ANSI Z39.48-1984. ∞™

Library of Congress Catalog Card Number 92-19190
ISBN 0-8103-7595-8

Contents

Plan of the Series

. . . Almost the most prodigious asset of a country, and perhaps its most precious possession, is its native literary product—when that product is fine and noble and enduring.

Mark Twain*

The advisory board, the editors, and the publisher of the *Dictionary of Literary Biography* are joined in endorsing Mark Twain's declaration. The literature of a nation provides an inexhaustible resource of permanent worth. We intend to make literature and its creators better understood and more accessible to students and the reading public, while satisfying the standards of teachers and scholars.

To meet these requirements, *literary biography* has been construed in terms of the author's achievement. The most important thing about a writer is his writing. Accordingly, the entries in *DLB* are career biographies, tracing the development of the author's canon and the evolution of his reputation.

The purpose of *DLB* is not only to provide reliable information in a convenient format but also to place the figures in the larger perspective of literary history and to offer appraisals of their accomplishments by qualified scholars.

The publication plan for *DLB* resulted from two years of preparation. The project was proposed to Bruccoli Clark by Frederick C. Ruffner, president of the Gale Research Company, in November 1975. After specimen entries were prepared and typeset, an advisory board was formed to refine the entry format and develop the series rationale. In meetings held during 1976, the publisher, series editors, and advisory board approved the scheme for a comprehensive biographical dictionary of persons who contributed to North American literature. Editorial work on the first volume began in January 1977, and it was published in 1978. In order to make *DLB* more than a reference tool and to compile volumes

that individually have claim to status as literary history, it was decided to organize volumes by topic, period, or genre. Each of these freestanding volumes provides a biographical-bibliographical guide and overview for a particular area of literature. We are convinced that this organization—as opposed to a single alphabet method—constitutes a valuable innovation in the presentation of reference material. The volume plan necessarily requires many decisions for the placement and treatment of authors who might properly be included in two or three volumes. In some instances a major figure will be included in separate volumes, but with different entries emphasizing the aspect of his career appropriate to each volume. Ernest Hemingway, for example, is represented in *American Writers in Paris, 1920-1939* by an entry focusing on his expatriate apprenticeship; he is also in *American Novelists, 1910-1945* with an entry surveying his entire career. Each volume includes a cumulative index of the subject authors and articles. Comprehensive indexes to the entire series are planned.

With volume ten in 1982 it was decided to enlarge the scope of *DLB*. By the end of 1986 twenty-one volumes treating British literature had been published, and volumes for Commonwealth and Modern European literature were in progress. The series has been further augmented by the *DLB Yearbooks* (since 1981) which update published entries and add new entries to keep the *DLB* current with contemporary activity. There have also been *DLB Documentary Series* volumes which provide biographical and critical source materials for figures whose work is judged to have particular interest for students. One of these companion volumes is entirely devoted to Tennessee Williams.

We define literature as the *intellectual commerce of a nation:* not merely as belles lettres but as that ample and complex process by which ideas are generated, shaped, and transmitted. *DLB* entries are not limited to "creative writers" but extend to other figures who in their time and in their way influenced the mind of a people. Thus the series encompasses historians, journalists, publishers, and screenwriters. By this means

---

*From an unpublished section of Mark Twain's autobiography, copyright © by the Mark Twain Company

readers of *DLB* may be aided to perceive literature not as cult scripture in the keeping of intellectual high priests but firmly positioned at the center of a nation's life.

DLB includes the major writers appropriate to each volume and those standing in the ranks immediately behind them. Scholarly and critical counsel has been sought in deciding which minor figures to include and how full their entries should be. Wherever possible, useful references are made to figures who do not warrant separate entries.

Each *DLB* volume has a volume editor responsible for planning the volume, selecting the figures for inclusion, and assigning the entries. Volume editors are also responsible for preparing, where appropriate, appendices surveying the major periodicals and literary and intellectual movements for their volumes, as well as lists of further readings. Work on the series as a whole is coordinated at the Bruccoli Clark Layman editorial center in Columbia, South Carolina, where the editorial staff is responsible for accuracy of the published volumes.

One feature that distinguishes *DLB* is the illustration policy—its concern with the iconography of literature. Just as an author is influenced by his surroundings, so is the reader's understanding of the author enhanced by a knowledge of his environment. Therefore *DLB* volumes include not only drawings, paintings, and photographs of authors, often depicting them at various stages in their careers, but also illustrations of their families and places where they lived. Title pages are regularly reproduced in facsimile along with dust jackets for modern authors. The dust jackets are a special feature of *DLB* because they often document better than anything else the way in which an author's work was perceived in its own time. Specimens of the writers' manuscripts are included when feasible.

Samuel Johnson rightly decreed that "The chief glory of every people arises from its authors." The purpose of the *Dictionary of Literary Biography* is to compile literary history in the surest way available to us—by accurate and comprehensive treatment of the lives and work of those who contributed to it.

The *DLB* Advisory Board

Foreword

The twentieth century has been a time of enormous dramaturgic activity in the German-speaking lands. Some of the seminal playwrights of the century wrote in German and influenced the stage not only in Central Europe but all over the world. The best known of these dramatists is Bertolt Brecht, but there are many other significant writers whose innovative and sometimes drastic aesthetic tenets have transformed modern theater. One thinks especially of the expressionists, such as Georg Kaiser, Ernst Toller, and Fritz von Unruh; of the incomparable stylist Hugo von Hofmannsthal; and of Max Frisch and Friedrich Dürrenmatt. Earlier volumes of the *Dictionary of Literary Biography* devoted to twentieth-century German-language authors (*DLB 56, 66, 69, 75, 81,* and *85*) intentionally limited treatment of the dramatic production of these writers, reserving the discussion of their plays for this volume and the forthcoming *DLB 122: Twentieth-Century German Dramatists, 1919-1992.*

The date of a dramatist's first publication was usually the determinant in placing the writer in the earlier or later periods treated in the two volumes. This structuring principle may seem arbitrary; but it is more sensible than a line of demarcation according to literary movements, since the majority of the dramatists belonged to more than one literary movement. The starting date for this volume, 1889, is the year of the breakthrough of naturalist drama and theater in Germany; 1918 is, of course, the year when World War I ended and, with it, the German and Austro-Hungarian monarchies. Given the profound changes in Central Europe in 1918, the date is by no means capriciously chosen.

Each entry in this volume starts with the rubric PLAY PRODUCTIONS, listing the first performances of an author's dramas. This information, in the case of several of the authors, can be found in no other reference work. PLAY PRODUCTIONS is followed by the primary bibliography of the author's works, the most important section of which is a chronological listing of all of the author's book publications. The text of the entry is a thorough account of the author's life

and work that tries to show his or her place in the history of German drama and theater. A secondary bibliography and a statement about the author's literary estate (Nachlaß) end the entry.

The contributors to the two volumes, chiefly Germanists from the United States, Canada, and Britain, are experts on their respective authors. Their entries combine readability with factual rigor.

The appendix to this volume is an essay by Professor Roy C. Cowen on the development of German drama and theater from the advent of naturalism in 1889 to the Nazi takeover of Germany in 1933. This wide-ranging survey obviates the need for a lengthy foreword. Still, a few words should be said by way of orientation. Readers unfamiliar with the cultural scene in Central Europe should understand that theater during the decades covered in these volumes occupied an influential position in the cultural life of those countries. While there were some commercial theaters, there was—and still is—a tradition of government subsidy in the German-speaking countries that resulted in practically every German city having a well-equipped and well-staffed theater. The opportunities for public recognition as well as for material rewards provided a strong incentive for the writing of dramas. The relative financial security of the theaters also meant that productions were not restricted to commercially profitable plays. Thus, dramas were written and performed that reflect these countries' political, economic, and social problems, and the theater was often an arena where the great political and ideological debates of the age were continued. Some of the major themes presented were the inability of human beings in the modern industrialized age to determine their own fate; the struggle between capitalism and socialism; changing sexual mores; generational conflict, especially between fathers and sons; democracy versus totalitarianism; war and exile; and the clash of socially progressive, big-city modernism in art and literature with politically conservative or reactionary—often sentimental—ruralism or provincialism. Nevertheless, demand for pure entertainment also produced dramas untouched by the turbulent times.

Cinematic production by the dramatists is touched on in the entries, as are the contributions of many dramatists as drama critics. A list of books for further reading appears at the end of the volume.

—*Wolfgang D. Elfe*
James Hardin

Acknowledgments

This book was produced by Bruccoli Clark Layman, Inc. Karen L. Rood is senior editor for the *Dictionary of Literary Biography* series. Philip B. Dematteis was the in-house editor.

Production coordinator is James W. Hipp. Projects manager is Charles D. Brower. Photography editors are Edward Scott and Timothy C. Lundy. Layout and graphics supervisor is Penney L. Haughton. Copyediting supervisor is Bill Adams. Typesetting supervisor is Kathleen M. Flanagan. Systems manager is George F. Dodge. The production staff includes Rowena Betts, Steve Borsanyi, Teresa Chaney, Patricia Coate, Rebecca Crawford, Gail Crouch, Henry Cuningham, Margaret McGinty Cureton, Bonita Dingle, Mary Scott Dye, Denise Edwards, Sarah A. Estes, Robert Fowler, Avril E. Gregory, Ellen McCracken, Kathy Lawler Merlette, John Myrick, Pamela D. Norton, Thomas J. Pickett, Thomasina Singleton, Maxine K. Smalls, and Jennifer C. J. Turley.

Walter W. Ross and Dennis Lynch did library research. They were assisted by the following librarians at the Thomas Cooper Library of the University of South Carolina: Jens Holley and the interlibrary-loan staff; reference librarians Gwen Baxter, Daniel Boice, Faye Chadwell, Jo Cottingham, Cathy Eckman, Rhonda Felder, Gary Geer, Jackie Kinder, Laurie Preston, Jean Rhyne, Carol Tobin, Virginia Weathers, and Connie Widney; circulation-department head Thomas Marcil; and acquisitions-searching supervisor David Haggard.

Acknowledgments

Dictionary of Literary Biography® • Volume One Hundred Eighteen

Twentieth-Century German Dramatists, 1889-1918

Dictionary of Literary Biography

Hermann Bahr
(19 July 1863 - 15 January 1934)

Dieter Wolfgang Adolphs
Michigan Technological University

See also the Bahr entry in *DLB 81: Austrian Fiction Writers, 1875-1913.*

PLAY PRODUCTIONS: *La marquesa d'Amaëgui,* Linz, Landschaftliches Theater, 1 March 1888;

Die neuen Menschen, Berlin, Deutsche Bühne, 18 January 1891;

Die häusliche Frau, Berlin, Lessingtheater, 8 June 1891;

Aus der Vorstadt, by Bahr and Carl Karlweis (Karl Weiss), Vienna, Deutsches Volkstheater, 11 March 1893;

Die Nixe, Munich, Gärtnertortheater, 1896;

Juana, Berlin, Neues Theater, 24 September 1896;

Das Tschaperl, Vienna, Carltheater, 27 February 1897;

Josephine, Vienna, Deutsches Volkstheater, 23 December 1897;

Der Star, Vienna, Deutsches Volkstheater, 10 December 1898;

Wenn es euch gefällt, by Bahr and Karlweis, Vienna, Etablissement Ronacher (Deutsches Volkstheater), 24 March 1899;

Der Athlet, Vienna, Deutsches Volkstheater, 7 October 1899;

Wienerinnen, Vienna, Deutsches Volkstheater, 3 October 1900;

Der Franzl, Linz, Landschaftliches Theater, 16 February 1901;

Der Apostel, Vienna, Burgtheater, 8 November 1901;

Der Krampus, Linz, Landschaftliches Theater, 23 November 1901;

Unter sich: Ein Arme-Leut'-Stück, Munich, Schauspielhaus, 6 November 1903;

Der Meister, Berlin, Deutsches Theater, 1904;

Sanna, Berlin, Kleines Theater, 10 March 1905;

Die Andere, Munich, Schauspielhaus, 4 November 1905;

Der arme Narr, Vienna, Burgtheater, 29 November 1906;

Ringelspiel, Berlin, Deutsches Theater, 18 December 1906;

Die gelbe Nachtigall, Berlin, Lessingtheater, 10 December 1907;

Das Konzert, Berlin, Lessingtheater, 23 December 1909;

The Concert, translated by Leo Dietrichstein, New York, Belasco Theater, 10 October 1910;

Die Kinder, Leipzig, Schauspielhaus, 23 December 1910;

Das Tänzchen, Berlin, Lessingtheater, 6 January 1912;

Das Prinzip, Breslau (now Wroclaw, Poland), Schauspielhaus, 9 June 1912;

Das Phantom, Darmstadt, Hoftheater, and Stuttgart, Schauspielhaus, 4 December 1913;

Der muntere Seifensieder, Stuttgart, Hoftheater, 18 January 1914;

Der Querulant, Munich, Schauspielhaus, 16 October 1914;

Die Stimme, Cologne, Schauspielhaus, 18 October 1916;

The Master, translated and adapted by Benjamin F. Glazer, New York, Fulton Theater, 5 December 1916;

Josephine, translated and adapted by F. E. Washburn Freund, New York, Knickerbocker

Hermann Bahr; sketch by Emil Orlik, 1905 (Bildarchiv der Österreichischen Nationalbibliothek)

Theater, January 1918;

Der Unmensch, Munich, Residenztheater, 4 December 1919;

Ehelei, Berlin, Kleines Schauspielhaus, 7 November 1920;

Der Selige, Berlin, Kleines Theater, 17 December 1920;

The Mongrel, translated by Frances C. Fay, adapted by Elmer L. Rice, New York, Longacre Theater, 15 December 1924;

Altweibersommer, Vienna, Akademietheater, 21 January 1925.

BOOKS: *Rodbertus' Theorie der Absatzkrisen: Ein Vortrag* (Vienna: Konegen, 1884);

Ueber Rodbertus: Vortrag (Vienna: Verlag der "Unverfälschten Deutschen Worte," 1884);

Die Einsichtslosigkeit des Herrn Schäffle: Drei Briefe an einen Volksmann als Antwort auf "Die Aussichtslosigkeit der Sozialdemokratie" (Zurich: Schabelitz, 1886);

Henrik Ibsen (Vienna: Verlag der "Deutschen Worte," 1887);

Die neuen Menschen: Ein Schauspiel (Zurich: Schabelitz, 1887);

La marquesa d'Amaëgui: Eine Plauderei (Zurich: Schabelitz, 1888);

Die große Sünde: Ein bürgerliches Trauerspiel (Zurich: Schabelitz, 1889);

Die gute Schule: Seelenstände (Berlin: Fischer, 1890);

Zur Kritik der Moderne: Gesammelte Aufsätze (Zurich: Schabelitz, 1890);

Fin de Siècle (Berlin: Zoberbier, 1891);

Die Mutter (Berlin: Sallis, 1891);

Russische Reise (Dresden & Leipzig: Pierson, 1891);

Die Überwindung des Naturalismus: Als zweite Folge von "Zur Kritik der Moderne" (Dresden & Leipzig: Pierson, 1891);

Aus der Vorstadt: Volksstück, by Bahr and Carl Karlweis (Karl Weiss) (Vienna: Konegen, 1893);

Dora (Berlin: Fischer, 1893);

Die häusliche Frau: Ein Lustspiel (Berlin: Fischer, 1893);

Neben der Liebe: Wiener Roman (Berlin: Fischer, 1893);

Der Antisemitismus: Ein internationales Interview (Berlin: Fischer, 1894);

Caph (Berlin: Fischer, 1894);

Studien zur Kritik der Moderne (Frankfurt am Main: Rütten & Loening, 1894);

Juana: Schauspiel (Munich: Rubinverlag, 1896);

Die Nixe: Drama in vier Akten, nach dem Russischen des Spashinskij (Munich: Rubinverlag, 1896);

Gerhart Hauptmanns Märchendrama "Die versunkene Glocke" (Königsberg: Teichert, 1897);

Renaissance: Neue Studien zur Kritik der Moderne (Berlin: Fischer, 1897);

Theater: Ein Wiener Roman (Berlin: Fischer, 1897);

Das Tschaperl: Ein Wiener Stück in vier Aufzügen (Berlin: Fischer, 1898);

Josephine: Ein Spiel (Berlin: Fischer, 1899);

Die schöne Frau; Leander (Berlin: Fischer, 1899);

Der Star: Ein Wiener Stück in vier Akten (Berlin: Fischer, 1899);

Wenn es euch gefällt: Wiener Revue in drei Bildern und einem Vorspiel, by Bahr and Karlweis (Vienna: Konegen, 1899);

Wiener Theater, 1892-1898 (Berlin: Fischer, 1899);

Der Athlet: Schauspiel in drei Akten (Berlin, Cologne & Leipzig: Ahn, 1900);

Bildung: Essays (Berlin & Leipzig: Insel, 1900);

Secession (Vienna: Wiener Verlag, 1900);

Der Apostel: Schauspiel in drei Aufzügen (Munich: Langen, 1901);

Der Franzl: Fünf Bilder eines guten Mannes (Vienna: Wiener Verlag, 1901);

Rede über Klimt (Vienna: Wiener Verlag, 1901);

Der Krampus: Lustspiel in drei Aufzügen (Munich: Langen, 1902);

Premièren: Winter 1900 bis Sommer 1901 (Munich: Langen, 1902);

Wirkung in die Ferne und Anderes (Vienna: Wiener Verlag, 1902);

Rezensionen: Wiener Theater 1901 bis 1903 (Berlin: Fischer, 1903);

Dialog vom Tragischen (Berlin: Fischer, 1904);

Der Meister: Komödie in drei Akten (Berlin: Fischer, 1904); translated and adapted by Benjamin F. Glazer as *The Master* (Philadelphia: Brown, 1918);

Unter sich: Ein Arme-Leut'-Stück (Vienna: Wiener Verlag, 1904);

Dialog vom Marsyas (Berlin: Bard, Marquardt, 1905);

Sanna: Schauspiel in fünf Aufzügen (Berlin: Fischer, 1905);

Die Andere (Berlin: Fischer, 1906);

Der arme Narr: Schauspiel in einem Akt (Vienna: Konegen, 1906); translated by F. E. Washburn

Freund as *The Poor Fool: A Play in One Act*, in *One Act Play Magazine* (May 1938): 3-33;

Josef Kainz (Vienna: Wiener Verlag, 1906);

Die gelbe Nachtigall (Berlin: Fischer, 1907);

Glossen zum Wiener Theater (1903-1906) (Berlin: Fischer, 1907);

Grotesken: Der Klub der Erlöser; Der Faun; Die tiefe Natur (Vienna: Konegen, 1907);

Ringelspiel: In drei Akten (Berlin: Fischer, 1907);

Wien (Stuttgart: Krabbe, 1907);

Buch der Jugend (Vienna & Leipzig: Heller, 1908);

Die Rahl: Roman (Berlin: Fischer, 1908);

Dramatische Reise (Berlin: Fischer, 1909);

Drut: Roman (Berlin: Fischer, 1909); republished as *Die Hexe Drut: Roman* (Berlin: Sieben Stäbe-Verlags- und Druckereigesellschaft, 1929);

Das Konzert: Lustspiel in drei Akten (Berlin: Reiss, 1909); translated by Leo Dietrichstein as *The Concert: A Comedy in Three Acts* (New York: Rosenfield, 1910); translated by Bayard Quincy Morgan as *The Concert: A Comedy in Three Acts*, in *Chief Contemporary Dramatists: Second Series*, edited by T. H. Dickinson (Boston, New York & Chicago: Houghton Mifflin, 1921), pp. 505-567; German version, edited by Joseph Wiehr (New York: Prentice-Hall, 1931);

Der Roman der XII, by Bahr, Otto Julius Bierbaum, and others (Berlin: Mecklenburg, 1909);

Stimmen des Bluts: Novellen (Berlin: Fischer, 1909);

Tagebuch (Berlin: Cassirer, 1909);

O Mensch! Roman (Berlin: Fischer, 1910);

Austriaca (Berlin: Fischer, 1911);

Die Kinder: Komödie (Berlin: Fischer, 1911);

Das Tänzchen: Lustspiel in drei Akten (Berlin: Fischer, 1911); translated as *The Little Dance: Comedy in Three Acts* (New York: Rosenfield, 1911);

Wienerinnen: Lustspiel in drei Akten (Bonn: Ahn, 1911);

Bayreuth, by Bahr and Anna Bahr-Mildenburg (Leipzig: Rowohlt, 1912); translated by T. W. Makepeace as *Bayreuth and the Wagner Theatre* (London: Unwin, 1912);

Essays (Leipzig: Insel, 1912);

Inventur (Berlin: Fischer, 1912);

Parsifalschutz ohne Ausnahmegesetz (Berlin: Schuster & Loeffler, 1912);

Das Prinzip: Lustspiel (Berlin: Fischer, 1912);

Erinnerung an Burckhard (Berlin: Fischer, 1913);

Das Hermann-Bahr-Buch: Zum 19. Juli herausgegeben (Berlin: Fischer, 1913);

Das Phantom: Komödie in drei Akten (Berlin: Fischer, 1913);

Dostojewski: Drei Essays, by Bahr, Dmitri Mereschkowski, and Bierbaum (Munich: Piper, 1914);

Der Querulant: Komödie in vier Akten (Berlin: Fischer, 1914);

Salzburg (Berlin: Bard, 1914); republished, with English translation by G. M. R. Biddulph (Vienna: Agathon, 1947);

Kriegssegen (Munich: Delphin, 1915);

Der muntere Seifensieder: Ein Schwank aus der deutschen Mobilmachung (Berlin: Fischer, 1915);

Das österreichische Wunder; Einladung nach Salzburg (Stuttgart: Die Lese, 1915);

Expressionismus (Munich: Delphin, 1916); translated by R. T. Gribble as *Expressionism* (London: Henderson, 1925);

Himmelfahrt: Roman (Berlin: Fischer, 1916);

Rudigier (Kempten & Munich: Kösel, 1916);

Die Stimme: Schauspiel in drei Aufzügen (Berlin: Fischer, 1916);

Der Augenblick: Lustspiel nach Goethe (Berlin: Ahn & Simrock, 1917);

Schwarzgelb (Berlin: Fischer, 1917);

Um Goethe (Vienna: Urania, 1917);

Vernunft und Wissenschaft (Innsbruck: Tyrolia, 1917);

Der Augenblick Österreichs (Munich: Volksvereins-Druckerei, 1918);

1917: Tagebuch (Innsbruck: Tyrolia, 1918);

Adalbert Stifter: Eine Entdeckung (Zurich, Leipzig & Vienna: Amalthea, 1919);

1918: Tagebücher 2 (Innsbruck: Tyrolia, 1919);

Die Rotte Korahs: Roman (Berlin: Fischer, 1919);

Spielerei: Drei Stücke (Berlin: Ahn & Simrock, 1919) —comprises *Spielerei, Der Selige, Der Umsturz*;

Der Unmensch: Lustspiel in drei Aufzügen (Berlin: Reiss, 1919);

Burgtheater (Vienna & Berlin: Wiener literarische Anstalt, 1920);

Ehelei: Lustspiel in drei Akten (Berlin: Reiss, 1920);

1919 (Leipzig: Tal, 1920);

Bilderbuch (Vienna & Leipzig: Wiener Literarische Anstalt, 1921);

Summula (Leipzig: Insel, 1921);

Kritik der Gegenwart (Augsburg: Haas & Grabherr, 1922);

Schauspielkunst (Leipzig: Dürr & Weber, 1923);

Selbstbildnis (Berlin: Fischer, 1923);

Sendung des Künstlers (Leipzig: Insel, 1923);

Altweibersommer: Ein Liebesschwank in drei Aufzügen (Berlin: Ahn & Simrock, 1924);

Liebe der Lebenden: Tagebücher 1921-1923, 3 volumes (Hildesheim: Borgmeyer, 1925);

Notizen zur neueren spanischen Literatur (Berlin: Stilke, 1926);

Der Zauberstab: Tagebücher von 1924 bis 1926 (Hildesheim: Borgmeyer, 1926);

Der inwendige Garten: Roman (Hildesheim: Borgmeyer, 1927);

Adalbert Stifters Witiko (Saint Gallen: Tschudy, 1928);

Himmel auf Erden: Ein Zwiegespräch (Munich: Müller, 1928);

Die Tante: Lustspiel in drei Aufzügen (Berlin: Ahn & Simrock, 1928);

Labyrinth der Gegenwart (Hildesheim: Borgmeyer, 1929);

Österreich in Ewigkeit: Roman (Hildesheim: Borgmeyer, 1929);

Mensch, werde wesentlich: Gedanken aus seinen Werken, edited by Anna Bahr-Mildenburg (Graz: Styria, 1934);

Salzburger Landschaft: Aus den Briefen an seine Frau Anna Bahr-Mildenburg und aus seinen Tagebüchern (Innsbruck: Rauch, 1937);

Das junge Österreich (Jerusalem: Verkauf, 1945);

Meister und Meisterbriefe um Hermann Bahr: Aus seinen Entwürfen, Tagebüchern und seinem Briefwechsel mit Richard Strauss, Hugo von Hofmannsthal, Max Reinhardt, Joseph Kainz, Eleonora Duse und Anna Bahr-Mildenburg, edited by Joseph Gregor (Vienna: Bauer, 1947);

Österreichischer Genius: Grillparzer, Stifter, Feuchtersleben (Vienna: Bellaria, 1947);

Wirkung in die Ferne: Eine Auswahl der Prosa-Dichtungen (Vienna: Bauer, 1947);

Kulturprofil der Jahrhundertwende: Essays, edited by Heinz Kindermann (Vienna: Bauer, 1962);

Theater der Jahrhundertwende: Kritiken, edited by Kindermann (Vienna: Bauer, 1963);

Sinn hinter der Komödie, edited by Rudolf Holzer (Graz: Stiasny, 1965);

Zur Überwindung des Naturalismus: Theoretische Schriften, edited by Gotthart Wunberg (Stuttgart: Kohlhammer, 1968);

Prophet der Moderne: Tagebücher 1888-1904, edited by Reinhard Farkas (Vienna: Böhlau, 1987).

OTHER: Carl Karlweis, *Wien das bist du!*, preface by Bahr (Stuttgart: Bonz, 1903);

Die Bücher zum wirklichen Leben, introduction by Bahr (Vienna: Heller, 1908);

Margarete von Schuch-Mankiewicz, *Mein Skizzenbuch: Gedichte*, preface by Bahr (Vienna: Fromme, 1908);

Gustav Mahler: Ein Bild seiner Persönlichkeit in Widmungen, contribution by Bahr (Munich: Piper, 1910);

Walt Whitman, *Ich singe das Leben*, preface by Bahr (Leipzig: Tal, 1919);

Briefe von Joseph Kainz, edited, with a preface, by Bahr (Vienna: Rikola, 1921);

Gegen Klimt, preface by Bahr (Vienna: Eisenstein, 1921);

Egon Friedell, *Das Jesusproblem*, preface by Bahr (Vienna: Rikola, 1921);

Festschrift zum 60. Geburtstag Gerhart Hauptmanns, contribution by Bahr (Berlin: Mosse, 1922);

Goethes sämtliche Werke, volume 10, introduction by Bahr and Jakob Wassermann (Berlin: Ullstein, 1923-1924);

Martha Berger, *Das Leben einer Frau*, preface by Bahr (Vienna: Rikola, 1925);

150 Jahre Burgtheater: 1776-1926, contributions by Bahr (Vienna: Kristall, 1926);

Ernest Hello, *Ludovik: Erzählung*, epilogue by Bahr (Leipzig: Insel, 1927);

Das junge Wein: Österreichische Literatur- und Kunstkritik, 2 volumes, edited by Gotthart Wunberg, contributions by Bahr (Tübingen: Niemeyer, 1976).

Hermann Bahr was one of the most active and important Austrian intellectuals of his time. What made his position unique was his involvement in virtually all aspects of cultural life: he was a prolific dramatist and novelist, a producer of plays, and a literary as well as a cultural critic. This combination of the creation, management, and critique of art made him a highly influential and powerful cultural figure far beyond Vienna; but it also made him the main target of prominent opponents, above all of the journalist and satirist Karl Kraus. Kraus spent much of his life trying to discredit Bahr, and it is largely due to the success of this campaign that shortly after Bahr's death his outstanding accomplishments fell into almost complete oblivion. The awakened interest in intellectual and artistic movements of the turn of the century, however, and the editorial and critical efforts of scholars such as Donald G. Daviau, Reinhard Farkas, and Gotthart Wunberg have laid the groundwork for a positive reevaluation of Bahr. Even so, the fame of most of his plays has faded; only a few of his comedies are still performed. *Das Tschaperl* (The Fool; performed, 1897; published, 1898), *Wienerinnen* (Viennese Women; performed, 1900; published 1911), *Der Krampus* (The Devil; performed, 1901; pub-

lished, 1902) *Der Meister* (1904; translated as *The Master*, 1918), *Das Konzert* (1909; translated as *The Concert*, 1910 and 1921), and *Die Kinder* (The Children; performed, 1910; published, 1911) have deservedly held their ground in the history of literature. Yet Bahr's activities as a playwright must be seen as part of his overall goal of radically changing Austria's intellectual life. Through his all-encompassing efforts to reach this goal, Bahr was largely responsible for the introduction into Austria and Germany of the most important literary currents of his time. Any attempt to review the origins of decadence, impressionism, and expressionism in these countries must recognize the decisive influence of Hermann Bahr.

Hermann Anastas Bahr was born on 19 July 1863 in Linz, the capital of the Austrian province of Oberösterreich (Upper Austria). His father, Dr. Alois Caspar Julius Bahr, a lawyer and notary public, was a highly respected local politician who also served as supervisor of the province's school system. He and his wife, Wilhelmine (Minna), née Weidlich, descended from Silesian flax spinners and linen weavers, and Minna Bahr's family also had served as state functionaries. In his excellent autobiography, *Selbstbildnis* (Self-Portrait, 1923), Bahr describes his parents as having opposing personalities. While his father was content with the world, actively supporting social progress and in full agreement with the tradition of nineteenth-century liberalism and the accomplishments of the constitutional monarchy, his mother considered her marriage a misalliance and was dissatisfied with her personal life as well as with humanity in general. She suffered from depression and frequent headaches, and her greatest pleasure was in mocking friends of the family and local celebrities in their absence. Bahr had a great deal of sympathy for his mother, whom he considered a victim of her upbringing and environment; she served as a model for many female figures in his plays, including the title character in *Die Mutter* (The Mother, 1891).

Although he was an excellent student at the Benedictine school in Linz, Bahr did not feel challenged by his teachers but despised them. He followed in his mother's footsteps by using his family as an audience for his mockery and buffoonery. What later would become a worldview of decadence had already germinated in young Bahr's personality, as described in *Selbstbildnis*: self-elevation and the pathos of being different, the desire to unmask the frailty of others, yet also sudden attacks of disillusionment and self-disgust.

When Bahr was fifteen, he was sent to Salzburg to work toward his Matura diploma (school-leaving certificate required for admission to a university) from the Benedictine school there. This move had a liberating effect on Bahr, and it also brought him together with an educator he deeply admired: Joseph Steger, a professor of classical Greek. In October 1881 he enrolled at the University of Vienna to study classical philology, but he soon lost interest in this field and shifted to law. He also became involved in politics and joined Georg Ritter von Schönerer's pan-German and anti-Semitic movement. In March 1883, on the occasion of Richard Wagner's death, he gave a speech in favor of the unification of Austria and Germany and was dismissed from the university.

Alois Bahr never gave up hope of steering his son toward a respectable career and supported his legal studies in Czernowitz (now Chernovtsy, Ukraine) in 1883-1884 and then in Berlin. In Berlin, Bahr studied economics and met the second educator who deeply impressed him: Professor Adolf Wagner, an advocate of Prussian chancellor Otto von Bismarck's politics. Although Bahr enjoyed the unrestricted student life-style, his academic career ended when his dissertation was rejected in April 1886. His diverse theoretical and political aspirations could be expressed more appropriately in the journalistic genre. At this point Bahr, pinning his hopes for a better world on socialism, met Viktor Adler, who invited him to become a contributor to his weekly newspaper *Die Gleichheit* (Equality). In May 1887 Bahr left Berlin to serve a compulsory year of military service in Vienna.

Bahr's first published plays not only witness the disappointment of his political ambitions but also show the increasing influence of Henrik Ibsen, writers from the school of French decadence such as Paul Bourget and Joris-Karl Huysmans, the Belgian poet and dramatist Maurice Maeterlinck, and especially Maurice Barrès, whom Bahr regarded as his spiritual twin.

Bahr's drama *Die neuen Menschen* (The New People, performed, 1891) was published in 1887. The play shows the disillusionment of the protagonist, Georg, with politics as well as with love. Serving the socialist revolution, Georg is married to his comrade Anne. One day he feels pity for Hedwig, a prostitute, and offers her shelter at his home. Hedwig, grateful for having been rescued from the street, falls in love with Georg. She fi-

nally convinces him to leave Anne and abandon politics. A year and a half later Anne visits Georg at his villa at Lake Garda; both of them have aged considerably in appearance in that time. Anne, too, has given up politics and has been secretly watching Georg and Hedwig's happiness. At the time of Anne's visit Hedwig has left on a boat ride to Malcesine with her and Georg's acquaintance Lothar. Georg tells Anne that he has come to realize that the days of their love are numbered: Hedwig is falling in love with Lothar but would not be capable of betraying Georg. This situation, he says, will result in complete despair for all of them. After listening to Georg, Anne looks across the lake and sees the boat turn over, leaving Hedwig and Lothar to drown. Georg and Anne can hardly bear their conviction that politics and love are illusions. Their attempt to become "new people" who will change society and liberate humanity has failed. The play has many shortcomings, including extremely long monologues and using long time lapses between acts instead of depicting character changes.

After his year of military service Bahr paid a visit to his artistic idol, Ibsen, in Munich and then went to Paris, where he stayed for more than a year. His father continued to support him, hoping for his son's artistic success. Bahr was immediately attracted to the decadence movement and the life-style of the Parisian bohemia. He presented his impressions of Parisian social life to the readers of the *Wiener Salonblatt* (Vienna Parlor Paper), using an entertaining conversational tone. In March 1888 his play *La marquesa d'Amaëgui* was performed in Linz, to the great pleasure of his father. Subtitled *Eine Plauderei* (A Chat), the one-act comedy reflects Bahr's early wavering between politics and the arts. The politician Hanns Berner (based on Bahr's friend Engelbert Pernerstorfer, a deputy to the national parliament) and his wife, Stella (modeled after Adler's wife, Emma), meet the writer Heinrich Wolf and his sister, Anna, during a vacation in the mountains. Hanns and Heinrich feel obliged to play the roles that fit their public images, which are the opposite of their true personalities. They can only begin to enjoy their vacation after they drop their facades: instead of acting the part of the pessimistic poet and the ever-active politician, they end up playing cards.

In 1889 Bahr made a second attempt to write a tragedy. He deliberately placed himself in the tradition of Friedrich Hebbel by designating *Die große Sünde* (The Great Sin) a "bürgerliches

Trauerspiel" (bourgeois tragedy). Instead of limiting the number of characters to three or four, *Die große Sünde* aims to draw a representative picture of society. The protagonist, Dr. Richard Heyden, was raised in isolation from society. Now that his parents have died, he tries to become more socially involved. Lacking any knowledge of human nature, he is extremely impressed with the political ideals of the Opposition Club and marries Elsa Lindheim, the daughter of one of the club's members. After three years he has become the leader of the movement, admired by everyone for his idealism and honesty. When the government dissolves the parliament and he tries to stir up public unrest and establish true political freedom, he realizes that the political slogans of his friends are nothing but empty phrases. Disenchanted and weakened after a three-month stay in prison, he returns to his wife, only to learn that she wants to leave him to avoid disgrace. Like Georg and Anne in *Die neuen Menschen*, he is disillusioned by both politics and love. In a rage he brutally kills Elsa and is put in an insane asylum. He escapes and shows up at an orgy of the Opposition Club, confessing to his former friends that he is guilty of a terrible offense: he has sinned against dishonesty. As he is taken back to the asylum, he shouts: "Es lebe die Lüge!" (Long live the lie!)—thereby losing his last admirer, the wholesaler Walters, who had thought of him as the only "wirklicher Mensch" (true human being). Bahr did not want his play to allow for the slightest faith in human values and hopes.

Bahr wrote to his father that he was determined to become immortal through his next drama, *Die Mutter*, his third experiment with tragedy. Here he completely departs from politics and turns to the circle of artists, a subject that would preoccupy him for the rest of his life. For the first time Bahr follows the classical model of unity of time, depicting the action of a single night. The protagonist of *Die Mutter* is a young man, Edi, who tries to liberate himself from his mother, an egotistical, forty-year-old actress. Edi has fallen in love with Terka, who leads a free and luxurious life. Before leaving for the theater, his mother beseeches him to dissociate himself from Terka. The second act takes place in Terka's boudoir. Edi experiences the erotic fulfillment he has desired so much; but he finds out that Terka is only using him to take vengeance on his mother, who turns out to be Terka's former lesbian lover. In the meantime Edi's mother

has left the theater in the middle of the play to try to rescue her son from Terka's clutches. When Edi is asked to choose between the two viragos, he decides to stay with Terka. In desperation Edi's mother flings an armchair at Terka's head and dashes her to the ground. After being dragged home by his mother, Edi is confined to bed in rapidly deteriorating health. His mother cares for him as if he were a child. He realizes that he, like his father, must die young. His mother, symbolically standing for all women, has denied both men the satisfaction of their need for love. After Edi dies in total despair, a circus clown who is the intellectual life companion of Edi's mother keeps her from committing suicide by distracting her with his tricks and pranks.

In Bahr's early plays, politics and art create ideals such as freedom and love that turn the heads of the protagonists, who realize only too late that they have fallen victim to illusions. Bahr does not necessarily intend to express a genuine worldview. Instead, he aims to demonstrate his disapproval of a particular aspect of naturalism, the developing artistic movement of those days: the idea that human actions are determined by outer circumstances. In Berlin he had toyed with the Marxist idea that character can be influenced by economics and the social environment, but he rejected this view and chose the other extreme. A statement by the title character in *Die Mutter* is typical of Bahr's early plays: "Alle Frauen sind Mörderinnen am Manne. Es ist in der Natur. Da läßt sich nichts dagegen machen" (All women are murderers of men. It is part of nature. Nothing can be done about it). Bahr had given up his hope of changing the world through reason and had become an impressionist who believes in the power of emotions. It was Bahr's conviction that through the course of civilization the emphasis on reason has dulled the feelings. In his early plays human beings are victims of their predetermined dispositions, and their conflicting personalities lead to fatal clashes. Of Bahr's early attempts at tragedy only *Die neuen Menschen* was performed, and it fell flat.

Following his stay in Paris, Bahr traveled through southern France, Spain, and Morocco. During this time he worked on an autobiographical novel, "Das spanische Buch" (The Spanish Book), which remained unfinished and is now part of his literary remains. This manuscript and a selection of Bahr's diaries from 1888 until 1904 published by Reinhard Farkas in 1987 show that he went through several severe psychological crises, which manifested themselves in serious threats to his physical health. *Die Mutter* can be seen as a cryptographic attempt to express and overcome his personal distress and fears.

Bahr returned to Berlin in May 1890. There he founded the journal *Die freie Bühne für modernes Leben* (The Free Stage for Modern Life) with Arno Holz and Otto Brahm. Brahm was the first chairman of the newly founded "Freie Bühne" (Free Stage), a private club devoted to the performance of naturalist plays that would have been censored on public stages.

For the readers of his time Bahr's early works, especially *Die Mutter*, the novel *Die gute Schule* (The Good School, 1890) and a collection of audacious novellas, titled *Fin de Siècle* (1891), were nothing but scandalizing. This response pleased their author, who was deeply impressed by Friedrich Nietzsche's motto, "épater les bourgeois" (shock the middle class). While the public still hesitated to accept the works of naturalist artists, Bahr was already preparing to go beyond naturalism and introduce the decadence movement to Berlin. The city was in a process of dramatic change: in 1888 both Emperor Wilhelm I and his successor, Friedrich III, had died, and Friedrich's ambitious son Wilhelm II had taken the throne. Wilhelm, who dismissed Bismarck on 20 March 1890, aimed for Germany to become a world power. As the capital, Berlin soon became a major center of intellectual and artistic life. It was Berlin where in 1889 Brahm had inaugurated the naturalist drama by producing Ibsen's *Ghosts* (1881) and Gerhart Hauptmann's *Vor Sonnenaufgang* (Before Dawn, 1889). The young publisher Samuel Fischer had a flair for spotting talent; he supported young authors such as Hauptmann who would ensure the fame of his publishing house. Fischer financed *Die freie Bühne für modernes Leben*; he also published *Die gute Schule* and many of Bahr's other works.

Bahr promoted young artists and modernist intellectual currents in his essays and reviews. His collections of essays *Zur Kritik der Moderne* (Criticism of Modernity, 1890) and *Die Überwindung des Naturalismus* (The Overcoming of Naturalism, 1891) influenced the next generation of artists, including Thomas Mann. But Bahr's interest in Berlin soon faded. He realized that the city was the center of a German form of modernity that contrasted with the French decadence movement he was trying to promote. After a trip to Saint Petersburg, Russia, he decided that Vienna was where he really belonged, and he moved there in Octo-

ber 1891. For the next twenty years he devoted himself to radically changing the intellectual life of the city. At the Café Griensteidl he and such artists as Hugo von Hofmannsthal, Arthur Schnitzler, and Richard Beer-Hofmann formed the "Jung Wien" (Young Vienna) movement, with Bahr as the main organizer and spokesman. It was largely due to Bahr's influence that the Viennese modernist movement moved out of the shadow of Berlin by developing a distinctive style indebted not to naturalism but to French decadence and symbolism.

In his essay "Die Moderne" (Modernity, 1890), a programmatic introduction to the newly founded periodical *Moderne Dichtung* (Modern Literature), Bahr explains his view of modern art. Like many young artists and intellectuals of his time he is extremely critical of the older generation's reconciliation of liberalism and Catholicism, a reconciliation that appeared to be complacent and mendacious. He agrees with the Romantics that the unity of life and "Geist" (spirit) has been lost. What distinguishes the modernist artists from the Romantics is the conviction of the former that it is futile to lament this loss. The new reality calls for a new way of thinking, which must be initiated by an attitude of sensual receptiveness. The decadence movement is an attempt to bring about such receptiveness. Bahr never adopted decadence as his own worldview but remained true to the main principle of modernity: always to strive for new experiences. His ironic nickname, "der Mann von übermorgen" (the man of the day after tomorrow), was a criticism of modernity in general, not of Bahr personally.

It was his openness and adaptability which enabled Bahr to be the spokesman for the many modernist currents. Thus, he could introduce decadent art to Germany and Austria, play a decisive part in the Viennese Secessionist movement, and be one of the first promoters of expressionism. In his own literary works he was also open to new currents, even though he was always indebted to impressionism. His novels, short stories, and many of his plays are bound to the time of their origin, making them important as historical documents; on the other hand, the abundance of allusions to events of the day reduces the enjoyment of readers who do not have proper knowledge of such contexts. Critics who see Bahr as a chameleon fail to recognize that despite the many faces of his works he always remained true to modernism.

From 1892 until 1894 Bahr was a theater critic and feuilletonist for the *Deutsche Zeitung* (German Newspaper) in support of his campaign for modernity. In 1894, deciding that he could better serve this goal with his own periodical, he founded the weekly newspaper *Die Zeit* (Time) in collaboration with Isidor Singer and Heinrich Kanner. At the age of thirty-one he had become financially independent. It was also at this time that he discovered that his true dramatic talent lay in writing comedies rather than tragedies.

The four-act play *Die häusliche Frau* (The Domestic Wife, performed, 1891; published, 1893) marks the beginning of Bahr's career as a comedy writer. It comprises the major elements of his future plays: detailed stage instructions, including precise characterizations of the protagonists' personalities, and a middle-class setting. Anna Schlieben, a young woman with a zest for life, is dissatisfied with her husband Gustav, a simple-minded and pedantic lawyer who is absorbed in his work. The sculptor Hans Gude, a friend of the Schliebens and lover of their maid Rieke, tries to seduce Anna. Gude, who despises women, turns out to be Anna's instrument for teaching her husband to trust his wife and to enjoy life.

Bahr's strength lies in writing witty dialogue that not only serves the plot but is an end in itself. He is a master of brilliant exchanges of ideas and arguments, charming his audience with elegantly formulated aperçus rather than trying to prove his point by means of plot development.

Aus der Vorstadt (From the Suburb, 1893), a Viennese "Volksstück" (folk play) written with Carl Karlweis, was a failure, as were Bahr's next two plays, *Die Nixe* (The Mermaid, 1896) and *Juana* (1896). In 1898 Bahr revised *Die häusliche Frau*, changing the scene of the action from Berlin to Vienna; but this work, with the new title "Veilchen" (Violet), was never performed or published. Bahr also continued to be extremely active as an essayist. His third collection of essays, *Studien zur Kritik der Moderne* (Contributions to the Criticism of Modernity) was published in 1894; the next collection, *Renaissance: Neue Studien zur Kritik der Moderne* (Renaissance: New Contributions to the Criticism of Modernity, 1897), indicates a shift in his agenda from modernism in general to the more specific goal of revivifying Austrian culture. Bahr alluded to this goal by using the pseudonym "Caph," the alchemic sign for making gold, for many of his contributions to *Die Zeit.*

Bahr considered *Das Tschaperl* his first truly good dramatic work. The protagonists, Alois and Fanny Lampl, are modeled after Bahr's friends the actors Karl and Marianne Langhammer. In addition, they represent Bahr's new situation as a successful theater critic and playwright. The process of becoming established is satirically demonstrated by the change of scenes between the first and second acts: the Lampls have left their rather modest apartment and are in the process of decorating their luxurious new residence. Their success, however, is due not to Alois, a theater critic, but to his young wife, who has written the comic opera *Schneewittchen* (Snow White). Even though Alois enjoys the comfort and prestige of their new life-style, he reveals himself as a male chauvinist who has a hard time coping with his wife's success and constantly accuses her of being disloyal to him. Like that of Gustav in *Die häusliche Frau*, his distrust is unfounded. He has to learn that it is not his wife but he himself who deserves to be called "Tschaperl." In *Die Mutter* Bahr had accused women of dominating men; here, the situation is reversed. Fanny leaves her seemingly incorrigibly selfish husband after he raises his hand against her in an act of foolish jealousy.

Called simply "der alte Lampl" (the old Lampl), Alois's father is the true hero of the play; he represents the old-fashioned, unassuming, and prudent Viennese. Old Lampl does not begrudge his son and daughter-in-law their new wealth, but he looks at the ambitiousness of the younger generation as a sign of moral decline. With his help Alois might learn his lesson.

The play's premiere on 27 February 1897 at the Carltheater with Arnold Korff as Alois, Franz Ritter von Jauner as Lampl, and Gisela Pahlen as Fanny was received with great enthusiasm and opened the Viennese stage for Bahr's future works. When it was produced in Berlin eight months later, however, it was not well received. Alfred Kerr called *Das Tschaperl* a "Mehlspeisen-Nora" (Austrian-sweet-dish *Nora*), condescendingly implying that the play was a poor imitation of Ibsen's *A Doll's House* (1879; the play is called *Nora* or *Ein Puppenheim* in German) with superficially added Viennese color. While *Das Tschaperl* is indebted to Ibsen, its conciliatory attitude and Viennese amiability are by no means a shallow veneer but are genuine characteristics of Bahr's better plays. It is instrumental to the success of his plays that the actors convey Bahr's intention of humorously depicting human frailties rather than

11

condemning his protagonists. In the Viennese production Korff's brilliant performance demonstrated Bahr's talent for creating interesting dramatic characters. During the coming years Bahr would create roles expressly written for the major actors of the Deutsches Volkstheater (German People's Theater) in Vienna.

The years 1894 to 1899 mark the period of Bahr's greatest success as promoter of Jung Wien. In addition to his activities as an art critic, he developed close ties to Max Burckhard, the director of the Burgtheater, and Emmerich von Bukovics, director of the Deutsches Volkstheater. These relationships enabled him to advance the careers of actors of his choice and to have a decisive influence on the repertoire. He even introduced a new acting style in the Burgtheater. On 5 May 1895 he married Rosa Jokl, a twenty-three-year-old Jewish woman who played minor roles at the Volkstheater. Although he had considered himself an atheist since the days of his enthusiasm for Schönerer, it was at this time that he officially left the Catholic church. In the spring of 1897 the Vienna Secession was founded by Gustav Klimt and other painters and architects in protest against the artistic establishment. Together with Burckhard, Bahr edited the Secessionist periodical *Ver sacrum*.

Between 1898 and 1900 Bahr had many books published, including three collections of essays and theater critiques; the jointly published novellas *Die schöne Frau* (The Beautiful Woman) and *Leander* (1899); and several plays. *Wenn es euch gefällt* (If You Like It, 1899), written in collaboration with Karlweis, was unsuccessful. *Josephine* (performed, 1897; published, 1899), *Der Star* (The Star; performed, 1898; published, 1899), and *Der Athlet* (The Athlete; performed, 1899; published, 1900), follow the model of *Das Tschaperl*, aiming to maintain a balance between tragedy and comedy. *Josephine* is the most daring of these works, all of which express the idea Bahr had developed in *Die Mutter*: all human beings are victims of their predetermined and unchangeable psychological dispositions. In Bahr's comedies this determinism does not lead to tragedy but to misconceptions that dictate people's actions and determine their fates. As in *La marquesa d'Amaëgui*, Bahr's intention is to unmask these misconceptions. In *Josephine*, Napoleon is a "Tschaperl" who becomes a world leader simply to please Josephine. Josephine sends him to war with Italy because she can no longer bear his petty jealousy. After Napoleon has been driven by rage over Josephine's escapades in Paris to become a victorious commander in chief, he realizes that he has to learn how to appear as a hero so as to satisfy the expectations of the public. In what Heinz Kindermann, a historian of modern European drama, calls one of the most effective scenes in twentieth-century German comedy, the actor Talma teaches Napoleon how to assume the heroic pose that will become his mark of distinction. To Josephine's disappointment, Napoleon begins to appreciate this role; he is no longer a slave to her but to his public image.

Josephine was first performed at the Deutsches Volkstheater in Vienna on 23 December 1897 with Helene Odilon as Josephine and Leopold Kramer as Napoleon. The audience was sharply divided between supporters and opponents, and both sides loudly expressed their feelings. Twenty years later, when an English adaptation of the play by F. E. Washburn Freund was performed in New York, some viewers were appalled by the satirical depiction of Napoleon; others agreed with Bahr's friend Josef Kainz, who praised the attempt to show a hero as a human being with common frailties.

While *Josephine* is an enjoyable play, it also demonstrates Bahr's limitations. An intriguing beginning sets the tone for the play, which proceeds through various surprising turns of the action and ends with an amusing "punch line." While this structure is adequate for a comedy, it is the main flaw of Bahr's more ambitious dramatic attempts, including *Der Star*—the less successful dramatic counterpart to his novel *Theater* (1897)—and *Der Athlet*. The protagonist of *Der Star* is Lona Ladinser, an actress; the role was expressly written for Odilon, who was, in essence, allowed to play herself. In accordance with Bahr's concept of fate, Lona Ladinser fails to have a fulfilling relationship with the postal clerk Leopold Weisinger; she comes to the conclusion that this failure was inevitable because "meine Welt und seine—es ist halt anders" (my world and his—they are too different). The contrast between the simple-minded but happy and sexually satisfied "Bürger" (common citizen) and the spiritually elevated but personally unfulfilled artist was a common literary subject at the turn of the century.

In *Der Athlet* Bahr uses another antithesis to illustrate his concept of an unshakable fate. Baron Gustav von Handel attempts to change the life of the criminal Loisl so as to prove the power of his own will. Handel fails in his project, and he finally comes to terms with the limitation of his power when he learns that his wife has betrayed him. Through this experience he realizes that it is impossible to fight one's fate; he accepts his destiny, thereby achieving maturity. Even though the play, which premiered on 7 October 1899 at the Deutsches Volkstheater, had an excellent cast—Kramer, Alexander Girardi, Minna Laferenz, and Viktor Kutschera—*Der Athlet* was not well received. That month Bahr left *Die Zeit* to become a theater critic for the *Neue Wiener Tagblatt* (New Viennese Daily).

The choice of Upper Austria as the setting for *Der Athlet* indicates the beginning of Bahr's disillusionment with Vienna. By 1900 the initial public enthusiasm for the Jung Wien movement had begun to be replaced by a conservative reaction. Bahr saw himself in a more and more defensive position. In 1901 he took Kraus to court over his inflammatory campaign against Bahr. Kraus lost the lawsuit, but he continued his defamation of the Jung Wien movement. During the next few years Bahr put much effort into defending his friends, in particular Klimt and Schnitzler. He distanced himself from Vienna by moving into a house designed by the architect Joseph Olbrich in Ober Sankt Veit, a rural suburb.

Bahr's attempts to support Jung Wien ended in complete disenchantment. The plays he wrote during the next five years reflect this development. It became increasingly harder for him to assume that conciliatory attitude that was the basis of his artistically more successful works. The best plays of this period are *Wienerinnen* and *Der Franzl* (1901).

Even though Bahr continued to use urban life for his dramatic settings, he did so with an increasingly critical and ultimately cynical attitude. *Wienerinnen* is the first of only two true comedies of this period. Using a simple but convincing antithetical structure, Bahr holds the balance between undistanced glorification and plain rejection of his protagonists. The hero of this play is Joseph Ulrich, an architect from the Austrian provinces who marries Daisy, a superficial young Viennese woman. After a series of fights Joseph convinces Daisy that her support of ideas such as woman's emancipation and the rejection of traditional art and life-styles is based on fashion rather than true conviction; the couple overcome their superficial differences and discover their deep love for one another. This simple plot is carried out masterfully, with witty dialogue and humorous situations. *Wienerinnen* was first performed on 3 October 1900 at the Deutsches

Volkstheater; it has been revived several times and remains one of Bahr's best-received works.

The barely disguised model for Ulrich was Olbrich, who had left Vienna because he felt that there was not enough appreciation of his work. Like Johann Wolfgang von Goethe, with his utopian idea of a "pädagogische Provinz" (pedagogical province), Olbrich and Bahr pinned their hopes for a revived culture on the idea of a rural artists' colony where they could educate young people according to their own ideals. For financial reasons, Bahr was never able to translate his politico-cultural plans into action.

The subtitle of *Der Franzl* is *Fünf Bilder eines guten Mannes* (Five Views of a Good Man). As in *Der Athlet*, Bahr turns to the Upper Austrian province in search of new positive models. *Der Franzl* pays homage to the nineteenth-century Upper Austrian dialect writer Franz Stelzhammer. Five rather independent scenes, covering a span of fifty years, depict different passions of Stelzhammer's life. Bahr here falls back on an idea he had touched on in *Die große Sünde*: Stelzhammer is presented as an exemplary member of the rare species of "true human beings." *Der Franzl* was first performed in Linz on 16 February 1901. Despite its lack of dramatic action, this play was commended by the critics for its positive attitude toward the Austrian provinces.

Der Apostel (The Apostle, 1901) condemns Austrian bureaucracy and politics. Bahr, always fascinated by the interchangeability of theater and everyday life, here turns the stage into a caricature of the national parliament. To escape total negativity, the play conjures up another "true human being," the title character. *Der Apostel* falls short of Bahr's earliest dramatic attempts, documenting how the author's disenchantment with his fellow citizens had taken over his better judgment as a writer.

The protagonist of *Der Krampus*, which is set in the late eighteenth century, is Anastasius Ritter von Negrelli, a retired "Hofrat" (privy councillor) and thus a stereotypical Austrian character. The play concentrates on the private life of the Hofrat, who seems to be a perfectly loathsome tyrant. Bahr surprises his audience with the revelation that Negrelli is only playing a role to hide his overly sensitive personality; he has fallen victim to his dehumanizing profession. The plot development is carried out masterfully, and *Der Krampus* was one of Bahr's most successful comedies. He skillfully incorporates into it such ele-

Anna Bahr-Mildenburg, Bahr's second wife, as Klytemnestra in the premiere of the opera Elektra, *by Hugo von Hofmannsthal and Richard Strauss, at the Vienna Royal Opera House in 1909*

ments of the Volksstück as music, dance, and pantomime.

The years 1903 and 1904 marked a period of artistic crisis for Bahr that ultimately led to a turning point. Bahr's disillusionment with Vienna reached its climax, coinciding with a physical breakdown and a prolonged period of ill health. As it had twenty-five years earlier, traveling helped him to overcome this crisis. In September 1904 he went to Bayreuth and attended a performance of Richard Wagner's music drama *Tristan und Isolde* (1859), with Anna Mildenburg as Isolde. He was profoundly impressed by Wagner's work; he also fell in love with Mildenburg. Another important experience was his encounter with the world of antiquity during a trip to Athens. Finally, Bahr became increasingly attracted to the thought of Goethe. All of these influences laid the groundwork for his writings of the next ten years.

Unter sich: Ein Arme-Leut'-Stück (Among Themselves: A Poor-Folk Play; performed, 1903; published, 1904) is a grotesque one-act play that follows the pattern of *La marquesa d'Amaëgui*. A group of politicians has gone to a southern resort to escape the public and to recuperate from the roles they are expected to play. Bahr expounds his view of politics as unprincipled and removed from the concerns of the people. Some of the politicians in *Unter sich* express the need to overcome their distance from the common people, but Bahr unmasks such talk as empty, even ridiculing his own recent hopes of reviving politics through closer ties with the Upper Austrian province.

With *Der Meister* Bahr returns to his artistic strengths by concentrating on a single protagonist who is illuminated from various angles. The three-act play features the liberal rationalist Caius Duhr, who falls victim to his illusionary convictions. Duhr had to fight the medical establishment, including his own brother, to become the director of a clinic that uses innovative "American" surgical methods and treatments. He owes his success to a group of followers who have always believed in him, but at the height of his triumph the members of this group realize that they were only being used to serve their "master's" egotistical concerns, above all his psychopathic desire to be in charge. When his brother visits him to pay tribute reluctantly to his success, Caius reveals that his desire for success and his insistence on rationally planning his life were results of his unhappy childhood. Instead of believing in the principles he has been advocating, he has used them as a facade to conceal his vulnerable personality. When it becomes public that his wife has betrayed him with his best friend, he claims that the matter is of no consequence to him. Realizing that he is incapable of showing emotion, his wife leaves him. It is only then that he falls apart. Duhr follows the dictum "Nicht was uns geschieht, sondern wie wir es es empfinden, dies allein macht unser Glück oder Unglück aus" (Not what happens to us, but how we perceive it—this alone determines whether we are happy or unhappy). Through his spokesman in the play, the Japanese doctor Kokoro, Bahr criticizes such an attitude as escapism.

Bahr called *Der Meister* a comedy, but the play is really a melodrama—especially the penultimate scene, where Duhr has lost all of his friends and is left with only his dog. In the final scene Duhr realizes that it was pride that led to his failure. He now admits that fate is stronger than human will and says: "Vielleicht ist es wirklich nur eine tragische Vermessenheit, kein Wurstl zu sein" (Perhaps it is really only a tragic presumption not to be a fool). *Der Meister* was first produced in 1904 at the Deutsches Theater in Berlin with Rudolf Rittner and Irene Triesche and was awarded the Bauernfeld Prize.

Sanna (1905) is Bahr's most ambitious attempt at tragedy, but although he gives careful attention to the play's structure and dramatic details, the work is not convincing. Set in 1847, the play presents a commonplace subject of nineteenth-century literature: Sanna is a young woman who is not allowed to marry the man she loves because her family doubts that he can support her appropriately. Furnian, Sanna's eighty-year-old uncle, is a retired Hofrat who lives with her family. He has the financial means to help the young couple, but he is an embittered man who seems to live only to insure that the younger generation will not have a better life than he had. Facing the threat of having to marry the fifty-year-old Schulrat (school superintendent) Zingerl, a sadist and necrophile, Sanna kills herself. The Hofrat and Schulrat are metaphors for the Austrian state, which, in Bahr's view, had fallen ill. Reinhardt directed the first performance of the play at the Kleines Theater in Berlin on 10 March 1905, but *Sanna* did not become part of the repertoire.

The first act of *Die Andere* (The Other Woman, performed, 1905; published, 1906) depicts a liaison between Heinrich Heß, a thirty-nine-year-old professor, and the highly talented violinist Lida Lind, who is twenty years younger than Heß. It seems that Heß will be able to cure Lida of subconscious fears that stem from a previous relationship; but when her agent and former lover Amschl visits her, she immediately becomes his slave again. He brutally exploits her for a year before abandoning her, leaving her in total poverty. When Heß comes to rescue her, it is too late. Before she dies Lida confesses that she could not have acted differently: Amschl was the only one she had loved, and her end in despair is the necessary price for the few hours of happiness she was granted. As Schnitzler said in a letter to Bahr, *Die Andere* does not show Lida Lind's inner conflict but simply surprises the audience with an unmotivated plot twist.

Bahr ends the play in a manner that anticipates the expressionist drama. Heinrich Heß provides the audience with the theoretical background for Bahr's rejection of cultural reforms, telling his former students: "Ich hab Euch damals gelehrt: Reform! Zur Rettung unserer Kultur! Sonst kommen die Barbaren wieder. . . . Wie aber, wenn erst die Barbaren wiederkommen müssen? Wenn es eben diese Kultur ist, vielleicht, an der wir krank sind?" (I used to teach you: Reform! For the salvation of our culture! Otherwise the barbarians will come back. . . . But what if the barbarians have to come back? What if it is this culture that makes us sick?). Another character, August Tuch, announces the end of Western civilization. The final scene alludes to the Russian "Bloody Sunday" uprising of 22 January 1905. Like Georg in *Die neuen Menschen*, Heinrich Heß argues that existing civilization must be destroyed to give future generations the chance for a better life. Even though Bahr became an advocate of expressionism—his book *Expressionismus* (1916; translated as *Expressionism*, 1925) was one of his few works to be translated into English— *Die Andere* remains his most serious experiment with elements of the expressionist drama.

The one-act play *Der arme Narr* (The Poor Fool, 1906) combines themes from *Das Tschaperl*, *Der Meister*, and *Sanna*, integrated with ideas from Wagner, Nietzsche, and the philosopher Arthur Schopenhauer; the play also gives indications of a revived religious faith on Bahr's part. While Vinzenz Heißt's two younger brothers were allowed to enjoy their lives without worrying about their futures, Vinzenz tried to please his father by working toward a career. Vinzenz's father has also chosen the wealthy and upright but more than fifty-years-old Huster to marry Vinzenz's seventeen-year-old sister, Sophie. Vinzenz's only satisfaction is that his life has been so miserable that it will be easier for him to die than for his brother, Hugo, who has enjoyed his life so much. Hugo is a poetic genius who has been confined in an insane asylum. Like Lida Lind in *Die Andere*, Hugo exemplifies the philosopher Ernst Mach's theory of the "fluid ego" as well as Nietzschean vitalism. When Hugo is brought to Vinzenz's house, Vinzenz realizes that it is not Hugo but he himself who deserves to be called a "poor fool." Hugo is by no means afraid of dying; his faith teaches him that life and death are an everlasting cycle. Hugo also recognizes Sophie as one of his kind, who will not follow her father's wishes. Vinzenz has suffered a total defeat. Before the curtain falls, he asks himself: "Aber wozu denn dann? Wozu dann?" (But why? Why?).

Ringelspiel (Round Dance; performed, 1906; published, 1907), a drama in three acts, is a comic complement to Bahr's friend Schnitzler's *Reigen* (Round Dance, 1900). *Ringelspiel* is set in Venice, where Bahr vacationed from 1906 until 1911. Julius and Franzl Eggers have agreed to have an open marriage. They live apart from each other and go through a series of love affairs. This life-style is threatened when both of them become involved with people who demand monogamous relationships. The Eggers and their lovers agree to discuss this dilemma at the beach of Lido. The relaxed atmosphere of the international resort keeps the situation from taking a tragic turn. Julius's lover, Rune Dohn, realizes that Julius is not capable of giving up his wife. Franzl sees that Rune is the perfect mistress for her husband and convinces Rune that she would have to take the less satisfying role of Julius's wife if he were to divorce Franzl. Harald Sandel, Franzl's lover, who came to Venice to ask Julius for the hand of his wife, realizes that Franzl likes to listen to his idealistic theories on love and marriage but has no intention of marrying him. According to *Ringelspiel*, love has two sides, passion and partnership; unfortunately, it cannot serve both of these functions at the same time.

While Schnitzler's *Reigen* uses the motif of the round dance metaphorically, to unmask the social conventions which conceal the overwhelming power of carnal desire, Bahr actually presents a round dance on stage. The colorful dance is watched by Julius and Rune and gives rise to their final exchange in the play. Rune says: "Dies alles . . . ich weiß nicht. So wild, so bös" (All of this . . . I don't know. So wild, so evil). Julius responds: "So stark, so froh.—Denn wir haben uns doch lieb" (So strong, so happy.—Because we love each other, after all).

In October 1905 Bahr had been offered the position of director of the Schauspielhaus in Munich. When the contract was withdrawn before Bahr could assume his duties, Reinhardt offered him a similar position at the Deutsches Theater in Berlin. *Ringelspiel* was directed by Bahr himself as his first duty at the Deutsches Theater on 18 December 1906. The initial response was negative due to the false impression of the critics that the play was autobiographical. *Ringelspiel* nevertheless became a frequent part of the German and Austrian repertoires.

Die gelbe Nachtigall (The Yellow Nightingale, 1907), like *Der Star* and *Theater*, deals with the relationship between the world of the theater and everyday life. Bahr has modified the view he expressed in the earlier works: while he then believed that the two spheres represent entirely different worlds, *Die gelbe Nachtigall* is meant to show that both actors and ordinary people are simply playing roles. The advantage of the theater is that the actors only play their roles during the performance, while others are never allowed to "remove their makeup."

In 1908 Bahr returned to Vienna as Burgtheater critic for the *Neues Wiener Journal*. In May 1909 Bahr divorced Rosa Jokl, from whom he had been separated for several years; two months later, he married Anna Mildenburg. After the marriage the couple's place of residence was mostly dependent on Anna's operatic engagements; in 1909 they stayed in Bayreuth for two months.

The comedy *Das Konzert* was Bahr's greatest success. It presents the story of a forestalled seduction. The acclaimed forty-three-year-old pianist Gustav Heink has reached a point in his life at which the enthusiasm of the audience, especially that of young women, for his genius is turning into a burden. Even at home he is surrounded by a bevy of well-to-do young ladies who are eagerly waiting for their piano lessons. When the play opens his students are in a frenzy: they have just been told that their "master" is leaving for an unexpected concert and has canceled all lessons for the next three days. One student, Eva Gerndl, is suspicious. Eva is made up in the latest fashion, hiding her girlish nature behind a mask patterned after the demonic, snakelike beauties in Klimt's paintings. (Bahr is there making one of his best friends the target of his satire, ridiculing the superficial influence of Secessionist art on Viennese society.) Eva vows to her girlfriends that she will rescue her beloved Gustav from the clutches of Delfine Jura.

In the next scene Eva tearfully confesses to Heink's wife, Marie, that she sent an anonymous telegram to Delfine's husband, Dr. Jura, informing him of the time and place of the suspected tête-à-tête. Eva had hoped that Delfine would be killed by her outraged husband, but now she fears that Gustav might well become the victim of Dr. Jura's vengeance. When Marie meets Dr. Jura shortly thereafter, she immediately realizes that this man is no threat to Gustav's life; he is Bahr's favorite theatrical type, the rationalistic theorist. Like Caius Duhr in *Der Meister* and Jura's other predecessors, he holds that one must try to love as many people as possible and declares an open marriage the most logical form of the institution. While he claims to be glad for Delfine's weekend in the mountains, he raises concern about her immature attitude to love: the seventeen-year-old Delfine is used to life going her way and would be crushed should Gustav only be interested in a short-lived adventure. Dr. Jura flatters himself with the belief that his only desire is to save Delfine from such disappointment. Marie, the true heroine of *Das Konzert*, understands that regardless of his theories Dr. Jura is truly in love with Delfine, just as Marie herself deeply cares for Gustav. Having decided not to tolerate Gustav's escapades any longer, she devises a scheme: she proposes that she and Dr. Jura divorce their spouses and marry each other. He consents, and a few hours later they surprise Gustav and Delfine at Gustav's mountain cabin. During the next two acts Marie's cunning plan smoothly unwinds. Delfine and Dr. Jura are taught lessons that will strengthen their relationship. Dr. Jura has to depart from his fashionable theories, while Delfine learns to be less superficial and selfish. After the trying first year of their marriage the young couple is ready for a honeymoon and escapes "in den herrlichen Frühling hinein" (into the gorgeous spring).

A humorous complement and homage to Goethe's *Wahlverwandtschaften* (Elective Affinities, 1809), *Das Konzert* presents the theory that marriage must continuously stand the test of averting the temptation of adultery; couples should not carelessly jeopardize their marriage if their elective affinities lie, in fact, within their own partnership. For Heink, however, this lesson is in vain. As an artist, he has to play the role that is expected of him by the public. He is surrounded by female worshipers who see any social amenity as the beginning of an affair. He feels drawn into these short-lived romances like a chess player who has to obey routine game strategies such as the Spanish Opening or Queen's Gambit. He is not ready to resign from the game and admit that he is growing older. Just after Marie has gotten rid of Delfine, Eva Gerndl appears in a "Klimptian" Alpine costume and throws herself into Gustav's arms. As the curtain falls Heink embarks on his next affair, saying resignedly: "Ich muß, ich muß" (I must, I must). It is up to Marie to cope with her next rival. The circle is closed, and the game can start all over again.

Das Konzert shows Bahr, the master of brilliant dialogue and aperçu, at his best. Instead of repeating his usual antithetical confrontation of "good" and "bad" characters, he sympathetically portrays the various personalities. He humorously exaggerates the idiosyncrasies and frailties of his characters, but he gets the audience to love each of them. Even the minor roles are carefully depicted, especially the married couple taking care of Heink's mountain cabin. Herr Pollinger, only three years older than his master, is suffering even more from age. Troubled with gout, he is too proud to admit that carousing and poaching have become a torment to him. The contrast between the Heinks' upper-class diction and the provincial dialect of the Pollingers creates a comic effect, and showing that couples from widely divergent social classes have to cope with similar difficulties gives the drama more depth. *Das Konzert* combines a smooth unfolding of dramatic action with a brisk succession of brilliant speeches.

The play had its premiere on 23 December 1909 at the Lessingtheater in Berlin. On 19 February 1910 it was performed at the Deutsches Volkstheater in Vienna with Lili Marberg as Marie and Leopold Kramer as Gustav. It was an immediate success on Czech and Hungarian as well as German and Austrian stages, and within a few months it had received worldwide acclaim. On 10 October 1910 an English adaptation by the director Leo Dietrichstein, who also played Gustav, opened at the Belasco Theater in New York; it became one of the most celebrated productions of the New York season. As a theater critic Bahr had contributed to the success of the other Jung Wien writers on their home stages, but it was his own play, *Das Konzert*, that won international recognition for the Viennese drama. There were four film adaptations of *Das Konzert*, including the American production *The Concert* (1921), directed by V. L. Schertzinger. A translation by Bayard Quincy Morgan was published in *Chief Contemporary Dramatists* (1921), and a college edition for American students of German by Josef Wiehr was published in 1931. While these books have long been absent from the book market, the Reclam edition of *Das Konzert* was Bahr's only literary work in print in 1992.

Bahr's last highly successful comedy was *Die Kinder*. A comic complement to Frank Wedekind's drama *Frühlings Erwachen* (Spring's Awakening, 1891), the play is a humorous variation on a central literary theme at the turn of the century: the confusion and disorder that result when the awakening of sensuality in adolescence confronts conventional morality. A double adultery results in the births of Anna Scharitzer and Konrad Graf Freyn. After the two families have not seen each other for years, the eminent surgeon "Hofrat Professor Doktor" Ignaz Scharitzer takes his seventeen-year-old daughter to Castle Freyn in Upper Austria, where she is introduced to the twenty-four-year-old Konrad Graf Freyn. Anna prides herself on her peasant ancestry, wants to be addressed as "comrade," and looks down on the privileges and customs of the nobility. When Konrad formally courts her, she turns him down. He does not admit defeat but asks Hofrat Scharitzer for his daughter's hand. Scharitzer is forced to admit that Konrad is his illegitimate son; thus, it seems to be impossible for him to marry Anna. But then it is revealed that old Graf Freyn is Anna's father, and Konrad and Anna are free to fall in love. Both have learned their lesson: knowing about her own aristocratic descent, Anna abandons her pseudoemancipated stereotypes about nobility, while Konrad no longer feels obliged to follow the outdated etiquette of a tradition to which he does not really belong.

Die Kinder humorously unmasks the idea of racial purity as an illusion. The tasks and challenges that lie ahead of the new generation demand a departure from the dangerous liaison between racial mania and conventional morality. *Die Kinder* demonstrates Bahr's ability to criticize sympathetically fashionable attitudes with which he himself had once flirted: Anna is a satirical depiction of the emancipated behavior Bahr had copied from Ibsen's *A Doll's House*, Scharitzer ironically represents the Nietzschean idolization of human superiority, and Graf Freyn is a caricature of the decadent movement.

Die Kinder premiered on 23 December 1910 on twenty-eight stages, including the Schauspielhaus (Playhouse) in Leipzig. It became one of the most popular comedies of the European repertoire. It also marks the end of Bahr's artistic development. The thirteen plays he wrote from 1911 until he retired as a playwright in 1928 clearly fall short of his previous dramas, especially *Das Konzert*. In the years preceding World War I he wrote four comedies that proved to be less successful variations of his former works: *Das Tänzchen* (The Little Dance, published 1911, premiered 1912) is a reworking of *Die Kinder*; it is also reminiscent of *Der Apostel*, as is *Das Prinzip* (The Principle, 1912). Like *Der arme Narr*, both *Das Prinzip* and *Das Phantom* (The Phantom, 1913) document that Bahr was on his way to a revived religious faith. *Der Querulant* (The

Bahr in 1909; after an etching by Orlik

Grumbler, 1914) is the best of these plays. Like Heinrich von Kleist's novella *Michael Kohlhaas* (1808) and his comedy *Der zerbrochene Krug* (The Broken Jug, 1811), it concerns an unreasonable desire for justice by someone who has been wronged. In addition, *Der Querulant* uses a popular turn-of-the-century motif: the grumbling old dog owner who hates the world but loves his mongrel. Hias, a peasant who wants the forester who killed his dog punished for murder, is sympathetically depicted as a victim of society. With the assistance of a priest, he learns that he cannot find justice on earth, that all human beings are subject to God's mercy, and that people should not blame each other for their sins. *Der Querulant* was first produced at the Munich Schauspielhaus on 16 October 1914. It was the last of Bahr's plays to be performed in America, where, under the title *The Mongrel*, it had its premiere at the Longacre Theater in New York on 15 December 1924.

Except for a half year, beginning in September 1918, when Bahr shared responsibility for selecting plays and worked as a producer at the Burgtheater in Vienna, his residence from 1912 until 1922 was the Arenberg Castle in Salzburg. He continued to write essays and socio-critical novels; he was also an excellent speaker who was frequently invited to give lectures and readings. In addition, he kept an extensive diary. He had already begun to have excerpts published in the *Neues Wiener Journal* in 1906 and continued to do so at intervals until 1933. In 1909 his first book of diaries appeared, and from 1918 until 1927 his diaries were published intermittently in book form. The exchange of letters between Bahr and his friend Josef Redlich, a highly respected Austrian scholar of law and political science who became a professor at Harvard University in 1926, gives excellent insight into Bahr's personal life, especially for the period from 1904 until 1925; the correspondence was published in 1980.

Like the majority of Austrian and German intellectuals, Bahr hailed the outbreak of World War I as the beginning of a radically new era; but he soon saw that his vision of a united German nation that could revive European culture by following the model of the old Austro-Hungarian multiethnic empire was an illusion. His farce *Der muntere Seifensieder* (The Merry Soap Boiler, performed, 1914; published, 1915) ridicules the hysteria and confusion at the beginning of the war.

Bahr finally made peace with himself and the world by reconverting to Catholicism in 1914. At the same time, his view of history became more oriented toward the past, mourning the decline of the Austrian empire and glorifying its history, especially the baroque age. Even though this conservative turn was typical for many Jung Wien writers, especially Bahr's friend Hofmannsthal, who coined the expression *Konservative Revolution*, one must give him credit for abstaining from politics rather than climbing on the bandwagon of national socialism. *Die Kinder* remains proof of his critical attitude toward racial mania. He depicted his intellectual and spiritual development in the autobiographical novel *Himmelfahrt* (1916) and his last attempt at a serious play, *Die Stimme* (The Voice, 1916).

Bahr's last dramatic works are nothing but the finger exercises of a retired dramatist; the title of a collection of three one-act comedies, *Spielerei* (Trifle, 1919), frankly acknowledges this fact. With *Der Augenblick* (The Twinkling of an Eye, 1917) Bahr tries to deal humorously with marital fidelity. *Der Unmensch* (The Brute, 1919),

Ehelei (Marriage Game, 1920), *Altweibersommer* (Indian Summer, performed, 1925; published, 1924) and *Die Tante* (The Aunt, 1928) are unambitious variations of Bahr's former comedies.

In 1922 Bahr moved to Munich, where his wife was teaching at the Akademie für Tonkunst (Academy of Music). There he finished his autobiography, *Selbstbildnis*, one of his best works. Like that of many of his comedies, the tone of this retrospection is conciliatory. Bahr died in Munich on 15 January 1934 after a long illness. He is buried in Salzburg, the city he praised as the cradle of his intellectual life.

While Bahr's accomplishments as a promoter of modernism in Germany and Austria soon fell into oblivion, his better comedies held their position among the most popular plays of the European repertoire. The post-World War II audiences appreciated the conciliatory attitude of his works, and his early withdrawal from the events of the time and preference for inwardness corresponded to the postwar spirit. Legal problems concerning his estate, however, ultimately prevented most of his artistic works from appearing in new editions.

Bahr's work is of interest for at least three reasons. First, he helped to insure the prominence of Jung Wien, and his personal development is exemplary for the history of this important intellectual movement. Second, his early works introduced the German audience to the European decadence movement. His effort to establish a peculiar form of modernism in Vienna was a struggle against aesthetic conventionalism and nationalistic politics. Finally, recent artistic and intellectual developments define themselves in opposition to modernism, the very movement Bahr helped to establish. Ironically, Bahr, like the recent proponents of postmodernism, expressed deep skepticism about overconfidence in reason and progress. Thus, plays such as *Der Meister* and *Ringelspiel* can still be seen as timely.

Letters:

Meister und Meisterbriefe um Hermann Bahr, edited by Joseph Gregor (Vienna: Bauer, 1947);

"Hugo von Hofmannsthal und Hermann Bahr: Zwei Briefe," edited by Rudolf Hirsch, *Phaidros*, 1 (1947): 85-88;

Hermann Bahr: Briefwechsel mit seinem Vater, edited by Adalbert Schmidt (Vienna: Bauer, 1971);

The Letters of Arthur Schnitzler to Hermann Bahr, edited by Donald G. Daviau (Chapel Hill: University of North Carolina Press, 1978);

Dichter und Gelehrter: Hermann Bahr und Josef Redlich in ihren Briefen, 1896-1934, edited by Fritz Fellner (Salzburg: Neugebauer, 1980);

"Hermann Bahr und Josef Nadler: Dokumentation einer Brieffreundschaft," edited by Karl Hopf, *Adalbert Stifter Institut des Landes Oberösterreich: Vierteljahresschrift*, 33 (1984): 19-51;

The Unpublished Letters of Richard Beer-Hofmann to Hermann Bahr, with the Unpublished Letters between Beer-Hofmann and Theodor Herzl, edited by Jeffrey B. Berlin and Mark H. Gelber (New York: Lang, 1986);

Stefan Zweig, *Briefwechsel mit Hermann Bahr, Sigmund Freud, Rainer Maria Rilke und Arthur Schnitzler*, edited by Berlin and others (Frankfurt am Main: Fischer, 1987).

Bibliographies:

Kurt Thomasberger, "Bibliographie der Werke von Hermann Bahr," in *Hermann Bahr: Ein Leben für das europäische Theater*, by Heinz Kindermann (Graz & Cologne: Böhlau, 1954), pp. 347-368;

Hermann Nimmervoll, "Materialien zu einer Bibliographie der Zeitschriftenartikel von Hermann Bahr (1883-1910)," *Modern Austrian Literature*, 13, no. 2 (1980): 27-100.

References:

Andrew W. Barker, "Der große Überwinder: Hermann Bahr and the Rejection of Naturalism," *Modern Language Review*, 78 (1983): 617-630;

Roger Bauer, "Gänsefüßchendékadence: Zur Kritik und Literatur der Jahrhundertwende in Wien," *Literatur und Kritik* (1985): 21-29;

Egon W. Brecker, "Hermann Bahr and the Quest for Culture: A Critique of His Essays," Ph.D. dissertation, University of Wisconsin—Madison, 1978;

Frank W. Chandler, "The Austrian Contribution: Schnitzler, Bahr, Schönherr, von Hofmannsthal," in his *Modern Continental Playwrights* (New York & London: Harper, 1931), pp. 435-465;

Emile Chastel, "Hermann Bahr, son oeuvre et son temps," Ph.D. dissertation, University of Paris, 1974;

Herbert Cysarz, "Alt-Österreichs letzte Dichtung, 1890-1914," *Preußische Jahrbücher*, 211 (1928): 32-51;

Donald G. Daviau, "The Friendship of Hermann Bahr and Arthur Schnitzler," *Journal of the International Arthur Schnitzler Research Association*, 5 (Spring 1966): 4-37;

Daviau, *Hermann Bahr* (New York: Twayne, 1985);

Daviau, "Hermann Bahr and Decadence," *Modern Austrian Literature*, 10 (June 1977): 53-100;

Daviau, "Hermann Bahr and Gustav Klimt," *German Studies Review*, 3 (February 1980): 27-49;

Daviau, "Hermann Bahr and the Radical Politics of Austria in the 1880s," *German Studies Review*, 5 (May 1982): 163-185;

Daviau, "Hermann Bahr and the Secessionist Art Movement in Vienna," in *The Turn of the Century German Literature and Art: 1890-1915*, edited by Gerald Chapel and Hans H. Schulte (Bonn: Bouvier, 1981), pp. 433-462;

Daviau, "Hermann Bahr as Director of the Burgtheater," *German Quarterly*, 32 (January 1959): 11-21;

Daviau, "Hermann Bahr in seinen Tagebüchern," *Literatur und Kritik* (1985): 485-495;

Daviau, "Hermann Bahr, Josef Nadler und das Barock," *Adalbert Stifter Institut des Landes Oberösterreich: Vierteljahresschrift*, 35 (1986): 171-190;

Daviau, "Hermann Bahr und der Antisemitismus, Zionismus und die Judenfrage," *Literatur und Kritik*, 23 (1988): 21-41;

Daviau, "Hermann Bahr's Cultural Relations with America," in *Österreich und die angelsächsische Welt II*, edited by O. Hietsch (Vienna: Braumüller, 1968), pp. 482-522;

Daviau, "Hermann Bahr's *Josephine*: A Revisionist View of Napoleon," *Modern Austrian Literature*, 12 (June 1979): 93-111;

Daviau, "Hermann Bahr's Nachlaß," *Journal of the International Arthur Schnitzler Research Association*, 2 (Autumn 1963): 4-27;

Daviau, *Der Mann von Übermorgen: Hermann Bahr (1863-1934)* (Vienna: Österreichischer Bundesverlag, 1984);

Manfred Diersch, "Hermann Bahr: Der Empiriokritizismus als Philosophie des Impressionismus," in his *Empiriokritizismus und Impressionismus* (Berlin: Rütten & Loening, 1973), pp. 46-82;

Rainer Dittrich, *Die literarische Moderne der Jahrhundertwende im Urteil der österreichischem Kritik: Untersuchungen zu Karl Kraus, Hermann Bahr und Hugo von Hofmannsthal* (Frankfurt am Main: Lang, 1988);

William A. Drake, "Hermann Bahr," in his *Contemporary European Writers* (New York: Day, 1928), pp. 184-191;

Amelia V. Ende, "Literary Vienna," *Bookman*, 38 (September 1913-February 1914): 141-155;

Reinhard Farkas, *Hermann Bahr: Dynamik und Dilemma der Moderne* (Vienna & Cologne: Böhlau, 1989);

Farkas, "Das spanische Buch Hermann Bahrs: Zur Diagnose des Dilemmas der Dekadenz," *Modern Austrian Literature*, 22 (1989): 1-14;

Jens Malte Fischer, "Hermann Bahr: Die gute Schule," in his *Fin de Siècle: Kommentar zu einer Epoche* (Munich: Winkler, 1978), pp. 100-114;

Walter Grünzweig, " 'Mit dem Phallus philosophieren': Hermann Bahr's Vision of Walt Whitman's 'Erotokratie,' " *Modern Austrian Literature*, 21 (1988): 1-12;

Hans von Gumppenberg, "Die Entdeckung: Ein Seelenstand. Von einem guten Schüler Hermann Bahrs," in his *Das Teutsche Dichterroß: In allen Gangarten vorgeritten* (Munich, 1966), pp. 100-114;

Willi Handl, *Hermann Bahr* (Berlin: Fischer, 1913);

Otto Michel Hirsch, "Hermann Bahr, der Novellist und Dramatiker," *Xenien*, 2, no. 11 (1909): 279-289;

Hugo von Hofmannsthal, "Die Mutter," in his *Prosa 1* (Frankfurt am Main: Fischer, 1950), pp. 16-23;

Hofmannsthal, "Zum Direktionswechsel im Burgtheater," *Neue Freie Presse*, 5 July 1918, pp. 1-2;

Manfred Jahnichen, "Hermann Bahr und die Tschechen," in *Slavische-Deutsche Wechselbeziehungen in Sprache, Literatur und Kultur*, edited by J. Belic, W. Kraus and V. I. Borkovskij (Berlin: Akademie, 1969), pp. 363- 377;

Dieter Kimpel and Reinhold Grimm, *Hugo von Hofmannsthal: Dramaturgie und Geschichtsverständnis* (Wiesbaden: Athenaion, 1981);

Heinz Kindermann, *Hermann Bahr: Ein Leben für das europäische Theater* (Graz & Cologne: Böhlau, 1954);

Bernhard Kleinschmidt, *Die "gemeinsame Sendung": Kunstpublizistik der Wiener Jahrhundertwende* (Frankfurt am Main: Lang, 1989);

Erwin Koppen, *Dekadenter Wagnerismus* (Berlin: De Gruyter, 1973);

Karl Kraus, "Die Überwindung des Hermann Bahr," *Die Gessellschaft*, 9 (May 1893): 627-636;

Helmut Kreuzer, *Die Boheme: Beiträge zu ihrer Beschreibung* (Stuttgart: Metzler, 1968);

M. E. Kronegger, "L'écrivain dans une Societé en mutation: Le cas de Hermann Bahr," *Literaturwissenschaftliches Jahrbuch*, 20 (1979): 173-182;

Friedrich Lehner, "Hermann Bahr," *Monatshefte*, 39, no. 1 (1947): 54-63;

Mary M. Macken, "Chronicle: Hermann Bahr, 1863-1934," *An Irish Quarterly Review*, 23 (March 1934): 144-146;

Macken, "Hermann Bahr: His Personality and His Works," *An Irish Quarterly Review*, 15 (March 1926): 34-46;

Thomas Mann, "German Letter," *Dial*, 75 (October 1923): 369-375;

Monika Meister, "Das kulturgeschichtliche Österreich-Bild im Wiener fin de siècle—dargestellt an der Grillparzer-Rezeption Hermann Bahrs," *Maske und Kothurn*, 31 (1985): 193-202;

Wilhelm Meredies, *Hermann Bahr als epischer Gestalter und Kritiker der Gegenwart* (Hildesheim: Borgmeyer, 1927);

Meredies, "Hermann Bahrs religiöser Entwicklungsgang," *Das heilige Feuer*, 15 (March 1928): 270-278;

Karl Johann Müller, *Das Dekadenzproblem in der österreichischen Literatur um die Jahrhundertwende, dargestellt and Texten von Hermann Bahr, Richard von Schaukal, Hugo von Hofmannsthal und Leopold Andrian* (Stuttgart: Heinz, 1977);

Josef Nadler, "Hermann Bahr und das katholische Österreich," *Neue Rundschau*, 34 (1923): 490-502;

Nadler, *Literaturgeschichte Österreichs* (Salzburg: Müller, 1951), pp. 397-406, 414-416;

Nadler, "Vom alten zum neuen Europa," *Preußische Jahrbücher*, 193 (1923): 32-51;

Herbert Nedomovsky, "Der Theaterkritiker Hermann Bahr," Ph.D. dissertation, University of Vienna, 1949;

Karl Nirschl, "Hermann Bahrs Wandlungen, gesehen durch seine Romane und Novellen," Ph.D. dissertation, University of Vienna, 1934;

Nirschl, *In seinen Menschen ist Österreich: Hermann Bahrs innerer Weg* (Linz: Oberösterreichischer Landesverlag, 1964);

Victor A. Oswald, "The Old Age of Young Vienna," *Germanic Review*, 27 (1952): 188-199;

Josef Plöckinger, *Hermann Bahr—der Herr aus Linz: Eine Dokumentation in Zusammenarbeit mit dem Adalbert-Stifter-Institut des Landes Oberösterreich und dem Archiv der Stadt Linz* (Linz: Stadtmuseum, 1984);

Percival Pollard, "Bahr and Finis," in his *Masks and Minstrels of New Germany* (Boston: Luce, 1911), pp. 290-299;

Jens Rieckmann, *Aufbruch in die Moderne: Die Anfänge des Jungen Wien. Österreichische Literatur und Kritik im Fin de Siècle* (Königstein: Athenäum, 1985);

Rieckmann, "Hermann Bahr: Sprachskepsis und neue Erzählform, *Orbis Litterarum*, 40 (1985): 78-87;

Christiane Zehl Romero, "Die 'Konservative Revolution': Hermann Bahr und Adalbert Stifter," *Germanisch-Romanische Monatsschrift*, 56 (1975): 439-454;

H. F. Rubinstein, "The German Bernard Shaw," *Forum*, 53 (January-June 1915): 375-379;

Felix Salten, "Aus den Anfängen: Erinnerungsskizzen," *Jahrbuch deustcher Bibliophilen*, 18-19 (1932-1933): 31-46;

Klaus Schröter, "Chauvinism and Its Tradition: German Writers and the Outbreak of the First World War," *Germanic Review*, 43 (March 1968): 120-135;

Robert Edward Simmons, "Hermann Bahr as a Literary Critic: An Analysis and Exposition of His Thought," Ph.D. dissertation, Stanford University, 1956;

Josef Sprengler, "Hermann Bahr—der Weg in seinen Dramen," *Hochland*, 2 (1928): 352-366;

Imma Übleis, "Hermann Bahr als Romanschriftsteller," Ph.D. dissertation, Innsbruck University, 1947;

Reinhard Urbach, "Hermann Bahrs Wien," *Literatur und Kritik* (1985): 404-408;

Peter Vergo, *Art in Vienna 1898-1918* (New York: Phaidon, 1975);

Peter Wagner, *Der junge Hermann Bahr* (Gießen: Druck der Limberger Vereinsdruckerei, 1937);

Robert Waissenberger, *Die Wiener Secession* (Munich: Jugend und Volk, 1971);

Erich Widder, *Hermann Bahr: Sein Weg zum Glauben* (Linz: Oberösterreichischer Landesverlag, 1963);

Viktor Žmegač, "Hermann Bahr als sozialgeschichtlich interessierter Kritiker," *Jahrbuch für Internationale Germanistik*, 17 (1985): 64-72.

Papers:
Hermann Bahr's literary estate is in the Theater Collection of the National Library in Vienna.

Ernst Barlach

(2 January 1870 - 24 October 1938)

Jochen Richter
Allegheny College

See also the Barlach entry in *DLB 56: German Fiction Writers, 1914-1945.*

PLAY PRODUCTIONS: *Der arme Vetter*, Hamburg, Hamburger Kammerspiele, 20 March 1919;

Der tote Tag, Leipzig, Leipziger Schauspielhaus, 22 November 1919;

Die echten Sedemunds, Hamburg, Hamburger Kammerspiele, 23 March 1921;

Die Sündflut, Stuttgart, Württembergisches Landestheater, 27 September 1924;

Der blaue Boll, Stuttgart, Württembergisches Landestheater, 13 October 1926;

Der Findling, Königsberg, Neues Schauspielhaus, 21 April 1928;

Die gute Zeit, Gera, Reussisches Theater, 28 November 1929;

Der Graf von Ratzeburg, Nuremberg-Fürth, Städtische Bühnen, 27 March 1952.

BOOKS: *Figuren-Zeichnen* (Strelitz: Hittenkofer, 1895);

Der tote Tag: Drama in fünf Akten (Berlin: Cassirer, 1912);

Der arme Vetter: Drama (Berlin: Cassirer, 1918);

Die echten Sedemunds: Drama (Berlin: Cassirer, 1920);

Der Findling: Ein Spiel in drei Stücken (Berlin: Cassirer, 1922);

Die Wandlungen Gottes: Sieben Holzschnitte (Berlin: Cassirer, 1922);

Die Sündflut: Drama in fünf Teilen (Berlin: Cassirer, 1924);

Der blaue Boll: Drama (Berlin: Cassirer, 1926);

Ein selbsterzähltes Leben (Berlin: Cassirer, 1928);

Die gute Zeit: Zehn Akte (Berlin: Cassirer, 1929);

Zeichnungen (Munich: Piper, 1935);

Fries der Lauschenden (Othmarschen: Privately printed, 1936);

Fragmente aus sehr früher Zeit (Berlin: Riemerschmidt, 1939);

Der gestohlene Mond: Roman. Nach Ernst Barlachs nachgelassener Handschrift, edited by Frie-

Ernst Barlach

drich Droß (Berlin & Frankfurt am Main: Suhrkamp, 1948);

Seespeck: Nach Ernst Barlachs nachgelassener Handschrift, edited by Droß (Berlin & Frankfurt am Main: Suhrkamp, 1948);

Sechs kleine Schriften zu besonderen Gelegenheiten, edited by Friedrich Schult (Bremen: Heye, 1950);

Fragmente (Güstrow: Schult, 1950);

Der Graf von Ratzeburg: Drama. Nach Ernst Barlachs nachgelassener Handschrift, edited by Schult (Hamburg: Grillen-Presse, 1951);

Güstrower Fragmente (Bremen: Ernst Barlach Gesellschaft, 1951);

Drei Pariser Fragmente (Bremen: Ernst Barlach Gesellschaft, 1952);

Kunst im Krieg, edited by Droß (Bremen: Ernst Barlach Gesellschaft, 1953);

Zwischen Erde und Himmel: 45 Handzeichnungen, edited by Carl Georg Heise (Munich: Piper, 1953);

Werkverzeichnis, 2 volumes, compiled by Schult (Hamburg: Hauswedell, 1958-1960);

Plastik, compiled by Wolf Stubbe, photos by Friedrich Hewicker (Munich: Piper, 1959);

Two Acts from The Flood: A Letter on Kandinsky; Eight Sculptures; Brecht: Notes on the Barlach Exhibition (Northampton: Printed at the Gehenna Press for the *Massachusetts Review*, 1960);

Eine Steppenfahrt, edited by Werner Timm (Leipzig: Graphische Kunstanstalt, 1961);

Zeichnungen, compiled by Stubbe, photos by Hewicker (Munich: Piper, 1961);

Das schlimme Jahr, text by Franz Fühmann (Rostock: Hinstorff, 1965);

Ernst Barlach Fragmente (Hamburg: Ernst Barlach-Gesellschaft, 1970);

Ernst Barlach: Das Wirkliche und Wahrhaftige: Briefe, Grafik, Plastik, Dokumente, edited by Fühmann, photos by Gisela Pätsch (Rostock: Hinstorff, 1970);

35 (Munich: Piper, 1974);

Güstrower Tagebuch, edited by Elmar Jansen (Berlin: Union, 1978).

Collections: *Das dichterische Werk*, volume 1: *Die Dramen*, edited by Klaus Lazarowicz and Friedrich Droß (Munich: Piper, 1956); volume 2: *Die Prosa 1*, edited by Droß (Munich: Piper, 1958); volume 3: *Die Prosa II*, edited by Droß (Munich: Piper, 1959);

Ernst Barlach: Prosa aus vier Jahrzehnten, edited by Elmar Jansen (Berlin: Union, 1964).

Editions in English: *The Transformations of God: Seven Woodcuts by Ernst Barlach with Selections from His Writings in Translation by Naomi Jackson Groves* (Hamburg: Christians, 1962);

Three Plays, translated by Alex Page (Minneapolis: University of Minnesota Press, 1964)—comprises *The Genuine Sedemunds, The Flood, The Blue Boll*;

Fulfilled Moments on a Higher Plane: From the German of Ernst Barlach, Glücksmomente im höheren Reich, translated by Groves (Hamburg: Ernst Barlach Haus, Hermann F. Reemtsma Foundation, 1971).

One of the best-known German sculptors during the Weimar Republic, Ernst Barlach also achieved recognition as a playwright after World War I. Although audiences never responded with great enthusiasm to his plays, literary critics generally agree that Barlach's dramatic work counts among the most important of the expressionist period. His plays attracted such directors as Leopold Jessner and Jürgen Fehling and such actors as Fritz Kortner and Heinrich George, and his play *Die Sündflut* (1924; translated as *The Flood*, 1964) earned him the prestigious Kleist Prize. After World War II, despite the defamation and suppression of his work by the Nazis from 1933 to 1945, Barlach's plays were accorded repeated productions with long runs.

All of the plays center around men and women who are trying to leave their earthly and limited existence in search of new, unknown forms of being. The urge to break out of the prison of everyday life suddenly comes over the protagonists, and from that point on they are groping for explanations, words, and actions to find a way to their metaphysical core. Concepts such as *Werden* (becoming, growing) and metaphors centered around the notion of *Weg* (road, way) dominate the plays. Since Barlach's major concern is inner development and growth, his plays have little action. In a tormenting, probing way, the protagonists are questioning themselves and others for the right way toward a goal they do not know. At times, this persistent questioning seems to separate from the action and turn into a struggle with language itself as the characters try to articulate that which cannot be expressed in words. His plays do not allow for concessions to audiences expecting to be entertained.

Ernst Heinrich Barlach was born in Wedel, a small northern German town near Hamburg, on 2 January 1870; he was the oldest of four sons of a financially struggling country doctor, Georg Barlach, and the former Luise Vollert. In 1883 Barlach's mother was committed to a psychiatric clinic; shortly after her return home the father died of pneumonia, leaving behind an unprovided-for family. In his autobiographical sketch *Ein selbsterzähltes Leben* (A Self-Told Life, 1928) Barlach gives a vivid account of these childhood experiences, all of which found their way into his dramatic oeuvre. He also emphasizes the strong influence of the small-town, northern German atmosphere, an influence that can be traced throughout his work.

In 1888 Barlach finished the Realschule (a school comprising the fifth to tenth grades and leading to a graduation certificate intermediate between those of Hauptschule and a gymnasium) in Schöneberg, Mecklenburg, and enrolled in the Hamburg School for Applied Arts. Three

Self-portrait of Barlach, painted in 1902

years later he entered the Dresden Art Academy, where he studied sculpture. After graduating from the academy in 1895 Barlach drifted for eleven years, searching for a sense of direction, purpose, and accomplishment. Moving back and forth among Paris, Hamburg, Berlin, and Wedel, he sank into a state of deep psychological crisis. Dissatisfied with his work, searching for his own style of expression, unsuccessful and unhappy in a six-month effort to establish himself as an art teacher, and suffering from constant lack of money, he saw himself as a failure and for a time contemplated suicide.

In 1906, however, two events changed Barlach's life and allowed him to find his artistic voice. The first was a two-month trip through Russia. Barlach was overwhelmed by the landscape and the people. In *Ein selbsterzähltes Leben* he describes himself as a person awakening from death and adds: "Ich sah, daß das Feld schnittreif meiner harrte" (I saw that the field was waiting for me, ready to be harvested). On his return to Berlin in September he began to model his first successful sculptures after the peasants and beg-

gars he had sketched on his trip. As media, he used mainly porcelain, terra-cotta, and bronze. The exhibition of these pieces led to a generous contract with the Berlin art dealer and publisher Paul Cassirer. Barlach's time of financial misery and artistic self-doubt had finally passed.

The second significant event had taken place in his absence: an illegitimate son, Nikolaus, had been born on 20 August. Barlach felt that the mother, a woman who had modeled for him, would not adequately care for his son and sued for custody. In 1908 the suit was decided in his favor.

The experience of the court battle and his efforts to resolve his feelings about his parents, his former lover, and his son found expression in his first drama, *Der tote Tag* (The Dead Day). Barlach began working on the play in 1907 and finished the manuscript in 1910, but it was not published until 1912. The play is symbolic in its basic texture but mixes the symbolism with a realistically dark and despairing atmosphere that seems to reflect the artist's state of mind before 1906. The protagonist, the Son, is struggling to escape the narrow confines of his mother's realm to prove himself in life. In this struggle he is supported by his unknown, godly father, who has sent him the steed Herzhorn as a signal for his departure. Although Barlach brings to the play a host of personal experiences, it transcends the merely biographical and explores the position of humanity in general. The Son is caught between the physical forces represented by the Mother and a spiritual principle attributed to the hidden father. By concentrating on the conflict between Mother and Son, Barlach created an original variation on the father-son conflict that dominates the early expressionist drama.

The Mother is associated with the subterranean. She prefers darkness, murkiness, and gloom and triumphs each night when the day has died. She is oriented toward the past and preoccupied with keeping her son dependent on her, since his independence would rob her of her role as mother. She is engaged in feverish activity to keep control over her son while all the other characters appear to be incapable of action.

Supported by the invisible gnome Steißbart and the blind character Kule, the Son struggles to break the bonds of his possessive, domineering mother. He is associated with the sun, dreams, and bird imagery. But when he tries to destroy the Alb, the nightmare which haunts all human beings, and thereby rid the world of fear and suffering, he fails and ends up calling his mother for help. To prevent the son from gaining his independence, the mother kills the steed. When the son uncovers her misdeed with the help of Steißbart, she stabs herself. The Son, who lacks the strength to break away from her, follows her into death. Although the play ends in despair with the suicide of Mother and Son, Barlach appends an important commentary which points toward his subsequent plays: it is not the deliverance from suffering and the attainment of the world of the father that is important but the act of searching itself.

As the allegorical quality of the play suggests, there is little room for character development. Alb, Besenbein, a spirit who serves as a domestic, and Steißbart do not change; Kule has surrendered all striving and has become an embodiment of passivity; the Son never leaves home despite his ardent desire to depart; and the Mother is concerned to maintain the status quo. This lack of development and action combined with the ever-present gloom prescribed by the

stage directions are serious flaws in Barlach's first drama.

After *Der tote Tag* appeared in print, it was seven years before it was produced on stage. The first performance, on 22 November 1919 in the Leipziger Schauspielhaus (Leipzig Playhouse), took place under the careful direction of Friedrich Märker. Märker had cut the text to a manageable length and used a stage with a timeless, fairy-tale-like atmosphere. The production was a success with the critics; but the audience seems to have been at a loss what to make of it, and it had only a short run. The pattern repeated itself in productions at the Neues Volkstheater (New People's Theater) in Berlin in 1923 and in Munich, Aachen, and Vienna in 1924. Although several critics, among them Thomas Mann, wrote favorable reviews, the audiences did not understand or like the play.

While he was still working on *Der tote Tag* Barlach began carving his first successful wooden sculptures; for them he was awarded the Villa Romana Prize, which allowed him to work in Florence in 1909. On his return to Germany in 1910 he settled in the small northern German town of Güstrow, and a period of great productivity followed. Between 1910 and 1914 he carved some of his best-known sculptures, finished the lithographs to accompany the published version of *Der tote Tag*, composed a series of prose fragments, and began to work on a novel based on his experiences before 1906; never completed, the novel was posthumously published as a fragment under the title *Seespeck* in 1948. In 1911 Barlach began working on his second play, provisionally titled "Die Osterleute" (The Easter People); he finished it in 1914 under the title *Der arme Vetter* (The Poor Relation, 1918).

The drama begins with a suicide attempt by the main character, Hans Iver, on Easter Sunday. His wound does not appear to be deadly, and he is taken to a nearby inn. There the other characters are forced to come to grips with him and his deed. Most of them react with indifference or even hostility. Only Lena Isenbarn sides with Iver; her fiancé, Siebenmark, after an intense inner struggle, joins the ranks of the indifferent and coldhearted. At the end Fräulein Isenbarn and Siebenmark break up, and Iver dies of his self-inflicted wound.

Der arme Vetter, like *Der tote Tag*, ends with the death of the protagonist; but it goes beyond the earlier play in developing and deepening the expressionist theme of the new man. Whereas the Son dies in desperation because he cannot equal the gods, Iver sees death positively, as a means to overcome his human limitations and a way of liberation. Barlach grants his protagonists the freedom to decide their own fate, and he expresses his trust in the divine core of human existence. While most of the other characters represent the old "Rattenleben" (rat existence) characterized by egotism, materialism, and longing for security and pleasure, a new way of being is emerging in Iver, who says: "Lieber ordentlich nichts als zweimal Halb" (It is better to be thoroughly nothing than twice [only] half). Fräulein Isenbarn overcomes Iver's disgust with and rejection of life; her presence hints at the possibility that human existence might have a positive, though obscure, meaning. Even Siebenmark raises at least the hope that those who are entrenched in the old, materialistic existence might be capable of changing.

The realistic element in *Der arme Vetter* is much stronger than that in Barlach's first drama. The play is firmly grounded in the northern German geography, atmosphere, and language. At the same time, the realism is constantly undermined by indications of an existential level beyond that of everyday banality. In this way Barlach creates an ambiguous reality where an inn near the river Elbe turns into a metaphor for the world and a dance in the inn becomes the dance of life.

The proper balance of these two levels of reality is a major requirement for a successful staging of *Der arme Vetter*. The first production of the play—the first production of any Barlach play—at the Hamburger Kammerspiele (Hamburg Intimate Theater) beginning on 20 March 1919 under the direction of Erich Ziegler did not strike that balance, and the reception was mixed. Barlach himself, who attended one of the performances, criticized the stylized sets and the lack of local color and authenticity. The breakthrough came on 23 May 1923, when Fehling directed a performance in the Berlin Schauspielhaus with George as Siebenmark. Fehling found the balance between down-to-earth reality and symbolic background. Twelve successful performances followed, and by 1933 the play had been produced on fifteen stages. After 1945 it was performed repeatedly in both East and West Germany; productions were staged in Basel, Frankfurt am Main, and Cologne in 1977, and in Hamburg in 1981. The postwar productions have interpreted the play as a precursor to the work of Samuel Beck-

Title page designed by Barlach for his play about a young man who seeks liberation from human limitations through death

ett or Harold Pinter, emphasizing Barlach's idiosyncratic and grotesque humor.

At the outbreak of World War I in 1914, Barlach volunteered to work in a children's day-care center in Güstrow. In December 1915 he was ordered to join the reserves and spent two months in the basic-training camp Sonderburg near the Danish border. He felt utterly out of place in the military and became increasingly disillusioned about Germany's role in the war. As a result of a petition signed by some prominent painter friends, including Max Liebermann, August Gaul, and Max Slevogt, he was discharged in February 1916. After his discharge he worked mainly on drawings, lithographs, and woodcuts for book illustrations. In 1917 he began writing his third play, *Die echten Sedemunds* (The Genuine Sedemunds), a comedy based on the seventh chapter of the novel fragment *Seespeck*; the chapter had been written in 1914 and titled "Der Löwe ist los" (The Lion Is on the Loose). The play was finished in 1919 and published in 1920.

The comedy, which mixes black humor with grotesque elements and moves from a fairground to a cemetery, is built around the problems of the Sedemund family. Young Gerhard Sedemund is lured home by his father, who wants to have him committed to an insane asylum. But the son and his friend Grude thwart the plan and force old Sedemund to confess publicly that he caused the death of his wife. A rumor that a lion has escaped turns the small northern German town where the Sedemunds live upside down and exposes the pretentiousness and corruption of the inhabitants. At the end order returns, and young Sedemund voluntarily withdraws into the madhouse. He leaves behind a humbled father and a more honest and sober society.

Again, Barlach creates a realistic small-town atmosphere with seemingly loving care, and he adds a good dose of his idiosyncratic humor. At the same time, he exercises harsh judgment on the pretentious, callous, and corrupt community. As in the previous two plays Barlach's major concern is not social criticism but the depiction of a foolish world that cannot overcome its meanness, pettiness, and brutality. Although several characters change or have at least some insights, the basic human condition remains one of pain and suffering. Despite Grude's pronouncement at the end that everything will change and that a new world has arrived, young Sedemund's withdrawal into the madhouse does not suggest a happy ending.

The first performance of *Die echten Sedemunds* took place on 23 March 1921. Again, Ziegler directed the company of the Hamburger Kammerspiele. By this time Barlach's stylized sculptures had become well known and must have suggested to Ziegler an abstract, expressionistic presentation rather than a more realistic one stressing the small-town milieu; the premiere was not a success, and the play ran for only six performances. On 1 April Jessner took the trend toward abstraction and stylization even further when his production opened at the Berlin Schauspielhaus. A dismayed Barlach, who attended a performance of the Jessner production, claimed that he did not recognize his own play and added that he would have booed even louder than the scandalized spectators. Critics pointed out the incompatibility of text and staging and the lack of dramatic organization and concentration around either a central figure or theme. The poor reception by audiences and critics cut the play's Berlin run short. A production in Darmstadt in 1924 did not fare much better.

One in Altona in 1935 directed by Kurt Eggers-Kestner and stressing the humor and sensual reality of the play met with much more success but was cut short because Barlach had been declared unacceptable by the Nazis. Since 1945 the play has been performed in West Berlin in 1958, Hannover in 1963, Hamburg in 1963, Schwerin in 1986, and East Berlin in 1988. Most productions followed Eggers-Kestner in staging the play as a multilayered comedy, and most were moderately successful.

In 1919 Barlach accepted an invitation to join the prestigious Prussian Academy of the Arts but turned down professorships offered by the academies in Dresden and Berlin. In 1920 his mother, who had lived with him since 1910 and taken care of his household and his son, drowned herself.

In the same year he began work on *Der Findling* (The Foundling), a play in three acts that was published, with twenty woodcut illustrations by Barlach, in 1922. In trying to deal with the catastrophe of World War I and its consequences, Barlach harks back to *Der tote Tag*. There is little of the realistic atmosphere that characterized the two preceding plays; instead, there are strong echoes of a medieval passion play. *Der Findling* is centered around the idea of the "Ekelkur" (cure through disgust). The old world and its inhabitants literally need to be devoured so that a new, less materialistic and more humane order can be established. The members of the old society are exposed as gluttons whose only purpose is the satisfaction of their physical needs; they make "Wurst aus Geist" (spirit into sausage). By taking this idea to its ultimate cannibalistic consequence, the play tries to show the turning point which reverses the process. The action takes place at the end of an apocalyptic epoch during which the Red Emperor had ruled. When the play begins, a group of starving people gather around the fire of the Stonemason, who has just slain the Emperor. The Stonemason serves them the Emperor as a meal, intending to demonstrate how low they have sunk to cure them through self-disgust. A conversion takes place—not through the people degrading themselves by their cannibalism but through two characters, Thomas and Elise, who do not partake in the meal. They overcome their self-disgust and self-centeredness by adopting the Foundling, a diseased, incredibly ugly, and miserable child of Father and Mother Sorrow. When they take the creature into their arms, it turns into a radiantly beautiful infant.

With this action, it is pronounced at the end, all the miserable children within all people have been converted. The "Ekelkur" theme has been abandoned; salvation occurs as the consequence of the altruism of Thomas and Elise.

The play's metaphysical and mystical themes cannot be adequately expressed in language, as Barlach himself seems to realize. One character, the Worshipper, admits: "Es geht nicht mit Worten zu . . . es fängt mit Stillschweigen an" (It can't be done with words . . . it begins with silence); but then he draws the paradoxical conclusion: "Ich muß reden, weil ich nichts weiß!" (I have to speak because I know nothing!). It is, above all, the excessive use of words that renders the play almost unbearable. For the first time Barlach tried to write in dramatic verse, using free rhythm and rhymed doggerel; the result is that the language becomes independent of the action. The rank growth of synonyms, metaphors, and images leads to a word inflation that obscures the intended message.

It is easy to see why the play could not be successful on stage; Barlach himself expressed doubts whether it could be performed. The premiere, on 21 April 1928 at the Königsberg Neues Schauspielhaus, confirmed Barlach's fears. The play was performed only once; no other attempts were ever made to stage it.

While continuing his rich production of sculptures, drawings, and woodcuts, Barlach set to work on his fifth play. *Die Sündflut* was written in 1923 and published and performed in 1924. It earned the prestigious Kleist Prize in the latter year.

The play is based on Genesis, chapters 6 and 7; Barlach questions the biblical story and discusses various concepts of God. The main characters are Noah and Calan, the latter a creation of Barlach's. Noah considers himself to be in possession of the true belief; Calan is searching for a belief. Noah passively accepts everything that happens as God's will; Calan actively challenges Noah and his God, going so far as to have a shepherd's hands cut off while Noah watches helplessly. Calan attributes the guilt for his deed to Noah and his God, since they let it happen, but Noah feels that he is innocent. At the end Calan dies in the Flood; but he accepts his guilt and shows mercy by sparing his servant Chus a torturous death, whereas Noah and his God neither show mercy nor are willing to accept guilt. Although physically defeated and dying a slow and terrible death, Calan triumphs morally over

Noah. Noah pictures the world as the result of a unique act of creation by a perfect creator; his world does not need change or correction. Anyone or anything challenging this view is evil and has to be eliminated; therefore the Flood is necessary. Calan perceives an imperfect world and feels called upon to perfect it. His search for perfection leads him into guilt, but through his guilt he finds salvation. He accepts his death as just punishment for his cruelty to the shepherd. His attitude, however, does not drown with him; by saving a place on Noah's ark for Awah, who carries Calan's child, Barlach assures the survival of Calan's ideas, promises hope for the future, and demonstrates the absurdity of the biblical Flood.

Of all of Barlach's plays, *Die Sündflut* is the most accessible to audiences. It has a clear structure; the language is unambiguous; and the meaning, which Barlach usually hides under the surface events, is elucidated by a sequence of commentaries. *Die Sündflut* turned out to be his most successful play, at least as far as the number of performances is concerned. After a well-received opening in Stuttgart on 27 September 1924, the play was staged twenty times before 1933. The response to these productions, however, was varied. In many cases the text was mutilated in such a way that its message was the opposite of Barlach's intentions; Noah was frequently played as the positive protagonist and Calan turned into the villain. All too often, the play was produced as a discussion piece on a barren stage designed to remind audiences of the artist's sculptures. Even after the war, such expressionist performances continued to obscure the humor and humanity of the play. But those productions which stressed the everyday atmosphere and played down the pathos had successful runs, most notably at the Hamburg Schauspielhaus in 1946 and at the Hannover Landesbühne (Hannover Provincial Stage) in 1952.

In 1925 Barlach was made an honorary member of the Munich Academy of Arts. During that same year he met the sculptress Marga Böhmer, who was to share the rest of his life. His next play, *Der blaue Boll* (The Blue Mr. Boll), was written in three months in 1925 and published, after two revisions, in 1926. On 13 October 1926 it was staged in Stuttgart at the Württembergisches Landestheater. It and *Die Sündflut* count as Barlach's most successful plays.

As in *Die echten Sedemunds*, the action takes place in a small Mecklenburg town much like Güstrow. The two main characters are Squire

Drawing by Käthe Kollwitz of Barlach on his deathbed, October 1938 (Dr. Hans Kollwitz, Berlin)

Boll, called "the blue Boll" because he looks apoplectic due to his licentious life, and Grete Grüntal, the wife of a swineherd. Both undergo a change which affects the other characters of the play as well. The encounter with Grete causes Boll to doubt his old life of indulgence: she offers herself to him in exchange for poison with which she can free her children from life in the flesh. Her request saddles Boll with the responsibility for the lives of her children. Boll is tempted by the offer of Grete's favors; but he overcomes the temptation, and a process of *Werden*, of change, begins.

Grete's radical negation of life is as wrong as Boll's self-indulgence and materialism. At the end, she returns to her family ready to resume her role as mother and wife, and Boll is facing a life of striving, suffering, and effort that will lead to a new existence. With this solution, Barlach overcomes the despair and disgust with life that dominated his earlier plays. Although they both contemplate suicide, neither Boll nor Grete follows the Son and Hans Iver into death; nor do they withdraw into the madhouse, like young Sedemund. They are striving for a synthesis of body and spirit, of earthly being and godlikeness, and the striving for a better world—"das Werden" itself—becomes the goal.

Der blaue Boll finds a balance between overt realism and underlying symbolism. There is an ambiguity which constantly introduces a deeper meaning into the everyday, small-town milieu and at the same time treats the inconceivable as something commonplace. This mixture of levels and the densely woven atmosphere, together with the naturalistic dialect of the characters, make an expressionist performance almost impossible. For that reason, *Der blaue Boll* was warmly received by most audiences. After a premiere in Stuttgart which was followed by only two more performances, Fehling's production at the Berlin Schauspielhaus on 6 December 1930 brought the play success. It received excellent reviews and ran for twenty-eight performances. On 26 March 1934 Eggers-Kestner staged the play at the Altona Stadttheater (City Theater). By this time Barlach had been blacklisted by the National Socialists, but the play ran for twelve performances. After the war *Der blaue Boll* was staged with success in 1961, 1967, 1981, 1983, and twice in

1985. Most productions used Fehling's as a model.

With *Der blaue Boll*, Barlach had reached his peak as a playwright. From 1926 to 1932 large sculpture projects, mainly in the form of public monuments, consumed most of his time.

The first version of his seventh play, *Der Graf von Ratzeburg* (Count von Ratzeburg), was finished in 1927. In 1932 he reworked the play, but his revisions were subsequently lost. *Der Graf von Ratzeburg* was posthumously edited by Friedrich Schult from the 1927 draft and published in 1951. Set in the late Middle Ages, it depicts the transformation of a count from a powerful landowner and ruler into a humble, selfless man who surrenders his authority and dies a martyr's death for his son. The play continues the theme of *Werden* but is crowded with religious themes which obscure the basic meaning. Two productions in 1952, in Nuremberg-Fürth and in Darmstadt, were failures.

Barlach's final drama, *Die gute Zeit* (The Good Time), appeared in print in 1929. Again there is a strong religious component in the play; it is mixed in an unfortunate way with a satirical attack on the hedonistic values of the 1920s. Countess Celestine is pregnant with a deformed child and must choose between abortion and bearing a degenerate heir. In the course of the play she gains more and more self-knowledge, and her willingness to sacrifice herself grows. Finally, she dies voluntarily on a cross in the place of an innocent boy. Although her child dies with her, she gives birth symbolically by saving the innocent child through her sacrifice. The unfortunate mixture of religious fervor, frivolous parody, and serious social criticism gives the play a disjointed character. The language is intended to be poetic but often sounds trite or sentimental. The only performance was held at the Reussisches Theater in Gera on 28 November 1929.

Between 1927 and 1933 Barlach was commissioned to execute war memorials in Güstrow, Kiel, Magdeburg, Hamburg, and other cities. His depiction of suffering and the expression of his pacifist attitude brought on the wrath of right-wing patriotic organizations, and he had to withdraw from several projects because of public pressure. In 1933 Barlach protested against this pressure in a public broadcast, and he also wrote a letter objecting to the exclusion of Heinrich Mann and Käthe Kollwitz from the Prussian Academy of Arts. He was decorated with the order Pour le Mérite, the highest honor that can be bestowed on a German civilian, one month after the National Socialists came to power. Despite the honor, his monuments were removed and destroyed, the Altona production of *Die echten Sedemunds* was closed in 1935, and a volume of his drawings was confiscated before they could be distributed. In 1937 he was labeled a "degenerate artist," and 381 of his works in public collections were confiscated. Despite the mounting demagoguery and public pressure, Barlach continued his artistic work and spent the last two years of his life working on a novel, *Der gestohlene Mond* (The Stolen Moon, 1948), which remained fragmentary; it is in the tradition of Alfred Döblin's *Berlin Alexanderplatz* (1929) and Hermann Broch's *Die Schlafwandler* (The Sleepwalkers, 1931-1932). On 24 October 1938 Barlach died of pneumonia in a clinic in Rostock.

As a sculptor, he has undisputedly claimed his place in his period and in the history of art. As to his merits as a playwright the verdict is not equally obvious. No history of the German theater omits his plays, but in most cases there are reservations about them. With the exception of *Die Sündflut* and *Der blaue Boll*, none of the plays has fared well onstage. Maybe Barlach has suffered from the stylized expressionist productions which were so much in vogue during his time, but even the more authentic postwar reinterpretations have failed to draw large audiences. All of his plays, however, have an intense searching quality that continues to attract directors and to reach and haunt viewers.

Letters:

Die Briefe I: 1888-1938, 2 volumes, edited by Friedrich Droß (Munich: Piper, 1968-1969).

Biographies:

Paul Schurek, *Begegnungen mit Barlach: Ein Erlebnisbericht* (Augsburg: List-Bücher, 1949);

Hans Franck, *Ernst Barlach: Leben und Werk* (Stuttgart: Kreuz, 1961);

Henning Falkenstein, *Ernst Barlach* (Berlin: Colloquium, 1978).

References:

Heinz Beckmann, "Die metaphysische Tragödie in Ernst Barlachs Dramen," *Veröffentlichungen der Ernst Barlach Gesellschaft* (1964-1965): 338-358;

Wolfgang Brekle, "Die antifaschistische Literatur in Deutschland (1933-1945)," *Weimarer Beiträge: Zeitschrift für Literaturwissenschaft, Aesthe-*

tik und Kulturtheorie, 16, no. 6 (1970): 67-128;

Edson M. Chick, *Ernst Barlach* (New York: Twayne, 1967);

Helmut Dohle, *Das Problem Barlach: Probleme, Charaktere seiner Dramen* (Cologne: Verlag Christoph Czwiklitzer, 1957);

Manfred Durzak, *Das expressionistische Drama: Ernst Barlach, Ernst Toller, Fritz von Unruh* (Munich: Nymphenburger Verlagshandlung, 1979);

Willi Flemming, *Ernst Barlach: Wesen und Werk* (Bern: Sammlung Dalp, 1958);

Karl Graucob, *Ernst Barlachs Dramen* (Kiel: Mühlau, 1969);

Margarethe Heukäufer, *Sprache und Gesellschaft im dramatischen Werk Ernst Barlachs* (Heidelberg: Winter, 1985);

Elmar Jansen, "Barlachs *Ein selbsterzähltes Leben*," *Marginalien: Zeitschrift für Buchkunst und Bibliophilie*, 52 (1973): 1-15;

Jansen, ed., *Ernst Barlach: Werk and Wirkung. Berichte, Gespräche, Erinnerungen* (Frankfurt am Main: Athenäum, 1972);

Klaus Günther Just, "Ernst Barlach," in *Deutsche Dichter der Moderne*, edited by Benno von Wiese (Berlin: Schmidt, 1975), pp. 456-475;

Herbert Kaiser, *Der Dramatiker Ernst Barlach* (Munich: Fink, 1972);

Helmut Krapp, "Der allegorische Dialog," *Akzente*, 1 (1954): 3, 210-219;

Otto Mann, "Ernst Barlach," in *Expressionismus: Gestalten einer literarischen Bewegung*, edited by Herrmann Friedmann and Otto Mann (Heidelberg: Rothe, 1956), pp. 296-313;

Walter Muschg, "Ernst Barlach als Erzähler," in his *Von Trakl zu Brecht: Dichter des Expressionismus* (Munich: Piper, 1963), pp. 244-263;

Muschg, "Ein Opfer: Ernst Barlachs Briefe" and "Der Dichter Ernst Barlach," in his *Die Zerstörung der deutschen Literatur* (Bern: Francke, 1958), pp. 84-109, 231-261;

Wolfgang Paulsen, *Deutsche Literatur des Expressionismus* (Frankfurt am Main: Lang, 1983);

Paulsen, "Zur Struktur von Barlachs Dramen," in *Aspekte des Expressionismus*, edited by Paulsen (Heidelberg: Winter, 1968), pp. 103-132;

Ernst Piper, *Ernst Barlach und die nationalsozialistische Kunstpolitik: Eine dokumentarische Darstellung zur 'entarteten Kunst'* (Munich & Zurich: Piper, 1984);

Jochen Richter, "Die Konzeption des 'Neuen Menschen' in Ernst Barlachs dramatischem Schaffen," Ph.D. dissertation, Syracuse University, 1975;

Wolfgang Rothe, "Ernst Barlach," in *Christliche Dichter im 20. Jahrhundert*, edited by Mann (Bern: Francke, 1970), pp. 269-285;

Friedrich Schult, *Barlach im Gespräch* (Wiesbaden: Insel, 1948);

Hans Schwerte, "Über Barlachs Sprache," *Akzente*, 1 (1954): 3, 219-225;

Ilhi Synn, "*Culpa Patris* in Barlach's Dramas," *Literatur in Wissenschaft und Unterricht*, 4 (1972): 158-166;

Synn, "The Language in Barlach's Dramas," *Revue des Langes Vivantes*, 37 (1971): 723-730.

Papers:

Ernst Barlach's manuscripts, diaries, and letters are at the Ernst Barlach Haus, Hamburg; the Barlach Memorial, Ratzeburg; and the Barlach Museum, Güstrow.

Ferdinand Bruckner
(Theodor Tagger)

(26 August 1891 - 5 December 1958)

Richard Critchfield
Texas A & M University

PLAY PRODUCTIONS: *Harry oder Die Komödie vom Untergang der Welt*, as Theodor Tagger, Halle, Stadttheater, 13 December 1920;

Annette, as Tagger, Vienna, Kammerspiele des deutschen Volkstheaters, 16 December 1920;

Te Deum, as Tagger, Berlin, Neues Theater am Zoo, 1 February 1922;

Esther Gobseck: Schauspiel in vier Akten nach Balzac, as Tagger, Berlin, Renaissance-Theater, 8 May 1923;

Krankheit der Jugend, Hamburg, Kammerspiele, 17 October 1926;

Die Verbrecher, Berlin, Deutsches Theater, 23 October 1928;

Die Kreatur, Munich, Kammerspiele, 27 February 1930;

Elisabeth von England, Berlin, Deutsches Theater, 1 November 1930;

Timon, Vienna, Burgtheater, 23 January 1932;

Heinrich von Kleist, *Die Marquise von O*, adapted by Bruckner, Darmstadt, Landestheater, 25 February 1933;

Die Rassen, Zurich, Schauspielhaus, 30 November 1933;

Napoleon der Erste, Prague, Tschechisches National-theater, 9 March 1937;

Gotthold Ephraim Lessing, *Nathan the Wise*, translated and adapted by Bruckner, New York, Belasco Theater, 3 April 1942;

Denn seine Zeit ist kurz, Bern, Städtische Bühnen, 5 September 1945;

Die Befreiten, Zurich, Schauspielhaus, 13 September 1945;

Heroische Komödie, Vienna, Volkstheater, 12 September 1946;

Fährten, Vienna, Burgtheater, 8 May 1948;

Simon Bolivar, Dresden, Stadttheater, September 1948;

Pyrrhus und Andromache, Zurich, Schauspielhaus, 16 February 1952;

Ferdinand Bruckner

Früchte des Nichts, Mannheim, Nationaltheater, 19 April 1952;

Die Buhlschwester, Berlin, Theater am Kürfürst-endamm, 23 December 1954;

Der Tod einer Puppe, Bochum, Schauspielhaus, 14 October 1956;

Der Kampf mit dem Engel, Brunswick, Staats-theater, 4 September 1957;

King Shūdraka, *Das Irdene Wägelchen*, adapted by Bruckner, Essen, Staatstheater, 29 October 1957.

BOOKS: *Von der Verheißung des Krieges und den Forderungen an den Frieden: Morgenröte der Sozietät,* as Theodor Tagger (Munich: Müller, 1915);

Die Vollendung eines Herzens: Eine Novelle, as Tagger (Berlin: Hochstim, 1917);

Das neue Geschlecht: Programmschrift gegen die Metapher (Berlin: Hochstim, 1917);

Über einen Tod: Eine Untersuchung, as Tagger (Berlin: Hochstim, 1917);

Der Herr in den Nebeln: Gedichte, as Tagger (Berlin: Hochstim, 1917);

Das neue Geschlecht: Programmschrift gegen die Metapher, as Tagger (Berlin: Hochstim, 1917);

Der zerstörte Tasso: Ausgewählte Gedichte, as Tagger (Leipzig: Wolff, 1918);

Auf der Straße, as Tagger (Vienna: Strache, 1920);

1920 oder die Komödie vom Untergang der Welt: Ein Zyklus, as Tagger, 2 volumes (Berlin: Osterheld, 1920)—comprises *Harry: Eine Komödie in fünf Akten; Annette: Komödie in drei Akten;*

Krankheit der Jugend: Schauspiel in drei Akten (Berlin: Fischer, 1928);

Die Verbrecher: Schauspiel in drei Akten (Berlin: Fischer, 1929);

Die Kreatur: Schauspiel in drei Akten (Berlin: Fischer, 1930);

Elisabeth von England: Schauspiel (Berlin: Fischer, 1930);

Timon: Tragödie (Berlin: Fischer, 1932);

Die Marquise von O: Schauspiel (Berlin: Fischer, 1933);

Die Rassen: Schauspiel (Zurich: Oprecht & Helbling, 1934); translated by Ruth Langner as *Races* (New York: Knopf, 1934);

Mussia: Erzählung eines frühen Lebens (Amsterdam: De Lange, 1935);

Denn seine Zeit ist kurz: Schauspiel (Zurich: Steinberg, 1945);

Simon Bolivar: Der Kampf mit dem Engel; Der Kampf mit dem Drachen (New York: Aurora, 1945);

Die Befreiten: Schauspiel in zwei Teilen (Zurich: Steinberg, 1945);

Fährten: Schauspiel (Vienna: Schönbrunn, 1948);

Heroische Komödie (Emsdetten: Lechte, 1955);

Der Tod einer Puppe; Der Kampf mit dem Engel (Cologne: Kiepenheuer & Witsch, 1956).

OTHER: *Marsyas,* edited by Bruckner, as Theodor Tagger, 1-6 (July-August 1917);

Psalmen Davids: Ausgewählte Übertragungen, translated by Bruckner, as Tagger (Berlin: Hochstim, 1918);

Blaise Pascal, *Größe und Nichtigkeit des Menschen,* translated by Bruckner, as Tagger (Munich: Müller, 1918);

Arthur Miller, *Der Tod des Handlungsreisenden,* translated by Bruckner (Berlin: Fischer, 1949).

SELECTED PERIODICAL PUBLICATIONS—
UNCOLLECTED: "Bizet," as Theodor Tagger, *Allgemeine Musikzeitung,* 35, no. 43 (1908);

"Hugo Wulfs Instrumentalkompositionen," as Tagger, *Allgemeine Musikzeitung,* 36, no. 11 (1909): 1f;

"Die französische Musik der Gegenwart," as Tagger, *Allgemeine Musikzeitung,* 36, nos. 33-39 (1909);

"Wiener Moderne," as Tagger, *Allgemeine Musikzeitung,* 38, no. 9 (1911): 1f;

"Der erste Bibliophil," as Tagger, *Die neue Rundschau,* 24 (1913): 880-883;

"Vom Tode," as Tagger, *Die neue Rundschau,* 24 (1913): 1046-1048;

"Brief an einen Juden," as Tagger, *Die weißen Blätter,* 2 (1916): 250-253;

"Leben in der Anoymität," *Querschnitt,* 2 (1929): 77-80;

"Gessler: Entwurf zu einem Film," *Das Wort,* 3 (1938): 10-20;

"Über Friedensziele," *Freies Deutschland,* 5 (1942): 9-10;

"Negerlieder in Amerika," *Ost und West: Beiträge zu kulturellen und politischen Fragen der Zeit,* 2 (1948): 21-30;

"Der alte Kasten," *Blätter der freien Volksbühne,* 4 (1955): 9-11;

"Einer neuen Tragödie entgegen," *Prisma: Blätter des Schauspielhauses Bochum,* 4 (1956-1957): 37;

"Symbole des Tragischen," *Wort in der Zeit,* 3 (1957): 18-24;

"Zum heutigen Stand der Tragödie," *Volk und Kunst: Zeitschrift der Volksbühne München,* 43 (1958): 3-4;

"Zu einer Umfrage über die Pariser Theateravangardisten," *Maske und Kothurn,* 1 (1958): 6.

In 1926 Theodor Tagger, writing under the pseudonym Ferdinand Bruckner, was acclaimed for the play *Krankheit der Jugend* (Sickness of Youth). It was at once Tagger's first great success as a dramatist and the beginning of a new career as Bruckner. Ferdinand Bruckner, who never again wrote under his real name, would go on to become one of the most prominent playwrights of the Weimar Republic. In taking his pen name from the playwright Ferdinand Raimund and the composer Anton Bruckner, Tagger was paying homage to both Austrian drama and Austrian music.

Theodor Tagger was born on 26 August 1891 in Sofia, in present-day Bulgaria, to a French mother and an Austrian father. His parents, who had been living in Constantinople, were on their way to Vienna at the time of his birth. The future playwright's childhood was not a happy one. His father was a businessman and a pragmatist, very much a man of the world. In family matters he was a strict authoritarian, and his plans for his son included a career in business. Tagger's mother, who worked as a translator, was interested in the arts, and it was she who kindled in him an abiding interest in literature. After her divorce from Tagger's father she married a French officer and moved to France. The artistically inclined Tagger, whose interests reflected those of his mother, clashed with his father over the question of his future profession. Attempting to become independent of his father, Tagger turned as a young man to free-lance journalism, writing articles on literature, philosophy, and music; for several years he worked unhappily as a reader for a German publishing house, a position he likened to a prison sentence.

Though he was equally attracted to music and to writing, Tagger studied piano and composition at the Paris Conservatory and in Berlin. The first turning points in his life and career occurred around 1916, when the impact of expressionism led Tagger to cease studying music and sell his piano. Expressionism first occurred in poetry and was highly subjective, often expressing the poet's internal visionary experiences. Tagger wrote a series of poems in this vein, and in 1917 he started an expressionist magazine, *Marsyas*, in Vienna. After World War I he turned to expressionist drama, with its satirical rejection and repudiation of bourgeois values.

In 1920 Tagger married Bettina Neuer. The same year brought the premieres of his comedies *Harry* and *Annette*, which were published together that year under the title *1920 oder die Komödie vom Untergang der Welt* (1920; or, The Comedy of the Downfall of the World). Both plays satirize the materialistic values of the German bourgeoisie in the early years of the Weimar Republic. Germany was undergoing the transition from monarchy to democracy and was in the beginning stage of a period of unprecedented inflation; the fixation on money of the figures in both plays must be seen against this background. Political and economic uncertainties tended to undercut the moral fabric of society, leading in the early 1920s to hedonism and materialism.

The plays, for all their shortcomings, are harbingers of later works by the mature Bruckner, particularly with their emphasis on the fate of youth victimized by a disoriented and decadent society. As the action of *Harry* begins to unfold it becomes apparent that the hallmark of postwar German society is a relentless and grotesque pursuit of money. Harry, the son of an unscrupulous moneylender, is a product of his time. But after a debauched night of gambling and drinking with money stolen from his father, he realizes that the intoxication of money, like that of alcohol, is of no lasting value. He decides to dedicate his life to hard, honest work. Harry's rebellion against the decadent world about him is futile, for his example finds no echo in a society consumed by greed; and his theft of his father's money, ironically, allows his heavily insured father to realize a profit. *Harry* points out a depraved and rampant materialism, but provides no solution to the problem; its figures lack depth and are types rather than well-defined characters.

Annette also focuses on the excessive and morally corrosive materialism of the time. The young and beautiful but calculating servant girl Anna marries an older man purely for financial gain. Following her husband's death and a sizable inheritance, she falls in love with Messerschmidt, a musician and a self-proclaimed idealist who ostensibly has dedicated his life to art and stands above the base materialism of the time. A caricature of the expressionist aesthete who scorned the prosaic realities about him while ensconcing himself in a world of art, he is in fact an unscrupulous opportunist; his sole interest in Anna is her money. In the end, Anna, whose social ascent rested on calculation and the repression of her feelings, becomes the victim of her love for Messerschmidt. The play depicts a demoralized society that allows no room for genuine human emotions.

Annette suffers from the same weaknesses as *Harry*. Its figures tend to be one-dimensional types, and the play fails to offer solutions to society's malaise. Still, these two early works reflect the playwright's interest in the questionable moral position of Germany's younger generation.

In 1923 Tagger and his wife moved to Berlin and founded the Renaissance-Theater, which still exists today. In addition to producing plays by Gabriele D'Annunzio, George Bernard Shaw, August Strindberg, and Luigi Pirandello, Tagger translated and adapted a series of French works for his theater. In addition, he wrote for his theater *Esther Gobseck*, drawing heavily on Honoré de Balzac's novel *Splendeurs et Misères des Courtisanes* (1838-1847). The work was performed in 1923, and while it was well received by the public, it was denounced by critics as shallow and offensive and as an exploitation of Balzac. Fearing that the critics were prejudiced against the name Tagger, he brought out his next play, *Krankheit der Jugend*, under the pseudonym Ferdinand Bruckner, the name he would use until his death; his true identity would remain an enigma for years to come.

Productions in Hamburg and Breslau in 1926 of *Krankheit der Jugend* were highly successful. The playwright had not only assumed a different name but he had begun to write in the style of "Neue Sachlichkeit" (New Objectivity), with its stress on a factual and objective and realistic rendering of social and political reality. An important influence on Bruckner's play was Sigmund Freud's psychoanalytic theory, with its focus on sexual drives and eroticism, a theme that also captured the interest of German and Austrian playwrights such as Arthur Schnitzler, Frank Wedekind, and Bertolt Brecht.

Krankheit der Jugend was acclaimed for its trenchant depiction and analysis of tormented and disoriented German youth. According to the critic Kurt Pinthus, no contemporary German dramatist had so convincingly and poignantly presented the torments and sickness of Germany's youth as had Bruckner. Looking back years later, Bruckner applauded himself for his perspicacious rendering of a generation destined to self-destruction and the destruction of the world about them. The play is set in a student residence in Vienna. Two of the principal characters are female medical students, the problematical countess Desiree and the middle-class Marie, who is a diligent student. The countess Desiree, a lackadaisical student and a lesbian, is disillusioned with life. The serious and diligent Marie cares for her friend Petrell, an unsuccessful poet and weakling. Another female student, the ambitious and manipulative Irene, seduces Petrell, where-

Drawing of Bruckner by Bato (from Hans Kaufmann, ed., Geschichte der deutschen Literatur 1917 bis 1945 [1973])

upon Marie, trying to compensate for her loss, is drawn to the seemingly stronger Desiree. The other male characters include the cynical, brutal, and eternal student, Fredel, who turns the servant girl Lucy into a prostitute. The play culminates in Desiree's suicide and Marie's desperate self-ordained murder at the hands of Fredel. *Krankheit der Jugend* presents the moral aberrations of a younger generation caught in a vicious and tragic world of seduction, murder, and suicide.

The production in 1928 in Berlin of *Die Verbrecher* (The Criminals) at the Deutsches Theater in Berlin met with even greater popular success and critical acclaim than had *Krankheit der Jugend*. The theme of *Die Verbrecher* is not the sickness of Germany's youth but the malaise of a whole society. Much more than *Krankheit der Jugend*, Bruckner's second play conforms to the literary tenets of Neue Sachlichkeit in treating a crisis in the justice system. Many other German dramatists and novelists were then attacking the legal system in the Weimar Republic, from the death penalty to the prohibition of abortion. *Die*

Verbrecher portrays a criminal justice system incapable of differentiating between true criminals and the victims of social injustice and poverty who transgress the law in moments of desperation. The play is set against the background of the unprecedented inflation that was impoverishing Germany in the 1920s. Its action takes place in a Berlin apartment building in which the true criminals live side by side with the innocent. The perpetrators of theft, extortion, murder, and the homosexual seduction of young men go unpunished, while a man is condemned to death for a murder he did not commit and a woman who kills her baby in a moment of desperation because she no longer has the money to feed the child is sentenced to a long prison term. The play is a protest not only against the courts but against the capitalistic and materialistic society which, in Bruckner's view, was ultimately responsible for the criminal acts his work portrays and in which those who have money or know how to acquire it go unpunished. Moreover, in *Die Verbrecher* Bruckner scrutinizes the very essence of the law, indicating that life contains a natural law governing its actions but that the fear of anarchy has led to the promulgation of laws which run counter to people's natural needs and aspirations. In its analysis of the problem of law, *Die Verbrecher* transcends its immediate theme of an inequitable justice system.

The three-story house used for the set of *Die Verbrecher* exemplifies a staging technique called *Simultanbühne* (simultaneous stage), which enabled the dramatist to present several story lines running parallel to each other. When the curtain went up the audience saw several separate rooms in which the stories of the various characters were about to unfold. Bruckner's use of the set also had a metaphorical significance: the separate rooms were meant to show that in the Weimar Republic people lived side by side but did not live together as a community. As a young judge in the play puts it, crime can be seen as a "dull, egocentric, side by side existence, of watching, of nonparticipation. Those are the only real crimes, since they have their origin in a complacency of the heart, an inertia of the spirit—thus a total denial of the principle of life and the idea of community."

In May 1930 Bruckner completed the historical drama *Elisabeth von England* (Elizabeth of England). The play was performed throughout Germany to universal acclaim and went on to become an international success. It depicts the power struggle between Protestant England and Catholic Spain, which ended victoriously for England in 1588 with the sinking of the Spanish Armada. The Simultanbühne is employed to present the two antithetical worldviews and the fates of Elisabeth and Philip of Spain. Reflecting the influence of Lytton Strachey's biography *Elisabeth and Essex*, Bruckner emphasizes Elisabeth's indecisiveness, moodiness, and sensuality, but also her realism and intellectuality. Her adherence to the dictates of reason is manifested above all in her commitment to peace in a world dominated by men who urge her to war. Philip is portrayed as an ascetic, fanatical exponent of Catholicism and as a king enamored of his own power. His irrationality and fanaticism are reflected in his statement that he would rather rule over corpses than heretics.

For dramatic effect, Bruckner conflates the struggle between England and Spain, which ended in 1588, with a subplot concerning the relationship of Elisabeth and her lover, the younger and ambitious Earl Essex, which terminated in 1601 with his execution. Essex, having unsuccessfully petitioned the queen to make his friend Francis Bacon a councillor of the crown, becomes a key player in an ill-fated attempt to overthrow Elisabeth. After signing his death sentence she is tormented by feelings of hate, repentance, and love. Disillusioned and overwhelmed by a need for revenge, she declares that she is ready to enter the war with Spain that she had so much wanted to avoid. Elisabeth emerges in Bruckner's play as a tragic figure in both her private and public lives, a woman deceived by the man she loved and a ruler who has entered a war she had tried so hard to prevent.

In 1931 Bruckner's interest was drawn to the issue of the artist's responsibility to society. The fruit of Bruckner's reflections on this eternal problem was *Timon* (1932). Bruckner took his material from William Shakespeare's *Timon of Athens* (1623), from Plutarch's *Alcibiades* and *Antonius*, and Lucian's *Timon; or, the Misanthrope*. The end product, however, was a very Brucknerian work, with a quite different message from the one in Shakespeare's play about the spendthrift who loses his money and his friends and withdraws into isolation and misanthropy. Looking back years later, Bruckner said that *Timon* was perhaps his most important play; it was certainly one of his most timely works. At the center of the play is the conflict of the aesthete with reality, or, put more precisely, the conflict of the artist with society. Timon, for whom the intellect is his most important possession, lives in a world of idealism, denying the prosaic realities about him. Seen from today's perspective, Bruckner's rendering of Timon was an apt and cogent analysis of the failure of the bourgeois intellectuals in the Weimar Republic to combat the rise and ultimate victory of Nazism. Timon, the intellectual and aesthete who desires to exist in the world of the mind, a world of splendid isolation, is superfluous in moments of political upheaval. Bruckner sets the action of his play at the time of Alexander the Great, the period of the political and cultural decay of Athens. The Athenians are preparing to wage a war against Alexander, who has in no way attempted to limit their freedom. Bruckner is clearly referring to the Weimar Republic and its eventual demise at the hands of the National Socialists and their supporters in industry. Unbridled nationalism, the longing for a heroic age, and the interest of the business class in militarism and war are characteristics Bruckner's Athenians share with the Germans of his day. As for Timon, it is only at the moment of death that he realizes that he has led a totally ineffectual life; in effect, he destroys himself by his self-ordained isolation. *Timon* was not as well received by critics and audiences as *Elisabeth von England*. The preponderance of dialogue over action and the play's didacticism may have contributed to its mixed reception.

With the victory of the National Socialists in 1933 Bruckner's worst fears became reality. His books were banned and burned. Like so many other intellectuals, against whom *Timon* was directed, Bruckner was forced into exile, returning only after the total collapse of Germany that *Timon* had symbolically prophesied. In 1933 Bruckner went to Austria and then to Paris, where he wrote the antifascist drama *Die Rassen* (published, 1934; translated as *Races*, 1934). The play was first performed at the end of November 1933 at the Züricher Schauspielhaus (Zurich Playhouse). Bruckner's intention was to show the political and psychological situation in Germany in March and April 1933, the period of the consolidation of Nazi power following the burning of the Reichstag in February. It was during this period that the first harassment and persecution of the Jews began to take place. The intellectual but apolitical medical student Karlanner is in love with Helen, the daughter of the wealthy Jewish industrialist Marx. But Karlanner is soon influenced by his fellow medical student Tessow into becoming

a Nazi, whereupon he breaks his engagement with Helen. Karlanner and Tessow are seduced by the promise that the Nazis are going to resurrect the glory of the German Empire, which was destroyed at the end of World War I. Karlanner submerges himself for a time in the mass hysteria and irrationalism of the Nazi movement; but he undergoes a second transformation when he becomes aware of the fanaticism and inhumanity of the Nazis. Ordered to arrest Helen, who is in the resistance, he rescues her instead—fully cognizant what his fate will be at the hands of the Nazis. Bruckner's criticism in *Die Rassen* is directed, on the one hand, against the irrationalism and anti-intellectuality then rampant in Germany and, on the other, against conservative German Jews. Helen's father belongs to the German National party and believes, as many wealthy Jews did at the time, that one can do business with the Nazis. He even assumes a racist stand, describing Eastern European Jews as inferior to their western counterparts. While *Die Rassen* holds out little hope for German youth in Nazi Germany, the play does challenge the Jews to action, namely to emigration. Helen leaves Germany; and the Jewish student Siegelman, after being tortured by the Nazis, decides to immigrate to Palestine, even if it means starting a new life as a farm laborer. Bruckner suggests that in Palestine the Jews will find a true community and a homeland. As *Races*, the play was performed in 1934 by the Theatre Guild in Philadelphia but met with little success. A Broadway production planned for the same year never took place.

Bruckner immigrated to the United States in 1936, settling in Hollywood; he moved to New York in 1937. Bruckner attempted to adapt his earlier works for the American stage, but he was never truly successful. Pressed by dwindling finances, he became a free-lance journalist and taught European theater at Brooklyn and Queens Colleges. In Bruckner's opinion one of his most important accomplishments in America was his translation and adaptation of *Nathan der Weise* (1779), the play on religious tolerance by Gotthold Ephraim Lessing. Directed by Erwin Piscator, *Nathan the Wise* was successfully performed in 1940 in New York. With *Nathan the Wise* Bruckner had wanted to show that a German had been one of the great and eloquent advocates of religious tolerance. In adapting the play Bruckner, at a time of German aggression and fanaticism, was drawing attention to the humanistic tradition of Germany which he and many of his fellow German writers, then living in such American cities as New York and Los Angeles, sought to present.

Bruckner wrote several plays during his exile in the United States, one of the most important of which, particularly for Americans, is *Die Befreiten* (The Liberated, 1945). Based on newspaper reports, the work deals with problems encountered by the American occupying forces with the populace of Italy. Written in autumn 1944, the play was first performed in Zurich in 1945. While the liberators and the liberated are united by the victory over Fascism, they are divided by their different psychological needs and their perceptions of the political realities of Italy.

The play takes place in an Italian town, whose patriots have helped to arrest and drive out the Fascists. But most of the town's populace has been adversely affected by the years of Fascism. The Americans, having the best intentions, wish to begin with the democratic reconstruction of the town and the punishment of former Fascists. Above all, they wish to establish "law" and "order." But such concepts as law and order, morality, and humaneness were overshadowed by the brutality of Fascism. The patriots of the town can only regain their self-respect and integrity by coming to grips with their Fascist past and the Fascists, who have still not been apprehended and brought to justice. Communication between the Americans and the Italians is further thwarted by formal American law, which has been imposed on the liberated town. Thus, while a former freedom fighter sits in jail, a former Fascist policeman and torturer goes free because he is a star witness in the trial of the town's Fascist commandant. This concept of law is totally alien to the Italians, who want the policeman brought immediately to justice. The patriots and former freedom fighters argue that the liberators have changed nothing with their concept of law and order: the Fascists continue to move about the town freely and are active in the black market, illegally purchasing ration cards. As in the past, they profit from the misery of others. Moreover, as a young girl emphasizes, Fascism was not only the political doctrine of Italy but a way of life: "In jeder Pore spure ich ihn. . . . Er klebt auf der Haut. Er sitzt in der Brust. Er sürgt am Hals" (it is in the pores of the people, in their bosoms, it sticks to their skin, it hangs about their necks). The central message of the play is that only the Italians can truly liberate themselves from Fascism. It is only after the Italians, in a civil court, condemn the former city commander to death that a young Italian

woman can say to an American lieutenant: "Jetzt sind wir wirklich auch: 'Befreite'" (Now we are truly liberated). The play is a reminder to the Germans that after they have been physically liberated from oppression, only they must still liberate themselves from a political ideology that has destroyed the moral fabric of their society through indoctrination, intimidation, and fear.

During a stay in Paris in 1950 Bruckner translated and adapted Arthur Miller's *Death of a Salesman* (1949) for the German stage; it was the first time a work by Miller had been translated into German. In 1953 Bruckner settled in Berlin, where he worked as a dramaturgical consultant at the Schiller Theater. He continued to write plays and adapt those of other dramatists until his death on 5 December 1958.

Letters:
"Briefe aus dem Exil," *Alternative*, 52 (1967): 7-15.

References:
Friedrich Baukloh, "Ein Forscher der Wirklichkeit: Der Dramatiker Ferdinand Bruckner," *Wort in der Zeit*, 2 (1956): 449-455;

Peter Bauland, *The Hooded Eagle: Modern German Theater on the New York Stage* (Syracuse, N.Y.: Syracuse University Press, 1968), pp. 117-118, 148-150;

Pia Buonomo, "Das Theater Ferdinand Bruckners: Die Hauptideen in den dramatischen Werken," Ph. D. dissertation, University of Naples, 1955;

Roy C. Cowen, "Das Positive im Negativen: Ein Problem der frühen Exilliteratur erläutert am Beispiel von Ferdinand Bruckners *Die Rassen*," *Kontroversen, alte und neue*, 5 (1986): 215-219;

Franz Theodor Csokor, "Größe und Nichtigkeit des Menschen: Zum Hinscheiden des Dichters Ferdinand Bruckner," *Wort in der Zeit*, 5 (1959): 3-6;

Doris Engelhardt, "Ferdinand Bruckner als Kritiker seiner Zeit: Standortsuche eines Autors," Ph. D. dissertation, Technische Hochschule, Aachen, 1984;

Anthony J. Harper, "Ferdinand Bruckner's Treatment of the Timon Theme," *German Life and Letters*, 17 (1963-1964): 259-269;

Karin Hörner, *Möglichkeit und Grenzen der Simultandramatik, unter besonderer Berücksichtigung der Simultandramen Ferdinand Bruckners* (Bern: Lang, 1986);

Wulf Koepke, "Die Wirkung des Exils auf Ferdinand Bruckners aktuelle Dramen," *Jahrbuch für Internationale Germanistik*, 3 (1981): 103-112;

Christiane Lehfeldt, *Der Dramatiker Ferdinand Bruckner* (Göppingen: Kümmerle, 1975);

Otto Mann, "Ekurs über Ferdinand Bruckner," Deutsche Literatur im 20, Jahrundert, edited by Mann and Hermann Friedmann (Heidelberg: Rothe, 1961), pp. 162-178;

Dennis M. Mueller, "Ferdinand Bruckner," in *Deutsche Exilliteratur seit 1933*, volume 2, part 1, edited by John M. Spalek and Joseph Strelka (Bern: Francke, 1989), pp. 161-177;

Maria Lay Piscator, *The Piscator Experiment: The Political Theater* (London: Feffer & Simon, 1967), pp. 136-137, 168-169;

Helene Scher, "British Queens in German Drama: Elizabeth and Mary in Plays by Schiller, Bruckner and Hildesheimer," *Theatrum Mundi: Essays on German Drama and German Literature dedicated to Harold Lenz on His Seventieth Birthday, September 11, 1978*, edited by Edward R. Haymes (Munich: Fink, 1980), pp. 353-370;

Fritz Schiefert, "Ferdinand Bruckner," *Maske und Kothurn*, 4 (1958): 358-370;

Sibylle Selbmann, "Die dramaturgischen Prinzipien Ferdinand Bruckners," Ph.D. dissertation, Freie Universität, Berlin, 1970;

Walter H. Speidel, "Tragik und Tragödie in der dichterischen Entwicklung Ferdinand Bruckners," Ph.D. dissertation, University of Utah, 1960;

Peter Szondi, *Theories of the Modern Drama*, translated and edited by Michael Hays (Minneapolis: University of Minnesota Press, 1987), pp. 73-76;

Hans-Christoph Wächter, *Theater im Exil. Sozialgeschichte des deutschen Exiltheaters 1933-1945* (Munich: Hanser, 1973), pp. 172-175.

Papers:

Manuscripts, unpublished letters, diaries, and other materials of Ferdinand Bruckner are at the Akademie der Künste (Academy of Arts), Berlin.

Paul Ernst

(7 March 1866 - 13 May 1933)

Jürgen G. Sang
University of Hawaii

See also the Ernst entry in *DLB 66: German Fiction Writers, 1885-1913*.

PLAY PRODUCTIONS: *Lumpenbagasch*, Berlin, Theater der Urania, 27 March 1898;

Im Chambre séparée, Berlin, Theater der Urania, 14 May 1899;

Die schnelle Verlobung, Berlin, Dramatische Gesellschaft, 14 May 1899;

Wenn die Blätter fallen, Berlin, Dramatische Gesellschaft, 14 May 1899;

Demetrios, Weimar, Nationaltheater, 5 March 1910;

Eine Nacht in Florenz, Düsseldorf, Schauspielhaus, 20 September 1910;

Ninon de Lenclos, Dresden, Schauspielhaus, 31 March 1911;

Brunhild, Munich, Residenztheater, 7 April 1911;

Der Hulla, Dresden, Schauspielhaus, 9 November 1911;

Ariadne auf Naxos, Weimar, Nationaltheater, 26 February 1914;

Ritter Lanval, Friedrichroda, Freilichtbühne, 3 July 1914;

Preußengeist, Weimar, Nationaltheater, 27 November 1915;

Über alle Narrheit Liebe, Nuremberg, Stadttheater, 30 January 1918;

Manfred und Beatrice, Frankfurt am Main, Schauspielhaus, 27 February 1918;

Canossa, Stuttgart, Landestheater, 1918;

Chriemhild, Mannheim, Nationaltheater, 15 February 1924;

Der heilige Crispin, Bonn, Schauspielhaus, 5 November 1927;

Kassandra, Weimar, Nationaltheater, 11 April 1931;

Pantalon und seine Söhne, Königsberg, Neues Schauspielhaus, 10 September 1933;

York, Aachen, Stadttheater, 11 October 1933.

BOOKS: *Leo Tolstoi und der slavische Roman* (Berlin: Brachvogel, 1889);

Paul Ernst

Die Arbeiterschutzgesetzgebung und ihre internationale Regelung (Berlin: Buchhandlung "Vorwärts," 1890);

Pêle Mêle (Berlin, 1892);

Der Capitalismus fin de siècle, by Ernst and R. Meyer (Vienna: Austria, 1894);

Die gesellschaftliche Reproduktion des Kapitals bei gesteigerter Produktivität der Arbeit (Berlin-Wilmersdorf: Teistler, 1894);

Lumpenbagasch; Im Chambre séparée: Zwei Schauspiele (Berlin: Sassenbach, 1898);

Polymeter (Berlin: Sassenbach, 1898);

Die schnelle Verlobung: Lustspiel in einem Akt (Berlin: Entsch, 1899);

Sechs Geschichten (Leipzig: Insel, 1900);

Friedrich Nietzsche (Berlin: Gose & Tetzlaff, 1900);

Wenn die Blätter fallen; Der Tod: Zwei Trauerspiele (Berlin: Sassenbach, 1900);

Die Prinzessin des Ostens und andere Novellen (Leipzig: Insel, 1903);

Beatrice und Deflores: Trauerspiel in vier Aufzügen (Berlin: Deutsche Bühne, 1904);

Henrik Ibsen (Berlin: Schuster & Loeffler, 1904);

Der schmale Weg zum Glück: Roman (Stuttgart: Deutsche Verlags-Anstalt, 1904);

Demetrios: Tragödie in fünf Akten (Leipzig: Insel, 1905);

Eine Nacht in Florenz: Lustspiel in vier Aufzügen (Leipzig: Insel, 1905);

Sophokles (Berlin: Schuster & Loeffler, 1905);

Das Gold: Trauerspiel in vier Aufzügen (Berlin: Bard, 1906);

Der Hulla: Lustspiel in vier Aufzügen (Berlin: Bard, 1906; revised edition, Berlin: Meyer & Jessen, 1912);

Ritter Lanval: Lustspiel in drei Aufzügen (Leipzig: Insel, 1906);

Merope oder vom Wesen des Tragischen: Eine Abhandlung (Berlin: Bard, 1906);

Der Weg zur Form: Ästhetische Abhandlungen vornehmlich zur Tragödie und Novelle (Leipzig: Insel, 1906; revised edition, Berlin: Hyperion, 1915);

Der Harz (Stuttgart: Krabbe, 1907);

Canossa: Ein Trauerspiel in fünf Aufzügen (Leipzig: Insel, 1908; revised edition, Munich: Müller, 1922);

Brunhild: Trauerspiel in drei Aufzügen (Leipzig: Insel, 1909);

Die selige Insel: Ein Roman (Leipzig: Insel, 1909);

Über alle Narrheit Liebe: Lustspiel in drei Aufzügen (Leipzig: Insel, 1909);

Ninon de Lenclos: Trauerspiel in drei Aufzügen (Leipzig: Insel, 1910);

Ariadne auf Naxos: Ein Schauspiel in drei Aufzügen (Weimar: Gesellschaft der Bibliophilen, 1912);

Ein Credo, 2 volumes (Berlin: Meyer & Jessen, 1912);

Der Tod des Cosimo (Berlin: Meyer & Jessen, 1912);

Der heilige Crispin: Lustspiel in fünf Aufzügen (Berlin: Meyer & Jessen, 1913);

Die Hochzeit: Ein Novellenbuch (Berlin & Vienna: Meyer & Jessen, 1913);

Manfred und Beatrice: Schauspiel in drei Aufzügen (Berlin: Verlag der Neuen Blätter, 1913);

Preußengeist: Schauspiel in drei Aufzügen (Leipzig: Reclam, 1915);

Saat auf Hoffnung: Roman (Berlin: Hyperion-Verlag, 1916);

Die Taufe: Novellen (Munich: Müller, 1916);

Kassandra: Schauspiel in fünf Aufzügen (Munich: Müller, 1916);

Pantalon und seine Söhne: Lustspiel in drei Aufzügen (Munich: Muller, 1916);

Gesammelte Werke, 13 volumes (Munich: Müller, 1916-1922);

Die Zerstörung der Ehe (Darmstadt: Falken, 1917);

Chriemhild: Trauerspiel in drei Aufzügen (Munich: Müller, 1918);

Der Zusammenbruch des Marxismus (Munich: Müller, 1919); enlarged as *Grundlagen der neuen Gesellschaft*, volume 5 of *Gesammelte Werke* (Munich: Müller, 1930);

Komödiantengeschichten (Munich: Müller, 1920);

Spitzbubengeschichten (Munich: Müller, 1920);

Die Venus: Novellen (Heidelberg: Meister, 1920);

Geist, werde wach! Ein Aufruf zur Revolution (Munich: Müller, 1921);

Fünf Novellen (Leipzig: Insel, 1921);

Bemerkungen über mein Leben (Chemnitz: Gesellschaft der Bücherfreunde, 1922);

Occultistische Novellen (Munich: Müller, 1922);

Zusammenbruch und Glaube (Munich: Beck, 1922);

Das Kaiserbuch: Ein Epos in drei Teilen. Teil I: Die Sachsenkaiser (Munich: Hueber, 1923);

Geschichten aus dem Süden (Berlin: Deutsche Buchgemeinschaft, 1925);

Das Kaiserbuch: Die Sachsenkaiser II (Ebersberg: Vereinigung für die Paul-Ernst-Spende, 1926);

Der Schatz im Morgenbrotstal: Roman (Berlin-Grunewald: Horen-Verlag, 1926);

Das Kaiserbuch: Die Frankenkaiser, 2 volumes (Ebersberg: Vereinigung für die Paul-Ernst-Spende, 1927);

Das Kaiserbuch: Die Schwabenkaiser, 2 volumes (Ebersberg: Paul-Ernst-Spende, 1928);

Geschichten von deutscher Art (Munich: Müller, 1928);

Gesammelte Werke, 21 volumes (Munich: Müller/Langen-Müller, 1928-1942);

Die Troubadourgeschichten: Das Liebesabenteuer der beiden Frauen (Berlin: Deutsche Buchgemeinschaft, 1929);

Der Heiland: Ein Epos in Versen (Munich: Müller, 1930);

Jugenderinnerungen (Munich: Müller, 1930);

Jünglingsjahre (Munich: Müller, 1931);

Die Kraft zum Leben (Chemnitz: Gesellschaft der Bücherfreunde, 1931);

Beten und Arbeiten: Gedichte (Munich: Müller, 1932);

Mein dichterisches Erlebnis (Berlin: Buchholz & Weißwange, 1933);

Das Glück von Lautenthal: Roman (Munich: Langen-Müller, 1933);

Religion (Berlin: Buchholz & Weißwange, 1933);

Deutsche Geschichten (Munich: Langen-Müller, 1934);

York: Schauspiel, completed by Adolf Potthoff (Munich: Langen-Müller, 1934);

Gedichte und Sprüche (Munich: Langen-Müller, 1935);

Aus dem Nachlaß (Chemnitz: Gesellschaft der Bücherfreunde zu Chemnitz, 1935);

Der unvollendete letzte Roman (Langensalza: Beltz, 1935);

Politische Studien und Kritiken: Aufsätze aus den Jahren 1894-1902 (Langensalza: Beltz, 1938);

Völker und Zeiten im Siegel ihrer Dichtung, volume 1: *Aufsätze zur Weltliteratur* (Munich: Langen-Müller, 1940); volume 2: *Aufsätze zur deutschen Literatur* (Munich: Langen-Müller, 1942); volume 1 revised as *Gedanken zur Weltliteratur: Aufsätze*, edited by Karl August Kutzbach (Gütersloh: Bertelsmann, 1959);

Childerich: Trauerspiel in drei Akten (Düsseldorf: Paul-Ernst-Gesellschaft, 1959).

OTHER: *Altitaliänische Novellen*, 2 volumes, translated and edited by Ernst (Leipzig: Insel, 1902);

Achim von Arnim, *Isabella von Aegypten*, edited by Ernst (Leipzig: Insel, 1903);

Des Knaben Wunderhorn: Alte deutsche Lieder, collected by Achim von Arnim and Clemens Brentano, edited by Ernst (Leipzig & Berlin: Meyer, 1903);

Bettina von Arnim, *Die Günderode*, 2 volumes, introduction by Ernst (Leipzig: Insel, 1904);

Annette von Droste-Hülshoff, *Die Judenbuche*, afterword by Ernst (Leipzig: Insel, 1904);

Friedrich Hölderlin, *Gedichte*, edited by Ernst (Jena: Diederichs, 1905);

Stephen Phillips, *Paolo und Francesca: Trauerspiel in vier Akten*, translated by Ernst (Düsseldorf: Düsseldorfer Schauspielhaus, 1905);

Jörg Wickram, *Der Goldfaden*, edited by Ernst (Munich: Piper, 1905);

Bettina von Arnim, *Clemens Brentanos Frühlingskranz*, 2 volumes, introduction by Ernst, (Leipzig: Insel, 1907);

Hans Jakob Christoffel von Grimmelshausen, *Simplicianische Schriften*, afterword by Ernst (Leipzig: Insel, 1907);

Johann Gottfried Schnabel, *Der im Irrgarten der Liebe herumtaumelnde Cavalier*, edited by Ernst (Munich: Müller, 1907);

Wilhelm Meinhold, *Maria Schweidler, die Bernsteinhexe: Historischer Roman*, edited by Ernst (Leipzig: Insel, 1908);

Johannes Praetorius, *Rübezahlgeschichten*, edited by Ernst (Leipzig: Insel, 1908);

Joseph von Eichendorff, *Gesammelte Werke*, volume 1: *Der Gedichte erster Band*, edited by Ernst (Munich & Leipzig: Müller, 1909);

Altfranzösische Novellen, 2 volumes, translated by Paul Hansmann, edited by Ernst (Leipzig: Insel, 1909);

Tausend und ein Tag: Orientalische Erzählungen, 4 volumes, translated by F. P. Greve and Hansmann, edited by Ernst (Leipzig: Insel, 1909);

Johann Christoph Biernatzki, *Die Hallig*, edited by Ernst (Berlin: Meyer & Jessen, 1910);

Jakob and Wilhelm Grimm, *Kinder- und Hausmärchen*, 3 volumes, edited by Ernst (Munich: Müller, 1910);

Geschichten aus dem alten Pitaval: Herausgegeben nach der von Schiller getroffenen Auswahl und um weitere Stücke vermehrt, 3 volumes, edited by Ernst (Leipzig: Insel, 1910);

Spielmanns-Geschichten, edited by Ernst (Munich: Müller, 1910);

Hans Christian Andersen, *Märchen und Geschichten*, 2 volumes, edited by Ernst (Weimar: Kiepenheuer, 1911);

Bibliothek der Romane, 10 volumes, edited by Ernst (Leipzig: Insel, 1911);

Das Buch der Liebe, 2 volumes, edited by Ernst (Munich: Müller, 1911); revised as *Die deutschen Volksbücher*, 1 volume (Berlin: Deutsche Buchgemeinschaft, 1927);

Meinhold, *Sidonia von Bork, die Klosterhexe*, 2 volumes, edited by Ernst (Leipzig: Insel, 1911);

1001 Nacht: Auswahl in vier Bänden, 4 volumes, edited by Ernst (Leipzig: Insel, 1911);

Des Herrn von Münchhausen Tischgespräche, edited by Ernst and Hansmann (Munich: Müller, 1912);

Ginés Pérez de Hita, *Die Geschichte der Bürgerkriege von Granada*, 2 volumes, translated by Ernst and P. Weiland, foreword by Ernst (Munich & Leipzig: Müller, 1913);

Altdeutsche Mären und Schwänke, edited by Ernst (Munich & Leipzig: Müller, 1913);

Johann Georg Lichtenberg, *Sittenbilder*, 2 volumes, edited by Ernst (Weimar: Kiepenheuer, 1913);

Erzählungen aus Tausendundeine Nacht, edited by Ernst (Weimar: Kiepenheuer, 1913);

William Makepeace Thackeray, *Die Geschichte des Henry Esmond,* translated by Else von Schorn, afterword by Ernst (Leipzig: Insel, 1913);

Johann Wolfgang von Goethe, *Novellen und Märchen,* foreword by Ernst (Berlin: Cassirer, 1914);

Herodotus, *Orientalische Königsgeschichten,* introduction by Ernst (Berlin & Vienna: Ullstein, 1916);

Longus, *Daphnis und Chloë,* translated by Friedrich Jacobs, introduction by Ernst (Weimar: Kiepenheuer, 1917);

Griechische und albanesische Märchen, 2 volumes, collected and translated by J. G. von Hahn, foreword by Ernst (Munich: Müller, 1918);

"Der sittliche Mut," in Wilhelm Schäfer, *An mein Volk* (Jena: Diederichs, 1918);

Sindbad der Seefahrer; Die Geschichte der Prinzessin von Deryabar, edited by Ernst (Potsdam: Müller, 1920);

Ludwig Tieck, *Märchen und Geschichten,* 2 volumes, edited by Ernst (Berlin: Propyläen, 1921);

Goethe, *Dramen der Mannesjahre,* introduction by Ernst (Berlin: Ullstein, 1923);

Henry Fielding, *Tom Jones: Die Geschichte eines Findlings,* translated by Paul Baudisch, afterword by Ernst (Leipzig: List, 1925);

Lily Hohenstein, *Das Kind und die Wundmale: Roman,* foreword by Ernst (Berlin: Deutsche Buchgemeinschaft, 1929).

There is no doubt about Paul Ernst's talent for writing novellas and short stories. His dramas, however, are not of equal value with his narrative works. The meaning behind the plots of his more than two dozen colorful one-act plays, comedies, and tragedies often eludes readers and viewers alike. The dramas present an ideologically erratic spirit which was also reflected in Ernst's personal struggles with political and aesthetic issues.

Karl Friedrich Paul Ernst was born on 7 March 1866 in Elbingerode to Johann Christian Friedrich Wilhelm Ernst, a mine foreman, and Charlotte Dittmann Ernst. In 1885 he studied theology and philosophy at the universities of Göttingen and Tübingen. In the fall of 1886 he moved to Berlin, where he joined the literary society "Durch" (Through) and became involved in the socialist movement. He studied history, litera-

ture, and economics at the universities of Berlin and Bern, receiving his doctorate from the latter institution in 1892. In 1895 he became a freelance writer in Berlin, where he associated with Arno Holz, Johannes Schlaf, Bruno Wille, and Richard Dehmel. His earliest plays were naturalistic in character, but in 1900, after a trip to Italy, he turned briefly to neoromanticism and then to neoclassicism. At about the same time, he renounced his leftist political views. He lived in Weimar from 1903 to 1914, except for the years 1904-1905, which he spent as a dramaturge in Düsseldorf. In 1914 he returned to Berlin. He lived from 1918 to 1925 in Upper Bavaria, and from 1925 until his death on 13 May 1933 in Sankt Georgen, Austria.

When Ernst started to have his dramatic writings published he was past thirty. He had committed himself to search for a new dramatic form; this quest became an existential battle to define individual ethics in a God-forlorn world. In the process Ernst had given up on Shakespeare, the German classics, naturalism, the psychological theater, and mime because they did not reflect the idea of ethical purification he wanted to express. Most of Ernst's plays were performed during the 1920s and 1930s. They were successful only when expertly directed and performed by a superb cast.

Lumpenbagasch (Riff-raff) is one of two plays published together in 1898 that still display the author's early socialism. Written in heavy Saxon dialect, it excels in showing the nature of the frightening, the ridiculous, and the profane. A tailor and the mayor of a small farming village try to exploit two poor villagers by inducing them to marry so that the tailor and the mayor can pocket the saved welfare money. Luise and Sebastian, however, catch on to the ruse and refuse to sell themselves cheaply. The play premiered on 27 March 1898 at the Theater der Urania in Berlin. The other play is set in a Berlin cabaret, the Chambre séparée. The characters—the owner of the cabaret, Mr. and Mrs. Süssmilch, a manager, a philistine comic, the singers Margot and Fifi, the guest, and the waitress—are based on people Ernst had met, and their Berlin jargon is copied from life. An evening of carousing is highlighted by corrupt business deals, manipulations, and boasting. *Im Chambre séparée* was first performed on 14 May 1899 at the Theater der Urania. Continuing in this vein is *Die schnelle Verlobung* (Quick Engagement, 1899), a satire about seemingly honest but corrupt bourgeois hypocrites.

At this time Ernst began to see himself as a dramatist with no proper stage for his works and no audience capable of understanding him. In his depression he burned more than fifteen plays. Still, he managed to compile two one-act plays from material saved from a larger work, "Liebe" (Love). *Wenn die Blätter fallen* (When the Leaves Fall; performed, 1899; published, 1900) presents the conversations of the dying Marie with her likewise ailing admirer, Reinhold. The play makes use of heavy-handed symbolism such as the dripping of blood from opened veins onto a carpet covered with white carnations. Only a singularly talented actress such as Louise Dumont was ever able to overcome such theatrics. The tragedy *Der Tod* (Death), published with *Wenn die Blätter fallen* but not performed, contains another deathbed conversation. The characters are Adele, who has just lost a child; her husband, Richard; and their friend Carl, who has been accused of adultery. The melodramatic exchanges fit neither the title nor the indicated genre of the play.

In 1910 Ernst's *Eine Nacht in Florenz* (A Night in Florence; published, 1905) was a success at Düsseldorf. Some critics praised the play as a hilarious comedy, while others thought it required a greater production effort than it was worth. The play deals with the quarreling noble houses of the Bardi and the Buendelmonti in Renaissance Florence. The entertainment is provided by contrasting good and bad characters, a mixture of verse and prose, and a traditional plot complete with love affairs and fencing scenes.

Just when Ernst seemed to have mastered the comic form, he chose to write a tragedy, *Demetrios* (published, 1905; performed, 1910). The critic Alfred Kerr credited *Demetrios* with power, passion, and intelligent organization; yet there are as many ideas as there are characters—rulers, nobility, soldiers, slaves, demagogues, and gods. Ernst admitted to irregularities in style and meter. In addition, many anachronisms detract from the tragedy of Demetrios, who sacrifices himself for the gods of the state. The tragedy *Das Gold* (published, 1906) also shows stylistic unevenness and many intentional anachronisms in its story of an egotistical king gambling his small Spanish realm against the invading Moors.

Ernst's comedy *Der Hulla* (The Beggar; published, 1906) was performed in many cities after premiering in Dresden in 1911. The play consists of four acts of Arabian Nights-style fairy tales in which fantasy and imagination win out over reality and worldly power. The humor is often flat and the dialogue at times is plain, but the material is rich enough to give audiences an evening's entertainment.

Ernst turned again to historical and political subjects with the tragedy *Canossa* (published, 1908; performed, 1918). This treatment of the confrontation between the emperor Henry IV and Pope Gregory VII pits two opposite conceptions of worldly rule. In Ernst's view Gregory is the true tragic hero because he accepts fate.

The comedy *Über alle Narrheit Liebe* (Love above All Folly; published, 1909; performed, 1918) depicts a battle of the sexes between the disenchanted fifty-year-old governor of Ephesus, Palamedes, and his wife, Pankrato; two quarreling young lovers, Apollinios and Glykerion; and Apollinios's and Glykerion's respective slaves, Syros and Mysis. The play contains pranks, odd metaphors, hilarious anachronisms, and gender-specific clichés.

Ernst's admirers consider *Brunhild* (published, 1909), about a superhuman being who descends to earth and accepts the limitations of human existence, his masterpiece. This revival of mythological material centers on Ernst's concept of the tragic individual who overcomes guilt through inner strength. The young critic Georg Lukács praised the premiere in Munich in 1911. Lukács's appreciation was important for Ernst's self-esteem; the public reception of *Brunhild* had been unfavorable. Because of the many flaws in character development, actors did not warm to the drama.

Undaunted, Ernst wrote *Ninon de Lenclos* (published, 1910; performed, 1911), a tragedy in three acts. The play strives to build a conflict between the emancipated Ninon's rights to free love and happiness and a traditional bourgeois morality of double standards for men and women. Clichés about the life of a prostitute abound, and Ernst's moral position is lost more than once in twisted logic.

Ernst next turned to a "redemptive" play. *Ariadne auf Naxos* (Ariadne on Naxos, 1912) was first performed at the Nationaltheater in Weimar in 1914 and also had seven performances in Berlin. The drama, which forgoes psychological character motivation, presents a mixture of mythology and Christian belief with pragmatic ethical ideas.

Der heilige Crispin (Saint Crispin; published, 1913; performed, 1927) is a well-constructed comedy mixing prose and verse, parodies, and colorful medieval farce. The comedy works because of

„Demetrius", Tragödie von Paul Ernst.
Uraufführung auf dem Großherzoglichen Hoftheater zu Weimar.

Scene from the premiere of Ernst's Demetrios *at the Nationaltheater, Weimar, in 1910*

its witty language and its openly irreverent attitude.

In *Manfred und Beatrice* (1913) Beatrice, the daughter of a king deposed by three princes, loves the middle brother, Manfred. For two acts Manfred and Beatrice strive for the highest ethics, only to become hideous characters in the third act. The play was first performed in 1918 in Frankfurt am Main. Its reception was less than enthusiastic; even Ernst's staunch admirer Lukács questioned its style and the motivations of the characters.

Ernst's *Preußengeist* (Prussian Spirit; published, 1915) premiered in Weimar on 27 November 1915 but was later banned from performance anywhere in Prussia. The play's nationalistic praise of the Prussian ethic of duty went awry because of its untheatrical and, above all, its unhistorical form.

Turning for the last time to Greek mythology, Ernst wrote *Kassandra* (published, 1916). The god Apollo redeems the heroine, who then gives birth to a Homer-like poet. His singing of a metaphysical truth and the aesthetics of suffering provided an open invitation for the coming ideological exploitation of Ernst by the Nazis. Performances of *Kassandra* were few and far between; the first performance was given at Weimar's Nationaltheater on 11 April 1931 and the second on 15 January 1938 in Berlin at the Deutsches Theater (German Theater), which was then under the stewardship of Hermann Goering.

Ernst's last major comedy, *Pantalon und seine Söhne* (Pantalon and His Sons; published, 1916), was also destined to be performed on the stages of the Third Reich. The play's first performance was at the Neues Schauspielhaus (New Playhouse) in Königsberg on 10 September 1933, followed by a production in Berlin under the direction of Walter Felsenstein. The love-story plot deals with confused identities at a masquerade during a night of Venetian carnival.

Chriemhild (published, 1918) was performed at the Nationaltheater in Mannheim on 15 February 1924. Uncharacteristically for Ernst, the play is a psychological study of an indecisive character who wavers between insight and betrayal of herself and others. Ernst's version of the Nibelungen myth did not meet much approval, and perfor-

Scene from a production of Ernst's Kassandra *at the Deutsches Theater in Berlin in 1938*

mances of the play were rare prior to the advent of the Third Reich.

Although he had been working since 1922 on another Germanic tragedy, *Childerich* (published, 1959), the work was not published during Ernst's lifetime. He put the drama aside after he received unfavorable comments on it from Lukács. The developing ideological alienation between Ernst and his most ardent supporter, Lukács, contributed to Ernst's decision to give up dramatic writing. But above all, the German theaters had given up on Ernst and denied his dramatic works, particularly his great tragedies, access to the stage.

This situation temporarily changed when the national and state theaters under the Nazi government took an interest in Ernst. His presentation of a catalogue of ethical values such as love, faith, loyalty, inner strength, beauty, purity, discipline, and willpower, and his heroes' struggles to accept life's suffering as predestined, suited the National Socialist agenda. Rising dramatists in the Hitler Youth learned from Ernst; the academic community also took note of him, as lectures at the Berlin University by Robert Stumpfl document. This Nazi sponsorship was a major factor in Ernst's being ignored by postwar German literary criticism and in his plays being banished from the stage. While Ernst's comedies, when expertly produced, were successful, his tragedies were ill conceived and flawed; they failed to prove their dramatic value either during Ernst's lifetime or after 1945.

References:
H. Brening, "Paul Ernst and Schiller," Ph.D. dissertation, University of Michigan, 1938;

Norbert Fuerst, *Ideologie und Literatur: Zum Dialog zwischen Paul Ernst und Georg Lukács* (Emsdetten: Lechte, 1970);

Fuerst, *Paul Ernst, der Haudegen des Geistes* (Munich: Nymphenburg, 1985);

Fuerst, *Paul Ernsts Dramatik: Holzweg oder Kreuzweg?* (Emsdetten: Lechte, 1980);

Jane F. Goodloe, "In Defense of Certain 'Fanatics' and a Tribute to Paul Ernst," *American German Review*, 5 (1939): 10-12;

Erich Härlen, *Unterschiedliche Versuche vornehmlich an Paul Ernst* (Bonn: Bouvier, 1982);

Karl August Kutzbach, "Die heutige Beurteilung von Paul Ernst," *Les Litteratures de Langues Europeennes*, 2 (1984): 99-108;

Kutzbach, *Paul Ernst heute* (Emsdetten: Lechte, 1980);

Kutzbach, *Paul Ernst und Georg Lukács: Dokumente einer Freundschaft* (Emsdetten: Lechte, 1974);

Curt Langenbeck, *Wiedergeburt des Dramas aus der Zeit* (Munich: Langen/Müller, 1940);

W. M. Marr, "Theory and Practice in the Drama of Paul Ernst," Ph.D. dissertation, Indiana University, 1956;

J. W. McFarlane, "The Theory of Tragedy in the Works of Paul Ernst," Ph.D. dissertation, Oxford University, 1948;

H. J. Meesen, "Kassandra als Endform in Paul Ernsts religiöser Dramatik," *Monatshefte*, 43 (1951): 187-192;

Meesen, "Paul Ernst's Transition from the Drama to the Epic," *Monatshefte*, 32 (1941): 113-119;

Günther Rühle, *Zeit und Theater: Diktatur und Exil 1933-1945* (Berlin: Junker & Dünnhaupt, 1953);

Robert Stumpfl, *Unser Kampf um ein deutsches Nationaltheater* (Berlin: Junker & Dünnhaupt, 1935);

Hermann Wanderscheck, *Deutsche Dramatik der Gegenwart* (Berlin: Bang, 1940).

Papers:

Paul Ernst's papers are in the Deutsches Literaturarchiv (German Literature Archive), Marbach am Neckar.

Bruno Frank
(13 June 1887 - 20 June 1945)

Thomas A. Kamla
University of Scranton

PLAY PRODUCTIONS: *Die treue Magd*, Frank-furt am Main, Neues Theater, 5 November 1916;

Die Schwestern und der Fremde, Munich, Kammerspiele, 7 December 1917;

Bibikoff, Berlin, Deutsches Theater, 20 June 1918;

Die Trösterin, Munich, Schauspielhaus, 10 October 1919;

Das Weib auf dem Tiere, Breslau, Lobetheater, 27 September 1921; translated and adapted by Hubert Griffith and Benn W. Levy as *Young Madame Conti: A Melodrama*, London, Savoy Theatre, 19 November 1936; New York, Music Box Theater, 31 March 1937;

Henne im Korb, Berlin, Komödienhaus, 11 October 1922;

Zwölftausend, Munich, Kammerspiele, 22 April 1927; translated and adapted by William A. Drake as *Twelve Thousand*, New York, Garrick Theater, 12 March 1928;

Perlenkomödie, Berlin, Komödienhaus, 19 March 1929;

Sturm im Wasserglas, Dresden, Staatstheater, 29 August 1930; translated and adapted by James Bridie as *Storm in a Teacup*, London, Royalty Theatre, 5 February 1936, and as *Storm over Patsy*, New York, Theater Guild, 8 March 1937;

Nina, Dresden, Schauspielhaus, 3 September 1931; translated and adapted by Griffith as *Nina: A Comedy in Three Acts*, London, Criterion Theatre, 17 September 1935;

Der General und das Gold, Munich, Kammerspiele, 5 October 1932.

BOOKS: *Aus der goldenen Schale: Gedichte* (Heidelberg: Winter, 1905); revised as *Gedichte* (Heidelberg: Winter, 1907);

Im dunkeln Zimmer (Heidelberg: Winter, 1906);

Die Nachtwache: Roman (Heidelberg: Winter, 1909);

Flüchtlinge: Novellen (Munich: Langen, 1911);

Die Schatten der Dinge: Gedichte (Munich: Langen, 1912);

Bruno Frank

Gustav Pfizers Dichtungen (Tübingen: Kloeres, 1912);

Requiem (Munich: Langen, 1913);

Strophen im Krieg: Ein Flugblatt (Munich: Langen, 1915);

Die Fürstin: Roman (Munich: Langen, 1915);

Der Himmel der Enttäuschten: Novellen (Munich: Langen, 1916);

Die treue Magd: Komödie in drei Akten (Berlin: Drei Masken, 1916);

Bibikoff: Lustspiel in drei Akten. Frei nach einer Humoreske Dostojewskis (Munich: Drei Masken, 1918);

Die Schwestern und der Fremde: Schauspiel in zwei Aufzügen und einem Vorspiel (Munich: Müller, 1918);

Die Trösterin: Schauspiel in drei Akten (Munich: Musarion, 1919);

Die Kelter: Ausgewählte Gedichte (Munich: Musarion, 1919);

Ein Abenteuer in Venedig: Novelle (Munich: Musarion, 1919);

Von der Menschenliebe (Munich: Musarion, 1919);

Gesichter: Gesammelte Novellen (Munich: Musarion, 1920);

Alkmene: Eine Erzählung (Leipzig: Quelle & Meyer, 1921);

Leidenschaften und andere Geschichten (Berlin: Ullstein, 1921);

Das Weib auf dem Tiere: Ein Drama (Munich: Drei Masken, 1921); translated and adapted by Hubert Griffith and Benn W. Levy as *Young Madame Conti: A Melodrama* (London: French, 1938);

Bigram: Neue Erzählungen (Munich: Musarion, 1921)—includes "Der Goldene," translated by Basil Creighton as "The Golden Beetle," in *Tellers of Tales* (New York: Doubleday, Doran, 1939), pp. 1082-1105;

Henne im Korb: Lustspiel in drei Akten (Berlin: Drei Masken, 1922);

Tage des Königs (Berlin: Rowohlt, 1924); translated by H. T. Lowe-Porter as *The Days of the King* (New York & London: Knopf, 1927);

Die Melodie (Stuttgart: Fleischhauer & Spohn, 1925);

Trenck: Roman eines Günstlings (Berlin: Rowohlt, 1926); translated by Eden and Cedar Paul as *Trenck: The Love Story of a Favourite* (New York: Knopf, 1928);

Erzählungen (Berlin: Rowohlt, 1926);

Ein Konzert: Novellen (Potsdam: Kiepenhauer, 1927);

Zwölftausend: Schauspiel in drei Akten (Berlin: Rowohlt, 1927); translated by William A. Drake as *Twelve Thousand: A Play in Three Acts* (New York: Knopf, 1928);

Politische Novelle (Berlin: Rowohlt, 1928); translated by Lowe-Porter as *The Persians Are Coming* (New York & London: Knopf, 1929);

Perlenkomödie: Ein Spiel in vier Akten (Munich: Drei Masken, 1929);

Der Magier: Novelle (Berlin: Rowohlt, 1929);

Sturm im Wasserglas: Komödie in drei Akten (Munich: Drei Masken, 1930); translated by James Bridie as *Storm in a Teacup* (London: Constable, 1936);

Nina: Komödie in drei Akten (Berlin: Drei Masken, 1931);

Der General und das Gold: Schauspiel in einem Prolog und acht Bildern (Berlin: Drei Masken, 1932);

Cervantes: Ein Roman (Amsterdam: Querido, 1934); translated by Lowe-Porter as *A Man Called Cervantes* (London: Cassell, 1934; New York: Viking, 1935);

Der Reisepass: Ein Roman (Amsterdam: Querido, 1937); translated by Cyrus Brooks as *Closed Frontiers: A Study of Modern Europe* (London: Macmillan, 1937); translation republished as *Lost Heritage* (New York: Viking, 1937);

Sechzehntausend Francs (Amsterdam: Querido, 1940; Los Angeles: Privately printed, 1943); translated by Elizabeth Meyer as "16,000 Francs: A Novelette," *Decision*, 1 (April 1941): 44-52; (May 1941): 22-35; (June 1941): 28-39;

Ehre Vater und Mutter (Stockholm: Bermann Fischer, 1942); translated as "Honor Thy Father and Thy Mother," in *The Ten Commandments: Ten Short Novels of Hitler's War against the Moral Code*, edited by Armin L. Robinson (New York: Simon & Schuster, 1943), pp. 181-225;

Die Tochter: Roman (Mexico City: El Libro Libre, 1943); translated by Claire Trask as *One Fair Daughter* (New York: Viking, 1943);

Die verbotene Stadt: Ein Schauspiel in drei Akten (Berlin: Bloch, 1951).

Collections: *Aus vielen Jahren* (Amsterdam: Querido, 1937);

Ausgewählte Werke: Prosa, Gedichte, Schauspiele, introduction by Thomas Mann (Hamburg: Rowohlt, 1957).

Editions in English: "The Suitcase," translated by Barbara Hallewell, in *Heart of Europe: An Anthology of Creative Writing in Europe 1920-1940*, edited by Klaus Mann and Hermann Kesten (New York: Fischer, 1943), pp. 692-702;

The Magician, and Other Stories, translated by Hallewell, Willard B. Trask, and others, introduction by W. Somerset Maugham (New York: Viking Press, 1946).

MOTION PICTURES: *Heart's Desire*, screenplay by Frank, L. Du Garde Peach, Roger Burford, Jack Davies, Jr., and Clifford Grey (British International/Wardour, 1937);

The Hunchback of Notre Dame, screenplay by Frank and Sonya Levien, RKO, 1939;

A Royal Scandal, screenplay by Frank and Edwin Justis Mayer, 20th Century-Fox, 1945.

OTHER: Louis Verneuil, *Karussell: Lustspiel in drei Akten*, translated by Frank (Berlin: Drei Masken, 1920);

Friedrich der Grosse als Mensch im Spiegel seiner Briefe, seiner Schriften, zeitgenössischer Berichte und Anekdoten, edited by Frank (Berlin: Deutsche Buchgemeinschaft, 1926);

Marcel Achard, *Das Leben ist schön: Eine optimistische Komödie in drei Akten*, translated by Frank (Berlin: Drei Masken, 1929);

"Die Monduhr," in *Novellen deutscher Dichter der Gegenwart*, edited by Hermann Kesten (Amsterdam: De Lange, 1933); translated as "The Moon Watch," *Story*, 10, no. 54 (1937): 86-102.

SELECTED PERIODICAL PUBLICATIONS—
UNCOLLECTED: "Zu Thomas Manns neuem Werk *Die Geschichten Jakobs*," *Das Neue Tagebuch*, 1 (November 1933): 503-504;

"The Dressing Case," *Golden Book Magazine*, 20 (November 1934): 543-550;

"Meerfahrt mit Thomas Mann," *Das Neue Tagebuch*, 3 (April 1935): 375-377;

" 'Red' Scare Fails to Scare Speakers," *Hollywood Now*, 26 August 1938, pp. 1-2;

"Juden müssen die deutsche Sprache bewahren," *Aufbau* (New York), 27 December 1940, p. 9;

"The Very Friends of the American People: Revised Statement before the Congressional Committee for Investigation of Defense Migration (Tolan Committee) on March 7, 1942 at Los Angeles, Calif.," *Aufbau* (New York), 20 March 1942, pp. 17, 19;

"Ein Hollywood im 16. Jahrhundert," *Aufbau* (New York), 18 August 1944, p. 15;

"Selbstdarstellungen deutscher Dichter," in *Zeitgemäßes aus der "Literarischen Welt" von 1925-1932*, edited by Willy Haas (Stuttgart: Cotta, 1963), pp. 314-316.

Novelist, short-story writer, poet, and dramatist, Bruno Frank envisioned as his life's ideal the type of the "humane gentleman" represented by such writers as Leo Tolstoy, Ivan Turgenev, and Friedrich Hölderlin—an ideal that suggested warm compassion, high artistic culture, and an aristocratic sense of universal justice. Many writers who knew Frank, among them his lifelong friend Thomas Mann, felt that he was the embodiment of these attributes, and that a "humane gentleman" was reflected in his own works just as much as it was in those of his literary models.

Nothing was more foreign to Frank's way of thinking than German philistinism, whose narrow-mindedness he found worthy of a hearty laugh before it turned malicious and portended the ominous during the rise of fascism in the 1920s.

Born in Stuttgart on 13 June 1887 into a well-to-do family of German-Jewish bankers, Frank studied law, philosophy, and history at Tübingen, Munich, Leipzig, and Strasbourg universities before switching to language and literature at Tübingen, where he was awarded a doctoral degree in 1912 with an examination of the works of Gustav Pfizer. On completing his studies he traveled extensively in France, Spain, and Italy, then served in World War I on the Western Front and in Russia until illness forced his release from the service.

After the war Frank lived for several years as a free-lance writer in the countryside of southern Bavaria. In 1924 he settled in Munich, where he married Elisabeth Pallenberg-Massary, the daughter of the actress Fritzi Massary and stepdaughter of the comedian Max Pallenberg. Frank's career as a successful author and playwright was cut short by the Nazi rise to power in 1933. The day after the burning of the Reichstag he and his wife went into exile in Austria, Switzerland, France, and finally England, where they planned to stay until they could return to Germany. In 1937, however, Frank received an offer to come to Hollywood, and in the fall of that year they moved to Los Angeles, where he became associated with several of the large film studios. Never to return to the "true Germany" he vociferously defended during the war years, Frank died of a heart attack at his home in Beverly Hills on 20 June 1945, one month after the collapse of the Third Reich. He was fifty-eight.

Frank was a respected lyric poet before World War I and, then and later, a novelist and short-story writer recognized at home and abroad. Yet he has never received the serious critical attention his works deserve. With his first publication, *Aus der goldenen Schale* (Out of the Golden Bowl, 1905), he established himself as a precocious lyricist. The poems, modeled on those of Rainer Maria Rilke, are predominantly intellectual and exhibit an astonishing mastery of form. In contrast, a more personal, often melancholy tone of almost epigrammatic brevity pervades the collection *Die Schatten der Dinge* (The Shadows of Things, 1912), while *Requiem* (1913), written in memory of a deceased woman, is a rhythmically controlled cycle of stanzas. A selection of Frank's lyrical oeuvre appeared in 1919 under the title *Die Kelter* (The Winepress).

The best known of Frank's work is his fiction. What distinguishes his novels and short stories is their unity of content and form, of weight and lightness. The smooth and effective style of his prose shows a cultured and sensitive writer. These qualities are in evidence in the short stories in his early volume *Flüchtlinge* (Refugees, 1911), in which people attempt in vain to liberate themselves from the constraints of everyday existence, only to become reconciled with it after a sudden reawakening. In the award-winning "Pantomime," for example, two lovers find their way back to life following an unsuccessful attempt at suicide on the wrong railroad track, while a Berlin banker in "Abenteuer in Venedig" (Adventure in Venice) flees back to the home he had ignored. *Der Himmel der Enttäuschten* (The Heaven of the Disenchanted, 1916), *Gesichter* (Faces, 1920), *Bigram* (1921), and *Ein Konzert* (A Concert, 1927) are other early collections. The story "Der Goldene" (translated as "The Golden Beetle," 1939) in *Bigram* represents one of his most mature and profound contributions. Dealing with moral responsibility and humane sympathy, a recurring theme throughout Frank's work, it is the story of a man who, on his discharge from prison, waylays his inhuman former warder, whom he throttles but at the last moment releases, thus restoring an inner sense of freedom that would have been compromised had the act been carried out.

Frank's subtle character studies reveal the compassion and understanding of a true humanist who, as W. Somerset Maugham said in the introduction to Frank's *The Magician, and Other Stories* (1946), "was more apt to see the good than the evil in his fellow creatures." Frank is at his best when treating the fates of historical characters. *Tage des Königs* (1924; translated as *The Days of the King*, 1927), about Frederick the Great, is a masterpiece in the historical-novel genre that captures the lonely greatness and suffering of the man behind the legend. Frederick is also featured in *Trench: Roman eines Günstlings* (1926; translated as *Trench: The Love Story of a Favourite*, 1928), about an officer whose destiny is molded by his infatuation for the king's sister. Frank was attracted to Frederick the Great by the humaneness, genius, and strength of the monarch, traits that are also displayed in Frank's play *Zwölftausend* (1927; translated as *Twelve Thousand*, 1928).

Frank's insights into the precarious political and cultural situation of his time are reflected in his *Politische Novelle* (Political Novella, 1928; translated as *The Persians Are Coming*, 1929), an appeal to his readers not to forsake the common cultural heritage of Europe and a warning against the threats posed by fascism, the soul-killing materialism of the West, and the collectivist uniformity of the East. Mann thought the novella to be as ethically courageous and insightful as it was poetic. The novella *Der Magier* (1929; translated as "The Magician" in *The Magician, and Other Stories*), in which a world-renowned theater director (based on Max Reinhardt) abandons fame and, by becoming a director of poor black actors, returns to the origins of his creative talent, reveals Frank's affection for the stage.

The most significant work to emerge from Frank's years in exile was the biographical novel *Cervantes* (1934; translated as *A Man Called Cervantes*, 1934), which, in the contrast between the hero's roles as warrior and poet, becomes a symbol of the preservation of inner freedom over servitude and misery. The semi-autobiographical *Der Reisepass* (The Passport, 1937; translated as *Closed Frontiers* and as *Lost Heritage*, 1937) deals with an antifascist refugee's effort to complete work on his magnum opus, a history of European portraiture, whose only reader, as it turns out, is the author himself. Frank's final major prose work, *Die Tochter* (The Daughter, 1943; translated as *One Fair Daughter*, 1943), revolves around anti-Semitism and is an affectionate roman à clef about the author's wife. Frank's involvement with drama was restricted to the years in which he resided in Germany. As an expatriate he lost contact with the German stage and his native audience, and his dramatic production virtually ceased after 1933.

Frank's first play, the comedy *Die treue Magd* (The Loyal Maid; published, 1916), premiered in Frankfurt am Main on 5 November 1916. Günther Sohnrey, the son of the prominent businessman Hermann Sohnrey, attempts to cover his gambling debts by signing over notes to Georg Laturner under the name of his father's firm. Interceding on Günther's behalf is Hermann's maid Mathilde. The play revolves around Laturner's plan to reveal to Hermann the nature of his son's transactions and the son's anxiety over the repercussions that this revelation will have.

To shed light on the relationship between Hermann Sohnrey, Laturner, and Mathilde,

Frank flashes back some twenty-five years to a time when the two men were bachelors and business associates and had Mathilde in their employ. Laturner had gambled away his partner's money, and Sohnrey had dissolved their relationship. Mathilde, who was secretly in love with Sohnrey, had pleaded on Laturner's behalf, an act which dissuaded Sohnrey, who was also in love with Mathilde, from asking her to marry him. Twenty-five years later Laturner sees in the debts Günther has been accruing a way of getting back at his former partner. The loyal, virtuous, and tolerant servant Mathilde, through her winning personality, finally brings about a reconciliation between Hermann Sohnrey and Laturner. Men of extremes, both become humanized by Mathilde's appeal to decency and moderation.

One scene in the play, regarded by some reviewers as an unnecessary digression, is a discussion on literature between Hermann Sohnrey and the writer Albrecht Hildebrand, the lover of Sohnrey's daughter Ruth. The opinionated Sohnrey is characteristically skeptical about most contemporary writing, which he sees as overly subjective. In his view, literature should reveal less of the writer's inner life and be more concerned with the reader. Sohnrey is voicing opposition to the movement dominating the German literary scene at the time, expressionism, with its emphasis on distortion, abstraction, and inner vision. Literature, he says, should be readily intelligible to the average reader, deal with universal human virtues and failings, and have at its basis a clearly defined code of morality. By arguing this way Sohnrey reveals himself as Frank's mouthpiece, for the play is entirely traditional in its characterization and staging. This traditionalism can be seen in Frank's portrayal of women as exercising a humanizing influence on others; *Die treue Magd* invokes an almost Goethean perception of the feminine as a vehicle of harmony and moderation in the affairs of men.

The play was well received by the Frankfurt audience, as well as by audiences in Dresden and Krefeld. A moving family drama written during one of Europe's darkest periods, it was felt to exude, through the figure of Mathilde, a kind of poetic healing in the face of wholesale destruction. Often more critical of its native Swabian dramatists than of those from other regions, the Stuttgart press gave *Die treue Magd* a somewhat negative review, saying that its characterization of the maid was too noble to be credible. In general, though, the press regarded the play as good, entertaining theater, noting particularly the polished dialogue and conversational style which were to become Frank's trademarks.

Still hardly a household name in theater circles, Frank was elated when he learned in late 1917 that Otto Falckenberg, the eminent director of the Munich Kammerspiele (Intimate Theater), had agreed to include *Die Schwestern und der Fremde* (The Sisters and the Stranger; published, 1918) in his repertoire. The drama, which premiered on 7 December 1917, opens with a ballroom scene in which two of the dancers, Rudolf Dorguth and Cordula von Gallas, meet and fall in love. It then moves to an afternoon social gathering of all of the play's protagonists: Frau von Gallas, her daughters Cordula and Judith, and their respective fiancés, Dorguth and Dr. Hoffmeister. Hoffmeister harbors an almost intuitive dislike for Dorguth; Judith cannot understand this attitude, since she considers Dorguth an honorable person. Hoffmeister accuses Dorguth of being a swindler and a coward; the imperturbable, almost benevolent manner in which Dorguth responds to this vilification totally disarms his attacker, with the result that the three women are only strengthened in their conviction that he is above reproach. Indeed, Judith is so provoked by this defamatory assault on her sister's betrothed (with whom she is secretly in love) that she seizes it as an opportunity to break off her engagement to Hoffmeister.

After the marriage of Cordula and Dorguth is cut short by Cordula's death, the grief-stricken mother showers praise on her son-in-law for the constant solicitousness that made her daughter unspeakably happy during her final days. In a conversation with Judith, however, Dorguth confesses that all his life he has been burdened with guilt and shame by the adulation that others have bestowed on him for his virtues. He regards his existence as a lie, since these virtues were always feigned and were never a true reflection of his character. Judith attempts to refute this admission, averring that such self-condemnation is unjustified in the light of all the good he has done. But when Dorguth continues to reveal the coldness, insensitivity, and apathy fundamental to his nature, she can hear no more; she flees, abandoning him to his loneliness.

Die Schwestern und der Fremde is a gripping drama of an individual struggling to become what he appears to be, to make the virtues for which he is extolled a part of himself. As it turns out, Hoffmeister's diatribe was not totally un-

Frank (left) with another young writer, Wilhelm Speyer, in 1906. At this point in his career Frank was known as a lyric poet.

founded: Dorguth was a swindler of sorts due to an impoverishment of his basic humanity. He sought to rectify this failing with each new encounter, but the result was only a reaffirmation of his emptiness.

Initial reviews of the premiere performance were anything but laudatory. Many believed the play lacked dramatic quality owing to Frank's predilection for psychological analysis and for evoking atmosphere and mood—things he excelled at in the narrative and lyrical genres, to which they were better suited. The theme of compassionate goodness praised in the first play is undercut by a coldness that impacts in kind on the audience. The new psychological depths reached in the work accentuated the tragic nature of human existence, but they contributed little to the element of action so essential to the dramatic genre. Reviewers again drew attention to Frank's finely polished dialogue but concluded that *Die Schwestern und der Fremde* lacked a satisfying ending and that the confessional aspect of the play rendered it too subjective.

The play was more positively received in Berlin, Wiesbaden, and Frankfurt and ran until early 1919. But in Frank's hometown of Stuttgart the director of the Landestheater (Provincial Theater), Wilhelm von Scholz, refused to stage *Die Schwestern und der Fremde* on the grounds that it was destructive rather than constructive. It was with reluctance that the theater had put on *Die treue Magd*, and the director was determined not to repeat the mistake. This decision was attacked by the critics, who thought that the play might have dramaturgical merits in spite of its theme.

With *Bibikoff* (published, 1918), which premiered at the Deutsches Theater (German Theater) in Berlin on 20 June 1918, Frank returns to comedy; actually, the play might more accurately be labeled a farce. A free adaptation of a humorous sketch by Fyodor Dostoyevski, the work centers on the adventures of the title character, an insanely jealous husband whose distrust of his wife gets him into the most ridiculous predicaments. Bibikoff's hapless escapades culminate in a scene in which he believes he has caught his wife in a compromising situation; instead, he finds himself in the bedroom of a totally strange woman from whose husband, who is about to return home, he seeks refuge under the bed. He is not alone, however, for an unexpected companion—the woman's lover—also has sought out the first accessible hiding place. Bibikoff might have been spared the embarrassment of discovery had it not been for the woman's lap dog, who, yapping, joins him and the stranger under the bed. Humiliated, he realizes the foolishness of his senseless jealousy.

Reviewers speculated that the scattered hissing and whistling at the close of the curtain would have turned into a storm of protest had not Pallenberg played Bibikoff; the renowned comic actor salvaged the play. Critics viewed the production less as a play than as a showcase for Pallenberg's talent. It was soon dropped from theater repertoires.

Die Trösterin (The Consoler; published, 1919) continues the series of familial conflicts, both humorous and serious, around which Frank's plays had revolved since he took up the genre. It premiered at the Schauspielhaus (Playhouse) in Munich on 10 October 1919. Dr. Brandenberger, a surgeon, sees in his wife, Sibylle, his only source of happiness; Sibylle's friend Lena, a spinster, pines for release from her loneliness; and the painter Rottacker has never known real happiness because his work, although not lacking in quality, can never measure up to the standards of true greatness. A traditionalist rather than a subscriber to avant-garde movements such as expressionism, he is in the twilight of his career and laments the fact that he is out of touch with the spirit of the time. Sibylle enters into a nonsexual liaison with the painter to lessen his anguish and to reinstill in him a sense of worth. The spiteful and envious Lena hints to Brandenberger that his wife is being unfaithful to him. At first indignant, Brandenberger changes his attitude when he discovers that Sibylle was not a party to a sordid affair but a "consoler" whose humanity, far from being degraded, is ennobled by the uniqueness of the liaison. Like Mathilde in *Die treue Magd*, Sibylle is a self-giving woman who brings out the human qualities of men. As a result, Rottacker's cynicism toward life and art yields to a renewed joy in creating, while Brandenberger's penchant for prejudging, like Sohnrey's too-rigid moral code, is replaced by tolerance.

Die Trösterin* was also performed in Berlin, Hamburg, Stuttgart, and Hannover and had a rather mixed reception from the critics. Frank's cultivated dialogue was given due recognition, but some critics thought that the play ought to be read rather than acted on the stage. Scholz of the Stuttgart Landestheater, who had rejected *Die Schwestern und der Fremde*, almost did the same with *Die Trösterin* but decided to give it a chance. He saw in the figure of the woman whose love for others is motivated by pity and an altruistic desire to make them happy a case of intellectual and moral infantilism. Others considered Frank's portrayal of the benevolent female too sentimental. The criticisms notwithstanding, the play enjoyed a good deal of success with audiences.

Frank's next play, *Das Weib auf dem Tiere* (The Woman on the Animal; published, 1921), premiered at the Lobetheater in Breslau on 27 September 1921 under the direction of Wilhelm Lichtenberg. It was later translated and adapted by Hubert Griffith and Benn W. Levy as *Young Madame Conti*, which premiered on 19 November 1936 at the Savoy Theatre in London and on 31 March 1937 at the Music Box Theater in New York, with the original British cast and with Levy directing both productions; the English-language version was published in 1938. The play is a courtroom drama. Nella Conti, a prostitute, is on trial for the murder of her lover, Stephen Horka. Conti testifies that she had overheard him telling a friend that he had not loved her but had led her on for the purpose of reaping the profits of her profession. What made her decide to shoot

Horka was the mocking manner in which he belittled their relationship. The jury seems to debate Conti's case more on emotional than on legal grounds (some of them have firsthand knowledge of the accused's profession). In a visionary scene, Conti presides as judge and the judge becomes the accused. Although she is sentenced to death by hanging, she escapes the gallows by taking poison. Frank leaves the audience sympathizing with the criminal, who is also a victim. Once again, he depicts a woman giving totally of herself—in this case, both physically and emotionally.

In the Breslau production of *Das Weib auf dem Tiere* the audience comprised part of the jury. Critics regarded this feature as a theatrically effective technique for drawing the theatergoers into the moral decision-making process of the play. In Berlin, one reviewer noted that playwrights long before Frank had exhausted the dramatic possibilities of the exploited-prostitute theme; other Berlin critics praised the quasi-expressionistic scene in which Conti becomes the judge, suggesting at least a moral victory for the accused.

Whereas *Das Weib auf dem Tiere* consists of six acts, a prologue and epilogue frame the three acts that comprise *Young Madame Conti*. The epilogue fills in more details of the confrontation—undramatized in the original—that leads to Horka's death, garnering even more audience sympathy for the prostitute. The defense attorney in *Young Madame Conti* uses the most graphic language to describe the anguish the accused will go through in awaiting her execution—an element that is missing from *Das Weib auf dem Tiere*.

The London premiere of *Young Madame Conti* elicited mixed reactions. While both audience and reviewers considered it a moving and powerful drama, in part owing to the excellent performance by Constance Cummings, they felt that it was so violently presented as to leave the viewers themselves bruised and battered. Critics also felt that the melodramatic aspects of the play compromised Frank's effort to analyze seriously suffering and injustice. The same sentiments were expressed, to an even greater degree, by New York critics, who felt that the play flaunted the baseness of humanity, preened itself on sadistic detail, and dwelled unnecessarily on the horror of the girl about to be hanged. Because of her beauty and emotional power and the reticence with which she ennobled her suffering, Cummings saved what was regarded as an artistically and ethically weak play. It closed after twenty-two performances.

Henne im Korb (Chicken in the Basket; published, 1922), a short-lived burlesque that premiered at the Komödienhaus (Comedies House) in Berlin on 11 October 1922, concludes the first phase of Frank's dramatic production; turning again to his forte, he wrote over the next several years some of his best historical novels and novellas. In a later autobiographical sketch, he said that the year 1924 began the part of his literary production on which he could think back without discomfort. His best dramatic works date from his Munich years, among them *Zwölftausend*, an expression of republican Germany's contempt for the Führer (leader) principle of the state. *Zwölftausend* is the dramatic counterpart to his historical novels *Tage des Königs* and *Trenck*.

The most successful of Frank's serious plays, *Zwölftausend* premiered under Falckenberg's direction at the Munich Kammerspiele on 22 April 1927; an adaptation for the American stage opened at the Garrick Theater in New York on 12 March 1928. The petty duke of a German principality contracts with Faucitt, a representative of King George III, to supply twelve thousand troops for use against the rebels in America. The price, fifty talers for each mercenary, will provide funds for the private pleasures of the duke, who laughs with scorn as he reads the Declaration of Independence. On their way to America, the troops will have to pass through Prussian territory. The duke and Faucitt are aware of the risks involved, for Frederick the Great has expressed opposition to that kind of traffic. They plan with the greatest secrecy; but the duke's humble secretary, Piderit, whose roots are with the people and whose two peasant brothers have been pressed into service, conspires with the duke's mistress, Baroness Spangenberg, to use the duke's signet ring to transmit a sealed message to the king. On the eve of the farewell festival a Prussian colonel arrives with the message that the king will not allow the transportation of such troops through his dominion. The duke discovers Piderit's "treason" and condemns him to be hanged, but the colonel grants him safe conduct to America. Accepting the shrewd advice of the baroness, the duke saves face before his soldiers by pretending that he has changed his mind; the twelve thousand are permitted to return home.

Zwölftausend enjoyed a wide and enthusiastic reception and was performed in more than one

hundred German theaters, the last being in Hamburg in 1958. Its best performances were perhaps those under the direction of Reinhardt at the Deutsches Theater in Berlin, with Werner Krauss playing Piderit. Reviewers saw the play as a strong satire of little despots and a vigorous plea for democracy, noting that the viewer was scarcely conscious of the inherent propaganda until the play was over. William A. Drake's adaptation, *Twelve Thousand*, ran for sixty-four performances on Broadway. It opened in London on 15 September 1931.

Frank's next play, *Perlenkomödie* (Comedy of Pearls; published, 1929), premiered at the Komödienhaus in Berlin on 19 March 1929. Erwin Siethoff presents his mistress, Cora Petry, with a set of genuine pearls and gives his wife, Wera, an imitation set. A secret admirer of Wera's, Peter Mack, steals the fake pearls and, while paying a visit to his old girlfriend Cora, surreptitiously exchanges them for the real ones; he then gives the real pearls to Wera. Divorce is agreed to by both parties at the end, with Siethoff getting Cora and Wera winding up with the more deserving Peter.

While *Perlenkomödie* was touring the theater circuit, Frank gave an interview in which he said that to achieve the financial security that would allow him to write his novels he would compose one play each year purely as a source of income; his aim, he made it clear, was commercial and not artistic success. *Perlenkomödie* was, indeed, a hit with audiences in Berlin, Dresden, Kiel, and Stuttgart; in 1966 it was adapted for German television. Most critics did not share this enthusiasm, however, those in Stuttgart going so far as to describe the play as a piece of trash.

Sturm im Wasserglas (published, 1930; translated as *Storm in a Teacup*, 1936) premiered at the Staatstheater (State Theater) in Dresden on 29 August 1930 and became one of Germany's most successful comedies in the years immediately preceding the Nazi takeover. It is a satire about a pompous municipal official, Dr. Konrad Thoss, who aspires to higher office; his private life and habits, however, conflict with the ethical requirements of such a position. As the play opens, Franz Burdach, a journalist, has appeared at the Thoss residence to interview the official about the impending election, in which Thoss is running for mayor. While awaiting Thoss's arrival home, he chats with Thoss's wife, Viktoria. Mrs. Vogl, a poor flower lady, shows up and, seeing Burdach with Mrs. Thoss, assumes that he is the official. She complains that the authorities, through Thoss's influence, have impounded her dog Toni and threaten to put it to sleep if she fails to pay her long-overdue hound tax, and she begs for a remission of the assessment so that she can have Toni back. Burdach leaves to meet a press deadline, promising to come back to conduct the interview. Thoss arrives home and dismisses Mrs. Vogl in the most brutal fashion. Burdach returns just in time to witness this scene and offers to pay the dog tax for the woman; the gesture is rejected by Thoss as impertinent. Thoss throws the woman out; then, in the following interview, he expounds in the noblest of phrases on the social responsibility of public officials.

The interview is printed as conducted. But even though the editor supports Thoss's candidacy, Burdach sneaks into another section of the paper an account of Mrs. Vogl's case in which it is stated that a man capable of such behavior as that demonstrated toward the old flower lady ought never to become mayor. The desired effect is achieved: during a political rally the next day the candidate's speech, which centers on the rights of the individual and how he will work to guard them, is broken up by prolonged barking and yelping from the dog-loving electorate, and his career is ruined. Burdach, who has been fired by his editor, then shows up at Thoss's home and demands that he answer for his actions. Although Viktoria is initially furious at the journalist, she comes to realize that he has acted out of idealism and cannot help but respect him. Indeed, she betrays even stronger feelings for Burdach following another row by an incensed community, this time in front of Thoss's house. Thoss loses his equanimity and collapses.

Still insisting that justice be done, Burdach steals the dog from the city pound with the hope of returning it to its owner. At Thoss's instigation, he is brought to trial for theft. The courtroom scene is an uproarious bit of satire that includes the old flower seller, the dog, the keeper of the pound, a pompous judge speaking an amusing dialect, and a clever defense by Burdach. In the end Mrs. Vogl, who has been showered with donations following Burdach's newspaper article, regains possession of her dog; Burdach is acquitted and reinstated with the paper; and Viktoria divorces Thoss, leaving her free to marry the journalist.

Sturm im Wasserglas is probably Frank's best comedy in terms of unified action and character motivation. Its premiere in Dresden was a smashing success, as were productions in Munich, Stuttgart, and Berlin. Between 1966 and 1988 the play was revived in Ulm, Munich, Mannheim, Vienna, Stuttgart, and Bregenz, as well as on German television.

On 5 February 1936 the premiere of *Storm in a Teacup* was held at the Royalty Theatre in London at the express wish of King Edward VIII. The adaptation by James Bridie was skillful. Although the setting of the play was moved to Scotland, neither the plot nor the characters were changed. Critics noted that the work had all the vigor of an original play and none of the artificial mannerisms of translated comedy. It played in London for more than a year.

When the Theater Guild presented the play in New York on 8 March 1937, the only modifications it made to the Bridie text were to change the dog's name from Toni to Patsy and the title to *Storm over Patsy*. Most reviewers agreed that, although quite mild as a satire, the play was entertaining and funny. Others saw it as a languid and skimpy anecdote which the actors occasionally rescued from dullness. It closed after forty-eight performances.

In 1930, as Frank's mother-in-law embarked on a trip around the world, she lamented that she had no decent role to look forward to when she returned. Frank promised to create one for her, and thus came into being the drawing-room comedy *Nina* (published, 1931). The play deals with a cinema star, Nina Gallas, whose fiancé, Stefan Breuer, a successful inventor, wants her to give up her career so that they may have more time for one another after they are married. To facilitate the transition she approaches the director Paul Hyrkan with the suggestion that he allow her studio double, Trude Mielitz, to take her place. Hyrkan consents to the proposal. When Trude is informed of her rise to stardom she changes instantly from a fawning stand-in to a supercilious star who is carried away by conceit and a craving for publicity.

To insure that the substitution will go unnoticed, Hyrkan decides to produce his next film in Hollywood. The dupery is a resounding success. In the final act the former actress is living happily in Munich with her husband. The new "Nina" and Hyrkan, who are also married now, arrive in the city to promote her most recent release. Nina and Stefan are warned by their secretary, Eva Weininger, that Hyrkan and Trude intend to call at their residence, and Nina considers it best that she not be present when they arrive (Nina and Trude are played by the same actress). Instead, Stefan stays in the drawing room to receive them. When Trude realizes that Nina is snubbing her she is infuriated and attempts to enter Nina's room, but she is hindered by the ever-watchful Eva. Trude regains her composure, swallows her pride, and leaves.

Nina successfully premiered at the Dresden Schauspielhaus on 3 September 1931 under the direction of Joseph Gielen, but its best reception took place at the Deutsches Theater in Berlin, owing to the delightful performance by Massary in the dual role. Other than that, the play enjoyed only moderate success on the German stage; compared with *Sturm im Wasserglas*, it was considered too long-winded and conversational. It was revived in Stuttgart in 1950, and it appeared again on the stage in 1981 when the Ludwigshafen Theater in Pfalzbau featured Elke Sommer in the leading role. In 1982 the play was adapted for German television. On 17 September 1935 Hubert Griffith's English adaptation of *Nina* was presented at the Criterion Theatre in London. The German actress Lucie Mannheim played the double role of Nina and Trude, turning in a bravura performance. The play itself was, however, regarded by some London critics as trivial.

The last of Frank's plays to be staged in Germany during his lifetime, *Der General und das Gold* (The General and the Gold, 1932) is based on the life of John August Sutter, who settled in California before the gold rush and received a grant of land from the Spanish governor. The discovery of gold brings in a new era in the development and settling of California, and Sutter's claims to ownership of his land are ignored. The authorities, among them President Abraham Lincoln, agree in principle that he is the sole legal owner of the territory; they pay him a handsome sum for the injury he has suffered, but they realize that the movements of history are more powerful than any single individual's claim to justice. Sutter never gets his land back; the overly long play ends with his death at the age of eighty on the steps of the Capitol, where he has gone still hoping that the United States government will decide his case in his favor. Sutter achieves a kind of heroic stature by attempting to stand up to the inevitable.

With Falckenberg directing, *Der General und das Gold* premiered at the Kammerspiele in Munich on 5 October 1932. The play was well re-

ceived both by the audience and the critics, who saw in the affectionate portrayal of the hero a clear indication of Frank's humanity. It was staged in Stuttgart as late as February 1933, the year that forced all humanitarian drama in Germany into silence.

Frank's plays and novels are usually mentioned only in passing in literary histories and critical studies. Perhaps one reason his works have failed to receive serious scholarly attention is that they were overshadowed by the humble, solicitous, and humane personality of the writer himself. Discussions of his writings, therefore, have focused not on the work but on the reflection of the man in the work. Apart from reviews, published comments about the author have usually been rendered by acquaintances, well-wishers, and fellow authors, rarely by literary scholars. Those who have pronounced critically on Frank, however, have noticed that his comedies, which make up the bulk of his dramas, are not simply products of the time but contain formal elements that link them with the *Volksstück* (folk play) and the boulevard comedy.

The German *Volksstück* was a genre of sentimental popular comedy that focused on common people in a simple and straightforward style. The French boulevard comedy originated at the end of the nineteenth century; these light comedies were technically well constructed and frequently dealt with marital problems. Frank's comedies usually fall into the tradition of one or the other of these earlier forms. But in his most successful comedy, *Sturm im Wasserglas*, the two overlap, with the *Volksstück* action, centering on the flower vendor and her dog, meshing with the more elegant boulevard-comedy setting of the drawing room. The French influence can be detected in the delightful dialogues in many of Frank's comedies, especially *Perlenkomödie* and *Nina*.

Frank wrote only one play during his years in exile. In 1940 he completed the manuscript for *Die verbotene Stadt* (The Forbidden City), which deals with the Westernization of China from 1898 to 1900. It was published posthumously in 1951 but has never been performed. As one critic has said, "The varied and lavish settings necessary to present the play . . . proved an obstacle to its staging."

Frank's last work in Hollywood was a collaboration on the screenplay for the motion picture *A Royal Scandal* (1945), directed by Ernst Lubitsch. At the time of his death he was writing a novel about the eighteenth-century French moralist Nicolas Chamfort.

Bibliography:

Virginia Sease, "Bruno Frank," in *Deutsche Exilliteratur seit 1933*, edited by John M. Spalek and others (Bern: Francke, 1976), I:ii: 36-41, 172-173.

References:

Martin Gregor-Dellin, "Bruno Frank: Gentleman der Literatur," in his *Im Zeitalter Kafkas: Essays* (Munich: Piper, 1979), pp. 62-85;

Reinhold Grimm, "Gentlemanschriftsteller," in *Views and Reviews of Modern German Literature*, edited by Karl S. Weimar (Munich: Delp, 1974), pp. 121-132;

Grimm, "Neuer Humor? Die Komödienproduktion zwischen 1918 und 1933," in *Die deutsche Komödie im zwanzigsten Jahrhundert*, edited by Wolfgang Paulsen (Heidelberg: Stiehm, 1976), pp. 107-133;

Herbert Günther, "Bruno Frank," *Die Literatur*, 32 (1929-1930): 511-516;

Günther, *Drehbühne der Zeit: Freundschaften, Begegnungen, Schicksale* (Hamburg: Wegner, 1957);

Günther, "Erinnerungen an Bruno Frank," *Welt und Wort*, 1 (1946): 134-136;

Klaus Hermsdorf, "Anmerkungen zu Bruno Franks *Die Tochter*," in *Theatrum Europaeum*, edited by Richard Brinkmann and others (Munich: Fink, 1982), pp. 611-623;

Harold von Hofe, "German Literature in Exile: Bruno Frank," *German Quarterly*, 18 (March 1945): 86-92;

Thomas A. Kamla, "Bruno Frank's *Der Reisepass*: The Exile as an Aristocrat of Humanity," *Monatshefte*, 67 (1975): 37-47;

Erika and Klaus Mann, *Escape to Life* (Boston: Houghton Mifflin, 1939), pp. 289-295;

Klaus Mann, *Heute und Morgen: Schriften zur Zeit*, edited by Gregor-Dellin (Munich: Nymphenburger Verlagshandlung, 1969);

Irene Ruttmann, "Bruno Frank," in *Handbuch der deutschen Gegenwartsliteratur*, edited by Hermann Kunisch and Hans Hennecke (Munich: Nymphenburger Verlagshandlung, 1965), I: 210-211;

Virginia Sease, "Bruno Frank," in *Deutsche Exilliteratur seit 1933*, edited by John M. Spalek and others (Bern: Francke, 1976), I:ii: 352-370.

Papers:

Bruno Frank's papers are at the Deutsches Literaturarchiv, Marbach, Germany.

Leonhard Frank

(4 September 1882 - 18 August 1961)

Russell E. Brown
State University of New York at Stony Brook

See also the Frank entry in *DLB 56: German Fiction Writers, 1914-1945.*

PLAY PRODUCTIONS: *Karl und Anna*, Munich, Residenz-Theater; Frankfurt am Main, Schauspielhaus; Aachen, Stadttheater; Bochum, Stadttheater; Bremen, Städtisches Theater; Magdeburg, Wilhelm-Theater, 16 January 1929;

Die Ursache, Munich, Kammerspiele; Vienna, Deutsches Volkstheater; Hamburg, Deutsches Schauspielhaus, 8 March 1929;

Karl and Anna, translated by Ruth Langner, New York, Theater Guild, 7 October 1929;

Hufnägel, Düsseldorf, Schauspielhaus, 27 September 1930;

Ruth, Gera, Bühnen der Stadt Gera, November 1962.

BOOKS: *Fremde Mädchen am Meer und eine Kreuzigung* (Munich: Delphin, 1913);

Die Räuberbande: Roman (Munich: Müller, 1914); translated anonymously as *The Robberband* (London: Davies, 1928; New York: Cape & Smith, 1929);

Die Ursache: Eine Erzählung (Munich: Müller, 1915); translated by Cyrus Brooks as *The Cause of the Crime* (London: Davies, 1928); translation republished as *Clamoring Self* (New York & London: Putnam's, 1930);

Der Mensch ist gut (Zurich: Rascher, 1918);

Die Mutter (Zurich: Rascher, 1919);

Hermann Büschler, der Stattmeister zu Schwäbisch-Hall (Schwäbisch-Hall, 1922);

Der Bürger: Roman (Berlin: Malik, 1924); translated by Cyrus Brooks as *A Middle-Class Man* (London: Davies, 1930);

An der Landstraße: Erzählung (Berlin: Rowohlt, 1925);

Die Schicksalsbrücke: Erzählungen (Berlin: Rowohlt, 1925);

Im letzten Wagen: Erzählungen (Berlin: Rowohlt, 1925); translated by Brooks as *In the Last Coach and Other Stories* (London: Lane,

Leonhard Frank

1934); "Im letzten Wagen" revised as *Absturz: Novelle* (Leipzig: Reclam, 1929);

Das Ochsenfurter Männerquartett: Roman (Leipzig: Insel, 1927); translated by Brooks as *The Singers* (London: Grayson & Grayson, 1932; New York: Holt, 1933);

Karl und Anna: Erzählung (Berlin: Propyläen, 1927); translated by Brooks as *Carl and Anna* (London; Davies, 1929; New York: Putnam's, 1930); translation republished as *Beloved Stranger: The Story of Carl and Anna* (New York: Fischer, 1946); translation republished as "Desire Me," in *Desire Me, and Other Stories* (New York: Penguin, 1948);

60

Der Streber, und andere Erzählungen (Berlin: Deutsche Buchgemeinschaft, 1928);

Karl und Anna: Schauspiel in vier Akten (Leipzig: Insel, 1928); translated by Ruth Langner as *Karl and Anna: A Drama in Three Acts* (New York: Brentano's, 1929);

Bruder und Schwester: Roman (Leipzig: Insel, 1929); translated by Brooks as *Brother and Sister* (London: Davies, 1930; New York: Cape & Smith, 1930);

Die Ursache: Drama in vier Akten (Leipzig: Insel, 1929);

Die Entgleisten: Filmnovelle (Berlin: Hobbing, 1929);

Hufnägel: Schauspiel in drei Akten (Leipzig: Insel, 1930);

Von drei Millionen Drei: Roman (Berlin: Fischer, 1932); translated by Brooks as *Three of the Three Million* (London: Lane, 1936);

Traumgefährten: Roman (Amsterdam: Querido, 1936); translated by Maxim Newmark as *Dream Mates* (New York: Philosophical Library, 1946);

Gesammelte Werke in Einzelausgaben, 7 volumes (Amsterdam: Querido, 1936-1949);

Der Außenseiter: Komödie (Basel: Reiß, 1937);

Maria: Schauspiel (Amsterdam: Querido, 1939);

Mathilde: Roman (Los Angeles: Privately printed, 1943; Amsterdam: Querido, 1948); translated by Willard R. Trask as *Mathilde* (London: Davies, 1948; New York: Simon & Schuster, 1948);

Die Jünger Jesu: Roman (Amsterdam: Querido, 1949);

The Baroness, translated by Brooks (London & New York: Nevill, 1950); original German version published as *Deutsche Novelle* (Munich: Nymphenburger Verlagshandlung, 1954);

Links, wo das Herz ist: Roman (Munich: Nymphenburger Verlagshandlung, 1952); translated by Brooks as *Heart on the Left* (London: Barker, 1954);

Gesammelte Werke, 6 volumes (Berlin: Aufbau, 1957-1959);

Michaels Rückkehr (Leipzig: Reclam, 1957);

Schauspiele (Berlin: Aufbau, 1959);

Ruth (Munich: Desch, 1960);

Sieben Kurzgeschichten (Berlin: Aufbau, 1961);

Hans Fallada (Berlin: Volk & Wissen, 1962);

Gesamtwerk, 6 volumes (Munich: Nymphenburger Verlagshandlung, 1964);

Das Porträt: Eine Berliner Erzählung um 1946 (Berlin-Friedenau: Friedenauer Presse, 1968);

Die Summe, edited by Martin Gregor-Dellin (Munich: Nymphenburger Verlagshandlung, 1982).

Edition in English: *Desire Me, and Other Stories*, translated by Cyrus Brooks (New York: Penguin, 1948)—comprises "Desire Me," "The Clerk," "The Pusher," "The Bridge of Fate."

Leonhard Frank's fiction and dramas span expressionism and Neue Sachlichkeit (New Objectivity), the realistic literature of the Weimar period. He was a champion of the common people, a pacifist, an opponent of the death penalty, and a socialist. Pacifist and socialist themes are presented in his works sometimes in an earnest didactic mode, sometimes as sentimental melodramatic pathos. Social commitment is gradually displaced by Frank's great theme of grand passions, often of an illicit or socially disapproved nature, such as his novel of incestuous love, *Bruder und Schwester* (1929; translated as *Brother and Sister*, 1930), or the story *Karl und Anna* (1927; translated as *Carl and Anna*, 1929), in which a homecoming soldier replaces a comrade—who is still a prisoner of war—in the bed and heart of the latter's wife.

Frank suffered greatly from exile and the loss of contact with his native culture and society during the Nazi period. In spite of the honors heaped on him in both postwar German states, he never recovered his former powers and position in the cultural world. The East Germans, who published his collected works and sponsored dissertations on his writings, viewed him as an idealistic socialist who never moved to a commitment to communism. At the same time, his critique of Nazism and militarism (elements of which he believed had survived Adolf Hitler), of capitalism, and of nuclear armament in works such as the novel *Die Jünger Jesu* (The Disciples of Jesus, 1949) made him a suspect figure for many West Germans.

Frank was born in Würzburg on 4 September 1882, the fourth child of Johann Frank, a carpenter, and Marie Bach Frank. At age thirteen he was apprenticed to a mechanic, and he later held jobs as a bicycle repairman, chauffeur, factory worker, and housepainter.

In 1905 Frank left Würzburg for Munich to study painting under Otto Groß. A collection of colored lithographs published in Munich in 1913 is the only record of his career as an artist. The sale of some drawings enabled him to move in 1910 to Berlin, where he frequented the expres-

Frank in 1907

sionist meeting place, the Café des Westens. He married Lisa Erdelyi on 4 February 1914 and decided to pursue a career as a writer. In 1914 his first novel, *Die Räuberbande* (1914; translated as *The Robberband*, 1928), was awarded the prestigious Fontane Prize. In the same year Frank arranged for the publication of his mother's autobiography, *Der Lebensroman einer Arbeiterfrau* (The Life Story of a Worker's Wife), which she wrote under the pseudonym Marie Wegrainer to support her son financially.

When World War I began, Frank publicly announced his opposition to the war (he slapped a man who was celebrating the sinking of a passenger ship as a heroic deed) and then immigrated to Switzerland, where he joined a pacifist group led by the writer René Schickele and contributed short stories to the literary journal *Die Weißen Blätter* (The White Pages); the stories, which were collected in the volume *Der Mensch ist gut* (Man Is Good, 1918), ridicule patriotic fervor and the glorification of death on the battlefield for the fatherland, proposing instead a universal brotherhood. The collection was published in Zurich and had enormous popular success; a friend of Frank's who was in the diplomatic corps smuggled the

book into Germany, where it was distributed clandestinely by socialists. *Der Mensch ist gut* received the Kleist Prize in 1920.

When the war ended in November 1918, Frank returned to Germany and became a member of the revolutionary council of the Räterepublik (Soviet republic) in Munich. He moved to Berlin in 1920. His wife died in 1923; six years later he married Elena Maquenne.

In *Karl und Anna*, Karl and Richard are prisoners of war on the Siberian steppes. After listening for years to descriptions of Anna, Richard's young wife, Karl falls in love with her. Karl is released before Richard, returns to Germany, and persuades Anna to accept him as her husband. Although she is aware of his deception, she allows him to remain, falls in love with him, and becomes pregnant. When her real husband returns, Anna leaves with Karl. Thus a great love prevails over prosaic marriage, just as love overrules the incest taboo in *Bruder und Schwester*.

The popular success of *Karl und Anna* encouraged Frank to rewrite the story for the theater; the dramatic version was published in 1928 and performed in Frankfurt am Main and many other cities in January 1929. An English transla-

*The actress Charlotte London-Jäger in Aachen, circa 1930.
She became Frank's third wife in 1952.*

tion by Ruth Langner, *Karl and Anna*, appeared in New York later that year.

The play *Die Ursache* (The Motive), which was published and produced in 1929, is based on Frank's story of the same title that was published in 1915 (translated as *The Cause of the Crime*, 1928). An impoverished intellectual who had been emotionally crippled by a sadistic teacher returns to his hometown at age thirty-five to murder the teacher, who is still tormenting his pupils. The play is devoted to his trial and the hours before his execution by beheading. It met a cool reception from the critics and closed quickly.

Frank's play *Hufnägel* (1930) is the story of a poor mechanic who strews nails on the highway near his garage to get business repairing tires; as a result, a seven-year-old girl is killed in an accident. His wife despises him until he reacts in a manly way to the discovery of her infidelity. In a victory for true love like that of *Karl und Anna*,

the husband forgives his repentant wife, and the couple immigrates to America.

Frank resigned from the Preußische Akademie der Künste, Sektion für Dichtkunst (Prussian Academy of the Arts, Literature Section), to which he had been elected in 1928, after Hitler came to power in 1933. When his books were "verboten und verbrannt" (forbidden and burned) by the Nazis, Frank began his second immigration, traveling to Zurich, London, and Paris. The Nazis revoked his German citizenship in 1934. Frank was twice interned in France as an enemy alien in 1939, but managed to flee ahead of the Germans in 1940 to Spain, Portugal, and the United States. He was met at the pier in New York by a representative of Warner Brothers, who gave him two hundred dollars and instructed him to report to Hollywood to work as a script writer; among his new colleagues were Heinrich Mann, Alfred Döblin, and Carl Zuckmayer. Frank often visited Thomas Mann, and they sometimes read to each other from their manuscripts. In 1945 Frank moved to New York.

Frank returned to Germany in October 1950. His reception in his hometown of Würzburg was hostile, partly because of his 1949 novel about the Nazi period in Würzburg, *Die Jünger Jesu*, which condemned the smugness and hypocrisy of his former fellow citizens. Frank settled in Munich, divorcing his wife in 1952 and marrying Charlotte London-Jäger. An autobiographical novel, *Links, wo das Herz ist* (1952; translated as *Heart on the Left*, 1954) describes his ideals, disappointments, and alienation in exile and after his return to Germany; it ends with the prediction that socialism will replace capitalism by the year 2000.

During the last decade of his life Frank received many honors in both parts of divided Germany. He was elected to the Deutsche Akademie für Sprache und Dichtung (German Academy for Language and Literature) in 1950 and the Bavarian Academy in 1951. He received awards from Würzburg in 1952 and Nuremberg in 1953, as well as the Große Bundesverdienstkreuz (Commander's Cross of the Order of Merit) of the Federal Republic of Germany in 1957. East Germany awarded him the Nationalpreis erster Klasse (National Order of Merit First Class) in 1955, and he was elected to the Deutsche Akademie der Künste (German Academy of the Arts) in East Berlin the same year. He received an honorary doctorate from the Humboldt University in East Berlin in 1957. Despite his warm reception in East Ger-

Frank circa 1960, the year his play Ruth *was published*

many and his undiminished faith in socialism, Frank chose to live in West Germany.

Frank's comedy *Der Außenseiter* (The Outsider) had been published in 1937 in Basel but was never performed. He revised it as *Die Hutdynastie* (The Hat Dynasty) for the 1959 volume *Schauspiele* (Plays). *Die Hutdynastie*, about a family that owns a hat-manufacturing company, is intended as a criticism of capitalism and its "Geldwahnsinn" (money madness). The search for profit is the overriding motivation of the family. The firm produced military hats for Hitler's armies, thereby—according to Frank—helping pave the way for World War II and the Holocaust. Now in 1958, the company has begun producing uniform caps for the rearmament of West Germany—where, it is pointed out, atomic weapons are stationed.

In 1933 the owner's son-in-law disappeared, abandoning his domineering wife and an eight-hundred-thousand-mark share in the family business. He has been believed dead but has actually been a sailor for twenty-five years. He now returns from a more natural and authentic world, not distorted by greed and female domination,

and saves his son's marriage, stops the production of military hats, gets his father-in-law committed to a mental institution, and rescues his wife's second husband from her domination. He then returns to sea, leaving his recovered fortune to be used for a retired sailor's home.

Ruth (published, 1960; performed, 1962) is Frank's dramatization of his novel *Die Jünger Jesu*. The Jewish girl Ruth Bodenheim was sent from Auschwitz to work for a year in a military bordello in Poland. She returns to her hometown in 1950, kills the unpunished Nazi murderer of her parents, and is tried for murder. As in *Die Ursache*, the trial is presented onstage. Ruth is found innocent, and she leaves to marry her former fiancé, a young psychiatrist. The play describes the survival of Nazi criminals and Nazi attitudes in postwar Germany.

Frank, who had visited the Soviet Union in 1955, received that country's Tolstoy Medal in 1960. He died in Munich on 18 August 1961.

Letters:

"Aus seinem Briefwechsel mit dem Insel-Verlag," edited by Gerhard Hay, *Archiv für Geschichte des Buchwesens*, 14 (1973-1974): 134-162.

Bibliographies:

E. H. Samorajczyk, "A Bibliography of Leonhard Frank's Major Works," Ph.D. dissertation, University of Southern California, 1974;

Maritta Rost, Rosemarie Geist, and Jörg Armer, *Leonhard Frank: Auswahlbibliographie zum 100. Geburtstag* (Leipzig: Deutsche Bücherei, 1981).

References:

William Anders, "Der Heimkehrer nach zwei Weltkriegen im deutschen Drama," Ph.D. dissertation, University of Pennsylvania, 1951, pp. 182-185;

Otto F. Best, "Leonhard Frank," in *Deutsche Exilliteratur seit 1933*, edited by John M. Spalek and Joseph Strelka, volume 1, part 1 (Bern & Munich: Francke, 1976), pp. 371-382;

Richard Drews, "Er ging unbeirrt seinen Weg: Zu Leonhard Franks 70. Geburtstag," *Die Weltbühne*, 37 (1952): 11-77;

Christian Emmrich, "Problematik und Gestaltung der Würzburger Trilogie Leonhard Franks," Ph.D. dissertation, University of Jena, 1956;

Charlotte Frank, *Sagen, was noch zu sagen ist* (Munich: Nymphenburger Verlagshandlung, 1982);

Frank and Hanns Jobst, *Leonard Frank: 1882-1961* (Munich: Nymphenburger Verlagshandlung, 1962);

Martin Glaubrecht, *Studien zum Frühwerk Leonhard Franks* (Bonn: Bouvier, 1965);

Reinhold Grimm, "Leonhard Frank," in *Fränkische Klassiker: Eine Literaturgeschichte in Einzeldarstellungen*, edited by W. Buhl (Nuremburg: Nürnberger Presse, 1971), pp. 658-666;

Grimm, "Zum Stil des Erzählers Leonhard Frank," *Jahrbuch für fränkische Landesforschung*, 21 (1961): 165-195;

Harold von Hofe, "German Literature in Exile: Leonhard Frank," *German Quarterly*, 20 (March 1947): 122-128;

Friedrich Wilhelm Kaufmann, "Das Werk Leonhard Franks," *Germanic Review*, 7 (January 1932): 45-58;

Rudolf Kayser, "Leonhard Frank," *Die neue Rundschau*, 43 (1932): 425-426;

Wilhelm Knevels, "Über einige expressionistische Dramatiker," *Der Geisteskampf der Gegenwart*, 65 (1929): 455-461;

T. C. Mathey, "Das Sozialkritische in den Werken Leonhard Franks," Ph.D. dissertation, University of Southern California, 1968;

Heinz Neugebauer, *Leonhard Frank* (Berlin: Volk und Wissen, 1960);

Ernst Pentzoldt, "Leonhard Franks Würzburger Abenteuer: Zum Skandal um die Aufführung von 'Karl und Anna' in Würzburg," *Deutsche Rundschau*, 79 (1953): 75-77;

Robert Petsch, "Novelle und Drama: Bei Gelegenheit von L. Franks 'Karl und Anna,'" *Der Kreis: Zeitschrift für künstlerische Kultur*, 6 (1929): 572-581;

Jenny de Rouck, "Leonhard Frank: Liebe zur Menschheit in seinem Leben und Werk," Ph.D. dissertation, University of Ghent, 1961;

Christian Schmeling, *Leonhard Frank und die Weimarer Zeit* (Frankfurt am Main: Lang, 1989);

Walter H. Sokel, *The Writer in Extremis* (Stanford: Stanford University Press, 1959);

David Turner, "Expressionist Pathos and Psychological Analysis: Opposition to War in Leonhard Frank's *Der Mensch ist gut* and Stefan Zweig's *Der Zwang*," *Forum for Modern Language Studies*, 24 (1988): 301-320;

Zinaida Viktorovna Zhitomirskaia, *Leongard Frank* (Moscow: Kniga, 1967).

Papers:

The papers of Leonhard Frank are in the Literarisches Archiv der Deutschen Akademie der Künste (Literary Archive of the German Academy of Arts), Berlin, and the Deutsches Literatur-Archiv (German Literature Archive), Marbach am Neckar.

Reinhard Goering

(23 June 1887 - circa 14 October 1936)

Jochen Richter
Allegheny College

PLAY PRODUCTIONS: *Seeschlacht*, Dresden, Königliches Schauspielhaus, 10 February 1918;

Der Erste, Berlin, Kammerspiele des deutschen Theaters, 25 October 1918;

Scapa Flow, Frankfurt am Main, Neues Theater, 27 January 1920;

Der Zweite, Aachen, Stadttheater, 16 December 1923;

Die Südpolexpedition des Kapitäns Scott, Berlin, Staatliches Schauspielhaus, 16 February 1930;

Der Vagabund und das Mädchen, Oldenburg, Staatstheater, 23 April 1931;

Das Opfer: Oper, Hamburg, Staatsoper, 12 November 1937.

BOOKS: *Jung Schuk: Roman* (Munich: Delphin, 1913);

Seeschlacht: Tragödie (Berlin: Fischer, 1917); translated by J. M. Ritchie and J. D. Stowell as *Naval Encounter*, in *Vision and Aftermath: Four Expressionist War Plays* (London: Calder & Boyars, 1969), pp. 75-110;

Der Erste: Schauspiel (Berlin: Fischer, 1918);

Der Zweite: Tragödie (Berlin: Fischer, 1919); revised as *Dahin?* (Berlin: Fischer, 1919);

Die Retter: Tragisches Spiel (Berlin: Fischer, 1919);

Scapa Flow (Berlin: Fischer, 1919);

Die Südpolexpedition des Kapitäns Scott: Spiel in drei Teilen (Berlin: Propyläen, 1929);

Prost Helga!: Schauspiel (Berlin: Arcadia, 1930);

Der Vagabund und das Mädchen, by Goering and Robert Büschgens (Berlin: Fischer, 1931)—attribution to Goering is dubious;

Das Opfer: Oper, music by Winfried Zillig (Vienna: Universal-Edition, 1937);

Prosa, Dramen, Verse, edited by Dieter Hoffmann (Munich: Langen/Müller, 1961).

OTHER: *Das lyrische Jahrbuch 1912*, edited by Albert H. Rausch, contributions by Goering (Frankfurt am Main: Schirmer & Mahlau, 1912), pp. 173-182.

SELECTED PERIODICAL PUBLICATIONS— UNCOLLECTED: "Kriegerische Feier," *Neue Rundschau*, 30 (March 1918): 375-383;

"Gedichte," *Junges Deutschland*, 1, no. 2 (1918): 44;

"Vier Zeichnungen," *Junges Deutschland*, 1, no. 2 (1918): 48-49;

"Selbstbildnis," *Zuschauer*, 1, no. 2 (1920): 7;

"Zwei Zeichnungen und zwei Aquarelle," *Sturm*, 11, no. 4 (1920): 49, 55, 57; no. 11/12: 156;

"Andeutung zur Tanzfolge der Niddy Impekoven," *Zuschauer*, 1, no. 2 (1920): 8-9;

"Zur Uraufführung von *Scapa Flow*," *Zuschauer*, 1, no. 2 (1920): 3;

"Zwei Zeichnungen," *Sturm*, 12, no. 4 (1921): 77, 79;

"Der westliche Bhudda," *Neue Rundschau*, 37 (June 1926): 637-644;

"Gedichte," *Sturm*, 18, no. 9 (1927/1928): 134;

"Liedopfer," *Sturm*, 18, no. 10 (1927-1928): 137-144;

"Novelle Genua 1912," *Horen*, 5, no. 10 (1928/1929): 880-893;

"Gandhi," *Literatur*, 33 (1930-1931): 427-429;

"Rebellion," *Hochwart*, 2 (1932): 34-39;

"Arzt und Baukunst," *Medizinische Welt*, 6 (1932): 1115-1117;

"Der 'kranke' Nietzsche," *Literatur*, 35 (1933): 249-251;

"Erlöserprobe in Herrchenberg," *Querschnitt*, 14 (1934): 17-23;

"Der gnadenreiche Tobias," *Türmer*, 36 (1934): 505-512;

"Ein Mann erfährt Gerechtigkeit," *Neue Rundschau*, 48 (June 1937): 596-603;

"Die verlorene und wiedergefundene Musik," *Neue Rundschau*, 48 (June 1937): 591-594.

Although Reinhard Goering produced only a slim oeuvre consisting of some poetry, one novel, several short prose pieces, and eight published plays, he occupies an important place in German literature. Among his works, it is mainly his first play, *Seeschlacht* (published, 1917; performed, 1918; translated as *Naval Encounter*, 1969), and his last, *Die Südpolexpedition des Kapitäns Scott* (Captain Scott's Expedition to the South Pole, published, 1929; performed, 1930), on which his reputation rests. The former is considered one of the most important expressionist dramas dealing with World War I; the latter is counted among the outstanding dramatic examples of Die Neue Sachlichkeit (The New Objectivity).

Since the two plays did not conform to the aesthetic style prescribed by the National Socialists and since both dealt with the theme of de-feat, they disappeared from the German stage from 1933 to 1945. Goering's work was reprinted after 1945, and some of his plays were performed in the 1950s and 1960s, but his dramas shared the fate of those of other expressionist playwrights, such as Ernst Barlach, Walter Hasenclever, Georg Kaiser, Ernst Toller, and Fritz von Unruh: they never really recaptured the stage, although they still are considered part of the traditional canon.

Biographers have found it difficult to separate the facts of Goering's biography from his fiction. He was born at Castle Bieberstein, near Fulda, on 23 June 1887 to the *Regierungsbaumeister* (an architect employed by the state government) Friedrich Goering and Paula Treiß Goering. His father's suicide in 1895 led to his mother's mental breakdown; she spent most of the rest of her life in institutions. Relatives looked after Reinhard; Walter, born in 1888; and Lotte, born in 1889.

From 1894 to 1898 Goering attended primary schools in Brunswick, Münster, Oberstein, and Kaiserslautern. In 1898 he was enrolled in a boarding school in Traben-Trabach; he received his *Abitur*, qualifying him for study at a university, in 1906. He began studying law at the University of Jena in 1907 but soon switched to medicine. In the following four years he studied in Munich, Jena, Berlin, and Jena again. Although his field was medicine, his major areas of interest were art and literature. He wrote several unpublished plays and poems during this period. In 1910 he became engaged to Grete Braukmann; her father did not approve, and the engagement was broken off in 1911. In the same year Goering went to Paris to study sculpting and met Helene Gurowitsch, a Russian who was studying painting. On 11 November 1911 they were married, apparently because Helene was pregnant with their daughter Ulrike. The marriage was resented by both partners because it interfered with their artistic aspirations.

In 1912 Goering returned to the University of Munich to find that his financial support had been cut off because of his marriage. From this time on, he was constantly in debt. But 1912 also brought the first publication of Goering's poems, nine of which appeared in the anthology *Das lyrische Jahrbuch 1912* (The Poetical Almanac 1912). The poems are traditional in form and content and show no influence of the new expressionist movement. The editor of the anthology, Albert Rausch, whom Goering had met in 1907 and who wrote under the pseudonym Henry Benrath, opposed expressionism. It was Rausch who introduced Goering to the works of Stefan George, whose influence on Goering remained strong for the rest of Goering's life.

In 1913 Goering's only novel, *Jung Schuk* (Young Schuk), was published. It is patterned after Johann Wolfgang von Goethe's *Die Leiden des jungen Werthers* (The Sufferings of Young Werther, 1774; translated as *The Sorrows of W—*, 1779) and consists of an introduction by the "publisher" and the diary of young Schuk, who committed suicide. The novel uses specific autobiographical data, such as a stay on the island of Sylt in northern Germany and a trip to London which Goering took in 1910; it can also be read as an accurate psychograph of Goering. Schuk, like Goering, is torn between medicine and poetry. He shares his author's restlessness, his search for redemption and greatness, his self-torturing doubts mixed with arrogance and disdain for normal bourgeois existence. Elation and enthusiasm alternate with deep depression and despair; mystical experiences of harmony with nature are followed by horrifying feelings of emptiness, loneliness, and dislocation. Finally, although he would be older than the young Schuk when he did so, Goering, too, would commit suicide in an isolated location and not be discovered until sometime later.

The novel lacks structure and formal discipline. Some passages are embarrassing and tasteless in their strained effort to record Goering's most intimate feelings in an exalted tone; others are almost comical in their mixture of banality and idealism. But on the whole there is a sense of honesty and openness which is compelling.

In 1914 Goering moved to the University of Bonn to continue his study of medicine. When World War I broke out that year he was allowed to take a provisional examination and receive a medical license. After serving for four weeks as an army doctor in the Saarland, he contracted tuberculosis and was sent to Davos, Switzerland, for recuperation; his family joined him there. The four years he spent in Davos were the most stable and productive period in Goering's life. A second daughter, Susanne Ingrid, was born in 1915, and in 1916 he met Stefan George. In the same year he began writing *Seeschlacht* after reading an account of the Battle of Jutland between the fleets of Great Britain and Germany on 31 May 1916. One of the major naval encounters in modern history, the battle ended with heavy losses on both sides and without a clear victor. The first draft of *Seeschlacht* was finished within a week, and the play was published in 1917.

The play is set in the gun turret of a German destroyer before and during the Battle of Jutland. Each of the seven nameless sailors in the turret assumes a different attitude toward the events. The two main figures are "der Erste" (the First), who has a premonition of the death of the crew and is trying to find a hidden religious meaning in it, and "der Fünfte" (the Fifth), who rebels against the insanity of war, longs for a more humane world, and wants to realize "was sein kann zwischen Mensch und Mensch" (that which can be between people). To achieve this goal, der Fünfte is willing to mutiny; but before he can act, the battle erupts. He becomes intoxicated with the fighting and even assumes a commanding position. Dying together with the other sailors, he ends the play by posing a series of questions: "Ich habe gut geschossen, wie? Ich hätte auch gut gemeutert! Wie? Aber schießen lag uns wohl näher? Wie?" (I have shot well, haven't I? I would have mutinied well too! Wouldn't I? But shooting was more natural for us, wasn't it?).

With its confinement in space and time and its concentrated action, the play shows parallels to a Greek tragedy; for that reason, it has been argued that it does not classify as an expressionist drama. Most critics, however, agree that the intensity of the emotions expressed as well as the use of language are expressionist. The play was interpreted by some as a pacifist document and by others as a glorification of the seductive, intoxicating, Dionysian power of battle. It was dismissed as propaganda and praised as a tragedy portraying human reactions in an existential crisis. The sailors were seen as pigs who are butchered without control over their own destiny and as heroes who sacrifice themselves for their country. The play was attacked for defeatism, but the German navy lent its support by giving technical advice for the staging of the play. Most analyses try to prove that one of these positions reflects Goering's intentions, but it is precisely its ambivalence that made *Seeschlacht* a success. The same ambivalence in Goering's personal life made it possible for him both to show interest in communism and to join the National Socialist party.

The first performance of the play, on 10 February 1918 in Dresden, while World War I was still raging, used a realistic staging to a spectacular effect. One woman went into hysterics, and several spectators fainted. The second production, directed by Max Reinhardt in Berlin, included

Sketch by Ernst Stern of a scene from Goering's play Seeschlacht, *set in the gun turret of a German destroyer in World War I*
(Volk und Wissen Archiv, Berlin)

some of the best-known German actors, such as
Hermann Thimig, Conradt Veidt, Emil Jannings,
Paul Wegner, and Werner Krauß, and created a
different but equally strong response in the audience. Critics reported that at the end of the performance there was no applause: the audience
was so moved that it remained silent, and the atmosphere in the theater was compared to that in a
church.

Two years after its first appearance in print,
Seeschlacht had gone through eleven editions. In
1921 it shared the Schiller Prize with Fritz von
Unruh's *Ein Geschlecht* (A Generation, 1917). The
play remained successful until 1933. Several efforts to revive *Seeschlacht* after World War II, however, including a radio version produced by
Hans Lietzeau, met with little success.

In January 1916, about half a year before
writing *Seeschlacht*, Goering had written another
one-act play under the title "Keiner" (No One). It
was published in 1918 as *Der Erste* (The First
One) and premiered in Berlin on 25 October
1918. The play lacks the dramatic intensity of
Seeschlacht and is more lyrical in nature. There
are echoes of Hugo von Hofmannsthal's early lyri-

cal plays, although Goering's language does not
achieve the same artistic quality.

The idealistic priest Antonio saves Paula, a
young woman, from drowning herself, and they
fall in love. But Paula's love becomes obsessive,
and her demands interfere with Antonio's mission to help others. In a violent argument, he
strangles her. Paula's former lover appears immediately afterward, unaware that she is dead, and
splits her head with an axe, allowing Antonio to
blame him for her death. Antonio believes that
the murder and the cover-up are justified because of his mission to serve society. But when he
is confronted with the former lover, who is about
to be hanged for his alleged crime, he recognizes
that his convictions are based on delusions and offers himself as a sacrifice by confessing his murder. Although the plot seems to promise spectacular action, the play really does not move at all;
instead, it presents a superficial exploration of
the conflict between a person's duties to society
and his love for one person. The "double murder" of Paula is melodramatic and as unconvincing as Antonio's conversion at the end of the play
from Nietzschean superman to Christian martyr.

It was only the stunning success of *Seeschlacht* which led to the staging of *Der Erste*, and neither the critics nor the audiences responded favorably to the play. A second production, in Munich a year later, received similar negative reactions.

A variation of *Der Erste*, called *Der Zweite* (The Second One), was published in 1919. Where Antonio affirmed his duty to society by sacrificing Paula, his successor, Angelo, overcomes his egoistic aspirations through his willingness to forgive and serve his wife, Chloe. In the beginning, he is determined to leave Chloe because he cannot realize his own potential in their relationship. Under the tutelage of his sister, Esther, he learns that giving oneself, forgiving, service, and self-denial are higher values than self-fulfillment. He even forgives his wife's adultery, which he witnesses on his return home. As in *Der Erste*, the dialogue is forced to carry the abstract ideas, and the play lacks dramatic strength. *Der Zweite* was performed in 1923 in Aachen; no further effort was made to bring the play to the stage.

The periodical *Neue Rundschau* (New Review) published Goering's dramatic sketch "Kriegerische Feier" (Martial Celebration) in March 1918; the sketch was never performed on stage. It was written to commemorate the German soldiers killed in World War I and to strengthen the national resolve. After twenty months of fighting, the lancer Ullrich finds himself alone, tired, and desperate on the sandy plains of Poland. In visions he sees himself as a peaceful youth and then meets the ghosts of friends who have died in battle. They admonish him to hold to the spirit of 1914 and to continue the fight. At first Ullrich resists their beckoning, declaring that the bloodshed must end. But in a reversal similar to that of the fifth sailor in *Seeschlacht*, he rededicates himself to battle when he learns that his friend Richard has been shot by the enemy while swimming helplessly in the ocean.

On 21 June 1919 the German fleet, forced to surrender to the British, sank itself at Scapa Flow in the Orkney Islands off Scotland. *Scapa Flow*, Goering's play about the event, was published the same year. Goering may have hoped to repeat the stunning success he achieved with *Seeschlacht*, but the play did not succeed. *Scapa Flow* is intended to show the end of one era and the beginning of a new one, but it only bemoans the passing of the old world and fails to give a vision of the future. The first act is set on the ship of the German admiral and shows the paralyzed passivity and total demoralization of the sailors. They feel betrayed by their leaders and their country and long for action and the opportunity to prove themselves. The second act, set on the British flagship, contrasts the despair of the German sailors with the merriment of their English counterparts. Their mood abruptly changes when they witness the heroic scuttling of the German fleet. In a final speech the German admiral interprets the act as service to the fatherland and restoration of national honor. While in reality the British shot at the German sailors and took them prisoner, Goering's British sailors cannot help but admire the Germans' act of self-sacrifice.

The play consists mainly of isolated monologues; the interchangeable sailors and officers deliver speeches to the audience. As in "Kriegerische Feier," the message is clear: the Germans lost the war, but as long as there are Germans like these sailors at Scapa Flow there is hope for a return of past glories and the reemergence of a strong German nation.

Whereas he had not attended a performance of *Seeschlacht* and the publisher of the play could not even furnish a photograph of him, Goering directed the premiere of *Scapa Flow* at the Neues Theater (New Theater) in Frankfurt on 27 January 1920. The play failed: the lack of dramatic action and dialogue was criticized, as was the painful slowness of the performance. Productions in Frankfurt in 1922 and 1928 and in Bochum in 1938 fared no better.

Only with *Die Retter* (The Saviors), published in 1919, did Goering succeed in writing a play of similar quality to *Seeschlacht*. Ironically, it has not yet been performed on stage. In its concentrated, simple structure; its terse, formulaic language; and its depiction of an essential human condition, it anticipates some features of Samuel Beckett's theater of the absurd. Unlike *Der Erste*, *Der Zweite*, and especially *Scapa Flow*, it does not try to deliver a political or moral message but to present a general truth.

Two dying old men who have lived morally upright lives are forced into situations in which they cannot avoid doing evil. A mortally wounded man crawls into their room to kill his also mortally wounded attacker for the sake of justice. To save the man under his protection, the first old man has to strangle the avenger. The second man ends up in a similar situation. The title of the play turns out to be ironic: there are no saviors and no salvation.

After the two old men return to their death-beds in despair, a young man and woman dance into their room. In their effortless, carefree dance they symbolize existence as it could have been. At first the old men mourn that they are seeing this possibility too late; then they take solace in the fact that they have at least had the opportunity to see it; finally they die wondering whether they have been deceived again. Their doubts prove justified: the young dancers are shot to death. Even so, their dance demonstrates what might be possible between human beings.

After this amazing outburst of creativity, which had yielded six plays, some poetry, and several short prose pieces, a restless, vagrant life began for Goering. In the spring of 1918 he suddenly disappeared from Davos and spent the following two years wandering through Switzerland as an adherent of Buddhism. During his wanderings Goering met a fifteen-year-old dancer, Niddy Impekoven. In her autobiography, *Die Geschichte eines Wunderkindes* (The Story of a Child Prodigy, 1955), she credits him with curing her of anorexia. Her parents broke up the relationship when they found out that Goering was married and had two children.

After his experience with Buddhism, Goering became interested in Marxism. He is said to have joined the Communist party for a short time in 1920, but there is no documentation of his membership.

In 1922 he was practicing medicine in Brunswick, where he used such unconventional methods that other doctors had him confined in an insane asylum for six weeks. The writer Kasimir Edschmid, who knew Goering, gives an indication of what must have disturbed Goering's medical colleagues: "Seine Therapie war, die Patienten zu verprügeln, um ihnen die Hysterie auszutreiben.... Er legte die Neurotiker in Betten, die er im Wald aufschlug.... Seine Kinder ließ er nachts im Freien in Fischkästen mit Luftlöchern schlafen und erlaubte ihnen nicht, Schokolade zu essen" (His therapy consisted in beating his patients to cure their hysteria.... He put neurotics in beds in the open woods.... His children had to sleep outside in holding tanks for fish, and he did not allow them to eat chocolate). Also in 1922 he met Dagmar Öhrbom, a teacher from Finland who was eleven years older than he. They became lifelong friends, and he frequently visited her in Finland or traveled with her in Germany, Austria, and France. It was Öhrbom who persuaded him to

finish his medical degree, which he did in 1926 with a dissertation titled "Über einen Fall von *Aneurysma spurium*" (On a Case of Spurious Aneurysm), and it is through her handwritten "Aufzeichnungen aus meinem Tagebuch über meine Reisen mit dem Dichter Reinhard Goering von Sept. '23 bis Okt. '36" (Notes from My Diary about My Travels with the Poet Reinhard Goering from September 1923 to October 1936) that many details about Goering's life have been pieced together. A copy of these handwritten "Notes" is in the Deutsches Literaturchiv, Schiller Nationalmuseum (German Literature Archives, Schiller National Museum), Marbach am Neckar.

In 1926 Goering was divorced from his wife, but he remained in close contact with her and his daughters and stayed with them for short periods after the divorce and even after he remarried. For part of that year he lived in the home of the Berlin bookstore owner Carl Holzapfel, where he met Holzapfel's twelve-year-old daughter, Marlene; she would become his wife nine years later. He set up practice in Berlin in 1927, opened a sanatorium for intellectuals in Bad Fürsteneck the same year, worked in Bad Neuenahr as a general practitioner in May 1928 and as a surgeon in June, but in November he returned to Davos. There he worked on *Die Südpolexpedition des Kapitäns Scott*, which was published in 1929 and received the Kleist Prize in 1930. The play is based on the diary kept by Robert F. Scott during his tragic expedition to the South Pole in 1911-1912. After fifteen hundred kilometers of superhuman efforts and suffering, Scott and his four companions reach their goal—only to find that Roald Amundsen has already claimed the pole for Norway. Disappointed, the five turn back, only to die a short distance from their base camp. The play ends with the contrast between Amundsen's triumphant arrival in Tasmania and Lady Scott's desperate hope for her husband's return.

Since the plot does not lend itself to dramatic confrontation, Goering introduced epic elements into the play: a chorus presents the background information and comments on the events. In its essence, however, the play is a heroic tragedy. This combination of epic techniques and conventional tragic theater was objected to by many critics, who also pointed to a lack of dramatic conflict. Nevertheless, the original production, directed by Leopold Jessner in Berlin on 16 February 1930, was favorably received by the audience. The play was staged in Darmstadt and

Würzburg in the same year, and productions were presented in 1952 in Remscheid and in 1958 in Berlin.

The play *Prost Helga!* (Cheers, Helga!, 1930) advocates some of Goering's rather unorthodox ideas about education, such as nudity and fondling among children. The main character, a doctor, elopes with a woman and later with her daughter. The play, which was never performed on stage, might have been the major reason why in 1933 the Nazi propaganda chief Joseph Goebbels rescinded Goering's nomination to the Nationalsozialistischer Dichterkreis des Reichsbundes für Freilicht- und Volksspiele (National Socialist organization of writers for the theater).

While residing in Wiesbaden in 1930 Goering became acquainted with the bookstore owner Hans Joachim von Goetz. The extensive correspondence between the two, kept in the German Literature Archive in Marbach, is a major source of information about the last years of Goering's life. According to his letters to von Goetz, Goering started to participate in the activities of the Nazi party in 1931 and became a member of the party in December of that year. In the same year he was arrested for attacking a Bavarian policeman and sentenced to serve two weeks in prison, but there are no records indicating that he actually served the time.

From 1930 Goering spent much of his time living or traveling with Marlene Holzapfel. He organized a sanatorium in Spangenberg in 1931 and attempted to set up a medical practice in Freiburg in 1932. From October 1932 to April 1933 Goering and Marlene experimented in "natural" living in a small cottage without running water and electricity. A son, Reinhard, was born in December 1932. The experiment ended with all three suffering ill effects from their primitive living conditions. Goering tried to organize a sanatorium in Bad Ems in 1933. That year he experienced the first symptoms of what seems to have been intestinal cancer. An operation on 23 January 1934 was not successful. In April a second son was born and named Knut-Stefan, in honor of the Norwegian author Knut Hamsun and Stefan George. Goering worked as a general practitioner in Berlin in the fall of 1934 and near Koblenz in 1935.

On 6 April 1935 he married Marlene Holzapfel, who was then twenty-one. In May he was hospitalized, and in November he underwent a second operation. Neither the operation nor a subsequent fasting cure improved his health. The frequency of his visits to Öhrbom in Finland increased in 1936. On 11 October 1936 he disappeared from Berlin. On 4 November his body was found in a forest near Jena. The autopsy showed that he had committed suicide by slitting his wrists and injecting himself with poison about three weeks earlier. Shortly before his death Goering had reworked *Die Südpolexpedition des Kapitäns Scott* as a libretto for an opera tentatively titled "Die Pinguine" (The Penguins). The work was completed and set to music by the twelve-tone composer Winfried Zillig. It premiered under the title *Das Opfer* (The Sacrifice) on 12 November 1937 at the Hamburg Staatsoper and was produced again in November 1960 in Kassel.

Goering's was a restless, chaotic, and controversial life; success either as a doctor or as a writer eluded him. Nevertheless, just as Captain Scott in Goering's last play achieved a place in history even though he did not discover the South Pole, Goering owns a place in the history of the German theater. The uncompromising intensity and sincerity of the plays give his work a timeless quality.

Bibliography:

Michael C. Eben, "A Bibliography of Secondary Literature Concerning Reinhard Goering (1887-1936)," *Modern Language Notes*, 92 (April 1977): 609-614.

Biography:

Robert C. Davis, *Final Mutiny: Reinhard Goering, His Life and Art*, Stanford German Studies, volume 21 (New York: Lang, 1987).

References:

Otto F. Best, "Rebellion und Ergebung: Reinhard Goerings *Seeschlacht* als dreifache Demonstration," *Colloquia Germanica*, 2 (1973): 144-161;

Roy C. Cowen, "Reinhard Goerings *Seeschlacht*: Tendenzstück oder Dichtung?," *Zeitschrift für deutsche Philologie*, 91 (1972): 528-540;

Manfred Durzak, "Nachwirkungen Stefan Georges im Expressionismus," *German Quarterly*, 42 (May 1969): 393-417;

Friedrich Düsel, "Dramatische Rundschau," *Westermanns Monatshefte*, 74, no. 2 (1930): 179-181;

Kasimir Edschmid, *Lebendiger Expressionismus: Auseinandersetzungen, Gestalten, Erinnerungen* (Munich: Desch, 1961), pp. 294-297;

Reinhold Grimm, "Zwischen Expressionismus und Faschismus," in *Die sogenannten Zwanziger Jahre: First Wisconsin Workshop*, edited by Grimm and Jost Hermand, Schriften zur Literatur, 13 (Bad Homburg: Gehlen, 1970), pp. 15-45;

Niddy Impekoven, *Die Geschichte eines Wunderkindes* (Zurich: Rotapfel, 1955);

Eberhard Lämmert, "Das expressionistische Verkündigungsdrama," in *Literatur und Gesellschaft vom neunzehnten ins zwanzigste Jahrhundert*, edited by Hans Joachim Schrimpf (Bonn: Bouvier, 1963), pp. 309-329;

William J. Lillyman, "Reinhard Goering's *Seeschlacht*: The Failure of the Will," *German Life and Letters*, 22 (July 1969): 350-358;

Dorothy Sue Martin, "The Life and Literature of Reinhard Goering: A Study in Contradictions," Ph.D. dissertation, University of Illinois, 1980;

Franz Norbert Mennemeier, "Reinhard Goerings Tragödienversuch," in *Untersuchungen zur Literatur als Geschichte: Festschrift für Benno von Wiese*, edited by Vincent J. Günther, Helmut Koopmann, Peter Pütz, and Hans Joachim Schrimpf (Berlin: Schmidt, 1973), pp. 465-479;

Günter Rühle, *Theater für die Republik 1917-1933: Im Spiegel der Kritik* (Frankfurt am Main: Fischer, 1967), pp. 112-118, 1008-1014;

Rühle, *Zeit und Theater*, volume 1: *Vom Kaiserreich zur Republik 1913-1925* (Berlin: Propyläen, 1973);

Helmut Sembdner, ed., *Der Kleist-Preis 1912-1932: Eine Dokumentation* (Berlin: Schmidt, 1967);

Ingeborg H. Solbrig, ed., *Reinhard Goering: Seeschlacht. Seebattle-Tragedy. 1917*, Stuttgarter Textbeiträge, 2 (Stuttgart: Akademischer Verlag, 1977);

Janis Little Solomon, *Die Kriegsdramen Reinhard Goerings* (Bern: Francke, 1985).

Papers:

Most of Reinhard Goering's manuscripts and letters are in the Deutsche Literaturarchiv, Schiller Nationalmuseum (German Literature Archive, Schiller National Museum), Marbach am Neckar.

Max Halbe

(4 October 1865 - 30 November 1944)

John Hibberd

University of Bristol

PLAY PRODUCTIONS: *Eisgang*, Berlin, Freie Volksbühne, 7 February 1892;

Jugend, Berlin, Residenztheater, 23 April 1893;

Der Amerikafahrer, Berlin, Residenztheater, 3 February 1894;

Lebenswende, Berlin, Deutsches Theater, 21 January 1896;

Mutter Erde, Berlin, Deutsches Theater, 18 September 1897;

Der Eroberer, Berlin, Lessingtheater, 29 October 1898;

Die Heimatlosen, Berlin, Lessingtheater, 21 February 1899;

Das tausendjährige Reich, Munich, Residenztheater, 28 December 1899;

Haus Rosenhagen, Dresden, Königliches Schauspielhaus, 14 February 1901;

Walpurgistag, Dresden, Königliches Schauspielhaus, 13 October 1902;

Der Strom, Vienna, Burgtheater, 19 October 1903;

Die Insel der Seligen, Munich, Schauspielhaus, 9 December 1905;

Das wahre Gesicht, Hamburg, Schauspielhaus, 9 October 1907;

Blaue Berge, Munich, Schauspielhaus, 20 November 1908;

Der Ring des Gauklers, Munich, Residenztheater, 5 January 1912;

Freiheit, Munich, Schauspielhaus, 27 September 1913;

Schloß Zeitvorbei, Munich, Schauspielhaus, 18 January 1919;

Hortense Ruland, Mannheim, Nationaltheater, 28 November 1919;

Kikeriki, Magdeburg, Stadttheater, 11 March 1922;

Die Traumgesichte des Adam Thor, Munich, Residenztheater, 25 October 1927;

Meister Jörge Michel und seine Gesellen, Munich, Prinzregententheater, 15 May 1928;

Präsidentenwahl, Munich, Residenztheater, 28 September 1929;

Leben und Lieben in der Natur (Hahnentanz), Munich, Bonbonnière, October 1929;

Ginevra oder der Ziegelstein, Munich, Residenztheater, 7 June 1932;

Heinrich von Plauen, Marienburg, Festspiele, June 1933;

Erntefest, Danzig, Staatstheater, 3 October 1936;

Durch die Jahrhunderte, Elbing, Stadttheater, summer 1937;

Kaiser Friedrich II. Danzig, Staatstheater, 4 October 1940.

BOOKS: *Die Beziehungen zwischen Friedrich II. und dem päpstlichen Stuhl vom Tode Innocenz III. bis zum Goslarer Tage* (Berlin: Cynamon, 1888);

Friedrich II. und der päpstliche Stuhl, bis zur Kaiserkrönung (Berlin: Mayer & Müller, 1888);

Ein Emporkömmling: Sociales Trauerspiel (Norden: Fischer, 1889);

Freie Liebe: Modernes Drama (Guben: Krollmann, 1890);

Eisgang: Modernes Schauspiel (Berlin: Fischer, 1892);

Jugend: Ein Liebesdrama in drei Aufzügen (Berlin: Fischer, 1893); translated by Sara Tracy Barrows as *Youth* (Garden City, N.Y.: Doubleday, Page, 1916);

Der Amerikafahrer: Ein Scherzspiel in Knittelreimen (Dresden: Bondi, 1894);

Lebenswende: Eine Komödie (Dresden: Bondi, 1896);

Mutter Erde: Drama in fünf Aufzügen (Berlin: Bondi, 1897); translated by Paul H. Grummann as *Mother Earth*, in *The German Classics of the Nineteenth and Twentieth Centuries*, edited by Kuno Francke and W. G. Howard, volume 20 (New York: German Publication Society, 1915), pp. 111-233;

Frau Meseck: Eine Dorfgeschichte (Berlin: Bondi, 1897);

Der Eroberer: Tragödie in fünf Aufzügen (Berlin: Bondi, 1899);

Die Heimatlosen: Drama in fünf Aufzügen (Berlin: Bondi, 1899);

Max Halbe (lithograph by Karl Bauer)

Das tausendjährige Reich: Drama in vier Aufzügen (Berlin: Bondi, 1900);

Ein Meteor: Eine Künstlergeschichte (Berlin: Bondi, 1901);

Haus Rosenhagen: Drama in drei Aufzügen (Berlin: Bondi, 1901); translated by Grummann as *The Rosenhagens* (Boston: Badger, 1910);

Walpurgistag: Eine Dichterkomödie (Berlin: Entsch, 1902);

Der Strom: Drama in drei Aufzügen (New York: Lederer, 1903; Berlin: Bondi, 1904);

Die Insel der Seligen: Eine Komödie in vier Akten (Munich: Langen, 1906);

Das wahre Gesicht: Drama in fünf Akten und einem Vorspiel (Munich: Langen, 1907);

Blaue Berge: Komödie in vier Akten (Munich: Langen, 1909 [i.e., 1908]);

Der Ring des Lebens: Ein Novellenbuch (Munich: Langen, 1910);

Der Ring des Gauklers: Ein Spiel in vier Akten (Munich: Langen, 1911);

Die Tat des Dietrich Stobäus: Roman (Munich: Langen, 1911);

Freiheit: Ein Schauspiel von 1812, in drei Akten (Munich: Langen, 1913);

Jo: Roman (Berlin: Ullstein, 1917);

Hortense Ruland: Tragödie in drei Akten (Munich: Langen, 1917);

Schloß Zeitvorbei: Dramatische Legende (Munich: Langen, 1917);

Gesammelte Werke, 7 volumes (Munich: Langen, 1917-1923);

Kikeriki: Eine barocke Komödie in drei Akten (Munich: Langen, 1921);

Der Frühlingsgarten (Berlin: Mosaik, 1922);

Die Auferstehungsnacht des Doktors Adalbert: Osternovelle (Leipzig: Gesellschaft der Freunde der deutschen Bücherei, 1928);

Meister Jörge Michel und seine Gesellen: Spiel in einem Akt (Munich: Bruckmann, 1928);

Präsidentenwahl: Schauspiel in drei Akten (Berlin: Vertriebsstelle und Verlag Deutscher Bühnenschriftsteller und Bühnenkomponisten, 1929);

Die Traumgesichte des Adam Thor: Schauspiel in fünf Bildern (Berlin: Horen, 1929);

Ginevra oder der Ziegelstein: Komödie in fünf Akten (Berlin: Vertriebsstelle und Verlag Deutscher Bühnenschriftsteller und Bühnenkomponisten, 1931);

Generalkonsul Stenzel und sein gefährliches Ich: Roman (Munich: Langen, 1931);

Heinrich von Plauen: Schauspiel in fünf Akten (Marienburg: Grossnick, 1933);

Scholle und Schicksal: Geschichte meines Lebens (Munich: Knorr & Hirth, 1933); revised as *Scholle und Schicksal: Die Geschichte meiner Jugend* (Salzburg: Das Bergland-Buch, 1940);

Jahrhundertwende: Geschichte meines Lebens, 1893-1914 (Danzig: Kafemann, 1935);

Die Elixiere des Glücks: Roman (Leipzig: Payne, 1936);

Erntefest: Schauspiel (Berlin: Vertriebsstelle und Verlag Deutscher Bühnenschriftsteller und Bühnenkomponisten, 1936);

Kaiser Friedrich II.: Schauspiel in fünf Akten (Salzburg: Das Bergland-Buch, 1940);

Durch die Jahrhunderte: Festspiel zur Siebenhundert-Jahrfeier der Stadt Elbing (Essen-Bredery: West, 1952).

Collection: *Sämtliche Werke*, 14 volumes (Salzburg: Das Bergland-Buch, 1945-1950).

SELECTED PERIODICAL PUBLICATION—
UNCOLLECTED: "Berliner Brief," *Gesellschaft*, 5 (1889): 1171-1186; excerpts reprinted in *Dramen des deutschen Naturalismus*, edited by Roy C. Cowen (Munich: Winkler, 1981), pp. 621-624.

To some, Max Halbe ranks second to Gerhart Hauptmann among the dramatists of the German naturalist movement; to others, he is a minor figure whose significance lies in his evocation of the landscape and traditions of West Prussia. That dual reputation belies the brevity and looseness of his adherence to naturalism and the power of his best work; it has also meant that his nonnaturalist pieces have suffered oblivion. *Jugend* (1893; translated as *Youth*, 1916) made him a household name; it was a phenomenal success, for two decades the most frequently performed of all modern German plays. Further successes, *Mutter Erde* (1897; translated as *Mother Earth*, 1915), *Haus Rosenhagen* (1901; translated as *The Rosenhagens*, 1910), and *Der Strom* (The River, 1903; published 1904) followed. Along with *Eisgang* (The Ice Is Moving, 1892), they were established in the German repertoire in the years up to World War I. But in the general estimation of his contemporaries his later work (more than twenty plays, as well as stories and novels) never equaled *Jugend*, and the man who in the 1890s seemed about to become Germany's greatest living dramatist never fulfilled his early promise. His mystical bent, which came increasingly to

the fore after 1900, found little understanding. In the 1930s he was smiled on by the Nazis, for he wrote of rural life in his native region, stressed the claims of tradition and nature, and depicted the rootlessness of modern intellectuals and urban civilization; he could thus be seen as a forerunner of the "Blut und Boden" (blood and soil) literature that the Nazis favored, with its celebration of "healthy German" values. This association has not enhanced Halbe's standing since that time. His volume of memoirs, *Jahrhundertwende* (Turn of the Century, 1935), is a valuable record of the exciting cultural scene in Berlin and Munich from 1893 to 1914.

Halbe's family had long been established as farmers in the lowlands of the Vistula delta. They were proud, independent, dour, and often eccentric characters, with a strong sense of their dependence on the elemental forces of nature. That inheritance and the landscape of his youth constituted, he later concluded, an all-decisive, inescapable influence. The power of nature and recurring patterns in human life were never far from his thoughts. In his plays he was to draw on accounts of his forebearers' struggles to secure property and life against floods, evoking the atmosphere of the rural communities where Germans and Poles lived in close proximity. He was born on 4 October 1865 at Güttland, West Prussia (now Kozliny, Poland), a village then several hours' journey from Danzig (Gdansk). His father, Robert Halbe, who employed some twenty to thirty men and women, had married Bertha Alex, a farmer's daughter, in 1863. Their first child had died soon after birth. Halbe was the second, a difficult, oversensitive boy who resented the way his brother Felix soon monopolized their mother's affection. When the four-year-old Felix died in 1871, Halbe was plagued by guilt at his jealousy. His early years were spent without youthful companions. As Catholics in a Protestant community the Halbes had few contacts with neighboring landowners, and Halbe, who had a private tutor, was not encouraged to fraternize with the villagers. His life was dominated by the rhythm of the seasons and by imaginative brooding and reading encouraged by solitude. His Polish nanny regaled him with superstitions and ghost stories: they were, he later thought, not devoid of wisdom.

In 1875 he went to the grammar school in Marienburg (now Malbork). Among the other pupils, whose enmity to or envy of his academic brilliance he perceived or assumed, he was a lonely figure. In 1883 he gladly left for distant southern Germany to study law at Heidelberg University but transferred the next year to Munich and switched to German and history; in 1885 he moved to Berlin University. The country boy wanted to experience the modern city; the budding writer sought the centers of the newest developments in literature. In 1887 he returned to Munich University and in 1888 received the highest commendation for his doctoral thesis on the medieval emperor Frederick II's relations with the papacy. By then he had made contact with such leading figures in the new naturalist movement as Michael Georg Conrad, in whose Munich periodical *Gesellschaft* (Society) Halbe first appeared in print in 1887 with a scene from his *Ein Emporkömmling* (An Upstart, 1889), and the Friedrichshagen circle in Berlin.

Halbe sympathized with the naturalists' call for a new "scientific" literature. He was influenced by Charles Darwin and nineteenth-century materialist philosophy and was critical of the stifling conventions, moral hypocrisy, and social injustice in contemporary Germany. But *Ein Emporkömmling* is not a naturalist play, though it treats a social problem. Here Halbe's inspiration was Friedrich Hebbel, the great dramatist of an earlier realist generation. Halbe was, however, one of the first to proclaim the seminal importance of Henrik Ibsen; he did so in the *Gesellschaft* in 1889, stressing the need to treat contemporary issues. In that same year he witnessed the breakthrough of German naturalist drama, being present at the premieres of Gerhart Hauptmann's *Vor Sonnenaufgang* (1889; translated as *Before Dawn*, 1909) and Hermann Sudermann's *Die Ehre* (1890; translated as *Honor*, 1915) at the Freie Bühne (Free Stage) in Berlin. Yet neither his first play nor his *Freie Liebe* (Free Love, 1890) found entry to that or any other stage. *Freie Liebe* treats the strains of cohabitation outside marriage within a disapproving society. Before he married her in 1891 Halbe had such a relationship with Luise Heck, a farmer's daughter from Saxony whom he met in Berlin. He was adamantly opposed to the ties of bourgeois marriage, and later, as the father of three children (Robert, born in 1891; Anneliese, born in 1895; and Max Waldemar, born in 1896), he did not avoid erotic involvements. *Freie Liebe*, with its concentration on situation rather than action and its everyday language and incomplete sentences, stands under the influence of the story collection *Papa Hamlet* (1889), by Arno Holz and Johannes

Schlaf, a stylistic model for much naturalist writing. The play attacks narrow-mindedness and touches on women's liberation and the exploitation of the working class. But Halbe concentrates on the hero's inability to recognize real, binding values: this inability is, by implication, the crucial modern problem.

Despite Halbe's close connections with the Freie Bühne, he found no ally in its director, Otto Brahm (whom he dubbed naturalism's Oliver Cromwell). In February 1892, however, the Freie Volksbühne (Free People's Stage), recently founded to bring culture to the workers, put on *Eisgang* in a production directed by J. G. Stollberg. The reviews of the performance were mixed, but the audience applauded what they believed to be the work's announcement of the inevitable triumph of socialism. In fact, Halbe focuses not on the exploitation of the farmworkers but on the overwhelming conviction of Hugo von Tetzlaff, a young, would-be reformist landowner, that the guilt of a previous generation and the present circumstances (in other words, heredity and environment—central themes in naturalism) are forces so strong that his good intentions must come to nothing; he can only expiate the guilt as the victim of a historical process that is also a natural cataclysm. The well-managed crowd scenes point forward to Hauptmann's drama *Die Weber* (1892; translated as *The Weavers*, 1899); and the mixture of social realism, local color, psychological interest, sentiment, and symbolism ensured this tragedy considerable success after Halbe's name had become established.

In *Jugend* Halbe drew on an episode from his own youth. The young cousins Hans Hartwig and Annchen; their benign Uncle Hoppe, a Catholic priest in a country parish; and the severely ascetic Polish curate Gregor von Schigorski are based on real people and are convincingly true to life. The basis of the play's popular appeal was Halbe's ability to capture the feelings of the young lovers, a passion that finds obstacles in their own hopes and fears as well as in the attitudes of those around them. Annchen, whom Gregor is pressuring to enter a convent, sees in Hans her chance to escape from the stigma of her illegitimate birth. Hans fights against his love for Annchen, which he thinks will interfere with his ambition to seek a full life beyond the confines of bourgeois society and domesticity. In a bid to bind Hans to her, Annchen goes to his bedroom one night; this episode gave some theater managers qualms and made for a succès de

Scene from a 1935 production at the National Theater, Mannheim, of Halbe's 1893 play Jugend

scandale. At the end, Annchen's mentally retarded half-brother Amandus, jealous of Hans, shoots at him but kills Annchen. The theme of heredity versus environment and the detailed evocation of the West Prussian setting mark *Jugend* as a naturalist play. But the realistic dialogue verges on lyricism, and lighting effects underline the symbolic contrast of the enclosed house and the springtime outside. The real theme is the power of love: Hoppe, Gregor, and Amandus are as subject to erotic urges as the lovers themselves. In contrast to Frank Wedekind's *Frühlings Erwachen* (1891; translated as *The Awakening of Spring*, 1909), which has a similar theme, Halbe's dramatic technique is more traditional, his approach is more discreet, and he does not eschew sentiment; yet, like Wedekind, he questions conventional moral attitudes.

Paul Schlenther, who had taken over as director of the Freie Bühne, insisted that the play's ending was unsatisfactory, and many others later agreed that Amandus's fatal intervention was not properly motivated. Halbe believed that the ele-

mental forces at work were clear enough and refused to change the last scene. Time was to prove that the ending was good theater. Indeed, here as in his later pieces Halbe showed that he could rival anyone in dramatic effects; he was even accused of writing melodrama.

Jugend, written in 1892, was turned down by several directors and had to wait for its first performance until Siegmund Lautenburg, who was adding serious contemporary drama by such playwrights as Ibsen and August Strindberg to the repertory of farces at the Residenztheater in Berlin, finally scheduled the play for a single Sunday matinee in April 1893. This production, directed by Hans Meery, proved so successful that it was put on nightly; the play was soon taken up throughout Germany. The first Annchen, Vilma von Mayburg, made her name in the part, as did Centra Bré later. Leading actors such as Rudolf Rittner and Joseph Jarno played in *Jugend* many times. Until World War I the drama was a certain crowd-puller. It was chosen to open new theaters in Munich: the Deutsches Theater (German Theater) in 1896 and in 1898 the Schauspielhaus (Playhouse), which was to stage the piece more than three hundred times in the next ten years.

During the time when he was despairing that *Jugend* would ever reach the boards, Halbe, hurt by his treatment in Berlin theatrical and literary circles, wrote the farce *Der Amerikafahrer* (Off to America, 1894). With its doggerel, the play gave an early sign that he was not wedded to naturalism. It was a flop at Brahm's Neues Theater (New Theater) in Berlin in 1894. Halbe fled from Berlin, settling briefly in Switzerland before moving in 1895 to Munich. There, for almost two decades, he was a central figure in artistic circles on the bohemian fringe, forming literary groups, organizing beer-and-skittles evenings, promoting works that were ignored by established theaters (he played the lead role in the world premiere of Georg Büchner's *Leonce und Lena* [1850; translated as *Leonce and Lena*, 1919] in 1895), and mediating between the avant-garde and officialdom. As an author known to earn large royalties, he was approached for patronage by aspiring writers. He was essentially a private person, easily offended, for whom joyful company was an antidote to melancholy. His closest friends were the painter Lovis Corinth, the writer Count Eduard von Keyserling, and Wedekind. His relations with Wedekind were notoriously stormy, for each was jealous of the other's claim to be Munich's leading playwright and Hauptmann's rival as Germany's first dramatist.

Mutter Erde became Halbe's second most successful play. This dark tragedy reveals his disenchantment with Berlin and "advanced" intellectual women, yet it also gives a grim picture of his beloved rural homeland. Paul Warkentin hopes to regain purpose in life by returning to his family roots, but he is trapped between modern notions of progress and emancipation, on the one hand, and the call of tradition and the heart, on the other. These two worlds are associated with two women. His feminist wife, Hella, rejects his wish to remain on the family estate, and he is drawn to his former sweetheart Antoinette, now married to an alcoholic boor and petty tyrant. Hella will not set him free, and Antoinette, who loves him, cannot face the disapproval of society. The lovers, caught in a world of obstinate brutality, make a suicide pact. Halbe shows a masterful touch in the delineation and disposition of characters, in the management of a crowd scene, in directing the audience's sympathy and outrage, and in the creation of an atmosphere where, characteristically, local color and the symbolism of light

and dark play a central role. The 1897 premiere under Brahm at the Deutsches Theater (German Theater) in Berlin featured a strong cast with Else Lehmann, Rudolf Rittner, Hermann Müller, Paul Biensfeld, and Max Reinhardt. Many early critics insisted, at a time when such a dark picture of humanity was out of tune with intellectual trends, that the tragic ending was forced. But audiences were moved, and some critics have regarded *Mutter Erde* as Halbe's finest play.

Yet Berlin was again the scene of great disappointments for Halbe. His *Lebenswende* (Life's Turning Point, 1896) and *Die Heimatlosen* (Homeless People, 1899) were failures, the renaissance tragedy *Der Eroberer* (The Conqueror, 1898; published 1899) a scandalous flop. The Munich premiere of *Das tausendjährige Reich* (The Thousand-Year Empire, 1899; published 1900), directed by Josza Savits, was well received; but in Berlin, Brahm's determinedly naturalist production was abandoned after two performances: to Halbe's annoyance the central role, that of an articulate religious fanatic, was given to an actor known for playing heroes who stumble for words. *Haus Rosenhagen* was well received at its premiere, directed by Karl Zeiss in Dresden on 14 February 1901, and became established in the German repertory; but by this time it seemed that Halbe was condemned to approach the Prussian capital via the provinces. It was constantly asserted that he would never again produce a work of the standard of *Jugend*.

Halbe, a proud man who suffered from severe depressions and was always too nervous to watch the first performance of his works, did not cope well with the situation. The triumph of *Der Strom*, directed by Hugo Thimig at the prestigious Burgtheater (Palace Theater) in Vienna in 1903, did much for his morale. *Der Strom* soon moved to Berlin and to theaters throughout Germany. It is a powerful, concentrated family drama, in which the emotional entanglements grow to a crisis point: two brothers are attracted to the wife of their elder brother, who has falsified their father's will. The action points out social injustice; but guilt and fraternal conflict assume a mythical, existential dimension. The process of discovering an unpalatable truth and the evocation of dark atmosphere recall Ibsen, but in the violent confrontations of monomaniacal figures—actors fought to get the parts—he was working in the tradition of Hebbel.

Der Strom was the last great high point in Halbe's career. When he was fifty World War I

A meeting of the Working Committee of the Poetry Section of the Prussian Academy of the Arts in 1928; from left: Oskar Loerke, René Schickele, Ludwig Fulda, Halbe, Walter von Molo, Heinrich Mann

put an end to his world. *Jugend, Mutter Erde, Haus Rosenhagen,* and *Der Strom* no longer seemed topical. He continued to write symbolic dramas—historical, neoromantic and neoclassical, often in verse—some of which proved to be good theater; but none made a widespread impact, and his attempts at comedy were invariably failures. Nevertheless, during the 1920s he was still assured of performance—especially in Munich, whose Schauspielhaus treated him as its resident playwright. In Danzig, too, he was regarded with special love and respect. Rejecting utopianism and materialism, he clung to his own peasantlike, Catholic faith colored by Schopenhauerian pessimism. He turned for inspiration in his dramas as well as in his narrative prose to the fantastic world of E. T. A. Hoffmann, whose tales, together with the eccentric characters of Charles Dickens, he had loved since childhood. He had little in common with visionary expressionism or the brash realism of the 1920s. In 1924 he retired from Munich into the Bavarian countryside.

With the rise of the Nazis Halbe became an admired figure again; a 1940 production of *Der Strom* in Berlin was greeted with enthusiasm. But his thoughts centered on the past, and he was offended when the Nazi censor insisted that he make changes in a novel he was writing. The man who at the turn of the century had entertained his friends in Munich at dinner parties that lasted throughout the night, who was said to

look like a farmer whose crops have been destroyed and is telling nobody that the insurance company has paid, had become an aged, resigned, and increasingly lonely figure. On rare visits to Munich during World War II, unable to climb stairs, he waited on the street below a younger friend's window until he was noticed. That friend—Artur Kutscher—was the only representative of Munich's literary and artistic world present at Halbe's funeral in 1944. Since then there has been no Halbe revival, and his work has received little critical attention. It is easy to underrate his achievements. His really successful pieces were few, and they are traditional in construction. His box-office hits were overtaken by the advent of modernism in the theater, so that few have observed that his work conveys a modernist sense that human problems admit no final solutions.

Letters:

"Vor dem Ruhm: Aus unveröffentlichten Briefen Max Halbes," edited by Herbert Günther, *Welt und Wort,* 2 (1947): 102-104.

Bibliographies:

Ernst Metelmann, "Max Halbes Schriften," *Die Neue Literatur,* 43 (1942): 6-8;

Gero von Wilpert and Adolf Gühring, *Erstausgaben deutscher Dichtung: Eine Bibliographie zur deutschen Literatur 1600-1960* (Stuttgart: Kröner, 1967), pp. 479-480.

References:

Gottlob C. Cast, *Das Motiv der Vererbung im deutschen Drama des 19. Jahrhunderts* (Madison: University of Wisconsin Press, 1932), pp. 94-101;

Roy C. Cowen, *Der Naturalismus* (Munich: Winkler, 1973), pp. 198-206;

Wilhelm Emrich, "Max Halbe und die Progressiven," in his *Polemik: Streitschriften, Pressefehden und kritische Essays* (Frankfurt am Main: Athenäum, 1968), pp. 173-180;

Friedrich Erdmann, "Max Halbe als Heimatdichter," *Ostdeutsche Monatshefte*, 24 (1958): 57-59;

Otfried Graf Finkenstein, "Max Halbe," *Merian*, 4, no. 7 (1952): 52-56;

Werner Frizen, "Drei Danziger: A. Schopenhauer, M. Halbe, G. Grass," *Schopenhauer Jahrbuch*, 68 (1987): 147-168;

Hugh F. Garten, *Modern German Drama* (London: Methuen, 1959), pp. 48-49;

Anneliese Halbe, "Zur Gründung des Max Halbe-Archivs und der Max Halbe-Gesellschaft 2. Mai 1953," *Ostdeutsche Monatshefte*, 25 (1959): 881-882;

Sigfrid Hoefert, *Das Drama des Naturalismus* (Stuttgart: Metzler, 1968), pp. 36-38;

Hoefert, "E. T. A. Hoffmann und Max Halbe," *Mitteilungen der E. T. A. Hoffmann Gesellschaft*, 13 (1967): 12-19;

Hoefert, "Max Halbe: Pension Rosmersholm. Erstveröffentlichung einer Ibsen-Parodie," in *Analecta Helvetica: Festschrift für H. Boeschenstein*, edited by Armin Arnold (Bonn: Bouvier, 1979), pp. 276-290;

Hoefert, "Max Halbe und die Sprache," *Muttersprache*, 76 (1966): 164-167;

Hoefert, "Zur Nachwirkung Hebbels in der naturalistischen Ära: Max Halbe und Hebbel," *Hebbel Jahrbuch* (1970): 98-107;

Hoefert, "The Work of Max Halbe with Special Reference to Naturalism," Ph.D. dissertation, University of Toronto, 1963;

Wolfgang Kayser, "Zur Dramaturgie des naturalistischen Dramas," in his *Die Vortragsreise* (Bern: Francke, 1958), pp. 214-231;

Heinz Kindermann, *Max Halbe und der deutsche Osten* (Danzig: Rosenberg, 1941);

Gerhart Kluge, "Das verfehlte Soziale: Sentimentalität und Gefühlskitsch im Drama des deutschen Naturalismus," *Zeitschrift für deutsche Philologie*, 96 (1977): 195-234;

Artur Kutscher, *Frank Wedekind: Leben und Werk*, abridged by Karl Ude (Munich: Liszt, 1964), pp. 174-177;

Kutscher, *Der Theaterprofessor* (Munich: Ehrenwirth, 1960), pp. 65-66, 233;

Kurt Martens, "Max Halbe, Dichter der Bodenständigkeit," *Die neue Literatur*, 43 (1942): 2-6;

Edward McInnes, *German Social Drama 1840-1900* (Stuttgart: Heinz, 1976), pp. 162-187;

Franz Mehring, *Aufsätze zur deutschen Literatur von Hebbel bis Schweichel* (Berlin: Dietz, 1961), pp. 355-376;

Ostdeutsche Monatshefte, special Halbe issue, 16 (October 1935);

Winthrop H. Root, "New Light on Halbe's *Jugend*," *Germanic Review*, 10 (January 1935): 17-25;

R. O. Röseler, "Max Halbe," *Monatshefte für deutschen Unterricht*, 37 (1945): 110-113;

H. Schmeer, ed., *Max Halbe zum 100. Geburtstag* (Munich: Stadtbibliothek, 1965);

Albert Soergel, *Dichtung und Dichter der Zeit* (Leipzig: Voigländer, 1911), pp. 352-356;

Karl Ude, "Centenar-Ausstellung für Max Halbe," *Welt und Wort*, 20 (1965): 370;

Ude, "Glanz und Elend des Literaturbetriebes um 1900: Nach Dokumenten aus Max Halbes unveröffentlichtem Nachlass," *Welt und Wort*, 17 (1962): 271-274;

Friedrich Zillmann, *Max Halbe: Wesen und Werk* (Würzburg: Holzner, 1959).

Papers:

The literary estate of Max Halbe is in the Manuscript Division of the Stadtbibliothek (City Library), Munich.

Otto Erich Hartleben

(3 June 1864 - 11 February 1905)

Michael Winkler
Rice University

PLAY PRODUCTIONS: *Angele*, Berlin, Freie Bühne, 30 November 1890;

Hanna Jagert, Berlin, Lessingtheater, 2 April 1893;

Ein Ehrenwort, Breslau, Schauspielhaus, 24 November 1893;

Die sittliche Forderung, Berlin, Deutsches Theater, 6 April 1897;

Die Erziehung zur Ehe, Vienna, Deutsches Volkstheater, 11 September 1897;

Die Befreiten, Berlin, Lessingtheater, 29 November 1898; revised version, Berlin, Lustspielhaus, 1 October 1904;

Ein wahrhaft guter Mensch, Munich, Residenztheater, 24 October 1899;

Rosenmontag, Berlin, Deutsches Theater, 3 October 1900;

Im grünen Baum zur Nachtigall, Vienna, Hofburgtheater, 27 October 1904;

Diogenes, Hagen, Sommerschauspiele, 27 June 1908.

BOOKS: *Quartett: Dichtungen*, by Hartleben, Arthur Gutheil, and Alfred Hugenberg, edited by Karl Henckell (Hamburg: Meissner, 1886);

Studenten-Tagebuch 1885-1886, as Otto Erich (Zurich: Verlags-Magazin, 1886; revised and enlarged, 1888);

Zwei verschiedene Geschichten (Leipzig & Berlin: Fischer, 1887); republished as *Die Seréyni* (Berlin: Fischer, 1891);

Der Frosch: Familiendrama in einem Act. Deutsch von Otto Erich, as Henrik Ipse (Leipzig: Reissner, 1889);

Angele: Comödie (Berlin: Fischer, 1891);

Die Erziehung zur Ehe: Eine Satire (Berlin: Fischer, 1893);

Hanna Jagert: Comödie in drei Acten (Berlin: Fischer, 1893); translated by Sarah Elizabeth Holmes, *Poet Lore*, 24 (Winter 1913): 369-418;

Die Geschichte vom abgerissenen Knöpfe (Berlin: Fischer, 1893);

Ein Ehrenwort: Schauspiel in vier Akten (Berlin: Fischer, 1894);

Vom gastfreien Pastor (Berlin: Fischer, 1895);

Meine Verse (Berlin: Fischer, 1895);

Die sittliche Forderung: Comödie in einem Act (Berlin: Fischer, 1897); translated by Harald Harper as *The Demands of Society: A Comedy*, in *Fifty More Contemporary One-Act Plays*, edited by Frank Shay (New York: Appleton, 1928), pp. 219-227;

Der römische Maler (Berlin: Fischer, 1898);

Die Befreiten: Ein Einacter-Cyclus (Berlin: Fischer, 1899)—comprises *Die Lore, Die sittliche Forderung, Abschied vom Regiment, Der Fremde*;

Ein wahrhaft guter Mensch: Comödie (Berlin: Fischer, 1899; revised, 1905);

Rosenmontag: Eine Offiziers-Tragödie in fünf Acten (Berlin: Fischer, 1900); translated by Rudolf Bleichmann as *Love's Carnival: A Play in Five Acts* (Chicago: Dramatic Publishing Company, 1904; London: Heinemann, 1904);

Von reifen Früchten: Meiner Verse zweiter Theil (Munich: Langen, 1902);

Der Halkyonier: Ein Buch Schlußreime (Berlin: Fischer, 1904);

Liebe kleine Mama (Munich: Langen, 1904);

Im grünen Baum zur Nachtigall: Ein Studentenstück in drei Akten (Berlin: Fischer, 1905);

Diogenes: Szenen einer Komödie in Versen (Berlin: Fischer, 1905);

Meine Verse: Gesammtausgabe (Berlin: Fischer, 1905);

Tagebuch: Fragment eines Lebens (Munich: Langen, 1906);

Ausgewählte Werke in drei Bänden, 3 volumes (Berlin: Fischer, 1909);

Aphorismen: Nach der Handschrift des Dichters, edited by Fred Robert von der Trelde (Innsbruck: Trelde, 1920).

OTHER: Albert Giraud, *Pierrot Lunaire*, translated by Hartleben (Berlin: Verlag deutscher Phantasten, 1893);

Otto Erich Hartleben in 1899; engraving by Andreas Pickel, after a painting by Georg Ludwig Meyn

Johann Wolfgang von Goethe, *Goethe-Brevier: Goethes Leben in seinen Gedichten*, edited by Hartleben (Munich: Schüler, 1895);

Johannes Scheffler, *Angelus Silesius*, edited by Hartleben (Dresden: Bondi, 1896);

Enrico Annibale Butti, *Lucifer*, translated by Hartleben and Ottomar Piltz (Berlin: Fischer, 1904);

Friedrich von Logau, *Logaubüchlein*, edited by Hartleben (Munich: Langen, 1904).

Otto Erich Hartleben had a short and moderately successful career during the 1890s as a writer of gently satirical comedies. He was an accomplished craftsman with a talent for conversational dialogue and characterization and with a facility for imitating the conventions of the contemporary naturalist stage repertory. The one play, however, for which he is still remembered in literary histories is a turgid tragedy in five acts, *Rosenmontag* (1900; translated as *Love's Carnival*, 1904), a story of love and intrigue among officers in a Rhenish garrison. It is quite uncharacteristic of his style, and its sensational, albeit short-lived, success was a great surprise to its author. He also expressed irritation at the fact

that the notoriety he had gained so suddenly was due more to a misapprehension of his intent, which was primarily ironic, than to the play's artistic and social merits. After 1900 the play was performed in virtually every German and Austrian theater as well as in many cities in other European countries, making Hartleben financially secure for the rest of his life; but he considered *Rosenmontag* an improvisation in the popular taste of his time rather than a piece of subtle and psychologically engaging literature. Its success, at any rate, also marked the end of his creativity as a dramatist.

Hartleben was born on 3 June 1864 in the old mining community of Clausthal in the Harz mountains into a stolid family of Prussian civil servants. He was the oldest of six children. Their mother died in 1876 and their father, Hermann, three years later. A grandfather, then seventy-five years old, took over their education; later another relative, a Senator Angerstein in Hannover, became their guardian. Hartleben experienced the discipline these men imposed on the children as a severe imposition and suffered under their determined efforts to make him into a bureaucrat. He was sent to a gymnasium in

Celle, where he lived as a boarder in the house of a respected teacher, Dr. Seeback. After Hartleben's belated graduation in 1885 and with the help of a small inheritance from his grandmother, he prepared reluctantly for a career as a lawyer in the Prussian judicial system by studying law in Berlin, Leipzig, and Tübingen. His first post, in 1889, was that of court stenographer in Stolberg. After he was transferred to an equally modest and boring clerkship in Magdeburg, he decided in August 1890 to follow his true avocation and become a free-lance writer in Berlin.

Hartleben had started writing poetry and prose sketches as a gymnasium student, and he sought contacts with the new generation of writers who had gathered around Bruno Wille, Wilhelm Bölsche, and the brothers Julius and Heinrich Hart in Friedrichshagen, near Berlin. These writers thought of themselves as the New Moderns, socialist rebels against bourgeois philistinism, and they propagated through their work and their uninhibited life-style an aggressively critical attitude that may be loosely subsumed under the label of naturalism. There was no unity of purpose, consistent ideological orientation, or obligatory aesthetic program behind their pronouncements; they were inspired by a determined opposition to the staleness and pomp of official Prussian culture, and they engaged in a flurry of often short-lived literary ventures. Hartleben had a hand in nearly all of them: he wrote for M. G. Conrad's weekly *Gesellschaft* (Society), participated in founding Berlin's Freie Volksbühne (People's Free Stage) and its successor, the Neue Freie Volksbühne (New People's Free Stage), and helped start the Freie literarische Gesellschaft (Free Literary Society). He also became the friend of Samuel Fischer, who trusted Hartleben's advice in attracting many of the emerging writers to his new publishing house— among them Arthur Schnitzler, Hugo von Hofmannsthal, Gerhart Hauptmann, Hermann Hesse, and Thomas Mann.

Hartleben's career as a playwright started inconspicuously. Under the pseudonym Henrik Ipse he published at his own expense *Der Frosch* (The Frog, 1889), a short and rather flat-footed parody of his erstwhile idol Henrik Ibsen, whom he accused of having abandoned social criticism for a posture of symbolist pseudoprofundity. In 1891 Fischer published the fluffy "comedy" in two acts *Angele* (Angela), a story of love, deception, and contempt for women. A wealthy, aging, widowed bon vivant, cuckolded long ago by his beautiful wife, has an affair with the working-class lover of his "son" to avenge the deceptions of the Eternal Female. The anything-but-angelic Angele has another suitor, a poor and passionately sincere candidate for the ministry. When it appears that she only wanted to marry into money, she is expelled from polite society and advised to walk the streets. She accepts this suggestion with cool defiance: "Ja—das—kann ich" (Yes—I can do—that). The three men react to her self-assertion with moral protestations, haughty ridicule, and cynical contempt.

The right of a woman to a full and independent life of her own is also the central theme of Hartleben's first major play, *Hanna Jagert* (1893; translated, 1913), which had developed from a short burlesque alternatively subtitled "Die Begehrliche" (The Desirous Woman) and "Frauenmut" (Woman's Courage) into a full-fledged comedy with serious overtones. It was given helpful advance publicity when the Royal Prussian police commissioner for Berlin had the first performance, scheduled for 16 March 1892, canceled "in the interest of public probity." After several postponements the play opened to audience approbation, but the opinions of the critics were mixed. A few applauded its unabashed discussion of love, money, and the desire for individual self-realization; others (notably the advocates of the Social Democratic party) felt betrayed by Hartleben's flippant disregard for the proprieties of earnest socialist literature.

Hanna Jagert opens in March 1888, the year a popular crown prince becomes Emperor Wilhelm II amid widespread expectations that his youthful zest will inaugurate a period of social progress and institutional modernization. Hanna, the twenty-seven-year-old daughter of a bricklayer, is about to break out of her proletarian environment. She works as a salesgirl in a fashionable millinery shop and is engaged to a printer, Konrad Thieme, a fiery revolutionary and humanitarian. Returning home from incarceration for his political convictions, he claims her hand in marriage as a reward for his principled steadfastness. He is rebuffed by her because she no longer recognizes such claims; she has found a more pragmatic way to personal independence: financial self-sufficiency. Expelled from her home by an obstinately moralistic father, she starts her own fashion business with a loan from her devoted friend Alexander Könitz, owner of a chemical factory and holder of an M.D. degree. Hanna soon prospers through her benevolent egoism, combining concern for the welfare of her seamstresses with a sense of self-worth and the ambition to succeed through her own ingenuity. She acknowledges gratitude to her benefactor but does not confuse her appreciation with love, and at the end she leaves him amicably for a young French aristocrat.

On 2 December 1893 Hartleben married, and he and his wife, Selma, took a honeymoon trip through Italy to Tunisia. Thereafter he sojourned annually in Italy.

Hartleben succeeded in constructing workable plots when he could group his subsidiary characters around a versatile central figure, preferably a woman who uses her wits and an attitude of enlightened egoism to advance her fortunes in a world of dubious morality. His plots disintegrated into stereotypical schemes with predictable complications when he tried to make fun of the double standards of bourgeois family life. The topic of the mildly satirical *Die Erziehung zur Ehe* (Education for Marriage; published, 1893; performed, 1897), a comedy in three acts that he completed in less than a month in 1891, is the erotic confusions to which the grown children of a bank president's widow fall victim. An intrigue set in motion by an anonymous letter from a spurned lover who is a salesman of men's finery; an effete aristocrat's professions of sincerity; a dissolute uncle's recollections of his student days and his "healthy" appetites; and the mother's imperious insistence on the privileges of wealth all contribute to teaching the young people the difference between love and societal obligations. Erotic entanglements with a wily chambermaid and sweetly innocent bookkeeper provide harmless diversions before the dreaded marriage with a partner from one's social circle.

Plot conventions of this sort produce a sequence of short, quickly changing scenes, often with a surprising revelation or turn of events: a confession long held back or an insight that suddenly shatters all previous certainties destroys the placid surface of convention and exposes emotional complications that had been suppressed. Such episodes were particularly appropriate to a theatrical genre that was popular around the turn of the century: the one-act play. The four one-act plays collectively titled *Die Befreiten* (The Liberated; performed, 1898; published, 1899) are noteworthy more for the skill with which Hartleben handles the potential of what may be called a short story for the stage than for their themes. In *Die sittliche Forderung* (The Moral Im-

perative), for example, the famous concert singer Rita Revera, the daughter of a respected businessman, introduces an old hometown admirer to the pleasures of bohemian libertinage when he tries to convince her to return to the provincial conventions of married respectability. *Abschied vom Regiment* (Leaving the Regiment) dramatizes the final dissolution of an infantry captain's marriage: his wife's lover kills him to protect her from his assault. He succumbs in an aesthetically pleasing defeat: roses fall from his tunic where his opponent's saber pierced him.

Rosenmontag uses a similar material to equally sentimental effect. A young lieutenant, Hans Rudorff, is returning to his old regiment after a convalescence of half a year, determined to prove himself a dutiful soldier. He is received by his comrades with great fanfare but also amid whispers that something about his past is still a cause for dark apprehensions. When he announces at the regiment's casino ball his impending marriage to the daughter of a financier, all suspicions seem forgotten. Hans had previously had an extended love affair with an artisan's daughter, Gertrude Reimann; he believes that she betrayed him with one of his friends. But he learns that his cousins, to whom he had entrusted her in his absence, had instigated an intrigue that also led her to assume that he had deserted her for a woman of his own class. Her seducer, the callous Ferdinand von Grobitzsch, calls her a whore to Hans's face while she overhears his justification for the plot to separate the two lovers. Hans seeks a way to avenge his true love's humiliation, but she convinces him that it is nobler not to respond. After a final night of happiness during the revels of a masked ball they commit suicide on the morning of Rosenmontag, the Monday before Lent.

This sentimental unhappy ending no doubt contributed significantly to the play's popular success. So did the general perception that Hartleben had captured the milieu, language, and attitudes characteristic of Prussian officers' casinos. The English version was not so successful; a production of *Love's Carnival* at the St. James Theater in London in April 1904 was canceled after three performances, probably due to the miserable translation. A performance in German in New York in January 1901, on the other hand, fared considerably better. There were accusations of plagiarism when Hartleben's plot was discovered to show many similarities to two 1896 novels, *Leidenschaft* (Passion), by Felix von Stenglin, and *Die Geschichten des Majors* (The Major's Stories), by Hans Hopfen; but the public demand for stories of military life was strong, and original plots were not easy to come by.

In December 1901 Hartleben bought a house near Salò on Lake Garda, Italy, and renamed it Villa Halkyone; there he entertained his bohemian friends. Beginning in 1900 he received clinical treatment for alcoholism, an affliction that contributed to his decline as a writer and brought about his death at Salò at the age of forty on 11 February 1905.

Hartleben, after abandoning his early socialist sympathies and his attacks on bourgeois philistinism, devoted himself to a lighthearted literature that provided easy entertainment for an audience that wanted to be titillated and provoked, but in moderation and without the taint of scandal. This kind of writing required alert attention to rapidly changing fashions in a volatile market in which competition was fierce and success more often a matter of shrewd calculation than artistic integrity. Hartleben's satire was restrained; his ironic wit, while poking fun at social inequities, moral pomposity, and male self-importance, was never derisive or contemptuous. He scoffed at those foibles and faults that were the expected targets of an essentially respectful and thus harmless criticism. Erotic subjects were permissible, but politics was taboo. Hartleben was careful not to appear too serious or, worse yet, doctrinaire. He did not shirk controversy but was

loath to espouse what might have been rejected as boring convictions. He projected the image of a carefree bohemian who lived by his naive intuition; improvised hedonism rather than high principles was the defining mark of his persona. His ubiquitous presence on the artistic scene did more to secure his reputation than the abiding quality of his oeuvre. When he died, his work had already outlived its appeal. It quietly disappeared with him.

Bibliography:

Alfred von Klement, *Die Bücher von Otto Erich Hartleben: Mit der bisher unveröffentlichten ersten Fassung der Selbstbiographie des Dichters und hundert Abbildungen* (Salò, Italy: Halkyonische Akademie für unangewandte Wissenschaften [i.e., Regensburg: Published by the author], 1951).

Biographies:

Selma Hartleben, *"Mein Erich": Aus Otto Erichs Leben* (Berlin: Fischer, 1910);

Heinrich Lücke, *Otto Erich Hartleben: Der Lebenslauf eines Dichters* (Clausthal-Zellerfeld: Pieper, 1941).

Reference:

Hans Reif, "Das dramatische Werk Otto Erich Hartlebens," Ph.D. dissertation, University of Vienna, 1963.

Carl Hauptmann

(11 May 1858 - 4 February 1921)

Christoph Eykman
Boston College

PLAY PRODUCTIONS: *Die Austreibung*, Breslau, Lobe Theater, 18 November 1905;

Panspiele, Cologne, Stadttheater, 22 October 1910;

Die armseligen Besenbinder, Dresden, Königliches Schauspielhaus, 17 October 1913;

Die lange Jule, Hamburg, Deutsches Schauspielhaus, 20 November 1913;

Tobias Buntschuh, Berlin, Deutsches Theater, March 1917;

Krieg: Ein Tedeum, Gera, Reußisches Theater, 29 January 1922;

Moses, Koblenz, Stadttheater, 26 March 1924.

BOOKS: *Die Bedeutung der Keimblättertheorie für die Individualitätslehre und den Generationswechsel* (Jena: Dabis, 1883);

Beiträge zu einer dynamischen Theorie der Lebewesen, Teil 1: Die Metaphysik in der modernen Physiologie (Dresden: Ehlermann, 1893);

Marianne: Schauspiel (Berlin: Fischer, 1894);

Waldleute: Schauspiel (Stuttgart: Cotta, 1896);

Sonnenwanderer: Neun Erzählungen (Berlin: Fischer, 1897);

Ephraims Breite: Schauspiel (Berlin: Fischer, 1900); republished as *Ephraims Tochter: Schauspiel* (Munich: Wolff, 1920);

Aus meinem Tagebuch (Berlin: Fischer, 1900; enlarged edition, Munich: Callwey, 1910); enlarged edition, edited by Will-Erich Peuckert (Berlin: Horen, 1929);

Die Bergschmiede: Dramatische Dichtung (Munich: Callwey, 1902);

Aus Hütten am Hange (Munich: Callwey, 1902);

Mathilde: Zeichnungen aus dem Leben einer armen Frau (Munich: Callwey, 1902);

Unsere Wirklichkeit: Vortrag (Munich: Callwey, 1902);

Des Königs Harfe: Bühnenspiel (Munich: Callwey, 1903);

Die Austreibung: Tragisches Schauspiel (Munich: Callwey, 1905);

Miniaturen: Erzählungen (Munich: Callwey, 1905);

Carl Hauptmann

Einfältige: Eine Studie (Vienna: Wiener Verlag, 1906);

Moses: Bühnendichtung in fünf Akten (Munich: Callwey, 1906);

Einhart der Lächler: Roman, 2 volumes (Berlin: Marquardt, 1907);

Das Geheimnis der Gestalt: Vortrag, gehalten vor der Germanistischen Gesellschaft von Amerika am 2. 12. 1908 (New York: Columbia University Press, 1909);

Judas: Drei Erzählungen (Munich: Callwey, 1909);

Panspiele (Munich: Callwey, 1909);

Der Landstreicher (Munich: Callwey, 1910);

Napoleon Bonaparte, 2 volumes (Munich: Callwey, 1911);

Der Landstreicher und andere Erzählungen (Stuttgart: Die Lese, 1912);

Nächte (Leipzig: Rowohlt, 1912);

Die armseligen Besenbinder: Altes Märchen (Leipzig: Rowohlt, 1913);

Ismael Friedmann (Leipzig: Wolff, 1913);

Die lange Jule: Drama (Leipzig: Wolff, 1913);

Krieg: Ein Tedeum (Leipzig: Wolff, 1914); translated by J. M. Ritchie as *War: A Te Deum*, in his *Vision and Aftermath: Four Expressionist War Plays* (London: Calder & Boyars, 1969);

Schicksale: Erzählungen (Leipzig: Wolff, 1914);

Aus dem großen Krieg: Dramatische Scenen (Leipzig: Wolff, 1915);

Rübezahlbuch (Leipzig: Wolff, 1915);

Die uralte Sphinx: Kriegsvortrag (Leipzig: Wolff, 1915);

Tobias Buntschuh: Eine burleske Tragödie in fünf Akten (Leipzig: Wolff, 1916);

Dort, wo im Sumpf die Hürde steckt: Sonette (Leipzig: Wolff, 1916);

Die Rebhühner: Komödie (Leipzig: Wolff, 1916);

Gaukler, Tod und Juwelier: Spiel (Leipzig: Wolff, 1917);

Die goldnen Straßen: Eine Trilogie (Leipzig: Wolff, 1918);

Offener Brief an den Präsidenten der Vereinigten Staaten von Amerika, Woodrow Wilson (Jena: Diederichs, 1918);

Der schwingende Felsen von Tandil: Legende (Hannover: Steegemann, 1919);

Des Kaisers Liebkosende: Legende (Hannover: Steegemann, 1919);

Lesseps: Legendarisches Porträt (Hannover: Steegemann, 1919);

Musik: Spiel (Leipzig: Wolff, 1919);

Der abtrünnige Zar: Eine Legende (Vienna: Tal, 1919);

Eva-Maria: Eine Legende, edited by Künstlerdank (Berlin: Eigenbrödlerverlag, 1920);

Drei Frauen (Hannover: Banas & Dette, 1920);

Das Kostümgenie (Berlin: Collignon, 1920);

Der Mörder (Dresden: Dresdner Verlag, 1920);

Die lilienweiße Stute: Legende (Dresden: Kaemmerer, 1920);

Die arme Marie: Eine Legende (Berlin: Officina Serpentis, 1922);

Eine Heimstätte: Erzählung (Friedeberg: Iser, 1923);

Vom neuen Studenten: Rede an die deutschen Studenten (Erfurt: Gotik, 1923);

Von Verbrechern und Abenteurern (Berlin: Wegweiser Verlag, 1925);

Die Heilige: Musikalische Legende (Berlin: Funkdienst, 1927);

Tantaliden: Eine Romandichtung (Berlin: Horen, 1927);

Die seltsamen Freunde: Entwurf eines Romans (Leipzig: List, 1933);

Heimstätten und Schicksale: Mit einem Lebensbild des Dichters von Maria Hauptmann, edited by H. Krey (Berlin: Union, 1958).

OTHER: "Frank Wedekind," in *Das Wedekindbuch*, edited by J. Friedenthal (Munich: Müller, 1914), pp. 177-181.

SELECTED PERIODICAL PUBLICATIONS—
UNCOLLECTED: "Vom Wesen des Theaters," *Frankfurter Theateralmanach* (1917/1918): 19-20;

"Seele," *Der Leuchter* (1919): 241-271;

"Die erlöste Erde: Ein Tedeum" (Erster Teil), *Jahrbuch des Reußischen Theaters Gera* (1923): 45-58;

"Der ewig Junge: Mythe" (Zwei Akte), *Ostdeutsche Monatshefte*, 4, no. 11 (1923/1924): 562-573;

"Schwermut," *Horen*, 2 (1925): 48;

"Drei Szenen," *Horen*, 2 (1925): 247-255.

Carl Hauptmann's plays spanned two literary movements, to neither of which he fully belonged: naturalism and expressionism. Although his plays have naturalistic elements, he criticized naturalism because of its neglect of the human individual vis-à-vis the conditioning factors of heredity and social environment. He recognized expressionism as being akin to his own efforts, particularly his search for the human "soul" and his belief in a creative intuition based on an inner vision rather than on observation of the outside world. Thus Hauptmann's plays often have a mystical dimension. Many of his protagonists are seekers of timeless truths; they ponder the relationship of God and humanity, hoping for redemption from their impure and ephemeral existence as earthly creatures. He frequently offsets realistic portrayal of characters and events with dreamlike scenes enveloping the miserable struggle of everyday life with an aura of the fairy tale. Poverty and social injustice, though clearly recognized as painful realities, are almost never viewed as resulting from political, economic, and social developments but rather as God-given circumstances. Thus, in contrast to early works by his better-known brother Gerhart, social change is either not an issue in Hauptmann's work or else it is limited to a few isolated acts of lawbreaking necessitated by the struggle for survival. While the poor passively accept their fate, the wealthy and powerful arrogantly assume their positions in society and often are portrayed as strong-willed demons.

Carl Hauptmann was born in Salzbrunn, Silesia, on 11 May 1858 to Robert and Marie Straehler Hauptmann. From 1872 to 1880 he attended the high school Am Zwinger in Breslau. In 1880 he took up studies in philosophy, physiology, and biology at the University of Jena, where he was a student of the philosopher Rudolf Eucken and befriended the zoologist and philosopher Ernst Haeckel. He earned his doctoral degree with a dissertation titled *Die Bedeutung der Keimblättertheorie für die Individualitätslehre und den Generationswechsel* (The Significance of the Cotyledon Theory for the Principle of Individuality and the Alternation of Generations, 1883). After marriage to Martha Thienemann and a journey to Italy in 1884, he continued his study of science and philosophy at the University of Zurich under Richard Avenarius and Auguste Forel. From 1891 until his death he shared a house in Schreiberau, Silesia, with his brother Gerhart. In 1893 appeared the only volume of a projected four-volume work which was to prove the mechanistic structure of organic life while eradicating from science the concepts of soul, vital power, and will: *Die Metaphysik in der modernen Physiologie* (Metaphysics in Modern Physiology). But about this time his philosophical idealism began to undermine his scientific positivism, and he abandoned his plans for an academic career in the sciences in favor of the writer's pen. Having made that decision, he found himself more and more in pursuit of what he had once rejected: the human soul. His marriage ended in divorce in 1908, and Maria Rohne became his second wife.

Hauptmann's most ambitious play, *Napoleon Bonaparte* (1911), is a biographical panorama of grand proportions. Because of its length, the constant shifting of scenes, and the unusually large number of minor characters, the play defies any attempt at staging. It might be called a historiographic epic in dramatic guise. Hauptmann's Napoleon reveals himself as a leader possessed by his mission, a man of action commanding inexhaustible willpower and energy. He is convinced that he, the "Werkzeug des Himmels" (tool in a divine hand), has been called to greatness. He is ruthless and brutal, mercilessly sacrificing thousands of lives for his military objectives. He never

doubts that he is a born ruler; yet he knows that the legitimacy of his rule is open to challenge by the royalists at home in Paris, and he is troubled by his lack of descent from kings or emperors. He experiences doubt and emotional pain. The faces of the dead on the battlefields touch him deeply. Toward the end of his career he is tired of his fame, crushed under the burden of statesmanship, wondering whether his life and his victories were wasted. He prides himself on having breathed a new soul into France and on having made it the ruler of the continent, yet he also despises his people and admits that politics is nothing more than trivial life cloaked in ermine. He craves to be recognized as the one who freed France from the tyrannical rule of the aristocracy. France, in his view, is the outlawed Prometheus among nations, since she dared to steal the flame of liberty from the altar of the gods. Under his leadership, the enlightenment of the West has prevailed over the superstition of the East. Yet the realist in him knows that the struggle is ultimately one for power and territorial gain. Nagging questions torture his conscience: must there always be bloody battles? Is mankind still under the curse of Cain? In the last scene, though, the dying Napoleon, despite his growing self-doubt, expects to be united with his peers Alexander, Frederick the Great, and Caesar.

Hauptmann's *Die armseligen Besenbinder* (The Poor but Happy Broom Makers, 1913) represents a very different type of drama from *Napoleon Bonaparte*. It is set in Hauptmann's native region, the Riesengebirge of Silesia, and deals with the plight of the poor—a world totally apart from the splendor of political and military history. The old broom maker Raschke and his family live in poverty. Their clothes are rags; they are forced to steal to avoid starvation, and they occasionally land in prison. Yet this is not a work in the vein of the rebellious naturalism practiced by Hauptmann's brother Gerhart in his play *Die Weber* (1892; translated as *The Weavers*, 1899). Raschke never challenges the social and economic conditions of his life; he accepts misery as his unalterable destiny. The thought of reform or revolution never enters his mind.

Two psychological strategies enable Raschke to endure the drudgery of his daily life. The first is his absolute faith in God and divine justice. With one foot, he tells himself, we get ensnared time and again in sin and disgrace, but with the other we stand in the realm of expectation, faith, and hope. In a dream Raschke finds himself in front of the gate to Heaven. Only the higher social classes are allowed in; the poor old man with his heavy burden of brooms is rejected. Yet his faith remains unshaken, and Saint Peter holds out hope for him in announcing that those who were poor on earth shall become rich in Heaven.

Raschke's eternal optimism also has a secular source: his hope for a miracle here on earth. His son Johann, who had left home years before, returns immensely rich, half magician, half aristocrat, under the name Count Johannes Habundus. He claims to have come straight from the "Raven Mountains" in America, where huge diamonds lie about in the sand.

Here, as in other parts of the play, graphic naturalism gives way to the suspension of the laws of logic, probability, and reality typical of the fairy tale; indeed, the subtitle of the play is *Altes Märchen* (Old Fairy Tale). Is the miraculous return of Johannes Habundus a "real" event or merely a figment of Raschke's imagination, a form of psychological escapism? Its fantastic aspects are mirrored in the behavior of the mentally deranged old woman who lives in Raschke's attic and believes that she is the daughter of the king of Araucaria and that the families of the broom makers are her servants and ladies-in-waiting. Her illusion of a better life as "Prinzessin Trull" eclipses her true status as a wretched and penniless old woman. Like Raschke, she is "armselig": poor but happy.

Hauptmann, though keenly aware of the misery of the characters he presents, refuses to posture as a social revolutionary. Instead, he offers a highly sympathetic portrayal of the ingenious and creative ways in which the human mind compensates for the pains of the daily struggle for survival. By using contrasting images of squalid poverty and lustrous wealth and by weaving realistic strands into the fabric of the fairy tale, Hauptmann creates believable characters who live in both worlds. They are whole and yet they are split, accepting misery while compensating for it through a world of grand illusions or by their unshakable faith in a happier hereafter. The play was first performed on 17 October 1913 at the Königliches Schauspielhaus (Royal Playhouse) of Dresden under the direction of Arthur Holz and was positively received.

A village in the Riesengebirge is also the setting of *Die lange Jule* (Tall Jule, 1913). The play is a psychological study of a strong woman who will do anything to have her way. Jule Hallmann, the daughter of a wealthy farmer, becomes so ob-sessed with her goals that she ruthlessly manipulates others; yet she is capable of feeling genuine sorrow. Since Jule never got along with her father's second wife, her father had driven her from his farm and cursed her at the hour of his death. Now Jule's only desire is to buy the farm, on which the mortgage is held by the sinister Schuster Dreiblatt, and oust her stepmother. In one of the most entertaining scenes in the play, Jule tempts Dreiblatt both erotically and financially until he lets her have the farm. Just when Jule seems to be at the brink of victory, the farmhouse is destroyed by fire. Her lifelong goal of settling accounts with her father now out of reach, she commits suicide. Her hostility to her father is, of course, rooted in his rejection of her love; her suicide is her final attempt to impose a reconciliation on him. Her father's ghost appears briefly in the flames before she joins him in death.

Die lange Jule was first performed on 20 November 1913 at the Deutsches Schauspielhaus (German Playhouse) of Hamburg under the direction of Max Grube. The audience and the critics rejected the play, but subsequent performances in Vienna were received positively.

Hauptmann's best play, *Krieg: Ein Tedeum* (published, 1914; translated as *War: A Te Deum*, 1969), is also his most expressionistic one. The characters are either abstract types or fairy-tale creatures. Wearing animal costumes (including those of a bear, rooster, eagle, and whale), representatives of the nations gather to debate the impending war. Later in the play horrific figures with rat faces, wearing necklaces made of animal skulls and human bones, crowd the stage, and an army column of skeletons marches to funeral music. War is personified in the "ausgebrochener Staatsphantast" (Escaped Visionary), and an archangel represents the will of God. Instead of a plot, a panoramic view of the anticipated horrors of the war unfolds. The power of the play-wright's grim visions is all the more astounding when one considers that the play was written prior to the outbreak of World War I. War is viewed as a self-inflicted purge on the part of mankind, which finds itself in the grip of evil powers. War means the unleashing of human bestiality—hence the many animal figures in the play. The realistic viewpoint shifts during the course of the play to a metaphysical and religious one. War turns out to be the work of God, not of humanity. God not only makes war, he *is* war. The archangel proclaims God's intention to revitalize the tamed forces of animality in man, and the angel's prophet, Petrus Heissler, defines God as a vortex of men slaying each other. Humans are all too willing to accept war; they welcome it with shouts of "Hurrah" and are ready to squander their lives. Many soldiers fear that the war will end too soon. Hauptmann captures this naive attitude in the image of der goldene Prunkwagen (the Golden Carriage of War): according to the stage directions, the people pull it and push it from behind; it rolls across streams of human blood, crushing millions to death.

Yet the images in *Krieg: Ein Tedeum* are by no means exclusively images of doom and hopelessness. Petrus Heissler trusts that the hand of the Lord will raise him up and strip him of his bestiality. Even the Escaped Visionary dreams of a new and peaceful world. At the end of the fighting, nationalism and racism will have become obsolete, some characters predict. On the war-ravaged earth a monk builds a small temple, a symbol of hope and spiritual renewal. *Krieg: Ein Tedeum* was first performed on 29 January 1922 in Gera under the direction of Paul Medenwaldt and was positively received. Hauptmann had died nearly a year earlier, on 4 February 1921.

Letters:

Leben mit Freunden: Gesammelte Briefe, edited by Will-Erich Peuckert (Munich & Berlin: Horen, 1928);

Briefe mit Modersohn (Leipzig: List, 1935).

Biography:

Walter Goldstein, *Carl Hauptmann: Ein Lebensbild* (Darmstadt: Bläschke, 1978).

References:

Thomas Duglor, *Carl Hauptmann: Ein schlesischer Dichter* (Düsseldorf: Wegweiser, 1958);

Walter Goldstein, *Carl Hauptmann: Eine Werkdeutung* (Hildesheim & New York: Olms, 1972);

Heinrich Minden, *Carl Hauptmann und das Theater* (Kastellaun: Henn, 1976);

Karol Musiol, "Carl Hauptmann und Josepha Kodis: Ihr gegenseitiges Verhältnis im Spiegel des dichterischen Werkes," *Deutsche Vierteljahresschrift für Literaturwissenschaft und Geistesgegeschichte*, 34 (1960): 257-263;

Will-Erich Peuckert, "Carl Hauptmann's Anfänge," *Zeitschrift für deutsche Philologie*, 77 (1958): 113-130;

Hubert Razinger, *Carl Hauptmann: Gestalt und Werk* (Krummhübel: Bonavoluntas, 1928);

Anna Stroka, *Carl Hauptmanns Werdegang als Denker und Dichter* (Wroclaw: Zaklad Narodowy im. Ossolińskich, 1965).

Papers:

A collection of Carl Hauptmann's unpublished letters and diaries is at the Ossoliński Library in Wroclaw (formerly Breslau), Poland. Letters to and from Hauptmann are at the Staatsbibliothek Preußischer Kulturbesitz, Berlin. The Deutsches Literatur-Archiv, Marbach, has letters and literary manuscripts. Remnants of Hauptmann's literary estate are also at the Schlesische Bibliothek, Kattowitz, at the Hauptmann Archiv at Radebeul (Dresden), and at the Literaturarchiv of the Akademie der Künste, Berlin.

Gerhart Hauptmann

(15 November 1862 - 6 June 1946)

Roy C. Cowen
University of Michigan

See also the Hauptmann entry in *DLB 66: German Fiction Writers, 1885-1913*.

PLAY PRODUCTIONS: *Vor Sonnenaufgang*, Berlin, Lessingtheater, 20 October 1889;

Das Friedensfest, Berlin, Ostendtheater, 1 June 1890;

Einsame Menschen, Berlin, Residenztheater, 11 January 1891;

Kollege Crampton, Berlin, Deutsches Theater, 16 January 1892;

Die Weber, Berlin, Neues Theater, 26 February 1893;

Hanneles Himmelfahrt, Berlin, Königliches Schauspielhaus, 14 September 1893;

Der Biberpelz, Berlin, Deutsches Theater, 21 September 1893;

Florian Geyer, Berlin, Deutsches Theater, 4 January 1896;

Die versunkene Glocke, Berlin, Deutsches Theater, 2 December 1896;

Fuhrmann Henschel, Berlin, Deutsches Theater, 5 November 1898;

Schluck und Jau, Berlin, Deutsches Theater, 3 February 1900;

Michael Kramer, Berlin, Deutsches Theater, 21 December 1900;

Der rote Hahn, Berlin, Deutsches Theater, 27 November 1901;

Der arme Heinrich, Vienna, Hofburgtheater, 29 November 1902;

Rose Bernd, Berlin, Deutsches Theater, 31 October 1903;

Elga, Berlin, Lessingtheater, 4 March 1905;

Und Pippa tanzt!, Berlin, Lessingtheater, 19 January 1906;

Die Jungfern von Bischofsberg, Berlin, Lessingtheater, 2 February 1907;

Kaiser Karls Geisel, Berlin, Lessingtheater, 11 January 1908;

Griselda, Berlin, Lessingtheater, and Vienna, Hofburgtheater, 6 March 1909;

Die Ratten, Berlin, Lessingtheater, 13 January 1911;

Gabriel Schillings Flucht, Bad Lauchstedt, Goethes Theater, 14 June 1912;

Festspiel in deutschen Reimen, Breslau, Jahrhunderthalle, 31 May 1913;

Der Bogen des Odysseus, Berlin, Deutsches Künstlertheater, 17 January 1914;

Winterballade, Berlin, Deutsches Theater, 17 October 1917;

Der weiße Heiland, Berlin, Großes Schauspielhaus, 28 March 1920;

Peter Brauer, Berlin, Lustspielhaus, 1 November 1921;

Indipohdi, Dresden, Staatliches Schauspielhaus, 23 February 1922;

Festaktus zur Eröffnung des Deutschen Museums in München, Munich, Deutsches Museum, 7 May 1925;

Veland, Hamburg, Deutsches Schauspielhaus, 19 September 1925;

Dorothea Angermann, Vienna, Theater in der Josefstadt; Munich, Kammerspiele; Leipzig, Schauspielhaus; Brunswick, Landestheater; and thirteen other theaters, 20 November 1926;

Shakespeare: Hamlet, adapted by Hauptmann, Dresden, Staatliches Schauspielhaus, 8 December 1927;

Spuk: Die schwarze Maske, and *Hexenritt*, Vienna, Burgtheater, 3 December 1929;

Vor Sonnenuntergang, Berlin, Deutsches Theater, 16 February 1932;

Die goldene Harfe, Munich, Kammerspiele, 15 October 1933;

Hamlet in Wittenberg, Leipzig, Altes Theater; Altona, Stadttheater; and Osnabrück, Deutsches Nationaltheater, 19 November 1935;

Die Tochter der Kathedrale, Berlin, Staatliches Schauspielhaus, 3 October 1939;

Ulrich von Lichtenstein, Vienna, Burgtheater, 11 November 1939;

Iphigenie in Delphi, Berlin, Staatliches Schauspielhaus, 15 November 1941;

Iphigenie in Aulis, Vienna, Burgtheater, 15 November 1943;

Agamemnons Tod and *Elektra*, Berlin, Deutsches Theater, 10 September 1947;

Herbert Engelmann, adapted by Carl Zuckmayer, Vienna, Akademietheater, 8 March 1952;

Die Finsternisse, Göttingen, Studio, 5 July 1952;

Magnus Garbe, Düsseldorf, Schauspielhaus, 4 February 1956;

Herbert Engelmann (original version), Putbus/Rügen, Theater, 12 November 1962.

BOOKS: *Liebesfrühling: Ein lyrisches Gedicht* (Salzbrunn: Privately printed, 1881);

Promethidenloos: Eine Dichtung (Berlin: Ißleib, 1885);

Das bunte Buch: Gedichte, Sagen & Märchen (Leipzig & Stuttgart: Meinhard, 1888);

Vor Sonnenaufgang (Berlin: Conrad, 1889); translated by Leonard Bloomfield as *Before Dawn* (Boston: Badger, 1909);

Das Friedensfest: Eine Familienkatastrophe. Bühnendichtung (Berlin: Fischer, 1890); translated by Janet Achurch and C. E. Wheeler as *The Coming of Peace: A Family Catastrophe* (Chicago: Sergel, 1900);

Einsame Menschen (Berlin: Fischer, 1891); translated by Mary Morison as *Lonely Lives* (New York: De Witt, 1898);

Der Apostel; Bahnwärter Thiel: Novellistische Studien (Berlin: Fischer, 1892); "Bahnwärter Thiel" translated by A. S. Seltzer as "Flagman Thiel" in *Great German Short Novels and Stories*, edited by Bennett A. Cerf (New York: Modern Library, 1933);

College Crampton: Komödie (Berlin: Fischer, 1892); translated by Roy Temple House and Ludwig Lewisohn as *Colleague Crampton*, in *The Dramatic Works of Gerhart Hauptmann*, edited by Lewisohn, volume 3 (New York: Huebsch, 1914);

Die Weber: Schauspiel aus den vierziger Jahren (Berlin: Fischer, 1892); translated by Morison as *The Weavers* (New York: Russell, 1899); translated by F. Marcus as *The Weavers* (London: Methuen, 1980);

Der Biberpelz: Eine Diebskomödie (Berlin: Fischer, 1893); translated by Lewisohn as *The Beaver Coat*, in *The Dramatic Works of Gerhart Hauptmann*, edited by Lewisohn, volume 1 (New York: Huebsch, 1912);

Hannele Matterns Himmelfahrt (Berlin: Fischer, 1893); republished as *Hannele: Traumdichtung in zwei Teilen* (Berlin: Fischer, 1894); translated by William Archer as *Hannele* (London: Heinemann, 1894); translated by Charles Henry Meltzer as *Hannele* (New York: Doubleday, Page, 1908); original republished as *Hanneles Himmelfahrt: Traumdichtung* (Berlin: Fischer, 1896);

Florian Geyer (Berlin: Fischer, 1896); translated by Bayard Quincy Morgan as *Florian Geyer*, in *The Dramatic Works of Gerhart Hauptmann*, edited by Lewisohn, volume 9 (New York: Viking, 1929);

Die versunkene Glocke (Berlin: Fischer, 1897); translated by Mary Harned as *The Sunken Bell* (Boston: Badger, 1898);

Fuhrmann Henschel: Schauspiel (Berlin: Fischer, 1899); translated by Marion A. Redlich as *Drayman Henschel* (Chicago: Dramatic Publishing Co., 1910);

Helios: Fragment eines Dramas (N.p., 1899); translated by Lewisohn as *Helios (Fragment)*, in *The Dramatic Works of Gerhart Hauptmann*, edited by Lewisohn, volume 7 (New York: Huebsch, 1917);

Michael Kramer: Drama in vier Akten (Berlin: Fischer, 1900); translated by Lewisohn as *Michael Kramer*, in *The Dramatic Works of Gerhart Hauptmann*, edited by Lewisohn, volume 3 (New York: Huebsch, 1914);

Schluck und Jau: Spiel zu Scherz und Schimpf (Berlin: Fischer, 1900); translated by Lewisohn as *Schluck and Jau*, in *The Dramatic Works of Gerhart Hauptmann*, edited by Lewisohn, volume 5 (New York: Huebsch, 1916);

Der rote Hahn: Tragikomödie in vier Akten (Berlin: Fischer, 1901); translated by Lewisohn as *The Conflagration*, in *The Dramatic Works of Gerhart Hauptmann*, edited by Lewisohn, volume 1 (New York: Huebsch, 1912);

Der arme Heinrich: Eine deutsche Sage (Berlin: Fischer, 1902); translated by Lewisohn as *Henry of Auë*, in *The Dramatic Works of Gerhart Hauptmann*, edited by Lewisohn, volume 4 (New York: Huebsch, 1915);

Rose Bernd: Schauspiel in fünf Akten (Berlin: Fischer, 1903); translated by Lewisohn as *Rose Bernd*, in *The Dramatic Works of Gerhart Hauptmann*, edited by Lewisohn, volume 2 (New York: Huebsch, 1913);

Elga (Berlin: Fischer, 1905); translated by Harned as *Elga* (Boston: Badger, 1909);

Und Pippa tanzt! Ein Glashüttenmärchen in vier Akten (Berlin: Fischer, 1906); translated by Harned as *And Pippa Dances* (Boston: Badger, 1909);

Gesammelte Werke, 6 volumes (Berlin: Fischer, 1906);

Die Jungfern von Bischofsberg: Lustspiel (Berlin: Fischer, 1907); translated by Lewisohn as *The Maidens of the Mount*, in *The Dramatic Works of Gerhart Hauptmann*, edited by Lewisohn, volume 6 (New York: Huebsch, 1916);

Griechischer Frühling (Berlin: Fischer, 1908);

Kaiser Karls Geisel: Legendenspiel (Berlin: Fischer, 1908); translated by Lewisohn as *Charlemagne's Hostage*, in *The Dramatic Works of Gerhart Hauptmann*, edited by Lewisohn, volume 5 (New York: Huebsch, 1916);

Griselda (Berlin: Fischer, 1909); translated by Alice Kauser as *Griselda* (Binghampton, N.Y.: Binghampton Book Manufacturing Co., 1909);

Der Narr in Christo Emanuel Quint (Berlin: Fischer, 1910); translated by Thomas Seltzer as *The Fool In Christ Emanuel Quint* (New York: Huebsch, 1911);

Die Ratten: Berliner Tragikomödie (Berlin: Fischer, 1911): translated by Lewisohn as *The Rats*, in *The Dramatic Works of Gerhart Hauptmann*, edited by Lewisohn, volume 2 (New York: Huebsch, 1913);

Atlantis: Roman (Berlin: Fischer, 1912); translated by Adele and Thomas Seltzer as *Atlantis* (New York: Huebsch, 1912);

Gabriel Schillings Flucht: Drama (Berlin: Fischer, 1912); translated by Lewisohn as *Gabriel Schilling's Flight*, in *The Dramatic Works of Gerhart Hauptmann*, edited by Lewisohn, volume 6 (New York: Huebsch, 1916);

Gesammelte Werke: Volksausgabe in 6 Bänden, 6 volumes (Berlin: Fischer, 1912);

The Dramatic Works of Gerhart Hauptmann, edited by Lewisohn, 9 volumes (volumes 1-8, New York: Huebsch, 1912-1917, 1924; volume 9, New York: Viking, 1929);

Festspiel in deutschen Reimen (Berlin: Fischer, 1913); translated by Morgan as *Commemoration Masque*, in *The Dramatic Works of Gerhart Hauptmann*, edited by Lewisohn, volume 7 (New York: Huebsch, 1917);

Lohengrin (Berlin: Ullstein, 1913);

Der Bogen des Odysseus (Berlin: Fischer, 1914); translated by Lewisohn as *The Bow of Odysseus* in *The Dramatic Works of Gerhart Hauptmann*, edited by Lewisohn, volume 7 (New York: Huebsch, 1917);

Parsival (Berlin: Ullstein, 1914); translated by Oakley Williams as *Parsifal* (New York: Macmillan, 1915);

Winterballade: Eine dramatische Dichtung (Berlin: Fischer, 1917); translated by Willa and Edwin Muir as *A Winter Ballad*, in *The Dramatic Works of Gerhart Hauptmann*, edited by Lewisohn, volume 8 (New York: Huebsch, 1924);

Der Ketzer von Soana (Berlin: Fischer, 1918); translated by Morgan as *The Heretic of Soana* (New York: Huebsch, 1923; London: Secker, 1923);

Der weiße Heiland: Dramatische Phantasie (Berlin: Fischer, 1920); translated by Willa and Edwin Muir as *The White Saviour*, in *The Dramatic Works of Gerhart Hauptmann*, edited by Lewisohn, volume 8 (New York: Huebsch, 1924);

Indipohdi: Dramatisches Gedicht (Berlin: Fischer, 1920); translated by Willa and Edwin Muir as *Indipohdi*, in *The Dramatic Works of Gerhart*

Hauptmann, edited by Lewisohn, volume 8 (New York: Huebsch, 1924);

Anna: Ein ländliches Liebesgedicht (Berlin: Fischer, 1921);

Peter Brauer: Tragikomödie (Berlin: Fischer, 1921);

Das Hirtenlied: Ein Fragment (Berlin: Holten, 1921); translated by Lewisohn as *Pastoral (Fragment)*, in *The Dramatic Works of Gerhart Hauptmann*, edited by Lewisohn, volume 7 (New York: Huebsch, 1917);

Für ein ungeteiltes deutsches Oberschlesien: Öffentliche Protestversammlung zu Berlin (Berlin: Zentralverlag, 1921);

Sonette (Berlin: Voegel, 1921);

Deutsche Wiedergeburt: Vortrag (Vienna: Heller, 1921);

Gesammelte Werke: Große Ausgabe, 12 volumes (Berlin: Fischer, 1922);

Rußland und die Welt, by Hauptmann, Fridtjof Nansen, and Maksim Gorki (Berlin: Verlag für Politik und Wirtschaft, 1922);

Phantom: Aufzeichnungen eines ehemaligen Sträflings (Berlin: Fischer, 1923); translated by Morgan as *Phantom* (New York: Huebsch, 1922; London: Secker, 1923);

Fasching (Berlin: Holten, 1923);

Ausblicke (Berlin: Fischer, 1924);

Festaktus zur Eröffnung des Deutschen Museums, text by Hauptmann, music by H. Zilcher (Munich: Knorr & Hirth, 1925);

Die Insel der Großen Mutter oder Das Wunder von I'le des Dames (Berlin: Fischer, 1925); translated by Willa and Edwin Muir as *The Island of the Great Mother; or, The Miracle of I'le des Dames* (New York: Huebsch, 1925);

Veland: Tragödie (Berlin: Fischer, 1925); translated by Edwin Muir as *Veland*, in *The Dramatic Works of Gerhart Hauptmann*, edited by Lewisohn, volume 9 (New York: Viking, 1929);

Dorothea Angermann: Schauspiel (Berlin: Fischer, 1926);

Die blaue Blume (Berlin: Fischer, 1927);

Till Eulenspiegel: Ein dramatischer Versuch (Leipzig: Klinkhardt, 1927);

Des großen Kampffliegers, Landfahrers, Gauklers und Magiers Till Eulenspiegel Abenteuer, Streiche, Gaukeleien, Gesichte und Träume (Berlin: Fischer, 1928);

Gedanken an Walther Rathenau, by Hauptmann, Wilhelm Marx, Arnold Brecht, and Edwin Redslob (Dresden: Reißner, 1928);

Ansprache bei der Eröffnung der internationalen Buchkunst-Ausstellung Leipzig (Leipzig, 1928);

Wanda (Der Dämon): Roman (Berlin: Fischer, 1928);

Der Baum von Gallowayshire (Heidelberg: Kampmann, 1929);

Spuk: Die schwarze Maske, Schauspiel; Hexenritt: Ein Satyrspiel (Berlin: Fischer, 1929);

Buch der Leidenschaft, 2 volumes (Berlin: Fischer, 1930);

Drei deutsche Reden (Leipzig: Gesellschaft der Freunde der Deutschen Bücherei, 1930);

Die Spitzhacke: Ein phantastisches Erlebnis (Berlin: Fischer, 1931);

Die Hochzeit auf Buchenhorst: Erzählung (Berlin: Fischer, 1932);

Vor Sonnenuntergang: Schauspiel (Berlin: Fischer, 1932);

Um Volk und Geist: Ansprachen (Berlin: Fischer, 1932);

Das dramatische Werk: Gesamtausgabe zum siebzigsten Geburtstag des Dichters, 2 volumes (Berlin: Fischer, 1932);

Die goldene Harfe: Schauspiel (Berlin: Fischer, 1933);

Das Meerwunder: Eine unwahrscheinliche Geschichte (Berlin: Fischer, 1934);

Hamlet in Wittenberg: Schauspiel (Berlin: Fischer, 1935);

Das epische Werk, 2 volumes (Berlin: Fischer, 1935);

Im Wirbel der Berufung: Roman (Berlin: Fischer, 1936);

Das Abenteuer meiner Jugend, 2 volumes (Berlin: Fischer, 1937);

Ährenlese: Kleinere Dichtungen (Berlin: Fischer, 1939);

Die Tochter der Kathedrale: Schauspiel (Berlin: Fischer, 1939);

Ulrich von Lichtenstein: Komödie (Berlin: Fischer, 1939);

Iphigenie in Delphi: Tragödie (Berlin: Suhrkamp, 1941);

Der Schuß im Park: Novelle (Berlin: Fischer, 1941);

Der Dom (Dramenfragment) (Chemnitz: Gesellschaft der Bücherfreunde, 1942);

Magnus Garbe: Tragödie (Berlin: Fischer, 1942);

Der große Traum: Dichtung (Leipzig: Insel, 1942); enlarged, edited by Hans Reisiger (Gütersloh: Bertelsmann, 1956);

Das gesammelte Werk: Ausgabe letzter Hand zum achtzigsten Geburtstag des Dichters, 17 volumes (Berlin: Fischer, 1942);

Der neue Christophorus: Ein Fragment (Weimar: Gesellschaft der Bibliophilen, 1943); enlarged, edited by H.-E. Hass (Berlin: Propyläen-Verlag, 1965);

Iphigenie in Aulis: Tragödie (Berlin: Suhrkamp, 1944);

Neue Gedichte (Berlin: Aufbau, 1946);

Die Finsternisse: Ein Requiem, introduction by Walter A. Reichart (Aurora, N.Y.: Hammer, 1947);

Mignon: Novelle (Berlin: Suhrkamp, 1947);

Agamemnons Tod; Elektra: Tragödien (Berlin: Suhrkamp, 1948);

Galahad oder Die Gaukelfuhre: Dramatische Fragmente, edited by C. F. W. Behl (Lichtenfels: Fränkische Bibliophilengesellschaft, 1948);

Die Atriden-Tetralogie: Tragödie (Berlin: Suhrkamp, 1949);

Herbert Engelmann: Drama in vier Akten. Aus dem Nachlaß, completed by Carl Zuckmayer (Munich: Beck, 1952);

Winckelmann: Das Verhängnis. Roman, edited and completed by Frank Thiess (Gütersloh: Bertelsmann, 1954);

Der große Traum, edited by Reisiger (Gütersloh: Bertelsmann, 1956);

Sämtliche Werke: Centenar-Ausgabe zum hundertsten Geburtstag des Dichters 15. November 1962, edited by Hass, Martin Machatzke, and W. Bungies, 11 volumes (Frankfurt am Main & Berlin: Propyläen-Verlag, 1962-1974);

Italienische Reise: Tagebuchaufzeichnungen, edited by Machatzke (Berlin: Propyläen-Verlag, 1976);

Diarium 1917 bis 1933, edited by Machatzke (Berlin: Propyläen-Verlag, 1980);

Notiz-Kalender 1889 bis 1891, edited by Machatzke (Frankfurt am Main, Berlin & Vienna: Propyläen-Verlag, 1982);

Tagebuch 1892 bis 1894, edited by Machatzke (Frankfurt am Main, Berlin & Vienna: Propyläen-Verlag, 1985);

Tagebücher 1897-1905, edited by Machatzke (Frankfurt am Main: Propyläen-Verlag, 1987).

OTHER: Franz Stelzhamer, *Charakterbilder aus Oberösterreich*, foreword by Hauptmann (Vienna: Wiener Verlag, 1906);

Herman Georg Fiedler, ed., *The Oxford Book of German Verse*, foreword by Hauptmann (London: Oxford University Press, 1911);

Ludwig von Hofmann, *Rhythmen: Neue Folge. Zehn Steinzeichnungen*, foreword by Hauptmann (Leipzig: Dehne, 1921);

Heinrich Grünfeld, *In Dur und Moll: Begegnungen und Erlebnisse aus fünfzig Jahren*, introduction by Hauptmann (Leipzig: Grethlein, 1923);

Kurt Hielscher, *Deutschland: Baukunst und Landschaft*, foreword by Hauptmann (Berlin: Wasmuth, 1924);

Käthe Kollwitz, *Abschied und Tod: Acht Zeichnungen*, introduction by Hauptmann (Berlin: Propyläen-Verlag, 1924);

William Shakespeare, *Die tragische Geschichte von Hamlet Prinzen von Dänemark in deutscher Sprache*, translated and adapted by Hauptmann (Weimar: Cranachpresse, 1929);

Johann Wolfgang von Goethe, *Werke*, introduction by Hauptmann, 2 volumes (Berlin: Knaur, 1931);

R. Voigt, *Das Gesicht des Geistes*, introduction by Hauptmann (Berlin: Metzner, 1944).

SELECTED PERIODICAL PUBLICATIONS—
UNCOLLECTED: "Deutschland und Shakespeare," *Jahrbuch der deutschen Shakespeare-Gesellschaft*, 51 (1915): vii-xii;

"Hamlet: Einige Worte zu meinem Ergänzungsversuche," *Sächsische Stadttheater: Schauspielhaus Dresden 1927* (1927);

"Goethe," *Germanic Review*, 7 (1932): 101-122;

"Die Wiedertäufer: Romanfragment," *Gerhart Hauptmann-Jahrbuch*, 1 (1936): 12-37;

"Uber Tintoretto," *Die neue Rundschau*, 49 (1938): 209-226;

"Johann Winckelmanns letzte Jahre: Novelle (Fragment)," *Das XX. Jahrhundert*, 2 (1940): 331-334, 337;

"Das Märchen," *Die neue Rundschau*, 52 (1941): 686-694;

"Die Wiedertäufer," *Die neue Rundschau*, 53 (1942): 488-494.

Gerhart Hauptmann first attempted to express himself artistically as a sculptor. But once he had discovered his literary talents he explored, after a somewhat epigonic beginning, all possible literary forms: novellas, novels, epics and lyrical poetry, and drama. While he had artistic and popular success with his novellas and novels, Hauptmann achieved his broadest recognition as a playwright. He rapidly became the most prolific and most imitated dramatist since Friedrich Schiller, whose plays dominated German thinking about this genre up to the advent of naturalism. Without its success on the stages in Berlin, naturalism would probably have remained only a mildly disruptive occurrence on the German literary scene; and this success would have been impossible without Hauptmann's plays. On the other hand, without the emergence of naturalism, Hauptmann might never have found the proper vehicle for his talents, let alone gained such prominence and influence.

Today Hauptmann remains for most theatergoers and literary historians alike the outstanding representative of strongly realistic, character-oriented, socially critical plays. Not only did he achieve his first triumphs with them, but he continued to succeed in writing such dramas—interspersed with works in other genres and modes—long after radical realism had ceased to be in fashion. He gradually expanded the potential of realistic drama far beyond that recognized by his contemporaries during and after the period of naturalism. He accommodated it to his own changing views of human existence and incorporated into it elements of such subsequent developments as neoromanticism, symbolism, Jugendstil (art nouveau), and expressionism.

Robert and Marie Straehler Hauptmann, who were already the parents of three other children—Georg, Johanna (Lotte), and Carl—have never been viewed as being directly influential on the later artistic success of their youngest child, who was born on 15 November 1862 and was baptized in 1863 Gerhard (*sic*) Johann Robert Hauptmann. Nor did his formal education contribute to his receiving, in 1912, the Nobel Prize in literature as a successor to such learned countrymen as Theodor Mommsen, Rudolf Eucken, and Paul Heyse. Hauptmann's elementary schooling, which began in his birthplace, Ober-Salzbrunn (now Szczawno, Poland), and continued in Breslau (now Wrocław, Poland), ended abruptly in 1878 as a consequence of his father's loss of the resort hotel he owned.

Nonetheless, the indirect influence of these early years proved to be lasting. Hauptmann would gain literary immortality through his depiction of flesh-and-blood characters from all classes and environments. In his diary he wrote on 29 November 1898: "Erst Menschen, hernach das Drama. An ein Drama von Puppen kann niemand glauben" (First the people, then the drama. No one can believe a drama of puppets). Hauptmann was convinced that realistically portrayed characters would necessarily evoke a plot, and he always made his characters as heterogeneous as possible. At his father's hotel he was exposed as a child to such a mixed bag of social

Program for an early production of Hauptmann's first play, the first German naturalist play to be performed

classes, the wealthy bourgeoisie and to members of the German, Polish, and Russian nobility. Ober-Salzbrunn, situated in a rural area, provided Hauptmann's first contact with simpler people and farmers, which was augmented in 1878-1879 by his work as an agricultural trainee on the estates of his uncle Gustav Schubert in Lohning and Lederose. There he fell in love for the first time and was subjected to the pietism of the Herrnhut sect. During his formative years Hauptmann made the acquaintance of many people who would provide models for literary characters, such as Alfred Ploetz, the model for Loth in *Vor Sonnenaufgang* (1889; translated as *Before Dawn*, 1909), Alf in *Helios* (1899; translated, 1917), and Schmidt in *Atlantis* (1912; translated, 1912). Since these characters, albeit based on one real person, are so different, it is obvious that Hauptmann, when drawing on people he had known, would utilize only those traits he needed or could show within the confines of a given work.

In 1880 Hauptmann resumed his formal education at the Royal Art and Trade School in Breslau. He also tried his hand at writing; his products—poems, an alliterative epic, and several dramatic fragments—all betray the then-fashionable obsession with the Germanic and the influence of the very writers against whom the naturalists would soon take up arms. His efforts in art school resulted in failure and expulsion. He then began private instruction with the sculptor Robert Haertel, who first helped him to reenter the art school and then assisted him in enrolling at the University of Jena, where Hauptmann heard lectures by Eucken, Ernst Haeckel, and other eminent scholars. His studies remained unsystematic and ended after a year.

In 1883 his fiancée, Marie Thienemann, whose sisters married his brothers Georg and Carl, financed Hauptmann's trip to the Mediterranean; Málaga, Barcelona, Marseilles, Naples, Pompeii, Rome, and Florence were among the cities he visited. He went back to Germany only to return soon afterward to Rome, where he took up residence as a sculptor. But his efforts ended in failure in 1884, and six weeks of study at the Dresden Academy of Arts in the summer of that year likewise produced nothing. Two semesters at the University of Berlin in 1884-1885 provided no academic inspiration; thereafter, Hauptmann turned once and for all to creative writing. In retrospect one can recognize that academic success would have had little direct effect on his eventual achievement, for Hauptmann's most salient asset would prove to be his ability to observe and listen to the persons around him as human beings, not as representatives of ideas. In his greatest plays Hauptmann does let his characters express ideas and principles that transcend their immediate situations; nonetheless, these ideas are not necessarily Hauptmann's own beliefs. Instead, they are means of portraying a character with a definite personality and sometimes quite unique views. Moreover, Hauptmann never produced any theoretical writings of significance on his own or other writers' works. Art as life, not as art or as a vehicle for his own philosophical notions, would remain his strength. Yet the lack of a formal education left its mark on Hauptmann, who developed typically autodidactic strengths and weaknesses: great learning and many allusions in his works to both well-known and obscure subjects that serve primarily intuitive associations, not a systematic, logical approach.

On 5 May 1885 Hauptmann married Marie Thienemann and moved with her to Berlin. In September they moved to Erkner, a suburb of Berlin, where Hauptmann met many of the people who would reappear in his plays. He also encountered young writers such as Max Kretzer (later called the "Berlin Zola"); Wilhelm Bölsche, whose *Die naturwissenschaftlichen Grundlagen der Poesie* (The Scientific Foundations of Literature, 1887) would be one of the most important manifestos of German naturalism; and Bruno Wille, a strong advocate of the Social Democratic party. Since 1884 Hauptmann had been taking acting lessons from Alexander Heßler, who would provide the model for the politically and artistically conservative theater director Hassenreuter in *Die Ratten* (1911; translated as *The Rats*, 1913). This instruction, which lasted until 1886, offered Hauptmann insights into conventional modes of acting, the practical demands of the theater, and, as *Die Ratten* reveals, a clearly defined target against which his own first plays could be directed. In his mature years Hauptmann would direct many of his own and other playwrights' works, and he always demonstrated a concern for the practicalities of the stage.

In 1887 Hauptmann visited the new literary club "Durch" (Through), where he met yet more representatives of what later became known as naturalism. Although the theoretical discussions of this club—like those of the others springing up all over Berlin at that time—achieved little more than to keep alive the younger generation's demand for a new, modern, realistic literature, Hauptmann made an outstanding contribution befitting his own nontheoretical, practice-oriented thinking: he read to the members from the little-known works of Georg Büchner, one of the most important precursors of naturalism and subsequent literary movements such as expressionism and the theater of the absurd. Also in 1887 Hauptmann wrote his first two successful novellas: "Fasching" (Carnival) was based on a newspaper account and appeared the same year in *Siegfried*, an obscure magazine (it would be published in book form in 1923). "Bahnwärter Thiel" (1892; translated as "Flagman Thiel," 1933) appeared in 1888 in the first important journal of naturalism, *Die Gesellschaft* (Society), founded in 1885 in Munich. "Bahnwärter Thiel," strongly influenced by Büchner, proved to be a masterpiece and is still read in schools today.

Always interested less in the rational side of humanity than in its irrational side—emotions, psychological problems, mystical leanings—Hauptmann spent several weeks in 1888 studying under Auguste Forel, a prominent psychiatrist and director of a clinic in Zurich. There Hauptmann also associated with the playwright Frank Wedekind, who would later accuse Hauptmann of using in *Das Friedensfest* (1890; translated as *The Coming of Peace: A Family Catastrophe*, 1900) intimate details he had recounted from his own life. Wedekind would then seek revenge in his comedy *Die junge Welt* (The Young World, 1898), in which he satirized Hauptmann's "notebook" technique and naturalism in general.

The year 1889 was a turning point in the development of naturalism and also in Hauptmann's career. First came the publication of some of the most radically "realistic" prose thus far seen in Germany: *Papa Hamlet*, by Arno Holz and Johannes Schlaf. Until then, Hauptmann had been reading the works of foreign models for the new "realists" (the German naturalists seldom called themselves "naturalists"): Leo Tolstoy, Emile Zola, Ivan Turgenev, Fyodor Dostoyevski, and Walt Whitman. Then came the founding of the "Freie Bühne" (Free Stage), a club devoted to the performance of "modern" (naturalist) drama (a year later a periodical of the same name was founded, which later became the *Neue Rundschau* [New Review]; one member of the board was Samuel Fischer, whose publishing house brought out many plays of the young naturalists and published Hauptmann's works for many years). Its first chairman was Otto Brahm, who developed the naturalist style of stage direction and production that would dominate the German theater until Max Reinhardt came on the scene at the end of the century. Since the Freie Bühne was a private club, it could stage plays forbidden by the censor. With an eye for a proven theatrical success, Brahm began on 15 September 1889 with a production of *Ghosts* (1881), by Henrik Ibsen, whose *A Doll's House* (1879) had already become a rallying point for advocates of woman's emancipation. In August 1889 Hauptmann's own first mature, modern play, the social drama *Vor Sonnenaufgang*, had been published in Berlin and had caught the attention of many literary figures there. Needing a German playwright to make his undertaking a success, Brahm premiered Hauptmann's play on 20 October 1889. The work launched not only a series of imitations but also a frenzied conflict between conservative forces and the naturalists.

In some respects *Vor Sonnenaufgang* incorporates the innovations of Ibsen that characterize much of subsequent German naturalist drama; in other respects, however, Hauptmann goes far beyond Ibsen both in subject and in style. Ibsen's influence can be seen in the structure, which uses "analytic exposition"—the practice of beginning with a situation and gradually exposing what has led to it. A second technique, closely allied with the first and likewise perfected by Ibsen, is the use of a "messenger from the outside," a stranger who serves as a catalyst for the analytic exposition, sometimes without intending to do so. Alfred Loth, a journalist with an education in sociology and economics and an impassioned believer in social justice, abstinence, and the power of heredity, arrives at the farm of the Krause family, which has suddenly become wealthy through the discovery of coal and the exploitation of the other residents of the area. Loth looks up his old friend from his university days, the engineer Hoffmann. This reunion provides a "realistic" setting for revelations regarding their respective activities and changes in character since they last met: Loth's abortive attempt to establish a utopian community in the New World resulted in his imprisonment for supposedly collecting money for the socialists; Hoffmann, who now denies ever sharing Loth's idealism, has by devious means married into the Krause family and has been the driving force behind the manipulation and exploitation of the farmers and workers. Loth falls in love with Helene, Hoffmann's sister-in-law, who is apparently the sole uncorrupted member of the household. She falls in love with him, seeing in him the opportunity to escape her situation. But through Dr. Schimmelpfennig, another former friend from the university, Loth learns that Helene's sister and father are alcoholics. Believing first in his social mission, which includes not only the emancipation of women but also handing down his healthy genes to future generations, Loth writes a note to Helene and leaves. True to naturalist principles, Hauptmann strives for the greatest possible realism, which does not allow him to reveal any more about a character's thoughts and motives than a real person would reveal under the given circumstances. Thus, the characters are trapped in a closed, almost suffocating atmosphere, and the audience must watch for subtle gestures or chance words to gain insights into their various motives and intentions. Personalities, not principles, evoke most of the conflicts. Loth's fanaticism, coupled with his inability to effect any social reform, removes him from the conventional role of the playwright's spokesman. The play has remained a subject of lively critical debate mainly because of the questionable motives of Loth, Helene, and all the other characters. In fact Hauptmann scarcely ever created a "hero" or "heroine" who might be interpreted as his spokesperson; at the same time, as he himself said, he never created a true "villain."

What distinguishes *Vor Sonnenaufgang* from Ibsen's plays is, first, the frankness and crassness with which sexual and other manifestations of decadence and moral corruption are presented, as when Helene's drunken father grasps her in an lustful manner. Many contemporary naturalists in Germany had been calling for "truth" rather than beauty, and Hauptmann's play seems to respond to this demand. Second, Hauptmann incorporates the working-class and rural elements and lets them speak in dialect, a device he also uses with the Krause family to reveal how thin the veneer of culture acquired through wealth is. Hauptmann reveals his models for these innovations in his autobiography, *Das Abenteuer meiner Jugend* (The Adventure of My Youth, 1937): "Dieses Drama würde ohne *Thérèse Raquin* von Zola, ohne die *Macht der Finsternis* von Tolstoi und die Vehemenz des *Buches der Zeit* und seines Dichters wohl kaum entstanden sein" (This play would probably never have come about without *Thérèse Raquin* by Zola, *The Power of Darkness* by Tolstoy and the vehemence of the *Book of Time* and its author [Arno Holz]). It was especially Tolstoy's play, which was later performed by the Freie Bühne, that inspired Hauptmann to expand his realistic social drama to include not only the bourgeois hypocrisy that had been the subject of Ibsen's dramas but also the lot of farmers and laborers. Until then the general public had gleaned its literary images of country life from the Dorfnovellen and Dorfromane (village novellas and novels) that had flourished since the 1830s. In selecting locales for his works Hauptmann returns frequently to rural life in Silesia, but he does not idealize it.

During his lifetime Hauptmann had forty-one plays published, and five more appeared posthumously. His plays can be divided into three categories: at least seven have remained uncontested as literary masterpieces; twenty-two have evoked some degree of favorable critical and popular response or maintain interest because of their historical importance. Only seventeen have had relatively little popular or critical impact. While one might dispute the numbers in each category, one would certainly confer masterpiece status on *Die Weber* (published 1892; performed, 1893; translated as *The Weavers*, 1899), *Der Biberpelz* (1893; translated as *The Beaver Coat*, 1912), *Hannele Matterns Himmelfahrt* (Hannele Mattern's Ascension; published, 1893; performed as *Hanneles Himmelfahrt*, 1893; translated as *Hannele*, 1894), *Fuhrmann Henschel* (1899; translated as *Drayman Henschel*, 1910), *Rose Bernd* (1903; translated, 1913), *Die Ratten*, and *Vor Sonnenuntergang* (Before Sundown, 1932). Five of these works appeared before 1906, the year Hauptmann's seventeenth play, *Und Pippa tanzt!* (1906; translated as *And Pippa Dances*, 1909), was published. By this time Hauptmann had averaged one drama per year since his first appearance as a playwright. While he would complete another twenty-nine stage works, every one of these first seventeen falls into one of the first two categories. Given Hauptmann's succession of controversial or aesthetically interesting plays, it was only natural that the theatergoing public after 1906 awaited with enthusiasm every new drama from his pen. Only infrequently did his audience leave the theater disappointed. Nonetheless, Hauptmann's enduring fame depends primarily on the plays written by 1906. When Oxford University awarded him an honorary doctorate in 1905, it confirmed that Hauptmann's fame had become an international phenomenon.

Hauptmann's first six plays conform to the general goal of naturalism: to show people as products of their heredity and milieu. Yet *Die Weber* is both the extreme example of a supposedly strict adherence to such principles and is also theatrically unique. Throughout his life Hauptmann would be known not only as the foremost realist but also, more specifically, as the author of *Die Weber*. The naturalists had, from the beginning, denounced historical drama, a genre that dominated the serious stage following Schiller's death in 1805. *Die Weber* portrays the lot of Silesian weavers in the days leading up to their revolt on 3 June 1844, but it was considered by its first audiences a dramatization of almost contemporary events. The weavers' revolt had been crushed by government troops after only a few days, and their situation had not changed by 1891, when Hauptmann completed the first version of his play. Various literary works had kept alive the memory of the revolt, and newspapers throughout Germany were still publishing articles on the misery of the weavers.

Lithograph by Emil Orlik, drawn on the occasion of the Prague premiere of Hauptmann's Die Weber *in 1897*

True to the naturalist tendency toward ascertaining and reproducing all the sociopolitical details of a situation, Hauptmann traveled to the site of the revolt, where he spoke with survivors. He later recorded his impressions of what he saw on these visits: "Der Menschheit ganzer Jammer, wie man sagt, faßte mich nicht zum ersten Male an. Ich hatte in dieser Beziehung, wie das Buch meiner Jugend beweist, schon in Salzbrunn vieles gesehen. Grimmiger Treffendes dann in Zürich unter den Kranken des Burghölzli, der Kantonalirrenanstalt. Was sich in diesen Weberhütten enthüllte, war, ich möchte sagen: das Elend in seiner klassischen Form" (The entire suffering of humanity, as one says, did not seize me for the first time. In this connection I had, as the book of my youth proves, already seen much in Salzbrunn. More horribly moving things then in Zurich among the patients of Burghölzli, the Canton Insane Asylum. What was revealed in these huts of the weavers was, I would like to say, misery in its classical form). After recounting many details, he admits that he could never show the true depths of this misery in his play.

The censor, aware that the plight of the weavers was a live political issue, forbade Hauptmann's play as dangerous—first in its al-most incomprehensible original version in the Silesian dialect, then in the second version, which, as a concession to the Berliners, was written according to Hauptmann in a dialect "approaching High German" (dem Hochdentschen angenähert). The second version was performed by the Freie Bühne on 26 February 1893 and, after a court trial, elsewhere. A ban by the censor was not in itself remarkable; bans were often deliberately sought by the naturalists, who were intent on shocking contemporary audiences. What made—and still makes—*Die Weber* less political propaganda than a work of art is its aesthetic quality and its dramaturgical daring. There is no traditional "hero"; only one relatively minor character, who serves as a barometer for the rising emotional pressure among the weavers, appears in all five acts. The acts take place without any regard for the temporal and spatial limitations typical of most naturalist drama. At first glance, the play seems to consist of five individual one-act dramas, each with a different locale and with only occasionally recurring characters. Yet there is more than thematic unity, for the play does have a hero, albeit a new type: the weavers themselves as a collective, whose rising feelings of indignation lead to the revolt and whose heartbeat is heard throughout in the song "Das Blutgericht" (The Blood-Court), which was actually sung by the weavers in the 1840s. Hauptmann shows, through the collective, "misery in its classical form"; and, as in classical drama, the climax comes at the end of the third act, when one of the weavers says, "A jeder Mensch hat halt 'ne Sehnsucht" (Everyone has something he yearns for). Almost every character, even those speaking only a few lines, comes across as an individual. Yet despite its subtle, underlying adherence to traditional dramaturgical principles, *Die Weber*, unlike classical drama, ends on a note of ambiguity befitting the naturalist commitment to a "slice of life" having neither a real beginning nor a true conclusion. *Die Weber* is probably the greatest mass-drama in German literature and influenced all subsequent writers of such dramas, including the expressionists.

Hauptmann violates the rules of a well-made play by introducing a major character in the fifth act: Old Hilse, who voices trust in God and opposition to the no longer restrainable revolt occurring around him. In no other work does Hauptmann better show his ability to have a character express a thought that, while it purports to transcend the limitations of the immediate situation and the speaker, remains firmly anchored in the speaker's personality. Since Old Hilse's notions are typical of the religious attitudes prevalent among the weavers as a group, not the ideas but only their most persevering exponent can be seen as "new." Often interpreted as a representative of religion's function as what Karl Marx called an "opiate of the people," Old Hilse is killed by a stray bullet. Being accidental, his death cannot be viewed as a symbolic renunciation of the old ways that have kept the weavers in a state of self-enslavement. Hauptmann concludes his play on an ironic note that leaves the impression that the weavers will now triumph, but everyone in his audience knew that the real weavers were quickly defeated and forced back into their former life. While Hauptmann portrays the revolt as unavoidable, the play cannot be interpreted as a call for another revolt—unless deeper changes occur first in the people themselves.

Nonetheless, *Die Weber* was considered by many to be virtually seditious. When it was publicly performed for the first time, Kaiser Wilhelm II canceled his loge at the Deutsches Theater. And when Hauptmann was suggested for the prestigious Schiller Prize in 1896 and again in 1899,

Gerhart Hauptmann

Wilhelm personally rejected him both times. But Hauptmann had already exacted his revenge against the intolerance and stupidity of Wilhelminian officialdom with his masterful comedy *Der Biberpelz*, which uses as its heroine a washerwoman, Frau Wolff. Hauptmann changed his model, an honest washerwoman, into a petty thief who first poaches, then takes home carelessly stored firewood, and finally steals and sells a beaver coat—progressively greater crimes, which, because the victim is both wealthy and ludicrous, do not transgress the limits of a comedy. She commits them under the eyes of a local official, who is more concerned with the supposed danger of socialists, especially with one patently harmless character modeled after Hauptmann himself. The role of the thieving washerwoman is one of the most famous, and this comedy one of the most frequently performed, in German theatrical history.

Yet the initial reaction to *Der Biberpelz* was far from auspicious. The censor's office, substantiating Hauptmann's low opinion of public officials, allowed the play to be presented only because it was considered too boring to have a long run. The first audience remained in its seats after the last curtain because it expected a fifth act in which Frau Wolff would be discovered and punished. But the comedy ends with the official's reiteration of his belief in her innocence and good character and his reassertion of the danger of the suspected "socialist."

Der Biberpelz was Hauptmann's second comedy; the first was *Kollege Crampton* (performed 1892; published as *College Crampton*, 1892; translated as *Colleague Crampton*, 1914), a study of a drunken painter and teacher whose real-life counterpart Hauptmann had met in 1880 at the Breslau Art Academy. But the focus in the first comedy remained relatively narrow, and at the end the audience questions only the protagonist's ability to fulfill his good resolutions, not the social and political background. In his second comedy Hauptmann expands the comic potential of naturalism beyond the depiction of individual characters. While Crampton is an outsider or even a victim, Frau Wolff asserts her mastery over her environment. Always one step ahead of other characters and able to manipulate them, Frau Wolff appears as the rogue figure of many traditional comedies. At the same time she is always a realistically portrayed individual with a specific background and discernible limitations.

It was not popular morality, with its desire to see this "thief" punished, but the dictates of realism that led Hauptmann to write a sequel, *Der rote Hahn* (1901; translated as *The Conflagration*, 1912)—but as a tragicomedy, not a comedy. In the sequel Hauptmann shows that Frau Wolff's seemingly harmless, victimless crimes were motivated by capitalistic avarice; in the time since the end of the first play she has committed arson for profit. An innocent man is punished for her crime, but she refuses to confess. She dies at the end with the words: "Ma langt . . . Ma langt nach was" (One reaches . . . One reaches for something). Here is the culmination of Hauptmann's vision of his characters as individuals obeying their own instincts, drives, and emotions to the end, for the final, truly criminal acts of Frau Wolff were already implied by her personality in *Der Biberpelz*. The sequel has enjoyed neither the favorable critical reception nor the popularity of the original; but the consistency of thought and character connecting the two plays was noted by Bertolt Brecht, who tried to mold them into a single drama in his stage production *Bieberpelz und Roter Hahn* (1951).

To many, *Hanneles Himmelfahrt* seemed to initiate Hauptmann's break with naturalism. After *Die Weber* and *Der Biberpelz*, the lesser exponents of naturalism assumed that little else remained to be done technically and that subsequent works would distinguish themselves solely through new subjects and issues. *Hanneles Himmelfahrt*, however, reveals that Hauptmann had not abandoned the fundamental goals of naturalism but had expanded its artistic means.

The initial reception of *Hanneles Himmelfahrt* was not favorable. Paul Schlenther, one of the cofounders of the Freie Bühne and a close friend as well as first biographer of Hauptmann, commented that the overly pious members of the audience wanted to ascribe the play to the Social Democrats, while the Social Democrats found it too religious. The first of the two acts depicts in thoroughly naturalistic manner a poorhouse whose inhabitants take in the freezing young girl Hannele; a victim of poverty and maltreatment by her drunken stepfather, she has attempted to drown herself. In the second act the audience shares in Hannele's dream, in which Christ appears looking like her schoolteacher, and Hannele is prepared by angels for her wedding with him. At the end of the play the action returns to the real world, and the audience learns that Hannele has died.

Hauptmann incorporates in this play many aspects of the very literary tendencies—neoromanticism and Jugendstil—that were developing as reactions against naturalism's exclusion of everything not recognized by science and its emphasis on the banal and ugly side of life. Hannele's hallucination fulfills all the expectations of heaven that are implied by the traditional religious views of Old Hilse; consequently, there is some truth in those interpretations that consider *Hanneles Himmelfahrt* the second part of *Die Weber*. On the other hand, the irrationality of an obviously delirious dreamer, the erotic fantasies of an adolescent girl, and the sociological basis of her religious expectations do not exhaust the significance of the dream. Hauptmann's intention is to dramatize the creation of a work of art. In an April 1894 letter replying to one of his critics, Hauptmann asserts: "Wie das Märchen ist, suchte ich mir ein Aschenbrödel, um es, wiederum wie das Märchen tut, aus tiefstem Elend zu höchstem Glück zu führen. Gleich dem Märchen, welches nach Möglichkeit real zu sein versucht, suchte ich nun aber innerhalb des Märchenrahmens ebenfalls so viel mir möglich,

Hauptmann in 1916; lithograph by Johannes M. Avenarius

real zu sein. . . . Das Kind stellte für mich gleichsam ein Stückchen des Urbodens dar, aus dem alle Religion und alle Poesie entkeimt ist" (As in a fairy tale, I looked for a Cinderella in order to lead her, as a fairy tale does, out of the deepest misery to the highest happiness. Like the fairy tale, which tries as far as possible to be real, I now, however, likewise sought to be as real as possible within the framework of a fairy tale. . . . That child represented for me more or less a small piece of the mother earth from which all religions and all poetry have sprung). Hannele's dream, to be sure, represents the extreme example of personal escapism; but a similar desire to manipulate and transcend reality motivates all poetic expression.

Hauptmann's next attempt to dramatize such a line of thought, *Die versunkene Glocke* (performed, 1896; published, 1897; translated as *The Sunken Bell*, 1898), was more accessible to contemporary audiences. One of his most popular plays and the first one to earn a substantial amount of money for Hauptmann, *Die versunkene Glocke*, which bears the subtitle *Ein deutsches Märchendrama* (a German Fairy-Tale Drama) and is in verse, was its author's concession to bourgeois taste and to the fashion set by Maurice Maeterlinck; it is considered today to be a weak work.

Of far greater scope and of more lasting critical interest would, however, be the still frequently puzzling *Und Pippa tanzt!*, which begins almost as naturalistically as *Hanneles Himmelfahrt* but allows its nonrealistic elements even more autonomy. In fact, its almost allegorical tendencies mark it as a forerunner of expressionist drama.

After moving in 1889 to Charlottenburg, another suburb of Berlin, Hauptmann made a trip in 1890 to Zurich, Italy, and Monaco; in 1891 he traveled to Silesia for studies for *Die Weber*. By this time he and Marie had three sons—Ivo, born in 1886; Eckart, born in 1887; and Klaus born in 1889—and she had inherited enough money to make the family financially secure. In 1891 the Hauptmanns moved to Schreiberhau (now Szklarska Poreba, Poland) in Silesia. Hauptmann soon fell in love with the sister of Max Marschalk, the composer of the music for *Hanneles Himmelfahrt* and later for more of Hauptmann's works. Hauptmann had met Margarete Marschalk in 1889, when she was fourteen. She had later studied violin under Joseph Joachim but had had to give up a musical career. Hauptmann, who knew Gustav Mahler, Richard Strauss, and other prominent musical figures, was undoubtedly drawn to Margarete in part because of her musical talent. She reentered his life as a guest at the dinner Hauptmann gave after the premiere of *Hanneles Himmelfahrt* in September 1893. After spending the following days with Margarete in Berlin, he returned to his wife and children, who had remained in Silesia. Hauptmann confessed his new love to his wife. He returned shortly thereafter to Berlin, where he saw Margarete again. When he went to Paris for the opening of *Hanneles Himmelfahrt* there, Marie left for America, where she stayed with Alfred Ploetz in Meriden, Connecticut. Hauptmann hurried after her and a reconciliation was reached. Hauptmann gained mostly unfavorable impressions of the United States. Shortly after the failure of *Hanneles Himmelfahrt* in New York on 1 May 1894, he returned with his family to Germany.

The reconciliation did not last long; but Marie refused to give the playwright a divorce, even though Margarete gave birth to Hauptmann's son Benvenuto on 1 June 1900. In the fall of that year Marie and the children moved into a house in Dresden that Hauptmann had built for them, and he moved with Margarete into Wiesenstein, a house he had constructed for himself and his new family in Agnetendorf. Finally, in 1904, Marie divorced him, and in September of that year he married Margarete.

In September 1905 he met a sixteen-year-old girl, Ida Orloff, who became a threat to the new marriage. Hauptmann broke off his affair in 1906 or 1907. But while there are few figures in his works reminiscent of Margarete, Ida Orloff recurs frequently in his plays and fiction—sometimes in a positive, sometimes in a negative light—even long after he had stopped seeing her. One should not, however, ascribe such figures to her alone, for their occurrence in Hauptmann's works coincides with the obsession of many Jugendstil and symbolist poets for the *femme-enfant* and femme fatale. One could almost suggest that Hauptmann, through this affair, was unconsciously living out a current literary motif.

During these years Hauptmann suffered some artistic disappointments. The most notable came with the premiere of *Florian Geyer* (published, 1896; translated, 1929) on 4 January 1896. Although it has a "hero," this play about the Peasant Wars of 1524-1525 has much in common with *Die Weber*; to this day it represents the best attempt to write a thoroughly naturalistic drama on a historical subject of such remoteness in time. Hauptmann had begun his preliminary studies in 1891, while he was working on *Die Weber*; as in the case of *Die Weber* he went to the areas concerned, this time southern Germany. As a naturalist, Hauptmann always strives for a rigorously accurate phonetic reproduction of linguistic peculiarities and dialects, which allows his audience to pinpoint the educational and social level and regional background of a character. Opinions vary on Hauptmann's success in reproducing the language of the sixteenth century, but if he had not tried to reproduce it—including differentiations among the various characters and classes—then *Florian Geyer* would have been merely another costume piece, yet another play of the type the naturalists consciously rejected.

Moreover, the naturalist seeks the "complete" truth, not a "higher" or more poetic one. Hauptmann gathered an enormous amount of material on Geyer, his friends and enemies, and the times in general. Nonetheless, the play, admittedly not well staged or acted, was rejected by critics and public alike at its premiere. But in 1904 it was successfully performed with Rudolf Rittner in the title role, and thereafter it served as a vehicle for several other actors of stature. Yet such successes have, paradoxically, only emphasized a fundamental dilemma: did Hauptmann make a

Margarete Hauptmann in 1904, the year she became Hauptmann's second wife

politically inactive and historically unimportant historical figure too central to the work? Or do the events overcome and obscure not only the central character but also the myriad of others? In any case, *Florian Geyer* remains the only historical drama of note produced by naturalism.

Before 1906 Hauptmann created two more masterpieces, *Fuhrmann Henschel* and *Rose Bernd*. Both represent a refinement of naturalist technique rather than an expansion of it to previously untried subjects. At the same time, in both plays Hauptmann lets his audience feel that more than the forces of biological and sociological determinism produces the tragic outcome.

Returning to the themes of "Bahnwärter Thiel" and the Silesian milieu and dialect of *Vor Sonnenaufgang*, *Fuhrmann Henschel* portrays against the background of the industrial and economic changes of the contemporary world the unhappy marriage of a man to his former maid, a sexually active, domineering woman, after he promises his dying first wife that he will not marry her. Many contemporaries heard echoes in the play of the so-called fate tragedies of the early nineteenth century. But Hauptmann avoids the crudity of such plays' emphasis on a vague concept of fate: his protagonist commits suicide only after the audience has seen him destroyed by his guilt, the changes in the socioeconomic world, and his unfaithful second wife. The tragedy, which premiered on 5 November 1898 in Berlin, was an immediate success there and in Paris, where André Antoine, founder of the "théâtre libre," the model for the Freie Bühne, praised not only the presentation of the milieu but also the play's "clarity and sobriety." Many critics have subsequently likened it to Attic tragedy.

In 1897 and again in 1898 Hauptmann traveled to Italy, where he began several works on exotic subjects that, with the exception of material that was later integrated into *Der arme Heinrich* (Poor Henry, 1902; translated as *Henry of Auë*, 1915) and *Und Pippa tanzt!*, would not appear on the stage. Another drama in a realistic manner, if not a great one, followed: *Michael Kramer* (1900; translated, 1914) was rejected at its premiere on 21 December 1900, yet the fourth act, with Kramer's almost lyrical comments on death, found admirers in Rainer Maria Rilke and Thomas Mann.

Then another masterpiece, *Rose Bernd*, premiered on 31 October 1903 in Berlin. Although the theme of an unmarried mother killing her child had been a favorite of the Storm and Stress writers of the 1770s and had been given its most famous treatment by Johann Wolfgang von Goethe in *Faust I* (1808), Hauptmann's direct inspiration can be found neither in the past nor in the contemporary naturalist concern for fallen or victimized women. Instead, it came from his participation as a juror from 15 to 17 April 1903 at the trial of a waitress accused of murdering her child.

A criticism made of virtually all of Hauptmann's strongly realistic character dramas surfaced again in the case of *Rose Bernd*: that the play is too epic, that is, not "dramatic" enough. By 1903 the naturalist style of acting had dominated the stages of Germany for several years, and *Rose Bernd* seemed to many critics an anachronism. Moreover, despite the artistic liberties introduced by naturalism since 1889, the subject of *Rose Bernd* was still considered controversial enough for the play to be removed by royal order from the repertoire in Vienna.

Nevertheless, the tragedy gained in popularity and in 1919 became the first of Hauptmann's

plays to be filmed (his novel *Atlantis* had been filmed in 1913). There followed films of *Elga* (1905; translated, 1909) in 1919, *Die Ratten* and *Schluck und Jau* (1900; translated as *Schluck and Jau*, 1916) in 1921, *Die Weber* in 1927 and *Der Biberpelz* in 1928. After these silent films *Hanneles Himmelfahrt* initiated in 1934 a series of movies with sound: *Der Herrscher* (loosely adapted from *Vor Sonnenuntergang*), *Der Biberpelz*, and *The Rats* (based on *Die Ratten*) in 1937, and *Die Jungfern von Bischofsberg* (1907; translated as *The Maidens of the Mount*, 1916) in 1943. The years after the fall of the Nazi dictatorship, when a reborn German film industry was looking for uncontroversial but proven subjects, brought forth *Der Biberpelz* in 1949, *Die Ratten* in 1955, *Vor Sonnenuntergang* and *Fuhrmann Henschel* in 1956, *Rose Bernd* in 1957, and *Dorothea Angermann* (1926) in 1959. But none of the films contribute much toward an assessment of Hauptmann as a playwright. Almost without exception they take great liberties with his texts. Most are based on Hauptmann's realistic plays; yet despite the ability of the camera to show gestures and facial expressions crucial to naturalist acting but often not discernible to those seated at the back of a theater, most of these films are visually disappointing. Unlike Carl Zuckmayer, Brecht, and other playwrights, Hauptmann never wrote an original screenplay.

In 1907 Hauptmann traveled to Greece. The most immediate result of his sojourn there was his diary, *Griechischer Frühling* (Grecian Spring, 1908). In the years to come many critics would see this work as a turning point in Hauptmann's career, and one not in the right direction. Yet what Hauptmann says in *Griechischer Frühling* about Greek tragedy obviously stems from seeing it through the eyes of a dramatist schooled in the perspective and expectations of naturalism: "Tragödie heißt: Freundschaft, Verfolgung, Haß und Liebe als Lebenswut! Tragödie heißt: Angst, Not, Gefahr, Pein, Qual, Marter, heißt Tücke, Verbrechen, Niedertracht, heißt Mord, Blutgier, Blutschande, Schlächterei" (Tragedy means: friendship, persecution, hate and love as existential passion! Tragedy means: fear, misery, danger, anguish, torment, torture; means deception, crime, depravity; means murder, bloodthirstiness, incest, butchery). Hauptmann's works reflecting the forms and themes of antiquity remained for a long time mainly nondramatic ones; his only play on a classical source to appear before his old age would be *Der Bogen des*

Odysseus (1914; translated as *The Bow of Odysseus*, 1917), which he began during this trip but completed only after much work. The long genesis produced a play that relies more on characterization and the bucolic than on Homer, from whom Hauptmann takes only the plot. Despite its originality, the play enjoyed only moderate success.

By 1907 Hauptmann had become financially successful, although, as his correspondence reveals, he spent all his income. Public honors became more frequent: after an honorary doctorate from Oxford in 1905, he received another from the University of Leipzig in 1909. Invitations to lecture in major cities came frequently, and in 1912 he received the Nobel Prize in literature. The literary winds had turned increasingly away from naturalism, yet Hauptmann was frequently admired by and developed friendships with younger writers representing new literary movements, such as Hugo von Hofmannsthal, Rilke, Thomas Mann, and Georg Kaiser; James Joyce is said to have learned German just to read Hauptmann. During this time, however, his published works were mainly in fiction, and up to the advent of the Nazi dictatorship, his stage triumphs would become increasingly rare and would never duplicate those before 1906. He could, however, still create controversy. For example, he was commissioned to write a festival play to commemorate the centenary of the Wars of Liberation in 1813. The result, *Festspiel in deutschen Reimen* (Festival Performance in German Rhymes, 1913; translated as *Commemoration Masque*, 1917), applied not the expected blind reverence but a note of irony toward the revered figures of German history and caused a scandal. Nonetheless, at the outbreak of World War I in 1914 Hauptmann joined other writers in composing patriotic poems. While Hauptmann's attitudes and statements frequently contradict each other, on balance he is usually patriotic but not nationalistic or sycophantic toward the rulers.

In the years between *Rose Bernd* and World War I, Hauptmann, albeit largely occupied with fiction, wrote another truly great work for the stage, a tragicomedy that perhaps remains his most "modern" play. *Die Ratten* is the most complex and subtle play in Hauptmann's oeuvre. Its main plot is strongly naturalistic: Frau John, a cleaning woman who lives in a rat-infested former barracks, adopts the illegitimate child of a Polish maid but convinces her husband, a bricklayer, that she has given birth to it. She is discovered despite her brother's murder of the true mother

and commits suicide. The time of the play is 1884-1885—that is, before the theatrical breakthrough of naturalism with *Vor Sonnenaufgang*—and a second plot revolves around the acting school of Hassenreuter, which is housed in the same building. It provides an ironic, largely comic foil to the plot about Frau John. Hassenreuter, who is something of a philanderer, provides a sharp contrast to the cleaning woman, who tries to attain middle-class stability and happiness in her marriage but is driven to suicide by her husband's inflexible attitude toward her "crime." Hassenreuter is an exponent of Friedrich Schiller's classical, declamatory style of acting. His opponent in a series of arguments is his student Spitta, who advocates more reality—the naturalism that would soon put such people as Frau John on the stage as tragic heroes and heroines. Neither Hassenreuter nor Spitta notices that Frau John's plight has all the qualities of a tragedy in both the naturalistic and the classical senses, and they remain as ludicrous in their theoretical arguments as Frau John remains tragic in her real life. *Die Ratten* represents a reckoning both with the forces that made naturalism necessary and with the ultimate impotence of the naturalist as a reformer.

Few plays are recognized immediately as having the qualities of lasting greatness, and *Die Ratten* was no exception. After Hauptmann gained a court decision against a petty objection by the censor, the premiere took place on 13 January 1911 in Berlin. The reaction was subdued. Even Alfred Kerr, one of the most brilliant and perceptive theater critics, an exponent of naturalism, and an enthusiastic supporter of Hauptmann, had little to say about *Die Ratten* that was good. But five years later, when the play was performed again, another critic, Siegfried Jacobsohn, wrote: "Kritik ist Selbskritik. Weswegen bin ich 1911 vor diesen Ratten durchgefallen?" (Criticism is self-criticism. Why did I flop in 1911 when confronted by *Die Ratten*?). In retrospect, it can be seen that the cause of the rejection in 1911 is the very "modernity" and relevance of *Die Ratten*: its complex intertwining of the tragic and comic and its ironic, disquieting view of human existence and social values.

During World War I Hauptmann wrote little of note for the stage and certainly no overtly patriotic works. When peace came in 1918, Hauptmann welcomed it; the following year he also welcomed the Weimar Republic, which, in turn, li-

Hauptmann and his family with the family of the publisher Samuel Fischer in 1912: Fischer's son, Gerhart; Hauptmann; Margarete Hauptmann; the Hauptmanns' son, Benvenuto; Fischer's daughter, Brigitte; Fischer.

onized him to an extent previously unknown in Germany or elsewhere. His sixtieth and seventieth birthdays became events of national importance. Honorary doctorates from the German University in Prague in 1921 and Columbia University in 1932 show that his fame grew in foreign countries as well.

Between 1925 and 1936 Hauptmann was intensely preoccupied with William Shakespeare's *Hamlet*. He wrote an original play, *Hamlet in Wittenberg* (1935), which portrays the years before the beginning of Shakespeare's play. He also wrote an adaptation of the Shakespeare play (performed, 1927; published, 1929) and a novel, *Im Wirbel der Berufung* (Following My Calling, 1936), about staging the play. The purpose of all of these works was to show that Hamlet could not have been as passive and indecisive as he seems to be in Shakespeare's play. Hauptmann later said: "Überall ist er [Hamlet] um mich gewesen und hat sich dabei allmählich von den schönen Fesseln der Shakespearischen Dichtung ganz befreit. In unzähligen Stunden, Wanderungen durch Feld und Wald, Vigilien der Nächte meiner Gebirgsheimat, haben wir miteinander gesprochen und Meinungen ausgetauscht: Wo dann der Gedanke, ihn auch für andere nochmals sichtbar zu machen, sich beinahe mit Notwendigkeit ergab" (Everywhere he [Hamlet] was around me and thereby gradually freed himself from the fetters of the Shakespearean play. In countless hours, wanderings through field and forest, nocturnal vigils in my mountainous homeland, we spoke with one another and exchanged opinions: where then the thought of once again making him visible for others arose almost as a necessity). Here one can recognize a reversal of his creative process as a naturalist, where a character modeled after a real person reveals only a portion of his real-life counterpart; in contrast, Hauptmann sees Hamlet as only a portion of a real person and tries to conjure up the complete person that must have been on Shakespeare's mind. Yet his long study of *Hamlet* (including philological studies) and his "personal" relationship with its protagonist bore little fruit, for the critical reception of the Hamlet works was unfavorable.

Hauptmann's last unquestionably great and popular play, *Vor Sonnenuntergang*, which premiered in the midst of his Hamlet studies on 16 February 1932, grew out of an interest in another Shakespearean play. Hauptmann had set out to write a new *King Lear*, but soon the play embraced a multitude of other influences and stimuli. *Vor Sonnenuntergang* portrays the family conflicts that arise when Matthias Clausen, a dignified, cultured, and sensitive man of seventy, falls in love with his gardener's niece, Inken Peters, fifty years his junior. The main parallels to *King Lear* stem from the opposition of Clausen's sons and daughters to this union, which they oppose for financial reasons. In the printed version there is a fifth act in which Clausen commits suicide, but in the premiere and in many subsequent performances he dies of a heart attack in the fourth act.

The model for Matthias Clausen was Max Pinkus, a bibliophile and longtime friend of the author. Clausen quotes Goethe, has named his children after Goethe or Goethe's characters or friends, and is celebrating his seventieth birthday on the hundredth anniversary of Goethe's death. Moreover, everyone in the audience at the premiere probably remembered that the seventy-three-year-old Goethe had fallen in love with an eighteen-year-old girl. These parallels and allusions to Goethe are intended to reinforce the impression of Clausen as the last representative of a bygone concept of culture and humanism.

Vor Sonnenuntergang had its premiere the year before Adolf Hitler became chancellor. The more perceptive writers did not have to wait until the Nazis had actually assumed power to predict the manner and consequences of their rule. For example, in Thomas Mann's *Mario und der Zauberer* (1930; translated as *Mario and the Magician*, 1930) the stage technique of the demonic magician Cipolla shows great similarity to Hitler's observations on political rallies in *Mein Kampf* (My Struggle, 1925-1926). Also in 1932 Brecht was already working on his anti-Nazi play *Die Rundköpfe und die Spitzköpfe* (1957; translated as *Roundheads and Peakheads*, 1966). In his novella Mann proves himself to be especially adept in evoking the atmosphere that breeds a Cipolla and allows him to succeed. In the same way, Hauptmann's minor figures in *Vor Sonnenuntergang* represent an entire society's role in bringing about the "sundown" of traditional forms of family relationships and cultural values.

The "sundown" in the title of the play obviously alludes to Hauptmann's first success, which came just before a "dawn." On 20 July 1933, not quite five months after the burning of the Reichstag and less than a week after the creation of a one-party state in Germany, Hauptmann said to C. F. W. Behl: "Meine Epoche beginnt mit 1870 und endigt mit dem Reichstagsbrand" (My epoch begins with 1870 [the establishment of the Second Reich] and ends with the burning of the Reichstag). In other words, his time, the time that understood and revered culture, was over. Even if its prophetic implications had not been fulfilled through the dictatorship of the Nazis, *Vor Sonnenuntergang* would still capture the atmosphere of an era that bred radical opponents of traditional cultural values.

Many Jews and intellectuals left Germany in 1933 and the following years. But Hauptmann, who had turned seventy in 1932, felt himself too old to follow their lead. His remaining in Germany, his "inner emigration," subjected him to attacks from exiles such as his old friend Kerr. Even today this issue is occasionally raised as a stigma on his reputation. Hauptmann's attitude toward the new rulers can, however, be inferred from their policy toward him: he and his works were relegated to the status of museum pieces. Hauptmann did not publish a single artistic work that could be called an homage to the new masters.

Hauptmann and his wife were the only gentiles at the funeral of his Jewish friend Pinkus in 1934. Although Pinkus had been the model for the protagonist of *Vor Sonnenuntergang*, Hauptmann had ignored Pinkus's Jewishness in the play—even though Hauptmann had long wanted to write a drama about the mysteries of Judaism. In 1937 he finally accomplished this goal with *Die Finsternisse* (The Darknesses), which was inspired by Pinkus's funeral. In the last year of the war Hauptmann, fearing a police search, had the manuscript burned. But a copy found its way to the United States, where it was published in 1947 by Walter A. Reichart; it was first performed in 1952. Dramatically, this work leaves much to be desired; but it is an eloquent statement of Hauptmann's humanity. This play about a Jewish funeral documents not only Hauptmann's lifelong preoccupation with the "Magie des Todes" ("magic of death") but also his increasing tendency toward religious mysticism and interest in a "Zwischenreich" (middle kingdom between the real and mythical worlds).

During the Nazi years Hauptmann wrote a couple of minor stage works and some fiction. Then, almost eighty years old, he seemed to rise

Sketch by Orlik of Hauptmann and others watching a rehearsal of Hauptmann's Winterballade, *October 1917. Left to right: the director, Max Reinhardt; Hauptmann; Rainer Maria Rilke; Margarete Hauptmann (Federico Aborio Mella, Mailand).*

up like an awakening giant for one last great effort as a dramatist. This last creative surge began with *Iphigenie in Delphi* (1941). His inspiration was a passage in Goethe's *Italienische Reise* (1816-1817; translated as *Travels in Italy*, 1846) describing how Goethe would have written a sequel to his *Iphigenie auf Tauris* (1800; translated as *Iphigenia on Tauris*, 1851). But Hauptmann's Iphigenia, although she sacrifices herself to atone for the crimes committed by the house of Atreus, bears little resemblance to the Goethean personification of the all-too-human. Goethe adhered to J. J. Winckelmann's concept of Greek culture and art as representative of "edle Einfalt und stille Größe" (noble simplicity and quiet grandeur)." Hauptmann, on the other hand, remains true to what he said about Greek tragedy in *Griechischer Frühling*: that regardless of how it might be disguised, a human sacrifice is "die blutige Wurzel der Tragödie" (the bloody root of tragedy). Hauptmann in the meanwhile expanded this view of Greek tragedy to include *Hamlet* as well: he says in the novel *Im Wirbel der Berufung* that *Hamlet* is "ein antik-heroisches Leichenspiel" (an antique-

heroic play about a body) and that the ghost of Hamlet's father can be propitiated only by blood. Nonetheless, *Iphigenie in Delphi* ends on a conciliatory note, with the crimes of Agamemnon, Orestes, Klytemnestra, and Electra expiated. This outcome would seem to be consistent with Goethe's view that in his *Iphigenie auf Tauris* pure humanity atones for all human feelings.

Once he had completed his play, Hauptmann felt compelled to portray the events for which Iphigenia atones. He completed *Iphigenie in Aulis* (performed, 1943; published, 1944) in 1943, *Agamemnons Tod* (Agamemnon's Death; performed, 1947; published, 1948) in 1944, and *Elektra* (performed, 1947; published, 1948) in 1945 as the first three parts of a tetralogy. Of all the plays in the tetralogy, *Iphigenie in Aulis*, the second to be written but first in terms of the chronology of the plot, proved the most difficult for Hauptmann to complete and exists in the most manuscript versions; the two one-act dramas that fill out the intervening action of the tetralogy followed rather quickly. Hauptmann needed so long to finish *Iphigenie in Aulis* because he was free-

Hauptmann in 1922; etching by Orlik

ing himself of Goethe's influence and rethinking the implications of the legend within the framework of his own conception of Greek tragedy.

No critic has denied that the tetralogy represents a remarkable accomplishment for any playwright, especially for one in his eighties. But this has been the sole point of general agreement. Critics have condemned the language, the lack of dramatic qualities, and the naturalistic approach to the characters. The most damning criticism concerns the obvious differences in tone and in underlying attitude toward the human condition between *Iphigenie in Delphi*, which is usually interpreted as optimistic, and the three subsequently written parts, which take an essentially pessimistic view of the human ability to avert or rectify disaster.

Many critics see in the tetralogy Hauptmann's reckoning with the Nazi dictatorship and the war it brought about; in 1962 the director Erwin Piscator tried to stage the tetralogy (in much shortened form) as a symbolic representation of Nazi rule. But the texts themselves refute any direct equations of individual characters with contemporary historical personages. One can also demonstrate that Hauptmann was most inter-

ested in the Greek legend in itself, not as a vehicle for expressing essentially modern views.

When World War II ended, Hauptmann was a broken, tired man, although the Russians occupying Silesia treated the author of *Die Weber* with respect. He died on 6 June 1946 and was buried on the island of Hiddensee, where he had spent some of the most enjoyable times of his life and had, in 1930, bought the house "Seedorn" in Kloster. There are now Hauptmann museums in Kloster and Erkner maintained by the German government.

Letters:

Gerhart Hauptmann und Ida Orloff: Dokumentation einer dichterischen Leidenschaft (Berlin: Propyläen-Verlag, 1969);

Walter A. Reichart, "Gerhart Hauptmann and his British Friends: Documented in Some of Their Correspondence," *German Quarterly*, 50 (November 1977): 424-451;

Klaus Bohnen, "Briefwechsel zwischen Gerhart Hauptmann und Georg Brandes," *Jahrbuch der deutschen Schiller-Gesellschaft*, 23 (1979): 55-68;

Klaus W. Jonas, "Gerhart Hauptmann und Hans von Seeckt: Erinnerungen eines Sammlers und Bibliographen. Mit unveröffentlichten Briefen," *Imprimatur*, 9 (1980): 216-239;

Gerhart Hauptmann—Ludwig von Hofmann: Briefwechsel 1894-1944, edited by Herta Hesse-Frielinghaus (Bonn: Bouvier, 1983);

Otto Brahm—Gerhart Hauptmann: Briefwechsel 1889-1912, edited by Peter Sprengel (Tübingen: Narr, 1985).

Bibliographies:

Max Pinkus and Viktor Ludwig, *Gerhart Hauptmann: Werke von ihm und über ihn* (Neustadt/Schlesien, 1922; revised by Ludwig, 1932);

Walter Requardt, *Gerhart Hauptmann Bibliographie*, 3 volumes (Berlin: Selbstverlag, 1931);

C. F. W. Behl, "Gerhart Hauptmann-Bibliographie," *Gerhart Hauptmann-Jahrbuch*, 1 (1936): 147-162; 2 (1937): 150-160;

Walter A. Reichart, "Fifty Years of Hauptmann Study in America (1894-1944): A Bibliography," *Monatshefte*, 37 (1945): 1-31; 54 (1962): 297-310;

Reichart, "Bibliographie der gedruckten und ungedruckten Dissertationen über Gerhart Hauptmann und sein Werk," *Philobiblon*, 11 (June 1967): 121-134;

Reichart, *Gerhart-Hauptmann-Bibliographie* (Bad Homburg: Gehlen, 1969);

Klaus W. Jonas, "Gerhart Hauptmanns Manuskripte in Europa," *Börsenblatt für den deutschen Buchhandel*, 26 (28 July 1970): A121-A139;

Jonas, "Gerhart Hauptmann Collections in America and England," *Stechert-Hafner Book News*, 26 (February 1971): 77-82;

H. D. Tschörtner, *Gerhart-Hauptmann-Bibliographie* (Berlin: Deutsche Staatsbibliothek, 1971);

Rudolf Ziesche, *Der Manuskriptnachlaß Gerhart Hauptmanns* (Wiesbaden: Harrassowitz, 1977);

Sigfrid Hoefert, *Internationale Bibliographie zum Werk Gerhart Hauptmann*, 2 volumes (Berlin: Schmidt, 1986-1989).

Biographies:

Paul Schlenther, *Gerhart Hauptmann: Sein Lebensgang und seine Dichtung* (Berlin: Fischer, 1898; revised, 1912; revised by A. Eloesser, 1922);

C. F. W. Behl and F. A. Voigt, *Chronik von Gerhart Hauptmanns Leben und Schaffen* (Munich: Korn, 1957);

Wolfgang Leppmann, *Gerhart Hauptmann: Leben, Werk und Zeit* (Munich: Scherz, 1986).

References:

Neville Edward Alexander, *Studien zum Stilwandel im dramatischen Werk Gerhart Hauptmanns* (Stuttgart: Metzler, 1964);

Hermann Barnstorff, *Die soziale, politische und wirtschaftliche Zeitkritik im Werke Gerhart Hauptmanns* (Jena: Frommann, 1938);

Peter Bauland, Introduction to *Before Daybreak*, by Hauptmann, translated by Bauland (Chapel Hill: University of North Carolina Press, 1978), pp. i-xxiv;

C. F. W. Behl, *Wege zu Gerhart Hauptmann* (Goslar: Verlag Deutsche Volksbücherei, 1948);

Behl, *Zwiesprache mit Gerhart Hauptmann: Tagebuchblätter* (Munich: Desch, 1949);

Hans von Brescius, *Gerhart Hauptmann: Zeitgeschehen und Bewusstsein in unbekannten Selbstzeugnissen* (Bonn: Bouvier, 1976);

Joseph Chapiro, *Gespräche mit Gerhart Hauptmann* (Berlin: Fischer, 1932);

W. A. Coupe, "An Ambiguous Hero: In Defence of Alfred Loth," *German Life and Letters*, new series 31 (October 1977): 13-22;

Roy C. Cowen, *Das deutsche Drama im 19. Jahrhundert* (Stuttgart: Metzler, 1988);

Cowen, *Hauptmann-Kommentar zum dramatischen Werk* (Munich: Winkler, 1980);

Cowen, *Hauptmann-Kommentar zum nichtdramatischen Werk* (Munich: Winkler, 1981);

Cowen, *Der Naturalismus: Kommentar zu einer Epoche* (Munich: Winkler, 1973);

Hans Daiber, *Gerhart Hauptmann oder der letzte Klassiker* (Vienna: Molden, 1971);

C. T. Dussère, *The Image of the Primitive Giant in the Work of Gerhart Hauptmann* (Stuttgart: Heinz, 1979);

Gustav Erdmann, "Einige pommersch-rügensche Motive in Gerhart Hauptmanns Schaffen: Quellenkundliche Untersuchungen," *Greifswald-Stralsunder Jahrbuch*, 5 (1965): 211-277;

Ralph Fiedler, *Die späten Dramen Gerhart Hauptmanns* (Munich: Korn, 1954);

Hugo F. Garten, "Formen des Eros im Werk Gerhart Hauptmanns," *Zeitschrift für deutsche Philologie*, 90 (1971): 242-258;

Garten, *Gerhart Hauptmann* (Cambridge: Bowes & Bowes, 1954);

Garten, "Gerhart Hauptmann: A Revaluation," *German Life and Letters*, 3 (1949): 32-41;

Joseph Gregor, *Gerhart Hauptmann: Das Werk und unsere Zeit* (Vienna: Diana-Verlag, 1951);

Karl S. Guthke, *Gerhart Hauptmann: Weltbild im Werk* (Göttingen: Vandenhoeck & Ruprecht, 1980);

Frederick W. J. Heuser, *Gerhart Hauptmann: Zu seinem Leben und Schaffen* (Tübingen: Niemeyer, 1961);

Klaus Hildebrandt, *Gerhart Hauptmann und die Geschichte* (Munich: Delp, 1968);

Hildebrandt, *Naturalistische Dramen Gerhart Hauptmanns* (Munich: Oldenbourg, 1983);

Eberhard Hilscher, *Gerhart Hauptmann* (Berlin: Verlag der Nation, 1988);

James L. Hodge, "The Dramaturgy of 'Bahnwärter Thiel,'" *Mosaic*, 9 (Spring 1976): 97-116;

Sigfrid Hoefert, *Gerhart Hauptmann* (Stuttgart: Metzler, 1982);

Josef Hofmiller, *Zeitgenossen* (Munich: Süddeutsche Monatshefte, 1910);

Karl Holl, *Gerhart Hauptmann: His Life and His Work 1862-1912* (London: Gay & Hancock, 1913; Chicago: McClurg, 1913);

Jenny Christa Hortenbach, *Freiheitsstreben und Destruktivität: Frauen in den Dramen August Strindbergs und Gerhart Hauptmanns* (Oslo: Universitetsforlaget, 1965);

K. G. Knight and F. Norman, eds., *Hauptmann Centenary Lectures* (London: University of London Institute of Germanic Studies, 1964);

Ward B. Lewis, "O'Neill and Hauptmann: A Study in Mutual Admiration," *Comparative Literature Studies*, 22 (Summer 1985): 231-243;

Thomas Mann, *Gerhart Hauptmann* (Gütersloh: Bertelsmann, 1953);

Ludwig Marcuse, ed., *Gerhart Hauptmann und sein Werk* (Berlin & Leipzig: Schneider, 1922);

Alan Marshall, *The German Naturalists and Gerhart Hauptmann* (Frankfurt am Main & Bern: Lang, 1982);

Warren R. Maurer, *Gerhart Hauptmann* (Boston: Twayne, 1982);

Hans Mayer, *Gerhart Hauptmann* (Velber bei Hannover: Friedrich, 1972);

Edward McInnes, *Das deutsche Drama des 19. Jahrhunderts* (Berlin: Schmidt, 1983);

McInnes, *German Social Drama 1840-1900: From Hebbel to Hauptmann* (Stuttgart: Heinz, 1976);

Philip Mellen, *Gerhart Hauptmann and Utopia* (Stuttgart: Heinz, 1976);

Mellen, *Gerhart Hauptmann: Religious Syncretism and Eastern Religions* (Bern, Frankfurt am Main & New York: Lang, 1984);

Rolf Michaelis, *Der schwarze Zeus: Gerhart Hauptmanns zweiter Weg* (Berlin: Argon, 1962);

Rudolf Mittler, *Theorie und Praxis des sozialen Dramas bei Gerhart Hauptmann* (Hildesheim, Zurich & New York: Olms, 1985);

Irmgard Müller, *Gerhart Hauptmann und Frankreich* (Breslau: Priebatsch, 1939);

Siegfried H. Muller, *Gerhart Hauptmann und Goethe* (New York: King's Crown Press, 1949);

Muller, "Gerhart Hauptmann's Relation to American Literature and His Concept of America," *Monatshefte*, 44 (1952): 333-339;

Gerdt Oberembt, *Gerhart Hauptmann: Der Biberpelz* (Paderborn, Munich, Vienna & Zurich: Schöningh, 1987);

John Osborne, *The Naturalist Drama in Germany* (Manchester: Manchester University Press / Totowa, N.J.: Rowman & Littlefield, 1971);

Jill Perkins, *Joyce and Hauptmann: Before Sunrise* (San Marino, Cal.: Huntington Library, 1978);

Gerhart Pohl, *Bin ich noch in meinem Haus? Die letzten Tage Gerhart Hauptmanns* (Berlin: Lettner, 1953); translated as *Gerhart Hauptmann and Silesia* (Grand Forks: University of North Dakota Press, 1962);

Walter A. Reichart, *Einheben für Gerhart Hauptmann: Aufsätze aus dem Jahren 1929-1990* (Berlin: Schmidt, 1991);

Reichart, "Gerhart Hauptmann, War Propaganda, and George Bernard Shaw," *Germanic Review*, 33 (October 1958): 176-180;

Reichart, "Gerhart Hauptmann's Dramas on the American Stage," *Maske und Kothurn*, 8 (1962): 223-232;

Reichart, "Grundbegriffe im dramatischen Schaffen Gerhart Hauptmanns," *PMLA*, 82 (March 1967): 142-151;

Ilse H. Reis, *Gerhart Hauptmanns Hamlet-Interpretationen in der Nachfolge Goethes* (Bonn: Bouvier, 1969);

Walter Requardt and Martin Machatzke, *Gerhart Hauptmann und Erkner* (Berlin: Schmidt, 1980);

Hermann Schreiber, *Gerhart Hauptmann und das Irrationale* (Aichkirchen: Schönleiter, 1946);

Hans Joachim Schrimpf, ed., *Gerhart Hauptmann* (Darmstadt: Wissenschaftliche Buchgesellschaft, 1976);

Leroy R. Shaw, *Witness of Deceit: Gerhart Hauptmann as Critic of Society* (Berkeley & Los Angeles: University of California Press, 1958);

Peter Sprengel, *Gerhart Hauptmann: Epoche-Werk-Wirkung* (Munich: Beck, 1984);

Sprengel, "Todessehnsucht und Totenkult bei Gerhart Hauptmann," *Neue Deutsche Hefte*, 189, no. 33 (1986): 11-34;

Sprengel, " 'Vor Sonnenuntergang'—ein Goethe-Drama? Zur Goethe-Rezeption Gerhart Hauptmanns," *Goethe-Jahrbuch* (Weimar), 103 (1986): 31-53;

Sprengel, *Die Wirklichkeit der Mythen: Untersuchungen zum Werk Gerhart Hauptmanns aufgrund des handschriftlichen Nachlasses* (Berlin: Schmidt, 1982);

Sprengel and Philip Mellen, eds., *Hauptmann-Forschung: Neue Beiträge—Hauptmann Research: New Directions* (Bern, Frankfurt am Main & New York: Lang, 1986);

J. L. Styan, *Modern Drama in Theory and Practice*, volume 1: *Realism and Naturalism* (Cambridge, New York & Melbourne: Cambridge University Press, 1981);

Kurt Lothar Tank, *Gerhart Hauptmann in Selbstzeugnissen und Bilddokumenten* (Hamburg: Rowohlt, 1959);

Günther Taube, *Die Rolle der Natur in Gerhart Hauptmanns Gegenwartsdramen bis zum Anfang des 20. Jahrhunderts* (Berlin: Ebering, 1936; reprint, Nendeln / Liechtenstein, 1967);

H. D. Tschörtner, "Bertolt Brecht und Hauptmann," *Weimarer Beiträge*, 32, no. 3 (1986): 386-403;

Tschörtner, *Ungeheures erhofft: Zu Gerhart Hauptmann—Werk und Wirkung* (Berlin: Der Morgen, 1986);

Felix A. Voigt, *Antike und antikes Lebensgefühl im Werke Gerhart Hauptmanns* (Breslau: Maruschke & Berendt, 1935);

Voigt, *Gerhart Hauptmann der Schlesier* (Breslau: Schlesien-Verlag, 1942; revised, Goslar: Deutsche Volksbücherei, 1947);

Voigt, *Hauptmann-Studien: Untersuchungen über Leben und Schaffen Gerhart Hauptmanns* (Breslau: Maruschke & Berendt, 1936);

Voigt, "Die Schaffensweise Gerhart Hauptmanns," *Germanisch-Romanische Monatsschrift*, 32 (1950): 93-106;

Voigt and Reichart, *Hauptmann und Shakespeare* (Breslau: Maruschke & Berendt, 1938; revised, Goslar: Deutsche Volksbücherei, 1947);

Benno von Wiese, "Gerhart Hauptmann," in *Deutsche Dichter der Moderne*, edited by Wiese (Berlin: Schmidt, 1965), pp. 27-48;

Bernhard Zeller, ed., *Gerhart Hauptmann: Leben und Werk: Eine Gedächtnisausstellung des Deutschen Literaturarchivs zum 100. Geburtstag des Dichters* (Stuttgart: Turmhaus-Druckerei, 1962);

Theodore Ziolkowski, "Hauptmann's *Iphigenie in Delphi*: A Travesty?" *Germanic Review*, 34 (February 1959): 105-123;

Carl Zuckmayer, *Ein voller Erdentag: Zu Gerhart Hauptmanns hundertstem Geburtstag* (Frankfurt am Main: Fischer, 1962).

Papers:

Manuscript materials of Gerhart Hauptmann are at the Staatsbibliothek Preußischer Kulturbesitz, Berlin.

Hugo von Hofmannsthal

(1 February 1874 - 15 July 1929)

Michael Winkler
Rice University

See also the Hofmannsthal entry in *DLB 81: Austrian Fiction Writers, 1875-1913*.

PLAY PRODUCTIONS: *Madonna Dianora: Eine Ballade dramatisiert*, Berlin, Deutsches Theater, 15 May 1898;

Der Thor und der Tod, Munich, Theater am Gärtnerplatz, 13 November 1898;

Der Abenteurer und die Sängerin oder Die Geschenke des Lebens: Ein Gedicht in zwei Aufzügen, Berlin, Deutsches Theater and Vienna, Burgtheater, 18 March 1899;

Die Hochzeit der Sobeide: Dramatisches Gedicht in einem Aufzug, Berlin, Deutsches Theater and Vienna, Burgtheater, 18 March 1899;

Der Tod des Tizian: Ein dramatisches Fragment, Munich, Künstlerhaus, 14 January 1901;

Jules Renard, *Fuchs: Schauspiel in einem Akt*, translated by Hofmannsthal, Vienna, Burgtheater, 14 February 1901;

Elektra: Tragödie in einem Akt frei nach Sophokles, Berlin, Kleines Theater, 30 October 1903; revised as an opera, with music by Richard Strauss, Dresden, Hofoper, 25 January 1909;

Das gerettete Venedig: Trauerspiel in fünf Aufzügen, Berlin, Lessingtheater, 21 January 1905;

Oedipus und die Sphinx: Tragödie in drei Aufzügen, Berlin, Deutsches Theater, 2 March 1906;

Cristinas Heimreise: Komödie in drei Akten, Berlin, Deutsches Theater, 11 February 1910;

Sophocles, *König Ödipus: Tragödie*, translated and adapted by Hofmannsthal, Munich, Neue Musikfesthalle auf dem Ausstellungsgelände, 25 September 1910;

Die Heirat wider Willen: Komödie in einem Akt von Molière, neu übersetzt, Berlin, Deutsches Theater, 7 October 1910;

Der Rosenkavalier: Komödie für Musik in drei Aufzügen, music by Strauss, Dresden, Opernhaus, 26 January 1911;

Jedermann: Das Spiel vom Sterben des reichen Mannes erneuert, Berlin, Zirkus Schumann, 1 December 1911;

Hugo von Hofmannsthal circa 1924

Molière, *Der Bürger als Edelmann: Komödie mit Tänzen*, adapted by Hofmannsthal, music by Strauss, Stuttgart, Kleines Haus des Königlichen Hoftheaters, 25 October 1912;

Josephslegende, by Hofmannsthal and Harry Graf Kessler, music by Strauss, Paris, Opèra, 14 May 1914;

Die Schäferinnen, Berlin, Kammerspiele, 14 March 1916;

Alkestis: Ein Trauerspiel nach Euripides, Munich, Kammerspiele, 14 April 1916;

Die grüne Flöte: Ballettpantomime, music by Wolfgang Amadeus Mozart, Berlin, Deutsches Theater, 27 April 1916;

Die Lästigen: Ein Lustspiel, frei nach Molière, Berlin, Deutsches Theater, 27 April 1916;

Die Frau ohne Schatten: Oper in drei Akten, music by Strauss, Vienna, Staatsoper, 10 October 1919;

Dame Kobold: Lustspiel in drei Aufzügen von Calderon. Freie Bearbeitung für die neuere Bühne, Berlin, Deutsches Theater, 3 April 1920;

Der Schwierige: Lustspiel in drei Akten, Munich, Residenztheater, 8 November 1921;

Carnaval, getanzt nach der Schumann'schen Musik, Vienna, Operntheater, 12 June 1922;

Das Salzburger große Welttheater, music by Einar Nilson, Salzburg, Collegienkirche, 12 August 1922;

Der Unbestechliche: Lustspiel in fünf Akten, Vienna, Raimundtheater, 16 March 1923;

Szenischer Prolog zur Neueröffnung des Josefstädter Theaters, Vienna, Theater in der Josefstadt, 1 April 1924;

Die Ruinen von Athen: Ein Festspiel mit Tänzen und Chören, music by Strauss and Ludwig van Beethoven, Vienna, Operntheater, 20 September 1924;

Achilles auf Skyros: Ballett in einem Aufzug, music by Egon Wellesz, Stuttgart, Großes Haus des Landestheaters, 4 March 1926;

Das Theater des Neuen: Eine Ankündigung, Vienna, Theater in der Josefstadt, 21 March 1926;

Der Kaiser und die Hexe: Ein Spiel, music by Hans Pleß, Vienna, Urania, 16 December 1926;

Der weiße Fächer: Ein Zwischenspiel, Vienna, Akademietheater, 13 May 1927;

Der Turm: Ein Trauerspiel in fünf Aufzügen, Munich, Prinzregententheater and Hamburg, Schauspielhaus, 4 February 1928;

Gestern: Studie in einem Akt, in Reimen, Vienna, Die Komödie, 25 March 1928;

Die ägyptische Helena: Oper in zwei Aufzügen, music by Strauss, Dresden, Staatsoper, 6 June 1928;

Das kleine Welttheater oder Die Glücklichen, Munich, Residenztheater, 6 October 1929;

Das Bergwerk zu Falun, Vienna, Akademietheater, 20 December 1932;

Arabella: Lyrische Komödie in drei Aufzügen, music by Strauss, Dresden, Staatsoper, 1 July 1933;

Die Liebe der Danae, music by Strauss, Salzburg, Festspielhaus, 14 August 1952.

BOOKS: *Gestern: Studie in einem Akt, in Reimen*, as Theophil Morren (Vienna: Verlag der "Modernen Rundschau," 1891);

Theater in Versen (Berlin: Fischer, 1899)—comprises *Die Frau im Fenster, Die Hochzeit der Sobeide, Der Abenteurer und die Sängerin; Die Hochzeit der Sobeide* translated by Bayard Quincy Morgan as *The Marriage of Sobeide*, in *The German Classics of the Nineteenth and Twentieth Centuries*, edited by Kuno Francke and William G. Howard, volume 20 (New York: German Publishing Society, 1914), pp. 234-288;

Der Kaiser und die Hexe (Berlin: Insel, 1900);

Der Thor und der Tod (Berlin: Insel, 1900); translated by Elisabeth Walter as *Death and the Fool* (Boston: Badger, 1914);

Der Tod des Tizian: Ein dramatisches Fragment (Berlin: Insel, 1901); translated by John Heard as *The Death of Titian* (Boston: Four Seas, 1920);

Studie über die Entwickelung des Dichters Victor Hugo (Vienna: Verlag von Dr. Hugo von Hofmannsthal, 1901); republished as *Victor Hugo* (Berlin: Schuster & Loeffler, 1904); republished as *Versuch über Victor Hugo* (Munich: Bremer Presse, 1925);

Ausgewählte Gedichte (Berlin: Verlag der Blätter für die Kunst, 1903);

Das kleine Welttheater oder Die Glücklichen (Leipzig: Insel, 1903); translated by Walter Rather Eberlein as *The Little Theater of the World* (Aurora, N.Y.: Printed by Victor & Jacob Hammer, 1945);

Elektra: Tragödie in einem Aufzug frei nach Sophokles (Berlin: Fischer, 1904); translated by Arthur Symons as *Electra: A Tragedy in One Act* (New York: Brentano's, 1908);

Unterhaltungen über literarische Gegenstände, edited by Georg Brandes (Berlin: Bard, Marquardt, 1904);

Das gerettete Venedig: Trauerspiel in fünf Aufzügen (Berlin: Fischer, 1905); translated by Walter as *Venice Preserved: A Tragedy in Five Acts* (Boston: Badger, 1915);

Das Märchen der 672. Nacht und andere Erzählungen (Vienna & Leipzig: Wiener Verlag, 1905)—comprises "Das Märchen der 672. Nacht," "Reitergeschichte," "Erlebnis des Marschalls von Bassompierre," "Ein Brief"; "Reitergeschichte" translated by Basil Creighton as "Cavalry Patrol" in *Tellers of Tales*, edited by W. Somerset Maugham (New York: Doubleday, Doran, 1939), pp. 860-867; "Ein Brief" translated by Francis C. Golffing as "The Letter," *Rocky Mountain Review*, 6, no. 3-4 (1942): 1, 3, 11-13;

Ödipus und die Sphinx: Tragödie in drei Aufzügen (Berlin: Fischer, 1906); translated by Gertrude Schoenbohm as *Oedipus and the Sphinx*, in *Oedipus: Myth and Drama*, edited by Martin Kalisch and others (New York: Odyssey, 1968);

Kleine Dramen, 2 volumes (Leipzig: Insel, 1906-1907)—volume 1 comprises *Gestern, Der Tor und der Tod, Der weiße Fächer*; excerpt from *Der weiße Fächer* translated by Maurice Magnus as *The White Fan* in *Mask: The Journal of the Art of the Theater* (Florence), 1 (February 1909): 232-234; volume 2 comprises *Das Bergwerk zu Falun, Der Kaiser und die Hexe, Das kleine Welttheater*;

Die gesammelten Gedichte (Leipzig: Insel, 1907); translated by Charles Wharton Stork as *The Lyrical Poems of Hugo von Hofmannsthal* (New Haven: Yale University Press / London: Milford, 1918);

Die prosaischen Schriften gesammelt, 3 volumes (Berlin: Fischer, 1907-1917);

Vorspiele (Leipzig: Insel, 1908);

Hesperus: Ein Jahrbuch, by Hofmannsthal, Rudolf Alexander Schröder, and Rudolf Borchardt (Leipzig: Insel, 1909);

Cristinas Heimreise: Komödie (Berlin: Fischer, 1910; revised, 1910); translated by Roy Temple House as *Cristina's Journey Home: A Comedy in Three Acts* (Boston: Badger, 1917); German version revised as *Florindo* (Vienna & Hellerau: Avalun, 1923);

Jedermann: Das Spiel vom Sterben des reichen Mannes. Erneuert (Berlin: Fischer, 1911); translated by M. E. Tafler as *The Salzburg Everyman: The Play of the Rich Man's Death* (Salzburg: Mora, 1911); German version edited by Margaret Jacobs (London & Edinburgh: Nelson, 1957);

Grete Wiesenthal in Amor und Psyche und Das fremde Mädchen: Szenen (Berlin: Fischer, 1911);

Alkestis: Ein Trauerspiel nach Euripides (Leipzig: Insel, 1911);

Der Rosenkavalier: Komödie für Musik, music by Richard Strauss (Berlin: Fischer, 1911); translated by Kalisch as *The Rose-Bearer* (Berlin & Paris: Fürstner, 1912);

Die Gedichte und kleinen Dramen (Leipzig: Insel, 1911);

Ariadne auf Naxos: Oper in einem Aufzuge. Zu spielen nach dem "Bürger als Edelmann" des Molière, music by Strauss (Berlin & Paris: Fürstner, 1912); revised as *Ariadne auf Naxos: Oper in einem Aufzug nebst einem Vorspiel* (Berlin & Paris: Fürstner, 1916); translated by Kalisch as *Ariadne on Naxos: Opera in One Act, with a Prelude* (New York: Boosey & Hawkes, 1924);

Die Wege und die Begegnungen (Bremen: Bremer Presse, 1913);

Josephslegende, by Hofmannsthal and Harry Graf Kessler, music by Strauss (Berlin: Fürstner, 1914); translated by Kalisch as *The Legend of Joseph* (Berlin & Paris: Fürstner, 1914);

Prinz Eugen der edle Ritter: Sein Leben in Bildern, lithographs by Franz Wacik (Vienna: Seidel, 1915);

Die Frau ohne Schatten: Oper in drei Akten, music by Strauss (Berlin: Fürstner, 1916; London: Boosey & Hawkes, 1964);

Der Bürger als Edelmann: Komödie mit Tänzen von Molière. Freie Bühnenbearbeitung in drei Aufzügen, music by Strauss (Berlin: Fürstner, 1918);

Rodauner Nachträge, 3 volumes (Vienna: Amalthea, 1918);

Lucidor: Figuren zu einer ungeschriebenen Komödie (Berlin: Reiss, 1919); translated by Kenneth Burke as *Lucidor: Characters for an Unwritten Comedy*, in *Dial*, 73, no. 2 (1922): 121-132;

Die Frau ohne Schatten: Erzählung (Berlin: Fischer, 1919);

Der Schwierige: Lustspiel in drei Akten (Berlin: Fischer, 1921; edited by W. E. Yates, Cambridge: Cambridge University Press, 1966);

Reden und Aufsätze (Leipzig: Insel, 1921);

Gedichte (Leipzig: Insel-Verlag, 1922);

Das Salzburger große Welttheater (Leipzig: Insel, 1922);

Buch der Freunde (Leipzig: Insel, 1922); enlarged as *Buch der Freunde: Tagebuch-Aufzeichnungen* (Leipzig: Insel, 1929);

Die grüne Flöte: Ballettpantomime, music by Wolfgang Amadeus Mozart (Vienna & Leipzig: Universal-Edition, 1923);

Augenblicke in Griechenland (Regensburg & Leipzig: Habbel & Naumann, 1924);

Der Turm: Ein Trauerspiel in fünf Aufzügen (Munich: Bremer Presse, 1925; revised edition, Berlin: Fischer, 1927);

Die Ruinen von Athen: Ein Festspiel mit Tänzen und Chören, music by Strauss and Ludwig van Beethoven (Berlin: Fürstner, 1925);

Gedichte (Vienna: Johannes-Presse, 1926);

Szenischer Prolog zur Neueröffnung des Josefstädtertheaters (Vienna: Johannes-Presse, 1926);

Früheste Prosastücke (Leipzig: Gesellschaft der Freunde der Deutschen Bücherei, 1926);

Das Schrifttum als geistiger Raum der Nation (Munich: Bremer Presse, 1927);

Drei Erzählungen (Leipzig: Insel, 1927);

Die ägyptische Helena: Oper in zwei Aufzügen, music by Strauss (Berlin: Fürstner, 1928); translated by Kalisch as *Helen in Egypt* (Berlin: Fürstner / New York: Ricordi, 1928);

Loris: Die Prosa des jungen Hugo von Hofmannsthal (Berlin: Fischer, 1930);

Die Berührung der Sphären (Berlin: Fischer, 1931);

Wege und Begegnungen (Leipzig: Reclam, 1931);

Fragment eines Romans (Munich: Privately printed, 1931); enlarged as *Andreas oder Die Vereinigten: Fragmente eines Romanes* (Berlin: Fischer, 1932); translated by Marie D. Hottinger as *Andreas; or, The United: Being Fragments of a Novel* (London: Dent, 1936);

Arabella: Lyrische Komödie, music by Strauss (Berlin: Fürstner, 1933); translated by John Gutman as *Arabella: A Lyrical Comedy in Three Acts* (New York: Boosey & Hawkes, 1955; London: Boosey & Hawkes, 1965);

Semiramis; Die beiden Götter (Munich: Rupprecht-presse, 1933);

Prolog zur Feier von Goethes 50. Geburtstag am Burgtheater zu Wien (Vienna: Officina Vindobonensis, 1934);

Nachlese der Gedichte (Berlin: Fischer, 1934);

Dramatische Entwürfe aus dem Nachlaß, edited by Heinrich Zimmer (Vienna: Johannes-Presse, 1936);

Beethoven: Rede gehalten an der Beethovenfeier des Lesezirkels Hottingen in Zürich am 10. Dezember 1920, edited by Willi Schuh (Vienna: Reichner, 1938);

Festspiele in Salzburg (Vienna: Bermann-Fischer, 1938);

Gesammelte Werke in Einzelausgaben, 15 volumes, edited by Herbert Steiner (volumes 1-2, Stockholm: Bermann-Fischer, 1945-1948; volumes 3-15, Frankfurt am Main: Fischer, 1950-1959); reedited by Bernd Schoeller and Rudolf Hirsch as *Gesammelte Werke in zehn Einzelbänden*, 10 volumes (Frankfurt am Main: Fischer, 1979);

Das Theater des Neuen: Eine Ankündigung (Vienna: Edition Komödie im Bindenschildverlag, 1947);

Dem Gedächtnis des Dichters Theodor Storm, in der Handschrift des Dichters, edited by Lothar Hempe (Stuttgart: Hempe, 1951);

Aus dem Jugendwerk Hugo von Hofmannsthals (Loris), edited by Emmy Rosenfeld (Pavia, Italy: Editrice viscontia, 1951);

Danae oder die Vernunftheirat: Szenarium und Notizen, edited by Schuh (Frankfurt am Main: Fischer, 1952);

Österreichische Aufsätze und Reden, edited by Helmut A. Fiechtner (Vienna: Bergland, 1956);

Natur und Erkenntnis: Essays (Berlin: Deutsche Buch-Gemeinschaft, 1957);

Ausgewählte Werke, 2 volumes, edited by Hirsch (Berlin & Frankfurt am Main: Fischer, 1957);

Silvia im "Stern": Auf Grund des Manuskriptes, edited by Martin Stern (Bern & Stuttgart: Haupt, 1959);

Komödie (Graz & Vienna: Stiasny, 1960);

Das erzählerische Werk (Frankfurt am Main: Fischer, 1969);

Ausgewählte Werke, edited by Eike Middell (Leipzig: Insel, 1975);

Sämtliche Werke: Kritische Ausgabe, 19 volumes published, 38 volumes projected, edited by Rudolf Hirsch, Clemens Köttelwesch, Heinz Rölleke, and Ernst Zinn (Frankfurt am Main: Fischer, 1975-).

Editions in English: *Selected Writings*, volume 1: *Selected Prose*, translated by Mary Hottinger and Tania and James Stern (London: Routledge & Kegan Paul, 1952); volume 2: *Poems and Verse Plays: Bilingual Edition*, edited by Michael Hamburger, translated by John Bednall, Arthur Davidson, and others (London: Routledge & Kegan Paul, 1961; New York: Pantheon, 1961); volume 3: *Selected Plays and Libretti*, edited by Hamburger (New York: Pantheon, 1963; London: Routledge & Kegan Paul, 1964);

Three Plays, translated by Alfred Schwarz (Detroit: Wayne State University Press, 1966)—comprises *Death and the Fool, Electra, The Tower*.

OTHER: Arthur Schnitzler, *Anatol*, introduction by Hofmannsthal (Berlin: Fischer, 1901); translated by Trevor Blakemore in *Playing with Love* (Liebelei), by Schnitzler, translated by P. Morton Shand (London: Gay & Hancock, 1914);

Sophocles, *König Ödipus*, translated by Hofmannsthal (Berlin: Fischer, 1910);

Deutsche Erzähler, 4 volumes, edited by Hofmannsthal (Leipzig: Insel, 1912);

Österreichischer Almanach auf das Jahr 1916, edited by Hofmannsthal (Leipzig: Insel, 1915);

Franz Grillparzer, *Grillparzers politisches Vermächtnis*, edited by Hofmannsthal (Leipzig: Insel, 1915);

Pedro Calderón de la Barca, *Dame Kobold: Lustspiel in drei Aufzügen*, translated by Hofmannsthal (Berlin: Fischer, 1920);

Die Erzählungen aus den Tausendundeinen Nächten, 6 volumes, translated by Enno Littmann, introduction by Hofmannsthal (Leipzig: Insel, 1921-1928);

Griechenland: Baukunst, Landschaft, Volksleben, photographs by Hanns Holdt and others, introduction by Hofmannsthal (Berlin: Wasmuth, 1922); translated by L. Hamilton as *Picturesque Greece: Architecture, Landscape, Life of the People* (New York: Architectural Book Publishing Co., 1922; London: Unwin, 1923);

Neue Deutsche Beiträge, 6 volumes, edited by Hofmannsthal (Munich: Bremer Presse, 1922-1927);

Deutsches Lesebuch, 2 volumes, edited by Hofmannsthal (Munich: Bremer Presse, 1922-1923; enlarged, 1926);

Deutsche Epigramme, edited by Hofmannsthal (Munich: Bremer Presse, 1923);

Adalbert Stifter, *Der Nachsommer: Eine Erzählung*, afterword by Hofmannsthal (Leipzig: List, 1925);

Friedrich Schiller, *Schillers Selbstcharakteristik aus seinen Schriften*, edited by Hofmannsthal (Munich: Bremer Presse, 1926);

Wert und Ehre deutscher Sprache, in Zeugnissen, edited by Hofmannsthal (Munich: Bremer Presse, 1927).

What is perhaps most striking about Hugo von Hofmannsthal are contradictions that characterize his creative imagination. His poetic laboratory was filled with an ever-increasing multiplicity of images, themes, ideas, situations, and dramatis personae. In changing disguises and in new contexts they constitute a large repertoire of works in progress, some of which, often after long delays, came to fruition. Much more of his material, however, never developed beyond the stage of arrested inventiveness and was forced into shapes and patterns that defied the poet's quest for grace and civility. Hofmannsthal's plays, especially, either move along with an altogether irresistible ease and an unobtrusively natural momentum, every inflection of their dialogue perfectly coordinated, every character a convincing embodiment of his or her dramatic function, every scene a full realization of its inherent conflict; or they strike even the casual reader as laborious and stilted—as the futile products of a refined sensibility struggling against its better inclinations.

These contradictions haunted Hofmannsthal all his life and colored much of his posthumous reputation. They were a consequence both of his particular talent and, perhaps more so, of the cultural role he was expected if not forced to play, a role that was defined by the social and historical pressures of fin de siècle Vienna. To his early admirers Hofmannsthal represented the prodigiously talented aesthete; later critics saw in him the melancholy embodiment of an old order that had ceased to live long before its political demise, and his detractors attacked him as the propagator of a conservative ideology of cultural elitism. The brilliantly versatile virtuoso of the "beautiful life" had turned into an anachronism. What was missing between the artistic exuberance of his beginnings and the debilitating insecurities—even despair—of his final decade was an extended time of self-assured maturity. Hofmannsthal, like most of his literary creations, appears to have had an extended youth, during which he experienced all the privileges of a prodigy; and then he had to face the gravity of premature old age, with its agitated determination to maintain dignity or at least to preserve a posture of dignified resignation, perhaps even wisdom. He had to live with the awareness that at the age of forty he had become a part of history, and he had to turn this knowledge into a new source of inspiration. As early as the turn of the century, when he had reached the midpoint of his short life, Hofmannsthal's existence was defined by two contradictory burdens: that of an unfinished youth and that of representing the values of an old heritage. This paradox shaped his public persona and much of his creative work.

Hugo Laurenz August Hofmann, Edler von Hofmannsthal was born on 1 February 1874 in Vienna and was the only child of prosperous bourgeois parents. His father, Hugo August Peter Hofmann, was heir to part of a fortune that his own father, Isaak Löw Hofmann, had accumulated during the first half of the nineteenth century, primarily through improvements in the manufacture of silk and in the production of potash. Hugo August Peter Hofmann was a director of the Central-Bodencreditanstalt, a prominent investment bank. In 1873 he married Anna Maria Josefa Fohleutner, whose family came from Bavaria and the Sudetenland and whose wealth derived from agriculture and the brewing business. The Hofmanns' house at 12 Salesianergasse, a prestigious neighborhood, was four stories high and had an elegant neoclassical facade; it represented social solidity, urbane civility, discreet self-assurance, and the restrained opulence of old money. Hofmannsthal's paternal grandfather had converted from Judaism to Roman Catholicism on marrying the daughter of an Austrian court official in Milan. Hofmannsthal's parents considered themselves fully assimilated and put their confidence in religious tolerance, economic liberalism, the beneficence of the monarchy, and the inevitability of progress. They doted on the child, the mother often with nervous protectiveness and excessive solicitude; the father, a man of diverse cultural interests with a broad education and urbane manners, discreetly supervised his emotional and intellectual development and encouraged his precocious talents and artistic aspirations.

Hofmannsthal grew up in a world of undisturbed security and in an atmosphere of privileged insularity. Outside reality, in the forms of anti-Semitism, working-class poverty, nationalist extremism, and political demagoguery, seemed far away. But in the stock-exchange crash of 1873, a result of speculative manipulations of the bond market in connection with the Vienna World's Fair, Hofmannsthal's parents lost a major portion of their investments. They were still able, nevertheless, to give their son the best education, social contacts, and artistic experiences that established prominence in the cosmopolitan capital of the Austro-Hungarian Empire could provide, including riding and fencing lessons, opera tickets, a box at the Burgtheater (Imperial Theater), summer vacations in the Alps, and trips to the centers of Italian art.

Vienna's profusion of architectural traditions, its salons and cafés, and its divers other entertainments, as well as the atmosphere of its summer resorts, shaped the young Hofmannsthal no less than did his rigorous education. After preliminary studies with private tutors he was enrolled from 1884 until 1892 at the Akademisches Gymnasium, a public school with a tradition of Jesuit discipline and one of the three prominent institutions of humanistic learning in the city. He completed the study of law at the University of Vienna with his first juristisches Staatsexamen on 13 July 1894, then signed up for military service. He spent his obligatory year as a Freiwilliger (volun-

teer) with a regiment of dragoons garrisoned in the Moravian border town of Göding. He then resumed his academic career, which, after October 1895, centered around French literature. His dissertation on the language of the "Pléiade" poets was accepted in 1897, but he withdrew his study of Victor Hugo's development as a poet (1901) from consideration for an appointment to the faculty of the university. He had decided instead to make his living as a playwright and essayist.

Hofmannsthal's first publications were poems and analytical essays, often impressionistic in character, on the art and psychology of modern *décadence*; they are mellifluous and highly perceptive effusions of extraordinary versatility that describe various aspects of the mentality of fin de siècle Europe. Although they had to appear under pseudonyms (Loris, Loris Melikow, and Theophil Morren) because of university regulations, they quickly made him a literary sensation and gained him access to the circle of literati that became known as Young Vienna. The author and actor Gustav Schwarzkopf introduced him in the fall of 1890 to the writers gathering at Café Griensteidl, among them Arthur Schnitzler, Richard Beer-Hofmann, and Felix Salten (Siegmund Salzmann). Hermann Bahr, whom he met on 27 April 1891, was the most conspicuous spokesman of the group. Their artistic and cultural affinities, fostered in almost daily conversations of mutual encouragement and criticism, though hardly ever free of misunderstandings, personality conflicts, and jealousies, brought about a rejuvenation of Austrian letters and helped to introduce the style and attitudes of European symbolism to German literature.

The essential impulse behind their work was a predilection for refined sensations, nobly subdued and graceful gestures, and clusters of melodious words; such charms were expected to play out their most intoxicating effects on the stage of an intimate theater. Hofmannsthal's earliest symbolist playlet, written under the inspiration of this Viennese aestheticism, *Gestern* (Yesterday), was begun in early summer 1891 and was printed at his own expense in October of that year; it was not performed until 1928. In the Italian Renaissance, Andrea proclaims the attitude of hedonistic impressionism: he lives only for each moment's fleeting pleasures, fully conscious of every quickly changing mood and never able to preserve any sensory experience as an enduring value. He changes his attitude when Arlette, through a small act of infidelity, forces him to

Hofmannsthal (right) with the composer Richard Strauss, who collaborated with him on several operas

admit that past experience is an ineradicable part of his self. In this work the amorality of art for art's sake is subjected to criticism.

During his formative years as a poet Hofmannsthal was repeatedly frightened by the prospect of losing his inspiration. Periods of sustained and seemingly effortless creativity and enjoyment of life alternated with times of depression, even panic, and feelings of profound inadequacy. The ever-present reality of death, its accidental appearance in the midst of all the splendors of life and as the final intensification of life in a Dionysiac burst of vital energy, became a recurring preoccupation: in the fragmentary play *Der Tod des Tizian* (The Death of Titian, 1901), written during March and April 1892, in which a group of the old master's disciples experience the plague in Venice and their own voluntary deaths as an orgy of life heightened to its utmost sensuality; in *Der Thor und der Tod* (1898; published, 1900;

translated as *Death and the Fool*, 1914), written in March and April 1893), a one-act comedy in which the young nobleman Claudio, in melancholy withdrawal from the demands imposed on him by the world, at last welcomes death as the only true encounter among his fleeting contacts and one who teaches him to honor the value of life and fidelity; and in *Alkestis* (published, 1911; performed, 1916), written in February 1894, an adaptation of Euripides' play in which the rebirth of the noble king Admetos is made possible by his wife Alkestis's self-sacrificial death.

Hofmannsthal's personal life during these years was enriched by friendships with the poet Stefan George, whom he met in December 1891; with Marie Herzfeld, whom he met in March 1892; with the aged Josephine von Wertheimstein, whose death in July 1894 affected him deeply; and with the young poet and prospective diplomat Leopold von Andrian, whom he met in autumn 1893. Vacation trips took him to Switzerland and the south of France in September 1892, to the Salzkammergut region of Austria and Bavaria from August through October 1893; and to Venice in September 1895. He wrote an amazing variety of short pieces and read voraciously recent European and classical German literature, Latin poetry, the works of Honoré de Balzac and Guy de Maupassant, and Walter Pater on the Renaissance. During a bicycle tour through the Italian Alps in August 1897, many of his plans came to fruition in what he experienced as a miraculous outburst of lyrical intuition. Dramatic projects that had lingered during an earlier "very strong inner petrification and disorder" (letter to George of 3 June 1897) and were completed at this time include *Die Frau im Fenster* (The Woman in the Window, performed under the title *Madonna Dianora*, 1898; published, 1899); *Das kleine Welttheater oder Die Glücklichen* (The Little Theater of the World; or, The Happy Ones; published, 1903; performed, 1929; translated as *The Little Theater of the World*, 1945), completed by the end of August 1897 and inspired in part by Pedro Calderón de la Barca, a performance of whose *El gran teatro del mundo* (1655) in front of Vienna's courthouse Hofmannsthal had attended in June of that year; *Der weiße Fächer* (published, 1906; performed, 1927; excerpt translated as *The White Fan*, 1909); *Die Hochzeit der Sobeide* (1899; translated as *The Marriage of Sobeide*, 1914); and *Der Kaiser und die Hexe* (The Emperor and the Witch, published, 1900; performed, 1926).

All of these playlets portray characters who are connected to life with varying degrees of self-conscious hesitation and tentativeness and who must learn how to become worthy of fidelity and elicit trust. The most important of them is the *Das kleine Welttheater oder Die Glücklichen*. In a sequence of lyrical monologues different stages of humanity's removal from the "stream of life" are revealed. The play's central archetypal figure is "der Wahnsinnige" (the one who has lost his senses), who has surrendered his individuality to the mystery of an all-encompassing order.

By 1900 Hofmannsthal had found two publishers who would prove to be reliable advocates of his art: Samuel Fischer, who printed a collection of three of his verse plays as *Theater in Versen* (Theater in Verse, 1899); and Alfred Walter Heymel and Rudolf Alexander Schröder, the founders of the Insel Verlag (Island Publishing House), to whose journal, the *Insel*, Hofmannsthal frequently contributed and whose Insel-Bücherei, a series of exquisitely printed and illustrated small volumes, provided an appropriate format for his shorter theatrical works. *Der Thor und der Tod* became one of Insel's most successful titles. On the stage, however, Hofmannsthal's plays encountered many obstacles, hardly ever satisfied their author's expectations, and failed to meet with even a moderate measure of popular acclaim. A matinee performance of *Der Thor und der Tod* directed by Otto Brahms in Munich in 1898 was anything but memorable; the next attempt, the year after, proved even more disappointing: a presentation of *Die Hochzeit der Sobeide* together with a new "serious comedy," *Der Abenteurer und die Sängerin* (The Adventurer and the Singer, published, 1899), was canceled after three nights due to hostile reviews in the Berlin press. But Hofmannsthal's brief stay in Germany's theater and publishing capital was not without its benefits. He met Count Harry Kessler, a dilettante in various arts, energetic promoter of many cultural projects, diplomat, and man of the world; he renewed his acquaintance with Gerhart Hauptmann; and he solidified his friendship with Eberhard von Bodenhausen, a lawyer who would rise to prominent positions in German industry (including a directorship at Krupp), would acquire an expert knowledge of art history, and had served since 1895 as head of the literary society that financed the lavish art nouveau publication *Pan*. Through these connections Hofmannsthal was introduced to a world beyond Vienna that he was to cherish as personifying old

Scene from a 1926 Salzburg production of Hofmannsthal's Jedermann, *with Alexander Moissi as Everyman and Luis Rainer as Death*

Europe's cultural nobility at the time of its final glow. He was attracted to Helene and Alfred von Nostitz and to the much younger Ottonie von Degenfeld because of their moral integrity and their refined appreciation of the arts. The discreet elegance of Chateau Neubeuern, a possession of the Bodenhausen and Degenfeld families in the serenely beautiful countryside above the Inn River in southern Bavaria, became a congenial refuge from the pressures of his public life. It was there that Hofmannsthal, who was never able to fully free himself of snobbish affectations, preferred to meet his friends for year-end gatherings.

Der Abenteurer und die Sängerin, written between 22 September and 10 October 1898 in Venice, was inspired by an episode in Giovanni Giacomo Casanova's memoirs. The adventurous seducer Baron Weidenstamm is the first of several Casanova variations in Hofmannsthal's works. He persuades the musician Vittoria to overcome her submission to commercial success and bourgeois propriety and to rediscover the fire of inspiration that is his legacy as a "Lebens-künstler" (one who has made living a form of art). In finding herself she makes her music into a sublime elixir: the gift of life for others. The power of lyrical art to reverse the loss of identity and facilitate an imaginative access to the confusing multiplicity of worldly phenomena is advocated here for the last time.

By this point Hofmannsthal had become intensely suspicious of his own symbolist practice. This suspicion becomes apparent in a project which had begun to occupy him at the end of June 1899: a fairy-tale tragedy in five acts, *Das Bergwerk zu Falun* (The Mine at Falun, published, 1907; performed, 1932), based on a novella from E. T. A. Hoffmann's *Die Serapions-Brüder* (The Serapion Brotherhood, 1819-1821). The miner Elis Fröbom abandons his bride, Anna, for the Mountain Queen. His descent into the mountain from which he will not return symbolizes an intense process of introversion in which the reality of dreams obliterates all other possibilities of experience. Though revised several times, the play never achieved what Hofmannsthal was striving for: dramatic plasticity, the richness and immediacy of life, and external conflict. Its preponderance of subjectivity was a fundamental shortcoming. This failure is the central concern of "Ein Brief" (translated as "The Letter," 1942), written in 1901, published in the journal *Tag* (Day) in 1902 and in the collection *Das Märchen der 672. Nacht und andere Erzählungen* (The Tale of the 672nd Night and Other Stories) in 1905 and better known as the "Chandos Letter": the loss of coherent perception, conceptual systematization, and communicative competence when language represents only its own wealth of suggestive associations and abandons its discursive function.

Hofmannsthal embarked on a period of experimentation during which he sought to revitalize earlier genres of drama. He turned to ancient Greek tragedy, to the medieval mystery play, to the Spanish baroque practice of showing the world as a play before God (*teatro del mundo*), to the character comedies of Molière, to the Italian commedia dell'arte, to the Austrian Volkstheater, and to the opera buffa. In modernizing material from previous eras, Hofmannsthal at first relied heavily on elaborate stage designs and an excessive use of rhetorical language. These shortcomings disappeared as his mastery of the dramatic medium increased.

One of Hofmannsthal's most exhilarating experiences of this time was his sojourn from 10 February through 2 May 1900 in Paris, where his friend Georg Freiherr zu Franckenstein introduced him to the diplomatic elite and another friend, the painter Hans Schlesinger, introduced him to leading artists, among them Maurice Maeterlinck, Auguste Rodin, and Anatole France. On 8 June 1901 he married Gertrud Schlesinger, his friend's sister and the daughter of a bank official, with whom he had been acquainted for more than five years. The couple bought a villa in Rodaun, near Vienna, where they brought up their three children: Christiane, born in 1902; Franz, born in 1903; and Raimund, born in 1906. Apart from a small apartment in the city at Stallburggasse 2, the "Fuchsschlössel" (named after Countess Fuchs, the tutor of Empress Maria Theresa) became the place where he entertained such friends as Rudolf Alexander Schröder, Rudolf Borchardt, and Rudolf Kassner.

Hofmannsthal's turn away from the symbolist lyrical drama and his need to write plays of a larger compass—what he called "das große Stück" (the large play)—engendered a variety of projects: a never-completed tragedy, "Pompilia oder Das Leben" (Pompilia; or, Life), which was to have been built around a crime provoked by an act of marital infidelity (its plot, borrowed from Robert Browning, proved overcomplex because too many points of view had to be incorporated); *Elektra* (published, 1904; translated as *Electra*, 1908), conceived early in September 1901, finished two years later, and produced in 1903 by Max Reinhardt with Gertrude Eysoldt playing the title role at the Kleines Theater (Little Theater) in Berlin to strong critical and popular acclaim; a free adaptation of Calderón's *La vida es sueño* (1636) as "Das Leben ein Traum" (Life a Dream); a recasting of Thomas Otway's *Venice Preserved* (1682) as *Das gerettete Venedig* (1905), a first draft of which was finished at the end of November 1902, the final version in August 1904. Other plans included dramatizations of the myth of Jupiter and Semele; of an episode from the chapbook *Fortunatus* (1509); and an Oedipus trilogy, of which only one part, *Oedipus und die Sphinx* (1906; translated as *Oedipus and the Sphinx*, 1968) was finished. Plays dealing with King Kandaules, with Leda and the swan, and with Euripides' *The Bacchants* (circa 405 B.C.) were never completed. A plan to rewrite the English *Everyman* was first conceived in April 1903 and was revived in April 1906: the old morality play had become a drama in doggerel verse, *Jedermann: Das Spiel vom Sterben des reichen Mannes*

(1911; translated as *The Salzburg Everyman: The Play of the Rich Man's Death*, 1911).

Two new contacts Hofmannsthal made during this period developed into cooperative associations of lasting importance. In Reinhardt, whom he had met in Vienna in May 1903, he found an impresario and director who made the premieres of *Elektra* and *Jedermann* rousing successes. In Richard Strauss, whom he met on 2 February 1906 in Berlin, he found a composer with the talent to visualize what makes for effective theater; their cooperation during the next twenty years, though often tested by differences of temperament, style, and purpose, proved durable as Strauss coaxed and pushed the hesitant, fidgety, and ever-sensitive Hofmannsthal to complete some of his most balanced works for the opera stage. The need for frequent consultations with Reinhardt and Strauss made Berlin rather than Vienna his artistic headquarters. It was there that, at the end of February 1912, he met Sergey Diaghilev of the Russian Ballet; he attended the company's performances in Paris, most notably the premiere of Vaslav Nijinsky's *Afternoon of a Faun*, during his stay there from 25 March through 7 June. Their modernist dancing had such a strong impact on him that he wanted to become their principal scenarist, but the association did not materialize. He also failed to interest Strauss in writing the music for a tragic symphony for the company, to be titled "Orest und die Furien" (Orestes and the Furies). In partnership with Kessler, however, he wrote a short ballet, *Josephslegende* (1914; translated as *The Legend of Joseph* 1914), that was performed at the Paris Opéra on 14 May 1914.

By this time several other projects had taken hold of his imagination. A comedy, "Silvia im Stern" (Sylvia in the Star), was first outlined in August 1907 and occupied him intermittently during the following years; some of its themes were taken over into a new Casanova play in four acts, "Florindo," which was abandoned in December 1908 after its female protagonist, Cristina, had assumed central importance. *Cristinas Heimreise* (1910; translated as *Cristina's Journey Home*, 1917), completed on 6 December 1909, had to be shortened after its Berlin opening on 11 February 1910 for its performance by the troupe of Reinhardt's Deutsches Theater (German Theater) in Vienna, where in May 1910 it became a great success. By then, work on *Der Rosenkavalier* (1911; translated as *The Rose-Bearer*, 1912), which originated in a conversation with Kessler during the first half of February 1909 and which prof-

ited greatly from his suggestions, had progressed satisfactorily. Since its premiere on 26 January 1911 in Dresden, it has been the work with which Hofmannsthal's international reputation is most intimately connected. But new material pushed to the fore immediately thereafter: an opera about Ariadne replaced a plan for a drama to be titled "Das steinerne Herz" (The Heart of Stone). *Ariadne auf Naxos* (1912; translated as *Ariadne on Naxos*, 1924) was first performed as a one-act opera within Molière's *Le bourgeois gentilhomme* (1670)—translated into German as *Der Bürger als Edelmann*—on 25 October 1912 in Stuttgart; in later performances the play became a prelude to the opera. Work on *Die Frau ohne Schatten* (The Woman without a Shadow; published, 1916; performed, 1919) had not progressed much beyond the completion of act 2 when World War I broke out in 1914, but by the end of September 1915 the whole libretto was in Strauss's hands.

It may appear that during the decade before 1914 Hofmannsthal was exclusively absorbed in his work with Strauss. But this impression overlooks his concurrent fiction and essays. It also slights his attempts to write not only for the urban *haute bourgeoisie* who could afford to buy opera tickets and whose approval had made him a moderately wealthy man. He also wanted to speak to a broad audience of ordinary people, whom he called "die Menge" (the multitude) and "das Volk" (the people), and do so in a language that was simple without being condescending and complex without being idiosyncratic. He wanted to reclaim for the playwright and for the stage as a public institution something of their earlier relevance as sources of political education. Such a revitalization of art was not to be confused either with partisan sloganeering or with the nostalgic evocation of past cultural riches. Eschewing both naturalism and modernist experimentation, Hofmannsthal tried to recapture "Elementarerfahrungen" (fundamental human experiences) that he found most essentially expressed in religious mysteries and rituals. He knew how difficult it would be to resuscitate their mythic power in a secular society, but for Hofmannsthal the preservation of traditional religious values in the face of a general revaluation of all values was at stake. He came to consider it the poet's special obligation to show ways in which a mindless confidence in external possessions and materialism could be overcome. Christian allegory became his preferred means for expressing this concern.

Cartoon by Dolbin showing Hofmannsthal (right) and Strauss at a Vienna coffeehouse in the early 1920s. Standing in the rear are Arthur Schnitzler (left) and Richard Beer-Hofmann (from Alan Jefferson, Richard Strauss, *1975)*

As early as April 1903 he had read *Everyman*, and he consulted further relevant material, including Hans Sachs's Reformation play *Von dem reichen sterbenden Menschen* (Of the Rich Dying Man, 1549) as well as woodcuts and many other sources, throughout its slow transformation into *Jedermann: Das Spiel vom Sterben des reichen Mannes*. Its criticism of humanity's servitude to mammon owes a good deal to the sociologist Georg Simmel's *Philosophie des Geldes* (Philosophy of Money, 1900), which analyzes the destruction of individual differences and of subjectivity wrought by money as the mediating agency of all aspects of modern life. After experiencing how unreliable are the friendships that he had bought, Jedermann recognizes that what is required for a meaningful existence are the beauty of good deeds and faith in God's mercy.

The allegorical structure of *Jedermann* and its poetic archaisms reflect a dubious shift in Hofmannsthal's dramatic technique. He admitted that these features were impossible to duplicate in other plays. They were complemented by Reinhardt's highly modern directorial style, which absorbed the audience in a stunning dis-

play of meticulously coordinated effects of light, sound, movement, and costumes. In the final analysis, though, *Jedermann* was a dead end rather than a breakthrough to a sustainable new dramatic style. Linking *Elektra* with *Jedermann*, Hofmannsthal said that both plays ask what is left of human beings after everything has been taken away from them and that their answer is: "die Tat oder das Werk" (what one does or accomplishes). This affirmation of a law beyond the merely personal is the principal impulse behind his preoccupation with the theme of sacrifice; but Elektra's obsessions render her unable to act, and Jedermann's death has at best a minimal effect on the petrified world of objects around him.

Hofmannsthal turned to a form of drama whose peculiar mixture of styles and changing character constellations suggest that all things, even the most antagonistic and divergent elements, are connected with each other. In blending the ordinary with the fantastic and the sublime, in combining the humble with the pathetic, he wanted to show that in the midst of tumult and confusion it is still possible to find oneself. Persuaded that a pious Volksgeist (Spirit of the peo-

Hofmannsthal (left) and the director Max Reinhardt at a rehearsal for a 1925 production of Hofmannsthal's Das Salzburger große Welttheater

ple) was groping for modern confirmation, and encouraged by the popular acclaim of *Jedermann* after its performance on the Domplatz (Cathedral Square) on 22 August 1920 as part of the Salzburg Festival, he completed *Das Salzburger große Welttheater* (The Salzburg Great World Theater, 1922) in six weeks (1 October to 14 November 1921). Its central figure is the Beggar, who refuses to accept his position at the bottom of the secular hierarchy and whose rebellion threatens to turn the world upside down. But Wisdom raises her hands in prayer, neither for her own salvation nor for the protection of a corrupt order but to testify to the spiritual insignificance of wealth and power. The Beggar, converted by a miraculous insight, renounces revolutionary violence and becomes an obedient Christian.

This proclamation of conventional Christian morality was Hofmannsthal's answer to the dissolution of the Hapsburg empire, to Austria's impoverishment, and to uncertainty about the future. But his advocacy of traditional values and of the social institutions that make their survival possible goes back beyond 1914 and can be traced nowhere more clearly than in the various revisions of the Florindo-Cristina material, which was originally conceived as a comedic vindication of the artist-seducer. Florindo is a person without attachments who leaves his lovers with nothing but their memory of a moment of perfect erotic bliss; he arranges suitable marriages for them so that

he can escape the responsibilities of a husband. But more and more the naive country girl Cristina, secure in her moral convictions even though she becomes a victim of the seducer's designs, gains prominence. She overcomes the temptations of profligacy or despair by returning to her mountain village, where she will marry an old sea captain, Tomaso, a Ulysses figure. Their union will not fulfill her earlier expectations of love and happiness, but it is meant to be less a source of personal satisfaction than a testimony to the ethical values of marriage as an institution, of a covenant as permanent as the Alps where they will make their home.

Such a transformation of a somewhat frivolous idea into metaphysical seriousness overtaxed the potential of comedy. For this reason Hofmannsthal turned again to narrative prose, which proved to be a more appropriate form in which to express his concern with the need for loyalty and a willingness to subordinate personal desires to higher goals. The prose version of *Die Frau ohne Schatten* (1919), the story of an emperor's redemption through his wife's charitable honesty, is his most ambitious exemplification of what he meant by the "Triumph des Allomatischen" (triumph of the allomatic principle), the recovery of one's true self in another person. This principle is also a sustaining theme of Hofmannsthal's only novel, the fragmentary *Andreas oder Die Vereinigten* (1932; translated as *Andreas; or, The United*, 1936), which he worked on from 1907 to 1927 but most of which was written during 1912-1913. Such convictions also inspired his activities in support of the Austrian war effort. Hofmannsthal served in the Kriegsfürsorgeamt, a propaganda branch of the War Ministry, largely free to set his own agenda and convinced that his many articles, lectures, diplomatic missions, and especially his editions of representative documents from Austrian history would have a beneficial effect on the country's rapidly declining morale. For a while he believed that at last he had found a role that would satisfy his desire to contribute to the public good. In the end he realized that his cultural politics of a "konservative Revolution" and of a "schöpferische Restauration" (creative restoration) were the product of an idealistic illusion. But as late as 1927, in his speech of 10 January at Munich University that was published as *Das Schrifttum als geistiger Raum der Nation* (Literature as the Spiritual Homeland of the Nation, 1927), he suggested that literature would be able to replace the political institutions that had formerly

Scene from a performance of Das Salzburger große Welttheater *at the Salzburg Festival in 1925*

united the various German nations. His suspicion, however, that he was chasing a phantom had arisen long before the end of World War I made the full extent of the European catastrophe apparent. His evermore debilitating awareness that he was far removed from the forces that shaped the postwar world, that he had become an anachronism, was the cause of his increasingly frequent fits of depression. His correspondence between 1917 and 1922 with Rudolf Pannwitz, whose *Die Krisis der europäischen Kultur* (The Crisis of European Culture, 1917) made a profound impression on him, and the letters he exchanged with the young diplomat-scholar Carl Jakob Burckhardt reveal the depth of his disorientation.

The last decade of Hofmannsthal's life, when none of his new works found a responsive public, was characterized by a tenacious desire to show how social conflicts can be resolved. His premise was that such conflicts result from impulses and desires that, while disparate and antagonistic on the surface, converge at a deeper level. He achieved his purpose best in a type of comedy that combines three aspects in perfect fusion: the subtly ironic study of an inimitable char-

acter; a social portrait of that character's class, particularly of the evasive mannerisms of the aristocracy; and a conversational language that hides serious, even potentially tragic concerns behind a superficial ease. *Der Schwierige* (The Difficult One, 1921) is his only play set in the present. Its rather uneventful story takes place just after the war. Count Hans Karl Bühl decides to end his affair with Countess Antoinette Hechingen because he knows that her husband, his comrade during the war, is profoundly devoted to her. Bühl's sister, the widowed Countess Crescence Freudenberg, is afraid that Antoinette may seek to entrap her naively arrogant son Stani, and she asks Bühl to intervene as the young man's protector. Stani, meanwhile, reveals his intention of marrying Countess Helene Altenwyl, whose shy sensitivity has also attracted Bühl's affection. At a soiree at the Altenwyls' Bühl bids farewell to a desolate Antoinette and then, hesitant to put his feelings into words, speaks to Helene of an ideal marriage without mentioning that he would like to be the ideal husband. Tragic disappointments appear to be the order of the evening. But Helene puts an end to these confusions with a discreet confession of her love for Bühl, only to give rise to a new comedy of errors when Crescence assumes that her "irresistible" son is the cause of Helene's happiness—a mistake that an embarrassed Bühl must tactfully rectify.

With a perfectly balanced economy of means Hofmannsthal had realized, for the first time in his career, the theatrical potential inherent in his type of comedy, a comedy that reflects the futility of language and straightforward action at the same time as it shows their necessity. He had also succeeded in capturing the intimate interplay of the comedic with the tragic, a seemingly paradoxical amalgam that for him characterized the Austria—particularly its nobility—of his time.

No doubt in an attempt to capitalize on the mastery he had achieved in this genre, Hofmannsthal wrote another comedy during 1922. *Der Unbestechliche* (The Incorruptible One; performed, 1923) is a variation on the "servant as master" theme. Theodor, a Bohemian lackey who combines a crafty interest in his own advantages with virtuous dignity, has left the service of Baron Jaromir, a nobleman of questionable morals, to join the household of the latter's mother. When the presence of two of Jaromir's "prenuptial" lady friends on her estate endangers the baron's marriage, Theodor discreetly arranges events that impel the speedy departure of the unwelcome guests. Using the bedroom Jaromir had prepared for an amorous encounter for his own rendezvous with a young widow, the wily servant enjoys a double reward for his intervention on behalf of familial virtue. But his belief that he alone is in control of the little intrigues that save his master's marriage turns out to be erroneous. Ultimately a transcendent power, whose instrument he is, has to intervene at the critical moment to restore order to Jaromir's affairs.

At this time Hofmannsthal was concentrating on a drama in five acts that he had begun in the summer of 1902 as an adaptation of Calderón's *La vida es sueño*. It was originally intended to be an exploration of the "Höhlenreich des Selbst" (cavernous kingdom of the self), but the political implications of the plot assumed importance as early as 1904. *Der Turm* (The Tower, published, 1925; performed, 1928), as the play was renamed, appeared to have found its final shape in October 1924. But Reinhardt had reservations, especially considering its conclusion—the entrance of a child-king as the messianic representative of a new generation—unconvincing. At Reinhardt's residence, Schloß Leopoldskron near

Hofmannsthal's grave in the Kalksburg Cemetery, Vienna

Salzburg, the author and the director discussed a less mythic ending that gives prominence to Olivier, the unscrupulous master of power politics.

The play is set in a legendary Poland of the seventeenth century. Sigismund, the son of King Basilius, is imprisoned in a remote tower because of a prophecy that he will overthrow his father; he is unaware of his actual identity. Revolutionary upheavals persuade his guard, Julian, to conspire with a doctor to confront the king with his son. During the confrontation Sigismund questions the prerogatives of the old regime and strikes the king. Overpowered by courtiers, Sigismund and Julian are condemned to death. As the nobles turn against their absolutist monarch and the impoverished people accept the demagogue Olivier as their leader, a rebellion frees Sigismund as he is about to be executed. After the king's abdication, Sigismund, the new ruler, makes Julian his principal councillor. Julian warns the nobles not to oppose his plan of building a new kingdom with the support of the peasants. Even the new king rejects this program, fearing that it would lead to anarchy. When Olivier's masses turn against him, he realizes that Julian's attempt to restore legitimacy to the monarchy has failed. The divorce of power and spiritual values is absolute. Olivier, representing raw power without self-control, offers Sigismund a symbolic role in the victory parade; the king declines with aristocratic disdain. This assertion of his spiritual superiority seals his fate. He is discarded like a useless commodity after an assassin's bullet kills him from ambush. The play's language is freighted with an artificial seriousness and at the same time tries to appear simple and natural. It lacks dramatic intensity, precision, and concreteness.

During his last years Hofmannsthal traveled to the premieres of his plays, to Sicily, to northern Italy, to Paris, to Morocco, and to London and Oxford. There were bursts of renewed creativity, and he continued his involvement with the Salzburg Festival, but ever more frequently he complained of nervous exhaustion, depression, and of an inability to concentrate. While the general public respected him as a dignified representative of the "world of yesterday," he also could not help but notice that the next generation of writers barely knew his name. He died on 15 July 1929 of a stroke as he was preparing to go to his older son's funeral.

Letters:

Richard Strauss: Briefwechsel mit Hugo von Hofmannsthal, edited by Franz Strauss (Berlin & Leipzig: Zsolnay, 1926); translated by Paul England as *Correspondence between Richard Strauss and Hugo von Hofmannsthal, 1907-1918* (London: Secker, 1927; New York: Knopf, 1927);

Briefwechsel zwischen George und Hofmannsthal, edited by Robert Boehringer (Berlin: Bondi, 1938; enlarged edition, Munich: Küpper, 1953);

Briefwechsel: Richard Strauss/Hugo von Hofmannsthal. Gesamtausgabe, edited by Franz and Alice Strauss and Willi Schuh (Zurich: Atlantis, 1952); translated by Hanns Hammelmann and Edward Osers as *A Working Friendship: The Correspondence between Richard Strauss and Hugo von Hofmannsthal* (New York: Random House, 1961);

Hugo von Hofmannsthal/Eberhard von Bodenhausen: Briefe der Freundschaft, edited by Dora von Bodenhausen (Düsseldorf: Diederichs, 1953);

Hugo von Hofmannsthal/Rudolf Borchardt: Briefwechsel, edited by Marie Luise Borchardt and Her-

bert Steiner (Frankfurt am Main: Fischer, 1954);

Hugo von Hofmannsthal/Carl Jakob Burckhardt Briefwechsel, edited by Carl J. Burckhardt (Frankfurt am Main: Fischer, 1956);

Hugo von Hofmannsthal/Arthur Schnitzler: Briefwechsel, edited by Therese Nickl and Heinrich Schnitzler (Frankfurt am Main: Fischer, 1964);

Hugo von Hofmannsthal/Helene von Nostitz: Briefwechsel, edited by Oswalt von Nostitz (Frankfurt am Main: Fischer, 1965);

Hugo von Hofmannsthal/Edgar Karg von Bebenburg: Briefwechsel, edited by Mary E. Gilbert (Frankfurt am Main: Fischer, 1966);

Briefe an Marie Herzfeld, edited by Horst Weber (Heidelberg: Stiehm, 1967);

Hugo von Hofmannsthal/Leopold von Andrian: Briefwechsel, edited by Walter H. Perl (Frankfurt am Main: Fischer, 1968);

Hugo von Hofmannsthal/Harry Graf Kessler: Briefwechsel 1898-1929, edited by Hilde Burger (Frankfurt am Main: Insel, 1968);

Hugo von Hofmannsthal/Willy Haas: Ein Briefwechsel, edited by Rolf Italiaander (Berlin: Propyläen, 1968);

Hugo von Hofmannsthal/Josef Redlich: Briefwechsel, edited by Helga Fußgänger (Frankfurt am Main: Fischer, 1971);

Hugo von Hofmannsthal/Anton Wildgans: Briefwechsel, edited by Norbert Altenhofer (Heidelberg: Stiehm, 1971);

Hugo von Hofmannsthal/Richard Beer-Hofmann: Briefwechsel, edited by Eugene Weber (Frankfurt am Main: Fischer, 1972);

Briefwechsel mit Max Rychner; mit Samuel und Hedwig Fischer, Oscar Bie und Moritz Heimann, edited by Claudia Mertz-Rychner (Frankfurt am Main: Fischer, 1973);

Briefwechsel: Hugo von Hofmannsthal/Ottonie Gräfin Degenfeld, edited by Marie Thérèse Miller-Degenfeld and Weber (Frankfurt am Main: Fischer, 1974); revised as *Briefwechsel mit Ottonie Gräfin Degenfeld und Julie Freifrau von Wendelstadt* (Frankfurt am Main: Fischer, 1986);

Hugo von Hofmannsthal/Rainer Maria Rilke: Briefwechsel, edited by Rudolf Hirsch and Ingeborg Schnack (Frankfurt am Main: Insel, 1978);

Hugo von Hofmannsthal/Max Mell: Briefwechsel, edited by Margret Dietrich and Heinz Kindermann (Heidelberg: Lambert Schneider, 1982);

Ria Schmujlow-Claassen und Hugo von Hofmannsthal: Briefe-Aufsätze-Dokumente, edited by Claudia Albrecht (Marbach: Marbacher Schriften, 1982);

Hugo von Hofmannsthal/Paul Zifferer: Briefwechsel, edited by Burger (Vienna: Verlag der österreichischen Staatsdruckerei, 1983);

Hugo von Hofmannsthal: Briefwechsel mit dem Insel-Verlag 1901-1929, edited by Gerhard Schuster (Frankfurt am Main: Buchhändler-Vereinigung, 1985).

Bibliographies:

Horst Weber, *Hugo von Hofmannsthal: Bibliographie des Schrifttums. 1892-1963* (Berlin: De Gruyter, 1966);

Weber, *Hugo von Hofmannsthal: Bibliographie. Werke, Briefe, Gespräche, Übersetzungen, Vertonungen* (Berlin & New York: De Gruyter, 1972);

James E. Walsh, *The Hofmannsthal Collection in the Houghton Library: A Descriptive Catalogue of Printed Books* (Heidelberg: Stiehm, 1974);

Hans-Albrecht Koch, *Hugo von Hofmannsthal* (Darmstadt: Wissenschaftliche Buchgesellschaft, 1989).

Biographies:

Günther Erken, "Hofmannsthal-Chronik: Beitrag zu einer Biographie," *Literaturwissenschaftliches Jahrbuch*, new series 3 (1962): 239-313;

Werner Volke, *Hugo von Hofmannsthal in Selbstzeugnissen und Bilddokumenten* (Reinbek: Rowohlt, 1967).

References:

Richard Alewyn, *Über Hugo von Hofmannsthal* (Göttingen: Vandenhoeck & Ruprecht, 1958);

Norbert Altenhofer, *Hofmannsthals Lustspiel "Der Unbestechliche"* (Bad Homburg: Gehlen, 1967);

Gerhard Austin, *Phänomenologie der Gebärde bei Hugo von Hofmannsthal* (Heidelberg: Winter, 1981);

Lowell A. Bangerter, *Hugo von Hofmannsthal* (New York: Ungar, 1977);

Sibylle Bauer, ed., *Hugo von Hofmannsthal* (Darmstadt: Wissenschaftliche Buchgesellschaft, 1968);

Benjamin Bennett, *Hugo von Hofmannsthal: The Theatres of Consciousness* (Cambridge: Cambridge University Press, 1988);

Carlpeter Braegger, *Das Visuelle und das Plastische: Hugo von Hofmannsthal und die bildende Kunst* (Bern & Munich: Francke, 1979);

Gisa Briese-Neumann, *Ästhet - Dilettant - Narziss: Untersuchungen zur Reflexion der fin de siècle-Phänomene im Frühwerk Hofmannsthals* (Frankfurt am Main: Lang, 1985);

Hermann Broch, "Hofmannsthal und seine Zeit: Eine Studie," in his *Kommentierte Werkausgabe*, volume 9, edited by Paul M. Lützeler (Frankfurt am Main: Suhrkamp, 1975), pp. 111-275; translated by Michael P. Steinberg as *Hugo von Hofmannsthal and His Time: The European Imagination, 1860-1920* (Chicago & London: University of Chicago Press, 1984);

Brian Coghlan, *Hofmannsthal's Festival Dramas* (London: Cambridge University Press, 1964);

Károly Csúri, *Die frühen Erzählungen Hofmannsthals: Eine generativ-poetische Untersuchung* (Kronberg: Scriptor, 1978);

Donald G. Daviau and George J. Buelow, *The "Ariadne auf Naxos" of Hugo von Hofmannsthal* (Chapel Hill: University of North Carolina Press, 1975);

Manfred Diersch, *Empiriokritizismus und Impressionismus: Über Beziehungen zwischen Philosophie, Ästhetik und Literatur um 1900 in Wien* (Berlin: Aufbau, 1977);

Günter Erken, *Hofmannsthals dramatischer Stil: Untersuchungen zur Symbolik und Dramaturgie* (Tübingen: Niemeyer, 1967);

Karl G. Esselborn, *Hofmannsthal und der antike Mythos* (Munich: Fink, 1969);

Karen Forsyth, *"Ariadne auf Naxos" by Hugo von Hofmannsthal and Richard Strauss. Its Genesis and Meaning* (London: Oxford University Press, 1982);

Hanns Hammelmann, *Hugo von Hofmannsthal* (New Haven & London: Yale University Press, 1957);

Edgar Hederer, *Hugo von Hofmannsthal* (Frankfurt am Main: Fischer, 1960);

Hofmannsthal-Blätter: Veröffentlichungen der Hugo-von-Hofmannsthal-Gesellschaft, 1- (1968-);

Hofmannsthal-Forschungen, 1- (1971-);

Manfred Hoppe, *Literatentum, Magie und Mystik im Frühwerk Hofmannsthals* (Berlin: De Gruyter, 1968);

Corinna Jaeger-Trees, *Aspekte der Dekadenz in Hofmannsthals Dramen und Erzählungen des Frühwerks* (Bern & Stuttgart: Haupt, 1988);

Alan Jefferson, *Richard Strauss* (London: Macmillan, 1975);

Peter Christoph Kern, *Zur Gedankenwelt des späten Hofmannsthal: Die Idee einer schöpferischen Restauration* (Heidelberg: Winter, 1969);

Jacob Knaus, *Hofmannsthals Weg zur Oper "Die Frau ohne Schatten": Rücksichten und Einflüsse auf die Musik* (Berlin: De Gruyter, 1971);

Erwin Kobel, *Hugo von Hofmannsthal* (Berlin: De Gruyter, 1970);

Thomas A. Kovach, *Hofmannsthal and Symbolism: Art and Life in the Work of a Modern Poet* (New York: Lang, 1985);

Eva-Maria Lenz, *Hugo von Hofmannsthals mythologische Oper "Die ägyptische Helena"* (Tübingen: Niemeyer, 1972);

Wolfram Mauser, *Hugo von Hofmannsthal. Konfliktbewältigung und Werkstruktur: Eine psychosoziologische Interpretation* (Munich: Fink, 1977);

H. Jürgen Meyer-Wendt, *Der frühe Hofmannsthal und die Gedankenwelt Nietzsches* (Heidelberg: Quelle & Meyer, 1973);

David Holmes Miles, *Hofmannsthal's Novel "Andreas": Memory and Self* (Princeton, N.J.: Princeton University Press, 1972);

Wolfgang Nehring, *Die Tat bei Hofmannsthal: Eine Untersuchung zu Hofmannsthals großen Dramen* (Stuttgart: Metzler, 1966);

Eva-Maria Nüchtern, *Hofmannsthals "Alkestis"* (Bad Homburg: Gehlen, 1968);

Sherill Halm Pantle, *"Die Frau ohne Schatten" by Hugo von Hofmannsthal and Richard Strauss: An Analysis of Text, Music and Their Relationship* (Bern: Lang, 1978);

Karl Pestalozzi, *Sprachskepsis und Sprachmagie im Werk des jungen Hofmannsthal* (Zurich: Atlantis, 1958);

Gerhardt Pickerodt, *Hofmannsthals Dramen: Kritik ihres historischen Gehalts* (Stuttgart: Metzler, 1968);

Benno Rech, *Hofmannsthals Komödie: Verwirklichte Konfiguration* (Bonn: Bouvier, 1971);

William H. Rey, *Weltentzweiung und Weltversöhnung in Hofmannithals griechischen Dramen* (Philadelphia: University of Pennsylvania Press, 1962);

Hermann Rudolph, *Kulturkritik und konservative Revolution: Zum kulturellpolitischen Denken Hofmannsthals und seinem problemgeschichtlichen Kontext* (Tübingen: Niemeyer, 1971);

Rudolf H. Schäfer, *Hugo von Hofmannsthals "Arabella"* (Bern: Lang, 1967);

Friedrich Schröder, *Die Gestalt des Verführers im Drama Hugo von Hofmannsthals* (Frankfurt am Main: Haag & Herchen, 1988);

Jürgen Schwalbe, *Sprache und Gebärde im Werk Hofmannsthals* (Freiburg: Schwarz, 1971);

Egon Schwarz, *Hofmannsthal und Calderon* (Cambridge, Mass.: Harvard University Press, 1962);

Hinrich C. Seeba, *Kritik des ästhetischen Menschen: Hermeneutik und Moral in Hofmannsthals "Der Tor und der Tod"* (Bad Homburg: Gehlen, 1970);

Steven P. Sondrup, *Hofmannsthal and the French Symbolist Tradition* (Bern: Lang, 1976);

Rolf Tarot, *Hugo von Hofmannsthal: Daseinsformen und dichterische Struktur* (Tübingen: Niemeyer, 1970);

Cynthia Walk, *Hugo von Hofmannsthals großes Welttheater: Drama und Theater* (Heidelberg: Winter, 1980);

Waltraud Wiethölter, *Hofmannsthal oder die Geometrie des Subjekts: psychostrukturelle und ikonographische Studien zum Prosawerk* (Tübingen: Niemeyer, 1990);

Lothar Wittmann, *Sprachthematik und dramatische Form im Werke Hofmannsthals* (Stuttgart: Kohlhammer, 1966);

Michael Worbs, *Nervenkunst: Literatur und Psychoanalyse im Wien der Jahrhundertwende* (Frankfurt am Main: Athenäum, 1983);

Gotthart Wunberg, *Der frühe Hofmannsthal: Schizophrenie als dichterische Struktur* (Stuttgart: Kohlhammer, 1965);

W. E. Yuill and Patricia Howe, ed., *Hugo von Hofmannsthal (1874-1929): Commemorative Essays,* (London: Institute of Germanic Studies, 1981).

Papers:

Hugo von Hofmannsthal's papers are at the Bibliothek des Freien Deutschen Hochstifts (Library of the Free German Academy), Frankfurt am Main; at the Houghton Library at Harvard University; and in various private collections.

Arno Holz
(26 April 1863 - 26 October 1929)

Ward B. Lewis
University of Georgia

PLAY PRODUCTIONS: *Die Familie Selicke*, by Holz and Johannes Schlaf, Berlin, Die Freie Bühne, 7 April 1890;

Socialaristokraten, Berlin, Zentraltheater, 15 June 1897;

Heimkehr, by Holz and Oskar Jerschke, Berlin, Berliner Theater, 17 January 1903;

Traumulus, by Holz and Jerschke, Berlin, 23 September 1904;

Büxl, by Holz and Jerschke, Berlin, Neues Schauspielhaus, 11 October 1911;

Sonnenfinsternis, Hamburg, Thalia-Theater, 16 September 1913;

Ignorabimus, Düsseldorf, Schauspielhaus, 14 April 1927.

BOOKS: *Klinginsherz!* (Berlin: Arendt, 1883);

Deutsche Weisen, by Holz and Oskar Jerschke (Berlin & Leipzig: Parrisius, 1884);

Das Buch der Zeit: Lieder eines Modernen (Dresden: Reißner, 1884; revised Zurich: Verlags-Magazin, 1886; revised, Berlin: Fontane, 1892; revised, Munich: Piper, 1905; revised, Dresden: Sibyllen-Verlag, 1921);

Papa Hamlet, by Holz and Johannes Schlaf, as Bjarne P. Holmsen (Leipzig: Reißner, 1889);

Die Familie Selicke: Drama in drei Aufzügen, by Holz and Schlaf (Berlin: Issleib, 1890; Cambridge: Cambridge University Press, 1950);

Die Kunst: Ihr Wesen und Ihre Gesetze (Berlin: Issleib, 1891; revised, 1893);

Neue Gleise: Gemeinsames, by Holz and Schlaf (Berlin: Fontane, 1892);

Der geschundne Pegasus: Eine Mirlitoniade in Versen (Berlin: Fontane, 1892);

Socialaristokraten (Rudolstadt & Leipzig: Mänicke & Jahn, 1896); republished as *Sozialaristokraten* (Munich & Leipzig: Piper, 1905);

Phantasus, 2 volumes (Berlin: Sassenbach, 1898-1899; revised edition, 3 volumes, Dresden: Reißner, 1913; revised edition, 1 volume, Leipzig: Insel, 1916; edited by Jost Hermand, New York & London: Johnson Reprint, 1968);

Revolution der Lyrik (Berlin: Sassenbach, 1899);

Dr. Richard M. Meyer, Privatdozent an der Universität Berlin, ein litterarischer Ehrabschneider (Berlin: Sassenbach, 1900);

Johannes Schlaf: Ein nothgedrungenes Kapitel (Berlin: Sassenbach, 1902; revised and enlarged edition, Munich: Piper, 1905);

Die Blechschmiede (Leipzig: Insel, 1902); revised as *Die Blechschmiede; oder Der umgestürzte Papierkorb: Mysterium* (Dresden: Petzschke, 1917); revised as *Die Blechschmiede: Pandivinium, Pandämonium und Panmysterium* (Dresden: Sibyllen-Verlag, 1921);

Heimkehr, by Holz and Oskar Jerschke, as Hans Volkmar (Berlin: Sassenbach, 1903);

Lieder auf einer alten Laute: Lyrisches Portrait aus dem 17. Jahrhundert (Leipzig: Insel, 1903); revised as *Dafnis: Lyrisches Portrait aus dem 17. Jahrhundert* (Munich: Piper, 1904);

Traumulus: Drama in fünf Akten, by Holz and Jerschke (New York: Goldmann, 1904); republished as *Traumulus: Tragische Komödie* (Munich: Piper, 1905);

Frei! Eine Männerkomödie in vier Aufzügen, by Holz and Jerschke (Munich: Piper, 1907);

Sonnenfinsternis: Tragödie (Berlin: Sassenbach, 1908: revised edition, Berlin: Bong, 1919);

Gaudeamus! Festspiel zur 350jährigen Jubelfeier der Universität Jena, by Holz and Jerschke (Berlin: Sassenbach, 1908);

Büxl: Komödie in drei Akten, by Holz and Jerschke (Dresden: Reißner, 1911);

Ignorabimus: Tragödie (Dresden: Reißner, 1913);

Des berühmbten Schäffers Dafnis sälbst verfärtigte auffrichtige und Reue müthige Riesen-Bußthräne (Leipzig: Meißner & Buch, 1918);

Seltzsame und höchst ebentheuerlich Historie von der Insul Pimperle, daran sich der Tichter offt im Traum ergezzt (Berlin: Privately printed, 1919);

Fünf Abende in der Berliner Secession: Kurfürstendamm 232, music by Georg Stolzenberg (Berlin, 1919);

Flördeliese (Berlin: Privately printed, 1919);

Arno Holz

Das ausgewählte Werk (Berlin: Bong, 1919);

Die befreite deutsche Wortkunst (Vienna: Avalun, 1921);

Fünf neue Dafnis-Lieder (Berlin: Tieffenbach, 1921);

Das ist nun dein Leben! (Berlin: Officina Serpentis, 1921);

Neue Dafnis-Lieder, alß welche in des berühmbten Schäffers Dafnis Omnia mea das ist Sämbtliche höchst sündhaffte sälbst verfärtigte Freß- , Sauf- &

Venus-Lieder benebst angehänckten Auffrichtigen und Reue mühtigen Buß-Thränen biß anhero noch nicht enthalten sind (Dresden: Reißner, 1922);

Deutsches Dichterjubiläum (Berlin: Werkverlag, 1923);

Trio seraphicon (Berlin: Werkverlag, 1923);

Pronunciamento (Berlin: Werkverlag, 1923);

Kindheitsparadies (Berlin: Dietz, 1924);

Der erste Schultag (Berlin: Dietz, 1924);

Chinesischer Faun (Berlin: Holten, 1924);

Fern liegt ein Land (Berlin: Dietz, 1924);

Das Werk von Arno Holz, 10 volumes, edited by Hans W. Fischer (Berlin: Dietz, 1924-1925);

Zwölf Liebesgedichte (Berlin-Zehlendorf: Rembrandt-Verlag, 1926);

Entwurf einer Deutschen Akademie als Vertreterin der geeinten deutschen Geistesarbeiterschaft: Offener, sehr ausführlicher Brief und Bericht an die gesamte deutsche Öffentlichkeit (Berlin: Holten, 1926);

Das Werk: Monumental-Ausgabe in zwölf Bänden, 12 volumes (Berlin: Holten, 1926);

Zwei unveröffentlichte Gedichte (Chemnitz: Privately printed, 1927);

Mein Staub verstob: Wie ein Stern strahlt mein Gedächtnis!, edited by Alfred Richard Meyer (Nuremberg: Hesperos, 1943);

Werke, 7 volumes, edited by Wilhelm Emrich and Anita Holz (Neuwied am Rhein & Berlin-Spandau: Luchterhand, 1961-1964);

Kennst du das Land? Ein lyrischer Schriftwechsel mit Hans Schlegel/Arno Holz, edited by Klaus M. Rarisch (Düsseldorf: Eremiten-Press, 1977).

OTHER: *Emanuel Geibel: Ein Gedenkbuch*, edited by Holz (Berlin & Leipzig: Parrisius, 1884);

Aus Urgroßmutters Garten: Ein Frühlingsstrauß aus dem Rokoko, edited by Holz (Dresden: Reißner, 1903); published as *Von Günther bis Goethe: Ein Frühlingsstrauß aus dem Rokoko* (Berlin-Zehlendorf: Rembrandt, 1926).

Arno Holz was a highly visible literary personality of his time, and his work was remarkably diverse. In his verse he revived the baroque literary style of three centuries earlier, and from the middle 1880s he made a name for himself as a lyrical poet. Turning from poetry to prose and drama, he put into practice the aesthetic theories of naturalism, a movement dedicated to reducing the subjective element in art. Collaboration with Johannes Schlaf gave way to bitter hostility and jealousy regarding the importance of their respective roles. All his life Holz raged against critics and against authors he perceived as rivals.

Holz identified with Berlin. Although born in Rastenburg, East Prussia, on 26 April 1863 as the fourth of ten children, Arno Holz grew up in Berlin; his parents, Hermann Holz—a pharmacist—and Franziska Werner Holz, moved there when he was twelve. He attended the Humboldtgymnasium and then, from 1879 to 1881, the Königstädtisches Gymnasium, leaving

school at age eighteen with especially poor grades in Greek, French, and mathematics. He went to work for a newspaper and experienced the financial insecurity that would haunt him all his life. In 1883 he joined the literary club "Wartburg," where he met Oskar Jerschke; the following year they coauthored an anthology of verse, *Deutsche Weisen* (German Melodies).

In 1886 Holz cofounded the naturalist literary society "Durch" (Through). The same year a revised edition of his collection of socialist poetry, *Das Buch der Zeit* (The Book of Time), appeared; it had originally been published in 1884. The book was a failure. In the fall of that year Holz withdrew to Niederschönhausen, on the edge of the capital, and gradually moved from Marxism to a "natural" explanation of the development of history based on Darwinian evolutionary principles. Artistic styles, he decided, are born, flourish, and die in an evolutionary manner. The poet must respond to these laws of nature or become outdated. For the rest of his life Holz's polemics against literary contemporaries and critics were founded in his conviction that whoever created the new techniques that corresponded to the development emanating from the laws of nature was superior, and that those who did not change their techniques had abandoned themselves to the dustbins of history.

In the summer of 1889 Holz moved back to Berlin and accepted the post of managing editor of the journal *Die Freie Bühne für modernes Leben* (Free Stage for Modern Life), dedicated to the advancement of naturalism. He was compensated for literary essays he contributed to the *New-Yorker Staats-Zeitung* under the pseudonym Fritz Erdmann in 1889, and about this time he patented some children's toys that provided income. But for most of his life he was in debt or dependent on the financial support of friends.

The short-story collection *Papa Hamlet* (1889), by Holz and Johannes Schlaf, was published under the pseudonym Bjarne P. Holmsen. The work was written according to the concept of "konsequenter Naturalismus" (Consistent Naturalism) that the authors had formulated. The program combined art and science and prescribed maximum precision in the reproduction of minute details observable by eye and ear and captured in gestures and the tempo and pauses of speech. This technique came to be known as "Sekundenstil" (the style of seconds); it was a radical attempt to reveal inner states that are incapable of being conveyed by language.

Holz (left) in 1889 with Dr. G. Aschelm; Gerhart Hauptmann; Hauptmann's son, Ivo, and wife, Marie; Margarete Marschalk, who would become Hauptmann's second wife in 1904; and Margarete's brother, the composer Max Marschalk

Papa Hamlet awoke Gerhart Hauptmann to naturalism, which he popularized in his drama *Vor Sonnenaufgang* (1889; translated as *Before Dawn*, 1909), a work dedicated to "Holmsen." The name had been adopted to suggest Scandinavian origins associated with Henrik Ibsen, and the hoax succeeded until it was dispelled by the authors.

" . . . dann wird eben keine Frau, die auf Reputierlichkeit Anspruch erhebt, sich dort sehen lassen dürften und die Herren werden sich in diese Vorstellungen hineinstehlen müssen, wie man das beim Besuche zweifelhafter Lokale tut" (no woman then who has a claim to respectability will permit herself to be seen there, and gentlemen will have to steal into these performances as one visits a place of doubtful virtue), wrote a Berlin drama critic when it was announced that *Die Familie Selicke* (The Selicke Family, 1890), by Holz and Schlaf, had been accepted for production by the theater of the club "Die Freie Bühne." The work was presented at a matinee on Easter Monday, 7 April 1890, with Ida Stägemann in the role of the mother; the critics found her performance convincing. Wilhelm

Hock appeared as her husband, Eduard, and Agnes Müller as the daughter Toni. Toni's lover, the student Gustav Wendt, was portrayed by Emanuel Reicher; and Theodor Müller played Kopelke, a friend of the family, who was characterized by the critics as a figure truly representative of the people of Berlin. The performance was hailed the following day by the eminent novelist and drama critic Theodor Fontane as a new contribution to the field of dramatic art—a contribution that surpassed recent productions of works by Leo Tolstoy and Hauptmann, which had also severely strained the limits of conservative audience attitudes.

The three-act drama depicts, with minute attention to detail, a few hours of daily life in the modest living room of a Berlin family at Christmas. The Selicke family exists on the edge of society, is burdened by debt, and suffers from the father's authoritarianism and alcoholism. As the play opens he arrives home from work intoxicated and abuses the family. As he snores in drunken sleep his youngest daughter dies, having failed to receive proper medical treatment. Toni, the eldest, rejects the plea of their student roomer, Wendt, to flee with him to the country, where, as a pastor, he may regain the belief in God that he has lost in the inhumanity of metropolitan Berlin. She decides to remain with the family that needs her and to sacrifice herself in an attempt to achieve reconciliation.

In spite of his and Schlaf's attempt to link *Papa Hamlet* with the work of Ibsen, Holz insisted that *Die Familie Selicke* was the most German drama in the literature of that language and wholly devoid of any foreign influence. Never, he claimed, had there been a movement less influenced by foreign sources than konsequenter Naturalismus. The aesthetic principles of this movement are formulated in *Die Kunst: Ihr Wesen und Ihre Gesetze* (Art: Its Nature and Laws, 1891), in which Holz provides the equation: art = nature-x. X refers to the limitations of the artistic medium and the artist's skill in handling the medium. The work has been widely understood as advocating a photographically exact reproduction of the physical world, but Holz's meaning has been clarified by the interpretation of the critic Wilhelm Emrich in his introduction to Holz's works (1961-1964). *Nature* is to be understood as the complete intellectual, spiritual, social, and physical reality as seen, experienced, considered, imagined, and dreamed by any person. Art has the tendency to encompass this inner and external reality; it is kept from doing so only by the medium and the artist's use of the medium.

Although *Die Familie Selicke* had been greeted by Fontane as a breakthrough and has become significant in literary and dramatic history, it was rejected by the public. The two authors parted ways, becoming lifelong bitter enemies. It was not until six years after *Die Familie Selicke* that Holz turned his attention from verse back to drama to write *Socialaristokraten* (Social Aristocrats; published, 1896; performed, 1897) in three weeks. This play was conceived as the first of a cycle of works to be titled "Berlin: Das Ende einer Zeit in Dramen" (Berlin: The End of an Epoch in Dramas). In his introduction to the published version of the work, Holz says that the series will provide a comprehensive picture of the period.

Holz wished in *Socialaristokraten* to break out of the milieu of the little people as represented in the everyday tragedy of the Selicke family; he depicts a larger, more complex configuration of characters. The language of life, not the language of theater, is to be heard on the stage,

writes Holz in the preface, and plot is less important than the representation of human beings. *Socialaristokraten* unfolds as a bourgeois-philistine comedy centering on the founding of a journal. Taste is on the level of kitsch. Once-original ideas of figures such as the philosopher Friedrich Nietzsche are grotesquely caricatured in the speech and behavior of the populace, where they have reached the lowest common denominator. Stage directions describe the office of the editor, Oskar Fiebig: the walls are decorated with oleograph pictures of bathing nymphs and Swiss landscapes; there is a bust of Friedrich Schiller, a cardboard replica of the house where Albrecht Dürer was born, a wax apple on a glass plate.

With the introduction of Dr. B. Gehrke, author of *Lieder eines Übermenschen* (Songs of a Superman), the emphasis moves to political satire. Deserting Social Democracy with its mindless mass appeal, the vain and ambitious Gehrke propounds an unpolitical politics in which rational individuals govern; this is the theory of Social Aristocracy. Threatened by censorship after the appearance of his article "Die Freie Liebe im Lichte der Pädagogik" (Free Love in the Light of Pedagogy), Gehrke opportunistically becomes the candidate of the anti-Semitic People's Party.

Holz makes himself the object of satire when Fiebig relates that his verse drama *Die Blechschmiede* (The Tinsmiths; the title of a play by Holz published in 1902) might not constitute immortal poetry, but it *is* a money-maker. Fiebig also says that he introduced Holz and Schlaf to literature but rejected *Die Familie Selicke* as too depressing for the stage.

Socialaristokraten was first presented at the Zentraltheater in Berlin on 15 June 1897, after Holz unsuccessfully attempted to interest more prestigious theaters in the work. The author directed the production, and some of his friends acted in it—including the director Max Reinhardt, who played the American poet Frederick Bellermann. The work was panned by critics and closed after the three performances stipulated in Holz's contract.

Disappointed, Holz concentrated once again on his poetry. He did not return to drama until several years later, when he did so in collaboration with Jerschke. Between 1900 and 1908 Holz and Jerschke coauthored five dramas that appeared from 1903 to 1911. *Heimkehr* (The Return Home, 1903) is a lightweight comedy. A millionaire returns to his hometown and offers to contribute to charitable institutions on the condition that modern industry be held beyond the outskirts of the town. When this goal proves impossible to achieve, he marries an orphan and erects a wall about their home.

Success was achieved by *Traumulus* (The Dreamer, 1904), a five-act drama satirizing the secondary-school system. It bears similarities to Frank Wedekind's play *Frühlings Erwachen* (1891; translated as *The Awakening of Spring*, 1909), in which tyrannical pedagogues and puritanical, unenlightened parents bring about adolescent tragedy, and to Heinrich Mann's novel *Professor Unrat oder das Ende eines Tyrannen* (Professor Unrat; or, The End of a Tyrant, 1905; translated as *The Blue Angel*, 1931). In a break with the tradition of such satire, however, Holz and Jerschke present the school system not as excessively authoritarian but as too permissive. Professor Dr. Niemeyer, director of the gymnasium, devotes himself to teaching young men the classics and guiding them through adolescence with an indulgent understanding of their shortcomings; they seize every opportunity to go behind his back to satisfy their pubescent desires. His students refer to him by the Latin nickname "Traumulus." Because of a personal vendetta against Niemeyer by the Landrat von Kannewurf, the police conduct clandestine surveillance of the boys to gather evidence to force Niemeyer's dismissal. The "tragedy" in this comedy centers on the student Zedlitz: expelled from the gymnasium to face a future possibly as bleak as becoming a waiter somewhere in America, he kills himself. Meanwhile, Niemeyer's beautiful, much younger wife, Jadwiga, and his son, Fritz, live extravagantly, and old Niemeyer is devastated by the revelation that his son forged his signature on an IOU and by Jadwiga's decision to leave him rather than live on a reduced income after he loses his job.

Frei! Eine Männerkomödie in vier Aufzügen (Free! A Comedy for Men in Four Acts, 1907) is a satire on the legal profession. Wölbling, a lawyer and member of the board of directors of the Volkskreditbank (People's Credit Bank), opposes Dr. Bruck, also a lawyer and the director of the bank, when the latter endorses loans for worthless undertakings and receives attorney's fees for doing so. Wölbling intemperately attacks this practice in the press and in court as professionally unethical and a waste of the depositors' savings. He refuses to compromise his principles even after being fined and reprimanded by the court. When the other attorneys close ranks against him for his lack of collegiality, Wölbling resigns the profession to become "free." Anti-Semitism, which seems to reflect Holz's own views, is evident in the play: an old Jew who barges into Wölbling's consultation room is thrown downstairs for amusement by two men in the office, and Wölbling argues that the credit union was bound to fail because it could not compete with the Jews, who hold all the first mortgages and are directors of all the banks.

Gaudeamus! (1908), a festival play in observation of the 350th anniversary of the founding of the University of Jena, is a patriotic work set against the background of the Franco-German War of 1870-1871. Student fraternities quit fighting over their place in the pecking order of a ceremonial procession and recognize themselves first and foremost as sons of the German fatherland.

Holz interrupted his collaboration with Jerschke to turn once again to his dramatic cycle dealing with Berlin at the end of an epoch. The tragedy *Sonnenfinsternis* (Solar Eclipse; published, 1908; performed, 1913) took him two years to write. Hollrieder, a painter, has devoted himself to attempting to reproduce nature with the greatest possible fidelity. But what he has attained, he realizes with frustration, is only technique. A patch of grass in the sunlight or a color photograph reveals him by comparison as a miserable dauber.

He pursues a visionary inspiration: to paint the solar eclipse that he had seen in Berlin fifteen years before. Landscape, animals, and humans were dominated by a colossal, overwhelming force, which becomes the subject of his painting. Hollrieder achieves an artistic breakthrough on perceiving that it is not only technique—how he paints—that is important but also what he paints, and that dissatisfaction with his own work is necessary for the continued growth of an artist. Looking at his painting at an exhibition, Hollrieder recognizes that the means will always remain insufficient; the means remain the x that precludes the complete identity of art and nature. The director of the art gallery observes with amusement that Hollrieder has realized for the first time that a painted tree is not one growing with its roots in the soil.

The drama is excessively long. The stage directions are so detailed that they read like the prose of a novel; gestures, movements, and facial expressions are rigorously prescribed. The score of the D Minor Quartet (1824-1826) of Franz Schubert is provided in the text, to be played on a harmonium before the curtain rises.

Holz teamed up with Jerschke once again to write *Büxl* (1911). Aloisius Büxl, a swaggering Alsatian womanizer and adventurer in the French Foreign Legion who speaks terrible German interlaced with fragments of French, is sentenced to death for murder. With the help of the prestigious attorney Moritz Oppenheimer, he gains a delay of execution by accusing his best friend, who has fled to America. He then engineers a sensational escape with the aid of his girlfriend and ensconces himself high on the cliffs in the hunting lodge of the playboy Prince Buzzi, where he is besieged by the police and military for five days. Taking with him some incriminating love letters he has discovered, Büxl escapes across the border to France in the prince's automobile.

Büxl is by now world famous. He saves the lives of eighty-seven passengers when he halts a train that is about to collide with his stalled car. Kept by a beautiful, rich Parisian actress, he contracts to write his memoirs; they are to appear in seven languages. He relinquishes the love letters to Buzzi for a princely sum; Oppenheimer's beautiful wife, Tia, acknowledges by her guilty expression—unnoticed by her husband—that she wrote them. The drama concludes as French officials enter to grant Büxl the Legion of Honor.

The anti-Semitism and antipathy toward the legal profession that find expression in *Frei!* are turned about here. The State's Attorney makes a deprecating remark about Jewish attorneys, but he is made to appear unfair. Moritz Oppenheimer is depicted in a positive light; he is ethical, highly respected, and moves among the socially elite.

Even after his successes with Jerschke, Holz continued to pour out a torrent of letters and requests for help, donations, and subscriptions. He was a relentless self-promoter, commercially as well as artistically, among publishers, theater directors, and especially among critics who were negatively disposed to him.

Returning to his dramatic cycle about Berlin at the end of an epoch, Holz wrote the immense and difficult work *Ignorabimus* (published, 1913; performed, 1927). In *Socialaristokraten* he had depicted the literary and political situation at the turn of the century; in *Sonnenfinsternis* he had dealt with art from the perspective of naturalism. *Ignorabimus* examines the phenomena of spiritualism. The cycle, originally planned to consist of twenty-four works, then twelve, amounted ultimately to only three.

Ignorabimus bears some of the features of the Schicksalstragödie (Fate Tragedy), a genre in the German Romantic tradition dating back to the late eighteenth century. Prominent motifs of the genre are hereditary sin, the murder of a relative, a familial curse or a dire prophecy. The atmosphere is one of horror and suspense. The action takes place in the course of a day in various rooms in the home of the rector of the Friedrich-Wilhelms University on the outskirts of Berlin. The number of characters on stage is confined to five; several offstage characters are alluded to, the most important of whom is dead.

"Ignorabimus" (We shall never know [everything]) was the motto of the nineteenth-century physiologist Emil du Bois-Reymond, who opposed the Darwinist Ernst Haeckel and the optimistic belief that science might solve the problems of mankind and the riddles of the universe. In Holz's play academic figures devote themselves to experiments in spiritualism, supernaturalism, and the occult. Marianne is a medium who summons presences from the other world, reads people's thoughts, and experiences strange forebodings. In séances spirits are conjured, messages are received from the beyond, and melodramatic extremes of passion unleashed—especially anger. Three years previously, Marianne's twin sister, Mariette, believing herself to have been betrayed by her sister and her husband, had an affair and then killed herself and her children. After her death Mariette appeared to her sister in a dream and told her that three years hence she would be claimed by Mariette for the world of the spirits. Today is the fatal anniversary: as midnight approaches, the sins of the family are recalled. Marianne dies; the future looks equally bleak for the husband, who refuses to promise the departing Marianne that he will not fight a duel with Mariette's former lover.

In the course of the development of Holz's dramatic cycle, the works became increasingly less suited to production on the stage. The stage directions became more detailed: in *Ignorabimus*, as characters recall how the present-day outskirts of the metropolis were once the destinations for day trips from the city for picnics and visits to the lakes, sounds from outside can be heard even in the innermost rooms of the house. The songs of birds and barking of dogs, hoofbeats from the horses pulling carts and carriages, and the sound of bicycle horns and automobiles indicate the urbanization of the rural scene. Sometimes the directions are amusing, as when they call for the offstage barking of a black dog, or the sound of a tugboat with the timbre of the Hamburg port. The pronunciation of vowels is prescribed, as is the intention behind the utterance of lines. Descriptions are provided of facial expressions and gestures.

Whereas in *Socialaristokraten* characters could be recognized by their speech patterns, in Holz's later plays the dialogue becomes uniform and undifferentiated. In keeping with his taste in lyric poetry, Holz developed lengthy dramatic passages in a parody of baroque style, with accumulations of synonyms and superlatives, complicated subordinate sentence structures, and unusual choices of images. *Ignorabimus* is more than four hundred pages long and requires eight hours to perform. Holz would not allow it to be shortened; consequently, it has only once been seen by an audience, in a 1927 production in Düsseldorf directed by Bertold Viertel and starring Louise Dumont.

In 1926 Holz divorced Emilie Barczus, whom he had married in 1893 and by whom he had had three sons, and married Anita Tilk, whom he had met in Strasbourg while visiting Jerschke. He died in Berlin on 26 October 1929. The seven-volume edition of his works published from 1961 to 1964 and the notes by one of the editors, Emrich, suggesting the modernity of Holz's lyrical vision, have sparked a revival of interest in the writer.

Letters:

Briefe: Eine Auswahl, edited by Anita Holz and Max Wagner (Munich: Piper, 1948);

Aus dem Briefwechsel mit Arno Holz und Ernst Barlach (Munich & Zurich: Piper, 1979);

Die Akte Arno Holz, edited by Alfred Klein (Berlin & Weimar: Aufbau, n.d.).

References:

Ernst Alker, "Arno Holz," in *Lexikon der deutschsprachigen Gegenwartsliteratur*, edited by Hermann Kunisch (Munich: Nymphenburger Verlagshandlung, 1987), pp. 265-267;

Walter Beimdick, "Arno Holz: Berlin. Die Wende einer Zeit in Dramen (Untersuchungen zu den Werken des Zyklusfragments)," Ph.D. dissertation, University of Münster, 1966;

J. W. McFarlane, "Arno Holz's *Die Sozialaristokraten:* A Study in Literary Collaboration," *Modern Language Review*, 44 (October 1949): 521-533;

Helmut Motekat, *Arno Holz: Persönlichkeit und Werk* (Kitzingen: Holzner, 1953);

Helmut Scheuer, *Arno Holz im literarischen Leben des ausgehenden 19. Jahrhunderts* (Munich: Winkler, 1971);

Gernot Schley, *Die Freie Bühne in Berlin* (Berlin: Haude & Spener, 1967);

Gerhard Schulz, *Arno Holz: Dilemma eines bürgerlichen Dichterlebens* (Munich: Beck, 1974).

Papers:

The archives of Arno Holz are in the Amerika-Gedenkbibliothek (American Memorial Library), Berlin, and the Staatsbibliothek der Stiftung Preußischer Kulturbesitz (State Library of the Foundation for Prussian Cultural Property), Berlin.

Franz Jung

(26 November 1888 - 21 January 1963)

H.-J. Schulz
Vanderbilt University

PLAY PRODUCTIONS: *Wie lange noch?*, Berlin, Proletarisches Theater, 6 February 1921;

Die Kanaker, Berlin, Proletarisches Theater, 28 March 1921;

Legende, Dresden, Staatstheater, 13 November 1927;

Heimweh, Berlin, Studio der Piscatorbühne, 8 January 1928.

BOOKS: *Das Trottelbuch* (Leipzig: Gerstenberg, 1912);

Kameraden. . . ! Ein Roman (Heidelberg: Weißbach, 1913);

Sophie: Der Kreuzweg der Demut. Ein Roman (Berlin-Wilmersdorf: Verlag der Wochenschrift Die Aktion, 1915);

Opferung: Ein Roman (Berlin-Wilmersdorf: Verlag der Wochenschrift Die Aktion, 1916);

Saul (Berlin-Wilmersdorf: Verlag der Wochenschrift Die Aktion, 1916);

Gnadenreiche, unsere Königin (Leipzig: Wolff, 1918);

Der Sprung aus der Welt: Ein Roman (Berlin-Wilmersdorf: Verlag der Wochenschrift Die Aktion, 1918);

Jehan (Mülheim an der Donau: Verlag der Saturne, 1919);

Reise in Rußland (Berlin: Verlag der K.A.P.D., 1920);

Joe Frank illustriert die Welt (Berlin-Wilmersdorf: Verlag der Wochenschrift Die Aktion, 1921);

Der Fall Gross: Novelle (Hamburg: Hanf, 1921);

Die Kanaker; Wie lange noch?: Zwei Schauspiele (Berlin: Malik, 1921);

Proletarier: Erzählung (Berlin: Malik, 1921);

Die Rote Woche: Roman. Mit 9 Zeichnungen von George Grosz (Berlin: Malik, 1921);

Die Technik des Glücks, 2 volumes (Berlin: Malik, 1921-1923);

Arbeitsfriede: Roman mit 6 Zeichnungen von George Grosz (Berlin: Malik, 1922);

Annemarie: Ein Schauspiel in vier Akten mit Vorspiel und Nachspiel (Berlin: Malik, 1922);

An die Arbeiterfront nach Sowjetrußland: Zum Produktionskampf der Klassen (Berlin: Vereinigung Internationaler Verlags-Anstalten, 1922);

Hunger an der Wolga (Berlin: Malik, 1922);

Die Eroberung der Maschinen: Roman (Berlin: Malik, 1923);

Mehr Tempo, Mehr Glück, Mehr Macht: Ein Taschenbuch für Jedermann (Berlin: Malik, 1923);

Die Geschichte einer Fabrik (Vienna: Verlag für Literatur und Politik, 1924);

Der neue Mensch im neuen Rußland: Rückblick über die erste Etappe proletarischer Erzählungskunst (Vienna: Verlag für Literatur und Politik, 1924);

Das geistige Rußland von heute (Berlin: Ullstein, 1924);

Geschäfte: Eine Komödie (Potsdam: Kiepenheuer, 1927);

Der verlorene Sohn: Schauspiel in vier Akten (Berlin: Kiepenheuer, 1928);

Hausierer: Gesellschaftskritischer Roman (Berlin: Verlag Der Bücherkreis, 1931);

Der Weg nach unten: Aufzeichnungen aus einer großen Zeit (Neuwied: Luchterhand, 1961); republished as *Der Torpedokäfer* (Neuwied: Luchterhand, 1972).

Collections and Editions: *Joe Frank illustriert die Welt*, edited by Walter Fähnders, Helga Karrenbrock, and Martin Rector (Darmstadt: Luchterhand, 1972);

Die Eroberung der Maschinen, edited by Fähnders, Karrenbrock, and Rector (Darmstadt: Luchterhand, 1973);

Gott verschläft die Zeit: Frühe Prosa, edited by Klaus Ramm (Munich: Edition text + kritik, 1976);

Der tolle Nikolaus: Prosa, Briefe, edited by Cläre M. Jung and Fritz Mierau (Leipzig: Reclam, 1980; Frankfurt am Main: Röderberg, 1981);

Schriften und Briefe: In zwei Bänden, 2 volumes, edited by Petra and Uwe Nettelbeck (Salzhausen: Nettelbeck, 1981);

Werke, 12 volumes, edited by Lutz Schulenburg and others (Hamburg: Edition Nautilus, 1981-1991).

OTHER: *Die Revolution*, 1, no. 5, edited by Jung (1913);

Die Freie Straße, 1-6 (1915-1918);

Jack London: Ein Dichter der Arbeiterklasse, edited by Jung (Vienna: Verlag für Literatur und Politik, 1924);

"Das Erbe," in *Das Vier-Männer-Buch* by Max Barthel, Franz Jung, Adam Scharrer, and Oskar Wöhrle (Berlin: Bücherkreis, 1929), pp. 115-187;

Der Gegner, 1-3, edited by Jung (1931-1932);

"Die neue Bühnentechnik und ihr Einfluß auf das Schauspiel der Zukunft," in *Die Welt im Fortschritt*, volume 1 (Berlin: Herbig, 1935), pp. 129-175;

Ernst Fuhrmann, *Grundformen des Lebens: Biologisch-philosophische Schriften*, edited by Jung (Heidelberg: Schneider, 1962);

Heimweh, in *Spectaculum: Acht moderne Theaterstücke* (Frankfurt am Main: Suhrkamp, 1977), pp. 69-96;

"Von geschlechtlicher Not zur sozialen Katastrophe," in *Von geschlechtlicher Not zur sozialen Katastrophe*, by Otto Gross, edited by Kurt Kreiler (Frankfurt am Main: Robinson, 1980), pp. 125-148.

SELECTED PERIODICAL PUBLICATION—
UNCOLLECTED: "Puppenspiel," *Der Sturm*, 2 (1911-1912): 750.

Although Franz Jung did not identify with any of the literary movements of his time, his early prose works were hailed as major contributions to the literature of expressionism, and his plays and novels of the early 1920s set new standards for political theater and proletarian fiction. His literary work as a whole, however, embodies a revolutionary stance and an aesthetic which transcend the ideologies and literary styles of his age.

Jung was born on 26 November 1888 in Neisse (now Nysa) in Upper Silesia to Franz Josef Jung, a watchmaker, city councilman, amateur composer, and dramatist, and Clara Döhring Jung. After his graduation from the local gymnasium in 1907 Jung halfheartedly studied law and economics at the Universities of Leipzig, Jena, Breslau, and Munich, failing to complete a dissertation in economics. Between 1909 and 1915 he developed the unconventional life-style that he

was to maintain until his death: he experienced financial success as an insurance agent, economic journalist, and entrepreneur; and yet he believed in political anarchism, led a turbulent domestic life, and suffered financial destitution; his literary creativity came usually in short bursts, often while he was in prison for revolutionary activities. In 1909 he married Margot Rhein, a nightclub dancer, with whom he had a son, Frank, and a daughter, Dagny; their destructive relationship is one of the main themes of his prose until 1915. His second marriage, to Cläre Öhring, was childless. In 1912 he became a member of "Gruppe Tat" (Group Deed), the writer Erich Mühsam's circle of anarchists in Munich, and began his friendship with Otto Gross, an anarchist psychoanalyst. An army volunteer at the outbreak of World War I, he deserted after the battle of Tannenberg in 1914, was imprisoned, and was temporarily confined to a mental institution.

Jung's first book, *Das Trottelbuch* (The Book of Fools, 1912), was both a scandal and a critical success. It attracted the attention of Franz Pfemfert, editor of the journal *Die Aktion* (Action) and leader of a circle of revolutionary expressionists. Since many of Jung's subsequent works were published in the monograph series of *Die Aktion*, they came to be seen as a radical form of expressionist prose. Jung, however, went considerably beyond the innovations of his expressionist contemporaries. His early works, ironically called "Romane" (novels) or "Erzählungen" (stories), systematically subvert the principles of traditional narration and representation. They consist of repeated encounters of extreme emotional intensity, usually between a man and a woman; indecipherable parables; scenes of meaningless activity; and caustic tauntings of the reader. These works do not convey a sense of causality, individuality, milieu, or time, nor do they have a reliable narrative voice; their aim is not to represent a recognizable reality but to evoke through a rhythm of occurrences and intense emotions a deeper rhythm or "tempo" of existence, of a possible unalienated human life and communality. This utopian communal life is seldom positively present in Jung's work; its absence is felt through the intense suffering that comes with the recurring defeats of this ideal. Jung rejected the depiction of individual action and historical events in favor of an orchestration of rhythm, emotion, and atmosphere intended to energize the reader, not trigger rational cognitive processes.

Like many of the democratic intellectuals of his time, Jung became a political activist at the end of the war. He participated in revolutionary activities and joined the newly formed Communist party. Since Jung was an anarchist and believed in spontaneous actions of the masses as the proper form of revolution, he opposed the organizational control of the party. He was therefore dropped from its ranks and helped organize the radical Communist Workers party. To plead for admission of the new party into the Third Communist International, Jung—whose passport had been withdrawn—hijacked a fishing trawler to the Soviet Union. Advised by Lenin and others to seek a reconciliation between the two communist parties, Jung clandestinely returned to Germany, attempted such a reconciliation without success, and left the Communist Workers party. He remained allied with leftist organizations and supported them with propaganda and revolutionary actions. Arrested for the hijacking, he wrote many of his key proletarian works in prison.

Critics generally feel that Jung's conversion to political radicalism led to a break with the ideology and style of his earlier works, since he turned from what was seen as a concern with existential questions of the individual to a concern with the proletariat and its revolutionary struggle. The success of his proletarian writings, his association with Wieland Herzfelde's communist Malik publishing house, as well as his faithful representations of proletarian life do indicate a shift, but it is one to a new audience rather than to a new aesthetic. Jung turned to the proletariat as the most disadvantaged class, a group whose intense suffering had made it susceptible to the deep communal rhythms that he had evoked in his earlier writings. As his essays during these years show, Jung was not a Marxist, and he did not conceive of the class struggle as anything more than a symptom of a deeper struggle for communal experience and happiness. But since the novels and plays of this period were also meant as weapons in the specific social and economic battles of the day, they are informed by a tension between the ideology of the workers' movement—a materialist concept of social and economic progress and a historical utopianism—and a vitalist utopianism that, he thought, can be felt in the very texture of human experience.

In the German workers' movement, theater—especially as institutionalized in the socialist "Volksbühne" (popular theater) movement—had been a source of cultural education, but no prole-

tarian drama had been developed. When Jung's *Wie lange noch?* (How Much Longer?, 1921) and *Die Kanaker* (The Kanakas, 1921) were performed at Erwin Piscator's Proletarian Theater in early 1921, theater as an instrument of political consciousness-raising and agitation suddenly seemed possible. The plays were acclaimed in the socialist press as a new beginning of proletarian literature and were given special performances for political organizations and in factories—*Wie lange noch?* in Halle in fall 1921, *Die Kanaker* in a circus tent in Hamburg in May 1923 under the direction of Gustav von Wangenheim. Jung's plays, like all of his proletarian works, abandon a central character in favor of a group hero: he succeeds extremely well in presenting distinct individuals with their mixed motivations and hesitations, and at the same time assimilating them into a group character struggling for solidarity and identity in the fight against, and inevitable defeat by, the state. The failed uprisings are then used, in direct addresses to the audience, to demonstrate the need for solidarity. These direct appeals, which permitted interaction between actors and spectators, had—judging by contemporary accounts—a tremendous effect on the proletarian audience. "Durus" (Alfréd Keményi), the critic for the Communist party daily *Rote Fahne* (Red Flag), felt that in *Die Kanaker* Jung had achieved a new synthesis of art and propaganda—not by way of explicit didacticism but by convincing the spectators that everything that happened on stage concerned them directly. Jung's plays introduced the proletarian world as a scene of dramatic action, portrayed the proletariat as a dramatic and political agent, and suggested changing the theater from a place of passive reception to one of social interaction and community building.

What was not readily perceived by contemporary socialist critics was that Jung's plays neither advocate nor portray the class struggle in terms of organizational procedures and the rational tactics of "mastering" and accelerating a historical movement toward a classless society; rather, they emphasize defeat, suffering, and the spontaneous awakening of a communal vitality. This tension between portraying historical processes and an appeal to a utopian ideal becomes apparent in Jung's last proletarian drama, *Annemarie* (1922). Jung contrasts a group of capitalists with a suffering, inarticulate, combative, and finally defeated group of miners. The miners' growing solidarity is not primarily a form of political awareness but a quasi-religious communalization of suffering individuals. Their defeat, therefore, bears the marks of necessary martyrdom, of a sacrifice that invokes a paradisiacal other world. Jung gives a glimpse of this other world in a "Nachspiel" (postlude) to the play: it does not appear as the product of historical and political processes (processes long forgotten by its happy inhabitants) but as an ahistorical idyll of archaic communality. This idyll of simple vital rhythms does not stand at the end of class history as its necessary fulfillment; it is the projection of a timeless ideal. *Annemarie* was scheduled to be performed by the Volksbühne on Piscator's recommendation, but the production was canceled when Piscator withdrew from the organization.

In 1921 Jung had been arrested twice for revolutionary activities, the second time in Breda, Holland. Since he had acquired Soviet citizenship, the Dutch government permitted him to go to the Soviet Union, where he held various positions; he was particularly successful as the manager of two industrial installations. He left in November 1923, in part because he considered himself a victim of intrigues and bureaucratic incompetence; his enthusiasm for the Bolshevik revolution had waned considerably.

In his notes to *Annemarie* Jung rejected realistic representation, stressing atmosphere, rhythm, and a varied tempo. These remarks indicate a new conception of theater which Jung elaborated in several essays between 1927 and 1935 and attempted to realize in such plays as *Legende* (Legend, 1927) and *Heimweh* (Nostalgia, 1928). *Legende* was produced by Josef Gielen on 13 November 1927 at the Staatstheater (State Theater) in Dresden but was never published. In this play Jung radically deemphasizes plot and dialogue in favor of a rhythmicized atmosphere; the action has a counterpoint in the form of a film which is used not as background but as an integral part of the play. The portrayal of a deprived family's existence, the wife's killing of the husband, and her trial are used as catalysts for emotional explosions; the explosions, rather than the events depicted, are the focus of the play.

Heimweh is Jung's most concerted attempt to "deconstruct" the primacy and continuity of dramatic action. The play has no plot; its theme, nostalgia, is sounded in the vague and discontinuous dialogues of characters in a bar, on a tropical island, and again in the bar, but it is not presented primarily in verbal and dramatic action: Jung orchestrates all components of the theatrical

experience—language, vocal modulation, sound effects, silences, gestures, space, music, light, color, dance, and film—in a synesthetic "happening" that is to involve the audience in a communal rhythm. *Heimweh* was performed on 8 January 1928 on the experimental stage of Piscator's theater in Berlin. Jung had been promised a free hand as producer, but when some of his more radical ideas, such as foreign-language dialogue and circus numbers interspersed into the action, were vetoed, he walked out. A watered-down version, directed by Leonhard Steckel, was performed. The play was a failure, despite the set by John Heartfield and the music of Hanns Eisler, two of Piscator's most successful collaborators. Jung's intentions were not understood by his coproducers, the actors, or the critics; the play appeared to Piscator and others to be a technical experiment devoid of political intentions. Jung was being judged by the standards of his proletarian plays, but by this time he had pushed his attempt to vitalize the audience to what he considered a fundamental anthropological level, a level on which the primary cultic function of drama could be realized: that of inducing communal experience. The spectators who entered the theater as individuals were to leave it as a community. This conception of theater departed sharply from the Aristotelian aesthetics of representation and catharsis favored by socialist writers and theorists. Jung did not intend to *represent* communal action but to *induce* communality in the audience, and he hoped that a synesthetically orchestrated rhythm would have the hypnotic power to do so.

How strong and consistent this hope was is doubtful: two unperformed plays from this period, *Geschäfte* (Business, 1927) and *Der verlorene Sohn* (The Prodigal Son, 1928), have neither the intense political argument of his proletarian plays nor the synesthetic rhythm of *Heimweh*. *Geschäfte* consists of a series of dialogues between people whose business transactions can be seen as life and whose lives can be seen as business. Jung here attempts to exploit a grammar of verbal and nonverbal gestures, to create a business atmosphere as a paradigm of modern human relations. *Der verlorene Sohn* is a Pirandellesque playing with reality and appearance: the long-lost son who returns is a fraud, but the illusion has the power to shape reality. But Jung pushed beyond Luigi Pirandello's reality/illusion paradox: he wanted the play to be staged, he wrote in his autobiography, *Der Weg nach unten* (The Way Down, 1961), as a free-floating dialogue that contained nothing but an atmosphere of nothingness. Jung's highly experimental plays have completely disappeared from German stages.

Jung was arrested several times by German and Hungarian authorities during the Nazi years and was freed by the American army from a concentration camp in Bozen, Italy, in 1945. He spent the years 1948 to 1959 in the United States as an economics correspondent for several German newspapers and returned to Europe in 1960 to resume his literary career. The Germany of the economic miracle, however, was not susceptible to Jung's brand of utopianism. A rediscovery of Jung was triggered by the publication of his autobiography in 1961. He died on 21 January 1963 in Stuttgart.

References:

Armin Arnold, "Franz Jung," in his *Prosa des Expressionismus: Herkunft, Analyse, Inventar* (Stuttgart: Kohlhammer, 1972), pp. 57-107, 192-193;

Horst Denkler, "Der Fall Franz Jung: Beobachtungen zur Vorgeschichte der 'Neuen Sachlichkeit,'" in *Die sogenannten Zwanziger Jahre: First Wisconsin Workshop*, edited by Reinhold Grimm and Jost Hermand (Bad Homburg, Berlin & Zurich: Gehlen, 1970), pp. 75-108;

Walter Fähnders, "Proletarisches Theater 1919-1921," *Alternative*, 14 (1976): 25-32;

Arnold Imhof, *Franz Jung: Leben, Werk, Wirkung* (Bonn: Bouvier, 1974);

Werner Jung, "Der rasende Torpedokäfer: Ein biographisches und literarisches Portrait Franz Jungs," *Kürbiskern*, 3 (1983): 104-125;

Franz Loquai, "Politik auf der Bühne: Zum Verhältnis von politischem Bewußtsein und literarischer Tätigkeit bei Franz Jung," *Recherches germaniques*, 10 (1980): 156-182;

Harald Maier-Metz, *Expressionismus—Dada—Agitprop: Zur Entwicklung des Malik-Kreises in Berlin 1912-1924* (Frankfurt am Main, Bern, New York & Nancy: Lang, 1984);

Franz Norbert Mennemeier, "Paukenschlag-Ästhetik und utopische Idylle (Franz Jung)," in his *Modernes deutsches Drama* (Munich: Fink, 1979), pp. 205-212;

Theo Meyer, "Revolte und Resignation: Eine Analyse von Franz Jungs 'Torpedokäfer,'" *Jahrbuch der deutschen Schiller-Gesellschaft*, 23 (1979): 416-467;

Erwin Piscator, *Das politische Theater* (Reinbek: Rowohlt, 1963);

Martin Rector, "Franz Jungs literarische Arbeiten der 'roten Jahre,'" in *Linksradikalismus und Literatur: Untersuchungen zur Geschichte der sozialistischen Literatur in der Weimarer Republik*, by Rector and Fähnders (Reinbek: Rowohlt, 1974), I: 160-220;

Wolfgang Rieger, *Glückstechnik und Lebensnot: Leben und Werk Franz Jungs* (Freiburg: Ca-Ira-Verlag, 1987);

Rieger, "Der Torpedokäfer: Bemerkungen zu Franz Jung und seiner Wiederentdeckung," in *Stichtag der Barbarei: Anmerkungen zur Bücherverbrennung*, edited by Nils Schiffhauer and Carola Schelle (Hannover: Postskriptum, 1983), pp. 64-77;

Bärbel Schrader, "Wegstücke zur sozialistischen Literatur: Zum Leben und Schaffen von Franz und Cläre Jung," *Weimarer Beiträge*, 24, no. 11 (1978): 69-83.

Papers:

The main Franz Jung archive is in the Märkisches Museum, Berlin; additional papers are in the "Teilnachlaß" Franz Jung, Bockenem, and in the Deutsches Zentralarchiv (German Central Archiv), Potsdam.

Paul Kornfeld

(11 December 1889 - 25 April 1942)

Stephen Shearier
Muhlenberg College

PLAY PRODUCTIONS: *Die Verführung*, Frankfurt am Main, Schauspielhaus, 8 December 1917;

Himmel und Hölle, Berlin, Deutsches Theater, 21 April 1920;

Der ewige Traum, Frankfurt am Main, Schauspielhaus, 20 January 1923;

Palme oder Der Gekränkte, Berlin, Kammerspiele, 11 March 1924;

Kilian oder Die gelbe Rose, Frankfurt am Main, Schauspielhaus, 6 November 1926;

Impresario von Smyrna, Darmstadt, Landestheater, 18 February 1928;

Jud Süß, Berlin, Theater am Schiffbauerdamm, 7 October 1930.

BOOKS: *Die Verführung: Eine Tragödie in fünf Akten* (Berlin: Fischer, 1916);

Legende (Berlin: Fischer, 1917);

Himmel und Hölle: Eine Tragödie in fünf Akten und einem Epilog (Berlin: Fischer, 1919);

Der ewige Traum: Eine Komödie (Berlin: Rowohlt, 1922);

Palme oder Der Gekränkte: Eine Komödie in fünf Akten (Berlin: Rowohlt, 1924);

Sakuntala: Schauspiel in fünf Akten nach Kalidasa (Berlin: Rowohlt, 1925);

Kilian oder Die gelbe Rose: Eine Komödie in drei Akten (Berlin: Rowohlt, 1926);

Smither kauft Europa: Komödie in fünf Akten (Berlin: Oesterheld, 1928);

Jud Süß: Tragödie mit Epilog (Berlin: Oesterheld, 1930);

Blanche oder Das Atelier im Garten: Roman (Hamburg: Rowohlt, 1957).

OTHER: "Kokoschka," in program for the premiere of *Mörder, Hoffnung der Frauen*; *Hiob*; and *Der brennende Dornbusch*, by Oskar Kokoschka, Dresden, Albert-Theater, 3 June 1917.

Paul Kornfeld

SELECTED PERIODICAL PUBLICATIONS— UNCOLLECTED: "Der beseelte und der psychologische Mensch," *Das junge Deutschland*, 1, no. 1 (1918): 1-13;

"Wedekind," *Das junge Deutschland*, 1, no. 4 (1918): 99-100;

"Theater in Frankfurt," *Das junge Deutschland*, 1, no. 6 (1918): 202-204;

"Gerechtigkeit: Ein Fragment," *Jahrbuch für neue Dichtung und Wertung: Die Erhebung*, 2 (1920): 313-318;

"Forschungsreise ins innerste Darmstadt," *Das Tage-Buch*, 9, no. 36 (1928): 1497-1503;

"Der Roman der Durieux," *Das Tage-Buch*, 9, no. 37 (1928): 1549;

"Ein Zeuge des Staatsanwalts," *Das Tage-Buch*, 9, no. 44 (1928): 1850-1854;

"Der bestrafte Querulant," *Das Tage-Buch*, 9, no. 47 (1928): 1990-1995;

"Die Buchkritik," *Das Tage-Buch*, 10, no. 12 (1929): 562-566;

"Arnold Bronnen als Femesänger," *Das Tage-Buch*, 10, no. 25 (1929): 829-831;

"Der Bandit," *Das Tage-Buch*, 10, no. 28 (1929): 1160-1164;

"Schupo im Gerichtssaal," *Das Tage-Buch*, 10, no. 29 (1929): 1195-1198;

"Hamsun," *Das Tage-Buch*, 10, no. 31 (1929): 1282-1285;

"Der Schlauch," *Das Tage-Buch*, 10, no. 36 (1929): 1476-1478;

"Politisches Theater," *Das Tage-Buch*, 10, no. 37 (1929): 1519-1523;

"Der Gesichtspunkt," *Das Tage-Buch*, 10, no. 39 (1929): 1591-1593;

"Kochkunst," *Das Tage-Buch*, 10, no. 42 (1929): 1747-1750;

"Hermann Ungar," *Das Tage-Buch*, 10, no. 44 (1929): 1839-1840;

"Liebesromane," *Das Tage-Buch*, 10, no. 49 (1929): 2103-2108;

"Der Intendant," *Das Tage-Buch*, 10, no. 2 (1930): 56-57;

"Julien Green," *Das Tage-Buch*, 11, no. 4 (1930): 149-151;

"Das Dritte Reich," *Das Tage-Buch*, 11, no. 7 (1930): 272-274;

"Babbits Frau," *Das Tage-Buch*, 11, no. 10 (1930): 382-384;

"Die Entdeckung," *Das Tage-Buch*, 11, no. 11 (1930): 423-426;

"Die Geheimkonferenz," *Das Tage-Buch*, 11, no. 12 (1930): 461-465;

"Ein Statistiker im Südenpfuhl," *Das Tage-Buch*, 11, no. 13 (1930): 499-503;

"So ist die Welt," *Das Tage-Buch*, 11, no. 15 (1930): 589-591;

"Der Ästhet macht Weltrevolution," *Das Tage-Buch*, 11, no. 15 (1930): 596-597;

"Sport," *Das Tage-Buch*, 11, no. 17 (1930): 667-672;

"Kapitulation," *Das Tage-Buch*, 11, no. 22 (1930): 862-868;

"Ein Tonfilm," *Das Tage-Buch*, 12, no. 7 (1931): 256-258;

"Die Sektion für Dichtkunst," *Das Tage-Buch*, 12, no. 8 (1931): 304-307;

"Turnlehrer Loch," *Das Tage-Buch*, 12, no. 12 (1931): 459-463;

"Revolution mit Flötenmusik," *Das Tage-Buch*, 12, no. 19 (1931): 736-742;

"Die Todesstrafe," *Das Tage-Buch*, 12, no. 21 (1931): 815-818;

"Ungars Nachlaß," *Das Tage-Buch*, 12, no. 24 (1931): 945-946;

"Das Interessante," *Das Tage-Buch*, 12, no. 29 (1931): 1137-1142;

"Antwort an einen Photographen," *Das Tage-Buch*, 12, no. 30 (1931): 1181-1184;

"Philosophie der Barbarei," *Das Tage-Buch*, 12, no. 34 (1931): 1336-1341;

"Multifix und Schwenkkartei," *Das Tage-Buch*, 12, no. 37 (1931): 1453-1456;

"Ein Lebensbuch," *Das Tage-Buch*, 12, no. 41 (1931): 1597-1601.

In the remarkable constellation of literary personalities, including Franz Kafka, Franz Werfel, Max Brod, Rainer Maria Rilke, Egon Erwin Kisch, and Gustav Meyrink, that was known collectively as the Prague Circle, Paul Kornfeld, if not the most celebrated, was one of the most seminal of thinkers and for a brief period one of the most popular writers. In 1920, when his reputation was at its zenith, Kornfeld was the most discussed author in the German language next to Georg Kaiser and Carl Sternheim. At that time he had been writing for only a few years and had three plays and a handful of essays to his credit. Albeit short-lived, Kornfeld's fame was based equally on his theoretical and practical contributions to expressionist aesthetics, particularly in the area of drama. Of particular importance for historians of drama is his notion of ecstatic dramatic art. The theory was set forth in his essay "Der beseelte und der psychologische Mensch" (The Soulful and the Psychological Individual, 1918) and was realized in practice in his plays, particularly *Die Verführung* (The Seduction; published, 1916; performed, 1917) and *Himmel und Hölle* (Heaven and Hell; published, 1919; performed, 1920).

Kornfeld was born in Prague on 11 December 1889 into a family that was successful in commercial enterprise and placed great value on intelligence, knowledge, and philosophy. Kornfeld's great-grandfather, Ahron Kornfeld, was one of the most noted Talmudists in the Hapsburg Empire and the director of a well-known yeshiva in Golc-Jenikau. Kornfeld's father, Moriz, the proprietor of a Prague textile firm, was respected for his knowledge of philosophy, poetry, and Jewish theology.

Given this background, it is no surprise that Kornfeld's intellectual interests developed early. When his brother, an aspiring writer, died in 1905, he made a vow to carry on for him. As a pupil in the seventh class at the Gymnasium am Stephansplatz (University Preparatory School at Saint Stephen's Square) in Prague, where his fellow pupils included Werfel and Willy Haas, both of whom would go on to become noted writers, Kornfeld wrote fairy tales and submitted them to publishers. When these youthful efforts were rejected, the fledgling poet became lost in despair, an emotional state that would weigh upon Kornfeld throughout his life. Attempts to distance himself from his early failures resulted in complaints about his family's and his school companions' disregard of his talent. Self-pity reinforced his belief that he was "different" and may have contributed to the philosophy of transcendence he developed later in life.

Kornfeld rejected his father's demand that he study chemistry to prepare himself to enter the family textile business, a demand he considered tradition-bound, petit bourgeois, and unworthy of a thinking person. Despite this discord with his father, Kornfeld always referred lovingly to him in his diary and ignored the expressionist theme of the generational conflict in his dramas, where the expressionist authoritarian father is replaced by a hesitating, indecisive one. His mother, about whom little is known, was rarely mentioned, and then only in a negative context. This attitude is exceptional for Prague and for Jewish literary circles in general; it reflects a largely negative image of women that can be seen in several of his dramas.

Like his friends Kafka, Werfel, and Brod, over whom he exercised tremendous influence—especially through the séances he conducted with them at the Unicorn Pharmacy during the second decade of the 1900s—Kornfeld was interested in Jewish mysticism and was knowledgeable about the cabala. Unlike other members of the Prague Circle, however, he rarely discussed Judaism and took little interest in his ethnic background or in the idea of Zionism. Kornfeld also

steered clear of polemics and rejected politics in favor of art. Together with Werfel, Kornfeld became one of the leading representatives of the "anti-activist" position among the expressionists.

Like many other Jewish thinkers from the Hapsburg Empire, such as Hugo von Hofmannsthal, Edmund Husserl, Ludwig Wittgenstein, and Fritz Mauthner, Kornfeld developed a philosophical system that combines phenomenology and the aesthetics of impressionism. He wrote that only through continuous effort and investigation can "das Wahre" (the true) be discovered. His examination of the spiritual, emotional, and psychological aspects of his dramatic characters attests to his phenomenological or impressionistic method.

Kornfeld's first play, *Die Verführung*, written in 1913, premiered on 8 December 1917 at the Schauspielhaus (Playhouse) in Frankfurt am Main under the direction of Hans Hartung, with set designs by Conrad Felixmüller. The production, with Jakob Feldhammer and Fritta Brod in the lead roles, was a popular success, and Julius Bab and other critics felt that it was one of the most important events of the season. Having gone through five editions by 1921, it is probably Kornfeld's most influential play; it is considered, along with Reinhard Johannes Sorge's *Der Bettler* (The Beggar, 1912), to have introduced the expressionist movement in drama. The primary focus of this tragedy is the possibility of eternal friendship and love, a concern expressed in the essay "Der beseelte und der psychologische Mensch," whose main themes appeared in an afterword to the published version of the play under the title "An den Schauspieler" (To the Actor). The main figure, Bitterlich, falls at his sister's feet, declares his love for her, and attempts to embrace her. When the girl's fiancé, Josef, enters the room Bitterlich, who despises Josef's bourgeois nature, insults him, pushes him out of the room, and strangles him in the antechamber. Bitterlich arrogates the right to kill simply because he abhors a person. In his constant attempt to gratify his overblown ego he is undone by the tragic flaw of hubris. He flees with a woman named Ruth Vogelfrei and is killed by Ruth's brother, Wilhelm. One detects in Kornfeld's first drama typical expressionist elements such as suffering, the primal scream, the call for change, and hate of the secular world, of money, and of satiety. The distortion of reality through exaggeration as in a dream, where wish becomes deed and feeling becomes event, is also typically expressionist. The incorporation of dream conscious-

Sketch by F. K. Delavilla of the scene from the 1917 premiere of Kornfeld's Die Verführung *in which Bitterlich strangles his sister's fiancé (University of Cologne)*

ness remains fundamental throughout Kornfeld's oeuvre.

In 1916 Kornfeld left Prague for Frankfurt am Main. In Frankfurt he wrote his most influential work, "Der beseelte und der psychologische Mensch," which exemplifies in several respects the thinking of the expressionist generation. The premise of this influential work is that capitalism, with its presumed philosophy of competition and war, has brought about a catastrophic dehumanization process. Kornfeld promulgates transcendence as the only means to rediscover and salvage the essence of humanity, which he calls "die Seele" (the soul), and he suggests art as the appropriate avenue to transcendence. To art he delegates the monumental responsibility of leading humanity out of chaos. For him the highest of all art forms is the drama, which has the best possibility of offering models for humanity. Conventional theater persisted in the attempt to duplicate the surface, as opposed to the essence, of reality; the modern theater, according to Kornfeld, is to be self-conscious, to be aware of and even to draw attention to its artifice. The actor is to be nothing but a representative of thought, feelings, or fate; he or she is not to speak onstage as he or she speaks in ordinary life

and is not to pretend to reproduce reality. This call on the actor to go beyond "Natürlichkeit" (naturalness) to represent nature is the most poignant programmatic statement of expressionist aesthetics for the theater. The expressionist acting style, as found in exemplary works from this period such as Sorge's *Der Bettler* and Walter Hasenclever's *Der Sohn* (The Son, 1914), bears the indelible imprint of Kornfeld's aesthetic program.

Himmel und Hölle, Kornfeld's second drama, directed by Ludwig Berger in cooperation with the playwright and with sets designed by Rudolf Bamberger, premiered on 21 April 1920 at the Deutsches Theater (German Theater) in Berlin. Despite a stellar cast including Werner Krauß, Lina Lossen, Agnes Straub, and Paul Günther, the production was not a popular success and ran for only three performances. The dramatic realization of the theory laid out in his essay, the play met with a mixed reception by critics. Bab and Siegfried Jacobsohn felt that it spoke for an entire generation; but others, employing adjectives often used by opponents of expressionist drama, argued that the play was inherently undramatic or even antidramatic. Nevertheless, it went on to be produced in Frankfurt am Main, where it opened on 12 January 1922.

Count Ungeheuer, filled with self-hatred because his pride prevents him from showing his wife the affection she longs for, has invited the execrable prostitute Maria to live with him. The lowliest, most pitiable creature imaginable, Maria, like the Mother of God after whom she is named, is the redeemer, since she serves as the catalyst for deliverance from the horrors of the material world. When the tormented countess kills her own daughter, Maria, who desires death, claims responsibility for the deed. To join Maria in the afterworld her companion, Johanna, commits a murder so that she too may be condemned to death. The two are executed and are promptly joined by the count and countess, who also passionately yearned for the afterlife. The destructiveness of earthly existence is thus "overcome" by death. Jacob, the playwright's mouthpiece for his philosophy of transcendence, indefatigably urges all to join together in mass suicide.

Perhaps Kornfeld's happiest period was his marriage to Fritta Brod, whom he wed in 1919. During this marriage, which ended in divorce in 1926, he wrote three comedies and a "Schauspiel" (play—significantly, not a tragedy), as well as many essays. His first comedy, *Der ewige Traum* (The Eternal Dream; published, 1922), premiered on 20 January 1923 at the Schauspielhaus in Frankfurt am Main. The action takes place on two levels, represented by two stages. On the first stage intellectuals disjointedly ramble about ideological doctrines in a clubroom. Intellectual enlightenment, poetry, social responsibility, the family, Christianity, Buddhism, and socialism are hotly debated. The primary focus, however, is the definition of love. Suddenly, a voice offstage discredits this intellectual claptrap by stating that everything is garbage. Another offstage voice declares that man is on the threshold of a new age, while a third voice exclaims, "Liebe! Liebe!" (Love! Love!). A second stage then becomes visible, where a gesticulating speaker addresses an assembly of white-clothed girls and asserts that Nature and Reason struggle for existence and that the first commandment for women is to bear children.

In the next scene a group of older men engages a group of younger men in dialogue. Franz, the radical who thumbs his nose at justice, argues that only freedom, which he defines as individualism, is important. Carolus mentions the new ordinances governing sexual practices and declares his plan to bribe someone in the government so that he may mate with Anna. The scene changes to a room where Anna is being dressed by an old woman. Envious, the old woman asks what she might give Anna in order to be allowed to listen in on her mating. When Carolus enters and declares his love, Anna is filled with skepticism. In the following scenes it is revealed that the four-month union between Anna and Carolus has resulted in her extreme unhappiness and his ecstasy. Anna wants to die, while Carolus wants to be with her forever. Then, in a courtroom, a psychiatrist's assertion that Carolus must be imprisoned because he has fallen in love unleashes loud protests from the spectators.

A revolution follows, in which the crowd carries a banner with a red heart on a white background. One speaker calls for sexual freedom, while another states the need to deal with social questions. The mob cries, "Es lebe Carolus! Es lebe das erste Ehepaar!" (Long live Carolus! Long live the first married couple!) and "Hoch Anna! Es lebe die Liebe! Es lebe das Herz!" (Here's to Anna! Love lives! The heart lives!). A group of children shouts, "Nieder mit der Regierung! Hoch die Ehe!" (Down with government! Up with marriage!). Carolus and Anna reject revolution, claiming that they had no intention of changing society, that they cannot save humanity, and that they simply want to make each other happy. The play ends, as it began, in the clubroom, where there is heated discussion about the collective versus the individual. Some suggest that the family is to be nurtured to prevent war. One group, echoing the expressionist program, wants to disseminate posters with the simple message: "Menscheit!" (Humanity!). The president of the "Klub der geistigen Revolutionäre" (Club of Intellectual Revolutionaries) has the last word: he calms the contentious factions by announcing that the next meeting will pick up where this one left off. The "dream" is "eternal": there is no resolution, no utopia.

Palme oder Der Gekränkte (Palme; or, The Vexed One; published, 1924), Kornfeld's second comedy, premiered on 11 March 1924 at the Kammerspiele (Intimate Theater) of the Deutsches Theater in Berlin. Clara, a widow, stresses the need to transcend war and revolution; she argues that one should devote one's attention to more modest affairs and should smile, play, and laugh. Lauber, seeking to spoil her mood, warns Clara that Palme, whom she plans to marry, is not only too young and too poor for her but that he intends to marry her daughter, Helene. At this point Palme, the hypersensitive and unhappy embodiment of the tension between the longing for and the fear of love, enters and is embraced by Clara. It is clear that they are in love. Helene's reputation is not without blemish; Lauber believes her to be a whore, and Palme calls her "eien Bestie, ein Tiger, eine Hexe, Satan" (a beast, a tiger, a witch, Satan). But when she writes a letter to him in which she declares her love, Palme is convinced that Helene is an angel. These newfound feelings are quickly dashed when she leaves with Kimmich, one of Palme's rivals. In utter despair, Palme delivers a lengthy monologue about the evils of the world. When Clara enters, Palme accuses her of never having loved him and of having lied with every word, every kiss, every embrace. The play closes with Lauber's absurdly megalomaniacal monologue on how lucky Helene would be if he were to marry her. It is difficult to comprehend Kornfeld's reason for calling this work a comedy; *Palme* virtually cries out in despair.

Kornfeld's Schauspiel, *Sakuntala*, was published in 1925 but was never produced. The mythological play in prose and verse was inspired by Kornfeld's reading of an English version of an ancient Indian legend. King Duschmanta, who controls all the Earth surrounded by water, and Sakuntala, the daughter of a king and a heavenly nymph, are instructed to return to Earth, where they are to find and love one another. Thus, Kornfeld inverts the plot of *Himmel und Hölle*.

Kilian oder Die gelbe Rose (Kilian; or, the Yellow Rose, published, 1926), Kornfeld's third comedy and most successful play, premiered on 6 November 1926 at the Schauspielhaus in Frankfurt am Main under Richard Weichert's direction. The play begins with Erika expressing her longing for nightfall and "die Entfaltung der Kräfte" (the unleashing of powers) when she can give herself to dreams. Members of the intellectual circle led by Frau Samson, Erika's mother, begin to arrive. They are anticipating a visit from "der Meister" (the Master). Countess Ziegelturm, declaring her enthusiasm for the ideal of the "Übermensch" (Superman), another name for the eagerly anticipated guest, states that after reading all of the Master's experiences, she is unable to have any of her own. Julius, also excited by the guest's impending visit, is a former student who has given up his studies because he felt that his teachers offered him mere facts and nothing

Scene from a 1927 Berlin production of Kornfeld's comedy Kilian oder Die gelbe Rose

of the secrets and wonders of life. Schiroga, a fifty-year-old man who has seen life from many perspectives, claims that he has mystical experiences. For tonight's meeting he has brought his own bottle "um das körperliche Auge zu töten und das innere Auge zu erwecken" (in order to deaden the bodily eye and to awaken the inner eye). When Mantl, who upon entering is assumed by the others to be the awaited guest, denies that he is the Superman, Schiroga contends that Mantl *is* the Superman, if only for a moment, simply because he produced the impression of being such. Kilian, a bookbinder, arrives with the bound manuscripts of the Master's works; he, too, is mistaken for the Master. Kilian, whose knowledge rivals that of Frau Samson's circle, is challenged by Professor Kummer, who represents the scientific method gone mad. Like the crucified Christ, Kilian calls on God to save him from his torment. Jakob Natterer, the real Master, finally enters, and he and Kilian share their thoughts. Kilian realizes that they are virtually interchangeable except that he, Kilian, is not a Superman but a simple bookbinder. In the end Frau Samson, who still takes Kilian to be the Master, is pleased that he has made a visit and is now "zurück in jener Welt, aus der er kam" (back in the world from which he came). As the curtain falls, everyone goes to sleep. Kornfeld is here attacking the intelligentsia for postulating pseudoscientific theses; he is also ridiculing the interest in the occult of the literary salons, a movement in which he had played a central role.

In 1927 Kornfeld became dramaturge at the Hessisches Landestheater (Hessian Provincial Theater) in Darmstadt, where his unpublished play *Impresario von Smyrna* (Impresario of Smyrna), in which he poked fun at the European craze for Americans and the American craze for Europeans, premiered on 18 February 1928. The Darmstadt appointment was secure and lucrative, but life in the provinces did not agree with Kornfeld. From 1928 to 1931 he worked as a freelancer for Leopold Schwarzschild's *Das Tage-Buch* (The Diary), a leftist periodical.

Jud Süß (Jew Süß; published, 1930), the last of his plays to be produced, premiered on 7 October 1930 under Leopold Jeßner's direction at the Theater am Schiffbauerdamm in Berlin. In this tragedy in three acts and an epilogue Kornfeld deals with the theme of the outsider by tracing in realistic fashion the rise and fall of Josef Süß-Oppenheimer, financial adviser to Duke Karl Alexander of Württemberg in the early eighteenth century. Remarkably, instead of addressing the then current threat to Jews as a people, Kornfeld treats the problem of assimilation for an individual Jew. In the end, when Süß is to be executed, Kornfeld offers no solutions to the injustice exemplified by the sentence, nor are any means of combating racism posited.

Kornfeld did not consider Nazism, which by this time was gaining strength, to be a serious menace: "die Nazis haben ausgespielt, sind erledigt, wir werden es noch erleben, daß Hitler als eine historische Epoche betrachtet wird, höchstens ein Politiker sein wird wie irgend einanderer" (the Nazis have played themselves out. They're finished. We will see that Hitler will be a historical episode, at the most a politician like any other), he

said in a letter to his lover, Maria Czamska, on 12 September 1932. Earlier that year he had shown up at the publisher Ernst Rowohlt's Fasching party wrapped in a swastika flag, laughing gleefully. Kornfeld failed to perceive the danger National Socialism presented. His conviction that art and politics should remain separate resulted in his underestimating Nazism.

He returned to Prague in 1932. Later, instead of escaping to England with the rest of his family, he remained in a small room in an old house on the outskirts of town. In 1941 he was taken to the Lodz concentration camp. He died there on 25 April 1942.

Kornfeld's penchant for the metaphysical resulted in tragic misapprehensions about actual historical conditions. His desire for transcendence exemplifies the failure of expressionism to deal effectively with the complex cultural, social, and political reality of the 1920s.

References:

David Bathrick, "Marxism and Modernism," *New German Critique*, 33 (Fall 1984): 207-217;

Peter-Uwe Hohendahl, *Das Bild der bürgerlichen Welt im expressionistischen Drama* (Heidelberg: Winter, 1967);

Eva Kolinsky, *Engagierter Expressionismus* (Stuttgart: Metzler, 1970);

Manon Maren-Grisebach, ed., *Revolution mit Flötenmusik* (Heidelberg: Schneider, 1977);

Margarita Pazi, *Fünf Autoren des Prager Kreises* (Frankfurt am Main: Lang, 1978);

Paul Raabe, *The Era of German Expressionism* (Woodstock, N.Y.: Overlook, 1974);

James MacPherson Ritchie, *German Expressionist Drama* (Boston: Twayne, 1976);

Stephen Shearier, *Das junge Deutschland 1917-1920: Expressionist Theater in Berlin* (Bern: Lang, 1988), pp. 71-79, 205-214;

Walter H. Sokel, *Der literarische Expressionismus* (Munich: Langen/Müller, 1959);

Annalisa Viviani, *Das Drama des Expressionismus* (Munich: Winkler, 1970).

Papers:
Manuscripts of Paul Kornfeld are in the Akademie der Künste (Academy of Arts), Berlin.

Karl Kraus
(28 April 1874 - 12 June 1936)

Harry Zohn
Brandeis University

PLAY PRODUCTIONS: *Die letzte Nacht*, Vienna, Neue Wiener Bühne, 4 February 1923;
Traumstück, Berlin, Lustspielhaus, 25 March 1924;
Traumtheater, Berlin, Lustspielhaus, 25 March 1924;
Die Unüberwindlichen, Dresden, Residenztheater, 5 May 1929.

BOOKS: *Die demolirte Literatur* (Vienna: Bauer, 1897);
Eine Krone für Zion (Vienna: Frisch, 1898);
Maximilian Harden: Eine Erledigung (Vienna: Die Fackel, 1907);
Maximilian Harden: Ein Nachruf (Vienna: Rosner, 1908);
Sittlichkeit und Kriminalität (Vienna & Leipzig: Rosner, 1908);
Sprüche und Widersprüche (Munich: Langen, 1909);
Heine und die Folgen (Munich: Langen, 1910);
Die chinesische Mauer (Munich: Langen, 1910; revised edition, Vienna: Die Fackel, 1930);
Pro domo et mundo (Munich: Langen, 1912);
Nestroy und die Nachwelt: Zum fünfzigsten Todestage. Gesprochen im Großen Musikvereinssaal in Wien (Vienna: Jahoda & Siegel, 1912);
Worte in Versen, 9 volumes (volumes 1-5, Vienna: Verlag der Schriften von Karl Kraus; volumes 6-9, Die Fackel, 1916-1930);
Die letzte Nacht: Epilog zu der Tragödie Die letzten Tage der Menschheit (Vienna: Die Fackel, 1918);
Nachts (Leipzig: Verlag der Schriften von Karl Kraus, 1918);
Die letzten Tage der Menschheit: Tragödie in fünf Akten mit Vorspiel und Epilog, 3 volumes (Vienna: Die Fackel, 1918-1919; excerpts translated by Alexander Gode and Sue Ellen Wright as *The Last Days of Mankind*, edited by Frederick Ungar (New York: Ungar, 1974);
Peter Altenberg (Vienna: Lányi, 1919);

Die Ballade vom Papagei: Couplet Macabre (Vienna: Lányi, 1919);
Weltgericht, 2 volumes (Leipzig: Verlag der Schriften von Karl Kraus, 1919);
Ausgewählte Gedichte (Munich: Verlag der Schriften von Karl Kraus, 1920; Zurich & New York: Oprecht, 1939);

152

Literatur oder Man wird doch da sehn: Magische Operette in zwei Teilen (Vienna & Leipzig: Die Fackel, 1921);

Untergang der Welt durch schwarze Magie (Vienna & Leipzig: Die Fackel, 1922);

Traumstück (Vienna & Leipzig: Die Fackel, 1923);

Wolkenkuckucksheim (Vienna & Leipzig: Die Fackel, 1923);

Traumtheater (Vienna: Die Fackel, 1924);

Epigramme, compiled by Viktor Stadler (Vienna & Leipzig: Die Fackel, 1927);

Offenbach-Renaissance (Vienna: Die Fackel, 1927);

Die Unüberwindlichen: Nachkriegsdrama in vier Akten (Vienna & Leipzig: Die Fackel, 1928);

Literatur und Lüge (Vienna & Leipzig: Die Fackel, 1929);

Nächtliche Stunde, music by Eugen Auerbach (Vienna: Lányi, 1929);

Zeitstrophen (Vienna: Die Fackel, 1931);

Adolf Loos: Rede am Grab, 25 August 1933 (Vienna: Lányi, 1933);

Die Sprache, edited by Philipp Berger (Vienna: Die Fackel, 1937);

Die dritte Walpurgisnacht (Munich: Kösel, 1952).

Collections: *Werke*, 14 volumes, edited by Heinrich Fischer (volumes 1-10, Munich: Kösel, 1952-1962; volumes 11-14, Munich: Langen-Müller, 1963-1967);

Frühe Schriften 1892-1900, 2 volumes, edited by Johannes J. Braakenburg (Munich: Kösel, 1979);

Schriften, 13 volumes published, edited by Christian Wagenknecht (Frankfurt am Main: Suhrkamp, 1986-   ).

Editions in English: *Poems*, edited and translated by Albert Bloch (Boston: Four Seas, 1930);

In These Great Times: A Karl Kraus Reader, edited by Harry Zohn (Montreal: Engendra Press, 1976; Manchester, U.K.: Carcanet Press, 1984; Chicago: University of Chicago Press, 1990);

Half-Truths and One-and-a-Half Truths: Selected Aphorisms, edited and translated by Zohn (Montreal: Engendra Press, 1976; Manchester, U.K. & New York: Carcanet Press, 1986; Chicago: University of Chicago Press, 1990);

No Compromise: Selected Writings of Karl Kraus, edited by Frederick Ungar (New York: Ungar, 1977).

OTHER: *Die Fackel*, edited by Kraus, volumes 1-37, April 1899 - February 1936;

Johann Nestroy, *Das Notwendige und das Überflüssige*, adapted by Kraus (Vienna: Lányi, 1920);

Nestroy, *Der konfuse Zauberer oder Treue und Flatterhaftigkeit*, adapted by Kraus (Vienna: Lányi, 1925);

Jacques Offenbach, *Madame L'Archiduc*, adapted by Kraus (Vienna: Lányi, 1927);

William Shakespeare, *Timon von Athen*, adapted by Kraus (Vienna: Lányi, 1930);

Offenbach, *Perichole*, translated and adapted by Kraus (Vienna: Universal-Edition, 1931);

Peter Altenberg: Auswahl aus seinen Büchern, edited by Kraus (Vienna: Schroll, 1932);

Offenbach, *Vert-Vert*, translated and adapted by Kraus (Vienna: Die Fackel, 1932);

Shakespeares Dramen: Für Hörer und Leser bearbeitet, teilweise sprachlich erneuert, adapted by Kraus (Vienna: Lányi, 1934).

Karl Kraus, widely regarded as one of the greatest satirists of the twentieth century, was primarily a prose writer who produced thousands of critical essays and aphorisms. He also wrote a considerable amount of poetry that was collected in nine volumes between 1916 and 1930. The contents of most of Kraus's books first appeared in his journal, *Die Fackel* (The Torch), which was published from 1899 to 1936. Kraus, who forced the powerful and the pitiful alike to stand before the tribunal of his satire, was a legend in his lifetime, variously adored and vilified by his contemporaries. The key to his life and work is his relationship to language. As Erich Heller puts it, "Karl Kraus did not write 'in a language,' but through him the beauty, profundity, and accumulated moral experience of the German language assumed personal shape and became the crucial witness in the case this inspired prosecutor brought against his time." Kraus saw an absolute congruity between word and world, language and life; the unworthiness of his "sprachverlassenes" (language-forsaken) age was defined for him by its treatment—or abuse—of language. To Kraus, language was the moral criterion and accreditation for a writer or speaker. Joseph Peter Stern has termed this equation of linguistic obtuseness or dishonesty with moral torpor or degeneracy Kraus's "linguistic-moral imperative." Quotation is the hallmark of Kraus's satire, and in keeping with his conviction that what was most unspeakable about his age could be spoken only by the age itself he set out to fashion an imperishable profile of his time from such perishable materials as newspaper reports. Excoriating the press for its pollution of language, its poisoning of the human spirit, and its shameless invasions of privacy and civility, Kraus anticipated the judgment of present-day critics of the media.

Kraus's life and work were eminently theatrical. He served the theater as a critic, translator and adapter, playwright, reciter, and—last and definitely least—sometime actor. Kraus thought of himself as possibly the first writer who experienced his writings theatrically, the way a performer does: "Wenn ich vortrage, so ist es nicht gespielte Literatur. Aber was ich schreibe, ist geschriebene Schauspielkunst" (When I give a public reading, it is not acted literature. But what I write is written acting). Kraus's mode of thinking and writing was essentially theatrical, and *Die Fackel* may in itself be regarded as a stage, often taking the form of a pillory, on which Kraus dramatized himself and his ethical, didactic, aesthetic, and, above all, satiric mission. In his life and work criticism and showmanship, ethics and aesthetics were invariably linked, and his celebrated prose style is replete with expressive, rhetorical, theatrical elements. Many of Kraus's polemics and feuds were carried on with theater people, and he came to take a highly personal and polemical view of such celebrated actors as Otto Tressler, Joseph Kainz, Helene Odilon, Alexander Moissi (all negative); and Alexander Girardi, Adolf Sonnenthal, and Charlotte Wolter (all positive). All his life he championed and yearned for the old Vienna Burgtheater with its high style, dignity, integrity, artistry, and congruence of ethical and aesthetic purpose. He repeatedly evoked that theater's traditional style in programmatic and principled opposition to what he regarded as the corruption, commercialism, politicization, charlatanry, sensationalism, and feuilletonism (by which he meant slickness, shallowness, and meretriciousness) of the lavish productions of such directors as Leopold Jessner, Erwin Piscator, and Max Reinhardt. Kraus drew a distinction between "Buchdrama" (literary drama) and "Bühnendrama" (stage drama) and increasingly came to take a reader-centered view, regarding drama as literature in which language and ideas were paramount and the reader's imagination was enlisted. Kraus's half-dozen plays were intended to be read, possibly read aloud or recited, rather than given full-scale productions on a stage. "Most of Kraus's plays are closet dramas," writes Kari Grimstad, "and are not suitable for the three-dimensional reality of the stage."

Kraus in 1900; drawing by Emil Orlik (Historical Museum of the City of Vienna)

Kraus was born on 28 April 1874 in Jicin, a small Bohemian town northeast of Prague, the fifth son and ninth child of Jakob Kraus, a prosperous Jewish manufacturer of paper bags, and Ernestine Kantor Kraus, a physician's daughter. In 1877 the family moved to Vienna; Kraus was to spend the rest of his life in that city, with which he had a love-hate relationship. From 1884 to 1892 Kraus was a mediocre student at the Franz Josefs-Gymnasium. At his father's request he enrolled at the University of Vienna to study law. In 1893 he made an unsuccessful debut as an actor in Friedrich Schiller's *Die Räuber* (1781; translated as *The Robbers*, 1792), and his failure on the stage irrevocably turned him to journalism and literature. In 1894 he switched to courses in philosophy and German literature, but four years later he left the university without a degree. His first major satire, *Die demolirte Literatur* (Demolished Literature, 1897), was initially printed in the *Wiener Rundschau*, one of many Austrian and German journals to which the young Kraus contributed. In the form of a witty obituary of the Café Griensteidl, which was frequented by writers of the Young Vienna movement, it lampoons the coffeehouse culture of fin de siècle Vienna. The pamphlet *Eine Krone für Zion* (A Crown for Zion, 1898) attacks Zionism and its leader, Theodor Herzl, who was also the cultural editor of the *Neue Freie Presse* (New Free Press), a prestigious paper that became a frequent target of Kraus's satiric blasts after he turned down its offer of a position. *Eine Krone für Zion* is written from the standpoint of an assimilated European Jew in sympathy with socialism.

Because Kraus refused to become a sort of culture clown with the accursed popularity that a grinning Vienna bestows (as he put it), and because work within the Establishment seemed to be hedged in with multifarious taboos and considerations of a commercial and personal nature, Kraus founded his own satirical journal, *Die Fackel*; the first issue appeared on 1 April 1899. In October 1899 Kraus left the Jewish fold. After the death of his father in 1900 (his mother had died in 1891) Kraus detached himself from his family, but he continued to accept a subvention from the family fortune.

If Kraus's early writings were directed largely against standard aspects of corruption, the second period of his creativity may be dated from the appearance in *Die Fackel* in 1902 of his essay "Sittlichkeit und Kriminalität" (Morality and Criminal Justice), which focused on the glaring contrast between private and public morality and exposed the hypocrisy inherent in the administration of justice in Austria. This piece and related essays were published in book form in 1908.

After 1911 the irregularly issued *Fackel* contained Kraus's writings exclusively, though it continued to have many "contributors"—albeit unwitting and unwilling ones: the people who were copiously quoted in its pages and allowed to hang themselves with the noose of their own attitudes, statements, and actions. In 1911 Kraus was secretly baptized a Catholic; he would publicly break with the church in 1922. In 1913 he met Baroness Sidonie Nádherný, a Czech aristocrat to whom he unsuccessfully proposed marriage on several occasions. Despite her engagements and marriages to other men, Kraus's affectionate (and at times subservient) relationship with her continued until the end of his life.

The outbreak of World War I inspired the outraged and anguished pacifist and humanitarian Kraus to produce his most powerful and characteristic work, beginning with the address "In dieser großen Zeit" (In These Great Times),

Kraus in 1915 with Baroness Sidonie Nádherný, to whom he unsuccessfully proposed marriage several times

which was delivered in Vienna on 19 November 1914 and published in *Die Fackel* a few weeks later. The following year he began work on *Die letzten Tage der Menschheit* (1918-1919; excerpts translated as *The Last Days of Mankind*, 1974), a monumental dramatic repository of most of his satiric themes and techniques. Most of the 209 scenes of its five acts were first sketched during the summers of 1915, 1916, and 1917; the rhymed prologue dates from July 1915 and the epilogue—published separately as *Die letzte Nacht* (The Last Night, 1918)—from July 1917. In the preface to this early example of documentary drama, a type later popularized by Bertolt Brecht and Rolf Hochhuth, Kraus wrote that his drama was intended for a theater on Mars: its performance would, in earthly terms, require about ten evenings, and theatergoers of this world would not be able to bear seeing characters from an operetta enacting the tragedy of mankind. He refused offers by Reinhardt and Piscator to stage the play, permitting only performances of the epilogue in Vienna in 1923 and 1924 and Berlin in 1930; he also publicly read his own abridgment in 1930. Virtually the complete work was presented in Basel and Vienna in 1980 under the direction of Hans Hollmann, as well as in Edinburgh in 1983 by a Glasgow company under the direction of Robert David MacDonald.

Die letzten Tage der Menschheit begins with the voice of a newspaper seller and ends with the voice of God. It is set in the streets of Vienna and Berlin, in offices and barracks, churches and cafés, amusement places and military hospitals, railroad stations and army posts, "in hundert Szenen und Höllen" (in a hundred scenes and hells). The five hundred characters include pastors and prostitutes, chauvinists and showmen, professors and politicians, teachers and tradesmen, soldiers and sycophants, children and churchmen, inspectors and innkeepers, journalists and jesters, policemen and profiteers, editors and emperors. There are real persons as well as fictitious ones, and all of them reveal themselves by their authentic speech patterns, by what has been termed their "acoustical masks." The play is a striking amalgam of naturalistic and symbolic elements. The scenes are, by turns, lyrical and prosaic, tragic and comic; but even the comedy acquires a certain grimness in the context and usually appears as gallows humor. The play has no hero or plot in the conventional sense; it is episodic, with certain scenes recurring in cyclical patterns, and it inexorably grinds to a cataclysmic conclusion. The scenes range in length from one-line blackouts in the tradition of the cabaret to lengthy dialogues, monologues, dramatized editorials, and phantasmagoric tableaux. About half of this dramatic typology of inhumanity consists of quotes from actual newspaper articles, war communiqués, court judgments, advertisements, letters, and other documents, but even the scenes invented by Kraus reproduce with uncanny accuracy the language of the "great times." The play presents a Nietzschean vision of the disintegration of European culture and of a dying way of life.

Kraus's characters include two fatuous privy councillors who vie with each other in mangling one of the glories of German poetry, Johann Wolfgang von Goethe's "Wanderers Nachtlied" (Wanderer's Night Song, 1780); the Bavarian storyteller Ludwig Ganghofer, who yodels his way along the front, writes war reports for the *Neue Freie Presse*, and swaps jokes with an appreciative Kaiser; "patriotic" pastors of the "praise-the-Lord-and-pass-the-ammunition" variety, to whom Kraus gives the names of birds of prey; a judge who celebrates his hundredth death sentence;

two fat Berlin profiteers (Kraus calls them Gog and Magog) who disport themselves in the snows of the Swiss Alps; Alice Schalek, the first woman accredited to the Austrian army as a war correspondent, whose gushy effusions about the emotions of the common man, "das freigewordene Menschentum" (liberated humanity), and "das Fieber des Erlebens" (the fever of the adventure) and whose search for human-interest material amid degradation, destruction, and death made her a macabre joke and a frequent Krausian target; and the happy hangman, who appears on a picture postcard used as an illustration in the book edition of the play, holding his paws over the head of an executed man while the grinning, smug bystanders gather around the lifeless, dangling body. Another prime target of Kraus's satire (under the name "Maledikt") was Moriz Benedikt, the editor of the *Neue Freie Presse*, whom Kraus depicts as the "Herr der Hyänen" (lord of the hyenas) and the Antichrist. Old Man Biach, one of Kraus's fictitious characters and an assiduous mouther of Benedikt's editorials, dies of linguistic convolution and spiritual poisoning when even he can no longer reconcile the harsh reality with the journalistic double-talk and governmental doublethink. The twenty-three conversations between the Nörgler (Grumbler) and the Optimist function as the choruses of a tragedy; they represent oases of relative repose and reflection. In his running commentary the Nörgler constitutes the anguished conscience of the times and the voice of reason, presenting eschatological views rather than espousing realpolitik; he displays the kind of conscience, compassion, and consistency that might have saved European civilization.

While the prologue—which begins on 28 June 1914, the day on which the successor to the Austrian throne, Archduke Franz Ferdinand, and his wife were assassinated, and ends with their third-class funeral—shows with grim realism what lay underneath the veneer of the vaunted Austrian gemütlichkeit, surrealistic touches are introduced as the tragedy and the war rush toward their cataclysmic conclusion. Corybants and maenads spew forth verbal fragments, and there are choruses of gas masks, frozen soldiers, twelve hundred drowned horses, and the dead children of the *Lusitania*. The rhymed epilogue *Die letzte Nacht* is a harrowing poetic satire raised to a supernatural plane, in which many motifs of the play are recapitulated in cinematographic or operatic form, with actual and allegorical characters appearing in a ghastly procession. A moribund soldier screams that he is not dying for any emperor or fatherland; gas masks discuss their sexlessness and facelessness; a general riding over corpses in his flight still concerns himself with dress regulations; and a war correspondent is bent on recording the last sensations of a dying soldier. Other revolting specimens of homo sapiens include a dashing hussar who traffics in human material; a scientist who becomes a master of chemical warfare; and the human hyenas Fressack (Glutton) and Naschkatz (Sweettooth), who represent the parasitic commercial and industrial interests of the war. A typology of troops gives way to a dramatic confrontation between voices from above that speak the truth and voices from below that mouth the falsehoods of the "great times." After a stinging indictment of the planet a shower of meteors, accompanied by cosmic thunder, incinerates the earth. Following a silence, God's voice is heard speaking the words Kaiser Wilhelm II used at the beginning of the war: "Ich habe es nicht gewollt" (I did not will it so)—possibly a final glimmer of hope that humanity can yet redeem itself and work toward a better future. Parts of the play were published in special issues of *Die Fackel* and were read by the author at recitals.

The story of Kraus's postwar writings and polemics is the history of his disillusionment. The best that he could say about the Austrian republic, a truncated and scarcely viable country still bedeviled by what he discerned as the parasites remaining from the imperial age, was that it had replaced the monarchy and relieved the satirist of that burdensome companion, the other *K.K.*—the reference being to the abbreviation of *kaiserlich-königlich* (royal-imperial), the designation of many Austro-Hungarian institutions. *Literatur oder Man wird doch da sehn* (Literature; or, We'll See about That, 1921) is a "magische Operette" (magical operetta) that satirizes a literary movement in general and Franz Werfel, one of several Kraus apostles turned apostates, in particular. For the second time, Kraus had occasion to demolish a literature—expressionism rather than Young Vienna—this time not with witty glosses and aperçus but by letting it manifest its unworthiness and pronounce its own death warrant. Again the scene is a Vienna café—not the Griensteidl but the Central, a place that Kraus peoples with bourgeois bacchantes and meandering maenads. The Werfel figure is named Johann Wolfgang, and in true expressionistic fashion the

pretentious, pompous son rebels against his business-minded father. Kraus satirizes the effect that expressionist poets and playwrights, fashionable pseudophilosophical essayists, psychoanalysts, and other "redeemers" have had on the impressionable masses. This parodistic play includes one of Kraus's most successful chansons, "Das Lied von der Presse" (The Song of the Press), a concentrated account of Creation; it is sung by a character named Schwarz-Drucker (Ink-Printer), an operetta version of Benedikt. *Literatur* was presumably written in response to Werfel's "magical trilogy" *Spiegelmensch* (Mirror Man, 1920), in which the title character delivers a vulgar prose soliloquy that lampoons Kraus. Kraus first read his play in Vienna on 6 March 1921, a month before Werfel's play premiered at the Burgtheater.

In *Traumstück* (Dream Play; published, 1923; performed, 1924), a one-act verse drama written at Christmas 1922, lyric and grotesque elements intermingle. Kraus described this surrealistic fantasy as an amalgam of wartime experiences, the horrors of the postwar period, and his feelings about love, language, dreams, and psychoanalysis (a frequent target of his satire). A pessimistic monologue by the Dichter (Poet) is followed by a dream in which "Die Psychoanalen" (The Psycho-anals) identify themselves as killers of dreams, blackeners of beauty, compilers of complexes, and exhibitors of inhibitions—people to whom even Goethe's poems are nothing but badly repressed unconscious material. After several other visions and encounters, the Dichter awakens to the insight that the dream has clarified his mission to serve the Word and thus give permanence to his life.

The legacy of Annie Kalmar, an actress whom Kraus had admired and loved at the turn of the century and who had died young, shaped the one-act play *Traumtheater* (Dream Theater, 1924), which Kraus dedicated to her memory. Kraus has the beloved actress play love for him so that his love might be purged of jealousy. This improvisational philosophical-dramatic vignette consists of brief scenes in prose and verse that, in reality and in dreams, explore and illuminate the relationships between the Schauspielerin (Actress), the Dichter, the Regisseur (Director), Der alte Esel (The Old Ass—a member of the audience and a father symbol), and Walter, a secondary-school student.

Kraus regarded his reading of *Wolkenkuckucksheim* (Cloudcuckooland, 1923), a "phantastisches Versspiel in drei Akten" (fantastic verse play in three acts), as a fitting apotheosis of the republican idea. Kraus's play is indebted to Emil Schinck's German translation (1880) of Aristophanes' *The Birds* and reflects an old tradition of the Viennese popular theater: the travesty of classical motifs. Two Athenians, who find conditions in their native city (a barely disguised Vienna) unbearable, emigrate and become birds in a bird city. Soon enough, however, the coffeehouse culture, complete with prying journalists, avantgarde poets, psychoanalysts, and warmongers, catches up with them and sets the stage for the Last Days of Birdkind. The play has a happy ending, however; Die Lerche (the Lark) ends it with a Shakespearean monologue: all have been dreaming; the birds do not wish to be worshiped as gods; there will be no more violence or wars— "Wir träumten Macht. Wir leben Republik! . . . Nie wieder Krieg!" (We dreamed of power. We live in a republic! . . . No more wars!).

With his last play, *Die Unüberwindlichen* (The Unconquerables; published, 1928; performed, 1929), Kraus returned to the form of the documentary drama. The four-act play memorializes two of the satirist's feuds: with Imre Békessy, a corrupt, Hungarian-born press czar; and with Johannes Schober, Vienna's chief of police. Kraus accused Schober of collusion with Békessy and also held him responsible for the police riot of 15 July 1927 that followed the burning of the Ministry of Justice by a mob enraged by the acquittal of some killers. Kraus appears as Arkus and Békessy as Barkassy (*Barkasse* means "cash money"). Schober is made to sing the mordantly self-revealing "Schoberlied" (Schober Song) to a tune of the satirist's own composition. By the time the play was written Kraus had managed almost single-handedly to end Békessy's corrupt reign and make him flee the city; the slogan of his campaign had been "Hinaus aus Wien mit dem Schuft!" (Kick the crook out of Vienna!). Although such eminent actors as Peter Lorre, Ernst Ginsberg, Leonhard Steckel, and Kurt Gerron starred in the Berlin production of the play on 20 October 1929 and the influential critic Herbert Ihering reviewed it favorably, it was evident that plays of normal length were not Kraus's forte. Further performances were canceled at the behest of the Austrian embassy, but the play was revived in Leipzig two years later.

Kraus read his own works and major works of world literature, including plays and operettas in which he recited or sang all the parts. His first public readings took place in 1892, then ceased

until 1910. He gave 700 public readings in all, the last one on 2 April 1936; 414 took place in Vienna, 105 in Berlin, 57 in Prague, 17 in Munich, 10 in Paris, and the rest in various Austrian, German, Swiss, Czech, Hungarian, and Italian cities. Kraus read exclusively from his own writings on 260 occasions and exclusively from those of others on 302; 138 were mixed readings. Until 1925 these literary evenings were announced simply as "Vorlesung Karl Kraus" (Reading by Karl Kraus); beginning in 1925 Kraus used "Theater der Dichtung" (Theater of Poetry) as a subheading, and in the last few years of his life the programs were announced as "Theater der Dichtung; Darsteller Karl Kraus" (Theater of Poetry: Performer Karl Kraus). Despite the silent treatment given the satirist by the press in Vienna and other places, these spellbinding recitals usually attracted capacity audiences.

Between 1916 and 1936 Kraus recited his adaptations of thirteen of William Shakespeare's plays; seven of these adaptations, as well as Kraus's versions of Shakespeare's sonnets, were published in book form between 1930 and 1935. Since Kraus knew little English, he used existing translations as a basis for renditions that reflect his unerring dramatic, poetic, and above all, linguistic sense. For the 123 recitals devoted to the operettas of Jacques Offenbach, Kraus enlisted the services of a piano accompanist. Kraus had attended performances of Offenbach operettas at a summer theater as a child and came to regard the composer as the greatest musical dramatist of all time; he championed Offenbach's work in programmatic opposition to the "silver age" Austrian operetta, which he regarded as inane and deceitful. Kraus presented fourteen Offenbach operettas, and although he could not read music, he sang all the roles; he often included Zusatzstrophen (additional stanzas) of his own devising. Topical stanzas were also added to his readings of plays by Johann Nestroy, the nineteenth-century Viennese comic playwright and actor whom Kraus presented as a great dramatist and social satirist who, like Kraus himself, achieved his effects through an inspired use of language. Kraus regularly performed dramas of Gerhart Hauptmann, Bertolt Brecht, Goethe, Nikolai Gogol, Ferdinand Raimund, and Frank Wedekind. In 1905 he arranged the first Viennese performances of Wedekind's controversial *Die Büchse der Pandora* (1903; translated as *Pandora's Box*, 1914) and took a small role in it.

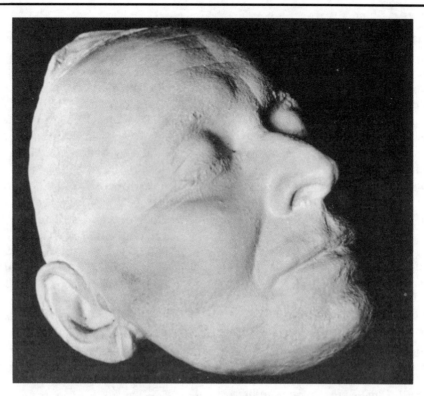

Death mask of Kraus (Landesbildstelle Wien-Burgenland)

"Mir fällt zu Hitler nichts ein" (I can't think of anything to say about Hitler) is the striking first sentence of Kraus's prose work *Die dritte Walpurgisnacht* (The Third Walpurgis Night), written in 1933 but not published in its entirety until 1952. That statement, which gave rise to misunderstandings and conflicts that were the bane of the satirist's existence in his last years, may be indicative of resignation, but it is also a hyperbolic device for depicting the witches' Sabbath of the time. Kraus sadly realized the incommensurability of the human spirit with the unspeakably brutal and mindless power structure across the German border. Once again language was in mortal danger, and the perpetrators of the new horrors were not characters from an operetta. In voicing genuine concern over Germany's pressure on his homeland, Kraus assumed the unaccustomed mantle of an Austrian patriot. Paradoxically, this stance led him to side with the clerico-fascist regime of Chancellor Engelbert Dollfuss, whose assassination in 1934 came as a severe blow to Kraus. Many of Kraus's adherents wanted him to join them in their struggle against the Nazis, perhaps expecting him to stop Hitlerism with a special issue of *Die Fackel*. By this time the journal was appearing at even more irregular intervals than before, and Kraus was content to reduce his

readership to those who not only heard the trumpets of the day, as he put it, but also cared about Shakespeare, Nestroy, Offenbach, and German style. Desiring to live "im sicheren Satzbau" (in the safe sentence structure), Kraus pathetically and futilely strove to pit the word against the sword. His death on 12 June 1936 of heart failure, at the end of a long period of physical and spiritual exhaustion and four months after the appearance of the last issue—number 922—of *Die Fackel*, saved Kraus from witnessing the Nazi takeover of Austria to the cheers of most of its population.

Letters:

Briefe an Sidonie Nádherný von Borutin, 1913-1936, 2 volumes, edited by Heinrich Fischer and Friedrich Pfäfflin (Munich: Kösel, 1974).

Bibliography:

Otto Kerry, *Karl Kraus-Bibliographie* (Munich: Kösel, 1970).

References:

Heinz-Ludwig Arnold, ed., *Sonderband Karl Kraus: Literatur und Kritik* (Munich: Edition text + kritik, 1975);

Helmut Arntzen, *Karl Kraus und die Presse* (Munich: Fink, 1975);

Walter Benjamin, "Karl Kraus," in his *Reflections* (New York: Harcourt Brace Jovanovich, 1978), pp. 239-273;

Martina Bilke, *Zeitgenossen der Fackel* (Vienna & Munich: Löcker, 1981);

Mechthild Borries, *Ein Angriff auf Heinrich Heine: Kritische Betrachtungen zu Karl Kraus* (Stuttgart: Kohlhammer, 1971);

Donald G. Daviau, "Language and Morality in Karl Kraus's *Die letzten Tage der Menschheit*," *Modern Language Quarterly*, 22 (March 1961): 46-54;

Paul Engelmann, *Dem Andenken an Karl Kraus* (Vienna: Kerry, 1967);

Ludwig von Ficker, ed., *Rundfrage über Karl Kraus* (Innsbruck: Brenner, 1917);

Frank Field, *The Last Days of Mankind: Karl Kraus and His Vienna* (New York: St. Martin's Press, 1967);

Heinrich Fischer, "The Other Austria and Karl Kraus," in *In Tyrannos: Four Centuries of Struggle Against Tyranny in Germany*, edited by H. J. Rehfisch (London: Drummond, 1944), pp. 309-328;

Jens Malte Fischer, *Karl Kraus* (Stuttgart: Metzler, 1974);

Richard Flatter, *Karl Kraus als Nachdichter Shakespeares* (Vienna: Berger & Fischer, 1934);

Kari Grimstad, *Masks of the Prophet: The Theatrical World of Karl Kraus* (Toronto: University of Toronto Press, 1982);

Erich Heller, "Karl Kraus," in his *In the Age of Prose* (New York: Cambridge University Press, 1984), pp. 87-103;

Heller, "Karl Kraus: The Last Days of Mankind," in his *The Disinherited Mind* (New York: Farrar, Straus & Cudahy, 1957), pp. 235-256;

Wilma Abeles Iggers, *Karl Kraus: A Viennese Critic of the Twentieth Century* (The Hague: Nijhoff, 1967);

Allen Janik and Stephen Toulmin, "Language and Society: Karl Kraus and the Last Days of Vienna," in their *Wittgenstein's Vienna* (New York: Simon & Schuster, 1973), pp. 67-91;

Friedrich Jenaczek, *Zeittafeln zur "Fackel": Themen, Ziele, Probleme* (Gräfelfing: Gans, 1965);

Georg Knepler, *Karl Kraus liest Offenbach: Erinnerungen, Kommentare, Dokumentationen* (Vienna: Löcker, 1984);

Caroline Kohn, *Karl Kraus* (Stuttgart: Metzler, 1966);

Werner Kraft, *Das Ja des Neinsagers: Karl Kraus und seine geistige Welt* (Munich: Edition text - kritik, 1974);

Kraft, *Karl Kraus* (Salzburg: Müller, 1956);

Leopold Liegler, *Karl Kraus und sein Werk* (Vienna: Lányi, 1920);

Franz H. Mautner, "Kraus' *Die letzten Tage der Menschheit*," in *Das deutsche Drama*, volume 2, edited by Benno von Wiese (Düsseldorf: Bagel, 1958), pp. 357-382; abridged English translation by Sue Ellen Wright in Kraus's *The Last Days of Mankind*, edited by Frederick Ungar, translated by Wright and Alexander Gode (New York: Ungar, 1974), pp. 239-263;

Modern Austrian Literature, special Kraus issue, edited by Daviau, 8, no. 1/2 (1975);

Michael Naumann, *Der Abbau einer verkehrten Welt: Satire und politische Wirklichkeit im Werk von Karl Kraus* (Munich: List, 1969);

Alfred Pfabigan, *Karl Kraus und der Sozialismus: Eine politische Biographie* (Vienna: Europaverlag, 1976);

Sidney Rosenfeld, "Karl Kraus: The Future of a Legacy," *Midstream*, 20 (April 1974): 71-80;

Richard Schaukal, *Karl Kraus: Versuch eines geistigen Bildnisses* (Vienna: Reinhold, 1933);

Sigurd Paul Scheichl and Edward Timms, eds., *Karl Kraus in neuer Sicht: Londoner Kraus-Symposium* (Munich: Edition text + kritik, 1986);

Robert Scheu, *Karl Kraus* (Vienna: Jahoda & Siegel, 1909);

Paul Schick, ed., *Karl Kraus in Selbstzeugnissen und Bilddokumenten* (Hamburg: Rowoholt, 1978);

Franz Schuh and Juliane Vogel, eds., *Die Belagerung der Urteilsmauer: Karl Kraus im Zerrspiegel seiner Feinde* (Vienna: Edition S, 1986);

Thomas W. Simons, Jr., "After Karl Kraus," in *The Legacy of the German Refugee Intellectuals*, edited by Robert Boyers (New York: Schocken, 1972), pp. 154-173;

Mary Snell, "Karl Kraus' *Die letzten Tage der Menschheit*: An Analysis," *Forum for Modern Language Studies*, 4 (July 1968): 234-247;

Joachim Stephan, *Satire und Sprache: Zu dem Werk von Karl Kraus* (Munich: Pustet, 1964);

Max Spalter, "Karl Kraus," in his *Brecht's Tradition* (Baltimore: Johns Hopkins University Press, 1967), pp. 137-155;

Joseph Peter Stern, "Karl Kraus's Vision of Language," *Modern Language Review*, 61 (January 1966): 71-84;

Gerald Stieg, *Der Brenner und Die Fackel: Ein Beitrag zur Wirkungsgeschichte von Karl Kraus* (Salzburg: Müller, 1976);

Edward Timms, *Karl Kraus, Apocalyptic Satirist: Culture and Catastrophe in Habsburg Vienna* (New Haven: Yale University Press, 1986);

Berthold Viertel, *Karl Kraus: Ein Charakter und die Zeit* (Dresden: Kämmerer, 1921);

Christian Johannes Wagenknecht, *Das Wortspiel bei Karl Kraus* (Göttingen: Vandenhoeck & Ruprecht, 1965);

Nike Wagner, *Geist und Geschlecht: Karl Kraus und die Erotik der Wiener Moderne* (Frankfurt am Main: Suhrkamp, 1982);

Hans Weigel, *Karl Kraus oder Die Macht der Ohnmacht* (Vienna: Molden, 1968);

Cedric E. Williams, "Karl Kraus: The Absolute Satirist," in his *The Broken Eagle: The Politics of Austrian Literature from Empire to Anschluss* (New York: Barnes & Noble, 1974);

Harry Zohn, *Karl Kraus* (New York: Twayne, 1971);

Zohn, "Karl Kraus im englischen Sprachraum: Erfahrungen eines Übersetzers," *Literatur und Kritik*, 213-214 (April/May 1987): 112-121.

Papers:
Karl Kraus's papers were destroyed by the Nazis.

Heinrich Mann

(27 March 1871 - 12 March 1950)

Hans Wagener
University of California, Los Angeles

See also the Mann entry in *DLB 66: German Fiction Writers, 1885-1913*.

PLAY PRODUCTIONS: *Der Tyrann*, Berlin, Neues Deutsches Theater, 2 March 1910;

Variété, Munich, Zum großen Wurstl, 1910 (exact date unknown, but before 11 November);

Die Unschuldige, Berlin, Kleines Theater, 11 November 1910;

Schauspielerin, Berlin, Theater an der Königgrätzer Straße, 6 November 1911;

Die große Liebe, Berlin, Lessingtheater, 8 February 1913;

Madame Legros, Munich, Kammerspiele and Lübeck, Stadttheater, 19 February 1917;

Brabach, Munich, Residenztheater, 22 November 1919;

Der Weg zur Macht, Munich, Residenztheater, 21 October 1920;

Das gastliche Haus, Munich, Kammerspiele, 21 January 1927;

Bibi: Seine Jugend in drei Akten, Berlin, Theater im Palmenhaus, 22 October 1928;

Das Strumpfband, Celle, Schloßtheater, December 1965.

BOOKS: *In einer Familie: Roman* (Munich: Albert, 1894; revised edition, Berlin: Ullstein, 1924);

Das Wunderbare und andere Novellen (Paris, Leipzig & Munich: Langen, 1897);

Ein Verbrechen und andere Geschichten (Leipzig-Reudnitz: Baum, 1898);

Im Schlaraffenland: Ein Roman unter feinen Leuten (Munich: Langen, 1900); translated by Axton D. B. Clark as *In the Land of Cockaigne* (New York: Macauley, 1929); translation republished as *Berlin: The Land of Cockaigne* (London: Gollancz, 1929);

Die Göttinnen oder Die drei Romane der Herzogin von Assy, 3 volumes: *Diana; Minerva; Venus* (Munich: Langen, 1903); volume 1 translated by Erich Posselt and Emmet Glore as *Diana*

(New York: Coward-McCann, 1929);

Die Jagd nach Liebe: Roman (Munich: Langen, 1903);

Professor Unrat oder das Ende eines Tyrannen: Roman (Munich: Langen, 1905); republished as *Der blaue Engel* (Berlin: Weichert, 1951); translated anonymously as *The Blue Angel* (London: Reader's Library, 1931); translation republished as *Small Town Tyrant* (New York: Creative Age Press, 1944); retranslated by Wirt Williams as *The Blue Angel* (New York: New American Library, 1959);

Flöten und Dolche: Novellen (Munich: Langen, 1905); "Pippo Spano" translated by Basil Creighton, in *Tellers of Tales*, edited by W. Somerset Maugham (New York: Doubleday, Doran, 1939), pp. 780-808; "Drei-Minuten-Roman" translated by Victor Lange as "Three Minute Novel," in *Great German Short Novels and Stories*, edited by Lange (New York: Random House, 1952), pp. 396-400;

Eine Freundschaft: Gustav Flaubert und George Sand (Munich: Bonsels, 1905);

Mnais und Ginevra (Munich & Leipzig: Piper, 1906);

Schauspielerin: Novelle (Vienna & Leipzig: Wiener Verlag, 1906);

Stürmische Morgen: Novellen (Munich: Langen, 1906); "Abdankung" translated by Rolf N. Linn as "Abdication," *Spectrum*, 4 (Spring-Summer 1960);

Zwischen den Rassen: Ein Roman (Munich: Langen, 1907);

Die Bösen (Leipzig: Insel, 1908);

Die kleine Stadt: Roman (Leipzig: Insel, 1909); translated by Winifred Ray as *The Little Town* (London: Secker, 1930; Boston & New York: Houghton Mifflin, 1931);

Gesammelte Werke, 4 volumes (Berlin: Cassirer, 1909);

Heinrich Mann

Variété: Ein Akt (Berlin: Cassirer, 1910);

Das Herz: Novellen (Leipzig: Insel, 1910);

Die Rückkehr vom Hades: Novellen (Leipzig: Insel, 1911);

Schauspielerin: Drama in 3 Akten (Berlin: Cassirer, 1911);

Die große Liebe: Drama in 4 Akten (Berlin: Cassirer, 1912);

Auferstehung: Novelle (Leipzig: Insel, 1913);

Madame Legros: Drama in 3 Akten (Berlin: Cassirer, 1913); translated by Winifred Katzin in *Eight European Plays*, edited by Katzin (New York: Brentano's, 1927), pp. 247-303;

Die Novellen, 2 volumes (Munich: Wolff, 1916);

Brabach: Drama in 3 Akten (Leipzig: Wolff, 1917);

Gesammelte Romane und Novellen, 10 volumes (Leipzig: Wolff, 1917);

Die Armen: Roman (Leipzig: Wolff, 1917);

Bunte Gesellschaft: Novellen (Munich: Langen, 1917);

Der Untertan: Roman (Leipzig & Vienna: Wolff, 1918); translated by Ernest Boyd as *The Patrioteer* (New York: Harcourt, 1929); translation republished as *Little Superman* (New York: Creative Age Press, 1945); translation

republished as *Man of Straw* (London: Hutchinson, 1946);

Drei Akte: Der Tyrann; Die Unschuldige; Variété (Leipzig: Wolff, 1918);

Der Weg zur Macht: Drama in 3 Akten (Munich: Wolff, 1919);

Der Sohn: Novelle (Hannover: Steegemann, 1919);

Macht und Mensch (Munich: Wolff, 1919);

Der Ehrgeizige: Novelle (Munich: Roland, 1920);

Die Tote und andere Novellen (Munich: Recht, 1920);

Diktatur der Vernunft (Berlin: Die Schmiede, 1923);

Abrechnungen: Sieben Novellen (Berlin: Propyläen, 1924);

Der Jüngling: Novellen (Munich: Langes, 1924);

Das gastliche Haus: Komödie in 3 Akten (Munich: Langes, 1924);

Der Kopf: Roman (Berlin, Vienna & Leipzig: Zsolnay, 1925);

Kobes: Mit 10 Lithographien von Georg Grosz (Berlin: Propyläen, 1925);

Gesammelte Werke, 13 volumes (Berlin, Vienna & Leipzig: Zsolnay, 1925-1932);

Liliane und Paul: Novelle (Berlin, Vienna & Leipzig: Zsolnay, 1926);

Mutter Marie: Roman (Berlin, Vienna & Leipzig: Zsolnay, 1927); translated by Whittaker Chambers as *Mother Mary* (New York: Simon & Schuster, 1928);

Suturp (Berlin: Wegweiser-Verlag, 1928);

Eugénie oder Die Bürgerzeit: Roman (Berlin, Vienna & Leipzig: Zsolnay, 1928); translated by Arthur J. Asthon as *The Royal Woman* (New York: Macauley, 1930);

Sieben Jahre: Chronik der Gedanken und Vorgänge (Berlin, Vienna & Leipzig: Zsolnay, 1929);

Sie sind jung (Berlin, Vienna & Leipzig: Zsolnay, 1929);

Der Tyrann; Die Branzilla: Novellen (Leipzig: Reclam, 1929);

Die große Sache: Roman (Berlin: Kiepenheuer, 1930);

Geist und Tat: Franzosen 1780-1930 (Berlin: Kiepenheuer, 1931);

Ein ernstes Leben: Roman (Berlin, Vienna & Leipzig: Zsolnay, 1932); translated by Edwin and Willa Muir as *The Hill of Lies* (London: Jarrolds, 1934; New York: Dutton, 1935);

Das öffentliche Leben (Berlin, Vienna & Leipzig: Zsolnay, 1932);

Die Welt der Herzen: Novellen (Berlin: Kiepenheuer, 1932);

Das Bekenntnis zum Übernationalen (Berlin, Vienna & Leipzig: Zsolnay, 1933);

Der Haß: Deutsche Zeitgeschichte (Amsterdam: Querido, 1933);

Heinrich Mann und ein junger Deutscher: Der Sinn dieser Emigration (Paris: Europäischer Merkur, 1934);

Ihr ordinärer Antisemitismus (New York: Information & Service Associates, 1934);

Die Jugend des Königs Henri Quatre: Roman (Amsterdam: Querido, 1935); translated by Eric Sutton as *Young Henry of Navarre* (New York: Knopf, 1937); translation republished as *King Wren: The Youth of Henri IV* (London: Secker & Warburg, 1937);

Es kommt der Tag: Deutsches Lesebuch (Zurich: Europa-Verlag, 1936);

Hilfe für die Opfer des Faschismus: Rede 1937 (Paris: Überparteilicher deutscher Hilfsausschuß, 1937);

Die Vollendung des Königs Henri Quatre (Amsterdam: Querido, 1938); translated by Sutton as *Henri Quatre, King of France*, 2 volumes (London: Secker & Warburg, 1938-1939); translation republished as *Henry, King of France* (New York: Knopf, 1939);

Mut: Essays (Paris: Éditions du 10 mai, 1939);

Lidice: Roman (Mexico City: Editorial "El Libro Libre," 1943);

Ein Zeitalter wird besichtigt (Stockholm: Neuer Verlag, 1945);

Voltaire—Goethe (Weimar: Verlag Werden und Wirken, 1947);

Der Atem: Roman (Amsterdam: Querido, 1949);

Ausgewählte Werke in Einzelausgaben, edited by Alfred Kantorowicz, 13 volumes (Berlin: Aufbau, 1951-1962);

Geist und Tat: Ein Brevier, edited by Alfred Kantorowicz (Berlin: Aufbau, 1953);

Eine Liebesgeschichte: Novelle (Munich: Weismann, 1953);

Empfang bei der Welt: Roman (Berlin: Aufbau, 1956);

Das gestohlene Dokument und andere Novellen (Berlin: Aufbau, 1957);

Gesammelte Werke in Einzelausgaben, 14 volumes (Hamburg: Claassen, 1958-1966);

Die traurige Geschichte von Friedrich dem Großen: Fragment (Berlin: Aufbau, 1960);

Das Stelldichein; Die roten Schuhe (Munich: Dobbeck, 1960);

Gesammelte Werke, edited by the Akademie der Künste der DDR, 24 volumes published (Berlin: Aufbau, 1965-   );

Werkauswahl in zehn Bänden, 10 volumes (Düsseldorf: Claassen, 1976).

OTHER: Alfred Capus, *Wer zuletzt lacht . . . : Roman. Aus dem Französischen*, translated by Mann (Munich: Langen, 1901);

Anatole France, *Komödiantengeschichte: Roman. Aus dem Französischen*, translated by Mann (Munich: Langen, 1904);

Pierre Ambroise François Choderlos de Laclos, *Gefährliche Freundschaften*, translated by Mann, 2 volumes (Berlin & Leipzig: Verlag der Funken, 1905); republished as *Schlimme Liebschaften* (Leipzig: Insel, 1920); republished as *Gefährliche Liebschaften* (Leipzig: Insel, 1926);

Albert Jamet, *Der unbekannte Soldat spricht*, translated by Hermynia zur Mühlen, foreword by Mann (Vienna: Prager, 1932);

Gerhart Seger, *Oranienburg: Erster authentischer Bericht eines aus dem Konzentrationslager Geflüchteten*, foreword by Mann (Karlsbad: Graphia, 1934);

Hans A. Joachim, *Die Stimme Victor Hugos: Hörspiel*, afterword by Mann (Paris: Editions du Phénix, 1935);

Felix Fechenbach, *Mein Herz schlägt weiter: Briefe aus der Schutzhaft*, foreword by Mann (St. Gallen: Kulturverlag, 1936);

Manuel Humbert, *Adolf Hitlers "Mein Kampf": Dichtung und Wahrheit*, foreword by Mann (Paris: Pariser Tageblatt, 1936);

The Living Thoughts of Nietzsche, edited by Mann (London: Cassell, 1939);

Der Pogrom, foreword by Mann (Zurich & Paris: Verlag für soziale Literatur, 1939);

Deutsche Stimmen zu 1789, foreword by Mann (Paris: Deutsches Kulturkartell, 1939);

Ernst Busch, *Lied der Zeit: Lieder, Balladen und Kantaten aus Deutschland von 1914 bis 1945*, foreword by Mann (Berlin-Niederschönhausen: Verlag Lied der Zeit, 1946);

Morgenröte: Ein Lesebuch, introduction by Mann (New York: Aurora, 1947);

Victor Hugo, *Dreiundneunzig*, translated by Alfred Wolfenstein, afterword by Mann (Munich: List, 1968).

Heinrich Mann is known today as a writer who satirized and analyzed Wilhelminian and Weimar society, who understood where Germany was heading politically, and who warned in vain of the impending catastrophe of Nazism. His novels, essays, and plays display his development from a preoccupation with the problems of the artist to a concern with social and political criticism and the attempt to prevent the victory of national socialism.

Luiz Heinrich Mann was born on 27 March 1871 to Thomas Johann Heinrich Mann, a merchant and patrician citizen of the old Hanseatic city of Lübeck, and Julia da Silva-Bruhns Mann, who had been born in Brazil as the daughter of a German immigrant and his Brazilian wife. His younger brother was Thomas Mann, with whom his relationship would be close but at times difficult because of their political differences. Not wanting to take over the family's wholesale grain business, Mann became an apprentice to a Dresden bookseller in 1889; the following year he went to work for the Samuel Fischer publishing house in Berlin, where he also attended the university. When the family business was sold after his father's death in 1891, Mann became financially independent and decided to pursue a career as a writer. After spending a great deal of time in France and Italy, he settled in Munich in 1914. In August of that year he married the Czech actress Maria Kanová; in 1916 their daughter Leonie was born. The Manns moved to Berlin in

Poster, designed by Paul Rosié, for the 1929 film based on Mann's novel Professor Unrat

1928; Heinrich and Maria were divorced in 1930. On 21 February 1933, less than a month after the Nazis came to power on 30 January, Mann left Germany for the French Riviera. During the next seven years he condemned Nazism in French newspapers and journals and participated in antifascist rallies. In 1939 he married Nelly Kroeger. When Germany invaded France in 1940 he, his wife, his nephew Golo Mann, and their friends Franz Werfel and Alma Mahler-Werfel fled across the Pyrenees to Spain, then to Portugal, and from there to the United States, arriving on 13 October 1940. Joining his brother Thomas in southern California, Mann settled in a modest apartment in Santa Monica. Unsuccessful as a writer in the United States, he was supported by Thomas and, until her suicide in 1944, by his wife's work as a nurse. In 1949 the newly founded German Democratic Republic invited him to become the first president of the German Academy of the Arts in East Berlin. He accepted and was preparing to return to Germany when he died of a stroke on 12 March 1950.

Mann is almost exclusively known as a novelist, the author of such works as *Professor Unrat* (1905; translated as *The Blue Angel*, 1931), *Der Untertan* (The Underling, 1918; translated as *The Patrioteer*, 1929), and two novels dealing with the French king Henri IV (1935 and 1938). But he also wrote plays, several of which were quite successful. The majority of these stage works were written shortly before and during World War I, but a few were written during the period of the Weimar Republic. He later said in *Ein Zeitalter wird besichtigt* (An Age Is Examined, 1945): "Das Theater war, um unbedenklich zu sprechen, mein lustigster Abschnitt. Die paar kräftigsten Jahre um die Mitte des Lebens genügten meinem Bedürfnis nach den dramaturgischen Strapazen. Andere, die immer Stücke schrieben, konnten nicht erraten, wie anziehend die Verschiedenheit der neuen Arbeit von meiner vorigen war" ([The time when I wrote for] the theater was, I can say without hesitation, the happiest period of my life. The few strongest years at the prime of my life satisfied my need for dramaturgical forays. Others, who always wrote plays, were unable to guess how attractive the difference between the new work and the former one was). This statement is somewhat misleading: although Mann certainly enjoyed writing plays, several of them are important counterparts to the novels he was working on at the same time and should not be dismissed as mere diversions. Moreover, Mann often developed his characters through dialogue in his prose works as well as in his plays. His novel *Lidice* (1943) and the fragment *Die traurige Geschichte von Friedrich dem Großen* (The Sad History of Frederick the Great, 1960) rely so heavily on dialogue that they have much in common with drama.

Mann's first play, *Das Strumpfband* (The Garter), written in 1902, was a comedy; it remains unpublished and was not performed until 1965. His first published and performed dramas were adaptations of his novellas with few changes having been necessary to transform them into the new genre. *Der Tyrann* (The Tyrant, 1918) is based on a novella of the same title that was first published in the volume *Die Bösen* (The Wicked Ones, 1908). Typical of the early Mann—who, beginning with *Die Göttinnen oder Die drei Romane der Herzogin von Assy* (The Goddesses; or, The Three Novels of the Duchess of Assy, 1903) and ending with *Die kleine Stadt* (1909; translated as *The Little Town*, 1930), chose Italian themes and settings for his works—it introduces a nineteenth-century Italian duke who has the beautiful Raminga brought to his chambers so that he can make love to her. She, however, has come to kill him—not only as a political act but also because the duke has killed her brother, the tyrant's former friend. The duke seems to be moved by her arguments for political freedom, and he declares his willingness to set his people free. Raminga's feelings change to admiration and love, and she reveals her original intentions. The duke suddenly announces that she has to die because she now knows his innermost feelings. He calls the guards and turns his back as she is dragged off. The tyrant is unable to let Raminga live, because accepting her love would impair his absolute power. The drama is an incisive psychological study of the corrupting effect of power on an essentially weak man. His ancestors wielded their power without hesitation or bad conscience; he is torn between vice and virtue.

Mann's next one-act play, *Die Unschuldige* (The Innocent Woman; performed, 1910; published, 1918), is the dramatization of a novella first published in 1910 in the collection *Das Herz* (The Heart). Halland, an attorney, has won the acquittal of Gabriele, who had been accused of killing her husband. Now they are married, and on their wedding night Gabriele makes him believe that she is a murderess after all. Although she then tells him that she was just pretending, the doubt remains. Mann skillfully suggests character traits of Gabriele that might make it possible for her to commit murder; he gives motives, refutes proofs of her innocence, and demonstrates that she has knowledge of particulars of the crime that could be known by no one but the perpetrator. Halland can never again be sure of Gabriele's innocence, and her playacting was so convincing that she herself may not be sure what actually happened.

Unlike *Der Tyrann* and *Die Unschuldige*, *Variété* (1910) was written specifically for the stage. It was most likely inspired by the plays of Frank Wedekind, particularly by *Der Kammersänger* (The Court Singer, 1899). The satirical, grotesque one-act *Variété* shares the theme of reality versus acting with the two earlier dramas. The vaudeville actress Leda d'Ambre and her gifted musical accompanist Fred try to persuade the theater director Fein to engage them for his stage. Since Fein only wants Leda, she and Fred feign an attempted double suicide as a publicity stunt. As a result, Fein hires both of them at a fantastic salary. Mann probes into the characters of the two performers, their penchant for melodrama, their playacting in their relationship with each other, and the pretended popularity which they use to cover up their miserable state. Pretense and reality are as indistinguishable as in *Die Unschuldige*.

Der Tyrann was first performed on 2 March 1910 at the Neues Deutsches Theater (New German Theater) in Berlin. *Variété* was first performed during the same year (the exact date is unknown) in Munich at Zum großen Wurstl (At the Big Hanswurst), a vaudeville theater that later became the more serious Münchener Kammerspiele (Munich Intimate Theater). All three one-act plays were performed together on 11 November 1910 at the Kleines Theater (Little Theater) in Berlin by the avant-garde literary society "Pan," with Tilla Durieux in the lead roles. While the response to the other two plays was reserved, the audience was won over by *Variété*. The reviews had more praise for Durieux than for Mann.

The theme of the intermingling of life and art was continued in a serious counterpart to *Variété*, the three-act *Schauspielerin* (Actress, 1911). The actress Leonie Hallmann wants to give up her acting career and marry the young factory owner Harry Seiler. She says: "Ich will Frieden. Wärme will ich endlich und Sicherheit—oder nichts" (I want peace. I want warmth and security at last—or nothing). Seiler's bourgeois mother is violently opposed to the marriage, believing that the actress will squander the family's money. Leonie's former lover, Fork, also schemes against her. In contrast to the weak Harry, Fork is a brutal, cynical adventurer with an overpowering sensuality. He seduces Leonie again and makes her realize that she is an actress by nature and is unable to settle down. By acting the part of a sweet and modest girl, Leonie wins over Frau Seiler but ultimately commits suicide because she has become inextricably entangled in a conflict between acting and reality.

The drama is based on a 1906 novella of the same title. The name of the heroine is the same in both the novella and the drama; in the novella the weak fiancé is called Rothaus, and the brutal lover, Fork, does not yet exist. In the novella the heroine does not commit suicide but only pretends to do so. The tragic ending of the play seems to have had an autobiographical basis: Mann's sister Carla had wanted to become an actress, despite her apparent lack of talent; when

her fiancé, the son of rich parents, acceded to their wishes and terminated their relationship, she committed suicide in 1910. *Schauspielerin* was first performed on 6 November 1911 at the Theater an der Königgrätzer Straße (Theater on Königgrätzer Street) in Berlin.

Die große Liebe (The Great Love, 1912) continues the theme of art versus life only indirectly. Christoph Gaßner, a composer, falls in love with Liane Löwen, wife of the industrialist Franz Löwen. She lacks the courage to leave her well-meaning husband and the flirtatious life-style she leads at luxurious spas and hotels. Liane is not able to experience great love; she merely dreams of it. She becomes Gaßner's mistress, but she commits herself neither to him nor to Viktor Türk, another industrialist who also loves her. The drama was not successful, probably because it dissipates its thrust in two different directions: it is a psychological play about the love between an artist and a married woman, but it is also a satire on the bourgeoisie and the nobility. Mann was at a turning point in his literary career with this play, evolving from a writer who deals with love and other personal feelings into a social critic. At the same time that he was writing *Die große Liebe*, he was also working on his great social-critical novel *Der Untertan*. *Die große Liebe* was first performed on 8 February 1913 at the Lessingtheater, Berlin, to negative reviews.

Mann interrupted his work on *Der Untertan* to write the drama *Madame Legros* (published, 1913; performed, 1917; translated 1927), which was completed in a few weeks. The plot reflects Mann's new political concerns. In 1789 Madame Legros, the wife of a Paris linen dealer, finds a letter from a man named Latude who has been unjustly imprisoned in the Bastille for forty-three years. Spontaneously making his cry for help her own cause, she finally pleads his case to the queen, Marie Antoinette, at whose order Latude is released. Madame Legros receives the Virtue Prize from the Académie and returns to her husband. When the French Revolution arrives with the storming of the Bastille, Madame Legros fails to understand the action.

Madame Legros is not a revolutionary heroine; she is a simple, naive woman who acts out of her innate sense of justice. She risks her marriage, causes financial problems for herself and her husband, exposes herself to ridicule, is almost arrested for causing a public uprising, promises herself to the Chevalier d'Angelot if he will help her achieve her goal, betrays the name of an Austrian agent, and feigns an affair with Latude to arouse the queen's interest. Yet her heroism is bound to this personal act; she does not see the general injustice that leads to the revolution but only one injustice demanding rectification. Mann offers a satire of the corrupt ancien régime, the nobility who see Madame Legros and her cause as entertainment to relieve their boredom; but she is not a "pure" character herself: she offers herself freely, playacts when her emotional drive weakens, and is plagued with jealousy when one of the noble ladies reports having visited Latude. Madame Legros has recently lost her only child, and she may have transferred her maternal love to Latude. It is a love from a distance that increasingly takes on all the characteristics of an obsession. Mann's language is stilted, stylized, and full of pathos—particularly in the first act, which at times attempts to imitate French diction in German. It would be tempting to see the play as a political allegory, but there are no clear parallels to the situation of the Wilhelmine empire. Mann used as his source Jules Michelet's *Histoire de la Révolution française* (1847-1853), moving the action from 1784 to 1789 and placing Latude in the Bastille instead of the Bicêtre, a prison for thieves and blackmailers. His Madame Legros, unlike the historical figure, does not become the leader of her people, an embodiment of freedom, but remains a naive human being who responds to a need to rectify a specific case of injustice.

The play was first performed on 19 February 1917, simultaneously in the Kammerspiele in Munich and in the Stadttheater (City Theater) of Lübeck. In spite of the difficulty of identifying with the heroine, it received favorable reviews except from critics of the political right. In *Ein Zeitalter wird besichtigt* Mann considers *Madame Legros* his only drama equal to his novels.

Brabach (1917), begun in 1916, seems at first glance to be quite different from *Madame Legros* but actually has much in common with the earlier drama. Brabach, an aging bank teller, realizes that he has wasted his life caring for his sister who has recently died, and working at a boring job. He decides to use his money to support the young bank intern Wendlicher, who has taken the welfare of the masses to heart and speaks regularly at meetings of a proletarian party. But Brabach has chosen poorly: Wendlicher merely uses him and the widow of one of the bank's owners to get money to ruin the present owner of the bank, Privy Councillor von Beer, whose daughter Esther is in love with him. Brabach at last realizes his mistake, and in a fit of rage Wendlicher stabs him to death.

The parallel to *Madame Legros* is that both title characters want to do good for others. In Brabach this altruism is complemented by a psychological need to compensate for his failed life by seeing his dreams realized in someone else. *Brabach* was strongly influenced by the contemporary expressionist drama, not only in its theme of generational conflict and its concern about mankind but also in its sententious language. Brabach has been compared to the bank teller in Georg Kaiser's expressionist play *Von Morgens bis Mitternachts* (From Morning to Midnight, 1916). In contrast to expressionist treatments of the father-son theme, however, Mann's son figure turns out to be unworthy. His killing of the father figure marks the victory not of an idealistic new vision of mankind but of an insensitive, egotistical, brutal, and superficial one.

Probably because of its sententious dialogue and contrived situations, the drama failed. All of the characters, whether educated or not, speak in the same way and act as mouthpieces for moral positions, aphorisms, and maxims. The first performance on 22 November 1919 at the Munich Residenztheater was a complete failure, and the reviews were devastating.

The type of the young, ambitious man who wants to succeed at all costs recurs in *Der Weg zur Macht* (The Road to Power, 1919), written in 1917-1918. In 1795 the bloody phase of the French Revolution has been completed, and the bourgeoisie has begun to establish itself. The believers in the old ideals of the revolution, such as the honest Thureau, are killed. The noncommittal Bourienne; the corrupt Barras and Tallien; and the war profiteer Collot, who supplied the army with cardboard shoes, hope to be able to keep the reins of power in their own hands. They are outsmarted by the ambitious General Napoleon Bonaparte, who at age twenty-six is looking for an assignment and who is tolerated in the salons only because he is the protégé of beautiful women. At first he believes in brotherhood, equality, and liberty, but gradually these youthful ideals give way to the scheming of a power-hungry politician who uses military power and blackmail to control his enemies. He becomes the commander of Paris and of the Italian army, which he is determined to use to plunder that country.

Napoleon is characterized by Mann as an actor who uses everyone in order to achieve his

Mann in 1925; oil painting by Willi Geiger (Deutsche Akademie der Künste, Berlin)

goal of power. Thus he is a realistic counterpart to the great actor François-Joseph Talma, whom he encounters in two important scenes of the drama. As Talma's schemes succeed in capturing him the role of Caesar in Pierre Corneille's play *La mort de Pompée* (1642), Bonaparte's schemes, betrayals, and playacting will soon give him the status of a new Caesar in Europe.

When the play was first performed on 21 October 1920 at the Residenztheater in Munich, it could be viewed as a comment on the failure of the 1918 revolution; but Mann at that time was not interested in drawing parallels between contemporary and historical events. He was more intrigued by the relation of ideals and reality and by what constituted the presumed greatness of a historical hero. His preoccupation with Napoleon was a lifelong one, and his judgment of the French emperor changed several times. *Der Weg zur Macht* is, next to *Madame Legros*, one of Mann's best dramas.

War profiteers appear once again in Mann's *Das gastliche Haus* (The Hospitable House, 1924). Written in the inflation year 1923, it deals with

the social upheaval following World War I. Privy Councillor Schummer is an industrialist who sees himself as the representative of "befestigter Reichtum" (stabilized wealth) even though his family has only been rich since 1880. His house once belonged to Count Quasse who committed suicide. Schummer had thrown out the count's two children and sent them to America. Under the names of Count and Countess Cassini they have returned to seek revenge on Schummer and his own two children, the adulteress Diana and the bankrupt lawyer Ralph. The Cassinis befriend Ralph and propose to move in with Schummer. At the same time, the war profiteer and black marketeer Milbe and his wife Trinetraute, who have bought Schummer's estate, arrive to take possession. Newly rich and unable to adapt to the behavior of the upper classes, they are the butt of much ridicule. At the conclusion of the complex intrigues all decide to live together in Schummer's house. Says Schummer: "Das ideale Verhältnis wäre das einmütige Zusammenleben aller sozialen Schichten und Generationen— natürlich nur, soweit sie Besitzende sind" (The ideal relationship would be the harmonious living-together of all social classes and generations—of course only insofar as they are propertied). Milbe replies: "Immer feste gegen die, die nichts haben. Nur nicht ins Geschäft reinlassen" (Always be tough against those who do not own anything. Just don't let them participate in the business).

This comedy is Mann's allegorical description of what he saw occurring in Germany at the time: the "hospitable house" represents the Weimar Republic. The staccato language and the character types have reminded most critics of Carl Sternheim's dramas "aus dem bürgerlichen Heldenleben" (about the heroic life of the middle class). What distinguishes this drama from *Der Weg zur Macht* is that the representatives of the upper social classes are in open agreement about taking advantage of the lower classes. The play was performed for the first time on 21 January 1927 in the Munich Kammerspiele. By this time the great inflation had been quelled, and the unrest of the postwar years had given way to seeming prosperity; the middle-class citizens were able to laugh at themselves and their folly.

The last dramatic piece Mann completed was the operetta *Bibi: Seine Jugend in drei Akten* (Bibi: His Youth in Three Acts) which was published in 1929 together with several novellas in the collection *Sie sind jung* (They Are Young). It was dedicated to the actress Trude Hesterberg, with whom Mann was such close friends that one newspaper reported that he intended to marry her. Youthful characters of the title hero's type are also to be found in several of Mann's prose works written around this time, such as the novels *Die große Sache* (The Big Deal, 1930) and *Ein ernstes Leben* (A Serious Life, 1932; translated as *The Hill of Lies*, 1934). Bibi is a seventeen-year-old professional dancing partner who works in a bar. Women like him and he likes them. He and his friends change partners frequently in a merry-go-round of love that also includes a rich industrialist; a film star; the industrialist's mother, who is infatuated with Bibi; and his daughter, whom Bibi ultimately marries. The play depicts cabaret gaiety and quick success by young people after the end of the 1923 inflation. Allusions are made to the rootlessness of this generation, which has nothing but its youth and its wits to live on; but this serious undercurrent does not make the play a socially critical one. *Bibi* was first performed on 22 October 1928 in the Theater im Palmenhaus in Berlin.

Bronze bust of Mann on his grave in the Dorotheenstadt Cemetery, Berlin

Heinrich Mann's plays had no great impact on the history of German drama; he accomplished far more in the genre of the novel. Nevertheless, *Schauspielerin*, *Madame Legros*, and *Der Weg zur Macht* are powerful and insightful dramas and remain worthy of attention.

Letters:
Thomas Mann/Heinrich Mann: Briefwechsel 1900-1949, edited by Hans Wysling (Frankfurt am Main: Fischer, 1984).

Bibliography:
Edith Zenker, *Heinrich-Mann-Bibliographie: Werke* (Berlin & Weimar: Aufbau, 1967).

Biographies
Klaus Schröter, *Heinrich Mann* (Hamburg: Rowohlt, 1967);
Sigrid Anger, ed., *Heinrich Mann 1871-1950: Leben und Werk in Dokumenten und Bildern* (Berlin & Weimar: Aufbau, 1971);

Volker Ebersbach, *Heinrich Mann: Leben, Werk, Wirken* (Frankfurt am Main: Röderberg, 1978);

Nigel Hamilton, *The Brothers Mann: The Lives of Heinrich and Thomas Mann 1871-1950 and 1875-1955* (London: Secker & Warburg, 1978).

References:

Heinz Ludwig Arnold, ed., *Heinrich Mann: Sonderband aus der Reihe text + kritik* (Munich: Boorberg, 1971);

William Brust, "Art and the Activist: Social Themes in the Dramas of Heinrich Mann," Ph.D. dissertation, University of Minnesota, 1968;

Jürgen Haupt, *Heinrich Mann* (Stuttgart: Metzler, 1980);

"Heinrich Manns Einakter in der Vorstellung durch die Zeitschrift 'Pan,'" *Arbeitskreis Heinrich Mann: Mitteilungsblatt*, 11 (1978): 18-32; 14 (1978): 19-26;

"Heinrich Manns Einakter in späteren Aufführungen," *Arbeitskreis Heinrich Mann: Mitteilungsblatt*, 14 (1978): 26-29;

Alfred Kantorowicz, "Nachwort," in *Schauspiele*, by Mann (Düsseldorf: Claassen, 1986), pp. 622-655;

Uwe Rosenbaum, "Die Gestalt des Schauspielers auf dem Theater des 19. Jahrhunderts mit der besonderen Berücksichtigung der dramatischen Werke von Hermann Bahr, Arthur Schnitzler und Heinrich Mann," Ph.D. dissertation, University of Cologne, 1971;

Ulrich Weisstein, *Heinrich Mann: Eine historisch-kritische Einführung in sein dichterisches Werk* (Tübingen: Niemeyer, 1962), pp. 231-255;

Weisstein, "Heinrich Mann's Madame Legros—Not a Revolutionary Drama," *Germanic Review*, 35 (February 1960): 39-49.

Papers:

Most of the literary estate of Heinrich Mann is in the Literaturarchiv of the Akademie der Künste (Academy of the Arts), Berlin. Letters and other materials are also at the Deutsches Literaturarchiv (German Literature Archive), Marbach am Neckar; and the Deutsche Bibliothek (German Library), Frankfurt am Main.

Johannes Schlaf

(21 June 1862 - 2 February 1941)

Raleigh Whitinger
University of Alberta

PLAY PRODUCTIONS: *Die Familie Selicke*, Berlin, Freie Bühne, 7 April 1890;

Meister Oelze, Berlin, Freie Deutsche Volksbühne, 4 February 1894;

Gertrud, Berlin, Residenztheater, 24 April 1898;

Der Bann, Berlin, Berliner Theater, 20 October 1901.

BOOKS: *Papa Hamlet*, by Schlaf and Arno Holz, as Bjarne P. Holmsen (Leipzig: Reißner, 1889);

Junge Leute: Roman (Berlin: Zoberbier, 1890);

Die Familie Selicke: Drama in drei Aufzügen, by Schlaf and Holz (Berlin: Ißleib, 1890; Cambridge: Cambridge University Press, 1950);

Neue Gleise: Gemeinsames, by Schlaf and Holz (Berlin: Fontane, 1892);

Der geschundene Pegasus: Eine Mirlitoniade in Versen, by Schlaf and Holz (Berlin: Fontane, 1892);

In Dingsda (Berlin: Fischer, 1892);

Meister Oelze: Drama in drei Aufzügen (Berlin: Fischer, 1892; revised edition, Munich: Müller, 1908; revised edition, Weimar: Fink, 1922);

Frühling (Leipzig: Kreisende Ringe, 1896);

Sommertod: Novellistisches (Leipzig: Kreisende Ringe, 1897);

Walt Whitman; Lyrik des Chat noir; Paul Verlaine (Leipzig: Kreisende Ringe, 1897);

Gertrud: Drama in drei Aufzügen (Berlin & Paris: Sassenbach, 1898);

Die Feindlichen: Drama in vier Aufzügen (Minden: Bruns, 1899);

Helldunkel: Gedichte (Minden: Bruns, 1899);

Lenore und Anderes (Berlin: Fontane, 1899);

Stille Welten: Neue Stimmungen aus Dingsda (Berlin: Fontane, 1899);

Die Kuhmagd und Anderes (Berlin: Fontane, 1900);

Das dritte Reich: Ein Berliner Roman (Berlin: Fontane, 1900);

Jesus und Mirjam; Der Tod des Antichrist (Minden: Bruns, 1901);

Die Suchenden: Roman (Berlin: Fontane, 1902);

Der Narr und Anderes: Novellistisches (Leipzig: Seemann, 1902);

Noch einmal "Arno Holz und ich" (Berlin: Meßner, 1902);

Peter Boies Freite: Roman (Leipzig: Seemann, 1903);

Frühjahrsblumen und Anderes (Berlin: Fleischel, 1903);

Der Kleine: Berliner Roman (Stuttgart: Juncker, 1904);

Walt Whitman (Berlin & Leipzig: Schuster & Loeffler, 1904);

Die Nonne: Novellen (Vienna: Wiener Verlag, 1905);

Mein Roman "Der Kleine": Eine Glosse (Stuttgart: Juncker, 1905);

Mentale Suggestion: Ein letztes Wort in meiner Streitsache mit Arno Holz (Stuttgart: Juncker, 1905);

Emile Verhaeren (Berlin: Schuster & Loeffler, 1905);

Das Sommerlied: Gedichte (Stuttgart: Juncker, 1905);

Weigand: Drama in drei Aufzügen (Munich: Bonsels, 1906);

Christus und Sophie (Vienna: Akademischer Verlag, 1906);

Diagnose und Faksimile: Notgedrungene Berichtigung eines neuen, von Arno Holz gegen mich gerichteten Angriffes (Munich: Bonsels, 1906);

Kritik der Taineschen Kunsttheorie (Vienna & Leipzig: Akademischer Verlag, 1906);

Maurice Maeterlinck (Berlin: Bard, Marquardt, 1906);

Novalis und Sophie von Kühn: Eine Psychophysiologische Studie (Munich: Bonsels, 1906);

Walt Whitman Homosexueller? Kritische Revision einer Whitman-Abhandlung von Dr. Eduard Bertz (Minden: Bruns, 1906);

Frenderchen und Anderes: Novellen (Leipzig: Grethlein, 1907);

Der "Fall" Nietzsche: Eine "Überwindung" (Leipzig: Thomas, 1907);

Der Krieg (Berlin: Marquardt, 1907);

Johannes Schlaf

Die Kritik und mein "Fall Nietzsche": Ein Notruf (Leipzig: Thomas, 1907);

Hermelinchen (Berlin: Harmonie, 1907);

    Der Prinz: Roman in zwei Bänden, 2 volumes (Munich: Müller, 1908);

Bernoulli und der Fall Nietzsche: Ein Beitrag zu gegenwärtigen Nietzsche-Krisis (Leipzig: Thomas, 1908);

Von der Freiheit des "religiosen Erziehers" und der Vollendung der Religion: Eine Entgegnung auf Horneffers: Religion und Deutschtum (Leipzig: Verlag deutsche Zukunft, 1908);

Psychomonismus, Polarität und Individualität: Ein offener Brief an Herrn Professor Max Verworn (Leipzig: Eckardt, 1908);

Unser westeuropäisches Schisma: Ein Wort zu der modernistischen Bewegung (Leipzig: Eckardt, 1908);

Am toten Punkt: Roman (Munich: Müller, 1909),

Der alte Herr Weismann und andere Novellen (Berlin: Bondy, 1910);

Das absolute Individuum und die Vollendung der Religion: Zwei Teile in einem Band (Berlin: Oesterheld, 1910);

Aufstieg: Roman (Berlin: Bondy, 1911);

Religion und Kosmos (Berlin: Hofmann, 1911);

Mieze: Der Roman eines freien Weibes (Munich: Müller, 1912);

Das Recht der Jugend: Erzählung (Berlin: Janke, 1913);

Tantchen Mohnhaupt und Anderes (Leipzig: Reclam, 1913; edited by Clifford E. Gates, New York: Knopf, 1927);

Auffallende Unstichhaltigkeit des fachmännischen Einwandes: Zur geozentrischen Feststellung (Munich: Müller, 1914);

Professor Plassmann und der Sonnenfleckenphänomen: Weiteres zur geozentrischen Feststellung (Hamburg: Hephaestos, 1914);

Mutter Lise: Roman (Munich: Müller, 1914);

Vom Krieg, vom Frieden und dem Irrtum des Pazifismus (Munich: Bonsels, 1918);

Die Erde, nicht die Sonne: Das geozentrische Weltbild (Munich: Dreiländer, 1919);

Gedichte in Prosa (Berlin: Boll & Pickardt, 1920);

Miele: Ein Charakterbild (Leipzig: Reclam, 1920);

Vorfrühling: Die Greisin: Erzählungen (Hannover: Banas & Dette, 1921);

Neues zur geozentrischen Feststellung (Rothenfelde: Holzwarth, 1921);

Die Wandlung: Roman (Dessau: Dünnhaupt, 1922);

Ein freies Weib: Roman (Leipzig: Keils, 1922);

Das Gottlied (Querfurt: Jaeckel, 1922);

Radium: Erzählungen (Berlin: Mosaik, 1922);

Seele (Weimar: Fink, 1922);

Ein Wildgatter schlag' ich hinter mir zu: Vaterländisches aus Dingsda (Braunschweig: Graff, 1922);

Der Lilienstrauß und der Ruf: Novellen (Bremen: Schünemann, 1923);

Die Linden, by Schlaf and Charlotte Francke-Roesing (Querfurt: Jaeckel, 1923);

Der Weihnachtswunsch und anderes: Neue Erzählungen aus Dingsda (Querfurt: Burgverlag, 1924);

Die Nacht der Planeten (Querfurt: Jaeckel, 1925);

Deutschland (Querfurt: Jaeckel, 1925);

Die geozentrische Tatsache als unmittelbare Folgerung aus dem Sonnenfleckenphänomen (Leipzig: Hummel, 1925);

Die andere Dimension: Erzählungen (Berlin: Weltgeist-Bücher, 1926);

Dichtungen (Leipzig: Privately printed, 1927);

Die Mutter: Dichtung (Querfurt: Jaeckel, 1927);

Das Spiel der hohen Linien: Dichtungen (Weimar: Vimaria, 1927);

Kosmos und kosmischer Umlauf: Die geozentrische Lösung des kosmischen Problems (Weimar: Literarisches Institut H. Doetsch, 1927);

Die Sonnenvorgänge (Querfurt: Jaeckel, 1930);

Neues aus Dingsda (Querfurt: Jaeckel, 1933);

Ausgewählte Werke, edited by Ludwig Bäte (Querfurt: Jaeckel, 1934);

Zur Aprioritätenlehre Kants (Berlin-Steglitz: Dion, 1934);

Vom höchsten Wesen (Berlin: Dion, 1935);

Ein wichtigstes astronomisches Problem und seine Lösung (Berlin: Dion, 1937);

Aus meinem Leben: Erinnerungen (Halle: Hallische Nachrichten-Bücherei, 1941).

TRANSLATIONS: Walt Whitman, *Grashalme* (Leipzig: Reclam, 1907);

Henry Bryan Binns, *Walt Whitman: Ein Leben* (Leipzig: Haessel, 1907).

SELECTED PERIODICAL PUBLICATIONS—
UNCOLLECTED: "Realistische Romane?," *Freie Bühne für modernes Leben*, 1 (1890): 68-71;

"Prüderie," *Freie Bühne für modernes Leben*, 1 (1890): 161-164;

"Abber Paule!," by Schlaf and Arno Holz, *Freie Bühne für modernes Leben*, 1 (1890): 323-325;

"Krumme Windgasse 20," *Freie Bühne für modernes Leben*, 1 (1890): 351-360;

"Abseits," *Freie Bühne für modernes Leben*, 1 (1890): 579-584;

"Über die notwendige Einseitigkeit der Polemik," *Die Gesellschaft*, 7 (1891): 783-785;

"Walt Whitman," *Freie Bühne*, 3 (1892): 977-988;

"Moral, Kritik und Kunst," *Die Gesellschaft*, 7 (1897): 1168-1172;

"Vom intimen Drama," *Neuland*, 1 (1897): 33-38;

"Selbstbiographisches," *Die Gesellschaft*, 8 (1897): 166-167;

"Weshalb ich mein letztes Drama zerriß," *Die Zukunft*, 6 (1898): 564-567;

"Im Spiegel: Autobiographische Skizzen. XI. Johannes Schlaf," *Das litterarische Echo*, 4 (1901/1902): 1388-1391;

"Die Anfänge der neuen deutschen Literaturbewegung," *Zeitgeist: Beilage zum Berliner Tageblatt*, 4 August 1902;

"Arno Holz und ich," *Das litterarische Echo*, 4 (1902): 1624;

"Brief unter der Rubrik 'Notizbuch,'" *Die Zukunft*, 12 (1904): 465-466;

"Der Indizienbeweis," *Das neue Magazin für Literatur, Kunst und soziales Leben*, 73 (6 August 1904); 174-180;

"Noch ein Indizienbeweis," *Das neue Magazin für Literatur, Kunst und soziales Leben*, 73 (13 August 1904): 200-204;

"Kritik und Pamphlet," *Das neue Magazin für Literatur, Kunst und soziales Leben*, 73 (3 September 1904): 288-289;

"Die Vollendung des Naturalismus," *Die Güldenkammer*, 2 (1912): 204-213;

"Zur Vollendung des Naturalismus," *Die Güldenkammer*, 2 (1912): 517-528.

Johannes Schlaf's literary career falls into two phases that mark a move from the center of innovation in the 1890s to the periphery of significance in twentieth-century literature. First came his partnership with Arno Holz between 1888 and 1892, and with it the emergence of German naturalist drama. With Holz, Schlaf wrote *Die Familie Selicke* (The Selicke Family, 1890); he then worked alone on *Meister Oelze* (Master Oelze; published, 1892; performed, 1894). Critics now consider these works seminal and typical, respectively, for the "konsequenter Naturalismus" (consistent naturalism) of that era and detect in them elements that anticipate trends of modern drama. The second phase followed Schlaf's break with Holz and his nervous breakdown in the 1890s; this phase was dominated by prose works. A long dispute with Holz, from 1898 to

1912 about their respective contributions to naturalism sheds light on that revolution's achievements. Schlaf wrote four postnaturalist dramas between 1898 and 1906 and worked on the staging and revising of *Meister Oelze*. But during this period others led German literature in new directions, building on the modernity embryonic in the naturalist plays. Schlaf retreated, with mystical novels and intimate dramas, into an older poetry from which the naturalist rebellion had only briefly broken free.

Schlaf was born on 21 June 1862 in Querfurt, near Merseburg, the third son of the merchant Ferdinand Schlaf and Luise Riegelmann Schlaf. He attended public schools in Querfurt and Magdeburg until 1884, when he went to Halle to study theology and philology. From 1885 to 1887 he studied philosophy, classical languages, and German in Berlin with an eye to a teaching career.

Schlaf's literary interest flourished in his last two years of school. Hermann Conradi, a boyhood friend and later a prominent critic and essayist, was an important influence. Conradi awakened Schlaf's enthusiasm for the French naturalism of Emile Zola; he also introduced him into the literary circles of poets who soon became known as the "Jüngstdeutschen" (Newest Germans). The "Bund der Lebendigen" (League of the Living) club and the "Durch" (Through) literary circle put him in contact with Holz as early as 1885.

A coincidence of crises late in 1887 resulted in the partnership that gave birth to German naturalist drama. Schlaf had had only a few sketches published; he was struggling with a novel based on his student days. With the failure of his anthology of revolutionary poems, *Das Buch der Zeit* (The Book of Time, 1884), Holz had turned to a realistic novel based on his childhood, "Die Goldenen Zeiten" (The Golden Years). Rich in ideas about a type of realism transcending that of Zola, whom he found too idealistic, Holz was hoping to contribute to an "Umwälzung der Kunst" (artistic revolution); but he was struggling to find plots to convey his views. He invited Schlaf to his quarters in Niederschönhausen, where, from March through the summer of 1888, the two reworked Schlaf's sketches into provocatively realistic pieces.

Papa Hamlet was the first fruit of this collaboration. It contained the novella of that title, plus revisions of Schlaf's sketch "Ein Tod" (A Death) and Holz's "Der erste Schultag" (The First Day at School). It appeared in January 1889 under the pseudonym "Bjarne P. Holmsen," with an introduction by "Bruno Franzius," the alleged translator from the original Norwegian. With this fiction the authors satirized the era's blind enthusiasm for Scandinavian writers.

Early in 1890 Schlaf and Holz completed the drama *Die Familie Selicke*. It premiered at the Freie Bühne (Free Stage) in Berlin on 7 April 1890, directed by Hans Meery.

The collection *Neue Gleise* (New Tracks, 1892) included *Die Familie Selicke* and the stories from *Papa Hamlet*, along with other sketches that anticipated those longer works in technique and subject matter. *Der geschundene Pegasus* (Pegasus Abused, 1892), a collection of Holz's poems with drawings by Schlaf, marked the end of the collaboration.

With their interweaving of social and poetic themes, the early sketches published in *Neue Gleise* anticipated both Gerhart Hauptmann's *Vor Sonnenaufgang* (1889; translated as *Before Dawn*, 1909) and *Die Familie Selicke*. The shorter prose works integrated naturalist literary polemics into the realistic depiction of social squalor and emphasized the gap between those harsh realities and the illusory ideals of traditional poetry. These works also anticipated Schlaf and Holz's move to drama: the narrative voice fell away and the reader was forced to confront every pause and stammer of realistic dialogue.

Here Holz was clearly the instigator. Yet critics who fault the sentimentality of Schlaf's sketches or see him only as the supplier of the raw material for Holz's new techniques are unjust. The pieces in *Neue Gleise* that Schlaf revised on his own—Holz was soon engrossed in his theoretical writings—coincide on these points with the revision of his "Dachstubenidyll" (A Garret Idyll) into "Papa Hamlet." Throughout, the poses and rhetoric of tragic poetry are treated as an ineffectual flight from real problems. The sentimental scenes and poetic clichés highlight rather than mitigate the contrast between the squalor depicted and the high-flown phrases of the literary tradition.

Schlaf also proved adept at continuing Holz's move away from the mediating narrator and toward starkly realistic dialogue. "Die papierne Passion" (The Paper Passion Play) especially speaks for Schlaf's progress and contributions as a naturalist. Of all the pieces in *Neue Gleise* it comes closest to *Die Familie Selicke* in dramatic form and theme. Its nondialogue portions stand apart in a different typeface, like stage directions. The work juxtaposes the hardship of Berlin tenement life with a paper artwork that expresses Christian ideals, thereby reflecting critically and self-consciously on art's tendency to idealize real suffering. A paper cutout of Christ on the cross, with its promise of redemption and paradise, is destroyed by the grim reality of a tenement brawl and the ensuing outbreak of a fire. "Die papierne Passion" is an early example of naturalist works that give prominent place to figures intensely involved in artistic activity.

Inspired by *Papa Hamlet*, Hauptmann dedicated his sensational dramatic debut, *Vor Sonnenaufgang*, to "Bjarne P. Holmsen." That success and Otto Brahm's founding of the innovative Freie Bühne quickened the dramatic interests of Holz and Schlaf. In early 1889 the pair had discussed a possible collaboration with Hauptmann on a drama. By February of that year Schlaf had completed "Eine Mainacht" (A Night in May), a prose sketch about the Selicke household. With "Die papierne Passion," it formed the basis for *Die Familie Selicke*. By late 1889 Schlaf had completed a draft. Holz made changes to the first and last acts, probably incorporating that tendency to self-consciousness and metapoetic reflection that is so evident in *Papa Hamlet*. Holz also oversaw the staging of the play.

The three acts of *Die Familie Selicke* are set in the tenement flat of the downwardly mobile petit-bourgeois Selickes on Christmas Eve and early Christmas morning. For the better part of two acts the mother and children await the arrival of the father, Eduard, a bookkeeper and heavy drinker. The self-centered, complaining mother and the selflessly altruistic older daughter, Toni, worry over the bedridden youngest daughter, Linchen. Eduard arrives after midnight, drunk and full of venom for his wife, whom he blames for the decline of his fortunes. He harangues her and Toni before Linchen's death reduces him to stuporous grief. Suspense arises in this static atmosphere through Gustav Wendt, a theology student renting a room from the Selickes. He hopes to rescue Toni from this hopeless oppression by taking her to his new parsonage in the country. Each act moves toward a scene that promises a choice on Toni's part. At first she is swayed by Wendt's picture of the idyllic pastor's life and resolves to leave if Linchen recovers. As act 2 ends she embraces her grief-stricken father as Wendt looks on from his doorway. At the end of the play she resolves to

stay with her family. Departing but promising to return, Wendt hails this decision as a sign of selfless moral strength.

The play's mixture of provocative innovation and traditional elements generated confusion and objection from the start. Contemporary audiences rejected the radical affront to traditional dramatic expectations. They felt that the emphasis on character and situation over action rendered the work undramatic. Both the original production at the Freie Bühne and later stagings at the Deutsche Volksbühne (German People's Stage) were short lived, and subsequent performances were rare. Yet some influential reviewers responded favorably—Theodor Fontane saw the play as "Neuland" (new literary terrain)—and the printed version went through four editions by 1892. Other critics questioned the play's naturalism, claiming that it depicted individuals who were suffering not because of socioeconomic realities but due to self-indulgence: money is at hand for fine clothes for the son, Albert, and for Eduard's drink, while Linchen's health is neglected. But more recent critics, such as Dieter Kafitz, Gerhard Schulz, and Klaus Müller-Salget, have pointed out how Toni succumbs to the accurately portrayed sociopsychological realities of the times. Urbanization and industrialization brought a decline in lower bourgeois status and self-esteem; in response, people like the Selickes clung to the illusion of their role in the existing order that was fostered in traditional art and poetry. The trappings of the Selicke household show this imagined role as pillars of nation and culture: pictures of the Kaiser and Otto von Bismarck hang on the walls; busts of Johann Wolfgang von Goethe and Friedrich von Schiller frame a lithograph depicting a scene of domestic bliss from a Goethe novel. Toni, too, clings to such images and is unable to break free.

Critics have long found the play inconsistent. For some, it sets out to paint a realistic picture of the social situation but retreats into the maudlin sentimentality of Linchen's death and the noble vision of moral free will on Toni's part. This criticism erroneously accepts Wendt as the mouthpiece of the author's ideals and neglects the play's self-conscious, metapoetic element. From the start, the play's many references to art and poetry undermine its own sentimental and traditional aspects. When Toni makes her much-lauded "decision," the play has long since encouraged the audience to suspect that she is still in thrall to the illusions presumably upheld by traditional art and poetry. Throughout, the play presents sociopsychological problems that the grand phrases of traditional poetry are pointedly unable to solve. In this way it encourages further critical reflection on the problems left unsolved. For critics such as Schulz, Müller-Salget, and Hanno Möbius, this element anticipates aspects of Bertolt Brecht's Epic Theater.

While the extent of Schlaf's contribution to *Die Familie Selicke* will always arouse debate, *Meister Oelze* is his work alone. The play appeared in 1892, first serially in the journal *Freie Bühne für modernes Leben* (Free Stage for Modern Life) and then in book form. Basic elements of the plot recall Zola's *Thérèse Raquin* (1867). It is likely that Schlaf knew Zola's play even before its performance at the Freie Bühne in February 1891; he later called it a major influence on his naturalism. His play, like Zola's, concerns the revelation of a murder. The title figure is suffering from an advanced stage of lung disease. He lives with his aged mother, his wife Rese, and their adolescent son, Emil (the latter two names are allusions to Zola and his play). Years ago Oelze conspired with his mother to poison his stepfather and cheat his stepsister, Pauline, out of her inheritance. Now Pauline and her daughter, Marie, are visiting Oelze. They have fled Pauline's drunkard husband and the squalor of big-city life to which Oelze's crime has doomed them. Throughout the three acts Pauline tries to coax Oelze into confessing. She plays on his guilt and his superstitious fear that supernatural forces might reveal his crime. Act 2 ends with theatrical fireworks: Pauline tells tales of ghostly apparitions revealing crimes and then dares Oelze to go out alone into the stormy night. A door slammed shut by the wind brings on the seizure that dooms him. Yet through the night of act 3 the bedridden Oelze holds out. Although he comes near confessing in his feverish moments, his cynicism and stubbornness prevail to the end; he dies unrepentant. The morning sun shines on another day in an unchanged world.

While there may be echoes of Zola and Holz, *Meister Oelze* demonstrates Schlaf's gift for realistic and psychologically subtle dialogue. The play is provocatively undramatic. The promised revelation never occurs. Extraneous story lines retard the action and underline the impression of an unchanging world bereft of justice and order.

The play never enjoyed a long run. The first staging by the Freie Deutsche Volksbühne (Free German People's Stage) in Berlin on 4 February 1894 was followed by a Munich staging by the Litterarische Gesellschaft (Literary Society) on 4 and 5 February 1899, a performance in Magdeburg on Easter Monday 1900, a matinee at the Berliner Theater on 2 February 1901 for an audience of young female teachers in training, and a production in Osnabrück on Schlaf's sixtieth birthday in 1922. But the play awakened critical interest as a radicalization of Zola's naturalism: it depicts a world where order is not restored. Instead, the drive for survival triumphs over morality. The play deprives the audience of cathartic identification with the individual and stimulates—again anticipating Brecht—reflection on the problems left unsolved.

By the late 1890s Schlaf had joined critics who espoused the "heroic" view of Oelze. Like the writers Stefan Zweig and Richard Dehmel, Schlaf spoke of Oelze's "fester Manneswillen" (unshakable manly will) and saw him elevated by his love for his son. In 1908 Schlaf reworked the play, eliminating many naturalist elements. The later version reduces the revealing pauses and stammers, the strong local dialect, the detailed depiction of milieu, and the epic elements.

In 1892 Schlaf suffered a nervous breakdown. Nervous disorders that had threatened Schlaf since his student days were aggravated by tensions resulting from his collaboration with Holz, in which the dynamic Holz dominated the shy, malleable Schlaf. An unhappy love affair intensified Schlaf's resentment of Holz, who provided no help or understanding when Schlaf was unable to establish a relationship with a young lady of the Berlin literary circles. Living with Holz and his new bride forced Schlaf to feel his failure even more acutely. He was institutionalized from 1892 to 1896.

Schlaf's recovery involved a new self-assertiveness. He claimed that Holz's role in their joint works had been that of a mere technician and editor. At the same time, he developed a worldview that rejected as superficial naturalism's picture of the individual as determined by social factors; instead, he embraced an outlook—influenced by Nietzschean individualism and Ernst Haeckel's monism—that saw the individual as part of an inscrutable mystical unity of all things, determined by spiritual connections and movements of the soul lying beyond rational comprehension or the control of the conscious will.

Schlaf's new worldview had an impact on the structure and substance of his subsequent four plays: *Die Feindlichen* (The Enemies, 1899),

Schlaf (right) and Arno Holz, with whom he wrote several early naturalist works

Gertrud (1898), *Der Bann* (The Spell, 1901), and *Weigand* (1906). Only two of these plays have ever been performed: *Gertrud* opened at Berlin's Residenztheater on 24 April 1898 and *Der Bann* premiered and closed at the Berliner Theater on 20 October 1901. All four plays have attracted attention as documents showing how the "intimate drama" developed out of naturalism around 1900. They retain naturalism's attention to realistic detail and its conviction that factors other than free will dominate human behavior. Yet they focus less on concrete social problems and more on mysterious spiritual or parapsychological relationships. Schlaf saw this emphasis as a "Vollendung" (completion or fulfillment) of naturalism. With Max Halbe, August Strindberg, Rainer Maria Rilke, and Hugo von Hofmannsthal, he extended the naturalist drama's realistic language into the realm of soul, religion, and mysticism. But this inwardness was only a brief interlude between naturalism and the still more socially and politically engaged dramas of expressionism and Brecht.

The four plays deal with love triangles. In each play a married woman wrestles with the choice between her husband and an exotic outsider. She is tied by convention, yet attracted to a man of strong will, intellectual acumen, and creative talent. In *Gertrud* and *Der Bann* the protagonist eventually rejects the idea of flight. The title figure of the former play, Gertrud Baerwald, stays with her philistine husband, Fritz, despite her attraction to Albrecht Holm. The weak-willed Ottilie in *Der Bann* remains with her husband, Hubert, and forsakes the painter, Wenzel. In *Die Feindlichen* and *Weigand* the wife rebels. In *Die Feindlichen* Asta chooses the mercurial Heinrich over her stolid husband, Herbert. Heinrich convinces her that his power over her has nothing to do with posthypnotic suggestion: rather, it is a positive attraction. In *Weigand* Hermine von Wiesener arranges her husband's murder so that she can live with the title figure. *Gertrud* and *Der Bann* tend to retreat into convention; *Die Feinlichen* and *Weigand* are more complex and daring in form and content. But in each of the four plays the protagonist's struggle reflects the dilemma of a modern individual tied to a commonplace world that suppresses—even perverts—that individual's intellectual and emotional capabilities. The plays express cultural criticism and moral psychology reminiscent of the ideas of Friedrich Nietzsche, Sigmund Freud, and Carl Gustav Jung. Critics have also suggested a strong autobiographical element, seeing the central figures as representing Schlaf's situation as a creative writer tied to one literary convention yet attracted to other modes of thought.

Schlaf left the clamor of Berlin for Weimar in 1904. *Weigand* was his last contribution to the drama. After 1906 he produced mystical descriptions of nature, works on religion and philosophy, and studies of kindred spirits such as Walt Whitman, Maurice Maeterlinck, and Novalis. Schlaf's trend toward the mystical and irrational and away from sociocritical reflection indicates his retreat from the modern world. In 1937 he moved to Querfurt, a small provincial town where he was born. He died on 2 February 1941.

The initial third of Schlaf's literary career, which centered on the drama, merits a more charitable evaluation than it has often received. His and Holz's works are the most radical and consistent version of a mode of drama that Hauptmann's major naturalist successes express in more accessible, popular form. In addition to Hauptmann, Schlaf and Holz are the central figures of German naturalism.

Bibliographies:

Fritz Fink, *Johannes Schlaf-Bibliographie* (Weimar: Archiv der Deutschen Schillerstiftung, 1928);

Lothar Hempte, *Johannes Schlaf-Bibliographie: Verzeichnis der von 1889-1937 selbständig erschienenen Erstdrücke in chronologischer Reihenfolge* (Stuttgart: Privately printed, 1938);

Penrith Goff, *Wilhelminisches Zeitalter: Handbuch der deutschen Literaturgeschichte. Zweite Abteilung: Bibliographien*, volume 10 (Bern & Munich: Francke, 1970), p. 166.

Biography:

Ludwig Bäte and Kurt Meyr-Rotermund, eds., *Johannes Schlaf: Leben und Werk* (Querfurt: Jaekkel, 1933).

References:

Walter Ackermann, "Die zeitgenössische Kritik an den deutschen naturalistischen Dramen: Hauptmann, Holz, Schlaf," Ph.D. dissertation, University of Munich, 1965;

Ludwig Bäte, "Johannes Schlaf," *Deutsche Rundschau*, 70, no. 11 (1947): 117-120;

Bäte, Kurt Meyer-Rotermund, and Rudolf Borcherdt, eds., *Das Johannes-Schlaf Buch* (Rudolstadt: Greifen, 1922);

Siegwart Berthold, "Der sogenannte 'konsequenter Naturalismus' von Arno Holz und Johannes Schlaf," Ph.D. dissertation, University of Bonn, 1967;

Dieter Borchmeyer, "Der Naturalismus und seine Ausläufer," in *Geschichte der deutschen Literatur vom 18. Jahrhundert bis zur Gegenwart*, volume 2, edited by Viktor Zmegac (Königstein: Athenäum, 1980), pp. 153-233;

Heinz-Georg Brands, *Theorie des sogenannten "Konsequenten Naturalismus" von Arno Holz und Johannes Schlaf: Kritische Analyse der Forschungsergebnisse und Versuch einer Neubestimmung* (Bonn: Bouvier, 1978);

Roy C. Cowen, *Der Naturalismus: Kommentar zu einer Epoche* (Munich: Winkler, 1973);

Michaela Giesing, *Ibsens Nora und die wahre Emanzipation der Frau: Zum Frauenbild im Wilhelminischen Theater* (Frankfurt am Main, Bern & New York: Lang, 1984);

Reinhold Grimm, "Naturalismus und episches Drama," in *Episches Theater*, edited by Grimm (Cologne & Berlin: Kiepenheuer & Witsch, 1966), pp. 13-35;

Katharina Günther, *Literarische Gruppenbildung im Berliner Naturalismus* (Bonn: Bouvier, 1972);

Max Halbe, "Intimes Theater," *Pan*, no. 2 (1895): 106-109;

Rene Hartogs, "Die Theorie des Dramas im deutschen Naturalismus," Ph.D. dissertation, University of Frankfurt am Main, 1931;

Arno Holz, *Johannes Schlaf: Ein nothgedrungenes Kapitel* (Dresden: Reißner, 1909);

Lothar Jegensdorf, "Die spekulative Deutung und poetische Darstellung der Natur im Werk von Johannes Schlaf," Ph.D. dissertation, University of Bochum, 1969;

Dieter Kafitz, "Das Intime Theater am Ende des 19. Jahrhunderts," in *Theaterwesen und dramatische Literatur: Beiträge zur Geschichte des Theaters*, edited by Gunther Holthus (Bern/Munich: Francke, 1987);

Kafitz, "Struktur und Menschenbild naturalistischer Dramatik," *Zeitschrift für deutsche Philologie*, 97 (1978): 225-235;

Samuel Lublinski, *Die Bilanz der Moderne*, edited by Gotthart Wunberg (Tübingen: Niemeyer, 1974);

Lublinski, *Holz und Schlaf: Ein zweifelhaftes Kapitel Literaturgeschichte* (Stuttgart: Juncker, 1905);

Edward McInnes, *German Social Drama 1840-1890: From Hebbel to Hauptmann* (Stuttgart: Heinz, 1976);

Horst Meixner, "Naturalistische Natur: Bild und Begriff der Natur im naturalistischen deutschen Drama," Ph.D. dissertation, University of Freiburg, 1961;

Hanno Möbius, *Der Positivismus in der Literatur des Naturalismus: Wissenschaft, Kunst und soziale Frage bei Arno Holz* (Munich: Fink, 1980);

Klaus Müller-Salget, "Autorität und Familie im naturalistischen Drama," *Zeitschrift für deutsche Philologie*, 103 (1984): 502-519;

Müller-Salget, "Dramaturgie der Parteilosigkeit: Zum Naturalismus Gerhart Hauptmanns," in *Naturalismus: Bürgerliche Dichtung und soziales Engagement*, edited by Helmut Scheuer (Stuttgart: Kohlhammer, 1974), pp. 48-68;

John Osborne, "Naturalism and the Dramaturgy of the Open Drama," *German Life and Letters*, 23 (January 1970): 119-128;

Osborne, *The Naturalist Drama in Germany* (Manchester, U.K.: Manchester University Press, 1971);

Helmut Praschek, "Zum Zerfall des naturalistischen Stils: Ein Vergleich zweier Fassungen des *Meister Oelze* von Johannes Schlaf," in *Worte und Werte: Bruno Markwardt zum 60. Geburtstag*, edited by Gustav Erdmann and Alfons Eichstaedt (Berlin: de Gruyter, 1961), pp. 315-321;

Ernst Sander, "Johannes Schlaf und das naturalistische Drama," Ph.D. dissertation, University of Rostock, 1922;

Klaus R. Scherpe, "Der Fall Arno Holz: Zur sozialen und ideologischen Motivation der naturalistischen Literaturrevolution," in *Positionen der literarischen Intelligenz zwischen bürgerlicher Reaktion und Imperialismus*, edited by Scherpe and Gert Mattenklott (Kronberg: Taunus, 1973), pp. 121-178;

Helmut Scheuer, *Arno Holz im literarischen Leben des ausgehenden 19. Jahrhunderts (1883-1896): Eine biographische Studie* (Munich: Winkler, 1971);

Scheuer, *Interpretationen: Dramen des Naturalismus* (Stuttgart: Reclam, 1988), pp. 67-106, 147-177;

Scheuer, "Zwischen Sozialismus und Individualismus: Zwischen Marx und Nietzsche," in *Naturalismus: Bürgerliche Dichtung und soziales Engagement*, edited by Scheuer (Stuttgart: Kohlhammer, 1974), pp. 150-174;

Dieter Schickling, "Interpretationen und Studien zur Entwicklung und geistesgeschichtlichen Stellung des Werkes von Arno Holz," Ph.D. dissertation, University of Tübingen, 1965;

Gerhard Schulz, *Arno Holz: Dilemma eines bürgerlichen Dichterlebens* (Munich: Beck, 1974);

Schulz, "Zur Theorie des Dramas im deutschen Naturalismus," in *Deutsche Dramentheorien: Beiträge zu einer historischen Poetik des Dramas in Deutschland*, edited by Reinhold Grimm (Frankfurt am Main: Athenäum, 1971), pp. 394-428;

David Turner, "*Die Familie Selicke* and the Drama of German Naturalism," in *Periods in German Literature: Volume II: Texts and Contexts*, edited by J. M. Ritchie (London: Wolff, 1969), pp. 193-219;

Raleigh Whitinger, "Art Works and Artistic Activity in Holz / Schlaf 's *Die Familie Selicke*: Reflections on the Play's Naturalistic and Epic Consistency," *Michigan Germanic Studies*, 14 (1988): 139-150;

Stefan Zweig, "Johannes Schlaf," *Das Litterarische Echo*, 4, no. 20 (1902): 1377-1388.

Papers:
Johannes Schlaf 's papers are in the Goethe and Schiller Archive, Weimar, and in the Schlaf Museum of the Johannes Schlaf Society, Querfurt.

Wilhelm August Schmidtbonn

(6 February 1876 - 3 July 1952)

Karin Doerr
Concordia University

PLAY PRODUCTIONS: *Mutter Landstraße*, Dresden, Königliches Schauspielhaus, 14 June 1901;

Die goldene Tür, Munich, Schauspielhaus, 1904;

Der Graf von Gleichen, Düsseldorf, Schauspielhaus, 3 February 1908;

Hilfe! Ein Kind ist vom Himmel gefallen, Berlin, Kleines Schauspielhaus, 18 February 1910;

Der Zorn des Achilles, Cologne, Schauspielhaus, 6 December 1910;

Der spielende Eros, Vienna, Theater in der Josefsstadt, 22 September 1911;

Der verlorene Sohn, Berlin, Deutsches Theater, 24 September 1913;

1914, Berlin, Deutsches Theater, 25 September 1914;

Die Stadt der Besessenen, Leipzig, Altes Theater, 17 November 1917;

Der Geschlagene, Hamburg, Deutsches Schauspielhaus, 15 April 1920;

Die Passion, Munich, Künstler-Theater, 2 June 1920;

Die Schauspieler, Berlin, Lustspielhaus, 23 September 1921;

Die Fahrt nach Orplid, Bochum, Stadt-Theater, 18 January 1923;

Maruf, der tolle Lügner, Nuremberg, Stadttheater Altes Haus, 14 January 1925;

Der Pfarrer von Mainz, Aachen Stadt-Theater, 10 June 1925;

Bruder Dietrich, Kassel, Staatstheater, 16 February 1929.

BOOKS: *Mutter Landstraße: Das Ende einer Jugend: Schauspiel in drei Aufzügen* (Berlin: Fleischel, 1903);

Uferleute: Geschichten vom untern Rhein (Berlin: Fleischel, 1903);

Raben: Neue Geschichten vom untern Rhein (Berlin: Fleischel, 1904);

Die goldene Tür: Ein rheinisches Kleinstadtrama in drei Aufzügen (Berlin: Fleischel, 1904);

Der Heilsbringer: Eine Legende von heute (Berlin: Fleischel, 1906);

Wilhelm August Schmidtbonn

Der Graf von Gleichen: Ein Schauspiel (Berlin: Fleischel, 1908);

Der Zorn des Achilles: Eine Tragödie in drei Aufzügen (Berlin: Fleischel, 1909);

Hilfe! Ein Kind ist vom Himmel gefallen: Eine Tragikomödie in drei Aufzügen (Berlin: Fleischel, 1910);

Lobgesang des Lebens: Rhapsodien (Berlin: Fleischel, 1911);

Der spielende Eros: Vier Schwänke (Berlin: Fleischel, 1911);

Geschichten vom unteren Rhein (Wien: Hofverlag, 1911);

Der verlorene Sohn: Ein Legendenspiel (Berlin: Fleischel, 1912);

Das Glücksschiff: Geschichten vom Rhein (Stuttgart: Die Lese-Verlag, 1912);

Der Wunderbaum: dreiundzwanzig Legenden (Berlin: Fleischel, 1913);

Die Stadt der Besessenen: Ein Wiedertäuferspiel in drei Aufzügen (Berlin: Fleischel, 1915);

Menschen und Städte im Kriege: Fahrten aus dem Großen Hauptquartier an die Aisne, an die Küste, in die belgischen Städte (Berlin: Fleischel, 1915);

Krieg in Serbien: Mit einem deutschen Korps zum Ibar (Berlin: Fleischel, 1916);

Wenn sie siegten! (Stuttgart & Berlin: Deutsche Verlags-Anstalt, 1916);

Schlaraffenland: Die Feldbücher (Stuttgart: Deutsche Verlags-Anstalt, 1916); "Die Letzte" translated by Harry Steinhauer and Helen Jessiman as "Derelict," in *Modern German Short Stories*, edited by Harry Steinhauer (London: Oxford University Press, 1938), pp. 19-36;

Weihnachten 1916: Weihnachtsgruß der Heimat an die Front (Berlin: Kriegspresseamt, 1916);

Das kleine Kriegsbuch (Leipzig: Hesse & Becker, 1917);

Der Geschlagene: Schauspiel in drei Aufzügen (Munich: Wolff, 1919);

Die Flucht zu den Hilflosen; Die Geschichte dreier Hunde (Leipzig: Tal, 1919);

Die Schauspieler: Ein Lustspiel in drei Aufzügen (Munich: Wolff, 1920);

Uferleute: Rheinische Geschichten (Stuttgart: Deutsche Verlags-Anstalt, 1921);

Die Fahrt nach Orplid: Ein Drama unter Auswanderern in drei Aufzügen (Berlin: Reiss, 1922);

Garten der Erde: Märchen aus allen Zonen. Nacherzählt (Leipzig, Zürich, Wien: Tal, 1922);

Hinter den sieben Bergen: Erzählung (Stuttgart: Reclam, 1922);

Der Pfarrer von Mainz: Schauspiel in drei Aufzügen (Berlin: Reiss, 1922);

Das verzauberte Haus (Köln: Saaleck, 1923);

Vier Novellen (Köln: Saaleck, 1924);

Der Verzauberte: Seltsame Geschichte eines Pelzhändlers (Leipzig: Tal, 1924); republished as *Der Pelzhändler: Seltsame Geschichte eines Verzauberten* (Berlin: Deutsche Buch-Gemeinschaft, 1926);

Die unerschrockene Insel: Sommerbuch aus Hiddensee (Munich: Drei Masken, 1925);

Maruf, der tolle Lügner: Märchenkomödie in fünf Aufzügen aus Tausend und eine Nacht (Stuttgart: Deutsche Verlags-Anstalt, 1925);

Die Geschichten von den unberührten Frauen (Stuttgart: Deutsche Verlags-Anstalt, 1926);

Die siebzig Geschichten des Papageien: Nach dem Türkischen neu erzählt (Stuttgart: Deutsche Verlags-Anstalt, 1927);

Das Wilhelm Schmidtbonn-Buch: Eine Auswahl der Werke Schmidtbonns, edited by Max Tau (Lübeck: Quitzow, 1927);

Der Doppelgänger: Sechs Erzählungen (Berlin: Deutsche Buch-Gemeinschaft, 1928);

Mein Freund Dei: Geschichte einer unterbrochenen Weltreise (Stuttgart & Berlin: Deutsche Verlags-Anstalt, 1928);

Bruder Dietrich: Der Morgen eines Volkes (Berlin: Osterheld, 1928);

Rheinische Geschichten (Leipzig: Eichblatt, 1929);

Der kleine Wunderbaum: Zwölf Legenden (Leipzig: Insel, 1930);

Mörder: Kölner Hännenspiel in drei Bildern (Berlin: Bühnenvolksbund, 1932);

An einem Strom geboren: Ein Lebensbuch (Frankfurt am Main: Rutten & Loening, 1935);

Der Dreieckige Marktplatz: Roman (Berlin: Propyläen, 1935);

Lebensalter der Liebe: Drei Erzählungen (Bremen: Schünemann, 1935);

Die Geschichte dreier Hunde (Berlin: Kiepenheuer, 1936);

Hü Lü: Roman (Potsdam: Rütten & Loening, 1937);

Anna Brand: Roman (Berlin: Propyläen, 1939);

Die tapferen Heinzelmännchen: Eine Märchenerzählung (Cologne: Staufen, 1943);

Albertuslegende (Cologne: Pick, 1948).

OTHER: Arnoul and Simon Gréban, *Die Passion: Das Misterienspiel der Brüder Arnoul und Simon Gréban. Aus dem Französischen des Jahres 1452 frei übertragen*, translated and adapted by Schmidtbonn (Berlin: Fleischel, 1919);

"Gustav Wunderwald," in *Das festliche Haus: Das Düsseldorfer Schauspielhaus. Spiegel und Ausdruck der Zeit*, edited by Kurt Loup (Cologne: Kiepenheuer & Witsch, 1955), pp. 110-114.

SELECTED PERIODICAL PUBLICATIONS—
UNCOLLECTED: "Eisgang," *Masken*, 2 (September 1906-June 1907): 287-290;

Der Jude von Venedig: Eine kurze Szene, in *Masken*, 3 (9 September 1907): 33-38;

"Das Recht auf den Namen," *Die Schaubühne*, 8 April 1909, pp. 402-403;

"Der Flieger," *Die Zukunft*, 62 (1910): 221-224;

1914: Ein Kriegsvorspiel für die Bühne, in *Das literarische Echo*, 3 (11 January 1915): 151-157.

Wilhelm Schmidtbonn was active in German theater, but only a few of his plays were performed with success. Today neither his prose nor his dramatic works are part of the German literary canon or theatrical repertoire. As early as 1930 the literary critic Werner Mahrholz complained that Schmidtbonn's plays were not appreciated; he called Schmidtbonn a truly German writer whose time would come. In 1978 Irmgard Wolf also suggested that he would be recognized one day.

Schmidtbonn's oeuvre includes plays, novels, stories, fairy tales, radio dramas, autobiographical accounts, and theater critiques. His period of relative success started around 1910 and waned in the mid 1920s. He belonged to the school of expressionist playwrights who dealt with strong emotions and ecstatic visions. His name has also been associated with postexpressionism and neoromanticism. It is difficult to link him firmly to any one literary tradition because of his strong individualism. Because he excelled in the depiction of his native land and its people, he is often referred to as a "Heimatdichter" (regional storyteller). That he chose to add *Bonn* to his surname, Schmidt, demonstrates his desire to be attached spiritually to his hometown.

Schmidtbonn chose common people as his heroes and heroines. His sympathies lay with characters who erred and had to suffer the consequences of their actions. Human weakness and uncontrollable passion are part of his characters' innocence, an innocence that results in the protagonists' downfall and consequent punishment or self-punishment. Often these protagonists endeavor to reach an unrealistic state of happiness; no sooner are they within sight of the attainment of their goal than they are plunged into despair, sometimes death. Linked to this search for ultimate happiness is sensual love, often expressed as uncontrollable physical desire. Schmidtbonn's explicit depictions of such desire led frequently to censorship troubles. (His female protagonists were as strong as the males in their sexual desires, in contrast to the more conventional depiction of the passive female lover.) It is this striving for an ideal and the ecstatic emphasis that has linked Schmidtbonn to romanticism and expressionism.

Wilhelm August Schmidt was one of seven children of a wealthy Bonn fur merchant. In his autobiography, *An einem Strom geboren* (Born on a River, 1935), he draws a vivid picture of a child and young man enjoying his family's indulgent upbringing. He does not hesitate to depict himself as a troublesome child and youth who often

blurred the line between truth and fiction. His actions were frequently contrary to the wishes of people in authority, and he was at odds with almost all of the educational institutions he attended.

As a fifteen-year-old gymnasium pupil, he wrote plays, stories, and poems and composed music. Growing up a few houses from Ludwig van Beethoven's birthplace influenced his decision to study music. In 1892, two years after his father's death, he left the gymnasium at Bonn to attend the Conservatory of Cologne. But school discipline did not please him, and he left six months later. He was then placed in a private gymnasium that he also soon deserted. His mother was troubled by her son's escapades, but she accepted his desire to become a writer. Her only caveat was that his training be connected to a trade. Consequently, he was apprenticed to a small publisher and bookseller in the university town of Giessen, in Hesse, in 1896. After three months he resigned to gain the freedom to write a play. So as not to worry his family in Bonn, he pretended to have changed jobs. He invented a new workplace and co-workers and wrote entertaining stories about them to his mother—almost believing his fictional creations himself. After six months he sent his finished play, "Thomas: Ein Lied" (Thomas: A Song) to Professor Berthold Litzmann, a progressive Bonn literary historian who had gained a reputation for his lectures on contemporary poets and writers. (Schmidtbonn was impressed that Litzmann permitted women to attend his seminars.) Litzmann persuaded Schmidt's guardian, an uncle, to allow the twenty-one-year-old aspiring playwright to follow his chosen path, but the play remained unpublished.

Schmidtbonn began studying at the University of Bonn in 1897 and was particularly fascinated with Middle High German. But his sense of adventure, his desire for change, and his proclivity for self-indulgence once more gained the upper hand. He left Bonn for Berlin and after a year there moved on to the universities at Göttingen and Zurich. But his yearning for complete freedom and the lure of the mountainous Swiss countryside were more powerful than his desire for learning. He rode his bicycle, roamed with vagabonds, became a vegetarian, and abandoned all responsibilities. His youngest brother joined him in 1899 on a dangerous winter crossing of the Furka Pass. From this extreme he swung to another by volunteering for military service in 1899. Because of his love for the Alps he chose a Munich unit and served there for one year.

Completing his military service, he moved to Innsbruck, Austria, where he married Luise Freuer in December 1900 and wrote a second play, *Mutter Landstraße: Das Ende einer Jugend* (Mother Road: The End of Youth; published, 1903). He dedicated it to Litzmann. He wanted to have the play performed at the Innsbruck theater; but to his surprise, the director there sent the manuscript to Dresden, where the court actor Carl Wiese and the young dramatist Karl Zeiss staged it on 14 June 1901 at the Königliches Schauspielhaus (Royal Playhouse). Although the audience seemed to like it, the critics called it psychologically unclear and unpolished.

Mutter Landstraße takes place in the Bavarian mountains and is partly written in dialect. It deals with the theme of the Prodigal Son. Hans, who has been absent for ten years, returns home destitute, with a wife and a fatally ill child. He is convinced that his father will accept them; in fact, he demands his birthright. The father, however, is intransigent. The ecstatic prostration of the son, his self-debasing pleading, and his belief in the rightness of his actions reflect qualities of German neoromanticism, but his emotional outpouring is overstated and repetitive. The father refuses to take the son's outstretched hand and scorns him. In his only act of charity, the father decides to support Hans's young wife, Trude, and the sick child, but he chases the son away. The son, resigned to abandonment, then joins the Spielmann (street singer), introduced at the beginning of the play as the free spirit of the open road, and leaves singing a song of consolation. The target of Schmidtbonn's criticism is the father. The father-son conflict had been prominent in nineteenth-century German naturalist literature and became even more so during the expressionist period. The influential actor and director Max Reinhardt staged the play, with Reinhardt himself playing the father, on 27 February 1904 at the Kleines Theater (Little Theater) in Berlin. The last performance of the play was in Bad Godesberg on 7 November 1930.

A second play by Schmidtbonn premiered in Munich in 1904. *Die goldene Tür: Ein rheinisches Kleinstadtrama* (The Golden Door: A Rhenish Small-Town Drama; published, 1904) is set in a shoe factory where one of the office clerks, Elisabeth, is ostensibly a modern working girl who wants to stand on her own two feet. But it turns out that she covets all the material goods

and comforts traditionally desired by women, such as jewelry and beautiful clothes. All these treasures are behind the "golden door" of the shoe manufacturer. Baum, another clerk, is a man who, because of his inferior financial position, has never experienced happiness. Even the factory workers are better off than he is, he claims; they get married when they are twenty because their wives work, too. While revealing the emotional and spiritual emptiness of these low-paid white-collar people, Schmidt draws a compassionate picture of them. In the 1920s, with the arrival of the literary movement usually called "Neue Sachlichkeit" (New Objectivity), it became popular to elevate the lower middle class to literature and to treat its representatives sympathetically; thus, in 1904 Schmidtbonn was anticipating a later trend.

The play ends without anyone finding love or happiness. On her way to what she hopes will be a more successful life in the city, Elisabeth drowns; thus, she is punished for her desire for happiness. Baum thought that he had been close to finding his desire for love fulfilled by her, but now he is reconciled to a stable, uneventful life with his mother. True to his name, which is German for *tree*, Baum remains strong and immovable. This ending was received by the audience with laughter and mock applause, and the show closed after the premiere performance. The director Otto Brahm wrote to Schmidtbonn that the motivation for the actions of the characters was missing.

Driven by renewed restlessness, Schmidtbonn went back to enjoying Alpine nature, this time with his wife and his dog. For a year they were accompanied by Schmidtbonn's close friend, the painter Gustav Wunderwald, and Wunderwald's wife. As usual, Schmidtbonn found in nature inspiration to write.

In 1905 Schmidtbonn went to Düsseldorf, where Louise Dumont and Gustav Lindemann had just opened a theater, the Schauspielhaus (Playhouse). He accepted the post of dramaturge, which he shared with the poet Herbert Eulenberg. The two were editors of the weekly theater journal *Masken* from September 1906 to June 1908. The Düsseldorf theater became a center of creativity, with painters such as Wunderwald and August Macke designing imaginative and avant-garde stage sets.

Schmidtbonn gained fame with *Der Graf von Gleichen* (Count von Gleichen, 1908), his most successful drama. It premiered at the Schauspielhaus on 3 February 1908. *Der Graf von Gleichen* is a powerful depiction of love and suffering. In the prologue, Count von Gleichen is in a Turkish prison after the First Crusade, making a deal with a knight who represents Death. Gleichen promises to marry a Turkish girl, Nae"mi, in return for his freedom. Death may claim him after she dies. The first act shows the count back in his homeland of Thuringia a year later. By then he has fallen in love with Nae"mi and plans to keep her, in addition to his wife. But the countess wants her out of the house, and in the second act the pope decrees that Nae"mi must go into a convent. The count, however, is prepared to act against the pope because of his love for Nae"mi. He declares that he wants to be loved by both women and to love both of them. In the third act the countess kills Nae"mi, who is pregnant. On receiving the news, the count is beside himself; he calls his wife a devil and wants to murder her in turn. But she points out that she killed the other woman out of love. The count now perceives his own guilt and realizes that he has to meet his fate. The knight reappears and claims him. Schmidtbonn has once more linked the desire for ultimate happiness with the punishment of death. The play is written in a free iambic meter; the dialogue is realistic and sparse. At the Düsseldorf premiere, Dumont played the countess and Lindemann directed.

Deciding that his duties as dramaturge and editor of *Masken* left him too little time for his own creative writing, Schmidtbonn left Düsseldorf in 1908. After short stays in Berlin and Switzerland, he took up residence at the Villa Brand on the Tegernsee in Bavaria. He called his next play, *Hilfe! Ein Kind ist vom Himmel gefallen* (Help! A Child Has Fallen from Heaven!; published, 1910), a tragicomedy, but it is neither tragic nor funny. The play depicts two levels of society: the wealthy factory owner Vogelsang and his family, and the burglar Bischof and his friends. Bischof breaks into the country house of Vogelsang's daughter, Maria, intending to burglarize it, but instead he sleeps with and impregnates her. Vogelsang demands that the child be given up for adoption and promises to pay for his upkeep and education. But Maria refuses to obey her father; she wants to keep the child. The second act shows the abject environment of Bischof and his cronies. Maria appears and wants to make a deal with the father of her boy. Bischof agrees, for a substantial sum of money, to marry

Maria so as to legitimize the child and to leave immediately afterward. The final act takes place in the father's house. The wedding is over, and Bischof wants his money. But Vogelsang refuses; he puts out the story that Bischof is a wealthy man from America, thus saving face in society. Maria decides to remain with Bischof to spite her father; moreover, she seems to have discovered qualities in her new husband that had hitherto lain dormant. Vogelsang agrees to buy the tickets for the couple's passage to America, and more money will await them on their arrival. In this unlikely scenario, Schmidtbonn is trying to show sympathy for the underprivileged. But while Maria and Bischof wind up happy, Bischof's pregnant girlfriend, Lisa, is left behind to raise her illegitimate child in poverty. The viewer does not regard the father as the villain or Bischof as the hero, as Schmidtbonn intends. The play premiered at the Kleines Schauspielhaus (Little Playhouse) in Berlin on 18 February 1910 and ran for only two performances.

Schmidtbonn's *Der Zorn des Achilles* (The Wrath of Achilles, 1909) is based on Homer's *Iliad* but deviates from it in certain respects. During the Trojan War the Greek king Agamemnon demands for himself Briseis, a daughter of King Priam of Troy. She had been given to Achilles as spoils of war. Achilles then refuses to go into battle. Knowing that they will lose the war without their strongest hero, the Greeks coax Patroclus, Achilles' best friend, into battle; as they had planned, he is killed, thus provoking Achilles to come out of his tent and fight. Achilles slays Hector, who killed Patroclus, in spite of the Greeks' acceptance of the Trojans' peace offer. At the end of the play, Achilles is killed by his own people; he voluntarily walks toward his murderers, shaking his blond hair and uttering a war cry. Schmidtbonn has changed Achilles into a Germanic hero; he is the only Greek who is blond and blue-eyed. He is a Nietzschean superman; strong and lonely, he avoids the herd and detests the power of a state run by devious and weak men.

Der Zorn des Achilles premiered in Cologne on 6 December 1910 and ran for nine performances. The Deutsches Theater (German Theater) in Berlin, with which Schmidtbonn had a contract, postponed staging the play. After two and a half years Reinhardt offered Schmidtbonn compensation of fifteen hundred marks if he would agree not to insist on staging it. But the author was adamant, and the drama opened on 13 January 1912 under the direction of Felix Hollaender. Perhaps its only virtue was its set design by Wunderwald. After three performances, the main actor broke his ankle; this injury was used as the official reason for canceling the production. Up to 1925 there were a few more performances in Düsseldorf, Krefeld, and Leipzig.

Schmidtbonn's set of four one-act plays, *Der spielende Eros* (Playful Eros, 1911), deals with sexual attraction in a lighthearted manner. In *Die Versuchung des Diogenes* (The Temptation of Diogenes) Ino, a young woman, tries to seduce the reclusive philosopher. He succumbs, and what started out as a game turns serious when she decides to stay with him. The second play, *Helena im Bade* (Helen in the Bath), portrays Helen's vanity. Flattered that Aspalion, an old man, wants to see her naked in her garden, she allows him to spy on her through an opening in the fence. Salaciously, Helen commands her maid to report Aspalion's reaction to her. This segment of the quartet was forbidden by the Berlin censor. In *Der junge Achilles* (Young Achilles) Achilles disguises himself as a girl and attends a girls' school. One of the students, Alkme, is assigned to find out whether there is a male among them. She discovers Achilles, and they fall in love. Another girl who is in love with Achilles exposes him, but the rest of the group does not want to report him to the headmistress. They give him permission to leave only after he has kissed every one of them. The sketch ends when a young married woman from the neighborhood becomes indignant over such indecent behavior. *Pygmalion* is based on the myth of the sculptor who falls in love with his own statue of a beautiful woman. It turns to flesh through a passionate kiss; but to the artist's chagrin, it despises his humble abode and station in life. When his patron comes to pick up the statue, Pygmalion wants to destroy it rather than part from it. But the statue has a will of its own and chooses the better life of the patron. At this point Pygmalion's love evaporates; this change in his feelings causes the statue to turn into stone again. In typical Schmidtbonn fashion, a character is driven by an excessive love that is beyond control; but in this case he recovers his sanity and suffers no punishment. The premiere in Vienna on 22 September 1911 was successful, and there were performances of individual parts of *Der spielende Eros* in various German cities. The prominent character actor Emil Jannings played Diogenes in a Berlin production in 1918.

Der verlorene Sohn (The Prodigal Son, 1912) returns to the theme of Schmidtbonn's first published play. This time, however, the end is a fairy-tale-like reunion with the father and mother. The rebellious son has left home, squandered his inheritance, and committed criminal acts. He returns impoverished and sick, and all is forgiven. The other son, who had remained at home, had worked hard, and was loyal to his parents, suffers their harsh words. It seems that Schmidtbonn was writing a fantasy version of his own life; he considered himself a Prodigal Son. In both of his plays treating this subject, the sons abandon country life in favor of the corrupt city, then both return home and promise to become new men through the labor of their hands; but only in *Der verlorene Sohn* is there a second chance. Schmidtbonn called the work a "Legendenspiel" (Legend Play), thus emphasizing its lack of realism. Schmidtbonn took Reinhardt's suggestion and enhanced the dreamlike quality of the play for the premiere in Berlin on 24 September 1913 by the use of music, song, and dance.

The Schmidtbonns were childless; while they were contemplating adoption, they were asked to take care of the one-year-old daughter of Mrs. Schmidtbonn's widowed sister for a few months. The child, Lo, remained with the couple for fifteen years. Because of Lo's ill health, they traveled to Forte dei Marmi, on the coast of Italy, in the spring of 1914. When World War I broke out in the fall, they returned via Switzerland to Germany. Schmidtbonn expressed his patriotism in *1914: Ein Kriegsvorspiel für die Bühne* (1914: Prelude to War for the Stage, 1915). This play captures the prewar mood in Germany. Only seven pages long, it was published in the paper *Das literarische Echo* (The Literary Echo) and performed at various German theaters. It is expressionistic in content and form. The characters appear only as types, such as a young woman, a farmer, a worker, and so on, rather than as individuals. Death is personified and enters into a dialogue with the young woman. All the male figures are ready to fight for Germany. Here Schmidtbonn echoes many of his fellow poets who glorified the war, thinking it would result in a quick victory. The enemies are depicted as inferior: the French are vindictive and jealous, the Russians are rapacious, the English are shopkeepers. But the blond and blue-eyed Germans, though they may be of various social classes, share a common heritage; war is the unifier of workers and bourgeoisie. The sketch ends with a battle cry and the singing of the national anthem.

At the end of 1914 Schmidtbonn became a war correspondent for the *Berliner Tagblatt* (Berlin Daily Paper). His book *Menschen und Städte im Kriege: Fahrten aus dem Großen Hauptquartier an die Aisne, an die Küste, in die belgischen Städte* (People and Cities during War: Travel from the Headquarters on the Aisne, to the Coast, into the Belgian Cities, 1915) describes his experiences on the western front. The German soldier is depicted as ready to sacrifice his life for the Fatherland; the French are portrayed as an inferior race.

Schmidtbonn's play *Die Stadt der Besessenen* (The City of the Possessed, 1915) deals with the Anabaptists in Münster in 1534. Rich and poor embrace the new doctrine. Jan van Leiden, the Dutch leader of the Anabaptists, abolishes the traditional marriage laws in favor of free love because he desires his sister-in-law. When he is rejected, he changes his law by decreeing that every woman has to belong to the man who wants her. The resulting sex orgies turn Münster into a new Sodom. Schmidtbonn ends his play with the bishop of Münster ordering the fanatics to renounce their new belief. The play was banned by the war censorship; Schmidtbonn had to make drastic changes before it was allowed to go on stage in Leipzig on 17 November 1917, but even in that form it was rejected by theatergoers.

Schmidtbonn's next post as a war correspondent was not in the Alps, as he had requested, but in Serbia. In *An einem Strom geboren* he tells of the hardships suffered by the German army and the civilian population; he also describes the plight of the army horses. Suffering from malaria, he returned from Serbia in the fall of 1916 and spent the winter in Berlin. His observations of war in the East were published in the propaganda pamphlet *Wenn sie siegten!* (If They Won!, 1916) and in *Krieg in Serbien* (War in Serbia, 1916). Asked by the Kriegspresseamt (War Press Bureau) to write the official 1916 Christmas greeting for the German soldiers at the front, Schmidtbonn, a fervent nationalist, called the task a sacred office and wrote about twenty versions before he was satisfied. Three million copies of *Weihnachten 1916* (Christmas 1916) were printed. Some members of his family, who had long regarded him as a prodigal son, praised him for the first time. A collection of six of his stories appeared in the series of pocket-size Feldbücher (field books) for the soldiers at the front; it had

the soothing title *Schlaraffenland* (Land of Milk and Honey, 1916).

In 1917 Schmidtbonn was appointed artistic councillor of the German embassy in Switzerland. After the war he lived again on the Tegernsee, where he wrote the play *Der Geschlagene* (The Defeated One, 1919), which premiered at the Deutsches Schauspielhaus (German Playhouse) in Hamburg on 15 April 1920. Set in the Rhineland, the drama shows how a serious war injury affects a young couple. Josef Wacholder, a young and ambitious former pilot, has gone blind. His crime, he says, was that he flew too high and the light above burned his eyes. He believes that he has been punished for his hubris. Although he recognizes his affliction as just punishment, he also rages against it. He feels that he is not wanted any more—especially by his wife, Elisa, whom he suspects of having an affair with his brother David. His behavior becomes so unbearable that David strikes him. In the last act it is revealed that David and Elisa had been in love with each other, but that their love was unconsummated. Elisa tells her husband that perhaps he had to become blind for her to love him. The play ends with Josef gaining religious faith. The extreme emotions displayed in the play make it typical for Schmidtbonn. Its pathos, sparse dialogue, and limited number of characters show the influence of expressionism.

An adaptation of a mystical French passion play of 1452 by Arnoul and Simon Gréban, *Die Passion* (The Passion; published, 1919), accentuates the physical suffering of the crucifixion and presents Jesus as a fanatic. Schmidtbonn refused to make any changes in the play, and this refusal marked the end of his collaboration with the Deutsches Theater in Berlin. *Die Passion* premiered at the Künstler-Theater (Artist Theater) in Munich on 2 June 1920.

In the comedy *Die Schauspieler* (The Actors; published, 1920) a theatrical troupe wants to perform a play in a village, but nobody has bought tickets. The actors have no money but owe the rent for the reserved hall. A rich old gentleman appears and desires to view the performance by himself, but the group declines. He then asks one of the actresses to spend the night with him, in return for which he will pay the troupe's debt. Three of the other actresses thwart the man's intentions by showing up at his room in the course of the night, but one of them, Gemma, later returns to him, knowing how lonely he is. Gemma's lover learns of her visit and renounces her, but she explains how desperate the man was. The benefactor wants to marry Gemma and end her poverty-stricken existence, but she refuses. He leaves, envying the actors their freedom and happiness. The play premiered at the Lustspielhaus (Comedy House) in Berlin on 23 September 1921.

Die Fahrt nach Orplid (The Journey to Orplid; published, 1922) reflects postwar inflation and unemployment, but it upholds German nationalism and condemns the desire to emigrate because of hard times. Orphal, a blond superman who should have remained at home to create a better generation of Germans, dies on his way to Peru, but his daughter will start a new life in Germany with a young man. This drama, like *Mutter Landstraße* and *Der verlorene Sohn*, deals with young people who reject the values of the older generation. It premiered in Bochum in 1923 and was performed in various German cities up to 1929. But by the late 1920s its expressionistic visionary scenes were out of date.

In *Der Pfarrer von Mainz* (The Pastor of Mainz, 1922) a pastor meets a young prostitute, Charlotte, who has been injured in a fight between her pimp and a man they tried to rob. The pastor takes her home, treats her wound, and falls in love with her. He vows to protect her from the police; she expresses her gratitude but doubts whether she is worthy of such kindness. The pastor's mother fears his undoing; she wants Charlotte out of the house. The son explains that for the first time in his life he is able to breathe freely. While the pastor tries to convince the director of police to leave the girl alone, Charlotte flees from the back room with the pimp, who has come to get her. Discovering Charlotte's flight, the pastor becomes desperate and goes to look for her. He finds Charlotte and the pimp at an inn and tries to persuade her to leave with him. Charlotte repeats that she is unworthy of a decent life; at the same time, she praises her own life of freedom. The pimp tries to stab the pastor, but Charlotte throws herself between them and is killed. The play ends with the pastor confessing that he had wanted to save her, but that she had saved him. One of Schmidtbonn's worst plays, the work remained unperformed.

Schmidtbonn's next play, *Maruf, der tolle Lügner* (Maruf, the Mad Liar, 1925), is based on the *Thousand-and-One Nights' Entertainments*. Maruf is a poor shoemaker in Cairo who prefers daydreaming to making money to support his obstreperous wife, Zaria. Bugu, an earth spirit, trans-

poses Maruf to the place of his dreams, Nischapur. There Maruf pretends to be a rich merchant awaiting a caravan of goods. In anticipation of Maruf's riches, the influential townspeople shower him with money and invitations. The hero gives the money as alms to the poor. The sultan offers Maruf his daughter. During the wedding preparations Maruf nearly empties the sultan's treasury, distributing everything to the poor. When his fiancée asks about his caravan, Maruf admits the truth. She helps him escape the sultan's wrath. He plans to settle down elsewhere, work, and send for her when he is established. But he begins to regret his lies and decides to abandon the woman he loves as an act of atonement. Such self-sacrifice would make him a typical Schmidtbonn hero. But in a fairy tale, dreams come true: a leaderless caravan arrives with costly goods, and Maruf reenters the sultan's town a rich man. His first wife, having found a new lover, agrees to a divorce, and all ends happily. Far removed from the sparseness of expressionism, this colorful comedy, which premiered in Nuremberg on 14 January 1925 was a success.

In the early 1920s Schmidtbonn moved to Bad Godesberg, near Bonn. In 1926 he was awarded a prize of four hundred marks by the Gesellschaft der Bücherfreunde (Society of the Friends of Books) at Chemnitz. In 1927 he participated in the celebrations of the centenary of Beethoven's death in Bonn, where Beethoven's house had been bought by one of Schmidtbonn's uncles and other citizens.

Schmidtbonn's final play was *Bruder Dietrich: Der Morgen eines Volkes* (Brother Dietrich: Morning of a People; published, 1928). This story is based on the legend of Dietrich of Bern, or Dietrich of Verona, which in turn was based on the life of the fifth-and-sixth century Ostrogoth king Theodoric the Great. Dietrich is driven from his lands in Italy by his rival Ermenrich but returns to defeat the tyrant. Schmidtbonn draws an idealized picture of Dietrich as an honest, just, and capable leader. The play premiered at the Staatstheater (State Theater) in Kassel on 16 February 1929.

Forced by his asthma to live in a milder climate, Schmidtbonn took up residence at Ascona, Switzerland, on Lake Maggiore. In 1935 he was inducted into the Prussian Academy of Poets, and on his sixtieth birthday the University of Bonn conferred an honorary doctorate on him. His works have a strong nationalistic flavor and the Nazis found them suitable for publication. Schmidtbonn, however, was never actively involved in politics. He returned to Germany in 1939; in December 1941 he received the Rhenish Literary Prize, and in 1949 he became a member of the Academy of Science and Literature in Mainz.

Schmidtbonn died in Bad Godesberg on 3 July 1952. Up to his death he expressed the hope that his plays would someday be resurrected, a wish that some critics have repeated.

Letters:

Wilhelm Schmidtbonn und Gustav Wunderwald: Dokumente einer Freundschaft 1908-1929, edited by Hildegard Reinhardt (Bonn: Röhrscheid, 1980).

Bibliography:

Ernst Metelmann, "Schmidtbonns Bibliographie," *Die schöne Literatur*, no. 26 (1926): 58-62.

References:

Joseph Antz, "Erfülltes Dasein: Zu Wilhelm Schmidtbonns 60. Geburtstag," *Das deutsche Wort*, no. 12 (1936): 275-277;

Frederick Jackson Churchill, "Wilhelm Schmidtbonn—Heimatdichter oder mehr?," Ph.D. dissertation, New York University, 1952;

Max Fischer "Wilhelm Schmidtbonn—der Epiker: Zum 50. Geburtstag," *Ostdeutsche Monatshefte*, 11, no. 6 (1926): 1152-1155;

Oskar Maurus Fontana, "Wilhelm Schmidtbonn," *Der Merker*, 1, no. 17 (1910): 724-728;

Werner Mahrholz, *Deutsche Literatur der Gegenwart: Probleme, Ergebnisse, Gestalten* (Berlin: Sieben Stäbe, 1930), pp. 240, 254-257, 467;

Walter von Molo, "Rede auf Wilhelm Schmidtbonn," *Die Literatur*, no. 36 (1934): 622-625;

Trudis E. Reber, *Wilhelm Schmidtbonn und das deutsche Theater* (Emsdetten: Lechte, 1969);

Herbert Saekel, ed., *Chor um Schmidtbonn* (Stuttgart: Anstatt, 1926);

Benjamin Daniel Webb, *The Demise of the "New Man": An Analysis of Ten Plays from Late German Expressionism* (Göppingen: Kümmerle, 1973);

Irmgard Wolf, " 'Als käme er aus dem Zauberberg . . . ': Zum Werk des Dichters Wilhelm Schmidtbonn," *Bonner Geschichtsblätter*, (Bonn: Heimat- und Geschichtsverein and Stadtarchiv Bonn, 1978), pp. 122-132;

Stefan Zweig, "Wilhelm Schmidtbonn: 'Deutsch—ach, man hat beinahe Angst . . . '," *Das Programm: Blätter der Münchener Kammerspiele*, 12, no. 4 (1912): 46.

Papers:

Wilhelm Schmidtbonn's manuscripts and letters are at the City Archives, Bonn, and the Theater Museum of the Institute for Theater Sciences of the University of Cologne.

Arthur Schnitzler
(15 May 1862 - 21 October 1931)

Gail Finney
University of California, Davis

See also the Schnitzler entry in *DLB 81: Austrian Fiction Writers, 1875-1913.*

PLAY PRODUCTIONS: *Das Märchen*, Vienna, Deutsches Volkstheater, 1 December 1893;
Liebelei, Vienna, Burgtheater, 9 October 1895;
Freiwild, Berlin, Deutsches Theater, 3 November 1896;
Das Vermächtnis, Berlin, Deutsches Theater, 8 October 1898;
Paracelsus, Vienna, Burgtheater, 1 March 1899;
Die Gefährtin, Vienna, Burgtheater, 1 March 1899;
Der grüne Kakadu, Vienna, Burgtheater, 1 March 1899;
Der Schleier der Beatrice, Breslau, Lobe-Theater, 1 December 1900;
Lebendige Stunden, Berlin, Deutsches Theater, 4 January 1902;
Der Puppenspieler, Berlin, Deutsches Theater, 12 September 1903;
Der einsame Weg, Berlin, Deutsches Theater, 13 February 1904;
Der tapfere Cassian, Berlin, Kleines Theater, 22 November 1904;
Zwischenspiel, Vienna, Burgtheater, 12 October 1905;
Der Ruf des Lebens, Berlin, Lessingtheater, 24 February 1906;
Zum grossen Wurstel, Vienna, Lustspieltheater, 16 March 1906;
Komtesse Mizzi oder der Familientag, Vienna, Deutsches Volkstheater, 5 January 1909;
Der tapfere Kassian (Singspiel), music by Oscar Straus, Leipzig, Neues Stadttheater, 30 October 1909;
Der Schleier der Pierrette, music by Ernö Dohnányi, Dresden, Königliches Opernhaus, 22 January 1910;
Der junge Medardus, Vienna, Burgtheater, 24 November 1910;
Anatol, Vienna, Deutsches Volkstheater and Berlin, Lessingtheater, 3 December 1910;

Arthur Schnitzler

Das weite Land, Berlin, Lessingtheater; Breslau, Lobe-Theater; Munich, Residenztheater; Hamburg, Deutsches Schauspielhaus; Prague, Deutsches Landestheater; Leipzig, Altes Stadttheater; Hannover, Schauburg; Bochum, Stadttheater; Vienna, Burgtheater, 14 October 1911;
Professor Bernhardi, Berlin, Kleines Theater, 28 November 1912;
Komödie der Worte, Vienna, Burgtheater; Darmstadt, Hoftheater; Frankfurt am Main, Neues Theater, 12 October 1915;
Fink und Fliederbusch, Vienna, Deutsches Volkstheater, 14 November 1917;

Die Schwestern oder Casanova in Spa, Vienna, Burgtheater, 26 March 1920;

Reigen, Berlin, Kleines Schauspielhaus, 23 December 1920;

Komödie der Verführung, Vienna, Burgtheater, 11 October 1924;

Im Spiel der Sommerlüfte, Vienna, Deutsches Volkstheater, 21 December 1929;

Der Gang zum Weiher, Vienna, Burgtheater, 14 February 1931;

Anatols Größenwahn, Vienna, Deutsches Volkstheater, 29 March 1932;

Die überspannte Person, Vienna, Deutsches Volkstheater, 29 March 1932;

Halbzwei, Vienna, Deutsches Volkstheater, 29 March 1932.

BOOKS: *Anatol: Mit einer Einleitung von Loris* (Berlin: Bibliographisches Bureau, 1893); translated by Grace Isabel Colbron as *Anatol*, in *Anatol; Living Hours; The Green Cockatoo* (New York: Boni & Liveright, 1917, pp. 1-97); translated by Frank Marcus as *Anatol* (London: Methuen, 1982);

Das Märchen: Schauspiel in drei Aufzügen (Dresden & Leipzig: Pierson, 1894; revised edition, Berlin: Fischer, 1902);

Sterben: Novelle (Berlin: Fischer, 1895); translated by Harry Zohn as "Dying," in *The Little Comedy and Other Stories* (New York: Ungar, 1977), pp. 147-234;

Liebelei: Schauspiel in drei Akten (Berlin: Fischer, 1896); translated by Colbron as *The Reckoning* (New York, 1907);

Die Frau des Weisen: Novelletten (Berlin: Fischer, 1898);

Freiwild: Schauspiel in drei Akten (Berlin: Fischer, 1898); translated by Paul H. Grummann as *Free Game* (Boston: Badger, 1913);

Der grüne Kakadu; Paracelsus; Die Gefährtin: Drei Einakter (Berlin: Fischer, 1899); translated by Horace B. Samuel as *The Green Cockatoo and Other Plays* (Chicago: McClurg, 1913)—comprises *The Green Cockatoo: Grotesque in One Act, The Mate, Paracelsus*;

Das Vermächtnis: Schauspiel in drei Akten (Berlin: Fischer, 1899); translated by Mary L. Stephenson as *The Legacy: Drama in Three Acts*, in *Poet Lore*, 22 (July-August 1911): 241-308;

Der Schleier der Beatrice: Schauspiel in fünf Akten (Berlin: Fischer, 1901);

Leutnant Gustl: Novelle (Berlin: Fischer, 1901); translated by Richard L. Simon as *None But the Brave* (New York: Simon & Schuster,

1926); translation revised by Caroline Wellbery, in *Plays and Stories*, edited by Egon Schwarz (New York: Continuum, 1982), pp. 249-279;

Frau Bertha Garlan: Novelle (Berlin: Fischer, 1901); translated by Agnes Jacques as *Bertha Garlan* (Boston: Badger, 1913); translated by J. H. Wisdom and Marr Murray as *Bertha Garlan: A Novel* (London: Goschen, 1914);

Lebendige Stunden: Vier Einakter (Berlin: Fischer, 1902); translated by Grummann as *Living Hours: Four One-Act Plays* (Boston: Badger, 1913);

Reigen: Zehn Dialoge, geschrieben Winter 1896/97 (Vienna & Leipzig: Wiener Verlag, 1903); translated by L. D. Edwards and F. L. Glaser as *Hands Around: A Cycle of Ten Dialogues* (New York: Privately printed, 1920); translated by Sue Davies and adapted by John Barton as *La Ronde* (Harmondsworth, U.K.: Penguin, 1982);

Der einsame Weg: Schauspiel in fünf Akten (Berlin: Fischer, 1904); translated by Edwin Björkman as *The Lonely Way* (Boston: Little, Brown, 1904);

Die griechische Tänzerin: Novellen (Vienna & Leipzig: Wiener Verlag, 1905);

Marionetten: Drei Einakter (Berlin: Fischer, 1906);

Der Ruf des Lebens: Schauspiel in drei Akten (Berlin: Fischer, 1906);

Zwischenspiel: Komödie in drei Akten (Berlin: Fischer, 1906); translated by Björkman as *Intermezzo: A Comedy in Three Acts*, in *The Lonely Way; Intermezzo; Countess Mizzie: Three Plays* (New York: Kennerley, 1915), pp. 139-259;

Dämmerseelen: Novellen (Berlin: Fischer, 1907);

Der Weg ins Freie: Roman (Berlin: Fischer, 1908); translated by Samuel as *The Road to the Open* (New York: Knopf, 1923; London: Allen & Unwin, 1932);

Der tapfere Kassian: Singspiel in einem Aufzug, music by Oscar Straus (Leipzig & Vienna: Doblinger, 1909);

Der junge Medardus: Dramatische Historie in einem Vorspiel und fünf Aufzügen (Berlin: Fischer, 1910);

Der Schleier der Pierrette: Pantomime in drei Bildern, music by Ernö Dohnányi (Vienna & Leipzig: Doblinger, 1910);

Das weite Land: Tragikomödie in fünf Akten (Berlin: Fischer, 1911); translated by Edward Woticky and Alexander Caro as *The Vast Domain: A Tragi-Comedy in Five Acts*, in *Poet Lore*, 34 (September 1923): 317-407; translated by Tom Stoppard as *Undiscovered Country* (Boston & London: Faber & Faber, 1980);

Masken und Wunder: Novellen (Berlin: Fischer, 1912);

Professor Bernhardi: Komödie in fünf Akten (Berlin: Fischer, 1912); translated by Hetty Landstone as *Professor Bernhardi: A Comedy in Five Acts* (London: Faber & Gwyer, 1927); translated by Mrs. Emil Pohli as *Professor Bernhardi*, in *A Golden Treasury of Jewish Literature*, edited by Leo W. Schwarz (New York & Toronto: Farrar & Rinehart, 1937), pp. 468-504;

Frau Beate und ihr Sohn: Novelle (Berlin: Fischer, 1913); translated by Jacques as *Beatrice: A Novel* (New York: Simon & Schuster, 1926);

Gesammelte Werke in zwei Abteilungen, 7 volumes (Berlin: Fischer, 1913; enlarged, 9 volumes, 1922-1923);

Komödie der Worte: Drei Einakter (Berlin: Fischer, 1915); translated, with additions, by Pierre Loving as *Comedies of Words and Other Plays* (Cincinnati: Stewart & Kidd, 1917);

Fink und Fliederbusch: Komödie in drei Akten (Berlin: Fischer, 1917);

Doktor Gräsler, Badearzt: Erzählung (Berlin: Fischer, 1917); translated by E. C. Slade as *Dr. Graesler* (New York: Seltzer, 1923; London: Chapman & Hall, 1924);

Casanovas Heimfahrt: Novelle (Berlin: Fischer, 1918); translated by Eden and Cedar Paul as *Casanova's Homecoming* (New York: Seltzer, 1922; London: Brentano's, 1923); translation revised by Wellbery, in *Plays and Stories*, pp. 153-247;

Die Schwestern oder Casanova in Spa: Ein Lustspiel in Versen. Drei Akte in einem (Berlin: Fischer, 1919);

Komödie der Verführung: In drei Akten (Berlin: Fischer, 1924);

Fräulein Else: Novelle (Berlin, Vienna & Leipzig: Zsolnay, 1924); translated by Robert A. Simon as *Fräulein Else: A Novel* (New York: Simon & Schuster, 1925); translated by F. H. Lyon as *Fräulein Else* (London: Philpot, 1925);

Die Frau des Richters: Novelle (Berlin: Propyläen, 1925): translated by Peter Bauland as "The Judge's Wife," in *The Little Comedy and Other Stories*, pp. 85-145;

Traumnovelle (Berlin: Fischer, 1926); translated by Otto P. Schinnerer as *Rhapsody: A Dream*

Novel (New York: Simon & Schuster, 1927; London: Constable, 1928);

Der Gang zum Weiher: Dramatische Dichtung in fünf Aufzügen (Berlin: Fischer, 1926);

Spiel im Morgengrauen: Novelle (Berlin: Fischer, 1927); translated by William A. Drake as *Daybreak* (New York: Simon & Schuster, 1927);

Buch der Sprüche und Bedenken: Aphorismen und Betrachtungen (Vienna: Phaidon, 1927); excerpts translated by Dorothy Alden as "Aphorisms: From an Unpublished Book 'Proverbs and Reflections,'" *Plain Talk*, 2 (May 1928): 590; 3 (October 1928): 419; 4 (December 1928): 733; excerpts translated by Frederick Ungar as *Practical Wisdom: A Treasury of Aphorisms and Reflections from the German*, edited by Ungar (New York: Ungar, 1977);

Der Geist im Wort und der Geist in der Tat: Vorläufige Bemerkungen zu zwei Diagrammen (Berlin: Fischer, 1927); translated by Robert O. Weiss as *The Mind in Words and Action: Preliminary Remarks Concerning Two Diagrams* (New York: Ungar, 1972);

Die Erwachenden: Novellen (Berlin: Fischer, 1928);

Therese: Chronik eines Frauenlebens (Berlin: Fischer, 1928); translated by Drake as *Therese: The Chronicle of a Woman's Life* (New York: Simon & Schuster, 1928);

Im Spiel der Sommerlüfte: In drei Aufzügen (Berlin: Fischer, 1930);

Flucht in die Finsternis: Novelle (Berlin: Fischer, 1931); translated by Drake as *Flight into Darkness: A Novel* (New York: Simon & Schuster, 1931);

Traum und Schicksal: Sieben Novellen (Berlin: Fischer, 1931);

Anatols Größenwahn: Ein Akt (Berlin: Fischer, 1932); translated by Paul F. Dvorak as *Anatol's Delusions of Grandeur*, in *Illusion and Reality: Plays and Stories of Arthur Schnitzler* (New York, Bern & Frankfurt am Main: Lang, 1986), pp. 43-62;

Die Gleitenden: Ein Akt (Berlin: Fischer, 1932);

Die kleine Komödie: Frühe Novellen (Berlin: Fischer, 1932);

Die Mörderin: Tragische Posse in einem Akt (Berlin: Fischer, 1932);

Abenteurernovelle (Vienna: Bermann-Fischer, 1937);

Über Krieg und Frieden (Stockholm: Bermann-Fischer, 1939); translated by Weiss as *Some Day Peace Will Return: Notes on War and Peace* (New York: Ungar, 1972);

Meisterdramen (Frankfurt am Main: Fischer, 1955);

Gesammelte Werke: Die erzählenden Schriften, 2 volumes (Frankfurt am Main: Fischer, 1961-1962);

Gesammelte Werke: Die dramatischen Werke, 2 volumes (Frankfurt am Main: Fischer, 1962);

Das Wort: Tragikomödie in fünf Akten. Aus dem Nachlaß, edited by Kurt Bergel (Frankfurt am Main: Fischer, 1966);

Aphorismen und Betrachtungen, edited by Weiss (Frankfurt am Main: Fischer, 1967);

Jugend in Wien: Eine Autobiographie, edited by Therese Nickl and Heinrich Schnitzler (Vienna, Munich & Zurich: Molden, 1968); translated by Catherine Hutter as *My Youth in Vienna* (New York: Holt, Rinehart & Winston, 1970);

Frühe Gedichte, edited by Herbert Lederer (Berlin: Propyläen, 1969);

Zug der Schatten: Drama in 9 Bildern. Aus dem Nachlaß, edited by Françoise Derré (Frankfurt am Main: Fischer, 1970);

Meistererzählungen (Frankfurt am Main: Fischer, 1975);

Ritterlichkeit: Fragment. Aus dem Nachlaß, edited by Rena Schlein (Bonn: Bouvier, 1975);

Entworfenes und Verworfenes: Aus dem Nachlaß, edited by Reinhard Urbach (Frankfurt am Main: Fischer, 1977);

Gesammelte Werke in Einzelausgaben, 15 volumes (Frankfurt am Main: Fischer, 1977-1979);

Lesebuch/Schnitzler (Frankfurt am Main: Fischer, 1978);

Tagebuch 1909-1912, edited by Werner Welzig and others (Vienna: Verlag der Österreichischen Akademie der Wissenschaften, 1981);

Tagebuch 1913-1916, edited by Welzig and others (Vienna: Verlag der Österreichischen Akademie der Wissenschaften, 1983);

Tagebuch 1917-1919, edited by Welzig and others (Vienna: Verlag der Österreichischen Akademie der Wissenschaften, 1985);

Fräulein Else und andere Erzählungen (Frankfurt am Main: Fischer, 1987);

Tagebuch 1879-1892, edited by Welzig and others (Vienna: Verlag der Österreichischen Akademie der Wissenschaften, 1987);

Beziehungen und Einsamkeiten: Aphorismen, edited by Clemens Eich (Frankfurt am Main: Fischer, 1987);

Medizinische Schriften, edited by Horst Thomé (Vienna: Zsolnay, 1988);

Tagebuch 1893-1902, edited by Welzig and others (Vienna: Verlag der Österreichischen Akademie der Wissenschaften, 1989).

SELECTED PERIODICAL PUBLICATIONS—
UNCOLLECTED: "Er wartet auf den vazierenden Gott," *Deutsche Wochenschrift*, 4 (12 December 1886): 644;

"Sylvesterbetrachtungen," *Internationale klinische Rundschau*, 3 (6 January 1889): 35-36;

"Mein Freund Ypsilon: Aus den Papieren eines Arztes," *An der schönen blauen Donau*, 4, no. 2 (1889): 25-28;

"Amerika," *An der schönen blauen Donau*, 4, no. 9 (1889): 197; translated by Franzi Ascher as "America," *Decision*, 3 (January-February 1942): 35-36;

"Der Andere: Aus dem Tagebuch eines Hinterbliebenen," *An der schönen blauen Donau*, 4, no. 21 (1889): 490-492;

Alkandi's Lied: Dramatisches Gedicht in einem Aufzug, An der schönen blauen Donau, 5, no. 17 (1890): 398-400; no. 18 (1890): 424-426;

"Reichtum," *Moderne Rundschau*, 3 (1 September 1891): 385-391; (15 September 1891): 417-423; 4 (1 October 1891): 1-7; (15 October 1891): 34-40; translated by Helene Scher as "Riches," in *The Little Comedy and Other Stories* (New York: Ungar, 1977), pp. 37-73;

"Der Sohn: Aus den Papieren eines Arztes," *Freie Bühne für den Entwicklungskampf der Zeit*, 3 (January 1892): 89-94; translated by Peggy Stamon as "The Son," in *The Little Comedy and Other Stories*, pp. 75-83;

"Spaziergang," *Deutsche Zeitung*, 6 December 1893;

"Blumen," *Wiener Neue Revue*, 5 (1 August 1894): 151-157; translated by Frederick Eisemann as "Flowers," in *Viennese Idylls* (Boston: Luce, 1913), pp. 1-18; translated by Elsie M. Lang as "Flowers," in *Beatrice, a Novel, and Other Stories* (London: Laurie, 1926), pp. 121-136;

"Die drei Elixiere," *Moderner Musen-Almanach auf das Jahr 1894: Ein Jahrbuch deutscher Kunst*, 2 (1894): 44-49;

"Der Witwer," *Wiener Allgemeine Zeitung*, 25 December 1894, pp. 3-4; translated by Paul F. Dvorak as "The Widower," in *Illusion and Reality: Plays and Stories of Arthur Schnitzler* (New York, Bern & Frankfurt am Main: Lang, 1986), pp. 129-138;

"Die kleine Komödie," *Neue Deutsche Rundschau*, 6 (August 1895): 779-798; translated by George Edward Reynolds as "The Little Comedy," in *The Little Comedy and Other Stories*, pp. 1-36;

"Ein Abschied," *Neue Deutsche Rundschau*, 7 (February 1896): 115-124; translated by Eisemann as "The Farewell," in *Viennese Idylls*, pp. 121-152;

Die überspannte Person: Ein Akt, *Simplicissimus*, 1 (18 April 1896): 3, 6; translated by Dvorak as *The High-Strung Woman*, in *Illusion and Reality*, pp. 63-68;

"Die Frau des Weisen," *Die Zeit*, 2 January 1897, pp. 15-16; 9 January 1897, pp. 31-32; 16 January 1897, pp. 47-48; translated by Eisemann as "The Sage's Wife," in *Viennese Idylls*, pp. 19-52; translated by Lang as "The Wife of the Wise Man," in *Beatrice, a Novel, and Other Stories*, pp. 163-188;

Halbzwei: Ein Akt, *Gesellschaft*, 13 (April 1897): 42-49; translated by Dvorak as *One-Thirty*, in *Illusion and Reality*, pp. 69-76;

"Die Toten schweigen," *Cosmopolis*, 8 (October 1897): 193-211; translated by Courtland H. Young as "The Dead Are Silent," in *Short Story Classics: Foreign*, volume 3, edited by William Patten (New York: Collier, 1907), pp. 953-977;

"Der Ehrentag," *Die Romanwelt*, 5, no. 16 (1897): 507-516; translated by Agnes Jacques as "The Hour of Fame," in *Beatrice, a Novel, and Other Stories*, pp. 189-220; translated by Jacques as "The Jest," in *Rejections of 1927*, edited by Charles H. Baker (Garden City, N.Y.: Doubleday, Doran, 1928), pp. 171-194;

"Um eine Stunde," *Neue Freie Presse*, 24 December 1899, p. 29;

"Der blinde Hieronymo und sein Bruder," *Die Zeit*, 22 December 1900, pp. 190-191; 29 December 1900, pp. 207-208; 5 January 1901, pp. 15-16; 12 January 1901, pp. 31-32; translated by Eisemann as "Blind Geronimo and His Brother," in *Viennese Idylls*, pp. 53-106;

Sylvesternacht: Ein Dialog, *Jugend*, 1, no. 8 (1901): 118-119, 121-122; translated by Dvorak as *New Year's Eve*, in *Illusion and Reality*, pp. 77-85;

"Dämmerseele," *Neue Freie Presse*, 18 May 1902, pp. 31-33; translated by Eric Sutton as "The Stranger," in *Little Novels* (New York: Simon & Schuster, 1929), pp. 39-54;

"Andreas Thameyer's letzter Brief," *Die Zeit*, 26 July 1902, pp. 63-64; translated by Eisemann as "Andreas Thameyer's Last Letter," in *Viennese Idylls*, pp. 107-120;

"Die Griechische Tänzerin," *Die Zeit*, 28 September 1902; translated by Pierre Loving as "The Greek Dancer," *Dial*, 71 (September 1921): 253-264;

"Exzentrik," *Jugend*, 2, no. 30 (1902): 492-493, 495-496;

Der Puppenspieler: Studie in einem Aufzug, in *Neue Freie Presse*, 31 May 1903;

"Die grüne Krawatte," *Neues Wiener Journal* (25 October 1903);

"Das Schicksal des Freiherrn von Leisenbogh," *Neue Rundschau*, 15 (July 1904): 829-842; translated by Kenneth Burke as "The Fate of the Baron von Leisenbogh," *Dial*, 75 (December 1923): 565-582;

Der tapfere Cassian: Puppenspiel in einem Akt, in *Neue Rundschau*, 15, no. 2 (1904): 227-247; translated by Adam L. Gowans as *Gallant Cassian: A Puppet Play in One Act* (London & Glasgow: Gowans & Gray, 1914); translated by Moritz A. Jagendorf as *Gallant Cassian: A Puppet Play*, in *Poet Lore*, 33 (December 1922): 507-520;

"Der Fall Jakobsohn," *Die Zukunft*, 49 (17 December 1904): 401-404;

"Das neue Lied: Erzählung," *Neue Freie Presse*, 23 April 1905, pp. 31-34; translated by Burke as "The New Song," *Dial*, 79 (November 1925): 355-369;

Zum großen Wurstel: Burleske in einem Akt, in *Die Zeit*, 23 April 1905;

"Die Weissagung," *Neue Freie Presse*, 24 December 1905, pp. 31-38; translated by Marie Bush as "The Prophecy," in *Selected Austrian Short Stories*, edited by Bush (London: Milford, 1928), pp. 246-279; translated by Sutton as "The Prophecy," in *Little Novels*, pp. 79-118;

"Die Geschichte eines Genies," *Arena*, 2 (March 1907): 1290-1292;

"Der tote Gabriel: Novelle," *Neue Freie Presse*, 19 May 1907, pp. 31-35; translated by Sutton as "Dead Gabriel," in *Little Novels*, pp. 193-217;

"Der Tod des Junggesellen: Novelle," *Österreichische Rundschau*, 15 (1 April 1908): 19-26; translated by Sutton as "The Death of a Bachelor," in *Little Novels*, pp. 259-279;

Die Verwandlungen des Pierrot: Pantomime in einem Vorspiel und sechs Bildern, in *Die Zeit*, 19 April 1908;

Komtesse Mizzi oder der Familientag: Komödie in einem Akt, in *Neue Freie Presse*, 19 April 1908, pp. 31-35; translated by Edwin Björkman as *Countess Mizzie* (Boston: Little, Brown, 1907); translation revised by Caroline Wellbery, in *Plays and Stories*, edited by Egon Schwarz (New York: Continuum, 1982), pp. 117-151;

"Der Mörder: Novelle," *Neue Freie Presse*, 4 June 1911, pp. 31-38; translated by O. F. Theis as "The Murderer," in *The Shepherd's Pipe and Other Stories* (New York: Brown, 1922), pp. 81-120;

"Die dreifache Warnung," *Die Zeit*, 4 June 1911; translated by Barrett H. Clark as "The Triple Warning," in *Great Short Stories of the World: A Collection of Complete Short Stories Chosen from the Literatures of All Periods and Countries*, edited by Clark and Maxim Lieber (New York: McBride, 1925), pp. 284-285;

"Die Hirtenflöte: Novelle," *Neue Rundschau*, 22 (September 1911): 1249-1273; translated by Theis as "The Shepherd's Pipe," in *The Shepherd's Pipe and Other Stories*, pp. 15-80;

"Das Tagebuch der Redegonda: Novellette," *Süddeutsche Monatshefte*, 9 (October 1911): 1-7; translated by Sutton as "Redegonda's Diary," in *Little Novels*, pp. 181-192;

"Wohltaten, still und rein gegeben," *Neues Wiener Tagblatt*, 25 December 1931, pp. 27-28; translated as "Charity's Reward," *Living Age*, 342 (March 1932): 48-52;

"Der Sekundant," *Vossische Zeitung*, 1-4 January 1932; translated by Dvorak as "The Second," in *Illusion and Reality*, pp. 199-216;

"Der letzte Brief eines Literaten: Novelle," *Neue Rundschau*, 43 (January 1932): 14-37; translated by Dvorak as "The Last Letter of a Writer," in *Illusion and Reality*, pp. 177-198;

"Gedanken über Kunst: Aus dem Nachlaß," *Neue Rundschau*, 43 (January 1932): 37-39;

"Die Nächste," *Neue Freie Presse*, 27 March 1932, pp. 33-39;

"Welch eine Melodie," *Neue Rundschau*, 43 (May 1932): 659-663;

"Der Empfindsame: Eine Burleske," *Neue Rundschau*, 43 (May 1932): 663-669;

"Ein Erfolg," *Neue Rundschau*, 43 (May 1932): 669-678;

"Der Fürst im Haus," *Wiener Arbeiter Zeitung*, 15 May 1932;

"Frühlingsnacht im Seziersaal: Phantasie," *Jahrbuch deutscher Bibliophilen und Literaturfreunde*, 18-19 (1932-1933): 86-91;

"Gespräch, welches in der Kaffeehausecke nach Vorlesung der 'Elixiere' geführt wird," *Jahrbuch deutscher Bibliophilen und Literaturfreunde*, 18-19 (1932-1933): 91-93;

"Boxeraufstand: Fragment. Entwurf zu einer Novelle," *Neue Rundschau*, 68, no. 1 (1957): 84-87;

"Kriegsgeschichte: Ein Entwurf," *Literatur und Kritik*, 13 (April 1967): 133-134;

"Roman-Fragment," edited by Reinhard Urbach, *Literatur und Kritik*, 13 (April 1967): 135-183;

"Das Haus Delorme: Eine Familienszene," edited by Urbach, *Ver Sacrum* (1970), 46-55;

"Über Psychoanalyse," edited by Urbach, *Protokolle*, 2 (1976): 277-284.

Scarcely any playwright is as closely identified with turn-of-the-century Vienna as is Arthur Schnitzler. Once regarded as a one-sided writer whose perspective was limited to upper-crust Viennese society during the *belle époque*, Schnitzler has come to be appreciated as a keenly perceptive critic of his milieu whose moralism is tempered by his own abundant possession of the foibles he illuminates. The older critical commonplace of his narrowness is belied by the variety of dramatic genres in which he wrote: conventional three- and five-act comedies, tragedies, and tragicomedies; one-act plays; dramatic poems; verse plays; historical dramas; play cycles; pantomimes; and puppet plays. He was also an accomplished writer of fiction. In its diversity Schnitzler's work exhibits features of the artistic modes predominant in his day—naturalism and aestheticism—yet his oeuvre resists stylistic classification.

It is little wonder that Vienna served as the setting for the bulk of Schnitzler's work. Born there on 15 May 1862, he never lived anywhere else, although he made frequent trips within Europe, traveling most often to Berlin. At Vienna's Akademisches Gymnasium from 1871 to 1879 the young Schnitzler was a model student, completing his studies with distinction. His family background virtually predestined him for a medical career: his father, Johann, was a laryngologist; his mother, born Louise Markbreiter, was the daughter of a physician. In the same year he finished high school Schnitzler began studying medicine at the University of Vienna. After achieving the degree of Doctor of General Medicine in 1885 he decided to specialize in his father's field. In 1887 he became editor of the *Internationale klinische Rundschau*, a medical journal founded by his father, for which he wrote many book reviews; the following year he became an assistant in his father's clinic.

Schnitzler's path to a medical career was far from smooth, however. The vehement encouragement of his father, one of Vienna's most respected physicians, had to contend with Schnitzler's literary inclinations, and Schnitzler often abandoned the examining room for the literary cafés that were prominent in Vienna around the turn of the century. The literary ambition that was later to dominate Schnitzler was present quite early, as poems written during his youth attest. Although he continued during the 1880s to write poetry and also began trying his hand at short prose pieces and one-act plays, his breakthrough as a writer came with *Anatol* (1893; translated, 1917), a cycle of seven one-act plays composed between 1888 and 1891. Although most of the individual plays in the cycle were performed during the 1890s, the cycle was not produced until five of the plays were staged in December 1910 in Vienna and Berlin, the two cities whose theaters consistently did the most to promote Schnitzler's work.

Written in the tradition of French boulevard theater but infused with an atmosphere unmistakably Viennese and fin de siècle, *Anatol* did perhaps more than any other work to create the legend of Arthur Schnitzler. The tone of the cycle is established by the introductory poem, written by the eighteen-year-old Hugo von Hofmannsthal under his pseudonym Loris. Schnitzler had met Hofmannsthal in 1890 at the Café Griensteidl, where they became two of the key participants in the literary group "Jung Wien" (Young Vienna). A loosely established circle whose members gathered from 1890 to 1897 at the café to read and comment on each other's works, Jung Wien also included writers and critics such as Hermann Bahr, Richard Beer-Hofmann, Felix Dörmann, Peter Altenberg, and Felix Salten. In his introductory poem the lyric prodigy Hofmannsthal creates a scene filled with rococo trappings. The setting, conveyed through a series of delicate impressions appealing to several senses, is expressly compared both to the Vienna of the Italian artist Canaletto and to pastoral paintings by Antoine Watteau. The evocation of works of art is not gratuitous, since Hofmannsthal goes on to compare this scene to a theater:

Also spielen wir Theater,
Spielen unsre eignen Stücke,

Frühgereift und zart und traurig,
Die Komödie unsrer Seele.

(Thus it is we play at theater,
Perform our own plays,
Precocious, delicate, and sad,
The comedy of our souls.)

These lines serve as an apt introduction to *Anatol*, whose title character is prone to self-analysis and "performs" much of the time, especially with his lovers. Moreover, a poem as laden with atmosphere as "Einleitung" is appropriate for the depiction of a character who reveals in the play *Episode* that for him the true secret of love, the key to the mystery of woman, lies in creating the proper mood for romance. For this melancholy playboy it is not the individual women who are important; each is merely an episode, represented after the end of the relationship by a bundle of letters, a lock of hair, or a dried flower. The episodic structure of the plays comprising *Anatol*, consisting of brief, concentrated dialogues usually with only two or three characters, underlines their content.

Although in *Episode* Anatol compares the end of one affair with the loss of an umbrella which one leaves somewhere and remembers only several days later, he also insists that all his former women are "holy" because they have lain in his arms. This rhetoric, so contradictory as to be meaningless, is typical of his tendency to idealize women, to render them angelic in his mind, and to poeticize love and passion and the decay of those emotions. The playboy outdoes himself in *Anatols Hochzeitsmorgen* (translated as *The Morning of Anatol's Wedding*), in which he has great difficulty telling the girl with whom he has spent the night that he is scheduled to get married that day. Running off to the wedding, he leaves his friend Max to placate her.

The function here of Max, who pacifies the girl by reminding her that while Anatol is likely to deceive his wife, he can always come back to his mistress, is typical of the role he plays in five of the seven plays: that of the ironic, droll foil to the frothy Anatol. Examples of Max's dry, insightful wit include his observation in *Episode* that jealousy does not necessarily end when love does and his response to Anatol in *Agonie*, whose open portrayal of an adulterous woman kept it off the stage: when Anatol exclaims that "es gibt nichts Entsetzlicheres, als der Liebhaber einer verheirateten Frau zu sein!" (there is nothing more dreadful than being the lover of a married

Schnitzler in Bad Ischl, circa 1894

woman!), Max counters, "Oh doch . . . ihr Gatte wär' ich zum Beispiel weniger gern!" (Oh, I don't know . . . I'd much less rather be her husband, for example!).

Anatol's married lover and abandoned mistress are only two of the many women characters in the cycle, which, with its diversity of female roles, set a standard for Schnitzler's later work. Indeed, the unusually high number of parts for women often made Schnitzler's plays difficult to stage. Two of his most frequently portrayed female types are juxtaposed in *Weihnachtseinkäufe* (translated as *Christmas Shopping*), in which Anatol encounters a former flame while looking for a Christmas gift for his current girlfriend. The woman, who now regrets having resisted Anatol's advances because she was married, appears to be based on Olga Waissnix, a married woman who maintained a platonic relationship with Schnitzler from the time they met in 1886 until her death in 1897.

As one who appreciated and encouraged his writing, Waissnix differed markedly from the nonintellectual girls with whom Schnitzler had relationships during the same period, such as Jeanette Heger and Marie (Mizi) Glümer. Despite his love for Glümer, an aspiring actress who had been passed along to him by a friend, Schnitzler could not bring himself to marry her because of her past. But he immortalized her in the "süßes Mädel" (sweet girl), the second female type delineated in *Weihnachtseinkäufe*. In a highly poetic, idealizing description which glosses over the often difficult economic status of these petit bourgeois girls from the Viennese suburbs, Anatol characterizes the sweet girl—exemplified by his sweetheart of the moment—as graceful, skilled in love, and as charming as a spring evening, though not particularly beautiful, elegant, or intelligent.

To a considerable extent, Anatol's bevy of women reflects that of Schnitzler himself, a notorious ladies' man who confided to his diary in 1897 that his ideal would be to maintain a harem yet who did not approve of a similar sexual freedom in his partners. In contrast to many of his male contemporaries, however, Schnitzler recognized the double standard characterizing his thinking, and he often attempted to come to terms with it in his works. In *Anatol* both Max and the title figure repeatedly demonstrate a belief in the double standard as regards virginity at the time of marriage and fidelity in relationships. Yet Schnitzler undercuts their views, thus implicitly taking a critical stance on his own, through his portrayal of Anatol's partners. One of the best examples is found in *Abschiedssouper* (translated as *Farewell Supper*). When, in 1893, it became the first of the one-act plays from *Anatol* to be publicly performed, it brought on trouble with the censors, attacks from the critics, and financial difficulties, giving Schnitzler a taste of the problems he was to have with his plays from then on. It depicts the supper at which Anatol is planning to break off with his mistress, only to have her beat him to it. When Anatol attempts to regain the upper hand by dishonestly telling her he has already deceived her, she shocks him by saying that she would never have been so insensitive as to reveal that she has been doing the same thing to him.

The structure of *Abschiedssouper*, ending with a surprising, amusing punch line which encourages the spectator to rethink the moral codes of the playlet, is found in all the plays comprising *Anatol*. In *Denksteine* (translated as *Souvenirs*), for example, Anatol's fiancée calms him down by telling him that a ruby he has found by rummaging through her drawers is a souvenir of the day that "made her a woman"; but when she says that she has kept another jewel because of its value, he hurls it into the fire and calls her a whore. Similarly, in *Die Frage an das Schicksal* (translated as *The Question Put to Fate*) Anatol hypnotizes his beloved to ask her whether she has been faithful to him; in the end he is unable to put the question, preferring his own illusions to a possibly different reality.

The insight into hypnosis evident in this work and in the later one-act play *Paracelsus* (1899; translated, 1913) is only one of the reasons why Sigmund Freud was moved, in a 1922 letter to Schnitzler, to call the writer his double. The affinities between the two men are indeed striking. After becoming a general practitioner Schnitzler studied psychiatry and learned hypnosis at the clinic of Theodor Meynert, with whom Freud had also worked. Like Freud, Schnitzler was interested in dreams and in the use of hypnosis to treat hysteria. Many of his works resemble case studies in their fascination with troubled psyches. The playlet originally conceived as the final part of *Anatol, Anatols Größenwahn* (1932; translated as *Anatol's Delusions of Grandeur*, 1986), in which an older and seemingly wiser Anatol views himself as the supreme connoisseur of women but learns that he is, even now, capable of being deluded by them, points in its title to a key syndrome described by Freud.

Schnitzler moved increasingly toward writing and away from the practice of medicine, particularly following the death of his father in 1893. In 1894 he composed one of his most popular dramas, *Liebelei* (performed, 1895; published, 1896; translated as *The Reckoning*, 1907). (The play was made into an opera by Franz Neumann that premiered in 1910 in Frankfurt.) *Liebelei* presents two variations of the "sweet girl": Mizi and Christine are associated, respectively, with Theodor and Fritz, well-to-do students and men-about-town for whom the girls seem to be a mere pastime. The differences between the members of each pair become evident at a supper at Theodor's. (The detail with which the preparations for dinner and the setting are described sets the tone for Schnitzler's subsequent plays, which are akin to naturalist dramas in their extensive stage directions, carefully delineated characters, and attention to particulars of appearance and gesture.) In contrast to the rather cynical and worldly-wise Mizi, Christine is devoted to Fritz with all her heart. A middle-class girl, she laboriously copies music to bring in a bit of extra money; Fritz's visit to her room, the simplicity of which impresses him as a reflection of her own, is reminiscent of Faust's visit to Gretchen's in Johann Wolfgang von Goethe's *Faust I* (1808). The portrayal of Christine owes much to the young singing teacher Marie Reinhard, another of Schnitzler's sweet girls of the 1890s; although she was not a "fallen" woman like Mizi Glümer, he could not bring himself to marry her, either.

Distinctions between Theodor and Fritz parallel to a degree those between Mizi and Christine. Whereas Theodor is a playboy and aesthete who seems to be more concerned with the rituals of the table than with Mizi's feelings, Fritz is genuinely in love—albeit with a married woman, not with Christine. Although he is killed by the woman's husband in a duel, the tragedy of the play is not Fritz's but rather that of Christine and her father, Weiring. Guessing that Fritz has died because of another woman, Christine is shattered by her realization that her relationship with him was so inconsequential that he did not even tell her good-bye and that no one thought to invite her to his funeral.

The close relationship between Christine and Weiring, a widowed violinist of modest means, along with the motif of the virtuous middle-class girl seduced by an upper-class man, links *Liebelei* to the tradition of the bourgeois tragedy prevalent in German literature since the mid eighteenth century. Class difference has characteristic importance here; it is given voice by Christine's neighbor, Katharina Binder, who chides her for being so obvious about her affair with a gentleman. Her father's tragedy is that he is so concerned for her happiness that he does nothing to thwart the relationship that winds up bringing her only despair. The play's final spotlight is on Weiring, sobbing in his certainty that his daughter has run off to her death. As in the bourgeois tragedies of Gotthold Ephraim Lessing, Friedrich Schiller, Friedrich Hebbel, and Gerhart Hauptmann, the father's inability to protect his daughter can be seen as representative of the impotence of the bourgeoisie in relation to the upper classes.

The most turbulent of the scandals caused by Schnitzler's works was brought on by *Reigen* (Round Dance, 1903; translated as *Hands Around*, 1920). Consisting of ten dialogues, nine of which center around various acts of sexual intercourse, the play earned for Schnitzler the label of pornographer. It was not allowed access on stage until 1920, when the directors of the Kleines Schauspielhaus (Little Playhouse) in Berlin, Gertrud Eysoldt and Maximilian Sladek, courageously ventured a performance. They and the cast were tried for obscenity but acquitted. Subsequent performances of *Reigen* in several German cities and in Vienna unleashed demonstrations, riots, and hate campaigns, often openly anti-Semitic. By 1922 Schnitzler was so weary of the affair that he forbade further productions of the play, a ban his son Heinrich maintained until 1981.

The play's title refers to its structure, in which one of the partners in each scene has appeared in the previous scene and the other appears in the following scene—"Die Dirne und der Soldat" (The Prostitute and the Soldier), "Der Soldat und das Stubenmädchen" (The Soldier and the Parlormaid), "Das Stubenmädchen und der junge Herr" (The Parlormaid and the Young Gentleman), and so forth. The work's innovative structure and its use of type designations instead of proper names emphasize the extent to which sexual desire is all-embracing, cutting across boundaries of class. *Reigen* also reveals lust to cut across boundaries of gender, although the play's male characters would prefer to think otherwise. As with the male figures in *Anatol* and *Liebelei*, their moral views are dominated by a double standard.

The husband of die junge Frau (the Young Wife) is the play's most adamant exponent of this value system; he laments women who have sex before or outside of marriage, although he is guilty on both counts. Yet the conventional distinction he makes between the pure women one loves and the fallen women one desires is undermined when his wife expresses fascination with and even envy of the latter. Similarly, while the women figures in the play often exhibit shame, which Schnitzler considered a typically feminine attribute, this display is unmasked as role-playing and in fact serves to stimulate seduction. In like manner, whereas the female characters seem, in their concern for their partners' feelings for them, to live up to the stereotype that associates love with women and sex with men, Schnitzler overturns this convention as well. The Young Wife's expression of her sexuality with the Young Gentleman literally deflates his potency, and the sexual appetite of die Schauspielerin (the Actress) proves to be too much for der Graf (the Count). Even the Sweet Girl is bolder here than the male characters expect her to be, her independent nature distinguishing her from her counterparts in Schnitzler's earlier works.

Just as the medieval dance of death showed death to be the great leveler, Schnitzler's erotic round dance joins men and women, rich and poor beneath the sway of sexuality. The link between love and death implied by the structure of *Reigen* becomes explicit in its dialogue, which contains several references to mortality. These may, in part, reflect the temperament of the author, who tended toward hypochondria and was plagued even as a young man by frequent thoughts of death.

Schnitzler's association of love and death in *Reigen* further allies him with the founder of psychoanalysis. But the similarity of Schnitzler's perspective to Freud's is perhaps most evident in *Paracelsus*. It is different from most of Schnitzler's dramas in that it was written in verse, is set not in contemporary Vienna but in early sixteenth-century Basel, and is based on a historical personage. Yet the play treats many of the themes which perennially occupy Schnitzler: love and sex and the lies and games people invent because of them, the difficulties of marriage, the excitement and anguish of extramarital relations, dreams and the truth they reveal, and—embracing all of these—the workings of the psyche.

The main "opponents" in *Paracelsus* are Cyprian, a blacksmith who enjoys life unreflectively and believes his beautiful wife, Justina, to be devoted to him; and the title character, who left Basel some years before but has now returned as a kind of magician who stuns crowds with his miracle cures. Cyprian urges Paracelsus to try his arts on the blacksmith's ailing sister, Cäcilia; but she is unwilling, and Paracelsus hypnotizes Justina instead. In contrast to Anatol's experiment with hypnosis in *Die Frage an das Schicksal*, however, here the truth comes out: in her half-sleeping state Justina has a vision of herself in the arms of the attractive Junker, Anselm. Although she later professes no memory of this vision, she admits that she had loved Paracelsus so passionately before his departure from Basel that she would have abandoned Cyprian for him. Cyprian is thus made doubly aware of the fragile and deceptive nature of his marital happiness. Moreover, in a typically Schnitzlerian twist, Anselm is united not with Justina but with Cäcilia, whose illness is unmasked as love for him. Paracelsus's often-quoted final words sum up the actions of the characters not only in this play but in many of Schnitzler's works: "Wir wissen nichts von andern, nichts von uns; / Wir spielen immer, wer es weiß, ist klug" (We know nothing of others, nothing of ourselves; / We are always playing, he who knows this is wise).

None of Schnitzler's dramas better exemplifies Paracelsus's dictum than *Der grüne Kakadu* (1899; translated as *The Green Cockatoo*, 1913), designated a "Groteske in einem Akt" (Grotesque in One Act). Set in Paris on the evening of 14 July 1789, it explores the blurred line between illusion and reality. The title is the name of a tavern run by Prospère, a former theater director whose actors now pose as criminals to titillate the nobles who frequent the tavern. On this particular day, however, the actors' verbal battering of the aristocracy and the predictions of their demise take on a tone simultaneously comic and ominous. Schnitzler's depiction of the nobility as hedonistic, frivolous, lacking perceptiveness, and oblivious of their imminent fate seems to make an indirect comment on the upper classes of his own day. Perhaps the most decadent of the noble guests in the Green Cockatoo is the marquise, who not only deceives her husband at every available opportunity but is sexually stimulated by the sight of murder. As in *Reigen*, however, Schnitzler demonstrates that erotic drives cross class boundaries: the marquise has a lower-class counterpart in the promiscuous actress Léocadie.

The difficulty of distinguishing reality from illusion and life from art brings about the grotesque tragedy at the heart of the play. Having learned of an affair between Léocadie and the duke, Prospère believes Léocadie's husband, Henri, the troupe's star actor, when he claims to have murdered the duke. Thus made aware of his wife's infidelity, Henri proceeds to kill the duke in reality. But the greatest irony comes when Henri is celebrated as a hero of the people, who have just stormed the Bastille, although his murder of the nobleman was prompted not by political convictions but by personal passion.

Banned by the censors in Berlin, *Der grüne Kakadu* premiered in 1899 at the Burgtheater (Imperial Theater) in Vienna as part of a trilogy of one-act plays including *Paracelsus* and *Die Gefährtin* (1899; translated as *The Mate*, 1913), a portrayal of double infidelity. But the trilogy was soon removed from the program because the emperor's daughter objected to *Der grüne Kakadu*, showing her awareness that its attack on the aristocracy was not limited to late-eighteenth-century France. This incident marked the beginning of the friction which was to characterize Schnitzler's relations with the Burgtheater during the tenure

of Paul Schlenther, who had taken over as director in 1898.

Schnitzler's troubled association with Schlenther was counterbalanced by his felicitous working relationship with Otto Brahm, director of Berlin's Deutsches Theater (German Theater). It was there that Schnitzler's next group of one-act plays, *Lebendige Stunden* (1902; translated as *Living Hours*, 1913), premiered. These four playlets treat the role of the artist or the relationship between art and life. The title work, for instance, investigates the function and value of literature. A retired civil servant berates his neighbor, a young writer, because the writer's invalid mother, with whom the older man was in love, has taken her life to free her son to write. Yet the writer counters that only art can give permanence to the "living hours" which his mother lost through her suicide. By contrast, *Die letzten Masken* (translated as *The Last Masks*) depicts, in the person of the journalist Karl Rademacher, the writer's impotence. His final wish as he lies dying is to tell off a certain Weihgast, a much more successful man whom Rademacher has always scorned and whose wife has been Rademacher's mistress. When Weihgast arrives, however, Rademacher is incapable of anything but pleasantries; he dies without realizing his only chance for self-fulfillment.

The pattern of *Die letzten Masken* is typical of many one-act plays around the turn of the century, when the form was enormously popular. These plays often depict a moment of crisis, frequently the moment before death or before the revelation of a character's death, leaving little time for development. Hence, the genre is highly suited to demonstrating the belief in determinism by forces such as environment and heredity which was so pervasive at the time (for example, in the work of the naturalists). In *Die letzten Masken* the mood of tragic inevitability and victimization is expressed linguistically by silence, emphasized by stage directions which specify pauses in the dialogue, the ticking of a clock, and so forth. In its concentration and density this work is especially illustrative of Schnitzler's sovereign command of the one-act form.

A lighter look at the writer's role is provided by another of the playlets that make up *Lebendige Stunden*. One of Schnitzler's most humorous plays, *Literatur* (translated as *Literature*) satirizes the tendency of writers to draw on their own experience without reworking it. The play's humor derives initially from the resistance of the pretentious dandy Klemens, the lover of the aspiring writer Margarete, to her literary ambitions because of his fear that she will expose their private experiences to the public eye. The comedy escalates when her former lover shows up and it is revealed that both have included their love letters in the novels they have just completed, thus rendering anonymity impossible. Margarete ultimately destroys her novel rather than risk alienating Klemens, although only after a series of entertaining twists and turns in the plot.

The remaining one-act play in *Lebendige Stunden, Die Frau mit dem Dolche* (translated as *The Woman with the Dagger*), is distinct from the others in its partly historical setting and nonrealistic, mystical quality. As in *Paracelsus*, a woman's extramarital desires are realized in a nonwaking state: having resisted the elegant young Leonhard in actuality, Pauline has a dream in which they spend the night together. The dream is set in the Renaissance Italy of the title picture, which they viewed in an art gallery. Both the dream and the frame play present facets of the complex interaction between life and art, a favorite theme in turn-of-the-century literature. In the dream, it is Pauline's murder of Leonhard (in their Renaissance guises as Paola and Lionardo), committed to protect her husband, Remigio, which inspires Remigio to complete the title picture. At the play's end Pauline, as if in imitation of Paola, gives in to her attraction to Leonhard. The characteristically Schnitzlerian irony of the situation is that Pauline herself, in a projection of her own wishes, has endowed the woman in the picture, whom she physically resembles, with an adulterous history.

Schnitzler's emotional life during these years was dominated by the actress Olga Gussmann, whom he met in 1899. Like Olga Waissnix, she was able to appreciate his writing, and he eventually overcame his reservations about the twenty-year age difference between them. The forty-one-year-old bachelor married Gussmann on 26 August 1903; she had given birth to their son Heinrich on 9 August 1902. A daughter, Lili, was born on 13 September 1909. Although the marriage ended in divorce in 1921, Schnitzler's relationship with Gussmann was the most enduring and important of his life.

In the full-length drama *Der einsame Weg* (1904; translated as *The Lonely Way*, 1904) two issues—the creation of art and parenthood—are played off against each other. This intimately staged work, in which little happens externally, is

Schnitzler with his wife, the former Olga Gussmann, and their children, Lili and Heinrich, in 1910

set in contemporary Vienna and focuses on three artists: Julian Fichtner, a painter who has not lived up to his potential and is drifting; Professor Wegrat, the director of the art academy; and the middle-aged Stephan von Sala, a fatally ill, widowed writer given to poetic excess.

Wegrat's daughter, Johanna, is in love with Sala; after Wegrat's wife, Gabriele, dies early in the play, it is revealed that the real father of her grown son, Felix, is not Wegrat but Julian. Suffering a creative crisis, Julian takes a sudden interest in Felix in the hope that the boy will give his life meaning and restore his artistic powers. Yet Julian alienates Felix by telling him how Julian abandoned Gabriele, pregnant by him but engaged to Wegrat, because of his fear of losing his freedom. The viewer's sense of Julian's irresponsibility is magnified by the appearance of his former mistress, Irene Herms, who now regrets letting Julian talk her out of having his child at the time they were lovers—which coincided with the period of his affair with Gabriele.

Julian's self-centered treatment of others is contrasted with Sala's philosophy that "Lieben heißt, für jemand andern auf der Welt sein" (Love means being there for someone else). It is darkly ironic that these lines are followed by the revelation that Johanna has drowned herself in the pond in Sala's garden, a place associated with their love, because she had learned of his fatal illness. The somberness of this moment is only an extreme manifestation of the Chekhovian melancholy of the entire play, which exemplifies in case after case the truth of Sala's observation that each of us is alone, regardless of whether we have others around us or not: Irene Herms has never been granted that which she feels would have fulfilled her; Julian, having misused a succession of women and neglected his son, is thrown back completely on himself; and Sala, having lost his wife and child years ago and now Johanna as well, faces the prospect of an early death alone. Only the father-son bond between Wegrat and Felix, who are onstage when the curtain falls, offers a counterbalance to the play's many images of loss and abandonment and thus an inkling of hope.

The tragicomedy *Das weite Land* (1911; translated as *The Vast Domain*, 1923) had one of Schnitzler's most triumphant premieres, opening at nine stages in Germany and the Austro-Hungarian realm. One of the titles he considered for *Der einsame Weg*, "Die Egoisten" (The Egoists), would be suited to this drama, whose affluent characters wile away their time having tea and supper, playing tennis and climbing mountains, flirting with each other, and discussing love, death, and aging. The portrayal of their activities evokes most of the comedy in the play. The rejected title is particularly applicable to the main character. Although a successful manufacturer in his forties, Friedrich Hofreiter is an eternal adolescent, impulsive and self-indulgent. He takes frequent advantage of his attractiveness to women, having long since fallen out of love with his wife, Genia.

As in *Der einsame Weg*, the revelations of *Das weite Land* are motivated by a death, in this case the suicide of a young Russian pianist with whom Friedrich suspects Genia to have had an affair. But she divulges that he killed himself because she refused him in the hope that Friedrich would regain his feelings for her. In one of Schnitzler's most ironic twists, this information further alienates Friedrich, since he feels that he had no right to expect fidelity from her and that a man has died unnecessarily. In the escapade that follows,

at a resort in the Dolomites Friedrich's near-affair with an emancipated young woman rounds out the viewer's perception of his situation as what would today be termed a mid-life crisis. When Genia seizes an opportunity to make up for her mistake by having an affair with a young naval officer, Friedrich challenges him to a duel and wins, thus ending his wife's late, brief period of happiness. By his own admission Friedrich acts not out of hate, jealousy, rage, or love, but simply to avoid being the dupe.

The behavior of Friedrich, one of the most perplexing figures in all of Schnitzler's dramas, is partially illuminated by the words of Dr. von Aigner, who, as an attractive ladies' man with children by many women, is an older version of Friedrich. When Friedrich is puzzled by Aigner's admission that he deceived his wife even though he loved her, Aigner responds that "Das Natürliche . . . ist das Chaos. Ja— . . . die Seele . . . ist ein weites Land" (What is natural . . . is chaotic. Yes— . . . the soul . . . is a vast domain). But this explanation is countered by the views of another doctor in the play. Like many other stage physicians throughout theater history, Dr. Maurer functions as a critical commentator on the foibles of his fellow characters. He diagnoses Friedrich as characterized by a mixture of reserve and boldness, of cowardly jealousy and false composure, of raging passion and empty lust. The dynamics of the drama as a whole, however, discourage the spectator from taking either Aigner's rationalization or Maurer's condemnation as the last word, since both positions seem valid to a degree. It is Schnitzler's refusal to offer black-and-white solutions, his recognition of the complexities of human psychology, that makes his works endure.

Although *Das weite Land* was successful at Vienna's Burgtheater, the director, Alfred von Berger, received letters attacking him for putting on a play by a Jew. This occasion was only one of many on which Schnitzler was the object of anti-Semitism, which became the central theme of his powerful drama *Professor Bernhardi* (1912; translated, 1927). Taking place in the clinical milieu Schnitzler knew so intimately, the play is highly realistic and filled with medical detail. The title character, the Jewish director of Vienna's Elisabethinum Clinic, refuses to allow a priest to administer the last rites to a dying patient because he does not want to disturb her predeath euphoria. This incident triggers an anti-Semitic smear campaign against Bernhardi that leads to his resignation and a two-month prison sentence. Through it all Bernhardi shows himself to be a man of principle: offered two chances to avoid further persecution—first by expressing regret for his action and then by deciding in favor of an ill-qualified non-Jewish candidate for a position at the clinic—he rejects both opportunities.

In its depiction of Bernhardi's case as a media sensation, *Professor Bernhardi* emerges as a political work in an oeuvre often characterized as apolitical. The themes of many of Schnitzler's lighter drawing-room comedies—snobbery, hypocrisy, gossip and backbiting, deceptiveness, blind belief in hierarchy—appear here in a sociohistoric context. Schnitzler unmasks the anti-Semitic element in turn-of-the-century Viennese Catholicism—particularly in his portrayal of the priest, who ultimately admits to Bernhardi that although he thought the physician had been right, he had not stood up to defend him. But the problem Schnitzler explores extends beyond the anti-Semitism prevalent in Europe at the time; as one of Bernhardi's colleagues observes, "wir leben in einer so konfusen Zeit—und in einem so konfusen Land. . ." (we are living in such muddled times—and in such a muddled country. . .). Indeed, the issue transcends the political realm altogether, as is suggested by the education minister Flint's description of Bernhardi's case in terms of the eternal struggle between light and darkness. Rather, this drama is concerned in its largest sense with the demise of humaneness, an issue which some twenty-five years later would occupy center stage in a tragedy of unprecedented dimensions—the Holocaust.

Not surprisingly, *Professor Bernhardi* was banned by the censors in Vienna. It premiered at the Kleines Theater (Little Theater) in Berlin under the direction of Viktor Barnowsky, one of the most successful directors of the era. Yet eight years later the climate in Vienna had changed, and on 8 October 1920 Schnitzler was awarded the Volkstheater Prize for the play. His other awards include the Grillparzer Prize for the comedy *Zwischenspiel* (performed, 1905; published, 1906; translated as *Intermezzo*, 1915), received on 15 January 1908, and the Raimund Prize for the historical drama *Der junge Medardus* (The Young Medardus, 1910), awarded on 27 March 1914. Schnitzler's works were more accessible than those of Hofmannsthal and other contemporaries and hence had a wider reading public. His popularity extended into the cinema as well, and films made from his dramas and novellas, such as *The*

Affairs of Anatol (1921), *Liebelei* (1927 and 1932), *Fräulein Else* (1929), and *La Ronde* (1950), are still shown today.

In his later years Schnitzler was increasingly plagued by the death fantasies which had always haunted him, and following the suicide in 1928 of his daughter, Lili, whom he adored, he aged with alarming rapidity. He died in Vienna of a cerebral hemorrhage on 21 October 1931. Although interest in Schnitzler declined after his death, it experienced an upswing with the commemoration of his hundredth birthday in 1962 and has continued to flourish ever since. The cliché of Arthur Schnitzler as the "frivolous melancholic" has given way to a recognition of his psychological sophistication and ethical seriousness. As another turn of a century approaches, the works of this fin de siècle diagnostician shed a unique light on the complex morality of the present era.

Letters:

Briefwechsel mit Otto Brahm, edited by Otto Seidlin (Berlin: Gesellschaft für Theatergeschichte, 1953);

Sigmund Freud, "Brief an Arthur Schnitzler," edited by Heinrich Schnitzler, *Neue Rundschau*, 66 (1955): 95-106;

Georg Brandes und Arthur Schnitzler: Ein Briefwechsel, edited by Kurt Bergel (Bern: Francke, 1956);

"Briefe über das Theater," *Forum*, 3 (October 1956): 366-369;

"Briefe," edited by Schnitzler, *Neue Rundschau*, 68 (1957): 88-101;

"Rainer Maria Rilke und Arthur Schnitzler: Ihr Briefwechsel," edited by Schnitzler, *Wort und Wahrheit*, 13, no. 4 (1958): 283-298;

"Unveröffentlichte Briefe Schnitzlers an Brahm," *Kleine Schriften der Gesellschaft für Theatergeschichte*, 16 (1958): 44-45;

Hugo von Hofmannsthal/Arthur Schnitzler: Briefwechsel, edited by Therese Nickl and Schnitzler (Frankfurt am Main: Fischer, 1964);

"Briefe an Josef Körner," *Literatur und Kritik*, 2, no. 12 (1967): 79-87;

"Briefe zur Politik," *Neues Forum*, 15 (October 1968): 677-680;

"Karl Kraus und Arthur Schnitzler: Eine Dokumentation," edited by Reinhard Urbach, *Literatur und Kritik*, 49 (1970): 513-530;

Schnitzler and Olga Waissnix, *Liebe, die starb vor der Zeit: Ein Briefwechsel*, edited by Nickl and Schnitzler (Vienna, Munich & Zurich: Molden, 1970);

Schnitzler in 1925

"Arthur Schnitzler-Franz Nabl: Briefwechsel," edited by Urbach, *Studium Generale*, 24 (1971): 1256-1270;

Der Briefwechsel Arthur Schnitzlers mit Max Reinhardt und dessen Mitarbeitern, edited by Renate Wagner (Salzburg: Müller, 1971);

The Correspondence of Arthur Schnitzler and Raoul Auernheimer with Raoul Auernheimer's Aphorisms, edited by Donald G. Daviau and Jorun B. Johns (Chapel Hill: University of North Carolina Press, 1972);

"Briefe zum *Reigen*," edited by Urbach, *Ver Sacrum* (1974): 36-43;

"Arthur Schnitzler-Thomas Mann: Briefe," edited by Hertha Krotkoff, *Modern Austrian Literature*, 7, no. 1/2 (1974): 1-33;

Der Briefwechsel Arthur Schnitzler-Otto Brahm, edited by Oskar Seidlin (Tübingen: Niemeyer, 1975);

"Richard Schaukal-Arthur Schnitzler: Briefwechsel (1900-1902)," edited by Urbach, *Modern Austrian Literature*, 8, no. 3/4 (1975): 15-42;

"Vier unveröffentlichte Briefe Arthur Schnitzlers an den Psychoanalytiker Theodor Reik," edited by Bernd Urban, *Modern Austrian Literature*, 8, no. 3/4 (1975): 236-247;

Adele Sandrock und Arthur Schnitzler: Geschichte einer Liebe in Briefen, Bildern und Dokumenten, edited by Wagner (Vienna: Amalthea, 1975);

"Ein bisher unbekannter Brief Arthur Schnitzlers an Otto Brahm," edited by Urbach, *Modern Austrian Literature*, 10, no. 3/4 (1977): 19-21;

"Arthur Schnitzler an Marie Reinhard (1896)," edited by Nickl, *Modern Austrian Literature*, 10, no. 3/4 (1977): 23-68;

"Der Briefwechsel Fritz von Unruhs mit Arthur Schnitzler," edited by Ulrich K. Goldsmith, *Modern Austrian Literature*, 10, no. 3/4 (1977): 69-127;

The Letters of Arthur Schnitzler to Hermann Bahr, edited by Daviau (Chapel Hill: University of North Carolina Press, 1978);

Briefe 1875-1912, edited by Nickl and Schnitzler (Frankfurt am Main: Fischer, 1981);

Briefe 1913-1931, edited by Peter Michael Braunwarth, Richard Miklin, and others (Frankfurt am Main: Fischer, 1984);

Eine Korrespondenz ergänzt durch Blätter aus Hedy Kempnys Tagebuch sowie durch eine Auswahl ihrer Erzählungen, edited by Heinz P. Adamek (Reinbek: Rowohlt, 1984);

"Briefe an Wilhelm Bölsche," edited by Alois Woldan, *Germanica Wratislaviensia*, 77 (1987): 456-466.

Bibliographies:

Richard H. Allen, *An Annotated Arthur Schnitzler Bibliography: Editions and Criticism in German, French and English 1879-1965* (Chapel Hill: University of North Carolina Press, 1966);

Jeffrey B. Berlin, *An Annotated Arthur Schnitzler Bibliography 1965-1977* (Munich: Fink, 1978).

Biographies:

Hartmut Scheible, *Arthur Schnitzler in Selbstzeugnissen und Bilddokumenten* (Reinbek: Rowohlt, 1976);

Renate Wagner, *Frauen um Arthur Schnitzler* (Vienna & Munich: Jugend & Volk, 1980);

Wagner, *Arthur Schnitzler: Eine Biographie* (Vienna, Munich & Zurich: Molden, 1981).

References:

Friedbert Aspetsberger, " 'Drei Akte in einem': Zum Formtyp von Schnitzlers Drama," *Zeitschrift für deutsche Philologie*, 85 (1966): 285-308;

Joseph W. Bailey, "Arthur Schnitzler's Dramatic Work," *Texas Review*, 5, no. 4 (1920): 294-307;

Gerhart Baumann, *Arthur Schnitzler: Die Welt von gestern eines Dichters von morgen* (Frankfurt am Main: Athenäum, 1965);

Hans-Peter Bayerdörfer, "Vom Konversationsstück zur Wurstelkomödie: Zu Arthur Schnitzlers Einaktern," *Jahrbuch der deutschen Schillergesellschaft*, 16 (1972): 516-575;

Frederick J. Beharriell, "Schnitzler: Freud's Doppelgänger," *Literatur und Kritik*, 19 (1967): 546-555;

Giuseppe Farese, ed., *Akten des internationalen Symposiums "Arthur Schnitzler und seine Zeit"* (Bern, Frankfurt am Main & New York: Lang, 1985);

Gail Finney, "Theater of Impotence: The One-Act Tragedy at the Turn of the Century," *Modern Drama*, 28 (September 1985): 451-461;

Finney, *Women in Modern Drama: Freud, Feminism, and European Theater at the Turn of the Century* (Ithaca, N.Y.: Cornell University Press, 1989);

Erhard Friedrichsmeyer, "Schnitzlers 'Der grüne Kakadu,'" *Zeitschrift für deutsche Philologie*, 88 (1969): 209-228;

Alfred Fritsche, *Dekadenz im Werk Arthur Schnitzlers* (Bern: Herbert Lang / Frankfurt am Main: Peter Lang, 1974);

Barbara Gutt, *Emanzipation bei Arthur Schnitzler* (Berlin: Spiess, 1978);

Ansgar Haag, *Arthur Schnitzler: Reigen. Erinnerungen an einen Skandal* (Darmstadt: Roether, 1982);

Stephanie Hammer, "Fear and Attraction: *Anatol* and *Liebelei* Productions in the United States," *Modern Austrian Literature*, 19, no. 3/4 (1986): 63-74;

Hunter G. Hannum, " 'Killing Time': Aspects of Schnitzler's *Reigen*," *Germanic Review*, 37 (May 1962): 190-206;

Rolf-Peter Janz and Klaus Laermann, *Arthur Schnitzler: Zur Diagnose des Wiener Bürgertums im Fin de Siècle* (Stuttgart: Metzler, 1977);

Klaus Kilian, *Die Komödien Arthur Schnitzlers: Sozialer Rollenzwang und kritische Ethik* (Düsseldorf: Bertelsmann, 1972);

Hans Kohn, *Karl Kraus-Arthur Schnitzler-Otto Weininger: Aus dem jüdischen Wien der Jahrhundertwende* (Tübingen: Mohr, 1962);

Anna Kuhn, "The Romanticization of Arthur Schnitzler: Max Ophuls' Adaptations of *Liebe-*

lei and *Reigen*," in *Probleme der Moderne: Studien zur deutschen Literatur von Nietzsche bis Brecht. Festschrift für Walter Sokel*, edited by Benjamin Bennett and others (Tübingen: Niemeyer, 1983), pp. 83-99;

Herbert Lederer, "Arthur Schnitzler's Typology: An Excursion into Philosophy," *PMLA*, 78 (September 1963): 394-406;

Hans-Ulrich Lindken, *Arthur Schnitzler: Aspekte und Akzente. Materialien zu Leben und Werk* (Frankfurt am Main & Bern: Lang, 1984);

Christa Melchinger, *Illusion und Wirklichkeit im dramatischen Werk Arthur Schnitzlers* (Heidelberg: Winter, 1968);

Renate Möhrmann, "Schnitzlers Frauen und Mädchen," *Diskussion Deutsch*, 13 (1982): 507-517;

Wolfgang Nehring, "Schnitzler, Freud's Alter Ego?," *Modern Austrian Literature*, 10, no. 3/4 (1977): 179-194;

Gerhard Neumann and Jutta Müller, *Der Nachlaß Arthur Schnitzlers: Verzeichnis des im Schnitzler-Archiv der Universität Freiburg i. B. befindlichen Materials* (Munich: Fink, 1969);

Erika Nielsen, ed., *Focus on Vienna 1900: Change and Continuity in Literature, Music, Art and Intellectual History* (Munich: Fink, 1982);

Ernst L. Offermanns, *Arthur Schnitzler: Das Komödienwerk als Kritik des Impressionismus* (Munich: Fink, 1973);

Michaela L. Perlmann, *Arthur Schnitzler* (Stuttgart: Metzler, 1987);

Heinz Politzer, "Arthur Schnitzler: Poetry of Psychology," *Modern Language Notes*, 78, no. 4 (1963): 353-372;

Herbert W. Reichert and Herman Salinger, eds., *Studies in Arthur Schnitzler: Centennial Commemorative Volume* (Chapel Hill: University of North Carolina Press, 1963);

Theodor Reik, *Arthur Schnitzler als Psycholog* (Minden: Bruns, 1913);

William H. Rey, "Arthur Schnitzler," in *Deutsche Dichter der Moderne*, edited by Benno von Wiese, revised edition (Berlin: Schmidt, 1975), pp. 247-269;

Rey, *Arthur Schnitzler: Professor Bernhardi* (Munich: Fink, 1971);

Heinz Rieder, *Arthur Schnitzler: Das dramatische Werk* (Vienna: Bergland, 1973);

Felix Salten, "Arthur Schnitzler," in his *Gestalten und Erscheinungen* (Berlin: Fischer, 1913), pp. 49-63;

Hartmut Scheible, "Arthur Schnitzler-Figur-Situation-Gestalt," *Neue Rundschau*, 92, no. 2 (1981): 67-89;

Scheible, *Arthur Schnitzler und die Aufklärung* (Munich: Fink, 1977);

Scheible, ed., *Arthur Schnitzler in neuer Sicht* (Munich: Fink, 1981);

Jürg Scheuzger, *Das Spiel mit Typen und Typenkonstellationen in den Dramen Arthur Schnitzlers* (Zurich: Juris; 1975);

Gerd K. Schneider, "The Reception of Arthur Schnitzler's *Reigen* in the Old Country and the New World: A Study in Cultural Differences," *Modern Austrian Literature*, 19, no. 3/4 (1986): 75-89;

Brigitte Schneider-Halvorson, *The Late Dramatic Works of Arthur Schnitzler* (Bern: Herbert Lang / Frankfurt am Main: Peter Lang, 1983);

Heinrich Schnitzler, Christian Brandstätter, and Reinhard Urbach, eds., *Arthur Schnitzler: Sein Leben, sein Werk, seine Zeit* (Frankfurt am Main: Fischer, 1981);

Olga Schnitzler, *Spiegelbild der Freundschaft* (Salzburg: Residenz, 1962);

Carl E. Schorske, "Politics and the Psyche: Schnitzler and Hofmannsthal," in his *Fin-De-Siècle Vienna: Politics and Culture* (New York: Knopf, 1980), pp. 3-23;

Herbert Seidler, "Die Forschung zu Arthur Schnitzler seit 1945," *Zeitschrift für deutsche Philologie*, 95 (1976): 567-595;

Gunter Selling, *Die Einakter und Einakterzyklen Arthur Schnitzlers* (Amsterdam: Rodopi, 1975);

Peggy Stamon and Richard H. Lawson, "Love-Death Structures in the Works of Arthur Schnitzler," *Modern Austrian Literature*, 8, no. 3/4 (1975): 266-281;

Petrus W. Tax and Richard H. Lawson, eds., *Arthur Schnitzler and His Age: Intellectual and Artistic Currents* (Bonn: Bouvier, 1984);

Horst Thomé, "Sozialgeschichtliche Perspektiven der neueren Schnitzler-Forschung," *Internationales Archiv für Sozialgeschichte der deutschen Literatur*, 13 (1988): 158-187;

Reinhard Urbach, *Arthur Schnitzler* (Velber: Friedrich, 1968); translated by Donald G. Daviau (New York: Ungar, 1973); German version revised (Munich: Deutscher Taschenbuch Verlag, 1977);

Urbach, *Schnitzler-Kommentar: Zu den erzählenden Schriften und dramatischen Werken* (Munich: Winkler, 1974);

Bernd Urban, "Arthur Schnitzler und Sigmund Freud: Aus den Anfängen des Doppelgängers," *Germanisch-Romanische Monatsschrift*, 24 (1974): 193-223;

George S. Viereck, "The World of Arthur Schnitzler," *Modern Austrian Literature*, 5, no. 3/4 (1972): 7-17;

Renate Wagner and Brigitte Vacha, *Wiener Schnitzler-Aufführungen 1891-1970* (Munich: Prestel, 1971);

Luverne Walton, " 'Anatol' on the New York Stage," *Modern Austrian Literature*, 2, no. 2 (1969): 30-44;

Marc Weiner, *Arthur Schnitzler and the Crisis of Musical Culture* (Heidelberg: Winter, 1986);

Robert O. Weiss, "Arthur Schnitzler's Literary and Philosophical Development," *Journal of the American Arthur Schnitzler Research Association*, 2, no. 1 (1963): 4-20;

Harry Zohn, "Schnitzler and the Challenge of Zionism," *Journal of the American Arthur Schnitzler Research Association*, 1, no. 4/5 (1962): 5-7.

Papers:

The papers which were formerly in the possession of Heinrich Schnitzler in Vienna are now in the Deutsches Literaturarchiv (German Literature Archive) in Marbach am Neckar; the remainder of the Schnitzler Archive is at the University of Freiburg im Breisgau.

Karl Schönherr

(24 February 1867 - 15 March 1943)

Pamela S. Saur
Lamar University

PLAY PRODUCTIONS: *Der Judas von Tirol: Volksschauspiel in drei Akten*, Vienna, Theater an der Wien, 10 October 1897;

Der Bildschnitzer, Vienna, Deutsches Volkstheater, 13 September 1900;

Die Altweibermühle: Ein deutsches Fastnachtspiel, by Schönherr and Richard Greinz, Vienna, Kaiser-Jubiläumstheater, 22 January 1902;

Der Sonnwendtag, Vienna, Burgtheater, 10 April 1902;

Karrnerleut', Vienna, Theater in der Josefstadt, 1904;

Familie, Vienna, Burgtheater, 30 November 1905;

Erde, Vienna, Burgtheater, 22 February 1908;

Das Königreich, Vienna, Deutsches Volkstheater, 13 February 1909;

Über die Brücke, Vienna, Burgtheater, 27 November 1909; revised as *Der Komödiant*, Vienna, Burgtheater, 14 November 1924;

Glaube und Heimat, Vienna, Deutsches Volkstheater, 17 December 1910;

Der Weibsteufel, Vienna, Johann-Strauss Theater, 1915;

Volk in Not, Vienna, Deutsches Volkstheater, 2 July 1916;

Frau Suitner, Vienna, Burgtheater, 18 November 1917;

Narrenspiel des Lebens, Berlin, Das Deutsche Theater, 4 February 1919;

Kindertragödie, Vienna, Deutsches Volkstheater, 28 November 1919;

Vivat Academia, Vienna, Deutsches Volkstheater, 1 April 1922;

Es, Vienna, Deutsches Volkstheater, 23 December 1922;

Maitanz, Vienna, Burgtheater, 13 January 1923;

Der Armen-Doktor, Vienna, Deutsches Volkstheater, 26 January 1926;

Der Nothelfer, Innsbruck, Exl-Bühne, 13 August 1926;

Herr Doktor, haben Sie zu essen?, Vienna, Burgtheater, 29 March 1930;

Passionsspiel, Troppau, 23 October 1933;

Karl Schönherr

Das Lied der Liebe, Vienna, Burgtheater, 24 March 1936;

Die Fahne weht, Graz, Stadttheater, 7 April 1937.

BOOKS: *Innthaler Schnalzer: Gedichte in Tiroler Mundart* (Leipzig: Literarische Anstalt Schulze, 1895);

Allerhand Kreuzköpf': Geschichten und Gestalten aus den Tiroler Alpen (Leipzig: Haessel, 1895);

Tiroler Marterln für abg'stürzte Bergkraxler (Leipzig: Haessel, 1895);

Der Bildschnitzer: Eine Tragödie braver Leute (Vienna: Wiener Verlag, 1900);

Der Sonnwendtag: Drama in fünf Aufzügen (Vienna: Stern & Rosner, 1902); revised as *Der Sonnwendtag: Drama in vier Akten* (Vienna & Leipzig: Wiener Verlag, 1905);

Karrnerleut' (Vienna & Leipzig: Wiener Verlag, 1905);

Caritas (Vienna: Wiener Verlag, 1905); revised as *Schuldbuch* (Leipzig: Staackmann, 1913);

Familie: Schauspiel in drei Akten (Stuttgart: Cotta, 1906);

Erde: Eine Komödie des Lebens in drei Akten (Leipzig: Staackmann, 1908);

Das Königreich: Märchendrama in vier Akten (Stuttgart & Berlin: Cotta, 1908; revised edition, Leipzig: Staackmann, 1917);

Glaube und Heimat: Die Tragödie eines Volkes (Leipzig: Staackmann, 1910); translated by Edmund von Mach as *Faith and Fireside*, in *The German Classics of the Nineteenth and Twentieth Century*, volume 16, edited by Kuno Francke and W. G. Howard (New York: German Publication Society, 1914);

Aus meinem Merkbuch (Leipzig: Staackmann, 1911);

Tiroler Bauernschwänke (Berlin & Vienna: Ullstein, 1913);

Die Trenkwalder: Komödie in fünf Aufzügen (Leipzig: Staackmann, 1914);

Der Weibsteufel: Drama in fünf Akten (Leipzig: Staackmann, 1914);

Volk in Not: Ein deutsches Heldenlied (Leipzig: Staackmann, 1916);

Frau Suitner: Schauspiel in fünf Akten (Leipzig: Staackmann, 1916);

Narrenspiel des Lebens: Drama in fünf Akten (Leipzig: Staackmann, 1918);

Kindertragödie in drei Akten (Leipzig: Staackmann, 1919);

Der Knabe mit dem Fieber (Vienna: Lyra-Verlag, 1919);

Der Kampf: Ein Drama geistiger Arbeiter in drei Akten (Leipzig: Staackmann, 1920); revised as *Vivat academia: Komödie in fünf Akten* (Leipzig: Staackmann, 1922); revised as *Der Spurius: Österreichische Komödie in drei Akten* (Leipzig: Staackmann, 1922); revised as *Herr Doktor, haben Sie zu essen?* (Berlin: Bloch, 1930);

Maitanz: Drei Szenen (Leipzig: Staackmann, 1922);

Vivat academia: Komödie in fünf Akten (Leipzig: Staackmann, 1922);

Es: Schauspiel in fünf Akten (Leipzig: Staackmann, 1923);

Erzählungen (Vienna: Österreichisches Jugendrotkreuz, 1924);

Die erste Beicht' und andere Novellen, afterword by Anton Bettelheim, Reclams Universal-Bibliothek, 6459 (Leipzig: Reclam, 1924);

Der Komödiant: Ein Vorspiel und fünf Akte (Vienna: Steyrermühl, 1924);

Die Hungerblockade: Drama in drei Akten (Leipzig: Staackmann, 1925); revised as *Der Nothelfer: Schauspiel in drei Akten* (Leipzig: Staackmann, 1926); revised as *Der Armen-Doktor: Schauspiel in drei Akten* (Leipzig: Staackmann, 1927); revised as *Blockade: Schauspiel in drei Akten* (Berlin & Leipzig: Zsolnay, 1938);

Der Judas von Tirol: Volksschauspiel in drei Akten (Leipzig: Staackmann, 1927);

Gesammelte Werke, 4 volumes (Vienna & Leipzig: Speidel, 1927);

Passionsspiel in drei Akten (Leipzig: Staackmann, 1933);

Die Fahne weht: Schauspiel in drei Akten (Leipzig: Staackmann, 1937);

Gesammelte Werke, 2 volumes, edited by Vinzenz Chiavacci (Vienna: Donau Verlag, 1948);

Gesamtausgabe, 3 volumes, edited by Chiavacci and Franz Hadamowsky (Vienna: Kremayr & Scheriau, 1967-1974).

Karl Schönherr is the leading representative of folk drama in Tirol, the Alpine region that is one of Austria's nine "lands" or states. He is a major figure in Austrian Heimatliteratur (literature that glorifies a region, usually a rural one), and his plays are still occasionally performed in Austrian theaters. Schönherr blurred the barrier between "high" and "low" drama by bringing his regional plays to prestigious German-speaking stages; he enjoyed considerable popularity with audiences, although critical reception was mixed. Most of his plays are set in the Tirol and written in an authentic but understandable regional dialect. A physician, Schönherr was better educated than many regional writers, but he aimed at a broad audience with his unambiguous messages and unsophisticated emotional appeal. In addition to his skillful rendering of dialect, Schönherr's strengths as a dramatist include economy of words, actions, and characters; the use of powerful gestures and symbols; and memorable concluding scenes. In naturalistic fashion, he often portrays the harshness of life and faults of the common people in blunt language, but occasionally he combines such grim realism with sentimentality and melodrama. He elicits sympathy for the suffering of the poor and sick; frequent themes include peasants' love of the land, family tragedies such as infertility, moral dilemmas of actors and physicians, and the battle of the sexes. While Schönherr's plays are free of the anti-Semitism of some Heimatliteratur, he is said to have favored Nazi Germany's annexation of Austria in 1938.

Schönherr was born on 24 February 1867 in the village of Axams bei Innsbruck to Joseph Schönherr, a teacher, and Marie Suitner Schönherr. His father was transferred to Schlanders, in the Vintschgau area in North Tirol, a few years after Schönherr's birth. After the father's death the community gave his widow a small pension. Struggling heroically, she moved to Bozen and raised and educated her daughter and five sons. Schönherr attended the gymnasia in Brixen, Hall, and Bozen, graduating in 1886. After studying briefly at the University of Innsbruck, he enrolled at the University of Vienna in 1891. As a student, Schönherr began to have stories published in Tirolean newspapers. In 1895 a collection of his regionally flavored tales and two volumes of dialect poems—one of which went into a second edition—were published. A mediocre student, he persevered, received a medical degree in 1896, and opened a practice in Vienna.

His first drama, *Der Judas von Tirol* (Judas of Tirol), is one of the best known of more than a hundred folk plays about the Tirolean hero Andreas Hofer, who led an unsuccessful rebellion against Napoleon's occupation of the region in 1809 and was executed after his whereabouts were betrayed by a poor farmhand, Franz Raffl, for money. Raffl became an outcast, rejected even by his own family, and had to leave the Tirol. Schönherr's play focuses less on Hofer's martyrdom than on Raffl's motivation and the psychology of betrayal. The play emphasizes the villagers' poor treatment of Raffl, culminating in their insistence that he play Judas in the annual passion play, a role that ironically contributes to his becoming an actual traitor. The premiere of *Der Judas von Tirol* at the Theater an der Wien (Theater on the Vienna) in Vienna in 1897 was directed by Alexandrine von Schönerer. Its mere three performances and poor reception led Schönherr to burn the manuscript, but a copy was found and revised by Schönherr thirty years later. The less melodramatic 1927 version is today regarded as one of his major achievements. A major triumph of Schönherr's career was the

premiere of the play in Innsbruck, capital of the Tirol, in 1928 by the local Exl Troupe. The play was also the basis of a 1933 movie, the only film made from any of his works during Schönherr's lifetime.

After his initial disappointment in 1897 Schönherr waited two years before writing the successful *Der Bildschnitzer: Eine Tragödie braver Leute* (The Wood-carver: A Tragedy of Good People, 1900), in which a desperately poor wood-carver martyrs himself by refusing medical treatment so that his lifelong friend will be able to marry his wife and care for his family. The play's premiere at the Deutsches Volkstheater (German People's Theater) in Vienna met with praise for its intense compression and economy of words, closed structure, and realism. The play was produced in ten theaters in 1900-1901, including stages in Berlin and Hamburg. Less successful was *Die Altweibermühle: Ein deutsches Fastnachtspiel* (The Mill of Youth: A German Mardi Gras Play), coauthored with Richard Greinz. The humorous folk play about a dwarf tailor whose tyrannical mother is happily transformed by a magical mill premiered at the Kaiser-Jubiläumstheater (Emperor's Jubilee Theater) in Vienna on 22 January 1902. In the same year Schönherr for the first time had a play put on at the official court theater, the Burgtheater in Vienna. *Der Sonnwendtag* (Solstice Day; published, 1902) presents a conflict between the Catholic church and freedom of thought as well as a fratricide; in the controversial final scene the disillusioned mother destroys her house altar. *Karrnerleut'* (The Carters; performed, 1904; published, 1905) is a melodrama in which a policeman uses bread to tempt a hungry gypsy boy to betray the boy's father. Overcome by guilt, the boy jumps into the river and is killed by a paddle wheel despite the policeman's efforts to save him. *Familie* (Family; performed, 1905; published, 1906), Schönherr's first play not written in regional dialect, deals with the effects of parental sins on children. By 1905 Schönherr was successful enough as a writer to retire from medicine.

Erde (Earth, 1908) presents Schönherr's most memorable character: the tenacious peasant Grutz, a man with demonic, elemental power. The seventy-six-year-old Grutz is a fault-finding tyrant who belittles his forty-six-year-old son Hannes and keeps him in the position of a hired hand. Two aging maids on the farm, Mena and Trine, hope to marry Hannes someday. Injured by a stallion, Grutz plans his own funeral; but he recovers in the spring. The son, too meek and attached to the homestead to leave, tries to content himself with his meager lot. Mena is expecting Hannes's child, and Hannes carves a cradle and horse. But Mena, who wants her own household, marries a widower, moving to his mountainous, icy farm. Grutz concludes the play by chopping up his own coffin for firewood.

The story's fascination stems from the contrast it presents between the operation and perversion of natural law: the rhythms of nature prevail on the farm, but the tyrant Grutz refuses to accede to the natural claims of youth; hopes raised by the arrival of spring are dashed by Grutz's recovery. The peasants' talk throughout the play is quite blunt—Grutz's egotism and contempt for his son and everyone else's wishes for Grutz's death are plainly expressed—and the symbolism of cradle and coffin is rather blatant. While the play lacks subtlety, its irony and tragedy and the powerful character of Grutz make it dramatically effective even today.

Das Königreich (The Kingdom; published, 1908), a musical fairy tale in a Viennese tradition associated with Ferdinand Raimund, was Schönherr's first departure from the peasant world: a distraught prince is alternately charmed by the happiness of a poor man and tempted by the devil. Rejected for the court stage by Archduke Franz Ferdinand because of its depiction of the power of evil, the play was performed at the Deutsches Volkstheater in 1909. Schönherr rewrote this unsuccessful play at least fifteen times. Unpublished and unperformed versions written in the 1930s were titled "Das Lied im Mai" (May Song), "Die Wiedergeburt der Hölle" (The Rebirth of Hell)—an unrealized screenplay—and "Das Lied der Liebe" (The Song of Love).

A relatively unsuccessful play about the acting profession was written and revised under four different titles. Originally called "Scheidung" (Divorce), it premiered at the Burgtheater on 27 November 1909 as *Über die Brücke* (Over the Bridge) and was performed only five times. As *Der Komödiant* (The Comedian; published, 1924) it premiered at the Burgtheater on 14 November 1924 and was performed only nine times. It was rewritten as *Lorbeer* (Laurels) for the 1927 edition of Schönherr's collected works. Some of the revisions were made at the request of the Burgtheater director, Paul Schlenther; others were demanded by the court censor.

A high point in Schönherr's career was the 1910 premiere of *Glaube und Heimat* (published,

1910; translated as *Faith and Fireside*, 1914). The play won the Grillparzer Prize in 1911 and provoked lively debates on the definition of the folk play, the use of melodrama, criticism of the church, and the play's sources and historical accuracy. The play deals with the heartrending decision facing seventeenth-century Tirolean peasants forced by the emperor to convert to Catholicism or leave their homeland. An old man, Rott, plans to admit his Protestantism on his deathbed until he learns that if he does so he will be denied a Christian burial. He leaves his homestead with his son, Christoph, and Christoph's wife, who is Catholic but faithful to her husband. When Christoph's son, Spatz, learns that minors cannot leave with their "heretic" parents, he jumps off a bridge and is killed by a paddlewheel. The Sandperger family decides to convert, but before they can do so Mrs. Sandperger is stabbed by a soldier; dying, she comes on stage clutching her Lutheran Bible. She will be buried on unhallowed ground. Catholicism is represented by an evil, imposing soldier, "der wilde Reiter" (the wild rider) who is miraculously moved by the peasants' faith at the play's end; in one of Schönherr's powerful theatrical gestures, he breaks his sword in two. While some reviewers objected to the melodramatic scenes, most agreed that they were balanced by the effective, swift action. The play was performed throughout Austria and Germany. Wilhelm II had it performed during the Kiel festival of 1910.

Glaube und Heimat was followed five years later by another triumph, *Der Weibsteufel* (The She-Devil; published, 1914), which premiered at a charity performance at the Johann-Strauss Theater early in 1915 and opened on 8 April of that year at the Burgtheater, whose director had been unsure it would pass censorship. The archbishop of Munich and many other clergymen spoke against the sex and violence in the play, although their reactions were in part veiled attacks on *Glaube und Heimat*. The play is a masterpiece of concentration and psychological intensity: three actors perform for five acts without one dull moment. The play presents a love triangle involving a frail, sickly, but clever smuggler; his unhappy, childless wife; and a sentry assigned to investigate the smuggler's crimes by gaining the wife's favor. The woman succumbs to the sentry's advances but becomes enraged when she realizes his aims. She also feels used by her husband, who asks her to protect him by distracting the sentry. She avenges herself by stirring the men's pas-

Scene from a 1908 production of Schönherr's Erde

sionate and violent impulses, finally causing the
sentry to murder her husband. In expressionist style, the play presents typed characters—
named only "Mann" (Man), "Weib" (Wife), and
Grenzjäger" (Sentry)—engaged in irrational,
seemingly inevitable struggles. Once again,
Schönherr creates powerful visual scenes by
using symbolic gestures and objects. At one point
the sentry smashes open a trunk, revealing not
contraband but baby clothes symbolic of the
wife's secret longing. The couple's ambition is represented by a house in the marketplace; the
sentry's by a star he might earn.

The historical play *Volk in Not: Ein deutsches
Heldenlied* (A People in Distress: A German Heroic Song, 1916) could not be performed at the
Burgtheater during World War I because it emphasized the bereavement caused by war and
showed Bavarians and Saxons fighting Tiroleans
during the Napoleonic campaigns. But it was performed at the Deutsches Volkstheater in 1916,
and in 1917 Schönherr received the Grillparzer
Prize for the play. A popular and critical success
in book form, the play was difficult to produce because of its elaborate battle scenes.

Frau Suitner (published, 1916; performed,
1917) is a tragedy of infertility, like *Der Weibsteufel*; like *Der Bildschnitzer* it involves a love triangle culminating in self-sacrifice. A barren wife
drowns herself so that her husband can marry
the vital, life-affirming Gretl, who works in their
store. This intense three-character psychological
drama builds quietly but suspensefully to its conclusion.

Deeply affected by the suffering of World
War I, Schönherr was silent for two years before
writing a series of grim plays on hunger, illness,
and the limitations of the medical profession. In
the episodic *Narrenspiel des Lebens* (Life's Mad
Pranks; published, 1918) an eminent surgeon poi-
sons himself because he finds his demanding profession inadequate and thankless. Schönherr had
lost popularity in Vienna, but the play was produced, unsuccessfully, by Max Reinhardt in Berlin in 1919. In the same year, however, the triumph of *Kindertragödie* (Children's Tragedy), a
reworking of *Familie*, earned Schönherr the prestigious Grillparzer Prize. Critics admired its con-

Scene from a 1915 performance at the Kammerspiele in Berlin of Schönherr's Der Weibsteufel, *with (left to right) Max Pallenberg as Mann, Lucie Höflich as Weib, and Otto Hartmann as Grenzjäger*

centration: the play has only three characters, all children who suffer in different ways from their mother's adultery. Schönherr returned to medical issues in *Vivat academia* (1922), which deals with hunger and illness and protests against unjust medical professors. *Es* (It; performed, 1922; published, 1923) was the high point of Schönherr's theatrical economy, for it has only two characters: "Der Arzt" (The Doctor) and "Die Frau" (The Woman). The title character, who never appears onstage, is a fetus. The play, which features issues rather than characters or events, elicited more discussion than aesthetic appreciation. A young doctor, a promoter of eugenics, learns that he has tuberculosis and aborts his wife's child to avoid passing on the disease. The force of life triumphs, however, when she becomes pregnant again.

On 8 April 1922 the fifty-five-year-old Schönherr married Malvine Chiavacci, the widow of the humorist Vincenz Chiavacci. The couple maintained a home in Vienna and another in the village of Telfs in the Tirol.

Another play on tuberculosis, the heartbreaking melodrama *Maitanz* (May Dance), was published in 1922 and premiered in 1923. A young victim of the disease, Annerl, rises from her deathbed to attend a spring dance. Shocked by her pale appearance, her boyfriend, Hansl, turns away and dances with her friend Rosl. Annerl goes home, dances alone, prays, and dies. The play ran for only five performances at the Burgtheater. The medical dramas *Der Armen-Doktor* (The Doctor for the Poor; performed, 1926; published, 1927) and *Der Nothelfer* (The Helper in Need, 1926) were both revisions of the unperformed play *Die Hungerblockade* (The Hunger Blockade, 1925).

For his sixtieth birthday in 1927 Schönherr was persuaded to have his collected works published in four volumes. He left his prose works virtually intact but revised nearly every page of his dramas. That year he became a member of the Deutsche Dichter Akademie (Academy of German Writers) and an honorary citizen of Vienna, and a commemorative performance of *Glaube und Heimat* was staged at the Deutsches Volkstheater.

Passionsspiel (Passion Play, 1933) is Schönherr's transformation of the medieval village

Schönherr in later years (photo by Fayer)

play portraying Christ's suffering into an economical and well-structured drama. The play was approved by church authorities, and the 1933 premiere was attended by Cardinal Theodor Innitzer as well as government officials; but it was not a stage success.

Schönherr's seventieth birthday was celebrated by the premiere of his last play, *Die Fahne weht* (The Flag Waves, 1937), on 7 April 1937. *Die Fahne weht*, like his first play, interweaves the story of the Tirolean hero Andreas Hofer with a passion play. Unable to revise the script to suit the Burgtheater director, Hermann Röbbeling, Schönherr convinced Viktor Pruscha, director of the Stadttheater (City Theater) in nearby Graz, to stage the drama.

Since his death on 15 March 1943 Schönherr has been viewed as a minor Austrian author whose works are worth preserving. In 1968 the Burgtheater put on *Der Weibsteufel*, and

a film version of *Frau Suitner*, directed by Karlheinz Haberland, premiered at the Ring-Kino (Ring Cinema) in Graz. A three-volume collection of Schönherr's works was published between 1967 and 1974, and scholarly works on him have appeared each decade since his death. While contemporary theatergoers may not admire some of Schönherr's melodramatic plots and heartrending incidents, they can appreciate the theatrical effectiveness of his plays: the power and vividness of his symbols and gestures, the suspenseful pacing, and the striking conclusions. Schönherr's plays have outlived their author not only in Austrian literary history but on the Austrian stage as well. Schönherr will continue to be known primarily as a regional writer of national importance, who chronicled the history and suffering of the Tirolean people and gave expression to their values of home and homeland, family, tradition, and faith.

Biography:

Anton Bettelheim, *Karl Schönherr: Leben und Schaffen* (Leipzig: Staackmann, 1928).

References:

Margarethe Anklin, *Enrica von Handel-Mazzetti und Karl Schönherr: Gedanken zum neuesten Literaturstreit* (Berlin: Mecklenburg, 1911);

Anton Bettelheim, *Karl Schönherr und das österreichische Volksstück*, Österreichische Bücherei, 24 (Vienna: Hartleben, 1926);

Wilhelm Bortenschlager, "Die drei großen Alten: Franz Kranewitter, Karl Schönherr, Josef Wenter," in his *Tiroler Drama und Dramatiker im 20. Jahrhundert* (Sankt Michael: Bläschke, 1982), pp. 20-38;

Anton Dörrer, ed., *Festschrift zum Dr.-Karl-Schönherr-Tag: Axams, die Heimat Karl Schönherrs* (Innsbruck: Landesverkehrsamt für Tirol, 1937);

Johannes Eckardt, *Karl Schönherrs Glaube und Heimat* (Munich: Engl, 1911);

Lion Feuchtwanger, "Glaube und Heimat," *Die Schaubühne*, 7, no. 12 (1911): 313-317;

Josef Hofmiller, "Glaube und Heimat," *Süddeutsche Monatshefte*, 8 (March 1911): 363-371;

Norbert Hölzl, "Karl Schönherr zum 25. Todestag," *Österreich in Geschichte und Literatur*, 12 (1968): 159-165;

Hölzl, "Der Tiroler Dramatiker Karl Schönherr im Spiegel der Wiener Theaterkritik," *Tiroler Heimatblätter*, 10/12 (1966): 117-128;

Hermann Kienzl, *Karl Schönherr und seine wichtigsten Bühnenwerke: Eine Einführung*, Schneiders Bühnenführer, 23 (Berlin & Leipzig: Schneider, 1922);

Max Lederer, *Karl Schönherr der Dramatiker: Eine Studie* (Vienna & Leipzig: Deutscher Verlag für Jugend und Volk, 1925);

Lederer, "Karl Schönherr 1867-1943," *Books Abroad*, 18 (Winter 1944): 23-25;

Karl Paulin, *Karl Schönherr und seine Dichtungen* (Innsbruck: Wagner'sche Universitäts-Buchhandlung, 1950);

Wilmer D. Sanders, "Pessimism in the Works of Karl Schönherr," Ph.D. dissertation, Indiana University, 1963;

Toni Schuh, "Künstlerischer Wert der Mundart in Schönherrs Dramen," in *Germanistische Studien*, edited by Johannes Erben and Eugen Thurnher, Innsbrucker Beiträge zur Kulturwissenschaft, volume 15 (Innsbruck: Innsbrucker Gesellschaft zur Pflege der Geisteswissenschaft, 1960), pp. 237-247;

Richard Sedlmaier, *Karl Schönherr und das österreichische Volksstück* (Würzburg: Verlagsdrückerei, 1920);

Roderick Wald, "Karl Schönherr, deutscher Apotheker als Dichter und Denker," *Süddeutsche Apothekerzeitung*, 79, no. 16 (1939): 147-150.

Papers:

Most of Karl Schönherr's papers are in the Austrian National Library in Vienna. Some are at the Ferdinandeum in Innsbruck.

Reinhard Johannes Sorge

(29 January 1892 - 20 July 1916)

Christoph Eykman
Boston College

PLAY PRODUCTIONS: *Der Bettler*, Berlin, Deutsches Theater, 23 December 1917;

Metanoeite, Munich, Kammerspiele, 27 December 1917;

König David, Zurich, Katholische Jugendpflege, 8 October 1922.

BOOKS: *Der Bettler: Eine dramatische Sendung, fünf Aufzüge* (Berlin: Fischer, 1912);

Guntwar: Die Schule eines Propheten. Handlung in fünf Aufzügen, einem Vorspiel und einem Nachspiel (Kempten & Munich: Kösel, 1914);

Metanoeite: Drei Mysterien (Kempten: Kösel, 1915);

König David: Schauspiel (Berlin: Fischer, 1916);

Mutter der Himmel: Ein Sang in zwölf Gesängen (Kempten: Kösel, 1917);

Gericht über Zarathustra: Vision (Munich: Kösel & Pustet, 1921);

Mystische Zwiesprache (Munich: Kösel & Pustet, 1922);

Preis der Unbefleckten: Sang über die Begebnisse zu Lourdes (Leipzig: Vier Quellen Verlag, 1924);

Der Sieg des Christos: Eine Vision, dargestellt in dramatischen Bildern (Leipzig: Vier Quellen Verlag, 1924);

Werke: Auszug, edited by Martin Rockenbach (Munich-Gladbach: Führer Verlag, 1924);

Der Jüngling: Die frühen Dichtungen (Munich: Kösel & Pustet, 1925);

Nachgelassene Gedichte, edited by Rockenbach (Leipzig: Vier Quellen Verlag, 1925);

Bekenntnisse und Lobpreisungen, edited by Otto Karrer (Munich: Ars Sacra, 1960);

Sämtliche Werke, 3 volumes, edited by Hans Gerd Rötzer (Nuremberg: Glock & Lutz, 1962-1967).

SELECTED PERIODICAL PUBLICATIONS—UNCOLLECTED: "Werden der Seele: Abriss einer Konversion," *Hochland* (May 1914): 199;

"Drama des Expressionismus," *Nachrichten aus dem geistigen und künstlerischen Leben Göttingens* (1920): 170;

"Eines Narren Narrenlieder," *Deutscher Kulturwart* (February 1940): 10-16.

Reinhard Johannes Sorge is considered one of the earliest expressionist dramatists in Germany. Although his death on the battlefield in World War I put an abrupt end to an all-too-brief six-year period of intensive literary productivity, Sorge, who was only twenty-four years old at the time of his death, achieved recognition as one of Germany's foremost religious playwrights and poets, one whose poetic mission was inspired by his fervent quest for God and by an ecstatic mystical faith. Sorge's protagonists are either projections of his own self into a dramatic character who combines the role of the writer as leader and healer with that of the prophet and seeker of God's truth, or personal interpretations of key figures in the history of Christianity such as King David, Saint Francis of Assisi, and Martin Luther. None of his plays was performed during his lifetime.

Sorge, the son of a building inspector, Max Sorge, and Helene Sorge, was born on 29 January 1892 in Rixdorf, near Berlin. He was the oldest of three children. He had attended the Luisenstädter high school in Berlin for several years when his father was committed to a mental institution. Sorge had to leave school and work in a hardware store and a bank before he was able to transfer to the Kaiserin Augusta high school. There he read the works of William Shakespeare, Johann Wolfgang von Goethe, and Henrik Ibsen and developed a keen interest in the art of ancient Greece.

After the father's death in 1908 Sorge's family moved to Jena, where he attended a local gymnasium and read works by such disparate writers as Oscar Wilde, Georg Simmel, Maurice Maeterlinck, Friedrich Naumann, Knut Hamsun, August Strindberg, Richard Dehmel, Friedrich Nietz-

Sketch by Ernst Stern of a scene from the 1917 Berlin production of Sorge's Der Bettler *(from Lionel Richard,* Phaidon Encyclopedia of Expressionism, *translated by Stephen Tint, 1978)*

sche, and Gerhart Hauptmann. Among the literary figures who particularly shaped the young student's mind were the poets Stefan George and Rainer Maria Rilke. As early as 1910 Sorge expressed what later became the all-encompassing theme of his creative life: a deep longing for the eternal, unchanging, and unworldly. At this early stage the nature of his metaphysical yearning was not yet clearly defined in religious terms.

In April 1911 Sorge took acting lessons, but he soon realized that he would not find fulfillment in an acting career. During the summer he took courses in Greek philology at the University of Jena. In October he began work on *Der Bettler* (The Beggar; published, 1912; performed, 1917), which would become his best-known play. The first expressionist play to be written, it is about Sorge's own quest and, by extension, about the mission of the writer in general. The central character, "der Dichter" (the writer), pursues his career in almost fanatical fashion. He follows the imperative of his inner voice in an uncompromising, self-assured, and arrogant manner that ill becomes a fledgling playwright. He expects his mentor to build a theater for him and is devastated when the mentor refuses. Sorge's Dichter is

never plagued by doubt about his talent or his ability to achieve the renewal of the drama. Literature, according to his idealistic viewpoint, has healing and purifying powers that will have a beneficial effect on the working class. But he fails to explain how literature will solve the social and economic problems of the German proletariat in the early twentieth century. The writer's work remains unpolitical, spiritual, and lofty, anchored in God and not in the teachings or principles of any political party.

This blissful and beatific awareness of being an instrument in God's hands seems to elevate the writer above his fellow human beings. Yet in spite of all his self-assurance he suffers moments of self-doubt and anxious uncertainty about his role in society. He knows that only earthly suffering will yield the experience and maturity without which his writing will be sterile, naive, and shallow. He also knows that he will constantly be called on to justify and legitimize his mission in a social environment hostile to the artistic and creative mind. This lack of social recognition prompts the playwright to try his hand at a "normal" middle-class occupation as a journalist, only to give it up after a brief and frustrating trial period. His frustration results in a sweeping and emphatic rejection of ordinary professions, trades, and crafts, which he associates with aesthetically repulsive images such as mud, morass, rubble, waste, pus, and so forth. After this unsuccessful episode he feels more strongly than ever that his is a higher calling that will lead him toward God. Yet there is one even higher calling from which he feels he is—at least for now—barred: the priesthood. Artists and writers, strive as they may to be close to God, are only half saints or, worse, false saints.

The protagonist's insane father, a mentally deranged Faust figure whose mental energies are absorbed by a project of harnessing the powers of the canals on Mars for agricultural purposes on Earth, begs his son to kill him. The son obliges by making him drink poisoned wine. This incident reflects the autocratic way in which the writer relates to and disposes of his fellow human beings. Another case in point is his relationship with a girl who willingly sacrifices everything, even motherhood, to his career. The play's title expresses the writer's position vis-à-vis God, not his fellow human beings. The "beggar" is the highly stylized "New Man" whose coming would later be proclaimed by countless expressionists. He is the savior, the writer-priest-prophet, the Nietzschean superman who elevates the human soul above the inferior materialistic world of science, technology, and business.

In February 1912 Sorge traveled to the island of Norderney in the North Sea, where he experienced a religious vision that marked him for the rest of his life. He rejected much of the philosophical and religious framework of his younger years, including his Lutheran faith and the teachings—as he understood them—of Nietzsche.

The decision of the S. Fischer publishing house to print *Der Bettler* was the first sign of public recognition of Sorge's work. In November 1912 Sorge received the prestigious prize of the Kleist Foundation.

Between October and December 1912 Sorge completed his second play, *Guntwar* (1914), another self-portrait. Whereas the writer in *Der Bettler* still beseeches God to let him partake in the truth of the divine, Guntwar has already experienced his awakening and his illumination. He has taken on the role of a modern prophet who will work tirelessly toward the purification and sanctification of humanity. The play contains detailed references to Sorge's complex and troubled relationship with his friend and mentor Bernt

Grönvold and Grönvold's wife, who are called Peter and Mirjam in the play. While Peter has doubts as to Guntwar's claim to religious leadership and is unable to accept Guntwar's theosophical mysticism (Grönvold's wife had introduced Sorge to theosophy), Mirjam intuitively understands and shares Guntwar's beliefs and aspirations. Mirjam's desperate attempts to draw Peter into their mystical experiences fail. While Guntwar and Mirjam fly to the heights of religious ecstasy, Peter finds Christ only in death. Peter's inability to follow Guntwar and Mirjam on their path toward God is meant to show that the prophet will remain a stranger to most of his fellow humans.

The scenes involving Guntwar, Peter, and Mirjam alternate with interludes in which an imperfect and sinful society reveals its need for redemption. The themes of guilt, redemption, and sinful material greed figure prominently in the play's prelude, which pits Satan against God's love. The interlude that follows the third act develops the theme further by focusing on society's voracity, laziness, and lust for power. These scenes culminate in an apocalyptic vision of the Day of Reckoning, when the sinners pay for their failings with their lives. Their fall is followed by the rise of a new, pure generation of humans bathed in a beam of light, the symbol of God's grace. The visionary modes of presentation and the call for spiritual renewal are expressionist features of the play.

Guntwar's literary production has but one objective: to praise God and his creation. His uncompromising devotion to his calling as a writer-prophet and his claim to be a chosen servant of God lead him to ignore most rules of social behavior. The exceptional man must be judged by exceptional standards.

In late 1912 and early 1913 Sorge read Dante, Luther, the mystics, and the Bible. He married in February 1913 and traveled to Italy, where he was overwhelmed by the liturgical beauty of the Easter service he attended at Saint Peter's Cathedral in Rome. On 17 September he and his wife converted to Catholicism. A second journey to Italy in the fall of 1913 was followed by a visit to Lourdes, France. After his return to Germany, Sorge moved to the small town of Flüelen, Switzerland, and considered becoming a priest or a monk.

In January 1914 Sorge wrote a biblical play, *König David* (King David; published, 1916; performed, 1922), which allowed him to present a var-

Paul Wegener as the Dichter in the 1917 Berlin production of Der Bettler; *drawing by Bruno Paul (Max Reinhardt Forschungsstätte)*

iation of his archetypal character: the man of God who devotes his life to the service of God's glory. David is the chosen one, anointed by Jahwe. With Jahwe's help he slays the giant Goliath. King Saul, on the other hand, has fallen from Jahwe's grace because of his disobedience. In a last attempt to force Jahwe to acknowledge his independence, Saul visits a witch who has the power to make Satan appear. But even Satan condemns Saul's refusal to obey God. Desperate and dejected, Saul takes his own life as enemy troops approach.

No sooner has David assumed the throne than his failings begin to appear. His son Absalom extorts from him secret instructions given to David by Jahwe. David also incurs Jahwe's wrath by lusting after Bathseba and having her husband, Uria, killed. Jahwe's punishment is severe. David's son by Bathseba dies, and Absalom disgraces his father by sleeping with David's women. For this transgression Absalom has to pay with his life on the battlefield. Crushed by Jahwe's scorn and filled with contrition, David proclaims that Salomo will be his successor. At the end of the play, which contains several prophetic messages announcing the coming of Christ, David dies, reconciled with his God.

During the summer of 1914 Sorge completed *Der Sieg des Christos* (Christ's Victory, 1924), which consists of two separate sequences of scenes. The first, *Franziskus, der heilige Bettler* (Saint Francis, the Holy Beggar), is the story of the life of Saint Francis of Assisi. Francis, the repentant sinner, vows to live a life of poverty and gives away all his worldly possessions. After some initial hesitation, the pope recognizes him and his order. The imitation of Christ through poverty, the endurance of physical suffering, celibacy, love, and humility is the guiding principle of Francis's life. Before his death Francis receives the stigmata.

The second sequence of scenes, *Martin Luther—der ohne Reichtum* (Martin Luther—the One without Wealth), presents a negative image of Luther. The reformer is shown as a guilt-ridden man plagued by fear and shaken by seizures. He is unable to praise God and has no trust in humanity. Because of original sin, Luther believes, the human will is evil and unfree. Luther has discarded theological and philosophical erudition as a path to redemption and is convinced that faith alone can bring salvation. Brother John, Luther's antagonist and Sorge's spokesman in the play, claims that Luther's self-torture, his painful soul-searching with regard to sin and salvation, is useless, since a loving God—through Christ—has already cleansed humanity of its sins. Luther's struggle threatens the church and obscures the idea of redemption. Luther's marriage to Katharina von Bora shows, according to Brother John that the reformer is doing the devil's work. In the last scene the Archangel Michael puts an end to Luther's rebellion.

In early October 1915 Sorge, who had taken a philosophy course at the Maria Hilf Seminary near his Swiss home to prepare himself for the study of theology, volunteered for service in World War I. On 13 July 1916 he was wounded in battle, and he died on 20 July near Ablaincourt, France.

In Sorge's plays realistic scenes often alternate with scenes in which a gradual dissociation from realistic perception, a shift toward an idealized, stylized, even monumentalized presentation, takes place. This stylistic device pertains in particular to the characters who are writer-prophets, saints, seekers of God, the elect. Just as the expressionist preeminence of the idea or essence over the outer tangible reality necessitates an abstract style, so characters such as the beggar, Guntwar, David, and Saint Francis represent the embodiment of the highest ideal of human existence. They are not realistically portrayed people but carriers of noble ideals. In Sorge's language the abstract dominates the concrete; concrete images serve to illuminate abstract concepts. Sorge's religious impetus lends a highly dynamic quality to his imagery of visionary grandeur. Ecstatic mysticism, the exalted quest for a truth that transcends time and space and reaches beyond humanity's mortal and earthly existence, and the symbolic use of the imagery of light, fire, and height are also found in the works of other expressionists. But Sorge's unique fusion of religious fervor and expressionist style earned him a place in the history of twentieth-century German drama.

References:

Michel Becker, *Reinhard Johannes Sorge: Versuch einer Deutung* (Würzburg: Wolfram, 1924);

Werner Hüllen, "Der Expressionismus und Reinhard Johannes Sorge," *Begegnung*, 5 (1950): 198-200;

Marie S. Humfeld, *Reinhard Johannes Sorge: Ein Gralsucher unserer Zeit* (Paderborn: Schöningh, 1929);

Elizabeth Kawa, *Reinhard Johannes Sorge* (Meitingen & Augsburg: Kyrios, 1949);

Ward B. Lewis, "The Early Drama of Reinhard Johannes Sorge: A Poet's Search for the Inner Light," *Modern Drama*, 14 (February 1971): 449-454;

Peter Lincoln, "Aspects of Sorge's Imagery: A Reappraisal of His Position within Expressionism," *German Life and Letters*, 34, no. 4 (1981): 374-384;

O. Linden, "Reinhard Johannes Sorge," *Bücherwelt*, 26 (1929): 321-327;

Claire Lucques, *Le poids du monde* (Paris: Beauchesne, 1962);

B. Neidhart, "Reinhard Johannes Sorge," *Schweizer Rundschau*, 26 (1926): 40-46;

B. O'Brien, "From Nietzsche to Christ," *Irish Monthly*, 60 (1932): 713-722;

Martin Rockenbach, *Studien zu R. J. Sorges künstlerischem Schaffen unter Berücksichtigung der dramatischen Sendung "Der Bettler"* (Leipzig: Vier Quellen Verlag, 1924);

Hans Schumacher, "Reinhard Johannes Sorge," in *Expressionismus als Literatur: Gesammelte Studien*, edited by Wolfgang Rothe (Bern: Francke, 1969), pp. 560-571;

Susanne Sorge, *Reinhard Johannes Sorge: Unser Weg* (Munich: Kösel & Pustet, 1927);

Wilhelm Spael, *Reinhard Johannes Sorge* (Essen: Fredebeul & Koenen, 1920);

Richard Hinton Thomas, "Notes on Some Unpublished Papers of Reinhard Johannes Sorge: A Contribution Relating to the Genesis of Expressionism," *Modern Language Review*, 32 (July 1937): 423-429.

Papers:

The papers of Reinhard Johannes Sorge are at the Deutsches Literaturarchiv (German Literature Archive), Marbach am Neckar.

Carl Sternheim
(1 April 1878 - 3 November 1942)

Edson M. Chick
Williams College

See also the Sternheim entry in *DLB 56: German Fiction Writers, 1914-1945.*

PLAY PRODUCTIONS: *Auf Krugdorf,* Dresden, Königliches Sächsisches Hoftheater, 7 January 1902;

Die Hose, Berlin, Kammerspiele des Deutschen Theaters, 16 February 1911;

Die Kassette, Berlin, Deutsches Theater, 24 November 1911;

Don Juan, Berlin, Deutsches Theater, 13 September 1912;

Bürger Schippel, Berlin, Deutsches Theater, 5 March 1913;

Der Snob, Berlin, Kammerspiele des Deutschen Theaters, 2 February 1914;

Der Scharmante, Berlin, Kammerspiele des Deutschen Theaters, 26 February 1915;

Der Kandidat, Vienna, Volksbühne, 6 December 1915;

Ulrich und Brigitte, Darmstadt, Freie Literarische Künstlerische Gesellschaft, 19 March 1916;

Das leidende Weib, Berlin, Deutsches Theater, 30 October 1916;

Der Geizige, Berlin, Deutsches Theater, 16 April 1917;

Perleberg, Frankfurt am Main, Schauspielhaus, 10 September 1917;

1913, Frankfurt am Main, Schauspielhaus, 23 January 1919;

Tabula rasa, Berlin, Kleines Theater, 25 January 1919;

Die Marquise von Arcis, Frankfurt am Main, Schauspielhaus, 5 September 1919;

Der Abenteurer, Darmstadt, Landestheater, 13 February 1921;

Der entfesselte Zeitgenosse, Darmstadt, Hessisches Landestheater, 17 February 1921;

Manon Lescaut, Berlin, Theater in der Königgrätzer Straße, 15 October 1921;

Der Nebbich, Darmstadt, Hessisches Landestheater, 9 October 1922;

Das Fossil, Hamburg, Kammerspiele, 6 November 1923;

Carl Sternheim

Oskar Wilde, Berlin, Deutsches Theater, 31 March 1925;

Die Schule von Uznach, Hamburg, Deutsches Schauspielhaus / Cologne, Schauspielhaus / Mannheim, Nationaltheater, 21 September 1926;

Vom König und der Königin, Görlitz, Stadttheater, 12 October 1929.

BOOKS: *Der Heiland: Komödie in einem Aufzug* (Hamburg: Hoffmann & Campe, 1898);

Judas Ischariot: Die Tragödie vom Verrath (Dresden & Leipzig: Pierson, 1901);

Fanale! (Dresden & Leipzig: Pierson, 1901);

Auf Krugdorf: Schauspiel in zwei Akten (Berlin: Entsch, 1902);

Vom König und der Königin: Tragödie in fünf Aufzügen (Schandau: Petrich, 1905);

Ulrich und Brigitte: Ein dramatisches Gedicht (Düsseldorf: Müllern & Lehneking, 1907);

Don Juan: Eine Tragödie (Leipzig: Insel, 1909);

Die Hose: Ein bürgerliches Lustspiel (Berlin: Cassirer, 1911); translated by Eric Bentley as *The Underpants: A Middle-Class Comedy* (New York: Doubleday, 1957);

Die Kassette: Komödie in fünf Aufzügen (Leipzig: Insel, 1912); translated by Maurice Edwards and Valerie Reich as *The Strongbox*, in *Anthology of German Expressionist Drama*, edited by Walter H. Sokel (New York: Doubleday, 1963);

Bürger Schippel: Komödie in fünf Aufzügen (Leipzig: Insel, 1913; edited by Derrick Barlow, London: Oxford University Press, 1969); translated by M. A. L. Brown as *Paul Schippel Esq.: A Comedy*, in *Scenes from the Heroic Life of the Middle Classes: Five Plays* (London: Calder & Boyars, 1970), pp. 23-75;

Busekow: Eine Novelle (Leipzig: Wolff, 1914); translated by Eugene Jolas as *Busekow, Transition*, no. 1 (1927): 36-56;

Der Snob: Komödie in drei Aufzügen (Leipzig: Insel, 1914); translated by J. M. Ritchie and J. D. Stowell as *The Snob*, in *Scenes from the Heroic Life of the Middle Classes*, pp. 145-193;

Der Kandidat: Komödie in vier Aufzügen nach Flaubert (Leipzig: Insel, 1914);

1913: Ein Schauspiel in drei Aufzügen (Leipzig: Wolff, 1915); translated by Ritchie as *1913: Play in Three Acts*, in *Scenes from the Heroic Life of the Middle Classes*, pp. 195-244;

Das leidende Weib: Drama nach Friedrich Maximilian Klinger (Leipzig: Insel, 1915);

Der Scharmante: Lustspiel mit Benutzung einer fremden Idee (Leipzig: Wolff, 1915);

Napoleon: Eine Novelle (Leipzig: Wolff, 1915);

Die drei Erzählungen (Leipzig: Wolff, 1916);

Tabula rasa: Ein Schauspiel (Leipzig: Wolff, 1916);

Meta: Eine Erzählung (Leipzig: Wolff, 1916);

Der Geizige: Komödie in fünf Aufzügen nach Molière (Leipzig: Wolff, 1916);

Mädchen (Leipzig: Wolff, 1917);

Perleberg: Komödie in drei Aufzügen (Leipzig: Wolff, 1917);

Posinsky: Eine Erzählung (Berlin: Harz, 1917);

Ulrike: Eine Erzählung (Leipzig: Wolff, 1918);

Chronik von des zwanzigsten Jahrhunderts Beginn, 2 volumes (Leipzig: Wolff, 1918);

Vier Novellen: Neue Folge der Chronik vom Beginn des zwanzigsten Jahrhunderts (Berlin: Harz, 1918);

Prosa (Berlin-Wilmersdorf: Verlag der Wochenschrift Die Aktion, 1918);

Die Marquise von Arcis: Schauspiel in fünf Aufzügen nach Diderot (Leipzig: Wolff, 1919); translated and adapted by Ashley Dukes as *The Mask of Virtue: A Comedy in Three Acts* (London: Gollancz, 1935; New York & Los Angeles: French, 1935);

Die deutsche Revolution (Berlin-Wilmersdorf: Verlag der Wochenschrift Die Aktion, 1919);

Europa: Roman, 2 volumes (volume 1, Munich: Musarion, 1919; volume 2, Munich: Wolff, 1920);

Der entfesselte Zeitgenosse: Ein Lustspiel (Munich: Wolff, 1920);

Berlin; oder, Juste Milieu (Munich: Wolff, 1920);

Fairfax: Eine Erzählung (Berlin: Rowohlt, 1921); translated by Alfred B. Cutter as *Fairfax* (New York: Knopf, 1923);

Tasso; oder, Kunst des Juste Milieu: Ein Wink für die Jugend (Berlin: Reiß, 1921);

Manon Lescaut: Ein Schauspiel (Munich: Drei Masken, 1921);

Libussa, des Kaisers Leibroß (Memoiren) (Berlin-Wilmersdorf: Verlag der Wochenschrift Die Aktion, 1922);

Der Abenteurer: Drei Stückchen von ihm (Munich: Drei Masken, 1922);

Der Nebbich: Ein Lustspiel (Munich: Drei Masken, 1922);

Gauguin und van Gogh (Berlin: Die Schmiede, 1924);

Das Fossil: Drama in drei Aufzügen (Potsdam: Kiepenheuer, 1925); translated by Ritchie as *The Fossil: Drama in Three Acts*, in *Scenes from the Heroic Life of the Middle Classes*, pp. 245-285;

Oskar Wilde: Sein Drama (Potsdam: Kiepenheuer, 1925);

Lutetia: Berichte über europäische Politik, Kunst und Volksleben 1926 (Berlin, Vienna & Leipzig: Zsolnay, 1926);

Die Schule von Uznach oder Neue Sachlichkeit: Ein Lustspiel in vier Aufzügen (Berlin, Leipzig & Vienna: Zsolnay, 1926);

John Pierpont Morgan: Ein Schauspiel (Brussels: Privately printed, 1930);

Kleiner Katechismus für das Jahr 1930/31: Für die in Verwirrung heranwachsende deutsche Jugend aber auch für Ältere beiderlei Geschlechts, die ihn brauchen können (Starnbergersee: Privately printed, 1930);

Vorkriegseuropa im Gleichnis meines Lebens (Amsterdam: Querido, 1936);

Aus dem bürgerlichen Heldenleben, 2 volumes (Berlin: Aufbau, 1947); translated by Brown and others as *Scenes from the Heroic Life of the Middle Classes*;

Das dramatische Werk, 2 volumes (Berlin: Aufbau, 1948);

Gesamtwerk, 10 volumes, edited by Wilhelm Emrich and Manfred Linke (Neuwied: Luchterhand, 1963-1976).

OTHER: Ottomar Starke, *Schippeliana: Ein bürgerliches Bilderbuch*, foreword by Sternheim (Leipzig: Wolff, 1917).

SELECTED PERIODICAL PUBLICATIONS—
UNCOLLECTED: "Vincent van Gogh," *Hyperion*, no. 11/12 (1910): 110-113;

"Molière, der Bürger," *Blätter des Deutschen Theaters* (Berlin), no. 17 (13 April 1912): 259-260;

"Molière," *Berliner Tageblatt*, 14 April 1917;

"Kampf der Metapher," *Berliner Tageblatt*, 21 July 1917.

Because circumstances worked against him, Carl Sternheim's preeminent position among German expressionist playwrights was not established until after World War II, more than a decade after his death. The Berlin police office of theater censorship, critics ill equipped to appreciate plays not conforming to their expectations concerning comedy, actors and directors who sometimes distorted his work to soften its satiric bite, and a wartime mentality that sought to ban any public utterance threatening solidarity on the home front all stood in the way of proper recognition of Sternheim by audiences, theater people, and the reading public—especially during the period 1910 to 1920, when he was at the height of his productive powers. Political tensions and agitation by right-wing groups to discourage performance of "un-German" plays interfered seriously with his reception during the 1920s. And with the National Socialists' accession to power in 1933 his plays disappeared altogether from German theaters and bookstores. Not only had he vi-

ciously satirized the mentality that made Adolf Hitler possible but he was also a Jew with openly espoused socialist and pacifist convictions. It was not until the 1950s that his work became standard in the repertoires of Germany's great state and city theaters as well as on smaller provincial stages. The publication of his complete works, with notes and variant readings, starting in 1963 signaled his elevation into the literary and theatrical pantheon. It is now possible to gauge Sternheim's achievement: he created a series of topical satiric comedies, informed by an uncompromising prophetic vision of Europe before the Great War, economically and intricately structured, and presented in a language that at once captures the idioms of the time and exposes the mentality of those who speak them. His best plays have not only endured but seem to have improved with the years. No other German playwright of his generation can match his accomplishment.

Carl Sternheim was born in Leipzig on 1 April 1878 and was christened William Adolf Carl Francke because the union between his father, Jacob (called Carl) Sternheim—a Jewish merchant, banker, and publisher—and his Lutheran mother, Rosa Marie Flora Francke, had yet to be solemnized. Two years later the wedding took place, and Jacob Sternheim recognized his son and a daughter, Marie, born in the meantime, as legitimate offspring. After some five years in Hannover the family moved to Berlin, where Sternheim attended grade school and in 1888 entered the Friedrich Werder Gymnasium.

Among his schoolmates were the future great Social Democratic politician Karl Liebknecht as well as Siegfried Jacobsohn, who would become a respected critic and publicist in the 1910s and 1920s and whose essays and reviews of Sternheim's dramas, composed when they first appeared, are still among the best appreciations of his work. As a schoolboy Sternheim seemed more interested in writing plays and poems and in his social life than in schoolwork and was not promoted from the sixth to the seventh class. He attended three secondary schools before passing the final examination at the Königin Luisen-Gymnasium (Queen Luise High School) in September 1897 with a barely passing grade. In that same month he received Protestant baptism in the Sankt-Johannes-Kirche.

It was in Berlin, in plush upper-middle-class parlors and in the Bellealliance Theater belonging to his uncle, that Sternheim received his early

Woodcut of Sternheim by Conrad Felixmüller

of deathless verse dramas in the style of and on a plane with those of Johann Wolfgang von Goethe and Friedrich Schiller. He also craved personal recognition and influence that would enable him to move in the circles of important men. Finally, he yearned for erotic power and a career of sexual conquest on the order of Don Juan's. These fantasies, more in their sinister than in their pleasurable implications, form the groundwork for many of his plays.

Motivated by the desire for influence, prestige, and artistic immortality, he began at fourteen to compose narratives, poems, and plays with titles such as "Verkauft" (Sold), "Eva" (Eve), "Madonna," "Fallende Blätter" (Falling Leaves, a Napoleon drama), "Die Serenade," "Gespenster" (Ghosts), and "Das eiserne Kreuz" (The Iron Cross). He was able to pursue his ambitions through most of his life, undistracted by the need to earn a living. His father supported him until his second marriage, to a wealthy woman, provided him with the means to write and to move into the upper ranks of the social world.

Four of his first five published plays were printed at his or his father's expense by vanity presses. The earliest, *Der Heiland* (The Savior, 1898), was accepted by a major publisher but has yet to reach the stage. It is a one-act drawing-room comedy whose urbane wit and sophisticated, decadent eroticism owe much to Arthur Schnitzler. A professor's wife almost allows herself to be seduced by a young writer. She worships the artist in him and yearns to become his muse. The "savior" is her seven-year-old son, who accidentally discovers a photo in the writer's coat pocket showing him with another woman.

Sternheim enrolled at five universities—in Munich, Göttingen, Leipzig, Jena, and Berlin—but never studied for more than two semesters at any one. On 11 August 1900, in Düsseldorf, he married Eugenie Christine Marie Hauth in a Roman Catholic ceremony, after which they settled in Weimar. Always hoping to find the perfect landscape and home, Sternheim must have seen Weimar, the Athens of German culture, as the place where his talent would flourish. On 3 July 1901 Eugenie had a son, Carlhans, who, after a life plagued by mental illness, would be executed in December 1944 in the Brandenburg penitentiary for making treasonous remarks against the Nazi regime.

Like *Der Heiland*, Sternheim's second play, *Judas Ischariot: Die Tragödie vom Verrath* (Judas Iscariot: The Tragedy of Betrayal, 1901), has never

impressions of the magic power of the stage. He admired the newspaper publisher Hans Maske, a friend of the family who provided him with further opportunities to attend Berlin theater performances. Sternheim later paid Maske the tribute of assigning his surname to the leading characters of three of his best plays. He was also influenced by his well-to-do schoolfriends and their influential families, by the universal adulation of the Prussian military, by Prince Otto von Bismarck and Kaiser Wilhelm II. He became familiar with the showy, sometimes fraudulent nouveau-riche world of fin de siècle Berlin to which his father belonged and with the truly powerful elite in business, publishing, and the arts. He read carefully the lists of noble families in the *Almanach de Gotha* and the published list of army officers. His particular idol was Ernst von Schwabach, a young dandy of great wealth, partner in the Bleichröder banking house, and owner of a castle and hunting preserve in Silesia—a person of taste and influence who was the first to urge Sternheim to study French literature. His own father, a tyrannical, overfed, high-living entrepreneur and speculator, left his mark on Sternheim's plays.

Like his father he was ambitious, but with quite different aims. From an early age he dreamed of becoming a *Dichter* (poet), the author been performed. Sternheim's Judas is an uncompromisingly idealistic, revolutionary firebrand commanding the absolute worshipful adoration of Martha. In a painfully overwrought, affected, and inflated rhetoric decorated with inappropriate metaphors—"Ich will ein riesiges rotes Licht sein" (I want to be a gigantic red light), "Ich sauge den Regen deiner Worte auf" (I am sucking up the rain of your words)—Judas preaches the messianic message, overshadowing a limply sanctimonious Jesus. The latter is the one who perpetrates the betrayal, by proclaiming his kingdom to be the only legitimate one. Judas then delivers him to the authorities to save his people from tyranny.

Auf Krugdorf (In Krugdorf, 1902) has received a single stage performance, in a Dresden theater in January 1902; it was paired with a second short play, *Im Herbst* (In the Autumn), by Paul Eger. Sternheim had first offered the piece to Otto Brahm, Berlin's leading producer, who had declined. Benevolent reviewers thought Sternheim might have a future as a dramatist even though *Auf Krugdorf* was technically awkward, unconvincing, and uneconomical. The flimsy action—a devoted wife is asked by her husband to prove her fidelity—and the moralizing are sometimes painful. The audience liked and laughed at the impudent tone of the stage jargon derived from Schnitzler, Bernard Shaw, Oscar Wilde, and French marital farces of the time.

Though the trilogy was not published in toto until 1922, the first of the three short plays making up *Der Abenteurer: Drei Stückchen von ihm* (The Adventurer: Three Little Pieces about or by Him) was written around 1902 and appeared in 1908 in *Hyperion* under the pseudonym Hünni B. Maison. The sketches are the product of Sternheim's reading of the memoirs of Giovanni Giacomo Casanova, an adventurer after his own heart. In the first play Casanova altruistically cures a duchess of her adulterous fascination with one of her guards by feeding him well and robbing him of his ascetic, idealistic mien. The remaining two pieces are unexceptional farces of seduction and cuckoldry.

In March 1902 Sternheim moved his family to Berlin. In October he became a one-year volunteer in the First Squadron of the Cuirassier Regiment of Czar Nicholas I of Russia, stationed in Brandenburg, but after six months, one of them spent in a military hospital because of repeated fainting spells during mounted exercises, he was dismissed as unfit for cavalry service. In August

1903 they took up quarters in Munich. In 1904 Sternheim and Eugenie agreed to a separation. A few months earlier Sternheim had met one of Eugenie's former schoolmates, Thea Löwenstein, the wife of an attorney, Arthur Löwenstein, and had immediately asked her to be his wife. He saw in Thea his muse and inspiration; with their first encounter he had felt himself liberated and his creative powers restored. Thea responded by devoting herself without reservation to him and, more important, to his writing, sensing that their common yearning for the higher artistic life would cement the union. Sternheim would write his greatest plays in response to her encouragement and critical guidance, which she would continue to provide even after her disillusionment with him as a person and after their union had begun to dissolve.

Perhaps Sternheim's most ambitious early play—but, in his own judgment, the worst one he ever had published—is the verse drama *Vom König und der Königin* (On the King and Queen, 1905). His aim in writing it was to outdo two giants of German drama, Heinrich von Kleist and Friedrich Hebbel, and to match Goethe's *Faust* (1808, 1832) as well. He drew the plot from Hebbel's biblical tragedy *Judith* (1841); the more monstrous ideas derive from Kleist's particularly pathological scenes; the female protagonist is a mix of Goethe's Gretchen from *Faust I* together with Kleist's Penthesilea (from *Penthesilea*, 1808) and Käthchen (from *Das Käthchen von Heilbronn*, 1810) plus some of Hebbel's Judith. Her mission to kill the king in revenge for his atrocities is aborted when her hatred turns to passionate love. In act 4 the despairing king, a kind of Faustian Achilles, fails in his attempt at a murder-suicide. In act 5 she finally murders him in a mixture of terror and religious frenzy.

The event that finally brought Eugenie to sue for divorce, rather than go on waiting for Sternheim to take action, took place in Freiburg on 26 February 1906. On that day a hotel maid leaped in terror from the window of his hotel room and broke both legs. This act presumably followed a scene much like the one in Sternheim's *Don Juan* (published, 1909; performed, 1912) in which the don forces a woman, on peril of death, to kneel and worship him like a god. To escape prosecution, Sternheim consented to spend three months under treatment in the Freiburg University psychiatric clinic.

In this same year Thea inherited a large estate from her father and began to support

Sternheim, renting and furnishing for him a house in Bremen. They spent much time together though she still hesitated to separate from Löwenstein, who insisted that if she did so she must surrender custody of her two children, the older one by him and the younger, Dorothea, by Sternheim. Under emotional pressure from Sternheim, who complained of loneliness and depression, she finally consented to renounce her rights to both children, and by the beginning of 1907 they were in Munich planning the construction of a manor house in Höllriegelskreuth to be called Bellemaison. The Sternheims' divorce had become final on 14 July 1906. On 10 April 1907 Thea was divorced, and she and Sternheim were married in Munich on 13 July.

In *Ulrich und Brigitte: Ein dramatisches Gedicht* (Ulrich and Brigitte: A Dramatic Poem, 1907), a suffocatingly neoromantic piece, Sternheim employs a mix of meters but couches most of the drama in rhymed and unrhymed trochaic tetrameter, a meter found primarily in the so-called fate tragedies that were popular in Germany in the early nineteenth century. Brahm declined to produce the play because, he noted, no modern audience could listen long to this kind of verse, nor could it follow the complicated circumstances leading to the denouement. The "fate" operating here is tuberculosis, and the star-crossed lovers Ulrich and Brigitte have to die a Liebestod (love-death) for the sins of their father. The initial cause of the catastrophe is a marital misstep on the part of Ulrich's mother, the revelation of which clears the way for the lovers to marry—they are, after all, not brother and sister—and simultaneously seals their doom. Only twice has *Ulrich und Brigitte* reached the stage: the Freie Literarische Künstlerische Gesellschaft (Free Literary Artistic Society) of Darmstadt gave it its premiere on 19 March 1916, and it was performed once more by the Meiningen Court Theater on 26 November 1918.

On 2 January 1908 Thea bore a son, Klaus, who would commit suicide in Mexico City in 1946. They moved into Bellemaison and into Munich society, and around this time Sternheim began his association with the writer and publicist Franz Blei. Using Thea's capital, Sternheim and Blei founded the journal *Hyperion*, with Blei as editor. Blei functioned as Sternheim's intellectual guide and public supporter for many years, urging him to study French writers, particularly Molière; in 1909 he introduced Sternheim to the great Berlin impresario Max Reinhardt, who was to produce the premieres of most of his major works.

Sternheim struggled on into 1909 to complete *Don Juan*, a long verse drama in two parts that he had begun in 1904 and that had become a matter of life and death for him. He had conceived it as a tribute to Thea, reflecting her influence on him; it was to be his *Faust*, his artistic statement of faith, and the last word on love and the relationship between man and woman. By this time he had set himself the task of fusing two Don Juans: the one of Spanish legend and the historical Don Juan d'Austria, who, under Philip II of Spain, won the Battle of Lepanto against the Turks in 1571. Sternheim did intensive historical and philosophical research, and the play is larded with echoes of such writers as Charles-Pierre Baudelaire, Lord Byron, Miguel de Cervantes, Lorenzo Da Ponte, and Goethe. It was Sternheim's final grandiose attempt to master Western poetic dramatic tradition, and he paid Reinhardt's Deutsches Theater (German Theater) fifty thousand marks to mount a production. Felix Hollaender wrote the stage adaptation and directed; Alexander Moissi played the title role. The first of only two performances, on 13 September 1912, came to a premature end shortly after intermission when the audience began to demonstrate its outraged disapproval and the iron curtain had to be lowered.

The drama, mostly in blank verse, tells in part 1 of the don's Faustian passion for Maria, a figure similar to Gretchen in Goethe's play. The action is muddled and the language overwrought here as well as in part 2, in which Don Juan, still obsessed with Maria, becomes a military hero as well as a great lover. He is shown on board ship before and after the Battle of Lepanto and sings a duet on deck with Cervantes. When he learns that Maria, who had meanwhile become the mistress of Philip II, has committed suicide, he loses his mind.

Sternheim did not find his true genre and idiom until 1910, when he put aside a drama about Henry VIII and, in response to Blei's urging, set about completing a play based on Molière's *George Dandin* (1668). On Thea's suggestion he moved the setting from Paris to the world he knew best, the parlors of Wilhelmine Berlin. *Die Hose: Ein bürgerliches Lustspiel* (1911; translated as *The Underpants: A Middle-Class Comedy*, 1957) was the first of six great satiric comedies he composed in the middle years of his career and grouped under the heading "Aus dem bürgerlichen Heldenleben" (From the Heroic Life of the Middle Classes). Sternheim was bound in love and hate to the prewar epoch named after Kaiser Wilhelm II. It had determined his values, and it had frustrated him. In his satires he laid bare the arrogance, hypocrisy, impotence, and aggression of workers, petty bureaucrats, schoolteachers, social climbers, politicians, leaders of industry, and aristocrats, largely through the skillful use of their various modes of speech. Through nuances of expression, jargon, clichés, and military cadences delivered in a stylized fashion, these figures unmask themselves.

The plays depict the process of self-assertion through assimilation. No holds are barred in the Darwinian struggle for domination over others, but at the same time appearances must be preserved; ideology and morality serve as decorative or camouflage devices to further the fortunes of the good—that is, fanatic, brutal, and usually victorious—protagonist, who in most cases is a bourgeois or would-be bourgeois.

Die Hose begins like a French sex farce when Luise Maske's underpants come unfastened and she has to step out of them on the street at the very moment His Imperial Majesty is passing by. For people concerned with appearances, this accident is an unspeakable disgrace; her husband, Theobald, is enraged and fearful of losing his otherwise secure civil service position. Surprisingly, quite the opposite occurs. He lets two spare rooms at outrageous fees to two men drawn by the underpants incident: a hairdresser and a neurasthenic poet, neither of whom is capable of responding to Luise Maske's yearning for sexual adventure. He not only outsmarts these two idiots, who speak the intellectual jargon of the day, and solidifies his financial position but he also maintains complete control over his wife. His job is secure; he continues his own weekly trysts with the woman next door; and in the eyes of the world he is a solid citizen.

Die Hose premiered on 16 February 1911 in the Kammerspiele (Intimate Theater) of Reinhardt's Deutsches Theater and had a run of only eight performances. Its virtues were not fully recognized until the later 1920s, when it became a fixture in the repertories of major theaters—only to disappear in 1933 when the Nazi regime banned Sternheim's books and forbade the performance of his dramas. The first reviewers and audiences were disappointed in the play because its opening scene led them to expect a ribald story of cuckoldry in the vein of Giovanni Boccaccio. The ac-

tion was meager for their tastes, and the language often veered off into realms of the absurd. In short, *Die Hose* was dramatic satire of an unfamiliar sort.

The Berlin police censor had not helped matters by demanding changes and deletions of politically or morally offensive material; he almost banned the play outright because it had been an object of controversy since it appeared in print. Starting with *Die Hose* the censor examined all of Sternheim's plays closely, in part because his essays acidly critical of contemporary Germany had displeased veterans and right-wingers. One further explanation for the initially poor reception of *Die Hose* is that neither Reinhardt's directors nor the members of his acting company could meet the demands of this new kind of play, with its anticlimaxes, its stylized diction, and its cold, nonnaturalistic tone that discouraged audience empathy.

Die Kassette (1912; translated as *The Strongbox*, 1963) was moved after its premiere on 24 November 1911 under Hollaender's direction from Reinhardt's large Deutsches Theater to the Kammerspiele. It had only ten more performances, again because acts 1 to 3 raised expectations that were not fulfilled in the last two acts. The comic tradition of the miser and his pot of gold, starting with Plautus, dictates that the miser be defeated and the lovers be joined happily in marriage. Albert Bassermann, the male lead and one of Reinhardt's most respected actors, urged Sternheim to tack on an additional scene with a happy ending; Sternheim refused because his intent was to show up the aggression, impotence, and self-delusion of his protagonist, Oberlehrer (senior grade-school teacher) Krull, who believes that by groveling before his rich maiden aunt Elspeth he will be rewarded with the securities she keeps in her strongbox and will be able to force others, including his family, to grovel before him. The real winner in this vicious domestic war, however, is Aunt Elspeth. She bequeaths all her wealth to the Church but deceives Krull into believing that it will be in his hands, thus insuring that she will continue to dominate the family and he will go on kowtowing. The spineless and brutal Krull and his foppish, womanizing son-in-law are so transfixed by the box that they stand lost in dreams of prestige and dominance as the curtain falls. The satiric irony of the play excited a theater riot in Munich as late as 1960.

With *Bürger Schippel* (1913; translated as *Paul Schippel Esq.*, 1970), which premiered at the

Scene from a 1927 production in Frankfurt am Main of Sternheim's Die Kassette

Deutsches Theater under the direction of Reinhardt himself on 5 March 1913, Sternheim conquered the theater. The audience brought the author and actors back for curtain calls at the end of each act, but reviews complained of a confusion of styles, unnatural diction, and a poisonous psychology. Its popularity cannot be attributed to its inspirational qualities, for it is a linguistic tour de force that travesties and mocks everything the Wilhelmine middle class cherished: Shakespeare, Schiller, Carl Maria von Weber's *Der Freischütz* (The Marksman, 1821), Richard Wagner's *Die Meistersinger von Nürnberg* (The Mastersingers of Nuremberg, 1868), the kaiser, German song, and the chastity of German womanhood.

The main figures, provincial petit-bourgeois members of a vocal quartet, are incapable of honest emotion and hide their impotence behind theatrical poses and inappropriate phrases borrowed from various sources. Clashing styles, malapropisms, mixed metaphors, and sententious but misapplied lines from the classics expose, rather than conceal, the emptiness and misery of these seeming pillars of society. One wonders why Paul Schippel, the one proletarian in the play Sternheim once planned to title "Le prolétaire bourgeois," would want to abandon his caste for theirs. He gets his chance when the quartet's tenor dies and the group begins to woo him, with some loathing, for his beautiful voice.

Sternheim unmasks as mere attitudes unsupported by convictions not only bourgeois pride of station but also the scorn workers show for their superiors: the leader of the quartet offers his own sister in marriage as an enticement, but Schippel rejects the offer for the altogether bourgeois reason that the girl's honor has been compromised by the local prince. This affront to the bourgeois sense of honor can be compensated for only by a duel between Schippel and the sister's new bridegroom, both of whom have to be dragged quaking to the scene. In an episode milked for laughs in later productions, the two tremble and become incontinent before they can force themselves to fire. Schippel accidentally inflicts a slight wound on his opponent, an act all misinterpret as brave and noble, and he is welcomed to his new station with the assurance that he is now entitled to the "höheren Segnungen" (higher blessings) of the middle classes. Schippel, no wiser than before and blind to the irony of the phrase, says blissfully, just before the final curtain, "Du bist Bürger, Paul" (You are a bourgeois, Paul), and bows deeply to himself.

With the premiere on 2 February 1914 of *Der Snob* (1914; translated as *The Snob*, 1970) in the Kammerspiele under Reinhardt's direction, Sternheim's theatrical career reached its zenith. The production so pleased audiences that it was repeated fifty-five times, more than any other play performed that year on Reinhardt's stages. The censor had demanded few changes; reviews, while not glowing, were at least positive, although they noted a certain heartlessness, a cruel mimicry, and an inclination toward the grotesque not usually found in comedies. Paul Schlenther, the most discerning of the critics, called it a well-deserved success: a subtle, topical satiric character comedy reminiscent of works by Molière. The press praised Bassermann in the lead role and remarked on the presence in the front-row orchestra of the Crown Prince and his retinue, all of whom applauded vigorously.

Christian Maske, son of Theobald and Luise from *Die Hose*, has risen to the top in the business world and applies a social sheen to his financial power by marrying into the aristocracy. In all his machinations he behaves like his father: he is hard-nosed, selfish, and pathologically obsessed with appearances. The play begins with Christian receiving a lesson on how to tie a necktie in the latest fashion. He is a climber without a conscience. He pays off and dismisses the woman who helped him to success, and he sends his parents to Switzerland lest they embarrass him before his prospective in-laws. His desire for prestige leads him to sacrifice everything of real value; and the irony is that no sacrifice was needed. The count and his family, who are in straitened circumstances, have long since determined that the alliance is unavoidable. So Christian's struggles are mere shadowboxing, and it is clear that each party fully deserves the other. Christian's emptiness and moral bankruptcy are complete when, in the closing lines, he besmirches his recently deceased mother's good reputation, suggesting as he undresses on his wedding night that he is in truth the illegitimate son of a viscount. The censor blurred this point by insisting that the original "süße Mutter Ehebrecherin" (sweet adulterous mother) be replaced by "süße Mutter, wenn auch Ehebrecherin" (sweet mother though adulterous).

World War I marked the abrupt end of Sternheim's prominence in the theatrical world. The right wing had carried on a press campaign against him since the appearance of *Die Hose*. Then in 1915 the Military High Command, fearful of the effect of his satire on civilian morale and acceding to pressure from patriotic organizations, issued an edict banning the performance of the plays subsumed under the title "Aus dem bürgerlichen Heldenleben"—in other words, of his best work. Sternheim worked frantically to persuade theater managers to adopt his plays, traveling from city to city offering his services as director or adviser. His frustration grew more acute with the gradual dissolution of his marriage, which had begun as early as 1910 with Thea's loss of trust and accelerated in 1915 when she discovered his annotated "Leporello" list of sexual conquests with some ninety names. (A second list, the sequel to the first, was delivered to her by a Belgian friend in 1920.)

Sternheim used Thea's translation of Gustave Flaubert's 1874 comedy *Le Candidat* as the basis of the finest of his stage adaptations. He transferred the scene to prewar provincial Prussia, made the language and terminology fit the time and place, and thoroughly revised act 4 to suit his satiric purpose, which was to expose the machinations and hallucinations of the bourgeois unleashed on the field of politics. *Der Kandidat: Komödie in vier Aufzügen nach Flaubert* (The Candidate: Comedy in Four Acts Based on Flaubert, 1914) premiered on 6 December 1915 at the Vienna Volksbühne (People's Stage) under the direction of Herbert Ihering. The Austrian censor demanded only two deletions: a mention of Jewish reserve officers and the last word in the play, "Ehrenwort!" (Word of honor), which gives the curtain speech, an extended mad monologue, its resonance and sting. The candidate Russek, who has sacrificed his family and his decency in the pursuit of office, sinks to new depths in thoughtless word and empty gesture saying: "Ich glaube an dich, Gott. *Er hebt den Schwurfinger und brüllt:* Ehrenwort!!" (I believe in you, God! *He raises his forefinger and roars*: Word of honor!!). Like Sternheim protagonists before and after him, the candidate, obsessed with the image which he knows to be the key to success, sacrifices his moral self and prostitutes his wife and daughter for the sake of a chimera that can be created or destroyed at the whim of a newspaper editor. Sternheim judged *Der Kandidat* to be one of the four plays that most clearly represented his intentions.

Another of the plays Sternheim thought representative is *1913* (1915; translated, 1970), which first reached the stage as a well-reviewed private performance directed by Gustav Hartung, a strong Sternheim supporter, at the Frankfurt am Main Schauspielhaus on 23 January 1919. Its stage success never matched that of *Die Hose* or *Der Snob*, though its satiric power and vision were immediately evident to reviewers of the published text.

1913 is the third of the Maske plays. Baron Christian von Maske has become a leader of the German military-industrial complex. Though aware that he is dying, he fights to maintain his position of power in an intrafamilial battle with his daughter Sofie, who has learned from him the advantages of unprincipled egotism and is starting to outdo him at his own game. He defeats her by manipulating newspaper reports but dies before he can enjoy his triumph, which is in fact no more than the creation and destruction of a public image. He leaves behind the ideology of unscrupulousness and the world he created, both running out of control toward the catastrophe of 1914 and, later, Nazism. It is this prophetic, satiric message embedded in the rhetoric of Maske, his daughter, and the proto-Nazi revolutionary

Wilhelm Krey that chilled the spines of audiences after World War II.

After the ban by the censor in 1915 Sternheim and the Reinhardt organization sought ways to keep his reputation alive and hit on the idea of further adaptations. The first was *Das leidende Weib* (The Suffering Woman, 1915), in which Sternheim tried to transplant the action of Maximilian Klinger's 1775 Storm and Stress tragedy of the same title into an unspecified time that looks a bit like Wilhelmine Germany. Klinger's drama tells of a virtuous ambassador's wife, involved against her will in an amorous intrigue, who expires of sorrow when her true love, long since renounced, has to die for protecting her honor. Sternheim brought the piece up to date by adding messages in favor of pacifism and tolerance toward the French and deploring the senseless wartime slaughter of a heroic younger generation of aristocrats. Reinhardt directed the premiere, a closed matinee performance on 31 March 1916 in the Kammerspiele before an audience of critics and officials from the censor's office, who, it was hoped, would release the play for public performance. The effort succeeded; but when the drama became part of the regular repertoire on 30 October 1916 it earned uniformly negative reviews and was performed only four times.

The dramatic adaptation of Guy de Maupassant's "Au bord du lit" (At the Edge of the Bed, 1883), which Sternheim titled *Der Scharmante: Lustspiel mit Benutzung einer fremden Idee* (The Charming Man: Comedy Using Someone Else's Idea, 1915), fared even worse in the theater. Hollaender directed the first of only two performances in the Kammerspiele on 26 February 1915. Sternheim described the evening as a quiet failure, meaning that while the audience disliked the play, they did not whistle, boo, or throw things. De Maupassant's sketch is a frivolous marital joke wherein the relationship is revived and made more exciting when the wife accepts her husband as a lover on condition that he pay her what it has been costing him to maintain his mistresses. Sternheim complicates the plot, turning it into a psychologically involved, erotic power struggle in which Countess Charlotte indignantly throws the money back in the count's face. The remainder of the piece deals with an elaborate intrigue in which the countess plays the philandering husband off against the young man (the charmer) who wants to be her lover, exposing their folly and vanity and in the end rejecting both.

Tabula rasa (1916) is once more in Sternheim's nasty satiric vein, and it is one of the four plays he thought best revealed his true intentions. It premiered successfully on 25 January 1919 at Berlin's Kleines Theater under the direction of George Altman, a personal friend who, the following year, together with Karl Heinz Martin mounted the production of a Sternheim cycle that included *Tabula rasa*, *Die Hose*, *Der Snob*, and *1913*.

The protagonist of *Tabula rasa*, Wilhelm Ständer, is the proletarian counterpart to Theobald Maske in *Die Hose*. By slyly conforming, dissembling, and exploiting, this labor leader gets the better of everyone: liberal and radical socialists, capitalist entrepreneurs, and the hapless women in his life. At sixty he is able to retire and live in luxury on the securities he has accumulated. Unlike Maske, he is at the end in a position to wipe the slate clean—hence the title—by telling the fools to their faces what he thinks of them and what their ideologies are worth. Ständer is despicable, but no more so than the less perspicacious characters who drape themselves in moral slogans. As in his other first-rate plays, Sternheim's ear for cant and jargon of all colors serves him well.

In 1916 Sternheim was commissioned by Reinhardt to adapt Molière's *L'Avare* (The Miser, 1668), and before the year was out *Der Geizige* (The Miser) appeared in print. It departs little from the original except that the miser's profligate son plays a significant part in the action. The premiere on 16 April 1917 at Reinhardt's Deutsches Theater and under his direction, with Max Pallenberg as Harpagon, was a great success with audiences but got a sharply divided critical reception. Pallenberg later went on tour giving guest performances as Harpagon, but the adaptation has been played rarely since.

Later retitled *Der Stänker* (The Stinker) at Sternheim's insistence, *Perleberg* (1917) premiered on 10 September 1917 at the Frankfurt Schauspielhaus. It was a great popular success, but the critics did not know what to make of it; they noted that it had a conciliatory, sentimental quality they did not associate with Sternheim. It had been completed in 1905, long before he had found his mature voice. It tells of a stinker who is softened through the benign influence and sad death of a saintly tubercular schoolteacher. The play was last staged in 1924.

Sternheim in 1917

Die Marquise von Arcis (1919; translated as *The Mask of Virtue*, 1935) is an adaptation of the tale of Madame de La Pommeraye from Denis Diderot's *Jacques le fataliste et son maître* (1796). In Sternheim's play the Marquise von Pommeraye, enraged at having been rejected by the Marquis von Arcis, plots revenge. The elaborate intrigue takes up four acts, and the fifth brings a surprise bourgeois-sentimental denouement. Having deceived the marquis into marrying a middle-class young woman whose virtue has been compromised, the Marquise von Pommeraye begins to exult in her triumph when, to her dismay, true love wins out. The girl confesses her past and her love so movingly that the marquis is transformed into a doting middle-class husband.

Sternheim considered the play hackwork but put all his energy into making its staging a success lest his name and work be forgotten. The play is indeed a potboiler, but perhaps for that very reason it is one of his most successful in the theater and on television. Hartung directed the premiere, which took place on 5 September 1919 at the Frankfurt Schauspielhaus and was followed by some forty-four further productions on German-speaking stages. The great actors of the 1920s, among them Heinrich George and Emil Jannings, found the role of the marquis conge-

nial; Vivien Leigh played the ingenue in the 1935 London production.

Der entfesselte Zeitgenosse (The Contemporary Unleashed, 1920), on the other hand, was greeted with catcalls and hisses after acts 2 and 3 on opening night, 17 February 1921, at the Hessisches Landestheater (Hessian Provincial Theater) in Darmstadt. The director, Hartung, tried to accentuate the play's topicality and satiric points, but his efforts went for naught. The drama was recognized by reviewers as a piece of shameless kitsch. Sternheim sets up six straw men—an admiral, a diplomat, a publicist, a politician, a tenor, and a professor—and shows them to be greedy, egotistical, and overly cerebral. They are all suing for the hand of a young heiress, and they are all put in the shade by Klette, a "Zeitkind" (child of the times) and man of the future, unchained and spontaneous, in touch with his feelings. Acting without guile or plan, he wins the heiress's love and in the final scene climbs a ladder to join her in her bedroom, as the chords of an aeolian harp waft through the night.

Looking for another vehicle to convey his new message that emotion is a better guide than rational will, Sternheim chose Abbé Prévost's *Manon Lescaut* (1728-1731) as the basis for his next drama. With help from Thea, he wrote *Manon Lescaut* (1921) expressly for the great Berlin actress Maria Orska. She played the title role in the first production, premiering under the direction of Rudolf Bernauer at the Theater in der Königgrätzer Straße (Theater in Königgrätz Street), Berlin, on 15 October 1921. The audience was enthusiastic, but the reviews were predominantly negative. The critics castigated Sternheim for grafting an inappropriate antibourgeois, antirational social message onto one of the world's great love stories; and Thea complained in her diary that his revisions of her version of act 4, in which he lets the chevalier die at Manon's side rather than return to his aristocratic milieu, were "reichlich verkitscht" (sentimentally overdone). There were five additional productions, mainly in provincial theaters, up to 1927, and none thereafter.

Sternheim invested much creative effort in the composition of *Der Nebbich* (The Nebbish, 1922) and did his best to insure its stage success. He worked for more than a week with the director, Hartung, to pull the performance together; but the premiere on 9 October 1922 at the Hessisches Landestheater was a failure, "bis zur Unkenntlichkeit banal" (banal to the point of

Sternheim in 1921; engraving by Felixmüller

unrecognizability), according to Thea. In early 1924, however, a Berlin production under Sternheim's direction with his daughter Dorothea's stage design was a great theatrical event; the drama enjoyed several revivals in the 1950s and 1960s in theaters as well as on television.

It is, by Sternheim's standards, a relatively lighthearted satiric language farce in which he carries on his campaign against *Metapher* (metaphor), by which he meant an ideology, a received idea, or any cliché used to camouflage or embellish reality. An oversexed diva, Rita Marchetti, unaccountably becomes infatuated with Tritz, the nebbish, whose aim in life is to become postmaster of Garmisch-Partenkirchen. In that position, shielded by the bars on his window, he will be able to assert his power over customers by making them wait in line. Rita is incapable of an honest word or feeling; she speaks in quotes from Goethe and grand opera. In the brief span of their affair, before Tritz becomes concerned about his health and sexual powers, she transforms him into a walking metaphor in cutaway, spats, yellow gloves, and gold-headed cane. By training him to mouth the right phrase at the right time she equips him to impress, in a series of absurdly comic scenes, leaders in politics, diplomacy, jour-

nalism, and industry. In the end Tritz and Rita are tired of one another but can part only by reenacting a poignant scene of renunciation from Hugo von Hofmannsthal and Richard Strauss's *Der Rosenkavalier* (1911; translated as *The Rose-Bearer*, 1912).

In a last concerted effort to awaken the resonance his great plays of 1911 to 1914 had evoked and to give dramatic form to the great issues of the Weimar Republic, Sternheim resurrected two figures from the Maske trilogy: Christian's daughter Sofie and her husband, Otto von Beeskow. As the preliminary title, "1921," suggests, the drama was to have the prophetic intensity and sweeping social and political vision of *1913*. The play was ultimately called *Das Fossil* (1925; translated as *The Fossil*, 1970). The failure of its premiere at the Hamburg Kammerspiele on 6 November 1923 under Erich Schönlank's direction so affected Sternheim's nerves that he had to be sedated with morphine. A second production, directed by Hartung at Berlin's Renaissance-Theater, fared no better. A major effort by the Bochum Schauspielhaus under Frank Reichert's direction in 1962 was well received.

The play's central figure is a retired Prussian cavalry general who at the end of act 2 mounts his hobbyhorse in full regalia and, swinging his sword and riding hard, calls for a charge against enemy lines. Sternheim's point is that the military-industrial establishment of the Wilhelmine era—the general's son, Otto, was an arms manufacturer, and his granddaughter is developing new explosives in her cellar laboratory—may have disappeared from view, but it is prepared to return to power. The conflict begins with the appearance of a young Prussian aristocrat, Ago von Bohna, who has returned from a Russian prison camp converted to communism. Bohna's socialist platitudes—some of which are drawn from Sternheim's own tracts—are as ridiculous as the general's military jargon, and he is no match for the wiles of the chemist. As she seduces him, he lets her throw the manuscript of his revolutionary book into the fire. The arbitrary denouement follows when the general surprises the couple in flagrante delicto, shoots them dead, and surrenders to the police, well assured that Weimar justice will be easy on him.

The first reason for the play's failure is its structural incoherence; the second, more telling one is its diction. In his later essays, stories, and plays Sternheim cultivates an ever more abrupt, compressed, contorted manner in an effort to convey vital intensity. In *Das Fossil*, the general's speeches are couched in what seems a grotesque parody on this idiom and are so terse that audiences must have found them hard to follow.

Working with the German translation of Frank Harris's 1916 biography of Wilde, Sternheim put together *Oskar Wilde: Sein Drama* (Oscar Wilde: His Drama, 1925) and directed its premiere at the Deutsches Theater, Berlin, on 31 March 1925. The reviews, including one by his close friend Franz Pfemfert, were aggressively negative, and there were no further performances. The play has many defects, the worst of which are the abundance of talk about Wilde and a lack of dramatic structure and tension. In addition, Sternheim invests his protagonist with his own megalomania, self-pity, and ideas about the decline of the West. This Oscar Wilde is not up to the task of being *the* man of the times and the agent of world history. Nor was it a service to the real Wilde to suffuse his dying days in Paris with sugary kitsch.

In his late plays Sternheim seemed to be creating fictional worlds of little import. To correct this fault he chose to write something completely divorced from prewar Germany and resolutely up-to-date. Its topicality shines forth from the title, *Die Schule von Uznach oder Neue Sachlichkeit* (The School of Uznach; or, New Objectivity, 1926); *Neue Sachlichkeit* was the term coined by art critics to designate the latest antiexpressionist movement in the visual arts, probably best represented by the Bauhaus. Its timeliness is underscored by the presence of characters easily identified as the dancer Mary Wigman, Sternheim himself, his son Klaus, and well-known educators. The action takes place in a girls' school populated by sophisticated young flappers exuding insouciance and wit and talking in abstractions about "persönliche, radikale Deutlichkeit" (personal, radical clarity of being). Into this group bursts Mathilde Enterlein, whose last name suggests the ugly duckling. She soon wins the audience's hearts and the hero's as well with her naiveté and old-fashioned ways. Her radiance is so great that she converts her schoolmates to a belief in true love and marriage.

It is a tribute to the respect Sternheim still commanded from theater managers that the play premiered simultaneously and with great success on 21 September 1926 at three major theaters: the Deutsches Schauspielhaus, Hamburg, under Arnold Marlé, with stage design by Sternheim's daughter Dorothea; the Cologne Schauspielhaus

under Friedrich Neubauer; and the Mannheim Nationaltheater under Heinz Dietrich Kenter, with stage design again by Dorothea. The following April the faithful Hartung mounted a production in the Theater in der Königgrätzer Straße, Berlin, with costumes by Dorothea, that had an astounding run of 150 performances. Sternheim knew that, like *Die Marquise von Arcis*, this play was not by any means great drama, but he was pleased that he had hit on a formula for attracting audiences.

With *Die Schule von Uznach* Sternheim's theater career ended. The condition of his body and mind had been declining for years. His arrogance, brutal lack of restraint, and indiscriminate lecherousness had grown worse and worse over the last seventeen years of his marriage. As his creative powers slackened, he became more and more alienated from family, from friends and co-workers, and from Germany, for which he developed a loathing. Ultimately he could name only three or four persons he could tolerate. In 1912 Bellemaison had been abandoned in favor of a house in Belgium, and after the war he had lived off and on in Holland, Switzerland, Dresden, and Munich. In 1926 Dr. Gottfried Benn diagnosed his problem as a long untreated case of syphilis, but the cure prescribed had no noticeable effect. Thea divorced him in 1927. In December 1928 he had a complete mental and physical collapse from which he did not emerge for more than a year. Throughout his years of exile and decline he was afflicted with frequent blackouts and fits of depression. He moved to Brussels after his marriage to Pamela Wedekind, the daughter of the playwright Frank Wedekind, on 17 April 1930 and, with the exception of a short stay in London, remained there until his death. After Pamela divorced him in 1934 so that she could pursue her acting career in Berlin, he lived in an apartment with a housekeeper, cut off by Nazi edict from any income from books and plays, surviving by selling off valuables. He ceased writing in 1936. When German troops occupied Brussels in May 1940 he destroyed his journals and other papers that might have been used against him. Friends shielded him from harassment by the Nazis. When pneumonia came to take him, it was a painful struggle; his death throes continued for twenty hours before he died on 3 November 1942.

Letters:
"Carl Sternheim: Briefe," edited by L. M. Fied-

ler, *Hofmannsthal Blätter*, 4 (Spring 1970): 243-254;

"Carl Sternheim: Briefe an Franz Blei," edited by Rudolf Billetta, *Neue deutsche Hefte*, 18, no. 3 (1971): 36-69;

Briefe, edited by Wolfgang Wendler, 2 volumes (Darmstadt: Luchterhand, 1988).

Bibliography:

Rudolf Billetta, *Sternheim-Compendium: Carl Sternheim, Werk, Weg, Wirkung* (Wiesbaden: Steiner, 1975).

Biography:

Manfred Linke, *Carl Sternheim* (Reinbek: Rowohlt, 1979).

References:

Heinz-Ludwig Arnold, ed., *Text und Kritik: Zeitschrift für Literatur*, special Sternheim issue, 87 (July 1985);

Derrick Barlow, ed., *Sternheim, "Bürger Schippel"* (London: Oxford University Press, 1969);

R. Beckley, "Carl Sternheim," in *German Men of Letters*, edited by Alex Natan, volume 2 (London: Wolff, 1963), pp. 131-154;

Edson M. Chick, *Dances of Death: Wedekind, Brecht, Dürrenmatt, and the Satiric Tradition* (Columbia, S.C.: Camden House, 1984), pp. 47-79;

Eckehard Czucka, *Idiom der Entstellung: Auffaltung des Satirischen in Carl Sternheims "Aus dem bürgerlichen Heldenleben"* (Münster: Aschendorff, 1982);

Burghard Dedner, *Carl Sternheim* (Boston: Twayne, 1982);

Wilhelm Emrich, "Carl Sternheims 'Kampf der Metapher' und für die 'eigene Nuance,' " in his *Geist und Widergeist* (Frankfurt am Main: Athenäum, 1965), pp. 163-184;

Emrich, "Die Komödien Carl Sternheims," in *Der deutsche Expressionismus*, edited by Hans Steffen (Göttingen: Vandenhoeck & Ruprecht, 1966), pp. 115-137;

Winfried Freund, *Die Bürgerkomödien Carl Sternheims* (Munich: Fink, 1976);

Manfred Linke, "Dokumente der Krise: Erstveröffentlichung eines Tagebuch-Fragments von Carl Sternheim," *Jahrbuch der deutschen Schillergesellschaft*, 25 (1981): 104-132;

H. S. Reiss, "Sternheim: Ein Satiriker?," *Deutsche Vierteljahrsschrift*, 57, no. 2 (1983): 321-343;

Gunther Scholdt, "Gegenentwürfe: Zu Sternheims 'bürgerlichem Heldenzyklus' und zu

seinem Verhältnis zu Molière," *Jahrbuch der deutschen Schillergesellschaft*, 26 (1982): 296-324;

Jörg Schönert, ed., *Carl Sternheims Dramen: Zur Textanalyse, Ideologiekritik und Rezeptionsgeschichte* (Heidelberg: Quelle & Meyer, 1975);

Hans Schwerte, "Carl Sternheim," in *Deutsche Dichter der Moderne*, edited by Benno von Wiese (Berlin: Schmidt, 1965), pp. 420-434;

W. G. Sebald, *Carl Sternheim: Kritiker und Opfer der wilhelminischen Ära* (Stuttgart: Kohlhammer, 1969);

M. Helena Goncalves de Silva, *Character, Ideology and Symbolism in the Plays of Wedekind, Sternheim, Kaiser, Toller and Brecht* (London: Modern Humanities Research Association, 1985), pp. 29-54;

Albert Soergel and Kurt Hohoff, *Dichter und Denker der Zeit*, volume 2 (Düsseldorf: Bagel, 1963), pp. 222-237;

Walter H. Sokel, *The Writer in Extremis* (Stanford: Stanford University Press, 1964), pp. 62, 108, 121-123;

Wolfgang Wendler, *Carl Sternheim: Weltvorstellung und Kunstprinzipien* (Frankfurt am Main: Athenäum, 1966);

Wendler, ed., *Carl Sternheim* (Darmstadt: Luchterhand, 1980);

Rhys W. Williams, *Carl Sternheim: A Critical Study* (Bern: Lang, 1982);

Williams, "Carl Sternheim's Debt to Flaubert: Aspects of Literary Relationship," *Arcadia*, 15 (1980): 149-163;

Williams "Carl Sternheim's Image of Marx and his Critique of the German Intellectual Tradition," *German Life and Letters*, new series 32, no. 1 (1978/1979): 19-29;

Williams, "Carl Sternheim's Image of van Gogh," *Modern Language Review*, 72, no. 1 (1977): 112-124;

Williams, "Carl Sternheim's *Tasso; oder, Kunst des Juste Milieu*: An Alternative History of German Literature," *Modern Language Review*, 75, no. 1 (1980): 123-147.

Papers:

Carl Sternheim's papers are in the Deutsches Literaturarchiv, Schiller Nationalmuseum (German Literature Archive, Schiller National Museum), Marbach am Neckar.

Hermann Sudermann
(30 September 1857 - 21 November 1928)

Christopher L. Dolmetsch
Marshall University

PLAY PRODUCTIONS: *Die Ehre: Schauspiel*, Berlin, Lessingtheater, 27 November 1889;
Sodoms Ende: Trauerspiel, Berlin, Lessingtheater, 5 November 1890;
Heimat: Schauspiel, Berlin, Lessingtheater, 7 January 1893;
Die Schmetterlingsschlacht: Komödie, Berlin, Lessingtheater / Vienna, Burgtheater, 6 October 1894;
Das Glück im Winkel: Schauspiel, Vienna, Burgtheater, 11 November 1895;
Morituri: Teja; Fritzchen; Das Ewig-Männliche, Berlin, Deutsches Theater / Vienna, Burgtheater, 3 October 1896;
Johannes: Tragödie, Berlin, Deutsches Theater / Dresden, Königliches Hoftheater, 15 January 1898;
Die drei Reiherfedern: Dramatisches Gedicht, Berlin, Deutsches Theater / Dresden, Königliches Hoftheater / Stuttgart, Königliches Hoftheater, 21 January 1899;
Johannisfeuer: Schauspiel, Berlin, Lessingtheater, 5 October 1900;
Es lebe das Leben!: Drama, Berlin, Deutsches Theater, 1 February 1902;
Der Sturmgeselle Sokrates: Komödie, Berlin, Lessingtheater, 3 October 1903;
Stein unter Steinen: Schauspiel, Berlin, Lessingtheater, 8 October 1905;
Das Blumenboot: Schauspiel, Saint Petersburg, Alexandrinsky Theatre, 25 March 1906; Berlin, Lessingtheater, 5 October 1906;
Rosen: Margot, Der letzte Besuch, Die ferne Prinzessin, Vienna, Burgtheater, 3 October 1907; *Lichtbänder*, Stuttgart, Königliches Interimstheater, 26 October 1907;
Strandkinder: Schauspiel, Berlin, Königliches Schauspielhaus, 21 December 1909;
Der Bettler von Syrakus: Tragödie, Berlin, Königliches Schauspielhaus, 19 October 1911;
Der gute Ruf, Berlin, Deutsches Theater / Munich, Königliches Hoftheater, 7 January 1913;

Hermann Sudermann

Die Lobgesänge des Claudian: Drama, Hamburg, Deutsches Schauspielhaus, 20 January 1914;
Die entgötterte Welt: Szenische Bilder aus kranker Zeit (Die Freundin, Die gutgeschnittene Ecke, Das höhere Leben), Berlin, Lessingtheater / Munich, Schauspielhaus, 28 January 1916;
Regina, Berlin, Theater an der Königgrätzerstraße, 27 September 1919;
Die Raschhoffs: Schauspiel, Königsberg, Neues Schauspielhaus, 18 October 1919;
Notruf: Drama, Berlin, Theater in der Königgrätzerstraße, 18 August 1921;
Wie die Träumenden: Schauspiel, Königsberg, Neues Schauspielhaus, 6 November 1922;

Der Hasenfellhändler: Schauspiel, Hamburg, Deutsches Schauspielhaus, 1 December 1928.

BOOKS: *Im Zwielicht: Zwanglose Geschichten* (Berlin: Lehmann / Stuttgart: Cotta, 1886)—includes "Des Hausfreunds Silvesterberichte," translated by Grace I. Colbron as "A New Year's Eve Confession" in *Short Story Classics (Foreign)*, 5 volumes, edited by William Patten (New York: Collier, 1907), III: 917-928; translated by C. Collier as "A New Year's Eve Confession" in *The World's One Hundred Best Short Stories*, 10 volumes, edited by Grant Overton (New York & London: Funk & Wagnalls, 1927), IV: 89-96;

Frau Sorge: Roman (Berlin: Lehmann / Stuttgart: Cotta, 1888); edited by Gustav Gruener (New York: Holt, 1900); translated by Bertha Overbeck as *Dame Care* (New York: Harper, 1891; London: Osgood & McIlvaine, 1891);

Geschwister: Zwei Novellen (Berlin: Lehmann / Stuttgart: Cotta, 1888)—comprises "Die Geschichte der stillen Mühle," translated anonymously as *The Silent Mill* (New York: Brentano's, 1919); "Der Wunsch," translated by Lily Henkel as *The Wish* (London: Unwin, 1894; New York: Appleton, 1895);

Die Ehre: Schauspiel (Berlin: Lehmann / Stuttgart: Cotta, 1890); translated by Hilmar R. Baukhage as *Honor: A Play in Four Acts* (New York: French, 1915);

Der Katzensteg: Roman (Berlin: Lehmann / Stuttgart: Cotta, 1890); translated anonymously as *The Cats' Bridge* (New York: Collier, 1890); translated by Hettie E. Miller as *Regine* (Chicago: Weeks, 1894);

Sodoms Ende: Trauerspiel (Berlin & Stuttgart: Cotta, 1891);

Iolanthes Hochzeit: Erzählung (Berlin & Stuttgart: Cotta, 1892); translated by Adele S. Seltzer as *Iolanthe's Wedding* (New York: Boni & Liveright, 1918);

Heimat: Schauspiel in vier Akten (Berlin & Stuttgart: Cotta, 1893; New York: Lederer, 1893); translated by Charles Edward Amory Winslow as *Magda: A Play In Four Acts* (New York: Lederer, 1895);

Es war: Roman (Stuttgart: Cotta, 1894); translated by Beatrice Marshall as *The Undying Past* (London & New York: Lane, 1906);

Die Schmetterlingsschlacht: Komödie in 4 Akten (Berlin: Entsch, 1894); translated by A. H.

Schwarz as *The Battle of the Butterflies: A Play In Four Acts* (New York: Kraus, 1914);

Das Glück im Winkel: Schauspiel in drei Akten (Stuttgart: Cotta, 1896; New York: Goldmann, 1896); translated by William Ellery Leonard as *The Vale of Content* (Boston: Houghton Mifflin, 1915);

Morituri: Teja; Fritzchen; Das Ewig-Männliche (Stuttgart: Cotta, 1896); translated by Archibald Alexander as *Morituri: Three One-Act Plays* (New York: Scribners, 1910; London: Duckworth, 1912);

Fritzchen (New York: Goldmann, 1896);

Johannes: Tragödie in fünf Akten und einem Vorspiel (New York: Goldmann, 1897; Stuttgart: Cotta, 1898); translated by W. H. and Mary Harned as *Johannes, Poet-Lore*, 11, no. 2 (1899): 161-236; translated by Marshall as *John the Baptist: A Play* (London & New York: Lane, 1909);

Die drei Reiherfedern: Ein Dramatisches Gedicht in 5 Akten (New York: Lederer, 1898; Stuttgart: Cotta, 1899); translated by Helen T. Porter as *The Three Heron's Feathers, Poet-Lore*, 12, no. 2 (1900): 161-234;

Johannisfeuer: Schauspiel in vier Akten (Stuttgart: Cotta, 1900); translated by Charles Swickard as *The Fires of St. John: A Drama in Four Acts* (Boston: Luce, 1904); translated by Charlotte Porter and Helen T. Porter as *St. John's Fire, Poet-Lore*, 15, no. 4 (1904): 1-71; translated by Grace E. Polk as *St. John's Fire: A Drama in Four Acts* (Minneapolis: Wilson, 1905);

Drei Reden (Stuttgart: Cotta, 1900);

Es lebe das Leben!: Drama in fünf Akten (New York: Lederer, 1901; Stuttgart: Cotta, 1902); translated by Edith Wharton as *The Joy of Living (Es lebe das Leben): A Play in Five Acts* (New York: Scribners, 1902; London: Duckworth, 1903);

Verrohung in der Theaterkritik: Zeitgemässe Betrachtungen (Stuttgart: Cotta, 1902);

Der Sturmgeselle Sokrates: Komödie in vier Akten (New York: Herrmann, 1903; Stuttgart: Cotta, 1903);

Die Sturmgesellen: Ein Wort zur Abwehr (Berlin: Fontane, 1903);

Das Blumenboot: Schauspiel in vier Akten und einem Zwischenspiel (Stuttgart & Berlin: Cotta, 1905);

Stein unter Steinen: Schauspiel in vier Akten (Stuttgart: Cotta, 1905; New York: Herrmann, 1905);

Teja: Drama in einem Akt, edited by Herbert C. Sanborn (New York: Holt, 1905);

Rosen: Vier Einakter. Die Lichtbänder; Margot; Der letzte Besuch; Die ferne Prinzessin (Stuttgart: Cotta, 1907); translated by Grace Frank as *Roses: Four One-Act Plays* (New York: Scribners, 1909; London: Duckworth, 1912);

Das Hohe Lied: Roman (Stuttgart & Berlin: Cotta, 1908); translated by Thomas Seltzer as *The Song of Songs* (New York: Huebsch, 1909); translated by Marshall as *The Song of Songs* (London: Lane, 1913);

Strandkinder: Ein Schauspiel in vier Akten (Berlin: Bloch, 1909);

Der Bettler von Syrakus: Tragödie in fünf Akten und einem Vorspiel (Stuttgart & Berlin: Cotta, 1911);

Die indische Lilie (Stuttgart: Cotta, 1911); translated by Ludwig Lewisohn as *The Indian Lily, and Other Stories* (New York: Huebsch, 1911);

Der gute Ruf: Schauspiel in vier Akten (Stuttgart & Berlin: Cotta, 1913);

Die Lobgesänge des Claudian: Drama in fünf Aufzügen (Berlin: Vertriebsstelle des Verbandes deutscher Bühnenschriftsteller, 1913);

Die entgötterte Welt: Szenische Bilder aus kranker Zeit (Stuttgart: Cotta, 1915)—comprises *Die Freundin: Schauspiel; Die gutgeschnittene Ecke: Tragikomödie; Das höhere Leben: Lustspiel;*

Der Katzensteg: Ein deutsches Volksstück (Berlin: Vertriebsstelle des Verbandes deutscher Bühnenschriftsteller, 1916);

Die gutgeschnittene Ecke: Tragikomödie in fünf Akten (Berlin: Boll, 1916);

Litauische Geschichten (Stuttgart: Cotta, 1917)—comprises "Die Reise nach Tilsit," "Miks Bumbullis," "Jons und Erdme," "Die Magd"; translated by Lewis Galantiere as *The Excursion to Tilsit* (New York: Liveright, 1930)—comprises "The Excursion to Tilsit," "Miks Bumbullis," "Jons and Erdma," "The Hired Girl";

Der verwandelte Fächer und zwei andere Novellen (Leipzig: Reclam, 1918);

Das höhere Leben: Komödie in vier Akten (Stuttgart & Berlin: Cotta, 1919);

Romane und Novellen: Gesamt-Ausgabe in sechs Bänden, 6 volumes (Stuttgart: Cotta, 1919; revised and enlarged edition, 10 volumes (Stuttgart & Berlin: Cotta, 1930);

Die Raschhoffs: Schauspiel in fünf Akten (Stuttgart: Cotta, 1919);

Notruf: Drama in fünf Akten (Berlin: Vertriebsstelle des Verbandes deutscher Bühnenschriftsteller, 1919);

Die Freundin: Schauspiel in vier Akten (Berlin, 1920);

Jons und Erdme: Eine litauische Geschichte (Stuttgart: Cotta, 1921);

Das deutsche Schicksal: Eine vaterländische Dramenreihe (Stuttgart: Cotta, 1921)—comprises *Heilige Zeit: Szenische Bilder in vier Akten und einem Nachspiel; Opfer: Schauspiel in vier Akten; Notruf: Drama in fünf Akten;*

Das Bilderbuch meiner Jugend (Stuttgart & Berlin: Cotta, 1922); translated by Wyndham Harding as *The Book of My Youth* (London: Lane, 1923; New York & London: Harper, 1923); excerpts of *Das Bilderbuch meiner Jugend* published as *Zwischen den Wäldern: Auf eigener Scholle* (Langensalza: Beltz, 1924);

Wie die Träumenden: Schauspiel in vier Akten und einem Vorspiel (Berlin: Vertriebsstelle des Verbandes deutscher Bühnenschriftsteller, 1922);

Die Denkmalsweihe: Schauspiel in vier Akten (Berlin: Vertriebsstelle des Verbandes deutscher Bühnenschriftsteller und Bühnenkomponisten, 1923);

Dramatische Werke: Gesamtausgabe in sechs Bänden, 6 volumes (Stuttgart & Berlin: Cotta, 1923);

Der tolle Professor: Ein Roman aus der Bismarckzeit (Stuttgart & Berlin: Cotta, 1926); translated by Isabel Leighton and Otto P. Schinnerer as *The Mad Professor* (New York: Liveright, 1928; London: Lane, 1929);

Der Hasenfellhändler: Schauspiel in vier Akten (Stuttgart & Berlin: Cotta, 1927);

Die Frau des Steffen Tromholt: Roman (Stuttgart & Berlin: Cotta, 1927); translated by Eden and Cedar Paul as *The Wife of Steffen Tromholt,* 2 volumes (New York: Liveright, 1929);

Purzelchen: Ein Roman von Jugend, Tugend und neuen Tänzen (Stuttgart & Berlin: Cotta, 1928); translated by Eden and Cedar Paul as *The Dance of Youth* (New York: Liveright, 1930);

Die Entscheidung der Lissa Hart: Schauspiel in vier Akten (Berlin: Block, 1931);

Im Paradies der Heimat: Geschichten aus der Ostmark (Berlin: Francke, 1932);

Der schwankende Grund (Stuttgart: Deutsche Verlags-Expedition, 1939).

OTHER: *Deutsches Reichsblatt,* edited by Sudermann, volumes 1-2 (1881-1882);

"Mein erstes Drama: Aufsatz," in *Geschichte des Erstlingswerkes: Selbstbiographische Aufsätze*, edited by Karl Emil Franzos (Stuttgart: Cotta, 1894), pp. 269-281.

SELECTED PERIODICAL PUBLICATIONS—
UNCOLLECTED: "Zur Enthüllung des Scheffeldenkmals: Rede," *Cosmopolis*, 11 (1898): 259-264;
"Zum tollen Professor," *Vossische Zeitung* (Berlin), 7 November 1926.

Sudermann in younger years

Hermann Sudermann was considered by many of his contemporaries to be second among German naturalist writers only to the Nobel Prize-winning playwright Gerhart Hauptmann. His first drama, *Die Ehre* (performed, 1889; published, 1890; translated as *Honor*, 1915), won lavish praise when it premiered at Berlin's Lessingtheater within weeks of Hauptmann's first masterpiece, *Vor Sonnenaufgang* (1889; translated as *Before Dawn*, 1909). Sudermann is today placed among the lesser figures of turn-of-the-century German literature, perhaps because he failed to develop as a writer following his earliest successes. His preoccupation with such traditional themes as honor, fidelity, and the prodigal's return soon wearied audiences in an age of increased social consciousness and theatrical experimentation. Now his works are described as, at best, fine period pieces that generally lack modern relevance. Another reason for the decline of Sudermann's reputation was that some of the most prominent theater critics of his day, notably Alfred Kerr, Felix Maximilian Harden, and Hermann Bahr, vehemently attacked Sudermann as a plagiarist and a charlatan, with Kerr going so far as to remark that Sudermann's successes were the results of his mistakes.

Sudermann was born on 30 September 1857 at Matziken in the district of Heydekrug in Memelland, East Prussia. He was the first of four children of the brewer Johann Sudermann and Dorothea Raabe Sudermann. His father's family was of Dutch and western German Mennonite origin. Around 1857 many small-town German brewers were beginning to feel the adverse economic effects of modernization and consolidation within the trade. His own family's precarious financial condition affected Sudermann only briefly, when he was compelled to withdraw from secondary school in nearby Elbing. A short pharmacological apprenticeship followed, after which distant relatives from Russia sent him to a preparatory school in Tilsit. At eighteen Sudermann enrolled at the University of Königsberg to study modern languages and literatures. By this time he and his classmates had begun to read and discuss the works of the more radical philosophers and theorists of the day, including the physician-turned-novelist Max Nordau's *Die conventionellen Lügen der Kulturmenschheit* (1883; translated as *Conventional Lies of Our Civilization*, 1884). Sudermann's liberalism was a result of this formative period. On 31 March 1877 he left Königsberg to continue his studies at the University of Berlin. Although he enrolled in literature courses, his major interests seem to have included national economics and the history of philosophy. His academic notebooks were full of notations on lectures on positivism, materialism, early socialism, and Adam Smith, and comments from discourses by Professor Karl Eugen Dühring.

The theater attracted his attention, too. While still in Königsberg he had submitted a draft of a drama, "Die Tochter des Glücks" (The Daughter of Fortune), to the directors of the

Residenztheater in Berlin with the request that they use whatever parts of it they deemed of value. Having received no reply, Sudermann visited the theater on his arrival in the city and was handed back his manuscript minus the margins— presumably the only part considered of worth. It seems that Sudermann never tired of retelling this story once he had achieved fame, for it was recounted in several biographical profiles published during his lifetime. At the time, however, it must have come as a severe blow, particularly since he was in financial straits. That October he wrote to the Berlin author Hans Hopfen, frankly admitting his plight and begging a recommendation for "irgendeine Arbeitstellung innerhalb Berlins, die mir einen, wenn auch noch so bescheidenen Wirkungskreis eröffnet, eine Stellung, in der ich mein Leben friste, ohne jemanden zur Last zu Fallen, und deren Pflichten mir noch etwas Zeit übrig lassen, meinen Studien zu leben" (any kind of work in Berlin which offers me, modest as it may be, a position to support my existence, without being a burden to someone, where the duties still leave me with some time to pursue my studies). Hopfen himself hired the struggling student as a household tutor, with subsequent tutorial employment provided by an acquaintance in banking.

His monetary needs satisfied, Sudermann began attending sessions of the Reichstag (Parliament) in his spare time. There he met the liberal leader Heinrich Rickert, who offered him the editorship of a newly founded political weekly, the *Deutsches Reichsblatt* (German Parliamentary Newsletter). The two years (1881-1882) Sudermann spent writing and editing this periodical proved invaluable to him in that he was able to hone his literary skills while at the same time establishing useful contacts with members of Germany's ruling elite. At a time when most of his former student colleagues were still likely to be impoverished, Sudermann was being supported by affluent friends in extensive travels to Italy in 1886-1887, Silesia in 1888, and Helgoland and Italy in 1889.

It was during his first trip to Italy that Sudermann began his literary career, writing several short stories in a style that would have been appropriate for the popular bourgeois family magazine *Die Gartenlaube* (The Garden Bower). After his reputation was secured, he was to be soundly criticized for having written such drivel. Originally published in serial form, the stories were collected under the title *Im Zwielicht: Zwanglose Geschichten* (At Twilight: Unassuming Stories,

1886) by the prestigious Cotta press. But it was not until his second prose piece, the novel *Frau Sorge* (1888; translated as *Dame Care*, 1891), that the public started to take notice. A somber tale in the tradition of the nineteenth-century north German writer Fritz Reuter, it focuses on the wretched Paul Meyerhöfer, who grows up in the shadow of Frau Sorge, the personification of his family's cares and worries. To prevent his cruel father from committing arson and possibly murder, Paul burns down the family farm and faces prison. The happy ending, when Paul is released and can at last marry his lifelong love, contributed to the popularity of the book. A volume containing two short stories followed the same year. But Sudermann's reputation was not significantly advanced until the fall of the next year, when *Die Ehre* premiered at Berlin's Lessingtheater. The fortune this work brought him enabled Sudermann to live free from financial worries for the rest of his life.

Die Ehre was originally titled "Zweierlei Ehre" (Two Kinds of Honor) but was shortened at the insistence of the director Otto Brahm. Like Hauptmann's *Vor Sonnenaufgang*, it is still considered a quintessential work of German naturalism. Set in contemporary Berlin, it juxtaposes the lives of the rich, in their luxurious townhouses fronting on the broad boulevard, with those of the poor, in the ramshackle tenements directly behind. A member of the rich Mühlingk family, the vacuous Kurt, seduces Alma Heinecke of the tenements. Her well-educated brother Robert, who has just returned from serving his benefactor, Count Trast, abroad, challenges Kurt to a duel; but he is refused on the ground of his inferior status. Robert secretly begins courting Kurt's sister Lenore, who returns his affection.

The play ends happily when the unconventional and whimsical Count Trast makes Robert sole heir to his fortune. The critics were generally pleased; even the notoriously caustic Kerr praised the play, and he subsequently pronounced it part of Sudermann's "Periode des Glanzes" (period of brilliance). Only much later did some of those reassessing the play denounce it as contrived or as sentimental claptrap.

The immense success of *Die Ehre* virtually guaranteed a market for Sudermann's historical novel *Der Katzensteg* (1890; translated as *The Cats' Bridge*, 1890; translated as *Regine*, 1894). Set in East Prussia between April 1814 and June 1815, it, too, has honor as its theme. In 1807 Baron von Schranden betrays the Prussian troops who

Cartoon by H. Schlittgen from Fliegende Blätter, *no. 2650 (1896), showing Sudermann surrounded by admiring women*

are resisting the French advance: he compels the innocent young Regina Hackelberg to lead the French over the Katzensteg to attack the defenders from the rear. The subsequent wrath of the community leaves him a broken and destitute man, and his shame is shared by both his unwitting accomplice and his son Boleslav. Under an assumed name Boleslav distinguishes himself in the Prussian army in the Wars of Liberation, then returns home to bury his father. His initial contempt for the hapless Regina turns to compassion and pity, but too late to prevent her from being killed by her vengeful father. A remorseful Boleslav returns to battle and dies at Ligny. Although the attitude of unquestioning loyalty popularized by Otto von Bismarck had recently been ridiculed, most Germans of the day seem to have approved of Sudermann's sympathetic treatment.

As Sudermann's fame began to grow, so did his self-esteem. Of impressive stature, he grew an enormous beard that became not only his most distinguishing physical characteristic but also a car-

toonist's delight. A Wiesbaden barber who did not recognize his celebrated customer remarked in admiration that he had a genuine Sudermann beard. More evidence of Sudermann's waxing vanity emerges from the correspondence he maintained with his wife. Clara Lauckner (née Schulz), daughter of the mayor of Bartenstein in Prussia, had married the Königsberg waterworks director in 1885 and had borne three children by him prior to his death in 1891. A young widow with aspirations of becoming a writer, she married Sudermann on 14 October 1891. Barely six weeks thereafter Sudermann left for Paris and their extensive correspondence began. From the start the tone of their letters makes abundantly clear the subservient role Clara would play. On 4 December 1891 she wrote: "Jedenfalls gebe ich Dir nochmals die Versicherung, daß Dir nie irgendwelche Verantwortung oder Verpflichtung aus allem erwachsen soll, und ich gebe sie Dir aus wirklich liebevollem Herzen und in der Idee, Dich in der Freiheit, die Du Dir wünschest, in keiner Weise zu beeinträchtigen" (In any case I once more give you my assurance that you shall have no responsibility or obligation whatsoever, and I give you this from a truly loving heart and with the idea not to encroach in any way upon the freedom you wish for yourself). On 14 December Sudermann replied: "Wir sind nicht Eheleute wie andere, unser Bund setzt Notwendigkeiten und Bedürfnisse voraus, die in anderen Ehen nicht existieren" (We are not like other married people; our union presupposes necessities and needs not found in other marriages). A month before the birth of their only child, Hede, on 14 June 1892, Clara wrote her distant husband: "Ich will Dir schließlich nur sagen, daß ich in jeder Beziehung aus Deinem Leben schon jetzt zurücktrete. Du bist absolut frei in jeder Beziehung, frei von jeder Verantwortung" (Finally I want to tell you that I am withdrawing from your life now in every respect. You are absolutely free in every respect, free from all responsibility). Despite her subjugation, Clara Sudermann did pursue a career as a writer and, perhaps on the strength of her husband's fame, enjoyed modest success with the novels *Die Siegerin* (The Woman Victor, 1896) and *Am Glück vorbei* (Beyond Good Fortune, 1920) and the novella *An geöffneter Tür* (At the Open Door, 1913).

One contemporary critic suggested that the whole world was eagerly awaiting Sudermann's second drama, *Sodoms Ende* (performed, 1890; published, 1891) when it opened at Berlin's Lessingtheater on 5 November 1890. Even Sudermann's most ardent defenders found little to praise in it, however. The artist Willy Janikow's masterpiece, based on the biblical tale of Lot, changes from recognizable rendition into abstraction as Willy, corrupted by society women—most notably Frau Adah—seduces his foster sister and then dies of a pulmonary hemorrhage on hearing of her suicide.

Sudermann's third drama, *Heimat* (Homeland, 1893; translated as *Magda*, 1895), is considered by many to be his greatest work of naturalism. Magda, who left her father, the now retired Lieutenant Colonel von Schwartze, to pursue a career as the great prima donna dall'Orto, returns to her village, hoping for a reconciliation. Her plans are jeopardized by the revelation that she had an illegitimate child years before by the local aristocrat, Herr von Keller. Her father demands that she redeem herself through marriage, but Keller accepts the woman but not her child. When Schwartze forces the matter on his daugh-

ter at gunpoint Magda hints at other indiscretions, whereupon her father suffers a seizure and dies. Such was the immediate success of *Heimat* that virtually all of the great actresses of the period, from Eleonora Duse and Helena Modjeska to Mrs. Patrick Campbell and Sarah Bernhardt, wanted to take on the role of Magda.

The preeminent status Sudermann enjoyed among his peers at this time can be seen from his participation in the Deutsche Schriftsteller Genossenschaft (Fraternity of German Writers), which invited him to join in November 1893. The group sponsored struggling young artists, a mission continued by the Sudermann-Stiftung (Sudermann Foundation) after the writer's death, and vigorously defended artistic freedom. For the next thirty years Sudermann was deeply involved in promoting progressive cultural ideas, although he did not always subscribe to them himself.

The year 1894 brought the publication of *Es war* (It Was; translated as *The Undying Past*, 1906), a novel conceived nearly ten years before, and the publication and premiere of *Die Schmetterlingsschlacht* (translated as *The Battle of the Butterflies*, 1914), Sudermann's first attempt at comedy. Both were failures. The novel is a ponderous study in pessimism and gloom, clearly a reflection of Sudermann's darker student days; the play is a drawing-room farce about Frau Hergentheim, a woman living in genteel poverty, and her three marriageable daughters, Else, Laura, and Rosi. While the older two daughters spend their time scheming for husbands, Rosi supports the entire family by decorating and selling fans, one of which depicts the battle of the butterflies.

Attempting to ingratiate himself with his disappointed audience, Sudermann returned to a serious theme in his next play, *Das Glück im Winkel* (Modest Happiness; performed, 1895; published, 1896; translated as *The Vale of Content*, 1915). Elisabeth Wiedemann, who married for financial security, is pursued unsuccessfully by Baron von Röcknitz. In his frustration Röcknitz schemes to blackmail her by lying to her husband about an imaginary tryst. In her despair she plans to kill herself, but her husband tells her that he knows the truth and will protect her.

Das Glück im Winkel was the last Sudermann play that most critics considered of merit. Nevertheless, theater directors continued to see potential profit in the familiar name Hermann Sudermann, and many of his subsequent works were given copious stagings even after what had been termed his "brilliance" was gone. Sudermann had become a formula writer who could produce insipid, popular works at regular intervals. Although they contained a few moments of genius, most of the works during the next two decades broke little, if any, new literary ground.

A trilogy of one-act plays under the collective title *Morituri* (1896; translated, 1910) introduced audiences to Sudermann's growing interest in historical drama. *Teja* is a tragedy about the besieged king of the Goths, who learns from his bride the sweetness of life at the moment in which his death becomes certain. *Fritzchen*, a work that is reminiscent of Sudermann's first two dramas, depicts the farewell of the adored son of a retired major and his ailing wife prior to a duel of honor in which the son expects to die. *Das Ewig-Männliche* (translated as *The Eternal Masculine*)—the title is a comic reference to the expression das *Ewig-Weibliche* (the eternal feminine) in Johann Wolfgang von Goethe's *Faust II* (1832)—is a satirical comedy in verse and is fashioned like a fairy tale. The three pieces are not related either by theme or by treatment, and one might suspect that Sudermann combined them merely for convenience.

His next drama, the biblical tragedy *Johannes* (published, 1897; performed, 1898; translated, 1899), recounts the life of John the Baptist. Sudermann here forsakes naturalism for a historical epic reminiscent of the work of Friedrich Hebbel. While some critics applauded the change, Kerr was not among them: "Die Sage bringt den Täufer in Beziehungen zur Herodias; die Kirche blickt allein auf seine religiöse Sendung. Ein guter Künstler hätte beides nicht so unproportional verquickt, wie Sudermann" (The legend connects the Baptist to Herodias; the church looks only at his religious message. A good craftsman would not have mixed up the two so disproportionately as Sudermann). Other critics felt that John the Baptist was not suited to be the hero of a tragedy, while Felix Maximilian Harden argued that Sudermann had plagiarized Gustave Flaubert's story "Herodias" (1877)—a charge Sudermann vehemently denied. The play's Berlin premiere was the subject of vigorous protest and could only proceed after the emperor personally interceded.

Sudermann's next play was the dramatic poem *Die drei Reiherfedern* (published, 1898; performed, 1899; translated as *The Three Heron's Feathers*, 1900), a work similar to Hauptmann's *Die versunkene Glocke* (1897; translated as *The Sunken Bell*, 1898) and Ludwig Fulda's *Der Talisman* (1893; translated as *The Talisman*, 1912). Prince Witte wins three egret feathers, the first of which, when burned, reveals his beloved; the second brings her to him; and the third leads to her death. The central theme of the play has to do with the human failure to recognize what one truly desires and the impulse to destroy what one loves.

In *Johannisfeuer* (1900; translated as *The Fires of St. John*, 1904) Sudermann attempted to return to his earlier, more successful style and theme. Lauded by some as his best drama, it is set in the author's East Prussian homeland among the bonfires of Saint John's Eve and concerns the love triangle of the untamed Marikke, daughter of the thieving peasant woman Weszkalnene; the tormented Georg von Hartwig, heir to the Vogelreuter estate, where, like Marikke, he has been reared as part of the family; and the innocent Trude Vogelreuter, who is destined to marry Georg. Unfortunate for Sudermann was the understandable tendency of the critics to compare this work to his earliest plays. His overreliance on symbolism and his approbation of social obligation over self-fulfillment won him little praise.

As though trying to appease his reviewers, Sudermann in *Es lebe das Leben!* (published, 1901; performed, 1902; translated as *The Joy of Living*, 1902) came back to the familiar subject of Berlin's aristocracy in a drama charged with personal as well as political intrigue. In the heat of an electoral campaign old love letters revealing an affair between Beate von Kellinghausen and Baron Richard Völkerlingk, the longtime friend of her politically ambitious husband, have come to the attention of the opposition candidate. Only her suicide frees her husband from the threat of blackmail and insures his success. Interest in this work was especially keen among Berlin's theatergoers since many believed, despite Sudermann's protestations, that it was based on contemporary political figures. The critics were not so enthusiastic. Sudermann responded to their condemnation with a short essay, *Verrohung in der Theaterkritik* (Brutalization in Theater Criticism, 1902), in which he presented examples of what he considered recent abuses by the local theater critics. Their reaction was predictable: not one of his subsequent plays was to receive favorable notices.

Around the turn of the century the Sudermanns acquired a sizable country estate at Blankensee, near Trebbin, in addition to their Berlin villa. This second home provided a most peaceful retreat, although surviving correspondence suggests that the couple was rarely in residence there together. Dramas composed or completed at Blankensee in the next few years included the comedy *Der Sturmgeselle Sokrates* (Storm Companion Socrates, 1903), which was intended as a satire of misguided nationalism, the follies of democracy, and the lip service rendered to hollow idealism. The elderly dentist Albert Hartmeyer, called "Socrates" by his fellow revolutionaries in the secret society "Storm Companions," professes democratic beliefs while denying his wife any personal freedom and refusing to accept the modern clinical techniques of his older son Fritz. A younger son, Reinhold, who has defied his father by joining a social club rather than a political fraternity, returns from the university to be initiated with his brother into the secret organization. At the ceremony a former leader, the old Baron von Laucken-Neuhof, who is clearly Sudermann's mouthpiece in the drama, derides the empty rhetoric of the group. The lack of enthusiasm for the work when it debuted in Berlin in October 1903 was, for once, due more to popular misunderstanding than to the harshness of critics. The play seemed to ridicule the revolutionaries of 1848, depicting them as idiots and hypocrites, when Sudermann's target was the contemporary saber-rattling Junker class that was edging Germany ever closer to war. Somewhat similar concerns were echoed in 1981 when the play was revived as a commentary on the contemporary German reform movement.

Das Blumenboot (The Flower Boat; published, 1905; performed, 1906) is a confusing and twisted story of high society; the play dwells on the notion that love cannot exist within marriage, while at the same time passionate longing kills without marriage. *Stein unter Steinen* (A Stone among Stones, 1905) deals with problems of rehabilitation after incarceration. Struwe, a cunning and spirited repeat offender, and Biegler, a diligent and talented young man who once killed in self-defense, are employed as construction workers by the philanthropic master stonecutter Zarncke. The night watchman and the lazy but gifted sculptor Göttlingk plot to ruin the company and destroy Biegler but are foiled by him. While Biegler gains a wife and position, Struwe is banished for attempted theft. Although *Stein unter Steinen* was clearly not envisioned as "family fare" by its author, it scarcely warranted the public outcry and street demonstrations that accompanied its premiere. His next dramatic efforts, four

Sudermann in 1927; painting by Max Slevogt (Nationalgalerie, Berlin)

one-act plays published and performed under the title *Rosen* (1907; translated as *Roses*, 1909), were first staged in Vienna and Stuttgart. Neither *Rosen* nor Sudermann's next seven plays reversed the waning of his reputation as a dramatist. The historically based *Strandkinder* (Children of the Shore, 1909) and the verse tragedy *Der Bettler von Syrakus* (The Beggar from Syracuse, 1911) were among the last productions to attract more than a brief acknowledgment from reviewers.

In 1912 Kaiser Wilhelm II officially recognized Sudermann for his copious literary contributions. By this time his brand of liberalism was no longer thought of as radical, and he had become a leading cultural spokesperson for nationalistic causes. On the eve of World War I appeared *Der gute Ruf* (The Good Reputation, 1913) and *Die Lobgesänge des Claudian* (Claudian's Hymns; published, 1913; performed, 1914), which were highly reminiscent of Sudermann's earlier, more successful works. The former is a drama of conflict among urban social classes, with honor again as a principal motif; the latter is another rather unsuccessful historical depiction. Anticipating the coming war, on 1 August 1914 Sudermann wrote in his diary, "Nun kommt große Zeit. Wenn ich den Bericht dieses Monats schließe, wird das Schicksal Deutschlands sich schon zum Guten oder Schlechten gewendet haben. Weltwende wird es auf jeden Fall. Jetzt muß auch ich meinen Mann stehen" (Now comes [a] great time. By the time I complete the entry for this month, the fate of Germany will have been decided for better or for worse. In any case, it will have global consequences. Now I, too, must stand my ground).

Despite being a champion of patriotic causes—including the organization of a wartime cultural troupe, the Bund schaffender Künstler (Union of Creative Artists), for which he received the Iron Cross Second Class on 5 April 1918—Sudermann wrote one wartime drama, the trilogy *Die entgötterte Welt* (The World without God; published, 1915; performed, 1916), that bears the suggestive subtitle *Szenische Bilder aus kranker Zeit* (Scenic Tableaux from a Sick Age). There is, however, absolutely nothing unusual in the three vignettes, which deal with the progress in society of a cast of contemporary urban figures. *Die Freundin* (The Woman Friend), *Die gutgeschnittene Ecke* (The Well-Cut Corner), and *Das höhere Leben* (The Higher Life) had already been in progress before the war broke out, the collective title only being added later.

If Sudermann is still remembered for anything from this period in his career, then it is likely for his prose rather than for his dramas. The novel *Das Hohe Lied* (1908; translated as *The Song of Songs*, 1909) and the collection of short stories *Die indische Lilie* (1911; translated as *The Indian Lily, and Other Stories*, 1911) had a somewhat better reception than his concurrent plays. One of his most memorable works appeared in 1917. *Litauische Geschichten* (Lithuanian Stories; translated as *The Excursion to Tilsit*, 1930) is a collection of four short stories set in his East Prussian homeland. "Die Reise nach Tilsit" (translated as "The Excursion to Tilsit") tells of the well-to-do Lithuanian Ansas Balczus's plan to murder his wife, Indre, while in a boat under way to Tilsit. Recoiling at the last minute, he loses his life in saving hers. In "Miks Bumbullis" the foul murder of a forester is only solved when the title character confesses to the slain man's grandchild, whom he has come to love. "Jons und Erdme" (translated as "Jons and Erdma") recounts the endeavor of two smallholders to build a better life for their daughters in the desolate moors. The daughters'

laziness and ingratitude, however, lead Erdme to destroy everything, forcing their children to start from scratch. In "Die Magd" (translated as "The Hired Girl") the farmer's maid Marinke tries to drown herself after being seduced, but she is rescued and lives a happy life in a marriage with the man she loves. Many have found in this collection of stories some of Sudermann's most original and creative writing, and the book has frequently been reprinted. Next to *Die Ehre* and *Heimat*, it is his best-known work.

During the last decade of Sudermann's life the theatrical revival of some of his earliest works, including his own dramatization of *Der Katzensteg* as *Regina* (1919), was accompanied by the publication of several new novels, short stories, and plays. Among the half-dozen new dramas of the period only *Die Raschhoffs* (The Raschhoffs, 1919) gained much notice. This unpleasant little comedy about a perplexed and wayward young husband from East Prussia and his mistress in Berlin reflects a mode of behavior that was coming into serious question in post-World War I Germany. The trilogy *Das deutsche Schicksal* (The German Fate, 1921), which includes the dramas *Notruf* (Emergency Call; published separately, 1919; performed, 1921), *Heilige Zeit* (Holy Time), and *Opfer* (The Sacrifice), was Sudermann's final assessment of the war at a time when many Germans were trying to put painful memories behind; only *Notruf* was staged. His next two plays, *Wie die Träumenden* (As the Dreamers, 1922) and *Die Denkmalsweihe* (The Memorial Dedication, 1923), were originally printed by an independent literary organization in Berlin; Sudermann's publisher, Cotta, had not anticipated that the demand for copies would be very great. On the other hand, a six-volume collected edition of Sudermann's dramatic works was published by Cotta in 1923, most likely to capitalize on the continuing popularity of his earliest plays. His most notable writings of this period were, again, prose. His memoirs, *Das Bilderbuch meiner Jugend* (1922; translated as *The Book of My Youth*, 1923), and the autobiographical novels *Der tolle Professor* (1926; translated as *The Mad Professor*, 1928) and *Die Frau des Steffen Tromholt* (1927; translated as *The Wife of Steffen Tromholt*, 1929), the latter based on his own unconventional marriage and dedicated to the memory of his wife, were all popular.

Following Clara's death on 17 October 1924, sixteen days after a massive heart attack, Sudermann became increasingly reclusive. A portrait painted in honor of his seventieth birthday shows that he had forsaken his trademark beard in favor of a modest mustache. In 1926 he pointedly rejected what he felt was a long-overdue offer to join the prestigious German Academy of Arts. The same year the University of Königsberg decided against awarding him an honorary doctorate, giving one instead to the person who had nominated him. In the last year of his life he worked on several literary projects. *Der Hasenfellhändler* (The Dealer in Hare Skins; published, 1927; produced, 1928) and the posthumously published *Die Entscheidung der Lissa Hart* (Lissa Hart's Decision, 1931) were his final completed dramas. A novel, *Purzelchen: Ein Roman von Jugend, Tugend and neuen Tänzen* (Little Purzel: A Novel of Youth, Virtue and New Dances, 1928; translated as *The Dance of Youth*, 1930), and a collection of short stories were his last prose publications. Early in November 1928 he suffered a stroke from which he never recovered; he died on 21 November. His son-in-law, Hans Frentz-Sudermann, who, at Sudermann's request, had assumed the family name following marriage to Hede on 3 July 1918, reported that his final audible words were: "Children, it must be inconceivably beautiful—this eternal dreamless sleep!"

In a study of the author published the year before his death, Kurt Busse notes that Sudermann's greatest asset was his character, meaning his honesty and integrity. While he was not consistent as a writer, Sudermann was, Busse suggests, constantly underrated by the critics. Political circumstances since Sudermann's death, especially after World War II, have also contributed to his continued obscurity. His favorite themes of Heimat (homeland), Ehre (honor), Treue (faithfulness), Blut und Familienbande (blood and family ties), and Sittlichkeit (morality) have become suspect due to their appropriation and exploitation by the Nazis. While an honest appraisal of Hermann Sudermann would surely not rank him among the greatest of Germany's authors, he should be accorded his rightful place alongside many of his day who are more highly regarded and more widely read.

Letters:

Briefe Hermann Sudermanns an seine Frau (1891-1924), edited by Irmgard Leux (Stuttgart & Berlin: Cotta, 1932).

Bibliography:

Penrith Goff, "Hermann Sudermann (1857-1928)," in *Handbuch der Deutschen Literaturgeschichte, Zweite Abteilung: Bibliographien*, volume 10, edited by Paul Stapf (Bern & Munich: Francke, 1970), pp. 182-183.

Biography:

Kurt Busse, *Hermann Sudermann: Sein Werk und sein Wesen* (Stuttgart & Berlin: Cotta, 1927).

References:

Ida Axelrod, *Hermann Sudermann: Eine Studie* (Stuttgart & Berlin: Cotta, 1907);

Carl Bleibtreu, *Die Verrohung der Literatur: Ein Beitrag zur Haupt- und Sudermännerei* (Berlin: Schall & Rentel, 1903);

Thomas Duglor, ed., *Hermann Sudermann: Ein Dichter an der Grenzscheide zweier Welten (1857-1928)* (Troisdorff: Wegweiserverlag, 1958);

E. Heyse Dummer, "Hermann Sudermann: A Contributor to American Culture," *American-German Review*, 13, no. 3 (1947): 26-29;

Hans Frentz-Sudermann, "Hermann Sudermann: An Appreciation," *American-German Review*, 16 (October 1949): 24-26;

E. Beall Ginty, *Argument of Magda: Drama by H. Sudermann* (New York: Rullman, 1896);

Ludwig Goldstein, *Wer war Sudermann? Gedächtnisrede* (Königsberg: Gräfe & Unzer, 1929);

Klaus Hanson, "Hermann Sudermann," in *Critical Survey of Drama: Foreign Language Series*, volume 5, edited by Frank N. Magill (Englewood Cliffs, N.J.: Salem, 1986), pp. 1757-1770;

Otto Heller, "Hermann Sudermann," in his *Studies in Modern German Literature* (Boston: Ginn, 1905);

Theodor H. Kappstein, *Hermann Sudermann und seine 17 besten Bühnenwerke* (Berlin: Schneider, 1922);

Waldemar Kawerau, *Hermann Sudermann: Eine kritische Studie* (Magdeburg & Leipzig: Niemann, 1897);

Alfred Kerr, *Herr Sudermann, der D..Di..Dichter: Ein kritisches Vademecum* (Berlin: Helianthus, 1903);

Kerr, *Das neue Drama*, volume 1 (Berlin: Fisher, 1917), pp. 219-284;

Karl Knortz, *Sudermanns Dramen* (Halle: Mühlmann, 1908);

Ernst Koch, "The Key to Sudermann," *PMLA*,

51 (October 1936): 851-862;

Dorothea Kuhn, "Hermann Sudermann, Porträt und Selbstporträt," *Marbacher Magazin,* 10 (1978);

Kuhn, "Zum Nachlaß von Hermann Sudermann," *Jahrbuch der Deutschen Schiller-Gesellschaft,* 24 (1980): 458-470;

William F. Mainland, "Hermann Sudermann," in *German Men of Letters: Twelve Literary Essays,* volume 2, edited by Alex Natan (London: Wolff, 1963), pp. 31-53;

R. H. Mathers, "Sudermann and the Critics: An Analysis of the Criticism of Sudermann's Works and of His Revolt against Literary Criticism of His Time," Ph.D. dissertation, University of Southern California, 1951;

Anatole C. Matulis, *Lithuanian Culture in Modern German Prose Literature. Hermann Sudermann, Ernst Wiechert, and Agnes Miegel* (Vienna: Spies, 1966);

Wilhelm Matull, "Hermann Sudermann: 1857-1928," in *Große Deutsche aus Ostpreußen* (Munich: Gräfe & Unzer, 1970), pp. 168-174;

Gerhard Muschwitz, "Nachwort," in Sudermann's *Heimat: Schauspiel* (Stuttgart: Reclam, 1980), pp. 95-102;

Siegfried B. Puknat, "Mencken and the Sudermann Case," *Monatshefte,* 51 (April-May 1959): 183-189;

Walter T. Rix, ed., *Hermann Sudermann: Werk und Wirkung* (Würzburg: Königshausen & Neumann, 1980);

Hubert Walter, *Sudermann und die Franzosen* (Emsdetten: Lechte, 1930);

Elisabeth Wellner, "Gerhart Hauptmann und Hermann Sudermann im Konkurrenzkampf," Ph.D. dissertation, University of Vienna, 1949;

Paul K. Whitaker, "The Inferiority Complex in Hermann Sudermann's Life and Works," *Monatshefte,* 40 (February 1948): 69-81;

Whitaker, "A Key to Sudermann's *Die drei Reiherfedern,*" *Monatshefte,* 48 (February 1956): 78-87;

Bernd Witte, "Nachwort," in Sudermann's *Die Ehre: Schauspiel* (Stuttgart: Reclam, 1982), pp. 113-134;

Witte, "Realismus der mittleren Schicht: Zu den zwei Fassungen von Hermann Sudermanns erstem Schauspiel *Die Ehre,*" in *Literatur und Theater im Wilhelminischen Zeitalter,* edited by Hans-Peter Bayerdörfer, Karl Otto Conrady, and Helmut Schanze (Tübingen: Niemeyer, 1978), pp. 121-138.

Papers:

Manuscripts, typescripts, and correspondence of Hermann Sudermann are in the Cotta-Archiv, Schiller Nationalmuseum, Marbach am Neckar.

Fritz von Unruh
(10 May 1885 - 28 November 1970)

Volker M. Langbehn
University of California, Los Angeles

See also the Unruh entry in *DLB 56: German Fiction Writers, 1914-1945.*

PLAY PRODUCTIONS: *Jürgen Wullenweber*, Detmold, Hoftheater, 2 April 1909;
Offiziere, Berlin, Deutsches Theater, 10 November 1911;
Ein Geschlecht, Frankfurt am Main, Frankfurter Schauspielhaus, 16 June 1918;
Platz, Frankfurt am Main, Frankfurter Schauspielhaus, 3 June 1920;
Louis Ferdinand, Prinz von Preußen, Darmstadt, Hessisches Landestheater, 22 March 1921;
Stürme, Darmstadt, Darmstädter Hoftheater, 5 June 1922;
Rosengarten, Darmstadt, Darmstädter Hoftheater, 24 November 1922;
Heinrich aus Andernach, Cologne, Kölner Schauspielhaus, 5 June 1925;
Bonaparte, Frankfurt am Main, Frankfurter Schauspielhaus, 5 February 1927;
Phaea, Berlin, Deutsches Theater, 30 May 1930;
Zero, Frankfurt am Main, Frankfurter Schauspielhaus, 7 May 1932;
Wilhelmus, Prinz von Oranien, Constance, 29 October 1952;
Duell an der Havel, Wiesbaden, Staatstheater, March 1954.

BOOKS: *Offiziere: Ein Drama* (Berlin: Reiß, 1911);
Louis Ferdinand, Prinz von Preußen: Ein Drama (Berlin: Reiß, 1913; New York: Oxford University Press, 1933);
Vor der Entscheidung: Ein Gedicht (Berlin: Reiß, 1914);
Ein Geschlecht: Eine Tragödie (Leipzig: Wolff, 1917);
Opfergang (Berlin: Reiß, 1919); translated by C. A. Macartney as *Way of Sacrifice* (New York: Knopf, 1928);
Platz: Ein Spiel; Zweiter Teil der Trilogie Ein Geschlecht (Munich: Wolff, 1920);
Rosengarten (Munich: Wolff, 1921);

Fritz von Unruh

Stirb und Werde: Eine Ansprache zur Frankfurter Goethewoche (Frankfurt am Main: Englert & Schlosser, 1922);
Stürme: Ein Schauspiel (Munich: Wolff, 1922);
Vaterland und Freiheit: Eine Ansprache an die deutsche Jugend (Berlin: Schneider, 1923);
Reden (Frankfurt am Main: Frankfurter Societäts-Buchdruckerei, 1924);
Flügel der Nike: Buch einer Reise (Frankfurt am Main: Frankfurter Societäts-Buchdruckerei, 1925);
Bonaparte: Ein Schauspiel (Frankfurt am Main: Societäts-Buchdruckerei, 1927); translated

by Edwin Björkmann as *Bonaparte: A Drama* (New York: Knopf, 1928);

Phaea: Eine Komödie (Berlin: Bloch, 1930);

Zero: Eine Komödie (Frankfurt am Main: Societäts-Verlag, 1932);

Politeia, edited by Ernst Adolf Dreyer (Paris & Vienna: Bergis, 1933);

Europa erwache! Rede gehalten am Europa-Tag in Basel, 17. Mai 1936 (Basel: Verlagsgenossenschaft der Europa-Union, 1936);

Seid wachsam! Eine Goethe-Rede (Frankfurt am Main: Kramer, 1945);

The End Is Not Yet! A Novel of Hatred and Love; of Darkness and Light; of Despair and Hope; Death and Life; of War and a New Courage, translated by Willard R. Trask (New York: Storm, 1947); original German version published as *Der nie verlor: Roman von Haß und Liebe, Dunkelheit und Licht, Verzweiflung und Hoffnung, von Kreig und einem neuen Mut* (Bern: Hallwag, 1948);

Friede auf Erden! Peace on Earth! (Frankfurt am Main: Kramer, 1948);

Rede an die Deutschen: Mit einem Geleitwort von Eugen Kogon (Frankfurt am Main: Verlag der Frankfurter Hefte, 1948);

The Saint: A Novel, translated by Trask (New York: Random House, 1950); original German version published as *Die Heilige: Roman* (Brunswick: Kleine, 1952);

Fürchtet nichts: Roman (Cologne: Comel, 1952);

Wilhelmus, Prinz von Oranien: Ein Drama (Cologne: Comel, 1953);

Duell an der Havel: Ein Schauspiel (Berlin: Krüger, 1954);

Mächtig seid ihr nicht in Waffen: Reden (Nuremberg: Carl, 1957);

Der Sohn des Generals: Roman (Nuremberg: Carl, 1957);

Dramen: Bonaparte, Louis Ferdinand, Bismarck, Offiziere, Phaea (Nuremberg: Carl, 1960);

Wir wollen Frieden: Die Reden und Aufrufe 1960/61 (Düsseldorf: Monitor, 1961);

Friede in den USA? Ein Traum (Ulm: Hess, 1967);

Odysseus auf Ogygia (Frankfurt am Main: Societäts-Verlag, 1968);

Kaserne und Sphinx (Frankfurt am Main: Societäts-Verlag, 1969);

Sämtliche Werke, 7 volumes published, edited by Hanns Martin Elster (Berlin: Haude & Spener, 1970-   ).

Fritz von Unruh was one of the best-known and most outspoken dramatists of the German ex-pressionist movement. His career began with a work that glorified Prussian militarism, but his experiences in World War I made him a pacifist. In many impassioned speeches he opposed the rapidly expanding war machine and spoke out against fanatical nationalism. Despite later criticism of his style, which remained virtually unchanged since the height of his fame during the period 1910 to 1920, his contribution to the expressionist movement remains an important one.

Fritz Wilhelm Ernst von Unruh was born on 10 May 1885 in Koblenz. His father, Karl von Unruh, a Protestant and a colonel in the Prussian infantry, insisted that his sons be brought up as Protestants; his daughters were brought up in the Catholic faith of their mother, Mathilde Klehe von Unruh. The value that Unruh's parents attached to religious instruction is reflected in all of his works. Educated in a cadet corps in Plön, Schleswig-Holstein, Unruh received the typical education given to the elite of the Wilhelminian era, a schooling that demanded discipline and absolute obedience to the emperor. The repressive atmosphere of these years resulted in a suicide attempt by Unruh.

During his time in Plön, Unruh wrote his first drama, *Jürgen Wullenweber*, which was staged on 2 April 1909 at the Hoftheater (Court Theater) in Detmold. Set in the sixteenth century, *Jürgen Wullenweber* depicts a man in inner conflict between military heroism and humanism. His second drama, *Offiziere* (Officers; published, 1911) was produced by Max Reinhardt at the Deutsches Theater (German Theater) in Berlin on 10 November 1911. It, too, shows Unruh's doubts about the military system. In this play Schlichting, an officer, disobeys the order of a superior and rebels against the stiff and outmoded tradition of the Prussian army. His disobedience is meant to revitalize the static nature of the military hierarchy. Unruh's play ultimately glorifies Prussian militarism. Nevertheless, official displeasure led to Unruh's resignation from the military to become a free-lance writer.

His third drama was *Louis Ferdinand, Prinz von Preußen* (Louis Ferdinand, Prince of Prussia; published, 1913). Describing the fall of the Prussian monarchy during the Napoleonic wars, the play once again voiced strong warnings against militaristic ambition while still glorifying the imperial system. The planned premiere was forbidden by Kaiser Wilhelm II not only because of the play's political tone but also because of a law that prohibited showing members of the royal family onstage.

When World War I broke out Unruh enlisted in the cavalry. Experiencing the horrors of modern warfare firsthand caused a profound change in him: from the patriotic glorification of war he turned to an open condemnation of it. The poem *Vor der Entscheidung* (Before the Decision, 1914) was his first clear antiwar statement. The poem was circulated in the trenches and resulted in Unruh's being brought before a court-martial, but he was acquitted. Switzerland awarded the Bodmer Prize to Unruh for the poem in 1917, the first time the honor had ever been bestowed on a foreigner. Despite his outspokenness, in August 1917 Unruh informed his publisher: "Es wird Sie interessieren, daß ich Rittmeister geworden bin" (It will interest you [to know] that I have become a cavalry captain).

Ein Geschlecht (A Race; published, 1917; performed, 1918), the first in a projected trilogy of verse plays, shows the dehumanizing effect of the war and the vision of a new and better world. The action of the one-act tragedy takes place on a knoll overlooking a small military cemetery. Although the imperial censor forbade the performance of the work, some critics, artists, and politicians managed to stage a private showing at the Frankfurter Schauspielhaus (Frankfurt Playhouse) on 16 June 1918. The drama was dedicated to Unruh's younger brother, Erich, who had been killed in battle in 1915. In 1920 Unruh was awarded the Das Junge Deutschland (Young Germany) prize for the work; in 1922, three years after its performance at the Burgtheater in Vienna, he received the Austrian Grillparzer Prize. Part two of the trilogy, *Platz* (Square), followed in 1920; but part three, "Dietrich," remained a fragment and was never published.

This period in German literary history was the heyday of expressionism, and Unruh, along with such writers as Ernst Toller and Georg Kaiser, was one of its best-known dramatists. Their plays described decay, war, and the end of the world but also showed the possibility of new beginnings and happiness. The expressionists, strongly influenced by the philosophy of Friedrich Nietzsche, perceived themselves as the proclaimers and representatives of a new time, and a radical antibourgeois attitude was fundamental to their writings. Unruh led them in promoting the relationship between writing and the quest for political change.

Scene from the premiere of Unruh's Ein Geschlecht *in Frankfurt am Main in 1918*

Before helping to found the Republican party and winning a seat in the Reichstag in 1924, Unruh wrote two more dramas that present his vision of world harmony. *Stürme* (Storms, 1922) focuses on a noble-minded young prince who has plans for the improvement of the world. *Stürme* is heavy with rhetoric and has great variety in its structure, reflecting the obstacles the protagonist must overcome in finding a new system of living. The play premiered on 5 June 1922 at the Darmstädter Hoftheater (Darmstadt Court Theater) under the direction of Gustav Hartung. Again under the direction of Hartung, *Rosengarten* (Rose Garden, 1921) premiered on 24 November 1922 at the same theater. Unruh's main motifs are present: the unifying power of love, the renewal of humanity, and the demand that mankind renounce war.

Heinrich aus Andernach (Henry from Andernach, 1925), a festival play written at the request of the city of Cologne for the celebration of the millennium of the Rhineland, shows the conflict between the French and the Germans. Heinrich, a winegrower, is anxious for revenge against a French occupation soldier who beat him with a whip. But Heinrich is reminded by a blind soldier of the tragedies that were perpetrated on French civilians by German soldiers, and he gives up his hatred and embraces peace. The drama drew an enthusiastic response. In 1926 Unruh received the Schiller Prize.

In Unruh's *Bonaparte* (1927; translated, 1928) the Bourbon prince Enghien, Napoleon's rival for the French throne, is imprisoned because he is suspected of conspiring against the French Republic. Prince Enghien's mother tries to help her son by appealing to Napoleon as the embodiment of justice and the ultimate representative of the ideals of the French Revolution. But Napoleon does not listen to her desperate pleas; greedy for power, he orders the execution of the prince, whose guilt was never proven. Although Napoleon appears to be the victor, it is clear to the viewer that the dictator has been vanquished by his lust for power.

The comedy *Phaea* (1930), directed by Reinhardt, premiered on 30 May 1930 at the Deutsches Theater. The title is the acronym for Photographisch-Akkustische-Experimentelle-Aktiengesellschaft (Photographic-Acoustic Experimental-Stock Corporation); the play is a harsh attack on the German film industry, which Unruh considered reactionary and which he felt manipulated the masses.

The steady rise of the Nazis brought forth Unruh's most passionate and best-known speech against war and fascism, presented before twenty-four thousand people at the Berlin Sports Palace on 18 January 1932. In the address, titled "Die Front des Reiches" (The Forward Line of Defense of the Reich), Unruh said that "Die deutsche Republik ist für uns keine politische Phrase, sondern eine sittliche Forderung" (The German Republic for us is not a mere political phrase but a moral demand) and called for an "eiserne Front" (iron front) against war and fascism.

Zero (1932) was Unruh's last play that could be performed in Germany before World War II. At the premiere of this political comedy at the Frankfurter Schauspielhaus on 7 May 1932 under the direction of Alvin Kronacher, when the line "Deutschland will Raum" (Germany needs space) was responded to with "Dann wird es untergehen!" (Then it will perish!), chaos broke out in the theater. Unruh, with his fist in the air, went on stage and screamed at the audience: "Auf dem Potsdamer Platz werden Schafe weiden!" (Sheep will graze on Potsdamer Square! [Berlin's busiest square at the time]). The next day the Nazis demanded the cancellation of Unruh's right, as a veteran, to lifetime residence in the Frankfurter Rententurm, and the comedy was banned. Threatening letters forced him to move to Zoagli, Italy. After the Nazis came to power in 1933, Unruh was expelled from the Prussian Academy of Art for refusing to sign a pro-Nazi statement distributed by the writer Gottfried Benn. On 10 May 1933 the Nazis included his works in their bonfires.

In 1935 Italian Fascists raided his house in Zoagli because of his refusal to support Benito Mussolini. He fled to Menton, France, where he lived with distant relatives. In 1939 he moved to Arcachon, near Bordeaux. In May 1936 seven thousand people attended Unruh's speech, *Europa erwache!* (Europe Awake!), in Basel. It ended with a call to prevent war "Eh' es für immer zu spät [ist]" (Before it [is] forever too late). In 1938 he was stripped of his German citizenship, and his property was confiscated.

As a German refugee, Unruh was interned by the French government when the war broke out. During his confinement in Camp Libourne on the Dordogne he wrote a series of essays about camp life that were to be part of a planned autobiographical novel. When German troops approached Bordeaux in June 1940, the French authorities closed the camp and allowed the inmates to flee. Unruh had to leave his manuscripts behind; they would be discovered and sent to him in 1952. In Málaga, Spain, the American consul issued emergency visas via telegram enabling Unruh and his wife, the former Friederike Schaller, whom he had married in 1940, to leave for the United States. On 10 August 1940 they arrived in New York. To get permission to settle in the United States, Unruh cited his writings at a hearing in Washington, D.C., as proof of his democratic convictions. His immigration was supported by other prominent German refugees, among them Albert Einstein and Thomas Mann.

Manfred George, publisher of the New York exile magazine *Aufbau* (Reconstruction), provided Unruh with a small income by buying some of his poems. Unruh also received limited financial support from the Emergency Rescue Committee and the American Committee for Christian Refugees. Rediscovering an old interest, Unruh held an exhibition of his paintings at the Galerie St. Etienne in New York in November 1947. None of the twenty-five paintings were sold during the show, but Unruh claimed that some were later purchased privately.

Unruh's attempts to gain public recognition in America through his dramas failed. A few of his early works, including *Phaea*, were performed as experimental plays at the Dramatic Workshop of the New School for Social Research in New York, but none were produced commercially. Unruh continued to write theater works that were neither produced nor published, among them "Miss Rollschuh" (Miss Rollerskate) and "Gefängnis" (Prison). Denied access to the stage, he turned to prose. The first result was the translated novel *The End Is Not Yet!* (1947); the original German version was published in Switzerland in 1948 as *Der nie verlor* (He Who Never Lost). The work proved to be a financial disaster for Storm Publishers, which was run by Unruh's friend Alexander Goede von Aesch. His other novel published in the United States, *The Saint* (1950; original German version published as *Die Heilige*, 1952), was also unsuccessful.

Postwar Germany had begun to pay tribute to its authors in exile; Unruh received the Wilhelm Raabe Prize in Brunswick in 1946 and the Goethe Prize in Frankfurt in 1948. In 1952 he returned to Germany, where his drama *Wilhelmus, Prinz von Oranien* (William, Prince of Orange; published, 1953) was staged in Constance on 29 October; the work was unsuccessful and failed to reestablish him as a dramatist. The play, which deals with the War of Liberation in the Netherlands in the sixteenth century, is obscure and cluttered with Spanish, Italian, French, and Latin phrases.

At the end of 1953 the Fritz von Unruh Society was founded in West Germany. The society aimed to find a publisher for Unruh's complete works and to reestablish his reputation. In 1954 Unruh was unanimously selected to become a member of the Literary Society of the Hague because of his contribution to the promotion of understanding between nations. In March of that year the Staatstheater (State Theater) of Wiesbaden premiered Unruh's play *Duell an der Havel* (Duel on the Havel; published, 1954), in which contemporary issues are symbolized through historical tableaux. Frederick the Great, the powerful Prussian king, is visited by Colder, the head of an American trade delegation representing George Washington. The absolutism of the aristocratic Old World thus collides with the freedom

Scene from the premiere of Unruh's Platz, *the sequel to* Ein Geschlecht, *in Frankfurt am Main in 1920*

and democracy of the New. As had been the case with *Wilhelmus, Prinz von Oranien*, the play did not make it beyond the premiere, despite a rousing opening night. Also in 1954 Unruh wrote *Bismarck*, which was included in a collection of his dramas published in 1960. Never staged, the comedy portrays the conflict between the Prussian nobleman Otto von Bismarck and the democrat Onog as symbolic of the struggle of a reform-minded leader who cannot escape the prejudices of his environment. Unruh urged the director Erwin Piscator, who had also returned to West Germany from exile, to stage his plays, but Piscator declined because he felt that Unruh's dramatic style was hopelessly outdated.

Despite all his failures of the postwar years, Unruh was awarded the Great Service Cross of the Federal Republic and the Schiller Prize in 1955. Also in 1955 the city of Düsseldorf invited Unruh to give a memorial speech to young people on the occasion of the 150th anniversary of

Friedrich Schiller's death. At the last moment the youthful crowd was turned away, and the teachers of the Rhineland were ordered to come to Düsseldorf instead: the authorities feared that the controversial writer's speech might cause unrest. Despite this insult, Unruh gave the speech; but he added some harsh introductory remarks: "Wenn wir etwa schon wieder da angelangt sein sollten, wo einer wie ich, der im Trommelfeuer von Verdun 1916 seinen 'Opfergang' schrieb, und dessen Bücher das Hitler-Regime verbrannte, daß der jetzt in der demokratisch-schwarzrotgoldenen Bundesrepublik nicht mehr zur Jugend sprechen darf, weil sonst 'Wirbel von Angst' entstünde, dann rufen Sie sich bitte den deutschen Dichter, der (falls es solch einen gibt) irgendwem zu Gefallen reden kann! Ich jedenfalls kann es nicht!" (If we should have arrived at a point again, where someone like me, who wrote his *Opfergang* [1919; translated as *Way of Sacrifice*, 1928] in the artillery fire of Verdun in 1916, and whose books were burned by the Hitler regime, is no longer allowed in this democratic black, red, and gold Federal Republic to talk to the youth because it would cause a 'tornado of fear,' then please try to find a German poet who [if he exists at all] will tell you only what you want to hear. I cannot do it!).

Later that year Unruh returned to New York, disillusioned with the new Germany. In 1956 he moved to the French Riviera. For the next five years he spent most of his time in Europe, returning to his Riverside Drive apartment in New York for the winter months. In 1961 he moved to Atlantic City, New Jersey.

The destruction of his house in Atlantic City in 1962 by a flood resulted in Unruh's return to his family estate at Diez. He received the Kogge Literature Prize in 1963 and the Carl von Ossietzky Medal in 1966, and in 1967 he was made an honorary member of the German Academy for Language and Literature.

Unruh's last drama to be published was *Odysseus auf Ogygia* (Odysseus on Ogygia, 1968) which was given a reading at the West Berlin Academy of Art. He died on 28 November 1970 in Diez. Unruh's works are largely ignored by literary scholars today. But as Edith J. R. Isaacs wrote in 1947: "Perhaps some happy day, a new generation of Germans will read von Unruh and know what their ancestors missed by not listening to him. The plays are, truly, like prophecies. They might not play well in our swift-moving theaters; the speeches are too long, the action too slow.

Yet they have a concentration of beauty and power in their poetry or prose and a message of brotherhood among men which the world could well use today."

References:

Manfred Durzak, *Das expressionistische Drama: Ernst Barlach—Ernst Toller—Fritz von Unruh, 1904-1921* (Munich: Nymphenburger Verlagsgesellschaft, 1979);

Durzak, "Fritz von Unruh," in *Expressionismus als Literatur: Gesammelte Studien*, edited by Wolfgang Rothe (Bern: Francke, 1969), pp. 490-505;

Petra Goder, "Moralist der Appelle: Zur Exilproblematik im Werk Fritz von Unruhs," in *Die deutsche Exilliteratur 1933-1945*, edited by Durzak (Stuttgart: Reclam, 1973), pp. 499-508;

Alexander Gode von Aesch, "Fritz von Unruh," *Germanic Review*, 23 (April 1948): 149-154;

Ina Götz, *Tradition und Utopie in den Dramen Fritz von Unruhs* (Bonn: Bouvier, 1975);

Edith J. R. Isaacs, "Fritz von Unruh: Hero, Apostle and Poet," *Theatre Arts*, 31 (February 1947): 33;

Dieter Kasang, *Wilhelminismus und Expressionismus: Das Frühwerk Fritz von Unruhs 1904-1921* (Stuttgart: Akademischer Verlag Hans-Dieter Heinz, 1980);

Alvin Kronacher, *Fritz von Unruh* (New York: Schick, 1946);

Walter F. Mainland, "Fritz von Unruh," in *German Men of Letters*, edited by Alex Natan, volume 3 (London: Wolff, 1964), pp. 153-175;

Friederich Rasche, ed., *Fritz von Unruh: Rebell und Verkünder. Der Dichter und sein Werk* (Frankfurt am Main: Büchergilde Gutenberg, 1965);

Günther E. Salter, "Christian Symbolism and Concepts in Fritz von Unruh's Works," Ph.D dissertation, Vanderbilt University, 1970.

Papers:

Fritz von Unruh's letters, papers, and manuscripts are in the Storm Archives, State University of New York at Albany; and the Schiller-Nationalarchiv, Deutsches Literaturarchiv (Schiller National Archive, German Literature Archive), Marbach am Neckar, Germany.

Frank Wedekind

(24 July 1864 - 9 March 1918)

Steve Dowden
Yale University

PLAY PRODUCTIONS: *Der Erdgeist*, Leipzig, Krystall-Palast, 25 February 1898;

Der Kammersänger, Berlin, Neues Theater, 10 December 1899;

Der Marquis von Keith, Berlin, Residenztheater, 11 October 1901;

So ist das Leben, Munich, Schauspielhaus, 22 February 1902; revised as *König Nicolo oder So ist das Leben*, Leipzig, Schauspielhaus, 15 January 1919;

Liebstrank, Nuremberg, Intimes Theater, 24 October 1903;

Die Büchse der Pandora: Eine Tragödie in drei Aufzügen, Nuremberg, Intimes Theater, 1 February 1904;

Karl Hetmann: Der Zwerg-Riese, Munich, Schauspielhaus, 18 February 1905;

Lulu, Nuremberg, Intimes Theater, 18 April 1905;

Totentanz, Nuremberg, Intimes Theater, 2 May 1906; revised as *Tod und Teufel*, Berlin, Künstlerhaus Werkstatt der Werdenden, 29 April 1912;

Frühlings Erwachen, Berlin, Kammerspiele des Deutschen Theaters, 22 November 1906;

Musik, Nuremberg, Intimes Theater, 11 January 1908;

Die junge Welt, Munich, Schauspielhaus, 22 April 1908;

Die Zensur, Munich, Schauspielhaus, 27 July 1909;

Der Stein der Weisen, Vienna, Kleine Bühne, 23 January 1911;

Oaha: Die Satire der Satire, Munich, Lustspielhaus, 23 December 1911; revised as *Till Eulenspiegel*, Munich, Kammerspiele, 1 December 1916;

Franziska, Munich, Münchner Kammerspiele, 30 November 1912;

Simson oder Scham und Eifersucht, Berlin, Lessingtheater, 24 January 1914;

Felix und Galothea, Munich, Unionsaal, 25 July 1914;

Frank Wedekind in 1894

Der Schnellmaler oder Kunst und Mammon, Munich, Kammerspiele, 29 July 1916;

Schloß Wetterstein, Zurich, Pfauentheater, 17 November 1917;

Elins Erweckung, Hamburg, Kammerspiele, 16 March 1919;

Herakles, Munich, Prinzregententheater, 1 September 1919;

Das Sonnenspektrum, Berlin, Tribune, 23 September 1922;

Bismarck, Weimar, Deutsches Nationaltheater, 30 October 1926;

Die Büchse der Pandora: Eine Monstretragödie, Hamburg, Deutsches Schauspielhaus, 13 February 1988.

BOOKS: *Der Schnellmaler oder Kunst und Mammon: Große tragikomische Original-Charakterposse* (Zurich: Schabelitz, 1889);

Frühlings Erwachen: Eine Kindertragödie (Zurich: Gross, 1891); translated by Francis J. Ziegler as *The Awakening of Spring* (Philadelphia: Brown, 1909); translated by Samuel A. Eliot, Jr., as *Spring's Awakening*, in *Tragedies of Sex* (London: Henderson, 1923; New York: Boni & Liveright, 1923), pp. 1-110; translated by Frances Fawcett and Stephen Spender as *Spring's Awakening*, in *Five Tragedies of Sex* (London: Vision, 1952; New York: Theatre Arts, 1952), pp. 29-96; translated by Tom Osborn as *Spring Awakening* (London: Calder & Boyars, 1969); translated by Edward Bond as *Spring Awakening* (London: Methuen, 1980); translated by Eric Bentley as *Spring's Awakening*, in *Before Brecht*, edited by Bentley (New York: Applause, 1985);

Kinder und Narren: Lustspiel in vier Aufzügen (Munich: Warth, 1891); revised as *Die junge Welt: Komödie in drei Aufzügen und einem Vorspiel* (Paris: Langen, 1896);

Der Erdgeist: Eine Tragödie (Munich, Paris & Leipzig: Langen, 1895); translated by Eliot as *Erdgeist (Earth-Spirit): A Tragedy in Four Acts* (New York: Boni, 1914); translated by Spender as *Earth-Spirit*, in *Five Tragedies of Sex*, pp. 97-210; translated by Carl Richard Mueller as *Earth Spirit*, in *The Lulu Plays* (Greenwich, Conn.: Fawcett, 1967), pp. 27-106;

Die Fürstin Russalka (Munich: Langen, 1897); translated by Frederick Eisemann as *Princess Russalka* (Boston: Luce, 1919);

Der Liebestrank: Schwank in drei Aufzügen (Paris: Langen, 1899);

Der Kammersänger: Drei Szenen (Paris, Leipzig & Munich: Langen, 1899); translated by Albert Wilhelm Boesche as *The Court Singer*, in *The German Classics of the Nineteenth and Twentieth Centuries*, volume 20, edited by Kuno Francke and William G. Howard (New York: German Publication Society, 1914), pp. 360-397;

Der Marquis von Keith (Münchner Scenen): Schauspiel in fünf Aufzügen (Munich: Langen, 1901); translated by Beatrice Gottlieb as *The Marquis of Keith*, in *From the Modern Repertoire*, edited by Bentley, second series (Denver: University of Denver Press, 1952), pp. 123-176; translated by Mueller as *The Marquis of Keith*, in *Masterpieces of the Modern German Theater*, edited by Robert W. Corrigan (New York: Collier, 1967), pp. 236-310;

So ist das Leben: Schauspiel in fünf Akten (Munich: Langen, 1902); translated by Ziegler as *Such Is Life* (Philadelphia: Brown, 1912); revised as *König Nicolo oder So ist das Leben: Schauspiel in drei Aufzügen und neun Bildern, mit einem Prolog* (Munich: Müller, 1911); translated by Martin Esslin as *King Nicolo, or Such is Life*, in *The Genius of the German Theater*, edited by Esslin (New York: New American Library, 1968), pp. 459-522;

Mine-Haha oder Über die körperliche Erziehung der jungen Mädchen: Aus Helene Engels schriftlichem Nachlaß herausgegeben (Munich: Langen, 1903);

Die Büchse der Pandora: Tragödie in drei Aufzügen (Berlin: Cassirer, 1904; revised, 1906; revised edition, Munich: Müller, 1911); translated by Eliot as *Pandora's Box* (New York: Boni, 1914); translated by Spender as *Pandora's Box*, in *Five Tragedies of Sex*, pp. 211-302; translated by Mueller as *Pandora's Box*, in *The Lulu Plays*, pp. 107-166;

Hidalla oder Sein und Haben: Schauspiel in fünf Akten (Munich: Marchlewski, 1904); revised as *Karl Hetmann, der Zwerg-Riese (Hidalla): Schauspiel in fünf Akten* (Munich: Müller, 1911);

Die vier Jahreszeiten: Gedichte (Munich: Langen, 1905);

Totentanz: Drei Szenen (Munich: Langen, 1906); revised as *Tod und Teufel (Totentanz): Drei Szenen* (Berlin: Cassirer, 1909); translated by Eliot as *Damnation!*, in *Tragedies of Sex*, pp. 303-347; translated by Spender as *Death and Devil*, in *Five Tragedies of Sex*, pp. 303-336;

Feuerwerk: Erzählungen (Munich: Langen, 1906)— includes "Der greise Freier," translated by Ziegler as *The Grisley Suitor* (Philadelphia: Brown, 1911);

Die Zensur: Theodizee in einem Akt (Berlin: Cassirer, 1908);

Musik: Sittengemälde in vier Bildern (Munich: Langen, 1908);

Oaha: Schauspiel in fünf Aufzügen (Berlin: Cassirer, 1908); revised as *Till Eulenspiegel: Komödie in vier Aufzügen* (Munich: Müller, 1916);

Der Stein der Weisen: Eine Geisterbeschwörung (Berlin: Cassirer, 1909); revised as *Der Stein der Weisen oder Laute, Armbrust und Peitsche: Eine Geisterbeschwörung* (Munich: Müller, 1920);

In allen Satteln gerecht: Komödie in einem Aufzug (Munich & Leipzig: Müller, 1910);

Schauspielkunst: Ein Glossarium (Munich & Leipzig: Müller, 1910); translated by Mueller as

"The Art of Acting: A Glossary," in *The Modern Theatre*, edited by Corrigan (New York: Macmillan, 1964), pp. 126-159;

In allen Sätteln gerecht: Komödie in einem Aufzug (Munich & Leipzig: Müller, 1910);

In allen Wassern gewaschen: Tragödie in einem Aufzug (Munich: Müller, 1910);

Mit allen Hunden gehetzt: Schauspiel in einem Aufzug (Munich: Müller, 1910);

Felix und Galathea (Berlin: Meyer, 1911);

Franziska: Ein modernes Mysterium in fünf Akten (Munich: Müller, 1912);

Schloß Wetterstein: Schauspiel in drei Akten (Munich: Müller, 1912); translated by Spender as *Castle Wetterstein*, in *Five Tragedies of Sex*, pp. 337-434;

Lulu: Tragödie in fünf Aufzügen mit einem Prolog (Munich & Leipzig: Müller, 1913);

Simson oder Scham und Eifersucht: Dramatisches Gedicht in drei Akten (Munich: Müller, 1914);

Bismarck: Historisches Schauspiel in fünf Akten (Munich: Müller, 1916);

Herakles: Dramatisches Gedicht in drei Akten (Munich: Müller, 1917);

Überfürchtenichts (Munich: Müller, 1917);

Lautenlieder: 53 Lieder mit eigenen und fremden Melodien, edited by Artur Kutscher (Berlin: Drei Masken, 1920);

Rabbi Esra (Munich: Müller, 1924);

Ein Genußmensch: Schauspiel in vier Aufzügen (Munich: Müller, 1924);

Das arme Mädchen: Ein Chanson (Lindau: Thorbecke, 1948);

Chansons (Munich: Desch, 1951);

Gedichte und Chansons (Frankfurt am Main & Hamburg: Bücherei, 1968);

Die Tagebücher: Ein erotisches Leben, edited by Gerhard Hay (Frankfurt am Main: Athenäum, 1986);

Die Büchse der Pandora: Eine Monstretragödie, edited by Peter Zadek (Hamburg: Programmbuch des Deutschen Schauspielhauses, 1988).

Collections: *Gesammelte Werke*, 9 volumes, edited by Artur Kutscher and Joachim Friedenthal (Munich: Müller, 1912-1921);

Ausgewählte Werke, edited by Fritz Strich (Berlin: Volksverband der Bücherfreunde, 1923);

Werke in drei Bänden, 3 volumes, edited by Manfred Hahn (Berlin: Aufbau, 1969).

Editions in English: *Rabbi Ezra; The Victim: Two Stories*, translated by Francis J. Ziegler (Philadelphia: Brown, 1911);

Tragedies of Sex, translated by Samuel A. Eliot, Jr.

(London: Henderson, 1923; New York: Boni & Liveright, 1923);

Five Tragedies of Sex, translated by Frances Fawcett and Stephen Spender (London: Vision, 1952; New York: Theatre Arts, 1952); reprinted without *Spring's Awakening* as *The Lulu Plays & Other Sex Tragedies*, translated by Spender (London: Calder & Boyars, 1972; New York: Riverrun, 1977);

The Lulu Plays, translated by Carl Richard Mueller (Greenwich, Conn.: Fawcett, 1967).

OTHER: "Die Furcht vor dem Tode," in *Frank Wedekind und das Theater* (Berlin: Drei Masken, 1915), pp. 83-84.

SELECTED PERIODICAL PUBLICATION—UNCOLLECTED: *Die Büchse der Pandora: Eine Monstretragödie*, *Theater heute*, 17 (April 1988): 42-57.

From the standpoint of attitudes about women and eroticism, modernist sensibilities can be dated from Jack the Ripper's internationally notorious sex murders in 1888. His widely publicized crimes seized the imagination of all Europe, suddenly thrusting into public view a world that Wilhelmine Germany, like Victorian and Edwardian England, had passed over in silence. In the popular imagination the Ripper soon came to symbolize the demonic claims of sexual instinct, aggression, and domination, the destructive passions that seemed to threaten the orderly conduct of middle-class life. These same themes quickly spanned the geography of literary modernism, from D. H. Lawrence's England to Arthur Schnitzler's Austria-Hungary. In the German theater they are above all associated with the work of Frank Wedekind, whose well-known femme fatale, Lulu, dies horribly at the hands of Jack the Ripper.

In his most enduring works, *Frühlings Erwachen* (published, 1891; performed, 1906; translated as *The Awakening of Spring*, 1909) and the two Lulu plays, Wedekind probed sexual topics on the German stage with greater frankness and more humor than the naturalists had. Naturalism dominated German theater when Wedekind began making his mark in the 1890s, and its most celebrated representatives were Henrik Ibsen and Gerhart Hauptmann. But in its emphasis on social facts, detached objectivity, and a more or less scientist realism, the naturalist

Final scene of the 1906 Berlin production of Wedekind's Frühlings Erwachen, *with Wedekind as the man in the mask*

movement belonged to the nineteenth century. Though Wedekind shared its spirit of enlightenment and demystification, his aesthetic is that of nascent modernism. Not only does he favor sexual instinct and the irrational as thematic material and alienated nonconformists as heroes but he also begins the modernist break with the conventions of realistic representation on the stage. Wedekind's mannered, tragicomic style helped cut a path toward the spiritual style of expressionism, the alienation effects of Bertolt Brecht, and the tragicomic satire of Friedrich Dürrenmatt and Max Frisch. Wedekind's antipsychological theater made effective use of various nonrealistic devices—such as the grotesque, the fantastic, and highly stylized and richly ambiguous dialogue—and he exploited a seriocomic tone that treats grave issues with all due gravity yet manages to generate an undercurrent of comic, usually satiric, irony.

Wedekind's social stance was that of an implacable Aufklärer (enlightener): his theater aims to unmask the mendacity and illusions of his culture. He was emphatically antibourgeois, a bohemian moralist opposed to the middle-class morality of imperial Germany and Austria. His drama characteristically satirizes the German bourgeoisie's most delicate subjects: sex and money. The spirit of liberal opposition seemed to run in Wedekind's family. His father, Friedrich Wilhelm Wedekind, a physician disenchanted with the failed revolutions of 1848, left Germany in 1849 for political reasons. He lived for a time in the United States, where he met Emilie Kammerer, an Austrian singer then engaged at the German Theater in San Francisco. They married and returned to Europe. Their son, named Benjamin Franklin Wedekind in memory of the American years, was born in Hannover on 24 July 1864; but he grew up at Schloß Lenzburg in the canton of Aargau, Switzerland, where the family moved in 1872. He attended school in Switzerland and went to the Universities of Lausanne and Munich, where he was a less than earnest student of law. After his father cut off his funds in 1886, Wedekind became the head of advertising for the Maggi food company of Zurich. By this time he was also consorting with the intellectuals, artists, and socialists of Zurich's lively bohemian scene, including the naturalist playwright Gerhart Hauptmann.

Though Wedekind shared the great naturalist's basic social sympathies, he showed little interest in exploiting the working class or rural poor as a literary theme. Instead, Wedekind was attracted personally and intellectually to artists, circus performers, pickpockets, prostitutes, and other inhabitants of the fringe of bourgeois culture. He was not interested in realistic portraiture of social and political concerns; nor did he claim insight into the individual souls of his slightly outlandish characters. Rather, Wedekind explored the ambiguous moral world that lies beneath social appearances and beyond the individual's inner life. He did not explore personal subjectivity so much as its foundations in nature and society. Human nature itself is Wedekind's basic theme. He shows it to be endlessly flexible, especially in its sexual, dominating, and acquisitive instincts. Because modern culture has been distorted by decadent values, human nature can only be represented in alienated, exaggerated types such as the sexual monster Lulu or the artist-swindler the Marquis of Keith and their clash with social and moral conventions. His first play, *Kinder und Narren* (Children and Fools; published, 1891), written in 1889, lampoons the naturalist's obsession with impartial observation. The naturalist kisses his wife and makes notes for a play over her shoulder at the same time.

Wedekind perceived naturalism as the least truthful form of art. Art is by its nature not natural but reflective, at a critical remove from nature. (The play was first performed in its revised form as *Die junge Welt* [The Young World; published, 1896] in 1908.) The playwright Alwa Schön in *Die Büchse der Pandora* (performed, 1904; published, 1904; translated as *Pandora's Box*, 1914) speaks for Wedekind when he says, "Das ist der Fluch, der auf unserer jungen Literatur lastet, daß wir viel zu literarisch sind. Wir kennen keine anderen Fragen und Probleme als solche, die unter Schriftstellern und Gelehrten auftauchen. Unser Gesichtskreis reicht über die Grenzen unserer Zunftinteressen nicht hinaus. Um wieder auf die Fährte einer großen gewaltigen Kunst zu gelangen, müßten wir uns möglichst viel unter Menschen bewegen, die nie in ihrem Leben ein Buch gelesen haben, denen die einfachsten animalischen Instinkte bei ihren Handlungen maßgebend sind" (That's the curse that burdens present-day literature: we are much too literary. The only questions and problems we have are the ones that crop up among writers and scholars. Our field of vision doesn't reach beyond our vested interests. To get back on the track of a great and passionate art, we'd have to live as much as we can among people who have never in their lives read a book, among people whose actions are governed by the simplest ani-

mal instincts). Wedekind's own response to Alwa's injunction was to join the circus and travel throughout Europe, writing poems, skits, and stories. After his father died in 1888 Wedekind came into enough money to move to Munich in the summer of 1889 and take up residence among the people who interested him most: bohemians, cabaret artists, poets, and vamps.

His first published drama, *Frühlings Erwachen*, was written in the winter of 1890-1891. Children are a good example of people "governed by the simplest animal instincts," as Alwa Schön puts it. The play's theme is the disastrous results for children of middle-class prudery. In nineteen episodic scenes Wedekind follows several adolescents as they blunder toward sexual enlightenment through a maze of misapprehension, disinformation, and dimly understood emotions. Melchior Gabor seduces fourteen-year-old Wendla Bergmann, whose mother had been too embarrassed to tell her the facts of life. When she becomes pregnant her parents force her to undergo an abortion, which is botched, and Wendla dies. Melchior, the innocent seducer, is banished to reform school. Another boy, Moritz Stiefel, is driven to suicide by his teachers, grotesque and fatuous pedants who show Wedekind in his most satirical mode.

Frühlings Erwachen marked a distinct break with the theater of naturalism because of its mixture of lyrical, prosaic, and ironic language; its flights into the purely imaginary, as in the final scene when Moritz Stiefel returns from the dead; and its grotesque comedy, such as the high pathos of Hänschen Rilow, a masturbating bluebeard who takes pornographic photos of women with him into the lavatory, only to flush his discarded mistresses down the toilet—with a grand poetic flourish—once they have served him. But little Hänschen and his drowned Ophelias did not amuse everybody. The Wilhelmine authorities perceived in Hänschen and his friends an affront to public decency. *Frühlings Erwachen*, though a major theatrical success when it finally made its way past the censors onto the stage in 1906, still had to be presented in expurgated versions.

Between 1891 and 1895 Wedekind lived out his bohemian fantasies in Paris and worked on his Lulu plays. He originally composed the two dramas as a single five-act tragedy titled "Die Büchse der Pandora: Eine Monstretragödie" (Pandora's Box: A Monster Tragedy). But when he turned the manuscript over to Albert Langen, his

Wedekind as Dr. Schön and his wife, Tilly, as Lulu in a scene from Wedekind's Der Erdgeist

Munich publisher, only the first half was accepted for publication; the second half no doubt seemed too violent and sexually charged to escape censorship. Wedekind revised the first half and added a fourth act, and it was published under the title *Der Erdgeist* (translated as *Erdgeist [Earth-Spirit]*, 1914) in 1895; in later versions the title was shortened to *Erdgeist*. The original drama's final two acts, with a new first act added, were published in 1904 under the title *Die Büchse der Pandora*. The authorities speedily confiscated the edition and charged Wedekind and the publisher, Bruno Cassirer, with disseminating pornography; but the defendants were acquitted.

Wedekind's Lulu plays did not fare well at the beginning of their stage life. *Der Erdgeist* was only a modest success when it premiered in 1898, and the censors were unwilling to release *Die Büchse der Pandora* for public performance. The

piece was seldom staged, and most of the few productions were private presentations. The best known of these private productions was organized in 1905 at Vienna's Trianon Theater by the satirist Karl Kraus, who sympathized with what he considered to be Wedekind's progressive outlook on women and sexuality and was eager to promote their shared views. Wedekind, who frequently acted in his own works, played Jack the Ripper in Kraus's production. The original 1895 version had to wait almost a century to be staged: in 1988 the West German director Peter Zadek mounted a highly acclaimed production of the play in Hamburg and published the text, which had been available only in manuscript form, in the journal *Theater heute* (Theater Today).

Lulu has become an icon of fin de siècle feminine sexuality: a dangerous, man-devouring, mythical beast. In Wedekind's plays she is not

Wedekind performing at the Munich cabaret Elf Scharfrichter

(the conventional but hypocritical values of business and family) upsets and finally destroys that world. In a jealous rampage the otherwise cool and rational businessman tries to murder Lulu. In the end she kills him in a scene that is a fine example of Wedekind's blackest comedy.

Die Büchse der Pandora finds Lulu in jail for the murder of Schön; her escape is arranged by some of her friends. Without Schön's economic protection, Lulu is led to her destruction by her sexuality. Sexual passion leads her to death because, in Wedekind's view, it belongs to nature and cannot be reconciled with civilization. With Schön's death even the pretense of civilization falls away, and Lulu finds herself among savage men eager to buy and sell her. She flees to London and becomes a prostitute. Lulu's yearning for release—she dreams of falling into the hands of a rapist-murderer—reveals Wedekind's antifeminist notion of sexual emancipation. Like Kraus and Sigmund Freud, Wedekind understands women to be less than fully rational creatures; they are determined by their sexual essence, a force that sits uneasily in civilization. Jack the Ripper serves as the exponentially heightened image of bourgeois morality exacting vengeance on Lulu for her transgressions. Wedekind's intention is the emancipation of female sexuality, but Lulu's decline and horrifyingly brutal death militate against his purpose. Jack's butchery, like Lulu's sexuality, seems to be a mythic force of nature that is beyond history and culture and inaccessible to reason. Whether Wedekind intends it or not, Lulu's murder has the effect of a cautionary tale, a warning for all right-minded people to beware the female lust and the male aggression it elicits. Wedekind purchases sexual freedom for women at the price of their humanity.

Under the pseudonyms "Hieronymus" and "Hermann" he was a frequent contributor to the satirical journal *Simplicissimus*, founded in 1896 by his publisher Langen. When Kaiser Wilhelm II became the butt of Wedekind's satirical poetry, a warrant was issued for his arrest. Wedekind fled to Zurich and then to Paris. He turned himself over to the police in June 1899 and spent seven months in jail, convicted of lèse-majesté for his poems "Meerfahrt" (Sea Journey) and "Im Heiligen Land" (In the Holy Land), in *Simplicissimus*, volume three, numbers 31 and 32, which satirized the Kaiser's trip to Palestine. After his release from confinement in March 1900 Wedekind turned his attention more and

strictly an embodiment of sexual instinct; rather, she is the embodiment of sexual instinct that has been conditioned by economic circumstance. In *Der Erdgeist* her chief antagonist is Dr. Schön, the manipulative newspaper tycoon whose wealth, success, and self-esteem are predicated on his cold-blooded rationality and pretense of bourgeois respectability. If he is to prosper he must exclude the irrational, indecent Lulu from his world, and he attempts to hold her in abeyance by marrying her off to other men. Naturally, marriage proves too flimsy a vessel to contain Lulu's tantalizing sexuality. Schön further tries to secure himself from her by marrying a respectable woman of high social rank, but in the end Lulu prevails: the intrusion of the irrational (Lulu's irrepressible sexuality) into the autonomous rationality of his world

Scene from a 1926 Berlin production of Wedekind's Franziska

more to cabaret, a genre that had interested him since the mid 1890s. His act at the Elf Scharfrichter (Eleven Executioners), a cabaret that opened in Munich in 1901, was highly successful. It had been conceived as something of a nightclub counterpart to the irreverent journals *Simplicissimus* and *Jugend* (Youth) and featured political satire, social parody, pantomime, dancing, and songs. Wedekind, the "executioner" of Wilhelmine moral and sexual complacency, wrote and performed in skits and dialogues, sang his own compositions, and accompanied himself on the lute and guitar.

Wedekind's success as a cabaret performer kept him solvent and made his reputation with the public. But he regarded the work as a distraction from his true calling, writing plays. *Der Marquis von Keith* (1901; translated as *The Marquis of Keith*, 1952), which Wedekind finished during his house arrest, develops a theme that he had introduced in the Lulu plays: the collusion between commerce and art. The Marquis von Keith is a male version of Lulu. Her essence is sexual pleasure, which Wedekind links to art through her profession as a dancer. Keith's essence is similarly aesthetic: he is an amoral pleasure seeker involved in the business end of the art world. Both Lulu

and Keith live from the illusions they create for rich men. The Marquis von Keith, who claims to be of noble Scottish descent, is a swindler who by trickery and deceit is trying to fund a center for the arts. But Keith, the aesthete, cannot compete with the brutal forces of commerce. The least artistic figures of the play, vulgar tycoons, discover that Keith is a con artist and take the project away from him. Keith loses everything because he is a true artist. His life and identity, like Lulu's, are works of art in the spirit of Friedrich Nietzsche's dictum that the world can be justified only as an aesthetic phenomenon. When challenged to justify his existence, Keith exclaims to his moralist alter ego, Ernst Scholz: "Ich brauche keine Existenzberechtigung! Ich habe niemanden um meine Existenz gebeten und entnehme daraus die Berechtigung, meine Existenz nach meinem Kopfe zu existieren" (I don't need to justify my existence! I didn't ask to exist, which is precisely why I claim the right to exist as I choose). But an aesthetic life of the kind lived by Keith and Lulu is an illusion that founders on the reality principle of money.

Wedekind thought *Der Marquis von Keith* the best of all his plays, but when it premiered in 1901 it was received coolly. He complained that audiences, actors, and critics schooled in the conventions of naturalist theater failed to understand his analytic style. Wedekind argued that the psychological theater of naturalism did not require acting, since the performers were supposed to appear lifelike; the reason he frequently took to the stage in his own plays was to demonstrate the proper handling of them. But the critics failed to appreciate his style as an innovation, patronizingly regarding his exaggerated, mannered performance as dilettantish. Only gradually did the Wedekind style find acceptance. The major breakthrough came in 1906 when Max Reinhardt, one of the most prominent directors in Germany and Austria, staged the premiere of *Frühlings Erwachen* in Berlin. From that point Wedekind's fame and fortune rose. In 1906 he married the Austrian actress Tilly Newes, who had played Lulu in Kraus's Viennese production of *Die Büchse der Pandora*. Initially they lived in Berlin, but in 1908 they settled in Munich. The union produced two daughters, Pamela and Kadidja; but it was not a happy marriage, evidently because of Wedekind's possessive attitude toward Tilly.

The newfound success of the stage works taught the middle-aged bohemian that his fortune lay in play writing, which meant an end to his attempts at a major prose work. His novel *Mine-Haha* (1903), which deals with the sexual education of girls, remained a fragment. His copious output for the stage continued to explore variations on his main themes: art, sex, and money. Earlier works began to appear or reappear on stages around Germany and Austria, and new works were eagerly received—insofar as they were able to escape the censors. His popular comedy *Der Kammersänger* (1899; translated as *The Court Singer*, 1914) considers a philistine artist who panders to his adoring public. *So ist das Leben* (1902; translated as *Such Is Life*, 1912), which is in part Wedekind's reckoning with the lèse-majesté affair, also deals with the artist's life. After King Nicolo of Umbria is overthrown by a commoner, his aesthetic inner nature asserts itself, and he becomes a traveling performer. Unwilling to relinquish his right to the highest place in society, he is repeatedly mocked, jailed, and banished for claiming to be the true king. He dies as a court jester, struggling for recognition in a society that does not understand him. Like the unacknowledged King Nicolo, the scientist Karl Hetmann of *Hidalla* (1904; performed as *Karl Hetmann*, 1905) is a misunderstood artistic spirit.

Wedekind in the final year of his life

His grand design—a Nietzschean eugenics project that links sex, philosophy, and moral theory—is to create a race of physically and morally superior human beings. But Hetmann himself is a deformed dwarf—Wedekind's image of the alienated artist in late-nineteenth-century Germany. Betrayed by a businessman (modeled on Wedekind's publisher Langen), subjected to ridicule, declared insane, and institutionalized, Hetmann hangs himself when he is offered a job as a circus clown. Commentators have generally connected Wedekind's disillusioned artist figures with his own disillusionment over the role of art in society. Wedekind's never-ending wrangles with the censors and his conflicts with his publishers over money no doubt contributed to his pessimism.

Other dramas on the artist theme include *Die Zensur* (Censorship; published, 1908; performed, 1909), which measures the sensual claims of art against the claims of bourgeois culture, and *Oaha* (published, 1908; performed, 1911), which dramatizes the dealings of an opportunistic publisher who, once again, bears a strong resemblance to Langen. Still other plays of Wedekind's middle period stress his abiding interest in women and sexual morality. In *Totentanz* (Dance of Death, 1906; translated as *Damnation!*, 1923) a feminist attempts to liberate a prostitute from a bordello and is herself converted to sensuality, which is presented as a highly ambiguous value. Wedekind linked together three one-act plays to form *Schloß Wetterstein* (published, 1912; performed, 1917; translated as *Castle Wetterstein*, 1952), a meretricious farrago of the Lulu thematics in which the sensual prostitute Effie drinks acid to prove her love for the sadistic killer Tschamper. *Franziska* (1912) depicts an adventuress, a female Faustus, who experiments with the entire gamut of roles open to women. In the end she finds fulfillment in motherhood—a kind of mystical apotheosis promised in the play's subtitle, *Ein modernes Mysterium* (A Modern Mystery). Whether or not Wedekind intended the conclusion ironically has been a point of contention.

When World War I broke out in 1914, Wedekind was one of the few pacifists among German intellectuals. He supported the antiwar position of his friend Heinrich Mann, but he did not share Mann's republicanism; Wedekind believed that Germany was inherently disposed toward monarchy.

Late in 1914 a severe bout of appendicitis put Wedekind in the hospital. He was operated on at the end of December and again in April 1915. The wound could not be sutured and had to remain open. Wedekind's convalescence lasted until late in the summer of 1915, but even then the scar had not healed completely. By late fall it had become infected, forcing Wedekind back into bed until December. He returned to his acting and writing in 1916, responding to the nationalist fervor of the war years with his drama *Bismarck* (published, 1916; performed, 1926). The play takes a somewhat nostalgic view of Otto von Bismarck as the true German statesman, a clearsighted leader of the sort conspicuously absent in Wedekind's time. Bismarck's cunning statecraft, rich in intrigue, links him to Wedekind's trickster figures. Shortly after completing the *Bismarck* in 1916 he began work on another heroic figure. *Herakles* (Hercules; published, 1917; performed, 1919), his last major drama, depicts the heroic struggle of the individual against his fate, which

here takes the form of the passionate instincts of lust, violence, and revenge. Wedekind's friend and biographer Artur Kutscher emphasizes the element of autobiographical stylization in Wedekind's Hercules. The dramatist saw himself engaged in a similar heroic struggle over the years, not unlike King Nicolo and Karl Hetmann. During his career Wedekind fought for artistic self-determination, for his version of enlightened sexuality, and against hypocrisies of every sort.

By January 1917 another operation was necessary. Later in the year Wedekind seemed well enough to act and travel. By that time his marriage was breaking up; his wife attempted suicide, which was a severe blow to him. She recovered, but the incision from his operation still would not heal. On 2 March 1918 he was operated on for a final time. The operation was successful, but in his weakened state he caught a cold that developed into pneumonia. He died on 9 March.

Letters:
Gesammelte Briefe, 2 volumes, edited by Fritz Strich (Munich: Müller, 1924).

Bibliographies:
Ernst Stobbe, *Bibliographie der Erstausgaben Frank Wedekinds*, Almanach der Bücherstube auf das Jahr 1921 (Munich: Stobbe, 1920);
Hartmut Vinçon, *Frank Wedekind*, Sammlung Metzler, 230 (Stuttgart: Metzler, 1987).

Biographies:
Artur Kutscher, *Frank Wedekind: Sein Leben und seine Werke*, 3 volumes (Munich: Müller, 1922-1931);
Tilly Wedekind, *Lulu: Die Rolle meines Lebens* (Munich: Rütter & Loehning, 1969);
Günter Seehaus, *Frank Wedekind in Selbstzeugnissen und Bilddokumenten* (Reinbek: Rowohlt, 1974).

References:
Kathy Acker, "Lulu," *Performing Arts Journal*, 30, no. 10 (1986-1987): 102-117;
Theodor Adorno, "Über den Nachlaß Frank Wedekinds," in his *Gesammelte Werke*, volume 11 (Frankfurt am Main: Suhrkamp, 1974), pp. 627-633;
Ann Taylor Allen, *Satire and Society in Wilhelmine Germany: "Kladderadatsch" and "Simplicissimus" 1890-1914* (Lexington: University of Kentucky Press, 1984);

Peter von Becker, "Ästhetik und Ästhetisierung des Schreckens: Wie realistisch ist, wie präfaschistisch wirkt heute Wedekind?," *Theater heute*, 19 (1978): 21-26;

Alban Berg, *Lulu: Texte, Materialien, Kommentare*, edited by Attila Csampai and Dietmar Holland (Reinbek & Munich: Rowohlt/Ricordi, 1985);

Alan Best, *Frank Wedekind* (London: Wolff, 1975);

Gordon Birrell, "The *Wollen/Sollen* Equation in Wedekind's *Frühlings Erwachen*," *Germanic Review*, 57 (Summer 1982): 115-122;

Elizabeth Boa, *The Sexual Circus: Wedekind's Theatre of Subversion* (Oxford: Blackwell, 1987);

Bertolt Brecht, "Frank Wedekind," in *Brecht on Theatre*, edited by John Willett (London: Methuen, 1964), pp. 3-4;

Angela Carter, "Femmes Fatales," in her *Nothing Sacred: Selected Writings* (London: Virago, 1982), pp. 119-123;

Edson Chick, *Dances of Death: Wedekind, Brecht, Dürrenmatt, and the Satiric Tradition*, Studies in German Literature, Linguistics and Culture, 19 (Columbia, S.C.: Camden House, 1984);

Carol Diethe, *Aspects of Distorted Sexual Attitudes in German Expressionist Drama: Wedekind, Kokoschka, Kaiser* (Bern: Lang, 1988);

Friedrich Dürrenmatt, "Bekenntnisse eines Plagiators," in *Deutsche Literaturkritik der Gegenwart*, edited by Hans Mayer (Stuttgart: Goverts, 1971), pp. 426-432;

Wilhelm Emrich, "Immanuel Kant und Frank Wedekind," in his *Polemik: Streitschriften, Pressefehden und kritische Essays um Prinzipien, Methoden und Maßstäbe der Literaturkritik* (Frankfurt am Main: Athenäum, 1968), pp. 56-60;

Gail Finney, *Women in Modern Drama* (Ithaca, N.Y.: Cornell University Press, 1989);

Sander Gilman, "The Nietzsche Murder Case," *New Literary History*, 14 (Winter 1983): 359-372;

Sol Gittleman, *Frank Wedekind* (New York: Twayne, 1969);

Friedrich Gundolf, *Frank Wedekind* (Munich: Langen/Müller, 1954);

Edward Harris, "Freedom and Degradation: Frank Wedekind's Career as Cabaretist," in *The Turn of the Century: German Literature and Art 1890-1915*, edited by Gerald Chapple and H. H. Schulte, Modern German Studies, 5 (Bonn: Bouvier, 1981), pp. 493-506;

Wolfgang Hartwig, ed., *Der Marquis von Keith: Text und Materialien* (Berlin: De Gruyter, 1965);

J. L. Hibberd, "Frank Wedekind and the First World War," *Modern Language Review*, 82 (January 1987): 119-141;

Hibberd, "The Spirit of the Flesh: Wedekind's Lulu," *Modern Language Review*, 79 (April 1984): 336-355;

John Hibbert, "Frank Wedekind and Lassalle," *German Life and Letters*, 42 (January 1989): 113-128;

Hibbert, " 'Die Wiedervereinigung von Kirche und Freudenhaus': Wedekind's *Die Zensur* and His Ideas on Religion," *Colloquia Germanica*, 19 (1986): 47-67;

Alfons Höger, "Hetärismus und bürgerliche Gesellschaft im Frühwerk Frank Wedekinds," *Text und Kontext*, Supplement 12 (1981): 1-208;

Hans-Jochen Irmer, *Frank Wedekind: Werk und Wirkung* (Berlin: Henschelverlag, 1975);

Peter Jelavich, *Munich and Theatrical Modernism: Politics, Playwriting, and Performance 1890-1914* (Cambridge, Mass.: Harvard University Press, 1985);

Volker Klotz, *Dramaturgie des Publikums* (Munich: Hanser, 1976);

Karl Kraus, "Die Büchse der Pandora," *Die Fackel*, 7, no. 182 (1905): 1-18;

Anna K. Kuhn, "Der aphoristische Dialog im *Marquis von Keith*," in *Theatrum Mundi*, edited by Edward R. Haymes, Houston German Studies, 2 (Munich: Fink, 1980), pp. 80-92;

Robin Lenman, "Politics and Culture: The State and the Avant-Garde in Munich 1886-1914," in *Society and Politics in Wilhelmine Germany*, edited by Richard J. Evans (London: Croom Helm, 1978), pp. 90-111;

Heinrich Mann, "Erinnerungen an Frank Wedekind," in his *Essays* (Hamburg: Claasen, 1960), pp. 243-262;

Thomas Mann, "Über eine Szene von Wedekind," in his *Altes und Neues: Kleine Prosa aus fünf Jahrzehnten* (Frankfurt am Main: Fischer, 1961), pp. 31-36;

Kurt Martens, "Erinnerungen an Frank Wedekind, 1897-1900," *Der neue Merkur*, 4 (1920): 537-549;

Thomas Medicus, *"Die große Liebe": Ökonomie und Konstruktion der Körper im Werk Frank Wedekinds*, Reihe Metro, 11 (Marburg: Guttandin & Hoppe, 1982);

David Midgley, "Wedekind's Lulu: From 'Schauertragödie' to Social Comedy," *German Life and Letters*, 38 (April 1985): 205-232;

Libuse Monikova, "Das totalitäre Glück: Frank Wedekind," *Neue Rundschau*, 96 (1985): 118-125;

Marc Muylaert, *L'image de al femme dans l'œuvre de Frank Wedekind*, Stuttgarter Arbeiten zur Germanistik, 159 (Stuttgart: Heinz Akademischer Verlag, 1985);

Ronald Peacock, "The Ambiguity of Wedekind's Lulu," *Oxford German Studies*, 9 (1978): 105-118;

Henning Rischbieter, "Der wahre Wedekind: Lulu Furiosa," *Theater heute*, 17 (April 1988): 6-17;

Jeannie Schüler-Will, "Wedekind's Lulu: Pandora and Pierrot," *German Studies Review*, 7 (February 1984): 27-38;

Willy Schumann, "Frank Wedekind: Regimekritiker?," *Seminar*, 15 (1979): 235-243;

Günter Seehaus, *Wedekind und das Theater* (Munich: Laokoon, 1964);

Leroy Shaw, "Frank Wedekind's *Spring Awakening*," in *Alogical Modern Drama*, edited by Kenneth White (Amsterdam: Rodopi, 1982), pp. 25-37;

Peter Skrine, *Hauptmann, Wedekind and Schnitzler* (London: Macmillan, 1989), pp. 72-110;

Colbert Stewart, "Comedy, Morality, and Energy in the Work of Frank Wedekind," *Publica-tions of the English Goethe Society*, 56 (1987): 56-73;

Haucke Stroszeck, " 'Ein Bild vor dem man verzweifeln muß': Zur Gestaltung der Tragödie in Wedekinds Lulu-Tragödie," in *Literatur und Theater im Wilhelminischen Zeitalter*, edited by Hans-Peter Bayerdörfer (Tübingen: Niemeyer, 1978), pp. 217-237;

Edward Timms, "Pandora and the Prostitute," in his *Karl Kraus: Apocalyptic Satirist* (New Haven: Yale University Press, 1986), pp. 63-93;

Hartmut Vinçon, "Wie Wedekinds Lulu entstand und unterdruckt wurde," *Theater heute*, 17 (April 1988): 16-17;

Klaus Völker, *Frank Wedekind*, Friedrichs Dramatiker des 20. Jahrhunderts, 7 (Velber bei Hannover: Friedrich, 1965);

Hans Wagener, *Frank Wedekind*, Köpfe des 20. Jahrhunderts, 90 (Berlin: Colloquium, 1979);

Wagener, "Frank Wedekind: Politische Entgleisungen eines Unpolitischen," *Seminar*, 15 (1979): 244-250;

Androne B. Willeke, "Frank Wedekind und die Frauenfrage," *Monatshefte*, 72 (1980): 26-38.

Papers:

The Munich City Library has manuscripts and other documents of Frank Wedekind in its Wedekind Archive. Holdings are also available at the Wedekind Archive of the Aargau Canton Library in Switzerland.

Anton Wildgans

(17 April 1881 - 3 May 1932)

Ulrike Rainer
Dartmouth College

PLAY PRODUCTIONS: *In Ewigkeit, amen,* Vienna, Volksbühne, 24 May 1913;
Armut, Vienna, Deutsches Volkstheater, 16 January 1915;
Liebe, Vienna, Deutsches Volkstheater, 18 November 1916;
Dies irae, Vienna, Burgtheater, 8 February 1919;
Kain, Rostock, Stadttheater, 12 January 1921;
Moses-Fragment, Vienna, Burgtheater, 8 May 1932.

BOOKS: *Vom Wege: Gedichte* (Dresden: Pierson, 1903);
Herbstfrühling: Verse (Berlin: Juncker, 1909);
Und hättet der Liebe nicht: Ein Cyclus neuer Gedichte (Berlin: Juncker, 1911);
Die Sonette an Ead (Leipzig: Staackmann, 1913);
In Ewigkeit, amen: Ein Gerichtsstück in einem Akt (Leipzig: Staackmann, 1913);
Allerseelen: Ein Requiem für die gefallenen Helden (Vienna: Heller, 1914);
Armut: Ein Trauerspiel (Leipzig: Staackmann, 1914);
Das große Händefalten: Ein Gebet für Österreichs Volk und Kämpfer (Vienna: Heller, 1914);
Ihr Kleingläubigen! Eine Laienpredigt fur Daheimgebliebene (Vienna: Heller, 1914);
Legende: Aus dem Alltag des Krieges (Vienna: Heller, 1914);
Heilige Nacht! Ein zeitgemäßer Prolog zu einem alten Weihnachtsspiel (Vienna: Heller, 1914);
Vae victis! Ein Weihelied den verbündeten Heeren (Vienna: Heller, 1914);
Festschrift für Wilhelm Jerusalem zu seinem sechzigsten Geburtstag von Freunden, Verehrern und Schülern, by Wildgans and others (Vienna: Braunmüller, 1915);
Österreichische Gedichte (Leipzig: Insel, 1915);
Infanterie! Ein Gedicht, gewidmet dem Volke in Waffen (Vienna: Heller, 1915);
Liebe: Eine Tragödie (Leipzig: Staackmann, 1916);
Dreißig Gedichte (Konstanz: Reuß & Itta, 1917);
Mittag: Neue Gedichte (Leipzig: Staackmann, 1917);

Anton Wildgans

Dies irae: Eine Tragödie (Leipzig: Staackmann, 1918);
Kain: Ein mythisches Gedicht (Leipzig: Staackmann, 1920);
Ausgewählte Gedichte (Berlin: Juncker, 1921);
Wiener Gedichte (Vienna: Speidel, 1927);
Kirbisch oder Der Gendarm, die Schande und das Glück: Ein episches Gedicht (Leipzig: Staackmann, 1927);
Musik der Kindheit: Ein Heimatbuch aus Wien (Leipzig: Staackmann, 1928);
Gedichte um Pan (Vienna: Speidel, 1928);
Buch der Gedichte (Leipzig: Staackmann, 1929);
Rede über Österreich (Vienna: Speidel, 1930);

264

Gesammelte Werke, 5 volumes (Leipzig: Staackmann, 1930);

Ich beichte und bekenne: Aus dem Nachlasse, edited by Lilly Wildgans (Leipzig: Staackmann, 1933);

Sämtliche Werke: Historisch-kritische Ausgabe in acht Bänden, 8 volumes, edited by Wildgans (Vienna: Bellaria / Salzburg: Pustet, 1948-1958);

Gedichte (Vienna: Kremayr & Scheriau, 1953);

Hypodameia: Ein Jugendwerk (Vienna: Donauland, 1962).

TRANSLATION: *Sonnette aus dem Italienischen: Nachdichtungen* (Leipzig: Staackmann, 1924).

Anton Wildgans was born in Vienna on 17 April 1881 to Dr. Friedrich Wildgans, a lawyer, and Therese Charvot Wildgans, a former maidservant. His mother died in 1885; his father remarried the same year. When Wildgans was sixteen his father's health started to deteriorate due to an undiagnosed brain tumor. Until his death in 1906 Friedrich Wildgans suffered from a paralysis that spread slowly throughout his body. This prolonged and painful illness not only left a lasting mark on the son's psyche but also brought the family to the brink of destitution. Wildgans, who graduated from the demanding Piaristengymnasium, a school administered by the Piarist religious order, had to interrupt his studies to support himself. Until 1905 he worked as assistant editor on the Vienna daily newspaper *Die Zeit* (The Times), supplementing his income with jobs as secretary to the Vienna Hunting Club and as a private tutor. After a trip to India and Australia in 1905, he decided to follow a family tradition by entering the legal profession, a choice he made without much enthusiasm and to a large degree to honor the memory of his father. The need to settle down into a permanent and lucrative profession had, however, a more urgent reason: during the summer of 1906 he met and fell in love with Lilly Würzel, the daughter of a leather manufacturer. He began the study of law at the University of Vienna in October 1907, earned his degree in January 1909, married Lilly on 27 March, and assumed the post of an investigative judge at the Superior Court of Vienna. But, unhappy with his career and encouraged by the success of his first major volume of poetry, *Herbstfrühling* (Autumn-Spring, 1909), he resigned his post in 1912 to dedicate himself to writing.

At the present time it might be hard to imagine how popular Wildgans's poetry was in Austria and Germany during the first two decades of the twentieth century. His *Und hättet der Liebe nicht* (And Have Not Charity, 1911) was in its eleventh printing by 1918, and *Die Sonette an Ead* (The Sonnets to Ead, 1913) sold thirty-eight thousand copies by 1922. Influenced in his early youth by the poetry and writings of Hugo von Hofmannsthal and Arthur Schnitzler as well as the works of Sigmund Freud, Wildgans developed a more radical and cynical view of contemporary society than those of his literary mentors. Another source of inspiration was Mönichkirchen, a mountain village not far from Vienna that became his second home after a severe and extended illness at the age of eighteen left him with a recurring circulatory ailment. His poetry's predominant themes are an unsentimental but loving view of nature and landscapes; a deep understanding of the beauty of the city as well as its negative manifestations of poverty, crime, and moral dissolution; and compassion for the poor and oppressed. The moods of his poetry range from enthusiasm to pathos, melancholy, and pessimism. In his time, Wildgans's poetry was recited by actors and schoolchildren and fervently read in offices and factories from Vienna to Hamburg. To be sure, even then Wildgans had his critics—most notably the satirist Karl Kraus, who characterized his outpouring as empty and hollow, appealing to a petit bourgeoisie whose shallow intellectual level and unimportant strivings it reflected. Kraus took particular offense at the *Österreichische Gedichte* (Austrian Poems, 1915). Written at the beginning of World War I and first published as pamphlets, the poems were meant to spread courage and confidence among the population and the troops; Kraus discerned in them hidden chauvinism, false patriotism, and a thinly disguised appeal to continue an unjust conflict.

More than his poetry, the plays of Wildgans were influenced by the naturalist and expressionist movements and their most prominent practitioners, Gerhart Hauptmann, Henrik Ibsen, August Strindberg, and Frank Wedekind. But although Wildgans was an astute critic of social conditions and a passionate advocate for those on the margins of society, his focus was on the private sphere, on intrafamilial conflict. In addition, his view of sexuality was rooted in some of the beliefs of the era that were expressed most succinctly and eloquently in Otto Weininger's influential *Geschlecht und Charakter* (1903; translated as *Sex and Character*, 1906). Consequently, the women in Wildgans's plays rarely transcend stereotypical depiction and functions; they appear either as overpowering, all-consuming mothers, seductive prostitutes, or self-sacrificing sisters and wives. Nevertheless, when it was first performed, each play was a huge success, and Wildgans received some of the most coveted theater awards Vienna had to offer: the Volkstheaterpreis, the Bauernfeldpreis, and the Grillparzerpreis.

Wildgans's first play, *In Ewigkeit, amen* (Amen in All Eternity, 1913), echoes experiences from his days as a lawyer and shows its debt to the naturalists. Settings, costumes, and the physical appearance and actions of the protagonists are prescribed in great detail in the stage directions; there is little room for a director to change the play. The setting is a criminal court in which the old recidivist Anton Gschmeidler once more stands accused of a blatant act of violence. During the trial it is revealed that he continues to commit such crimes in order to be returned to jail, the only home he ever knew. The presiding judge, the prosecutor, and the lower-class witnesses speak in the vernacular appropriate for their places in society. The message that poverty and ignorance are as much to blame for crimes as the individuals who perpetrate them was, by 1913, not revolutionary; what is unique in the play is the deep compassion shown those whom life has treated unjustly and the uncompromising exposure of those in positions of power who cruelly misuse their offices. *In Ewigkeit, amen* indicts contemporary Austrian society by bringing into sharp focus its rigid, class-conscious, corrupt bureaucracy. It was a realistic depiction, and the audience could identify with the events onstage.

Encouraged by the drama's success in Vienna and Berlin and delighted by the birth of his first son, Friedrich, on 5 June 1913, Wildgans finished his next play, *Armut* (Poverty; published, 1914; performed, 1915), in a frenzy of creativity. In this tragedy, also, poverty and its consequences are the central theme; the tone and mood, however, have undergone a subtle but significant change. The play moves beyond a purely naturalistic depiction of an impoverished household to introduce elements of spirituality and metaphysics. The plot involves not merely the death of an insignificant postal employee and the catastrophic consequences for his wife and barely grown son and daughter but also a celebration of human endurance and strength. The harshness

of social reality is counterbalanced by the capacity for unselfish love and the basic decency of the children, who, in their different ways, prove that nearly unbearable conditions do not necessarily lead to hatred and cynicism. The son's point of view dominates the play. His superior education enables him to analyze the situation with insight and some intellectual detachment, but he is powerless to effect change. His sister's attempt at financial rescue by offering herself to a rich lodger does not succeed, but the author does not condemn it on moral grounds. In the end, the son's keen perception and the daughter's moral integrity point to hope for a new generation. Abandoning realistic dialogue, the two characters chant verses which transform poverty into a holy office to be administered chastely, wakefully, and precisely. Such an idealistic solution to social injustice seems insupportable today, and one could dismiss the play as hopelessly out of date were it not for some small but important touches. In one of the dying man's blissful last dreams the emperor thanks him warmly for his thirty years or more of faithful service. The irony is obvious: by exposing the backwardness of contemporary Austrian society, in which empty gestures or even the hope for them replace much-needed reforms, Wildgans, perhaps unconsciously, questions the notion of the nobility of poverty. No other Wildgans play was as successful as *Armut*. After seconds of stunned silence the premiere audience broke into wild cheers: it had understood the drama not only in its significance for the time but also as a document of humanity's struggle against hunger.

In May 1915 Wildgans and his family moved to Mödling, a suburb at the edge of the Vienna Woods. His next play, *Liebe* (Love, 1916), deals with the estrangement of a husband and wife and, in a larger context, with the abyss that separates the sexes. On the surface, the middle-class couple Anna and Martin lead an exemplary life, but on closer scrutiny the cracks beneath the smooth facade become visible. Bored with each other and with the routine of their day-to-day existence, the husband and wife lose the language of passion they had shared. They deal with this crisis along sharply defined gender lines: he tries to recapture love by visiting a sympathetic prostitute, while she encounters a long-lost admirer with whom she renews a nonsexual bond. Their respective breaches of faith—Martin's physical betrayal and Anna's spiritual deceit—force the couple to confront each other honestly, but whether their marriage will endure remains an open question. For Anna these episodes spell the end of love, while for Martin they point toward a new beginning. As in *Armut*, at the end a lyrical chant replaces the dialogue, and here a mystical orchestra removes the action from reality to a realm beyond the ordinary where, perhaps, opposites can be reconciled.

The cautious optimism that informs *Liebe* gives way to a despairing view of man and society in the tragedy *Dies irae* (Days of Wrath; published, 1918; performed, 1919). More expressionist than naturalist, this play exposes what Wildgans saw as the pathology of the age. The central conflict, between an authoritarian father who wishes his son to succeed at all costs and a son who struggles futilely to meet impossible expectations, reflects a society clinging to the bourgeois values of the nineteenth century despite the profound upheavals of World War I. In addition, the mother's support of her son's aspirations sets her against her husband, and the child becomes a pawn in a long-standing marital war. There is no possibility of reconciliation; even over the body of their son, who has committed suicide, the mother and father accuse each other. Act 5, titled "Phantasticus," offers an impassioned plea to the patriarchs of society to lift the chains of paternal expectations from their sons. Supported by a mystical chorus, the son's rebellious friend condemns the father and all like him of the spiritual murder of their children.

Started in 1918, Wildgans's largest dramatic project was a trilogy based on material from the Old and New Testaments. The heroes were to be Cain, Moses, and Christ, and the subject was to be the tragedy of human existence. Only *Kain* (Cain; published, 1920; performed, 1921) was completed. Ironically, the author's appointment to the directorship of Vienna's prestigious Burgtheater in January 1921 put an end to eight years of intensive dramatic production. *Moses* is only extant in fragmentary form, and Wildgans never found his way back to the genre in which he hoped to leave his most lasting mark. Although with *Kain* he appeared to abandon contemporary topics and subjects, this "mythisches Gedicht" (mythical poem) is strongly linked to *Dies irae*. Here Cain is the unloved son, not only rejected from the very beginning of his existence by his parents, Adam and Eve, but also by his divine Father. Defying God's law because of this rejection, he becomes a law unto himself. By killing Abel, the favored son, whose goodness has its source in

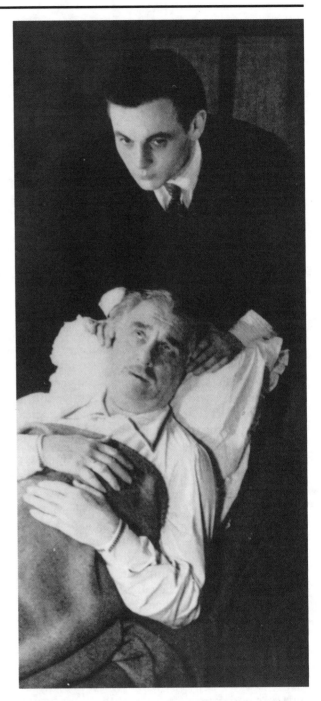

Heinrich Schweiger (top) as the son and Alfred Neugebaur as his dying father in a scene from a 1951 production of Wildgans's Armut *at the Akademietheater in Vienna*

unconditional love, he dooms humankind to eternal fratricide. Lacking the gift of love, the children of Cain will be greedy for wealth and power, and they will forever slay any new Abel born into the world. Cain challenges God to give him an answer to the question of why he exists, but he receives none. In the face of this silence, Cain declares himself a god. Close beneath the nihilistic surface lurks the wrenching incestuous longing of an unloved child. The drama focuses on the conflict between mother and son: only when Eve shows her abhorrence at the monster to which she gave birth does Cain turn to universal destruction. Nowhere else has Wildgans tried to bring together so densely all the preoccupations of his life and work, and nowhere else, except perhaps in his epic poem *Kirbisch* (1927), does he succeed as well in exposing the interrelatedness of metaphysical, sexual, and social constructs. To achieve such an effect Wildgans abandoned realistic dialogue in favor of a rhapsodic, lyrical mode of speech.

Fragile in health and prone to depression, Wildgans plunged into a crisis when he assumed the directorship, an office for which he was mentally unprepared. Only the birth of his second son, Gottfried, on 21 March 1921 brought him some joy. Wildgans was rooted in and bound to the traditions of the nineteenth century, but history and experience forced him to question his cherished beliefs. And it was probably not only his difficult, strife-ridden term at the Burgtheater from 1921 to 1923 that led to his abdication from the theater but also the realization that in the Vienna of the early 1920s the theater was no longer respected or used as a forum for intellectual challenges and social change. Between 1925 and 1927 Wildgans's poetic energies were almost exclusively devoted to *Kirbisch*. The only interruption in what was to become an almost obsessive preoccupation with this work was an extended lecture tour through Germany in the early months of 1925. But the highly acclaimed epic *Kirbisch*, written in hexameter, was more a critical than popular or financial success. In April 1927 Wildgans almost lost all he owned because of unpaid taxes. Throughout 1928 he suffered from heart trouble, high blood pressure, dizzy spells, and sleeplessness. Shattered in spirit and health after his first experience with the political intrigues and artistic rivalries of the Burgtheater, he took a long time to recover his creative and physical energies. Still, the first of what was intended to be a series of autobiographical writings appeared in 1928. *Musik der Kindheit* (Music of Childhood) was to have been followed by "Helldunkle Jugend" (Light-dark Childhood), but the latter never progressed beyond the planning stage. In 1929 Wildgans had to cancel a reading tour of Denmark, Norway, and Sweden after he collapsed at the Leipzig train station. Despite such an ill omen, he was pressed by financial neces-

sity to shoulder a burden that had proven too heavy for him before: in 1930 he agreed once more to manage the Burgtheater, and history repeated itself. His second directorship was as onerous as his first, and he was forced to resign toward the end of 1931. Physically worn out by his duties and mentally exhausted by the vicious attacks of Vienna's press, he died of heart failure on 3 May 1932 in his Mödling villa.

Had it not been for Wildgans's widow, the great Austrian poet of the early twentieth century might be no more than a footnote in literary history today. She was not only his inspiration but also his staunchest ally and supporter through good and bad times. Interest in his work diminished during the 1930s, and after World War II his poems and plays seemed to belong to another age. But Lilly Wildgans devoted the rest of her life to his memory and work. In 1932 she and other admirers founded the Anton-Wildgans-Gesellschaft (Anton Wildgans Society), and she preserved their house in Mödling as a museum and library. Thanks to her, manuscripts and letters were made accessible to scholars. When she died on 21 February 1968 at the age of eighty-two, Wildgans's son Gottfried took over the legacy (his older brother, Friedrich, had died in 1965). The present generation of Austrians may still recall Wildgans's name; but it will probably evoke no concrete associations, because it is difficult to recapture a sense of the decline of the Austro-Hungarian Empire or to appreciate the doomed political and social programs of the period between the world wars. And yet Wildgans's reflections on the human condition; psychological insights into family dynamics; and faith—tempered by a realistic estimation of the limits imposed by biology and social environment—in the capacity of individual men and women to alter the course of history deserve to be reevaluated. The writer's name lives on in the Anton Wildgans Prize, which was established in 1962. Among the recipients have been Fritz Hochwälder in 1962, Thomas Bernhard in 1967, Ingeborg Bachmann in 1971, Ernst Jandl in 1982, Peter Handke (who refused the honor) in 1984, and Christoph Ransmayr in 1988.

Letters:

Anton Wildgans: Briefe, edited by Lilly Wildgans (Vienna & Leipzig: Österreichischer Bundesverlag für Unterricht, Wissenschaft und Kunst, 1937);

Ein Leben in Briefen, 3 volumes, edited by Wildgans (Vienna: Frick, 1947);

Hugo von Hofmannsthal, Anton Wildgans: Briefwechsel, edited by Norbert Altenhofer (Heidelberg: Stiehm, 1971).

Biographies:

Lilly Wildgans, ed., *Vorfahren: Die Geschichte der Familie Wildgans* (Vienna: Sonderdruck der graphischen Lehr- und Versuchsanstalt, 1936);

Wildgans, *Anton Wildgans und das Burgtheater: Ein biographischer Beitrag, aus Dokumenten, Aufzeichnungen und Erinnerungen gestaltet* (Vienna: Kremayr & Scheriau, 1955);

Wildgans, *Der gemeinsame Weg: Mein Leben mit Anton Wildgans* (Salzburg & Stuttgart: Das Bergland Buch, 1960);

Wildgans, *Anton Wildgans und seine Freunde* (Mödling: Anton-Wildgans-Gesellschaft, 1977).

References:

Anton Dörfler, *Anton Wildgans und seine besten Bühnenwerke: Eine Einführung* (Berlin & Leipzig: Schneider, 1922);

Heinz Gerstinger, *Der Dramatiker Anton Wildgans* (Innsbruck: Universitätsverlag Wagner, 1981);

Joseph Gregor, *Geschichte des österreichischen Theaters* (Vienna: Donauverlag, 1948);

Franz Hadriga, *Drama Burgtheaterdirektion: Vom Scheitern des Idealisten Anton Wildgans* (Vienna: Herold, 1989);

Roland Heger, "Anton Wildgans als Dramatiker," Ph.D. dissertation, University of Vienna, 1947;

Norbert Leser, "Anton Wildgans, ein österreichisches Schicksal," *Die Republik: Beiträge aus der österreichischen Politik*, 9 (1973): 5-15;

Morgen: Kulturzeitschrift aus Niederösterreich, special Wildgans issue, 17 (June 1981);

Anton Pollak, ed., *Das Anton Wildgans Buch* (Vienna & Leipzig: Verlag für Jugend und Volk, 1934);

Friedrich Schreyvogl, "Rede auf Anton Wildgans," *Jahrbuch der Grillparzer Gesellschaft*, 3 (1960): 138-144;

Josef Soyka, *Das Buch um Anton Wildgans* (Leipzig: Staackmann, 1932);

Kenji Sugiura, "Anton Wildgans: Das Schicksal des 'österreichischen Menschen,'" *Doitsu Bungaku* (1988): 56-65;

Hans Vogelsang, *Österreichische Dramatiker des 20. Jahrhunderts* (Vienna: Braumüller, 1981);

Kenneth D. Weisinger, "Anton Wildgans' 'Kirbisch' and the Mock-epic Tradition," in *Austriaca: Beiträge zur österreichischen Literatur: Festschrift für Heinz Politzer*, edited by Winfried Kudszus and Hinrich C. Seeba (Tübingen: Niemeyer, 1975), pp. 339-351;

James F. de Young, "Anton Wildgans and His Relationship to the Austrian Countryside," *Modern Austrian Literature*, 4 (1971): 31-48.

Papers:

Manuscripts of Anton Wildgans are in the Austrian National Library, Vienna. Copies of all materials are in the Wildgans family villa in Mödling, Austria.

Stefan Zweig

(28 November 1881 - 22 February 1942)

Harry Zohn

Brandeis University

See also the Zweig entry in *DLB 81: Austrian Fiction Writers, 1875-1913.*

PLAY PRODUCTIONS: *Tersites*, Kassel, Hoftheater / Dresden, Hoftheater, 26 November 1908;

Der verwandelte Komödiant, Breslau, Lobetheater, 5 May 1912;

Das Haus am Meer, Vienna, Hofburgtheater, 26 October 1912;

Jeremias, Zurich, Stadttheater, 27 February 1918;

Legende eines Lebens, Hamburg, Deutsches Schauspielhaus, 25 December 1918;

Volpone, adapted by Zweig from the play by Ben Jonson, Vienna, Burgtheater, 6 November 1926;

Die Flucht zu Gott, Kiel, Städtisches Theater, 5 September 1928;

Das Lamm des Armen, Breslau, Lobetheater / Hannover, Schauspielhaus / Prague, Deutsches Theater, 15 March 1930;

Die schweigsame Frau, Dresden, Sächsische Staatsoper, 24 June 1935.

BOOKS: *Silberne Saiten: Gedichte* (Berlin & Leipzig: Schuster & Loeffler, 1901);

Die Liebe der Erika Ewald: Novellen (Berlin: Fleischel, 1904);

Verlaine (Berlin & Leipzig: Schuster & Loeffler, 1905); translated by O. F. Theis as *Paul Verlaine* (Boston: Luce, 1913; Dublin: Maunsel, 1913);

Die frühen Kränze (Leipzig: Insel, 1906);

Tersites: Ein Trauerspiel (Leipzig: Insel, 1907); revised as *Tersites: Trauerspiel in drei Aufzügen* (Leipzig: Insel, 1919);

Emile Verhaeren (Leipzig: Insel, 1910); translated by Jethro Bithell (Boston & New York: Houghton Mifflin, 1914; London: Constable, 1914);

Erstes Erlebnis: Vier Geschichten aus Kinderland (Leipzig: Insel, 1911); republished as *Die Kette: Ein Novellenkreis*, volume 1 (Leipzig: Insel, 1923);

Stefan Zweig

Das Haus am Meer: Ein Schauspiel in zwei Teilen (Leipzig: Insel, 1912);

Brennendes Geheimnis: Eine Erzählung (Leipzig: Insel, 1913); translated anonymously as *The Burning Secret, by Stephen Branch* (New York: Scott & Seltzer, 1919);

Der verwandelte Komödiant: Ein Spiel aus dem deutschen Rokoko (Leipzig: Insel, 1913);

Erinnerungen an Emile Verhaeren (Vienna: Reisser, 1917);

Jeremias: Eine dramatische Dichtung in neun Bildern (Leipzig: Insel, 1917); translated by Eden and Cedar Paul as *Jeremiah: A Drama in Nine Scenes* (New York: Seltzer, 1922; new edition, with preface by Zweig, New York: Viking Press, 1929; London: Allen, 1929; new edition, with new preface by Zweig, New York: Viking Press, 1939);

Das Herz Europas: Ein Besuch im Genfer Roten Kreuz (Zurich: Rascher, 1918);

Legende eines Lebens: Ein Kammerspiel in drei Aufzügen (Leipzig: Insel, 1919);

Fahrten: Landschaften und Städte (Leipzig: Tal, 1919);

Drei Meister: Balzac-Dickens-Dostojewski (Leipzig: Insel, 1920); translated by Eden and Cedar Paul as *Three Masters: Balzac-Dickens-Dostoeffsky* (New York: Viking Press, 1930; London: Allen & Unwin, 1930);

Der Zwang: Eine Novelle (Leipzig: Insel, 1920);

Angst: Novelle (Berlin: Hermann, 1920);

Marceline Desbordes-Valmore: Das Lebensbild einer Dichterin (Leipzig: Insel, 1920);

Romain Rolland: Der Mann und das Werk (Frankfurt am Main: Rütten & Loening, 1921); translated by Eden and Cedar Paul as *Romain Rolland: The Man and his Work* (New York: Seltzer, 1921; London: Allen & Unwin, 1921);

Die Augen des ewigen Bruders: Eine Legende (Leipzig: Insel, 1922);

Amok: Novellen einer Leidenschaft (Leipzig: Insel, 1922);

Sainte-Beuve (Frankfurt am Main: Frankfurter Verlags-Anstalt, 1923);

Die gesammelten Gedichte (Leipzig: Insel, 1924);

Passion and Pain, translated by Eden and Cedar Paul (London: Chapman & Hall, 1924; New York: Richards, 1925)—comprises "Letter from an Unknown Woman," "The Runaway," "Transfiguration," "The Fowler Snared," "Compulsion," "The Governess," "Virata; or, The Eyes of the Undying Brother";

Der Kampf mit dem Dämon: Hölderlin-Kleist-Nietzsche (Leipzig: Insel, 1925); translated by Eden and Cedar Paul as *The Struggle with the Demon* (New York: Viking Press, 1929; London: Allen & Unwin, 1930);

Volpone: Eine lieblose Komödie in drei Akten von Ben Jonson, frei bearbeitet (Berlin: Kiepenheuer, 1926); translated by Ruth Langner as *Ben Jonson's Volpone: A Loveless Comedy in Three Acts* (London: Allen & Unwin, 1928; New York: Viking Press, 1929);

Sternstunden der Menschheit: Fünf historische Miniaturen (Leipzig: Insel, 1927); edited by Felix Wittmer and Theodore Geissendoerfer (New York: Prentice-Hall, 1931); enlarged, translated by Eden and Cedar Paul as *The Tide of Fortune: Twelve Historical Miniatures* (New York: Viking Press, 1940; London: Cassell, 1955); enlarged German version published as *Sternstunden der Menschheit: Zwölf historische Miniaturen* (Stockholm: Bermann-Fischer, 1945);

Die unsichtbare Sammlung: Eine Episode aus der deutschen Inflation (Berlin: Privately printed, 1927);

Episode am Genfer See (Der Flüchtling) (Leipzig: Insel, 1927);

Verwirrung der Gefühle: Drei Novellen (Leipzig: Insel, 1927); translated by Eden and Cedar Paul as *Conflicts: Three Tales* (New York: Viking Press, 1927; London: Allen & Unwin, 1928);

Die Flucht zu Gott: Ein Epilog zu Leo Tolstois unvollendetem Drama "Das Licht scheinet in der Finsternis" (Berlin: Bloch, 1927);

Abschied von Rilke: Eine Rede (Tübingen: Wunderlich, 1927); translated by Marion Sonnenfeld as *Farewell to Rilke* (Fredonia, N.Y.: Friends of the Daniel Reed Library, State University College, 1975);

Reise nach Russland (Vienna: Österreichisches Journal, 1928);

Drei Dichter ihres Lebens: Casanova-Stendhal-Tolstoi (Leipzig: Insel, 1928); translated by Eden and Cedar Paul as *Adepts in Self-Portraiture: Casanova-Stendhal-Tolstoy* (New York: Viking Press, 1928; London: Allen & Unwin, 1929);

Thanks to Books, translated by Theodore Wesley Koch (Evanston, Ill.: Northwestern University Library, 1929);

Das Lamm des Armen: Tragikomödie in drei Akten (neun Bildern) (Leipzig: Insel, 1929);

Kleine Chronik (Leipzig: Insel, 1929);

Joseph Fouché: Bildnis eines politischen Menschen (Leipzig: Insel, 1929); translated by Eden and Cedar Paul as *Joseph Fouché: The Portrait of a Politician* (New York: Viking Press, 1930; London: Cassell, 1930);

Ausgewählte Gedichte (Leipzig: Insel, 1931);

Amok: A Story, translated by Eden and Cedar Paul (New York: Viking Press, 1931; London: Cassell, 1932);

Die Heilung durch den Geist: Franz Anton Mesmer-Mary Baker Eddy-Sigmund Freud (Leipzig: Insel, 1931); translated by Eden and Cedar Paul as *Mental Healers: Franz Anton Mesmer, Mary Baker Eddy, Sigmund Freud* (New York: Viking Press, 1932; London: Cassell, 1933);

Marie Antoinette: Bildnis eines mittleren Charakters (Leipzig: Insel, 1932); translated by Eden and Cedar Paul as *Marie Antoinette: The Portrait of an Average Woman* (New York: Viking, Press, 1933; London: Cassell, 1933);

Triumph und Tragik des Erasmus von Rotterdam (Vienna: Reichner, 1934); translated by Eden and Cedar Paul as *Erasmus of Rotterdam* (New York: Viking Press, 1934); translation republished as *Erasmus* (London: Cassell, 1934);

Maria Stuart (Vienna, Leipzig & Zurich: Reichner, 1935); translated by Eden and Cedar Paul as *Mary, Queen of Scotland and the Isles* (New York: Viking Press, 1935); translation republished as *The Queen of Scots* (London: Cassell, 1935);

Die schweigsame Frau: Komische Oper in drei Aufzügen frei nach Ben Jonson, music by Richard Strauss (Berlin: Fürstner, 1935);

Sinn und Schönheit der Autographen (Vienna: Reichner, 1935);

Arturo Toscanini: Ein Bildnis (Vienna: Reichner, 1935);

Die Kette (Vienna, Leipzig & Zurich: Reichner, 1936);

Kaleidoskop (Vienna, Leipzig & Zurich: Reichner, 1936);

Gesammelte Erzählungen (Vienna, Leipzig & Zurich: Reichner, 1936);

Castellio gegen Calvin oder Ein Gewissen gegen die Gewalt (Vienna, Leipzig & Zurich: Reichner, 1936); translated by Eden and Cedar Paul as *The Right to Heresy: Castellio against Calvin* (New York: Viking Press, 1936; London: Cassell, 1936);

The Old-Book Peddler and Other Tales for Bibliophiles, translated by Theodore W. Koch (Evanston, Ill.: Northwestern University, The Charles Deering Library, 1937)—comprises "Books Are the Gateway to the World," "The Old-Book Peddler: A Viennese Tale for Bibliophiles," "The Invisible Collection: An Episode from the Post-war Inflation Period," "Thanks to Books";

Georg Friedrich Händels Auferstehung: Eine historische Miniatur (Vienna, Leipzig & Zurich: Reichner, 1937); translated by Eden and

Cedar Paul as *George Frederick Handel's Resurrection* (London: Corvinus Press, 1938);

Der begrabene Leuchter (Vienna: Reichner, 1937); translated by Eden and Cedar Paul as *The Buried Candelabrum* (New York: Viking Press, 1937; London: Cassell, 1937);

Begegnungen mit Menschen, Büchern, Städten (Vienna, Leipzig & Zurich: Reichner, 1937);

Magellan: Der Mann und seine Tat (Vienna, Leipzig & Zurich: Reichner, 1938); translated by Eden and Cedar Paul as *Conqueror of the Seas: The Story of Magellan* (New York: Viking Press, 1938); translation republished as *Magellan: Pioneer of the Pacific* (London: Cassell, 1938);

Ungeduld des Herzens: Roman (Stockholm: Bermann-Fischer, 1939; New York & Toronto: Longmans, Green, Alliance Book Corp., 1939); translated by Phyllis and Trevor Blewitt as *Beware of Pity* (New York: Viking Press, 1939; London: Cassell, 1939);

Worte am Grabe Sigmund Freuds (Amsterdam: De Lange, 1939);

Brasilien, ein Land der Zukunft (Stockholm: Bermann-Fischer, 1941); translated by Andrew St. James as *Brazil, Land of the Future* (New York: Viking Press, 1941; London & Toronto: Cassell, 1942);

Schachnovelle (Buenos Aires: Pigmalion, 1942);

Amerigo: A Comedy of Errors in History, translated by St. James (New York: Viking Press, 1942); German version published as *Amerigo: Die Geschichte eines historischen Irrtums* (Stockholm: Bermann-Fischer, 1944);

The World of Yesterday: An Autobiography, translated by Benjamin W. Huebsch and Helmut Ripperger (New York: Viking Press, 1943; London: Cassell, 1943); German version published as *Die Welt von Gestern: Erinnerungen eines Europäers* (London: Hamilton & Stockholm: Bermann-Fischer, 1944);

Zeit und Welt: Gesammelte Aufsätze und Vorträge, 1904-1940, edited by Richard Friedenthal (Stockholm: Bermann-Fischer, 1943);

The Royal Game; Amok; Letter from an Unknown Woman (New York Viking Press, 1944); republished as *The Royal Game, with Letter from an Unknown Woman, and Amok* (London: Cassell, 1945)—comprises "The Royal Game" (*Schachnovelle*), translated by B. W. Huebsch, and "Amok" and "Letter from an Unknown Woman," translated by Eden and Cedar Paul;

Legenden (Stockholm: Bermann-Fischer, 1945); translated by Cedar Paul as *Jewish Legends*, edited by Jonathan D. Sarna (New York: Wiener, 1987);

Balzac: Der Roman seines Lebens, edited by Friedenthal (Stockholm: Bermann-Fischer, 1946); translated by William and Dorothy Rose as *Balzac* (New York: Viking Press, 1946; London: Cassell, 1947);

Ausgewählte Novellen (Stockholm: Bermann-Fischer, 1946);

Werke, edited by Friedenthal, 11 volumes (Frankfurt am Main: Fischer, 1954-1966);

Stories and Legends, translated by Eden and Cedar Paul and Constantine FitzGibbon (London: Cassell, 1955)—comprises "Twenty-four Hours in a Woman's Life," "A Failing Heart," "Episode in the Early Life of Privy Councillor D.," "The Buried Candelabrum," "The Legend of the Third Dove," "The Dissimilar Troubles";

Albert Schweitzer, Genie der Menschlichkeit, by Zweig, Jacques Feschotte, and Rudolf Grabs (Frankfurt am Main: Fischer, 1957);

Ausgewählte Werke, 2 volumes (Düsseldorf: Deutscher Bücherbund, 1960);

Fragment einer Novelle, edited by Erich Fitzbauer (Vienna: Verlag der Internationalen Stefan-Zweig-Gesellschaft, 1961);

Durch Zeiten und Welten, edited by Fitzbauer (Graz: Stiasny, 1961);

Im Schnee, edited by Fitzbauer (Vienna: Verlag der Internationalen Stefan-Zweig-Gesellschaft, 1963);

Der Turm zu Babel, edited by Fitzbauer (Vienna: Verlag der Internationalen Stefan-Zweig-Gesellschaft, 1964);

Die Dramen, edited by Richard Friedenthal (Frankfurt am Main: Fischer, 1964);

Frühlingsfahrt durch die Provence: Ein Essay, edited by Fitzbauer (Vienna: Verlag des Internationalen Stefan-Zweig-Gesellschaft, 1965);

Die Monotonisierung der Welt: Aufsätze und Vorträge, edited by Volker Michels (Frankfurt am Main: Suhrkamp, 1976);

Die Hochzeit von Lyon, edited by Fitzbauer (Vienna: Edition Graphischer Zirkel, 1980);

Das Stefan Zweig Buch, edited by Knut Beck (Frankfurt am Main: Fischer, 1981);

Das Geheimnis des künstlerischen Schaffens, edited by Beck (Frankfurt am Main: Fischer, 1981);

Menschen und Schicksale (Frankfurt am Main: Fischer, 1981);

Gesammelte Werke in Einzelbänden, edited by Beck, 25 volumes published (Frankfurt am Main: Fischer, 1982-   ).

OTHER: Paul Verlaine, *Eine Anthologie der besten Übersetzungen*, edited by Zweig (Berlin: Schuster & Loeffler, 1902);

Emile Verhaeren, *Ausgewählte Gedichte*, translated by Zweig (Berlin: Schuster & Loeffler, 1904);

Archibald B. H. Russell, *Die visionäre Kunstphilosophie des William Blake*, translated by Zweig (Leipzig: Zeitler, 1906);

Arthur Rimbaud, *Leben und Dichtung*, translated by K. L. Ammer, introduction by Zweig (Leipzig: Insel, 1907);

Honoré de Balzac, *Balzac: Sein Weltbild aus den Werken*, edited by Lothar Brieger-Wasservogel, introduction by Zweig, 2 volumes (Stuttgart: Lutz, 1908);

Verhaeren, *Ausgewählte Gedichte*, translated by Zweig (Leipzig: Insel, 1910);

Verhaeren, *Drei Dramen: Helenas Heimkehr–Philipp II–Das Kloster*, translated by Zweig (Leipzig: Insel, 1910);

Verhaeren, *Hymnen an das Leben*, translated by Zweig (Leipzig: Insel, 1911);

Lafcadio Hearn, *Das Japanbuch: Eine Auswahl aus Lafcadio Hearns Werken*, translated by Berta Franzos, introduction by Zweig (Frankfurt am Main: Rütten & Loening, 1911);

Verhaeren, *Rembrandt*, translated by Zweig (Leipzig: Insel, 1912);

Verhaeren, *Rubens*, translated by Zweig (Leipzig: Insel, 1913);

Romain Rolland, *Den hingerichteten Völkern (Aux peuples assassinés)*, translated by Zweig (Zurich: Rascher, 1918);

Rolland, *Die Zeit wird kommen (Le Temps viendra)*, translated by Zweig (Vienna & Leipzig: Tal, 1919);

Jean-Jacques Rousseau, *Emile oder Über die Erziehung*, introduction by Zweig (Potsdam: Kiepenheuer, 1919);

Madeline Marx, *Weib: Roman*, translated by Zweig and Friderike Zweig (Basel: Rhein, 1920);

André Suarès, *Cressida*, translated by Zweig and Erwin Rieger (Vienna: Tal, 1920);

Charles Baudelaire, *Die Blumen des Bösen*, eight poems translated by Zweig (Berlin: Oesterheld, 1921);

Franz Karl Ginzkey: Dem Dichter und Freunden zum 50sten Geburtstag, epilogue by Zweig (Vienna: Wiener Literarische Anstalt, 1921);

Zweig during his student years, circa 1901

Verlaine, *Gesammelte Werke*, edited by Zweig, 2 volumes (Leipzig: Insel, 1922);

Rolland, *Clérambault: Geschichte eines freien Gewissens im Kriege*, translated by Zweig (Frankfurt am Main: Rütten & Loening, 1922);

Charles Augustin Sainte-Beuve, *Literarische Portraits aus dem Frankreich des XVII.-XIX. Jahrhunderts*, edited by Zweig, 2 volumes (Frankfurt am Main: Frankfurter Verlags-Anstalt, 1923);

Hermann Bahr, *Die schöne Frau: Novellen*, epilogue by Zweig (Leipzig: Reclam, 1924);

François René Auguste, Vicomte de Chateaubriand, *Romantische Erzählungen*, edited by Zweig (Vienna, Leipzig & Munich: Rikola, 1924);

Franz Karl Ginzkey, *Brigitte und Regine und andere Dichtungen*, epilogue by Zweig (Leipzig: Reclam, 1924);

Max Brod, *Tycho Brahe's Weg zu Gott*, epilogue by Zweig (Berlin: Herbig, 1927);

Johann Wolfgang von Goethe, *Goethes Gedichte: Eine Auswahl*, edited by Zweig (Leipzig: Reclam, 1927);

Oskar Baum, *Nacht ist umher: Erzählung*, epilogue by Zweig (Leipzig: Reclam, 1929);

Maksim Gorky, *Erzählungen*, translated by Arthur Luther, introduction by Zweig (Leipzig: Insel, 1931);

Jean Richard Bloch, *Vom Sinn unseres Jahrhunderts*, translated by Paul Amann, introduction by Zweig (Berlin, Leipzig & Vienna: Zsolnay, 1932);

Luigi Pirandello, *Man weiß nicht wie*, translated by Zweig (Vienna: Reichner, 1935);

William Rose and G. Craig Houson, *Rainer Maria Rilke: Aspects of His Mind and Poetry*, introduction by Zweig (London: Sidgwick & Jackson, 1938);

Irwin Edman, *Ein Schimmer Licht im Dunkel*, translated by Zweig and Richard Friedenthal (Stockholm: Bermann-Fischer, 1940);

Stephan Zweig Presents the Living Thoughts of Tolstoy, essay by Zweig, translated by Barrows Mussey (Greenwich, Conn.: Fawcett, 1960).

In his lifetime the prolific Stefan Zweig was one of the most widely read writers in the world, his works having been translated into thirty languages. His star has dimmed somewhat in the Anglo-American realm, but his works are published in Germany in a manner befitting modern classics, and he has millions of readers in German-speaking and South American countries. Zweig is best known for his penetrating stories and his slightly fictionalized biographies of great historical and cultural figures. Lyric poetry does not loom large in his work, but several of his poems continue to appear in anthologies. Of his plays, only his wartime drama *Jeremias* (published, 1917; performed, 1918; translated as *Jeremiah*, 1922) and his adaptation of Ben Jonson's *Volpone* (1926; translated as *Ben Jonson's Volpone*, 1928) have had international dissemination, possibly because they are the only ones to have been translated into English. Friderike Maria Zweig wrote that her husband was uninterested in his plays once he had finished them, did not care for the footlights, was never completely at home in the world of the theater, and was always surprised by any stage success. In his posthumously published *The World of Yesterday* (1943) Zweig details the experiences with theaters, directors, and actors that made him suspect that his theatrical efforts were governed by an unlucky star. His goals as a dramatist were the same ones he sought to achieve in all his work. He was a translator in a wider and higher sense, a man who strove to inform, educate, inspire, and arouse appreciation and enthusiasm across literary, cultural, political, and personal boundaries. In his preface to a collection of his essays, *Begegnungen mit Menschen, Büchern, Städten* (Encounters with Persons, Books, Cities, 1937), Zweig speaks of "die unbeugsame Anspannung, auch das Fremdeste zu verstehen, immer Völker und Zeiten, Gestalten und Werke nur in ihrem positiven, ihrem schöpferischen Sinne zu bewerten und durch solches Verstehenwollen und Verstehenmachen demütig, aber treu unserem unzerstörbaren Ideal zu dienen: der humanen Verständigung zwischen Menschen, Gesinnungen, Kulturen und Nationen" (the determined effort to understand even what is most alien to us, always to evaluate peoples and periods, figures, and works only in their positive and creative sense, and to let this desire to understand and share this understanding with others serve humbly and faithfully our indestructible ideal: humane communication among persons, outlooks, cultures, and nations).

Zweig was born in Vienna on 28 November 1881, the second son of Moritz Zweig, a prosperous textile manufacturer, and Ida Brettauer Zweig. After graduating from the Wasa-Gymnasium he studied at the Universities of Vienna and Berlin. Taking what he called a flight into the intellectual from his father's stultifying bourgeois mentality and his mother's overbearing snobbishness, he had a cultural essay accepted by Theodor Herzl, the influential cultural editor of the prestigious *Neue Freie Presse* (New Free Press), and became a prominent member of the literary group known as "Jung Wien" (Young Vienna). His first book, a poetry collection titled *Silberne Saiten* (Silver Strings), appeared in 1901. In 1904 he took his doctorate at Vienna with a dissertation on Hippolyte Taine. Early trips to Germany, France, Belgium, Holland, England, Italy, Spain, India, and North America broadened the young man's intellectual horizon. But Zweig's evolution from an aesthetically oriented man of letters to what Jules Romains has called a "great European" was most decisively influenced by his encounter with the Flemish poet Emile Verhaeren, whose vibrantly contemporary, life-affirming poetry Zweig regarded as a lyrical encyclopedia of his age and whom he served as a translator, biographer, and popularizer until Verhaeren's death in 1916.

Zweig's first play, *Tersites* (published, 1907), was written in Italy in 1906. A three-act tragedy in blank verse, it focuses on the unhappiest and most downtrodden of the Greek warriors laying siege to Troy, a physically repulsive and widely de-

Zweig and his first wife, the former Friderike Maria von Winternitz, in the 1920s

spised doomsayer. The hapless protagonist unsuccessfully counsels Menelaus and Odysseus against wooing Achilles, who has been offended and has withdrawn from the war. Achilles spurns the friendship of the obsequious Thersites and remains inactive even when the Greeks are beaten. The deformed Thersites, who has never known the love of a woman, promises to fight for the freedom of Teleia, an Amazon princess who is Achilles' captive; he yearns to transmute his bitterness and hatred into noble deeds. But he comes to realize that Teleia is only using him to shock and hurt her master: she wishes to be Achilles' lover rather than his slave. After killing Teleia, the solipsistic Achilles for the first time muses about a human being he has slain. When Thersites brings Achilles the news that his friend Patroclus has been killed by the Trojan, Hector, Achilles kills the despised man and rushes out to do battle with Hector—ultimately to die at the hands of Paris.

In his first dramatic work, which abounds with eloquent speeches and ecstatic soliloquies, Zweig displays his empathy with those ill-favored by fortune and sounds one of his great themes, the moral superiority of the vanquished. Sigmund Freud praised the play in a letter to Zweig of 3 May 1908. The play was scheduled to be premiered at Berlin in March 1908, but after the death of Adalbert Matkowsky, who had been cast as Achilles, the play premiered simultaneously at theaters in Kassel and Dresden in late November 1908.

On commission from the actor Joseph Kainz, in 1910 Zweig wrote *Der verwandelte Komödiant* (The Transformed Actor, 1913). It was first performed in May 1912 in Breslau. The book edition is dedicated to the memory of Kainz, whose death from cancer had prevented him from playing a role that he had described as fitting him like a glove. Zweig described the one-act, five-scene play as "ein federleichtes Spiel aus dem Rokoko mit zwei eingebauten großen lyrisch-dramatischen Monologen" (a delicate rococo play that incorporates two big lyrical-dramatic monologues). In the play a young actor requests the patronage of a countess, who is herself the favorite of a prince and affects French diction and elegance. Having thought the actor was one of a troupe of boors performing crude plays on unworthy subjects, she is surprised to find that he is an educated man and promises to sponsor him. The actor realizes for the first time what it means to be an artist and to be able to inspire, awaken, and transform people. This discovery emboldens him to ask for the countess's love, but the aging woman, who has played at love too often to feel genuine passion, counsels him to be less passionate and more patient. The young man, now no longer a beggar, resolves to win her with his art.

Das Haus am Meer (The House by the Sea, 1912), completed in 1911, is a blank-verse drama in three acts and two parts (*Der Tausch* [The Exchange] and *Die Heimkehr* [The Homecoming]). This melodramatic play is redolent of naturalism and determinism. The house of the title is an inn near a German coastal town which is a way station for Germans being sold by their potentates to the British for service as mercenaries in the American Revolution. The inn is inhabited by Gotthold Krüger, an old river pilot; his nephew, Thomas; and the latter's wife, Katharina. A sergeant and a recruiter, who arrange billeting for the mostly unwilling soldiers-to-be, recognize Katharina as "rote Trine" (Red Kathy), a former prostitute. When Thomas is told about his wife's unsavory past, he decides to go to America as a mercenary even after he learns of his impending fatherhood. Twenty years later Thomas, now an American farmer known as Tommy Atkins, returns to find Katharina remarried to a wife-beater named Peter; his daughter, the slut Christine, is sleeping with her stepfather. Thomas takes his uncle's advice to leave the accursed house. After a fight on Peter's boat, which is taking Thomas to a transatlantic vessel, both men go to a watery grave.

Zweig's play was accepted by Alfred Berger, the director of the Hofburgtheater in Vienna, but Berger died before rehearsals could begin. After the play had been premiered there under the direction of Hugo Thimig, in 1912, performances at Munich, Hamburg, and Berlin followed. *Das Haus am Meer* was filmed in Germany in 1925 under the direction of Fritz Kaufmann and with Asta Nielsen as Katharina and Albert Steinrück as Thomas.

Zweig's European education was continued through his friendship, initiated in 1913, with the French writer, scholar, and humanist Romain Rolland, whose pacifistic activities during World War I were a great inspiration to the Austrian. While working at the Austrian War Archives in Vienna in 1915 and 1916 Zweig wrote his most powerful and most successful drama, *Jeremias*. An attempt to deal with the moral position of the individual in war, the play is Zweig's most mature statement of a position he had enunciated in *Tersites*: a rejection of the trappings of victory, power, and authority. The prophet Jeremiah has foreseen the fall of Jerusalem, but his laments have gone unheeded. After the disaster he feels that his prayer for guidance has not been answered, and he renounces his allegiance to God. When the victorious Chaldeans offer Jeremiah a high position in the service of Nebuchadnezzar, his prophetic gifts return; he foretells the downfall of the victors and assumes the leadership of the Jews, whom he convinces of the spiritual significance of their faith in an invincible and eternal holy city. Suffering has an ennobling effect; a sorely tried, vanquished, homeless people can find its way to God through faith. In the last scene, titled *Der ewige Weg* (The Everlasting Road), a choric recital of the wanderings and trials of the people of Israel culminates in Jeremiah's voice bidding his people to continue marching on the paths trodden by their forefathers to eternity. A Chaldean has the final in-

Zweig in Rio de Janeiro, circa 1940

sight: "Man kann ein Volk bezwingen, doch nie seinen Geist" (A nation can be controlled by force; its spirit, never). Zweig was convinced that it was the mission of the Jewish people to work toward a spiritual, supranational, eternal Jerusalem rather than striving, as the Zionists did, for a return to the real city. Only in this way could the Jews escape the self-destructive tendencies and hubris of those who believe in power.

It may be argued that *Jeremias* is not so much a Jewish drama as a pacifistic one, but in a letter to Martin Buber dated 8 May 1916 Zweig says he is working "an einem großen Jeremias-Drama, das ohne Liebesepisoden, ohne Theaterambitionen die Tragik des Menschen, dem nur das Wort, die Warnung und die Erkenntnis gegen die Realität der Tatsachen gegeben ist, auf dem Hintergrunde eines Entscheidungskrieges darstellt. Es ist die Tragödie und der Hymnus des jüdischen Volkes als des auserwählten—aber nicht im Sinn des Wohlergehens, sondern des ewigen Leidens, des ewigen Niedersturzes und der ewigen Erhebung und der aus solchem Schicksal sich entfaltenden Kraft" (on a great drama about Jeremiah that presents, against the background of a decisive war

and without love interests or theatrical ambitions, the tragedy of a man who has only words, warnings, and wisdom to pit against realities. It is the tragedy and the hymn of the Jewish people as the Chosen People—not in the sense of prosperity but in that of eternal suffering, eternal falling, and eternal rising, and of the strength deriving from such a fate). Friderike Zweig wrote that "of all his works, it was probably closest to his heart" and describes it as "a secondary matter that it was written for the stage." In a new preface to the book edition of 1939, marking the first American production by the New York Theatre Guild, Zweig revealed that his first sketches had involved a Cassandra figure, but that soon a great biblical figure had forced itself upon him. After years of neglect by an oblivious and over-optimistic Europe, he wrote, the undiminished timeliness of this play, as witnessed by productions in Palestine, Holland, and the United States, was a disturbing sign of the times.

Zweig's three-act prose play *Legende eines Lebens* (Legend of a Life; performed, 1918; published, 1919), written in 1918, uses elements from the lives of Friedrich Hebbel, Richard Wagner, Fyodor Dostoyevski, and Wagner's son Siegfried. The first act is set at the home of the celebrated writer Karl Amadeus Franck, who, a decade after his death, is the subject of a four-volume biography by his editor, Hermann Bürstein, and a cult presided over by his widow, Leonore. Bürstein and Leonore are preparing for a public reading from the works of Franck's son, Friedrich Marius (his name is a tribute to Zweig's future wife, Friderike Maria), an insecure young man who does not relish his status as a "crown prince" and feels so crushed by his father's fame that he has been trying to find a humanizing flaw in the icon. When the elderly Maria Folkenhof, Karl's former mistress, arrives from overseas, she is welcomed by Friedrich but rebuffed by Leonore, who, in an effort to retouch the great man's portrait, had told Bürstein that Maria was dead. The next day the editor and the son call on Frau Folkenhof. Friedrich learns that his impending birth was the reason for his father's abandonment of Maria and that the latter is his godmother. The son now recognizes himself in his father—not in the latter's greatness but in his cowardice and withdrawal. Grateful for his new self-knowledge, he resolves to be stronger than his father, whom he can now love in his human weakness. In his relationship with his lady friend, a lowly piano teacher, he has hitherto thought only of his own reputation and convenience; now he can love her fully and openly. When Bürstein tells Leonore of his resolve not to participate in the deception any longer, she at first vows to continue serving the legend; but then she realizes that Maria has been a victim. On their way to Karl's grave the two women decide to live together and share their memories.

In 1919 Zweig moved to Salzburg. The following year he married Friderike Maria Burger von Winternitz, whose first marriage had been annulled. The years in Salzburg with his wife and two stepdaughters were his most productive ones. The Zweigs' impressive mountainside home became a shrine to Zweig's central idea, the intellectual unification of Europe, and the mecca of a cultural elite.

Zweig modestly called the work he wrote during a trip to Marseilles in 1926 *Volpone: Eine lieblose Komödie in drei Akten von Ben Jonson, frei bearbeitet* (Volpone: A Loveless Comedy by Ben Jonson, Freely Adapted). Jonson's comedy *Volpone; or, The Fox*, first performed in 1605, had never been translated into German; Zweig's version, in which the adapter displays great comic talent, has been performed on hundreds of stages in Germany and elsewhere. Set in Renaissance Italy, Zweig's fast-paced comedy adopts the general outline of Jonson's plot but omits some of his characters and renames others. Thus Zweig gives the only two characters who are not deceitful and avaricious, Jonson's Bonario and Celia, the names Leone (Lion) and Colomba (Dove). The wealthy Volpone (Fox) contrives an elaborate scheme to outwit the fortune hunters who claim to be his friends: pretending to be at death's door, he exacts valuable gifts from them. His servant, Mosca (Gadfly), orchestrates this chorus of cupidity, inducing the old usurer Corbaccio (Raven) to disinherit his son, Leone, in favor of Volpone and persuades the merchant Corvino (Crow) to order his wife to sleep with Volpone to hasten the old man's demise. When Volpone makes Mosca his sole heir and pretends to be dead, the plot backfires as the lawyer Voltore (Vulture) helps to outfox the fox. A judge determines that his court has been duped, Volpone is sent packing to Smyrna, and Mosca, determined to end avarice, releases his gold for the sake of general merriment. In the end Mosca's poem about the restoration of gold to nature provides a counterpoise to Volpone's initial paean of praise to gold; and yet, as a musician's song heard at the beginning and

One of the last photographs taken of Zweig

at the end of the play indicates, it is in the nature of things that money will continue to rule the world.

Die Flucht zu Gott (The Flight to God; published, 1927; performed, 1928) is an epilogue in three scenes to Leo Tolstoy's unfinished autobiographical drama *And the Light Shineth in the Darkness*, begun in 1890. Zweig intended his play to be added to performances of Tolstoy's drama; he believed that he was supplying the last act that Tolstoy did not write but lived, in which he found the courage to unravel the tangled skein of his life and break out to freedom. Zweig gives the Russian writer, who called his protagonist Nikolai Mikhaelevich Zarynzev, his real name.

Zweig's play takes place in late October 1910. At Tolstoy's home, Yasnaya Polyana, two students challenge the novelist: why doesn't he join them as a revolutionary? He answers that even though he has demanded a complete social restructuring, he has never felt hatred and is unalterably opposed to violence. He realizes that he has been remiss in failing to act and blames himself for his weakness and vacillation, but he calls even

The grave of Zweig and his second wife, Elisabeth Charlotte Altmann Zweig, in the cemetery at Petrópolis, Brazil

the exploiters and cutthroats his brothers who need to be loved. His wife berates him for wasting his time with the youths, but their visit is the catalyst that spurs him to action at long last. After making a will that places his writings in the public domain, he tells his wife of forty-eight years that she has never shared his religious life. She replies that his religious beliefs have alienated him from his family. Even though she has promised to trust him, she rifles through his papers at night. Tolstoy takes this act as a sign that he should leave her. Bidding farewell to his daughter, he sets out for a monastery in the company of a physician friend. The final scene takes place three days later, when Tolstoy dies in peace at the Astapovo railway station.

In 1929 Zweig wrote *Das Lamm des Armen* (The Poor Man's Lamb; published, 1929; performed, 1930), a prose tragicomedy in three acts and nine scenes based on an episode from Napoleon's Egyptian campaign—the adultery supposedly committed by him in response to his wife's flirtation with a cavalry officer.

The first two acts are set in Cairo in 1798. Lieutenant François Fourès's fellow soldiers envy him his charming and spirited wife Pauline, called Bellilotte, who has managed to accompany him dressed in men's clothes. With the aid of Dupuy, his regional commander, and Berthier,

his adjutant, Napoleon plots Bellilotte's seduction after her husband is posted to Paris as a courier. But the British intercept Fourès's boat and release him, whereupon he returns to Cairo. When the plotters claim that Bellilotte wishes to divorce him, Fourès ruefully remembers the biblical tale about a poor man's only lamb that is taken from him by a rich man. His wife's only excuse for dishonoring his name is that there was no resisting Bonaparte. When Fourès criticizes Napoleon's desertion to Paris, he is discharged and returns to France as a civilian. The third act is set in Paris in 1799, shortly after a coup d'état has made Napoleon consul of the republic. Fourès continues to press for justice, but his quixotic quest makes him run afoul of Napoleon's police minister, Joseph Fouché. In the end Fourès is left only with the insight that little people always suffer when the mighty abuse their power and with the impotent rage that causes him to rip Bonaparte's portrait down from a wall.

In the last decade of his life Zweig, who wrote in his autobiography that as an Austrian, a Jew, a writer, a humanist, and a pacifist he had always stood at the exact point where the global clashes and cataclysms of his century were at their most violent, was bedeviled by the growing menace of Hitlerism. After 1933 the centrally located Salzburg became inhospitable and dangerously exposed. His move to England in 1934 marked the beginning of years of insecurity, restless globe-trotting, and mounting despair. Among the events and situations that oppressed the exile, who acquired British citizenship in 1940, were the breakup of his marriage and his ill-starred collaboration with Richard Strauss. The composer welcomed Zweig as a replacement for his longtime librettist Hugo von Hofmannsthal, who had died in 1929. Between September 1932 and January 1933 Zweig wrote the libretto for *Die schweigsame Frau* (The Silent Woman, 1935), a comic opera based on a motif by Ben Jonson. Morose, "a gentleman that loves no noise" in Jonson's play *Epicoene; or, The Silent Woman* (performed, 1609; printed, 1610) becomes Zweig's Sir Morosus Blunt, a retired admiral who, in his quest for a gentle wife, is tricked into favoring his nephew Henry, a singer who "rescues" his uncle from the not-so-silent Amida, who is really Henry's own wife. Strauss insisted that Zweig's name appear on the announcement of the opera's premiere at Dresden on 24 June 1935. Only four performances were permitted, and after the Nazi authorities intercepted an imprudent letter from Strauss to Zweig, the composer had to resign from his post as head of the Reichsmusikkammer (Reich Music Chancellory).

Profoundly depressed by the fate of Europe and fearing that the humanistic spirit of the "world of yesterday" was crushed forever, Zweig and his second wife, Elisabeth Charlotte Altmann Zweig, whom he had married in Bath in 1939, poisoned themselves at Petrópolis, near Rio de Janeiro, on 22 February 1942. The government of Brazil, a country Zweig had celebrated in *Brasilien, ein Land der Zukunft* (1941; translated as *Brazil, Land of the Future*, 1941), gave them a state funeral.

Letters:

Briefwechsel: Stefan Zweig-Friderike Zweig, 1912-1942 (Bern: Scherz, 1951); translated by Henry G. Alsberg and Erna McArthur as *Stefan and Friderike Maria Zweig: Their Correspondence* (New York: Hastings House, 1954); German edition republished as *Friderike Zweig-Stefan Zweig: Unrast der Liebe* (Bern: Scherz, 1981);

Richard Strauss-Stefan Zweig: Briefwechsel, edited by Willi Schuh (Frankfurt am Main: Fischer, 1957); translated by Max Knight as *A Confidential Matter: The Letters of Richard Strauss and Stefan Zweig, 1931-1935* (Berkeley: University of California Press, 1977);

Stefan Zweig: Unbekannte Briefe aus der Emigration an eine Freundin, edited by Gisella Selden-Goth (Vienna, Stuttgart & Zurich: Deutsch, 1964);

Maxim Gorki-Stefan Zweig; Briefwechsel, edited by Kurt Böttcher (Leipzig: Reclam, 1973);

Stefan Zweig: Briefe an Freunde, edited by Richard Friedenthal (Frankfurt am Main: Fischer, 1978);

The Correspondence of Stefan Zweig with Raoul Auernheimer and with Richard Beer-Hofmann, edited by Donald G. Daviau, Jorun B. Johns, and Jeffrey B. Berlin (Columbia, S.C.: Camden House, 1983);

Stefan Zweig-Paul Zech: Briefe 1910-1942, edited by Daviau (Frankfurt am Main: Fischer, 1985);

Rainer Maria Rilke: Briefwechsel mit Stefan Zweig, edited by Donald A. Prater (Frankfurt am Main: Insel, 1985);

Stefan Zweig und Meyer-Benfey: Bisher unveröffentlichte Briefe, edited by Claude Flor (Hamburg: Deutscher Literatur-Verlag Otto Melchert, 1986);

Stefan Zweig: Briefwechsel mit Hermann Bahr, Sigmund Freud, Rainer Maria Rilke, and Arthur Schnitzler, edited by Berlin, Prater, and Hans-Ulrich Lindken (Frankfurt am Main: Fischer, 1987);

Romain Rolland-Stefan Zweig: Briefwechsel 1910-1940, 2 volumes, translated by Eva Schewe, Gerhard Schewe, and Christel Gersch, edited by Waltraud Schwarze (Berlin: Rütten & Loening, 1987).

Bibliography:

Randolph J. Klawiter, *Stefan Zweig: A Bibliography* (Chapel Hill: University of North Carolina Press, 1965).

Biographies:

Erwin Rieger, *Stefan Zweig: Der Mann und das Werk* (Berlin: Spaeth, 1928);

Raul De Azevedo, *Vida e Morte de Stefan Zweig* (Rio de Janeiro: Aspectos, 1942);

Benjamin Jarnes, *Stefan Zweig: Cumbre Apagada* (Mexico: Editorial Proa, 1942);

Claudio De Souza, *Les Derniers Jours de Stefan Zweig* (Mexico: Editions Quetzal, 1944);

Alicia Ortiz Oderigo, *Stefan Zweig: Un Hombre de Ayer* (Buenos Aires: Editorial Nova, 1945);

Friderike Maria Zweig, *Stefan Zweig*, translated by Erna McArthur (New York: Crowell, 1946; London: Allen, 1948); German version published as *Stefan Zweig: Wie ich ihn erlebte* (Stockholm: Neuer Verlag, 1947);

Hans Hellwig, *Stefan Zweig: Ein Lebensbild* (Lübeck: Dr. I. M. Wildner Verlag, 1948);

Arnold Bauer, *Stefan Zweig* (Berlin: Colloquium, 1961);

Zweig, *Stefan Zweig: Eine Bildbiographie* (Munich: Kindler, 1961);

Elizabeth Allday, *Stefan Zweig: A Critical Biography* (London: Allen, 1972);

Donald A. Prater, *European of Yesterday: A Biography of Stefan Zweig* (Oxford: Clarendon Press, 1972); German version published as *Stefan Zweig: Das Leben eines Ungeduldigen* (Munich & Vienna: Hanser, 1981);

Prater and Volker Michels, eds., *Stefan Zweig: Leben und Werk im Bild* (Frankfurt am Main: Insel, 1981);

Joseph Strelka, *Stefan Zweig: Freier Geist der Menschlichkeit* (Vienna: Österreichischer Bundesverlag, 1981);

Hartmut Müller, *Stefan Zweig: In Selbstzeugnissen und Bilddokumenten* (Reinbek: Rowohlt, 1988).

References:

Hanns Arens, ed., *Der große Europäer Stefan Zweig* (Munich: Kindler, 1956);

Arens, ed., *Stefan Zweig im Zeugnis seiner Freunde* (Munich: Langen-Müller, 1968);

Arens, ed., *Stefan Zweig: sein Leben—sein werk. Mit Beiträgen von Walter Bauer* (Esslingen: Bechtle, 1949); translated by Christobel Fowler as *Stefan Zweig: A Tribute to His Life and Work, with Contributions by Walter Bauer and Others* (London: Allen, 1951);

Donald G. Daviau, "Stefan Zweig's Victors in Defeat," *Monatshefte*, 51 (1959): 1-12;

Robert Dumont, *Stefan Zweig et la France* (Paris: Didier, 1967);

Dumont, *Le Theatre de Stefan Zweig* (Paris: Presses Universitaires de France, 1976);

Erich Fitzbauer, ed., *Stefan Zweig: Spiegelungen einer schöpferischen Persönlichkeit* (Vienna: Bergland, 1959);

Marc H. Gelber, ed., *Stefan Zweig heute* (New York & Bern: Lang, 1987);

Pierre Grappin, ed., *Stefan Zweig: 1881-1942* (Paris: Didier, 1982);

Volker Henze, *Jüdischer Kulturpessimismus und das Bild des alten Österreich im Werk Stefan Zweigs und Joseph Roths* (Heidelberg: Winter, 1988);

Klaus Heydemann, "Das Beispiel des Erasmus: Stefan Zweigs Einstellung zur Politik," *Literatur und Kritik*, 169-170 (1982): 24-39;

Heinz Lunzer and Gerhard Renner, eds., *Stefan Zweig 1881/1981: Aufsätze und Dokumente* (Vienna: Zirkular, 1981);

Alfred Mathis, "Stefan Zweig as Librettist and Richard Strauss," *Music and Letters*, 25 (1944): 163-176, 226-245;

William H. McClain and Harry Zohn, "Stefan Zweig and Romain Rolland: The Literary and Personal Relationship," *Germanic Review*, 28 (December 1953): 262-281;

Modern Austrian Literature, special Zweig issue, edited by Daviau, 14, no. 3/4 (1981);

Donald Prater, "Stefan Zweig," in *Exile: The Writer's Experience*, edited by John Spalek and Robert Bell (Chapel Hill: University of North Carolina Press, 1982), pp. 311-322;

Jules Romains, *Stefan Zweig: Great European* (New York: Viking Press, 1941);

Marion Sonnenfeld, ed., *Stefan Zweig: The World of Yesterday's Humanist Today* (Albany: State University of New York Press, 1983);

Arthur Werner, ed., *Begegnung mit Stefan Zweig: Ein Buch der Erinnerung* (Vienna: Stefan Zweig-Gesellschaft, 1972);

Harry Zohn, "Stefan Zweig and Contemporary European Literature," *German Life and Letters*, 5 (1952): 202-212;

Zohn, "Stefan Zweig: Der Europäer, der Österreicher, der Jude," in his *Ich bin ein Sohn der deutschen Sprache nur* (Vienna: Amalthea, 1986), pp. 98-128;

Zohn, "Stefan Zweig: The European and the Jew," *Year Book XXVII of the Leo Baeck Institute* (1982): 323-336;

Friderike Maria Zweig, *Spiegelungen des Lebens* (Vienna, Stuttgart & Zurich: Deutsch, 1964);

Zweig, "Stefan Zweig," in her *Greatness Revisited* (Boston: Branden Press, 1972), 79-104.

Papers:

Stefan Zweig materials are at the Daniel Reed Library, State University of New York College at Fredonia; the Stefan Zweig Estate, London; the Austrian National Library, Vienna; and the Hebrew University Library, Jerusalem.

Appendix

German Drama from Naturalism to Fascism: 1889-1933

German Drama from Naturalism to Fascism: 1889-1933

Roy C. Cowen
University of Michigan

In German literary history most revolutionaries, reformers, and social critics have usually turned to drama—albeit often with little chance of success because of censorship. On the one hand, this phenomenon can be attributed to Germany's unique theatrical situation: in contrast to all other European countries, in Germany almost every city of any size had had a theater of some significance since, at the latest, the early eighteenth century. Thus, while in England and France theatrical developments were limited mainly to London and Paris, such cities as Hamburg, Frankfurt, Mannheim, Munich, Dresden, Leipzig, and Berlin must be considered in any account of German theatrical history. Drama was accorded a higher status in Germany than in any other country; the philosophers Georg Wilhelm Friedrich Hegel and Arthur Schopenhauer both characterize tragedy as the highest form of literature. On the other hand, this phenomenon stems from the aesthetically unique potential of drama: in this medium alone can a writer address an audience directly. The playwright finds out immediately how many people have seen a work and how they have reacted to it. By contrast, the author of an inflammatory pamphlet, a volume of poetry, or a piece of narrative prose may learn how many people have purchased the work but not how many have actually read, understood, or misunderstood it, or how many have simply received secondhand knowledge of its contents.

Moreover, drama is the only literary form of total immediacy—the only one that does not have the author as an intermediary who describes what he has already seen, heard, or felt. During the performance of a play, the audience sees the actions and hears the words at the very moment that they occur. Reading a play cannot substitute for experiencing its performance. The eternal present tense of dramatic action, including flashbacks and prophetic dreams, directly confronts the audience with the question: how well does what I am seeing conform to the world I know outside the theater? The historian of drama is concerned with the varying degrees to which a playwright or director tries to answer or suppress this question, for the stage offers a great potential for reproducing a given reality or creating a "new," perhaps completely alien one. Thus, any survey of historical developments in German drama and theater must attempt to answer two fundamental questions: What kind of relationship does the individual playwright try to establish with the audience? What is the implied relationship between the events and words on the stage and those in a world perceived by the audience as "real?"

Tendencies before 1889

The first plays of naturalism in 1889 brought a revolution to German stages. But neither the goals nor the impact of this revolution can be adequately understood without reference to the years between 1815, when Napoleon was defeated, and 1889. For, on the one hand, naturalism represents the culmination of several artistic and cultural tendencies during these seventy-four years. On the other hand, it marks the beginning of the modern period by its conscious revolting against many cherished artistic and sociopolitical values of the older generation. Thus, the German naturalists would call for, and see themselves as exponents of, "modern" literature; yet they would also associate their goals with the unfulfilled ones of unappreciated individuals and movements from as far back as the eighteenth century.

Germany produced more great dramatists in the nineteenth century than did any other European country. In literary histories of England scarcely any mention is made of playwrights between Richard Brinsley Sheridan and George Ber-

Cartoon in the satirical Berlin weekly Kladderadatsch *(1889) depicting the naturalist theater Die Freie Bühne*

nard Shaw, except for Oscar Wilde. In histories of France during the nineteenth century the ideas of Victor Hugo as a dramatist might be accorded some attention, and the names of Alexandre Dumas *fils* and Emile Augier might be saved from falling into total obscurity; but only Alfred de Musset is usually given any degree of critical attention today. The only dramatists from Scandinavia and Russia in the nineteenth century who still enjoy critical acceptance are precisely those who strongly influenced the German naturalists: Henrik Ibsen, Bjornstjerne Bjornson, August Strindberg, and Leo Tolstoy. Yet no history of the German-speaking area can ignore Franz Grillparzer, Christian Dietrich Grabbe, Georg Büchner, and Friedrich Hebbel as creators of great serious dramas, nor would such a history be complete without taking into account the two outstanding masters of Viennese popular comedy, Ferdinand Raimund and Johann Nestroy—quite aside from Richard Wagner, who considered his *Musikdramen* not operas but the dramas of the future.

Yet with the exceptions of Wagner and two Austrians, who represent the zenith and virtual end of a long tradition, none of the above-named German-language dramatists influenced contem-

porary or immediately subsequent theatrical developments; Grabbe's and Büchner's plays were not even performed until long after their deaths. Only Grillparzer achieved any measure of fame among his contemporaries; but in 1838, after the negative reception of his only comedy, the greatness of which is today unquestioned, he withdrew from the public stage and kept his last three plays from being published or performed until after his death. Hebbel experienced more notoriety than recognition because of his sexually excessive characters. What fame he did glean was frequently based on misunderstanding, and his most lasting contribution to German drama, his middle-class tragedy *Maria Magdalena* (1844), did not come into its own until critics dubbed Ibsen a "Hebbel redivivus." The reason for the lack of influence of these great dramatists is that from 1815 to 1889 German stages, like those of the rest of Europe, were dominated by mediocre works. Along with the works of foreigners such as Eugène Scribe, those by such Germans as Charlotte Birch-Pfeiffer and Ernst Raupach achieved great popularity. During this time, anyone with pronounced literary ambition tried his or her hand at verse tragedy, and anyone seeking fame and fortune on the stage had to write historical tragedies in the style of Friedrich Schiller. Yet Schiller's legacy was to prove fateful for the development of serious German drama, less because of what his works actually had to say than what people believed they heard in them and wanted to see in Schiller as their author.

In almost every period of literary history conflicting values have brought about at least one significant controversy. As far as dramatic theory and practice in Germany in the nineteenth century are concerned, the major such controversy revolved around the relative merits of Schiller and William Shakespeare as models for serious drama (Schiller had written no comedies). In popular thinking, Schiller represented idealism, Shakespeare realism. Büchner reflects this distinction in a letter of 28 July 1835 to his family: "Wenn man mir übrigens noch sagen wollte, der Dichter müsse die Welt nicht zeigen, wie sie ist, sondern wie sie sein solle, so antworte ich, daß ich es nicht besser machen will, als der liebe Gott, der die Welt gewiß gemacht hat, wie sie sein soll. Was noch die sogenannten Idealdichter anbetrifft, so finde ich, daß sie fast nichts als Marionetten mit himmelblauen Nasen und affectirtem Pathos, aber nicht Menschen von Fleisch und Blut gegeben haben, deren Leid und Freude mich mitempfinden macht, und deren Thun und Handeln mir Abscheu oder Bewunderung einflößt. Mit einem Wort, ich halte viel auf Goethe oder Shakspeare, aber sehr wenig auf Schiller" (If someone were to tell me that the poet should not depict the world as it is but as it should be, then I would answer that I do not want to make it better than God, who certainly made the world as it should be. As far as the so-called idealistic poets are concerned, I find that they have produced hardly anything besides marionettes with sky-blue noses and affected pathos, not human beings of flesh and blood, with whose sorrow and happiness I sympathize and whose actions repel or attract me. In a word, I think much of Goethe or Shakespeare, but very little of Schiller). Grillparzer, Grabbe, and Hebbel all expressed or implied their admiration for Schiller; Grabbe wrote an essay attacking the Romantic adulation of Shakespeare, and Grillparzer criticized the Romantic excesses of Ludwig Tieck's interpretations of Shakespeare. But all three, along with Büchner, stood closer in practice to the Englishman, for each reveals a pronounced tendency toward a realistic portrayal of characters and events that is missing in the majority of dramas during the nineteenth century.

For Grillparzer, Grabbe, Büchner, and Hebbel, "realism" dictated showing human beings caught up in a world that gave no indication of ultimate, immutable truths. At best, such truths could be found only in humanity's inability to control its destiny. In turn, they did not approach their audiences as interpreters of the real world. Grillparzer criticizes both Schiller and Johann Wolfgang von Goethe for creating dramas in which not the characters but an omniscient author is speaking; they do not portray the world as it is but interpret it for the audience by means of characters such as Goethe's Iphigenia and Schiller's Mary Stuart, who can rise above the turmoil and confusion surrounding them and grasp the higher principles or truths involved. Such characters are not talking to other characters but to the audience, and as a consequence, according to Grillparzer, they deprive the plays of their dramatic powers. Grillparzer says—and Grabbe, Büchner, and Hebbel imply—that people cannot escape the present but remain subject to their momentary emotions, notions, and lack of knowledge.

On the other hand, it follows that characters such as Iphigenia and Mary Stuart can recognize and realize ideal values. History becomes, for these characters and for the audience, the relative, changing background against which conflicts involving unchanging, timeless ideals are carried out. The world in which these characters are depicted is one in which mass movements, economic and social factors, lack of self-understanding, and chance events have little significance. As Büchner points out, this world is not the one the audience has left to enter the theater and must reenter on leaving the theater. It is a utopia and is addressed to the utopian expectations of the audience.

Hebbel's death in 1863 was followed by a hiatus in the development of German drama. No playwright of note emerged—the only possible exception is Ludwig Anzengruber—until the appearance of Gerhart Hauptmann's first work in 1889. Yet this quarter-century brought forth five of Germany's greatest writers, who are frequently designated as Poetic Realists: Gottfried Keller, Theodor Storm, Theodor Fontane, Conrad Ferdinand Meyer, and Wilhelm Raabe, all of whom excelled in the novella or novel, and most of whom also still enjoy critical recognition for their lyric poetry. Yet none of them wrote a play. A lack of talent alone does not suffice as an explanation, for all stressed the dramatic qualities of their narra-

Otto Brahm, the founder of Die Freie Bühne, in 1891

tive works. Keller carried on an extensive, illuminating correspondence about the state of drama at the time, and Fontane proved to be one of the most insightful, open-minded theater critics of his day. A more compelling explanation is the nature and social role of contemporary serious drama. These men were all literary realists writing at a time when the serious stage productions consisted primarily of historical plays displaying Schillerian idealism. Moreover, writing such plays would not only have gone against their artistic grain but would also have aligned them with groups from which they frequently distanced themselves and which they sometimes subtly or openly criticized. Schiller had become the national poet of nationalistically enthusiastic Germans and the bourgeoisie in general, and his imitators pandered to the values of these groups. The socially and politically symbolic significance that must be attributed to Schiller's name and to the type of drama he wrote and inspired is brought out most effectively by Gerhart Hauptmann in his tragicomedy *Die Ratten* (1911; translated as *The Rats*, 1913), which takes place in Berlin in 1883-1884—that is, shortly before naturalism

began its triumphant march across that city's stages. Although Hauptmann shows the inadequacies of naturalism and its proponents, he also makes evident how serious drama had by 1883-1884 excluded a large segment of the real world and become a vehicle for sustaining decadent social institutions.

During the nineteenth century, drama also lost more and more contact with the broader intellectual developments outside of the theater. The Poetic Realists were more closely attuned to the effects of new philosophical and scientific theories and discoveries than were the playwrights after Hebbel. These effects lay primarily in a radically altered view of reality. In turn, naturalism can be characterized both as a rejection of the old view still underlying much of the serious drama of the day and, in a positive light, as the greatest experiment in making art conform to what the nineteenth century had gradually come to understand as reality.

The great age of idealistic philosophy had ended with the death of G. W. F. Hegel in 1831, and his immediate supporters—the Young Hegelians such as Friedrich Theodor von Vischer and the Left Hegelians such as Karl Marx and Friedrich Engels—set about taking the speculative philosophy out of their mentor's system and substituting for it sociopolitical insights. In doing so, they anticipated the course of philosophy during the rest of the century, a century that increasingly abandoned speculation and abstractions in favor of observation and a metaphoric language drawn predominantly from the natural sciences, especially biology.

In many circles a new perspective on human nature and society was furnished by a new discipline: sociology. The anti-idealistic heritage of this new endeavor lies in its debt to the English school of empiricism. Linking the empirical, sociological, and naturalistic conceptions of humanity is the weight given to the environment at the cost of any inherent ability to recognize ideals. Sociology, as conceived by its founder, Auguste Comte, was to be a "social physics"; it would apply the methods of natural science to social relationships. This conception brought about a shift from qualitative measures of truth to quantitative ones: the more one knows about something, the more certain one can be of its truth. Understanding reality thus becomes a question of amassing details, not of attaining insights. When naturalism set about reproducing "reality," therefore, it strove for the "complete" truth, not a "higher" one. Moreover, from a sociological perspective moral values and ideals have validity not according to who asserts them but according to how many accept them. This perspective deprived any stage hero of the right to put forward his insights as absolute truths.

Another intellectual current that contributed to the erosion of the idealism implied by the serious drama before 1889 was Darwinism. Philosophical inroads had already been made against absolute religious values with the publication of *Das Leben Jesu* (The Life of Jesus, 1835), by David Friedrich Strauß, and *Das Wesen des Christentums* (The Essence of Christianity, 1841), by Ludwig Feuerbach. The former argued against the divinity of Christ, portraying him as an affable madman; the latter interpreted belief in the existence of God as a psychological necessity and a *Wunschbild* (wish-fulfillment). As the validity of religious truth was subjected to increasing skepticism, popular confidence grew regarding natural science's ability to provide answers to questions about human existence. Natural science seemed to live up to such expectations in 1859 with the publication of Charles Darwin's *The Origin of Species by Natural Selection; or, The Preservation of Favoured Races in the Struggle for Life*. The impact of Darwin's work was immediate, broad, and controversial. Even more important for naturalism than the issue of evolution—which had, in any case, been advanced by thinkers before Darwin—were the implications of natural selection as the result of the struggle for life. Parentage and heredity had played a role in literary works for centuries, but with the advent of naturalism, heredity and the influence of the environment emerged as the most crucial measures of the characters. Moreover, Darwin asserted that neither a divine plan nor logic manifests itself in evolution; only brute survivability determines the success or failure of a given species. Consequently, no ideal or moral inferences can be drawn from the survival or disappearance of a species. This view was rapidly applied to social interaction. The consequences for literature were obvious: any work purporting to reproduce real life could no longer indulge in poetic justice, nor could it allow the outcome of any conflict to be interpreted as more than the survival of the fittest.

By 1889, therefore, a new view of humanity had emerged. Since the social, biological, and physical sciences had provided this new conception, literature, if it was to be modern, had to portray humanity and society within the confines set by the sciences. Naturalism took many forms in different lands and even in the same country. Germany was the last country to develop a naturalist literature and perhaps as a consequence naturalism there became the most radical in its attitudes and experiments.

Naturalist Drama

The goals of literary naturalism could unquestionably have been best attained on the stage. But drama was the last genre to gain prominence as a medium of German naturalists. The naturalists recognized as their predecessors a succession of playwrights largely ignored or scorned by contemporaries: the dramatists of the Sturm und Drang (Storm and Stress) movement, notably Jakob Michael Reinhold Lenz and Heinrich von Kleist, along with Grabbe, Büchner, and Hebbel. They also recognized the efforts of foreign dramatists such as Ibsen and Strindberg in Scandinavia and Tolstoy in Russia. Yet the first significant publication by the German naturalists themselves was an anthology of their lyric poetry, *Moderne Dichter-Charaktere* (Modern Poet-Characters, 1885), which, perhaps aside from the poems by Arno Holz, simply documented their admiration for the so-called Young Germans of the period before 1848. Besides calling themselves the Moderns, the Germans also frequently eschewed the designation *naturalists* by referring to themselves as the *Jüngstdeutsche* (Youngest Germans). It remains questionable whether, within the confines set by naturalism, there can even be such a phenomenon as naturalist poetry. In any case, this collection represents at best a prelude to, not a realization of, the "modern" literature for which they were striving.

But probably the most important factor determining the course taken by the German naturalists was that Emile Zola, primarily a novelist and only secondarily a dramatist, provided the first important model who also could serve as a rallying point. Any "unacceptable" dramas by either Germans or foreigners could, of course, be ignored by the public stages or banned by the censor. On the other hand, Zola's "experimental novels," especially the long series *Les Rougon-Macquart* (1871-1893) that was based on a "scientific" approach through emphasis on heredity and environment, became a subject of bitter controversy on both sides of the Rhine. The spirited defense of Zola, whose works first evoked the use of naturalism as a designation, determined the direction to be taken by the Germans, who, until then, had been united solely by their dissatisfaction with the prevailing literature in their own country. Munich became their headquarters and their principal weapon the periodical founded there in 1885 by Michael Georg Conrad, *Die Gesellschaft* (Society), which was intended to offer "ein Organ des ganzen, freien, humanen Gedankens, des unbeirrten Wahrheitssinnes, der resolut realistischen Weltauffassung" (an organ of complete, free, humane thinking, an unerring sense of truth, and a resolutely realistic conception of the world) and declared war on the "Verlegenheits-Idealismus des Philistertums, der Moralitäts-Notlüge der alten Parteien—und Cliquewirtschaft auf allen Gebieten des modernen Lebens" (sham-idealism of the philistine, the moral white lies of the old parties and cliques in all areas of modern life). During its seventeen-year existence it would publish novellas by such significant writers as Gerhart Hauptmann and Thomas Mann. Nonetheless, the leadership of naturalism soon passed to Berlin, mainly because there a truly naturalist drama came into being and found a receptive audience.

Even in Berlin the stepping stone had to be provided in 1889 by a volume of prose works whose revolutionarily new style could, however, only lead to drama: *Papa Hamlet*, a collection of sketches by Arno Holz and Johannes Schlaf that was published in Berlin and Leipzig under the pseudonym of "Bjarne P. Holmsen" as "translated" by "Bruno Franzius" (thereby showing deference to the Norwegian and French pioneers). Previous naturalist prose works both in Germany and in other countries had maintained a relatively conventional narrative style and stance, despite purporting to be scientific, experimental, or simply objective. But Holz and Schlaf introduced two new qualities. In these sketches and their subsequent works they tried to eliminate the conventional narrator by an emphasis on dialogue and by onomatopoeic reproduction of sounds rather than descriptions. Since there must be some narration, they abandoned a fixed narrative stance and substituted narrations that seem to be coming from different perspectives and persons. The sketch "Papa Hamlet," for example, concludes with a comment expressed in the vocabulary and from the standpoint of the protagonist, who is already dead.

Holz later asserted "daß der Naturalismus eine Methode ist, eine Darstellungsart und nicht etwa 'Stoffwahl'" (that naturalism is a method, a manner of representation, not just some selection of a subject as such). While in the popular view naturalism had since its beginnings remained associated with specific subjects, Holz based his stylistic approach on a theory that he considered totally new yet obvious in its conclusions and applicable to any subject and any form of art. He developed a formula: "Die Kunst hat die Tendenz, wieder die Natur zu sein. Sie wird sie nach Maßgabe ihrer jedweiligen Reproduktionsbedingungen und deren Handhabung" (Art has the tendency to become reality again. It does so under the limitations of the given means of reproduction and their execution). He posits that it is not merely that the intention of the artist or writer is to duplicate reality but that the very essence of art tends toward a duplication of reality. But art will always remain art and reality will remain reality—a concession Holz expresses, with an algebraic equation: "Kunst= Natur - x" (art equals reality minus x). In other words, what is—due to the artistic medium—lacking between reality and the artistic reproduction of it cannot be eliminated entirely. But since it lies in the very nature of art to want to become reality, the artist, one must infer, should try to reduce the "x" to a minimum.

This difference or "x" exists most obviously in the artist's or writer's inability to reproduce enough details of his or her subject. In describing *Papa Hamlet*, Adalbert von Hanstein, the first historian of German naturalism, coins the expression *Sekundenstil* (second-style), which he defines as a technique of portraying space and time second by second, with every possible detail being recounted. But if so much detail is furnished, narrative, if it was to remain within reasonable dimensions, would have no room for a plot in a conventional sense. Only the stage allows a complete duplication of reality in all of its details without such a sacrifice: the audience instantly sees everything that a narrator must painstakingly describe.

Aside from such theoretical considerations, naturalists' desire to portray the contemporary world with absolute realism was motivated in large measure by their belief that it needed to be changed. But in 1889 strong censorship stood in the way of anyone attacking the established order and its values. A way had to be devised to circumvent the censor's office, and on 5 April 1889 a private club, "Die Freie Bühne" (The Free Stage) was founded. It sold nonvoting memberships that entitled the purchasers to performances of "modern" plays, which from the beginning was interpreted by the founders to mean naturalist

Cartoon from Kladderadatsch (1894) depicting the arrest of the naturalist dramatists (left to right) Gerhart Hauptmann, Henrik Ibsen, Ernst von Wildenbruch, and Hermann Sudermann

works. André Antoine had established a similar undertaking, the "théâtre libre," in Paris; but he had relied on amateur actors and on the sale of tickets—mistakes that the Germans did not repeat. Although the board of Die Freie Bühne had several prominent members, the two most responsible for the subsequent success were the president, Otto Brahm, and the treasurer, Samuel Fischer. Although he was not designated as the director on the programs, the former would be the guiding force in the development of naturalist staging and acting techniques; the latter would publish the most important plays and other works by the leading naturalists, above all Gerhart Hauptmann, and the journal *Die Freie Bühne* (later changed to *Die Neue Rundschau* [The New Review]).

By June there were 354 members; by the end of 1889, there were some 900, including many prominent theater directors and critics, as well as writers such as Ibsen, Fontane, and Anzengruber. The undertaking would be successful only if it offered good drama that was inaccessible on public stages. Brahm found just such a work to open the season on 29 September 1889: Ibsen's *Ghosts*. Banned in Berlin but already a proven stage success, *Ghosts* fulfilled all of Brahm's hopes. But Brahm realized that if it was to realize its full potential, Die Freie Bühne would have to premiere dramas by Germans. He found what he needed in Gerhart Hauptmann's first play, *Vor Sonnenaufgang* (published, 1889; translated as *Before Dawn*, 1909), which premiered on 20 October 1889 as the club's second offering. Hauptmann's play was viewed as a resounding success by the naturalists in Berlin; it also evoked so much controversy that its author, Brahm, and Die Freie Bühne became subjects of discussion throughout the country. (One of the leading Munich naturalists, Conrad Alberti, wrote a parody of it that was undoubtedly motivated by envy.) Although never officially committed to naturalism but only to "modern" plays, Die Freie Bühne provided the needed impetus for naturalism to take over the public stages. A series of court cases soon led to public performances of dramas forbidden by the censorship office; the best known of these cases was the one concerning Hauptmann's *Die Weber* (published, 1892; translated as *The Weavers*, 1899). *Die Weber*, which premiered on 26 February 1893, was the last of Hauptmann's four plays that had to be performed under the auspices of Die Freie Bühne: the club had become such a success that it had outlived its purpose. After 1893 its search for new and different dramas led it increasingly farther away from naturalist works.

By this time, largely through the efforts of such pseudonaturalists as Hermann Sudermann and some late converts, naturalist drama was becoming almost socially acceptable. Works such as Sudermann's appeared to be dealing with controversial, typically naturalistic issues and subjects, but they proffered resolutions fully in accord with the bourgeois values the naturalists attacked. Furthermore, they seldom went to the dramaturgical extremes or showed the theatrical daring that characterize the outstanding contributions of naturalism. Sudermann's plays still reflect the tradition of the "well-made play" of the period before 1889. Consequently, they have nothing in common either with Hauptmann's *Die Weber*, which probably represents the greatest naturalist drama, or with Holz and Schlaf's *Die Familie Selicke* (The Selicke Family; published, 1890); the later, which premiered on 7 April 1890 at Die Freie Bühne, was undoubtedly the most radically naturalistic play but was a total failure on the stage.

Without Brahm and his adept handling of Die Freie Bühne, Hauptmann might never have gained prominence as a playwright. On the other hand, German naturalism would never have captured such dominance over German stages without Hauptmann, who followed up his initial impact with a succession of provocative plays. The rapidity with which naturalism established itself on the stage can be attributed to the many young playwrights inspired by his example. Even though the dramas of these writers have proved unable to hold the attention of audiences no longer shocked by their novelty or interested in their topicality, they manifest the breadth and variety that naturalism attained. These playwrights include Holz and Schlaf, Max Halbe, Georg Hirschfeld, Otto Erich Hartleben, Max Dreyer, Emil Rosenow, Clara Viebig, Ernst Rosmer (pseudonym of Elsa Bernstein), Josef Ruederer, Karl Schönherr, and Oskar Panizza. To be seen more as "pseudonaturalists" are Sudermann and Paul Ernst, whose plays lack the convictions implied by the works of dedicated naturalists. The stage success achieved by these writers ranged from never seeing their plays performed to becoming, at least for a short time, rivals of Hauptmann. Moreover, several major writers not usually associated

with naturalism counted among their early works plays in an unquestionably naturalist mold: for example, Arthur Schnitzler's *Freiwild* (performed, 1896; published, 1898; translated as *Free Game*, 1913) and *Das Vermächtnis* (performed, 1898; published, 1899; translated as *The Legacy*, 1911) and Rainer Maria Rilke's *Im Frühfrost* (1897; translated as *Early Frost*, 1979).

German naturalism committed itself almost from its beginning to the portrayal of contemporary life, turning its back on the historical drama that was so popular on the stages of the time. Of course, earlier playwrights—including Gotthold Ephraim Lessing, those of the Sturm und Drang, Grabbe, Büchner, and Hebbel—had already realistically dramatized contemporary or almost contemporary life and events, albeit never exclusively.

Never in the history of the theater had such a complete and concentrated attempt been made to duplicate reality. Even in the most realistic works before 1889, the dialogue—especially in the dramas of Ibsen—attains in some cases a lyrical and symbolic quality, and in all cases it displays a terseness and succinctness that real persons, regardless of their station in life or education, seldom attain and scarcely ever sustain. Even in naturalist drama several characters speak their thoughts with unforgettable clarity and articulation—for example, Loth in *Vor Sonnenaufgang*, Old Hilse in *Die Weber*, and the protagonist of Hauptmann's *Michael Kramer* (1900; translated, 1914). Yet one innovation distinguishes the dialogue in a naturalist drama from that of previous plays: such a character is never surrounded by characters of equal articulateness and clarity of thought. It is therefore the totality of the play that Holz means when he declares: "Die Sprache des Theaters ist die Sprache des Lebens. Nur des Lebens! . . . Ihr Ziel zeichnet sich klar: . . . aus dem Theater allmählich das 'Theater' zu drängen" (The language of the theater is the language of life. Only of life! . . . Its goal is clearly outlined: . . . to gradually drive the "theater" out of the theater). The language of the stage had always seemed artificial because it strove for the articulation of ideas, self-description of characters, or inherent beauty of expression. These qualities, however, were detrimental to a re-creation of reality. The stage language of naturalism includes stammering, dialect, and everyday banalities.

Such complete realism in vocabulary and dialogue could be achieved only at the audience's expense. Not only do articulate characters disappear, but soliloquies, asides, and other stage conventions are also banned as "unrealistic." With the elimination of audience-oriented devices, the naturalist dramatist implies a new attitude toward the audience. In answer to critics of *Vor Sonnenaufgang*, Hauptmann wrote: "Schon oft hat man die alte Forderung wiederholt: die Bühne sei kein Katheder! und ich unterschreibe diese Forderung. Ich stellte sie auch an mich, als ich mein Stück begann ... und schrieb es durch, ohne an das Publikum nur zu denken, als ob die Bühne nicht drei, sondern vier Wände hätte" (One has already repeated the old demand often: Do not let the stage become a podium! I subscribe to this demand. I also made it of myself when I wrote my play ... and wrote it all the way through without thinking at all on the audience, as if the stage had not three but four walls). The audience, in other words, becomes the fourth wall or, more accurately, the person on the outside of a room who can only look into it through a keyhole. In turn, the audience must be ignored by the actors, just as real persons would be unaware of someone observing them through a keyhole.

Yet another crucial concession must be made to reality, according to the naturalists. Just as real life has no plot in a conventional, literary sense, with a definite beginning and a definite conclusion, neither may a realistic play be anything but open on both ends. When the play begins, the characters act and speak with a knowledge of many events about which the audience knows nothing and which it will never fully comprehend; and many naturalist plays end with little or no resolution of the characters' problems. At best, one of the main characters dies; but in real life no one person's death resolves all the problems of those around him or her. In many naturalist plays, one must doubt whether any change at all has been effected. For example, at the end of *Die Familie Selicke*, there is no assurance that Wendt will, as he promises, return to save Toni from her miserable situation, but neither can one be sure that he will not return or that Toni would go away with him if he did. The first audience of Hauptmann's *Der Biberpelz* (1893; translated as *The Beaver Coat*, 1912) remained seated at the end of the fourth act in expectation of a fifth, in which the real thief would be discovered and punished. But there was no fifth act. The thief, Mother Wolff, is the cleverest person in the play, and life is "survival of the fittest."

Such innovations in playwriting produced corresponding ones in acting. Since no single figure or group of figures addressed the audience directly, the emphasis shifted from individuals to the totality of the dramatic events. The ensemble became more important than the individual actors. The declamatory style gave way to understatement. All too frequently the results were drab and bleak.

Hauptmann, Holz and others assert over and over the primacy of character over plot as the key to understanding what the play has to say. The naturalist playwright describes the appearance of each character in minute detail. How a character looks frequently substitutes for what he or she must, because of the dictates of realistic dialogue, leave unsaid. Moreover, the actor, who no longer has monologues or asides at his disposal, must find nonverbal means to suggest a character's motives. At the same time, the characters are viewed by the naturalists as products of heredity and environment—so much so that they cannot gain an insight into their own situation without the assistance of an outside person. Commonly called "der Bote aus der Fremde" (the messenger from afar), this outsider becomes the catalyst who determines the structure of the play as one of "analytic exposition." A play based on this principle begins with a given situation and then reveals how this situation came into being. As old as Sophocles' *Oedipus Rex*, analytic exposition was the basis for naturalist plays beginning with *Ghosts*. But in keeping with modern views of human existence, the naturalist replaces fate or intrigue with the forces of heredity and environment.

In analytic exposition the audience's attention is necessarily directed toward the past, which can no longer be changed. It follows that since dramatic conflicts in the traditional sense arise only when the characters can still effect a change, such conflicts do not characterize dramas based on analytic exposition. When conflicts do arise, they come after the exposition and frequently seem anticlimactic. And since the characters' present situation and conduct have been determined by their heredity and environment, and since these causative factors have, after the process of analytic exposition, been made clear to the audience, the decisions reached by naturalist characters seldom come as a surprise. Consequently, critics, accustomed to conventional plots and conflicts involving characters still capable of change or unexpected actions, at first condemned naturalist drama as undramatic.

A good explanation of what gave naturalist drama its appeal and of why it was able to dominate the stage for more than a decade was given by Alfred Kerr (pseudonym of Alfred Kempner), probably the most incisive and influential theater critic of the time and a strong proponent of naturalist drama. Written during the heyday of naturalism, his essay "Technik des realistischen Dramas" (Technique of Realistic Drama) in the *Vossische Zeitung* (1891) helped to make naturalist goals and techniques more comprehensible and acceptable to his contemporaries and has lost little relevance today. Kerr recognizes the difficulties to be mastered by the author of a radically realistic play, especially that of time restrictions, and their effect on playwrights committed to indirect characterization instead of the older, conventional direct characterization. The time portrayed should not exceed twenty-four hours and should ideally coincide with the time needed to perform the play; where there are no skips in time, and therefore no implications of selectivity in what is shown, the guiding hand of the playwright is less evident. In this short time, however, characters must meet and reveal their own backgrounds and that of the situation in which they find themselves without any traditional contrivances. The audience will have access to only a limited amount of information from a limited number of sources, some of which might seem unreliable. In Kerr's eyes, just such limitations produce the "Reiz des Schlüsseziehens" (enjoyment of drawing conclusions) that sustains the audience's attention.

Obviously, this enjoyment of drawing conclusions can only be sustained as long as the plays offer characters and situations that awaken the audience's interest. To convince the audience that it is seeing reality, the naturalist must play on its preconceived notions—that is, must offer some stereotypical characters and situations—without losing sight of the basic premise of all realism: the individuality of whatever is being portrayed. From the beginning, however, Holz asserted that art is never based directly on reality but on our "Vorstellungsbild" (mental image) of it. Therefore, not only the rapid depletion of new and shocking subjects but also changes in how we form our mental images of reality would contribute to the disappearance of naturalism, which came into being as a response to modern images of human life.

Impressionism and Symbolism

The revolution in drama launched by Die Freie Bühne was so widespread and penetrating that the theater could never return to earlier forms. Instead, postnaturalist drama found itself following three lines, all of which confirmed the lasting impact of naturalism: the development of naturalist innovations toward impressionism and symbolism; the renewal of verse drama in general and the introduction of Jugendstil (art nouveau) in particular as a conscious rejection of naturalism; and the continuation of socially critical dramas that shared many themes and goals with naturalism but would later evolve into expressionism, which understood itself as the aesthetic and philosophical antithesis of naturalism. Even though the number of new plays in a naturalistic style fell markedly after 1900, what had been thought, said, and put into practice in the decade after 1889 had by and large closed the books on the nineteenth century's conception of drama. Aside from Lessing, Goethe, and Schiller, whose greatness was timeless, only those playwrights whom their contemporaries had ignored or scorned were heard in the twentieth century: Kleist, Grabbe, Büchner, Grillparzer, and Hebbel. Even in Austria, where naturalism never gained as much influence as in Germany, little besides the works of Raimund and Nestroy had much effect in the twentieth century.

The distinction between naturalism and either impressionism or symbolism in drama is often scarcely discernible, not only among various playwrights but also within many an individual's oeuvre. For example, while Ibsen was the first model for so much naturalist drama in Germany, by 1889, when Die Freie Bühne put on his *Ghosts*, Ibsen had already completed *The Wild Duck* (1884) and *The Lady from the Sea* (1888). The latter, especially, seems much closer to the works of impressionism and symbolism than to those that were yet to be produced by the German naturalists. And while German naturalism—beginning with *Papa Hamlet*—makes much use of allusions to underscore its own divergence from supposedly decadent and outlived literary conventions and expectations, none of its dramatic heroines demonstrates such self-conscious recognition of playing a literarily inspired role as does Ibsen's Hedda Gabler (1890), who thereby anticipates much of impressionism. On the other hand, Ibsens's *The Master Builder* (1892) makes no secret of its reliance on symbolism. In a like manner, one could trace Hauptmann's, Schlaf's or

Halbe's development away from the confines of a doctrinaire naturalism. (Hauptmann, however, returned to naturalism again and again, finding new ways to expand the potential inherent in many of its innovations.)

Impressionism in literature, as in painting, emphasizes the creator's perception of reality rather than the actual constitution of reality. Both intellectual circles and the general public had, by the turn of the century, accustomed themselves to a new view of their ability to perceive the world. Austrian physicist and philosopher Ernst Mach, for example, emphasized the relativity of our perceptions of reality. The writer Hermann Bahr, likewise an Austrian, agreed with Mach that *"Das Ich ist unrettbar"* (The ego is unsavable) and concluded: "Es gibt nichts als Verbindungen von Farben, Tönen, Wärmen, Drücken, Räumen, Zeiten, und an diese Verknüpfungen sind Stimmungen, Gefühle und Willen gebunden" (There is nothing but combinations of colors, sounds, warmths, pressures, spaces, times, and to these connections are tied moods, feelings and desires). Bahr thought that "Manet hätte wohl gelacht bei der Zumutung, daß er eine Philosophie gemalt haben soll; und es ist sehr leicht möglich, daß sich Mach, ein österreichischer Professor, durch die Beziehung auf den Impressionismus beleidigt fühlt. Ich zweifle aber nicht, daß man schon nach und nach ihre geistige Einheit herausspüren wird, und es dauert vielleicht gar nicht lange und man nennt die Weltanschauung Machs einfach die 'Philosophie des Impressionismus'" (Manet would probably have laughed at the idea that he is supposed to have painted a philosophy; and it is very easily possible that Mach, an Austrian professor, feels insulted by the reference to Impressionism. But I do not doubt that people will gradually sense out their spiritual unity, and it will perhaps not take long before Mach's worldview is simply called the "philosophy of Impressionism").

In 1874 Claude Monet had painted *Impression: Sunrise*, which emphasizes the ephemeral aspects of outdoor lighting and gave birth to the term *impressionism*. Edouard Manet had first established himself as a realistic painter and only later became associated with the newer group of impressionists. Other artists who are designated impressionists, post-impressionists, or neo-impressionists include Camille Pissarro, Alfred Sisley, Henri de Toulouse-Lautrec, Edgar Degas, Paul Gauguin, Georges Seurat, and Vincent van Gogh. Their painting represents a clear depar-

ture from a realism in art that corresponded to a movement in the theater away from the detailed images offered by naturalism.

If impressionism isolates a particular moment without regard for causal relationships, then symbolism isolates an object or event from its sociologically and hereditarily explicable context. Impressionism and symbolism have in common that their portrayal of reality stresses the quality of a moment, object, or event, not its quantitatively measurable placement in time and space. The necessary fragmentation of our image of reality that Mach and Bahr assert to be unavoidable absolves the playwright from the dictates of quantitative thinking and allows the return to qualitative distinctions.

Although Arthur Schnitzler was a friend of Otto Brahm and began his career with such naturalist dramas as *Das Vermächtnis*, his plays, more than those of any other one writer, define the basic approach of literary impressionism. He, like Mach and Bahr, was an Austrian; although impressionism was by no means limited to Austrian writers, Schnitzler's pictures of contemporary Vienna suggest an atmosphere in which the glorification of the moment offers the only meaning possible in life. In Schnitzler's *Liebelei* (performed, 1895; published, 1896; translated as *The Reckoning*, 1907), the protagonist, who, for the sake of honor, must fight a duel with the husband of his former lover, says to his new love, a simple girl who is unaware of the duel: "Du weißt doch nur eins, wie ich—daß du mich in *diesem* Augenblick liebst ... *Wie sie reden will:* Sprich nicht von Ewigkeit. *Mehr für sich:* Es gibt ja vielleicht Augenblicke, die einen Duft von Ewigkeit um sich sprühen ... Das ist die einzige, die wir verstehen können, die uns gehört" (Like me, you know only one thing—that you love me at *this* moment ... *When she wants to speak to him*: Don't talk about eternity. *More to himself*: There are perhaps moments that exude an aroma of eternity ... That is the only thing that we can understand, the only thing that belongs to us). The impressionist revives the prenaturalist notion that one experiences life not as the summation of all moments but as the recollection of a few significant ones. A fragmentation of the closed world of naturalism takes place, and the lives of characters are depicted in a series of vignettes. A classic example is Schnitzler's *Reigen* (published, 1903; performed, 1920; translated as *Hands Around*, 1920), which, moving up and back down the social ladder, shows a succession of love scenes, each of which includes one of the characters from the previous episode. A further example can be found in Schnitzler's one-act plays about Anatol (published, 1893; performed, 1910; translated, 1917), who recalls—sometimes incorrectly—his life as a series of episodes with different women.

In a like manner, the symbolist reminds us that although we see the totality of a given space, we focus on only single objects and events because these imply more than others. In a strictly naturalist drama such as *Die Familie Selicke*, the portrayed time and the time of the performance correspond almost completely; in *Liebelei*, single moments are isolated as meaningful for the characters, and this isolation makes them meaningful for the audience. In *Die Familie Selicke*, the objects in the room reveal the background and personalities of the characters but are never commented on by them; on the other hand, characters in *Liebelei* or *Anatol* single out objects and comment on them. Hauptmann's *Und Pippa tanzt!* (1906; translated as *And Pippa Dances*, 1909) demonstrates the trend toward symbolism. The first act is as naturalistic as anything Hauptmann ever wrote, but the last three acts abandon this realism and introduce characters who cannot be explained by reference to environment or heredity—that is, to an "objective," scientific view of the world. The elimination of realistic details leaves the audience no choice but to interpret the new figures by reference to their mythical implications. Wann is even characterized in the dramatis personae as "eine mythische Persönlichkeit" (a mythical personality), and when he appears in the third act he is ninety years old but has the strength of a youth. In act 1 Pippa is forced by her father to dance in a tavern; but she is abducted from this naturalistic milieu by Huhn, a brutish creature who reminds the viewer of Caliban in Shakespeare's *The Tempest*, and taken to the hut of the mythical Wann. Such symbolism seems to address primarily a small group of initiates. Consequently, playwrights such as Schlaf began to call for a new form of play, the "intimes Drama" (intimate drama).

The naturalist playwright challenged the viewer to find the scientifically verifiable explanation of the events depicted onstage. The symbolist playwright obligates the audience to find an explanation that gives events and characters meaning beyond the supposedly factual one. In an age that had become aware of the relativity of images of the so-called real world, it was held that each individual's experiences were important

insofar as they had meaning for that individual, even if this meaning may be different for others.

The Reactions against Naturalism

The most historically significant reaction against naturalism was the return to verse drama—not merely the elimination of naturalist banality and lack of articulation but the restoration of elevated diction—and, in particular, the emergence of Jugendstil. While the naturalist strives to create the impression of artlessness in art, this reaction emphasizes the art in art. The playwright is no longer the supposedly detached and impartial observer but the consciously artful creator. The theater thereby regains its function of producing a world distinct from the world of real life. It becomes a world of visual beauty and linguistic elegance, and it found its first great champion in the director Max Reinhardt, who eventually superseded Brahm as the dominant force in German theater.

Reinhardt began his theatrical activity under Brahm and acted in many naturalist works, including the premieres of Hauptmann's *Die Weber* in 1894, *Fuhrmann Henschel* (published, 1899; translated as *Drayman Henschel*, 1910) in 1898, and *Michael Kramer* in 1900. Reinhardt's breakthrough, however, came in 1903 with his Berlin production of Maurice Maeterlinck's *Pelléas et Mélisande*. Maeterlinck personifies the emergence of a symbolism and impressionism that are patently intended as rejections of naturalism. What the critics praised in Maeterlinck's play they could never have found in any of the plays that still reflected the influence of naturalism. Above all, the critics reviewing Reinhardt's production were quick to make the connection with contemporary developments in art. The sets were no longer merely the background for human conflicts; instead, they became the focus of attention, and the characters assumed a correspondingly lesser role. Irreality and the spectacular marked Reinhardt's productions, which attempted to make the inexplicable—that is, the mythical, symbolic, or allegorical—come alive before the audience.

In breaking the spell of Brahm and the dominance of naturalism, Reinhardt made possible the reemergence of verse drama on the stages of Germany; some of his own most significant productions included works by Sophocles, Shakespeare, Goethe, and Molière. His one film for Hollywood, which he made after his escape from Germany in 1933, was *Midsummer Night's Dream*

(1935), with James Cagney, Dick Powell, Olivia de Havilland, Joe E. Brown, and Mickey Rooney. Above all, the changes in staging that Reinhardt—in conjunction with the theories of the Swiss Adolphe Appia and the Englishman Edward Gordon Craig—inspired contributed to the theatrical success of both Jugendstil and expressionism.

The concept of literary Jugendstil is somewhat controversial. Like impressionism, it is borrowed from the graphic arts. Jugendstil was international both in its sources, which include the English Pre-Raphaelites and Japanese art, and in its manifestations, such as the illustrations of Aubrey Beardsley in England, those of Melchior Meyer in Germany, and the painting of Gustav Klimt in Austria. Jugendstil overlaps in popular thinking with such other phenomena as dandyism, *l'art pour l'art*, and decadence. Jugendstil is associated with a general movement toward the exotic, unreal, and decorative—all that represents the art-for-art's-sake attitude—combined with the implication that, as Oscar Wilde wrote in *The Soul of Man under Socialism* (1895), "art should never try to be popular. The public should try to make itself artistic." Mannerism and stylization are the means that the Jugendstil artists used to transform nature and to beautify it by human standards. They encountered their greatest challenges in beautifying death, but this challenge became an obsession. The "beautiful death" was a frequent theme of Jugendstil art and literature, as can be seen in Hauptmann's *Hanneles Himmelfahrt* (1893; translated as *Hannele*, 1894) and Hugo von Hofmannsthal's *Der Thor und der Tod* (performed, 1898; published, 1900; translated as *Death and the Fool*, 1914). A favorite figure in Jugendstil art and literature is the "femme fragile," such as Hauptmann's Pippa, who seems almost unreal in her delicacy; she symbolizes the short and threatened life of youth and beauty. Even when she is not placed against a background of the social evils of the times, such as crowded cities with their pollution and poverty, her popularity reflects a general reaction against these phenomena, which provided much of the subject matter of naturalism. Yet while naturalist drama often offered the promise of a rural setting as an escape from the ugliness of the big city, as in *Die Familie Selicke*, the Jugendstil artist or writer seeks out not the countryside but the park—nature "made beautiful" by human beings.

There are few dramas that can be completely ascribed to Jugendstil. Since Jugendstil had no underlying philosophy, its influence in drama remained restricted to a few themes and characters, but most of all to the staging of many works, including classical dramas.

Another type of drama that signaled a renunciation of naturalism was the attempt to write new classical plays in monumental style. Emphasizing the legendary and the historically remote, such dramas found their most notable champion in Paul Ernst, whose works garnered theoretical support from the writings of Samuel Lublinski and Wilhelm von Scholz. In his *Der Weg zur Form* (The Way to Form, 1906) Ernst coins the expression "Stilkunst" (style-art) for what he has in mind. Lublinski, in *Der Ausgang der Moderne* (The End of Modernism, 1909) maintains: "Die moderne Kunst wird monumental sein, oder sie wird gar nicht sein" (Modern art is going to be monumental, or it will not exist at all). Echoing the high ranking of drama by Schopenhauer and Hegel a century earlier, Lublinski claims: "Das Drama ist im Ästhetischen der vollkommenste Ausdruck für die Kraft, den Willen, die Leidenschaft und die Idealität einer Kultur" (In the aesthetic realm, drama is the most perfect expression for the strength, the will, the passion, and the ideals of a culture). Nonetheless, although Ernst understood his efforts as a refutation of impressionism and Jugendstil, his emphasis on "style" and "form" obviously link him with the latter. And the result was a group of plays that serve only the values of the Wilhelminian bourgeoisie. Today they have only historical and sociological significance, but they, too, reveal the public's dissatifaction with naturalism after 1905.

Socially Critical Drama after Naturalism

Of all the playwrights who rejected naturalism, only two wrote stage works of a socially critical slant before World War I that are still performed with any regularity: Frank Wedekind and Carl Sternheim. Wedekind and Sternheim shared the conviction that naturalism is boring. Why Wedekind is seen as a forerunner of expressionism is his love of the grotesque, bizarre, and tragicomic, of "lively" stage events. Wedekind's characters anticipate the angular distortion of human figures in paintings by Ernst Ludwig Kirchner and Karl Schmidt-Rottluff and the grotesque caricatures in George Grosz's paintings and drawings. They are not real people caught up in their everyday routines but characters living unusual, "exciting" lives. Wedekind sets his principal characters against a background that no longer functions as the formative, overpowering milieu of nat-

Scene from Frank Wedekind's Erdgeist

uralist drama. The literary lineage of such characters is easily recognized: one cannot overlook their resemblance to those in plays by Jakob Michael Reinhold Lenz, Grabbe, and Büchner.

For all his differences with naturalism, Wedekind's attack on that movement reflects a bitterness typical of an internecine conflict. One of Wedekind's earliest dramatic efforts was *Die junge Welt* (The Young World; published, 1896; performed, 1908), which first appeared as *Kinder und Narren* (Children and Fools) in 1891. Much has been made of Wedekind's portrayal of the writer Meier as an attack on Hauptmann, but it is a far more general satire of naturalism: Hauptmann was not the only naturalist who constantly carried a notebook to jot down authentic speech. Wedekind ridicules Holz's demand that the theater should be driven out of the theater. Wedekind, whose first plays were written during the heyday of naturalism and reflect a similar concern with controversial, socially critical subjects, thought of dramatic dialogue as "theatrical," albeit not in the nineteenth-century sense. It is not the elevated diction of the Schiller imitators but the witty, biting language of cabaret performers that is employed by Wedekind's characters, who both alienate and amuse the audience. As a playwright, Wedekind made few concessions to the de-

mands of motivation and background. As an actor in his own plays, he eschewed the naturalistic approach in favor of a distinctly wooden, unnatural style of presentation. His characters seem more like marionettes than people, and the audience, which is not treated like a "fourth wall" but feels itself directly addressed, assumes that a "higher" force is pulling the strings. But because Wedekind's plays do not maintain a uniform tone, his viewers cannot equate such a higher force with the playwright.

Die junge Welt revolves around women's emancipation, a theme introduced by Ibsen's *A Doll House* and favored by the German naturalists. But Wedekind ridicules this supposedly burning issue—at least as a sociological one. Justifiably or not, Wedekind soon became notorious as the dramatist of sex, and this issue permeated some of his most successful and influential plays: *Frühlings Erwachen* (published, 1891; performed, 1906; translated as *The Awakening of Spring*, 1909), *Erdgeist* (published, 1895; performed, 1898; translated as *Erdgeist* [*Earth-Spirit*], 1914), and *Die Büchse der Pandora* (1904; translated as *Pandora's Box*, 1914). Particularly in the last two—the so-called Lulu plays—he rejects any emancipation of women that would make them appear as "defeminized" competitors in a masculine world.

Instead, he elevates the feminine to mythical dimensions. But Lulu has nothing of the "eternal feminine" extolled at the end of Goethe's *Faust*. She is female sexuality incarnate, an unsolvable mystery not only to the male-dominated world surrounding her but also to herself. Neither the application of male stereotypes nor Lulu's striving through love affairs, marriage, lesbianism, and prostitution suffices to show her who she really is.

However one interprets Lulu, it cannot be denied that she is truly a theatrical character, much more so than her psychologically and sociologically realistic and therefore more limited counterparts in naturalist dramas. A naturalist character might destroy another person or a family; Lulu destroys an entire society. A like claim could be made for the rebellious youths in *Frühlings Erwachen*. Even the title character and his friend Scholz in *Der Marquis von Keith* (1901; translated as *The Marquis of Keith*, 1967) struggle with issues far more embracing than the socially realistic ones: they personify a conflict in existential modes that bears more comparison to Grabbe's Don Juan and Goethe's Faust or Büchner's Danton and Robespierre than to the characters in Hauptmann's *Einsame Menschen* (1891; translated as *Lonely Lives*, 1898) or Sudermann's *Die Ehre* (performed, 1889; published, 1890; translated as *Honor*, 1915).

Less biting and distorting in his portrayal of society, and seemingly more obligated to the demands of a realistic reproduction of events and people, Sternheim, like Wedekind, shuns proletarian issues and situations in favor of the middle class. But while Wedekind's portraits of the bourgeoisie are negative caricatures, Sternheim's best-known plays appeared under the collective title *Aus dem bürgerlichen Heldenleben* (Out of the Heroic Life of the Bourgeoisie). Since he intends to reveal the erring course taken by the middle class in its ludicrous attempt to emulate the aristocracy, one could assume irony in this title. Nonetheless, Sternheim reveals a latent admiration for the tenacity with which his bourgeois heroes quixotically pursue their goals, as vacuous and limited as those goals might be. One is left with the conclusion that a performance can emphasize either the satire or "heroization" of the bourgeoisie without being untrue to Sternheim.

Sternheim's plays present innovative dialogue that Burghard Dedner sees as a parody of the gradually emerging rhapsodic language of expressionism. Dedner's interpretation emphasizes

Scene from Georg Kaiser's expressionist play Gas

how "unrealistic"—that is, antinaturalistic—the language of Sternheim's plays is, despite their solid foundation in the world of social convention, capitalistic speculation, and hypocritical sexual mores.

Like Wedekind, Sternheim, while continuing many aspects of naturalist drama, provides a bridge to further developments by introducing not only a new type of distinctly theatrical dialogue but also a new concept of character. None of Sternheim's characters has the mythic dimensions of Lulu, but they reveal themselves as no less demonically obsessed than Wedekind's Marquis von Keith. Both playwrights used social conditions as the sources for their plays, but abandon the quantitative approach of naturalism: characters are no longer socially representative but individually interesting. The audience's attention is no longer directed toward the character's role in society but toward his or her conception of society. Thus, in Sternheim's *Die Kassette* (performed, 1911; published, 1912; translated as *The Strongbox*, 1963), Krull's obsession with the strongbox and Elsbeth's manipulation of his obsession interest the audience far more than the question of what might be contained in the box. In Sternheim's and Wedekind's plays, what the characters think they see is no longer played off against a verifiable reality, as was the case in naturalism, with its almost clinical view of eccentricities and aberrations. Instead, what these characters see, even when it is recognizable as a delusion, becomes far more important than the reality described by the physical and biological sciences. With this shift in perspective, the groundwork is laid for expressionism.

Expressionism

To the extent that a valid comparison can be made, expressionism represents the ultimate reaction against naturalism. But the validity of such a comparison is open to doubt. Literary historians may debate when naturalism began or ceased to be an important force on the literary scene and which writers should be considered naturalists; nonetheless, there is a basic conformity in their conception of the movement, a conformity that is made easier because naturalism left a lasting mark only on prose narration and especially on drama. Historically, one might speak of lyrical poetry by naturalists, but from a strictly aesthetic standpoint naturalist poetry seems to present a contradiction in terms. The definition of naturalist drama is simplified by the unquestionably salient role of Die Freie Bühne in promoting such drama. Moreover, naturalism in nonliterary forms of art is limited to the graphic arts and sculpture; no one has ever tried to espouse the possibility of naturalist music.

On the other hand, while most literary histories consider the years 1920 to 1925 as the period of literary expressionism in Germany, they have difficulty in agreeing on the common elements of literature during these years. Furthermore, unlike naturalism, expressionism left its mark on all literary genres, especially drama and lyric poetry; and the film came into its own as an artistic medium through expressionism, especially German expressionism, with *Das Kabinett des Dr. Caligari* (The Cabinet of Dr. Caligari, 1919), *Der Golem, wie er in die Welt kam* (The Golem: How He Came into the World, 1920), *Nosferatu: Eine Symphonie des Grauens* (Nosferatu: A Symphony of Horror, 1922), and *Metropolis* (1927). Moreover, expressionism is distinguished from other movements in German literary history by the outstanding role of prominent artists. To be sure, many prominent writers of earlier periods originally wanted to pursue careers in painting or sculpture or revealed talent as artists, among them Goethe, E. T. A. Hoffmann,

Gottfried Keller, and Gerhart Hauptmann. But at least three expressionists known today primarily as artists contributed significant stage works: Wassily Kandinsky, Ernst Barlach, and Oskar Kokoschka. Kandinsky's *Über das Geistige in der Kunst* (On the Spiritual in Art, 1910), which formulates the principles of abstract art, had an influence on literary expressionism. The most important groups of artists who were eventually to be known as *the* German expressionists were founded beginning in Dresden in 1905 with "Die Brücke" (The Bridge), formed by four architecture students: Ernst Ludwig Kirchner, Fritz Bleyl, Erich Heckel, and Karl Schmidt-Rottluff. In 1909 the "Neue Künstlervereinigung München" (New Artists' Alliance, Munich) was established by Wassily Kandinsky, Alexey von Jawlensky, and Gabriele Münter; after inner tensions led to the dissolution of the Neue Künstlervereinigung the better-known "Der Blaue Reiter" (The Blue Rider) was founded in 1911 by Kandinsky, Paul Klee, Franz Marc, and August Macke. Among the exhibitors at their first show was Arnold Schoenberg. The first use of *expressionisme* was by the painter Julien Auguste Hervé in describing works in a Paris exhibition of 1901; the first German occurrence of *expressionistisch* was in a catalogue by the "Berliner Sezession" for a 1911 showing of paintings by artists including Georges Braque, André Derain, Pablo Picasso, and Maurice de Vlaminck. The original uses of *expressionist* designated simply the opposite of *impressionist* but implied no definite program. Since these instances of *expressionist* as a designation were limited to graphic art and characterized not what these new paintings were but only what they were not, it is not surprising that works that might have been called "expressionist" in one country have received an entirely different designation in another.

In short, so many different forces from so many art forms and countries converged that one hesitates to apply one designation to cover them all. Gerhard P. Knapp suggests that *expressionism* be accepted not as an aesthetic designation but as a sociopolitical one covering all the manifestations of the will to revolt against contemporary situations and values.

As limited, therefore, as any comparison of expressionism with naturalism must remain, it can be said that drama after 1900 moved further and further from an important supposition of all naturalist drama; that theatrical characters and events should not violate the physical, psychologi-

Umfang acht Seiten Einzelbezug: 10 Pfennig

DER STURM

WOCHENSCHRIFT FÜR KULTUR UND DIE KÜNSTE

Redaktion und Verlag: Berlin-Halensee, Katharinenstrasse 5
Fernsprecher Amt Wilmersdorf 3524 / Anzeigen-Annahme und
Geschäftsstelle: Berlin W 35, Potsdamerstr. 111 / Amt VI 3444

Herausgeber und Schriftleiter:
HERWARTH WALDEN

Vierteljahresbezug 1,25 Mark ; Halbjahresbezug 2,50 Mark /
Jahresbezug 5,00 Mark / bei freier Zustellung / Insertions-
preis für die fünfgespaltene Nonpareillezeile 60 Pfennig

JAHRGANG 1910 BERLIN/DONNERSTAG DEN 14. JULI 1910/WIEN NUMMER 20

Zeichnung von Oskar Kokoschka zu dem Drama
Mörder, Hoffnung der Frauen

INHALT: OSKAR KOKOSCHKA: Mörder, Hoffnung
der Frauen / PAUL LEPPIN: Daniel Jesus / Roman /
ALFRED DÖBLIN: Gespräche mit Kalypso über die
Musik / SIEGFRIED PFANKUCH: Liegt der Friede in
der Luft / PAUL SCHEERBART: Gegenerklärung /
KARL VOGT: Nissen als Theaterdirektor / MINIMAX:
Kriegsbericht / Karikaturen

Mörder, Hoffnung der Frauen
Von Oskar Kokoschka

Personen:
Mann
Frau
Chor: Männer und Weiber.

Nachthimmel, Turm mit großer roter eiserner Käfig-
tür; Fackeln das einzige Licht, schwarzer Boden,
so zum Turm aufsteigend, daß alle Figuren relief-
artig zu sehen sind.

Der Mann
Weißes Gesicht, blaugepanzert, Stirntuch, das eine
Wunde bedeckt, mit der Schar der Männer
(wilde Köpfe, graue und rote Kopftücher, weiße,
schwarze und braune Kleider, Zeichen auf den
Kleidern, nackte Beine, hohe Fackelstangen,
Schellen, Getöse), kriechen herauf mit vor-
gestreckten Stangen und Lichtern, versuchen müde
und unwillig den Abenteurer zurückzuhalten, reißen
sein Pferd nieder, er geht vor, sie lösen den Kreis
um ihn, während sie mit langsamer Steigerung auf-
schreien.

Männer
Wir waren das flammende Rad um ihn,
Wir waren das flammende Rad um dich, Bestürmer
verschlossener Festungen!

gehen zögernd wieder als Kette nach, er mit dem
Fackelträger vor sich, geht voran.

Männer
Führ' uns Blasser!

Während sie das Pferd niederreißen wollen, steigen
Weiber mit der Führerin die linke Stiege herauf.

Frau rote Kleider, offene gelbe Haare, groß,

Frau laut
Mit meinem Atem erflackert die blonde Scheibe
der Sonne, mein Auge sammelt der Männer Froh-
locken, ihre stammelnde Lust kriecht wie eine
Bestie um mich.

Weiber
lösen sich von ihr los, sehen jetzt erst den Fremden.

Erstes Weib flüstern
Sein Atem saugt sich grüßend der Jungfrau an!

166

First page of an issue of the expressionist weekly Der Sturm *including Oskar Kokoschka's play* Mörder Hoffnung der
Frauen; *the drawing, which illustrates a scene from the play, is by Kokoschka*

cal, and sociological laws of the real world outside the theater. And while naturalism ignored the audience as the "fourth wall" and did not call upon it to "suspend its disbelief," the works staged after 1900 demanded that audiences accept people speaking in verse, the appearance of Death as a character, grotesque distortions of established institutions, and much more. Above all, the postnaturalist playwright abandoned the quantitative approach and interpreted reality by qualitative criteria in the form of unusual characters, exotic or even impossible situations, and highly abstract motivations.

Expressionism thus continued and radicalized a development that was already taking place before 1910. One cannot, as in the case of naturalism, point to one date, author, or play as the origin of expressionist drama. Likewise, its models are often not unique to expressionism; some, such as Grabbe and Büchner, had served as inspirations for the naturalists. August Strindberg's *To Damascus* (1898-1904) initiated the "Stationendrama" (drama in stations), one of the most characteristic forms of German expressionism. Other influences on German expressionism were Strindberg's *A Dream Play* (1902) and *The Spook Sonata* (1907). It has even been suggested that Hauptmann's *Die Weber*, an unquestioned masterpiece of naturalism, anticipated and served as a model for the mass-scene dramas of expressionism; And after the revival of *Und Pippa tanzt!* in 1919, Alfred Kerr commented: "Dies Werk war expressionistisch vor dem Expressionismus" (This work was expressionistic before expressionism). Thus, while the lineage of expressionist drama can be traced with a great degree of accuracy, this lineage is shared by the very individuals and groups to whom the expressionists saw themselves in opposition. Contemporaries such as Bernhard Diebold and Albert Soergel regarded Reinhard Johannes Sorge's *Der Bettler* (The Beggar; published 1912; performed, 1917) as the first truly expressionist drama. But later historians, such as Horst Denkler, go back to Alfred Döblin's *Lydia und Mäxchen* (Lydia and Little Max; performed, 1905; published, 1906), Kokoschka's *Mörder Hoffnung der Frauen* (performed, 1909; published, 1916; translated as *Murderer the Women's Hope*, 1963), and Kandinsky's *Der gelb Klang: Eine Bühnenkomposition* (The Yellow Sound: A Stage Composition, 1912), which Denkler calls "Vorläuferdramen" (precursor dramas). Also mentioned as predecessors of *Der Bettler* are works by Heinrich Lautensack,

Hermann Essig, Else Lasker-Schüler, Georg Kaiser, Carl Sternheim, and Fritz von Unruh. With the exception of the works by Döblin, von Unruh, and Sternheim, all of these dramas premiered *after* Sorge's; but *Der Bettler* was itself first performed *after* subsequently published plays such as Kokoschka's *Der brennende Dornbusch* (The Burning Bush, 1917), Walter Hasenclever's *Der Sohn* (The Son, 1914), and Kaiser's *Die Bürger von Calais* (published, 1914; performed, 1917; translated as *The Burghers of Calais*, 1970). Other writers generally counted among the expressionist dramatists are Johannes R. Becher, Ivan Goll, Ludwig Rubiner, Arnolt Bronnen, Reinhard Goering, Franz Werfel, Hanns Johst, Ernst Toller, August Stramm, and Paul Kornfeld.

Although Sternheim's comedies, beginning with *Die Hose* (1911; translated as *The Underpants*, 1957), were performed with success on the public stage before 1914, none of the first serious dramas of expressionism was presented onstage before that year. Many productions before the end of World War I took place, beginning in 1916, primarily in private theaters, such as Arthur Hellmer's Neues Theater (New Theater) in Frankfurt, Otto Falckenberg's Das jüngste Deutschland (Youngest German) in Munich, and Reinhardt's Das junge Deutschland (Young Germany) in Berlin. It was not until after the revolution of 1918-1919 that expressionist dramas began to be performed on public stages. The production of expressionist plays outlived the writing of such dramas by several years. In 1926 the director Leopold Jeßner called for an end to "Kunststücke . . . auf der Bühne" (tricks . . . on the stage) in favor of "die neue Sachlichkeit" (the new objectivity). "Neue Sachlichkeit" had already appeared on the stage in Toller's historical drama *Die Maschinenstürmer* (The Machinoclasts, 1922). Although expressionism was no longer a significant force in the theater by 1933, everything and everyone connected with expressionism in all of its manifestations were immediately forbidden by the Nazis.

In terms of the number of plays contributed to the modern theater repertoire, expressionism did not approach the impact of naturalism. Although the presence of the latter on stages after World War II can be attributed almost exclusively to the individual talent of Gerhart Hauptmann, not to the merits of the movement, it is still true that expressionism produced scarcely anyone of comparable talent. Only the works of the "Denkspieler" (player of ideas) among the

Mach and others brought into question the human ability to perceive reality. While the naturalist holds that the falling tree makes a sound even when no one is there to hear it, the expressionist contends that there is no *meaningful* sound without a listener. The opposition between naturalism and expressionism should not be exaggerated, however: the degree of objectivity in naturalism is attenuated when Arno Holz concedes that the artist or writer is reproducing only a "mental image" of reality, and the subjectivity of expressionism seems less pronounced when one takes into account that the expressionist is motivated by a desire to change the real world by changing the audience's view of it.

From the beginning, many—especially Marxists from Franz Mehring to Bertolt Brecht—condemned naturalism for its discouragingly deterministic view of the world. And it is true that most naturalist dramas end without showing any change in the initial situation—except, perhaps, for the deaths of some characters and a worsening of matters for the rest. The audience is treated as a "fourth wall"; it can merely observe the slice of life presented onstage and can do nothing to change it. The expressionists, on the contrary, wanted to shock the viewers into an awareness of their responsibility to the community. This result can only be achieved by alienating them from everything that evokes complacency, from the feeling that one is still in a familiar, comprehensible world. Every nook and cranny of the naturalist set was filled with everyday objects; expressionist staging rejected the quantitative completeness of naturalism in favor of the selectivity of the prenaturalist stage and indulged in an alienating distortion of the characters' environment. Such a distorted stage image corresponds to the rejection of traditional perspective and proportion in expressionist paintings: buildings threaten to tip over; objects fly through the air; people and objects in the background are drawn larger than those in the foreground. Naturalism showed its audiences people, things and circumstances that they had never seen before—for example, the huts of the weavers in Hauptmann's play—but as part of a familiar, "real" world; expressionism shocked its audiences into seeing the world as they had never seen it before. For example, in Kaiser's *Von morgens bis mitternachts* (published, 1916; performed, 1917; translated as *From Morn to Midnight*, 1920) the most familiar, everyday people and their surroundings appear strange and unnatural—so much so that the audience is not re-

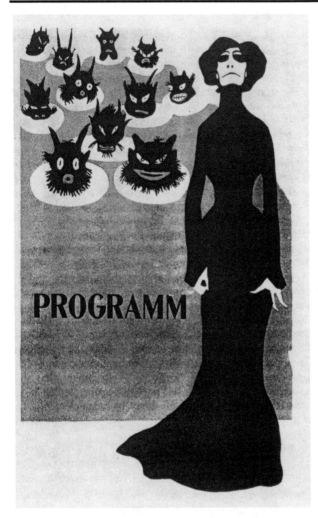

Program from 1903 for the Munich cabaret Elf Scharfrichter. Expressionist drama was influenced by the cabaret.

expressionists—Kaiser, who admitted having learned from Hauptmann and Wedekind—were reintroduced to the German theater after the war; the attempted renaissance of Kaiser's works did not succeed. Nonetheless, expressionist theories and innovations did influence later theatrical developments.

Although much had changed between 1889 and 1910, expressionism, no less than naturalism, represented a reaction against the society that had come into existence with the founding of the Second Reich in 1871 and would collapse after 1918. But how the expressionists viewed and reacted to social problems clearly distinguished them from the naturalists. The expressionists were less concerned with real changes in social reality than with a changed perception of the relationship of the individual to reality. In naturalist drama reality is accepted as factually given, but ally surprised when the cashier sees Death in a tree.

Expressionist drama reemphasizes the theatrical not only in its settings but also in its acting style: expressionist actors are not supposed to be like ordinary people. In the epilogue to his play *Die Verführung* (The Seduction; published, 1916; performed, 1917) Paul Kornfeld advises his actors to stretch their arms out wide and, with a sense of soaring, speak as they have never spoken in real life; he tells them not to be imitators or to seek their models in a world alien to the theater, not to be ashamed that they are acting; they should not try to feign reality. The actor should build his characters from his own experience of the emotion or fate he has to portray not from his recollections of people he has seen filled with these emotions or of victims of this fate. If he banishes such recollections, Kornfeld says, he will see that the expression of a feeling that is not genuine but has been artificially stimulated is purer, clearer, and stronger than one that has been prompted by a genuine stimulus. In other words, the actor must communicate an idea with greater clarity and intensity than could be found in real life. Kornfeld goes on to say that the expression of a real human being is never crystal clear because he himself is never crystal clear; he is never only *one* feeling. But the expressionist actor is not complex; each expressionist character is an intense abstraction of just one aspect of life or human relationships.

What Kornfeld calls for is realized in its simplest form by the rejection of personal names in favor of abstract or class designations. This practice is, of course, not new in the theater; it is as old as the appearance on the stage of the Devil as the personification of absolute evil. One could also point to the allegorical masques of the sixteenth and seventeenth centuries, to parts of Goethe's *Faust II*; to Shakespeare's comic use of such names as Snug, Bottom, and Flute in *A Midsummer Night's Dream* to suggest occupations; and to Büchner's use of the nameless doctor, captain, drum major, sergeant and others to represent Woyzeck's tormentors. But what was incidental to previous playwrights was an essential component of expressionist dramaturgy. One could almost dub a large segment of expressionist drama "plays of nameless characters."

Kaiser's list of characters in *Von morgens bis mitternachts*—Cashier, Mother, Wife, First Daughter, Second Daughter, Director, Salvation Army Girl, and so forth—does not contain a single per-

An example of Agitprop: poster announcing a guest appearance of the Soviet group "Blue Blouses" at Erwin Piscator's theater in Berlin in 1927

sonal name, not even a common, symbolic, or satirical one. Nonetheless, Kaiser's characters still participate in a real world of social and family relationships. On the other hand, the nameless characters in Sorge's *Der Bettler* seem to have real-life relationships, but these relationships are amorphous: the Poet of the first act, for example, appears in the second act as the Son.

The more a playwright tries to duplicate reality, as the naturalists did, the greater is the pressure on him to provide plausible motivations and events. But the farther the playwright moves from the real world to that of the theater, the less compelled he is to make such provisions. Theater in its purest form—that is, most removed from the dictates of reality—appears in the cabaret, revue, or variety show; in them no justification is needed for the inclusion of various performers or for the order in which they appear. The influence of these theatrical forms on expressionist theater can be seen in Sorge's *Der Bettler*, in which newspaper readers, pilots, and other characters suddenly appear onstage and speak. Moreover, unlike the chorus of Greek tragedy, they express ideas that have no direct connection with the main plot. The structure of an expressionist drama was determined by the playwright's thematic needs rather than by what nontheatrical reality would lead the audience to expect.

The Aftermath of Expressionism

Unlike naturalism, which dominated the stages for about ten years, expressionist drama evoked countercurrents soon after it appeared. The successors of expressionist drama were of three main kinds: revival of the Volksstück (a piece, often in dialect, about a specific region, drawing its characters mainly from the lower and middle classes); Neue Sachlichkeit (New Objectivity); and political stage works, which included those of the Agitprop (agitation and propaganda) groups, the theatrical innovations of Erwin Piscator, and the dramatic innovations of Brecht.

The Volksstück had never really vanished from the stage, and naturalism had given it new recognition in Hauptmann's pieces in dialect, as well as the plays by Max Halbe, Josef Ruederer, and Karl Schönherr. To the extent that expressionism was viewed as the total rejection of naturalism, the recurrence of the Volksstück as a dramatic form with serious intentions seemed to many to be a reaction against the excesses of expressionism. One of the first new Volksstücke to achieve wide success was Carl Zuckmayer's *Der fröhliche Weinberg* (The Happy Vineyard, 1925). Success with the Volksstück was also attained by Ödön von Horváth and Marieluise Fleißer. Zuckmayer, von Horváth, and Fleißer did not revert to the quantitative approach that characterized naturalism; yet in contrast to expressionism, they posited the existence of a verifiable social reality.

Neue Sachlichkeit designates not a movement or group but a rallying cry for those who wanted to move away from what they perceived as the subjectivity and arbitrariness of expressionism. It was a reaffirmation of material reality as distinguishable from the individual. Seen in this light, the New Objectivity corresponds to the spirit underlying the more ambitious Volksstücke. Thus Zuckmayer was able to make an easy transition from *Der fröhliche Weinberg* to the factually based *Der Hauptmann von Köpenick* (1930; translated as *The Captain of Köpenick*, 1932). The most

frequently mentioned representative of Neue Sachlichkeit is Ferdinand Bruckner, who began his career with expressionist lyrics but gained instant fame as a dramatist in 1926 with *Krankheit der Jugend* (Sickness of Youth; published, 1928) and followed it with *Die Verbrecher* (The Criminals, 1928; published, 1929). Bruckner's plays show the social commitment of Neue Sachlichkeit, as do Friedrich Wolf 's *Cyankali* (Cyanide, 1929) and *Die Matrosen von Cattaro* (The Sailors of Cattaro, 1930). In keeping with the goals of Neue Sachlichkeit there was a resurgence of historical drama. Probably the greatest success in this genre was achieved by Bruckner's *Elisabeth von England* (Elizabeth of England, 1930), which, like *Die Verbrecher*, employs a split stage that allows thematic contrasts but remains rooted in material reality.

While the Volksstück and many plays of Neue Sachlichkeit were socially critical, these works did not, in most cases, offer solutions to the problems they posed. But there also emerged a line of development on the political Left that did offer such solutions. One of the most influential forces in this development, which would culminate in the works of Brecht, was the director Piscator. For the Reichstag elections in 1924, Piscator staged his *Revue Roter Rummel* (Revue Red Carnival) for the Communist party. This event brought about the formation of Agitprop groups, whose number by 1930 had grown to more than two hundred in the big cities alone. For the Communist Party Day in 1925 Piscator staged a documentary drama under the title *Trotz alleden* (Despite All of That) with great success. In 1927 he was responsible for the successful staging of Toller's *Hoppla, wir leben!* (Whoopee, We're Alive!; published, 1927). Piscator, whose productions often used montages of films, speeches, photographs, documents, newspaper clippings, and other "nondramatic" materials, is given credit for originating Brecht's concept of Epic Theater. Such a fragmentation of the stage image by Piscator and later by Brecht would never have been possible without the pioneering efforts of the expressionists.

The years of the Weimar Republic were exciting ones in the theater. But the very people who made them so exciting—including Brecht, Zuckmayer, Bruckner, Toller, Kaiser, Reinhardt, and Piscator—were forced into exile in 1933 by the National Socialist regime.

Books for Further Reading

Allen, Ann Taylor. *Satire and Society in Wilhelmine Germany: Kladderadatsch and Simplicissimus 1890-1914*. Lexington: University of Kentucky Press, 1984.

Amman, Egon, and Eugen Faes, eds. *Literatur aus der Schweiz: Texte und Materialien*. Zurich: Suhrkamp, 1978.

Anz, Thomas, and Michael Stark, eds. *Expressionismus: Manifeste und Dokumente zur deutschen Literatur 1910-1920*. Stuttgart: Metzler, 1982.

Arnold, Armin. *Die Literatur des Expressionismus: Sprachliche und thematische Quellen*. Stuttgart, Berlin, Cologne & Mainz: Kohlhammer, 1966.

Arnold, Heinz Ludwig, ed. *Deutsche Bestseller—Deutsche Ideologie: Ansätze zu einer Verbraucherpoetik*. Stuttgart: Klett, 1975.

Arnold, ed. *Kritisches Lexikon zur deutschsprachigen Gegenwartsliteratur*. Munich: Edition text + kritik, 1978.

Bauland, Peter. *The Hooded Eagle: Modern German Drama on the New York Stage*. Syracuse, N.Y.: Syracuse University Press, 1968.

Baumann, Barbara, and Birgit Oberle. *Deutsche Literatur in Epochen*. Munich: Hueber, 1985.

Berg, Jan, and others. *Sozialgeschichte der deutschen Literatur von 1918 bis zur Gegenwart*. Frankfurt am Main: Fischer Taschenbuch Verlag, 1981.

Best, Alan, and Hans Wolfschütz, eds. *Modern Austrian Writing: Literature and Society after 1945*. London: Wolff, 1980; Totowa, N.J.: Barnes & Noble, 1980.

Bormann, Alexander von, and Horst Albert Glaser, eds. *Weimarer Republik—Drittes Reich: Avantgardismus, Parteilichkeit, Exil, 1918-1945*, Deutsche Literatur: Eine Sozialgeschichte, 9. Reinbek: Rowohlt, 1983.

Brands, Heinz-Georg. *Theorie und Stil des sogenannten "Konsequenten Naturalismus" von Arno Holz und Johannes Schlaf: Kritische Analyse der Forschungsergebnisse und Versuch einer Neubestimmung*. Bonn: Bouvier, 1978.

Brauneck, Manfred, ed. *Das deutsche Drama vom Expressionismus bis zur Gegenwart*. Bamberg: Buchners, 1972.

Brinkmann, Richard. *Expressionismus: Internationale Forschung zu einem internationalen Phänomen*. Stuttgart: Metzler, 1980.

Bronner, Stephen Eric, and Douglas Kellner, eds. *Passion and Rebellion: The Expressionist Heritage*. South Hadley, Mass.: Bergin, 1983.

Buck, Theo, and others, eds. *Tendenzen der deutschen Literatur zwischen 1918 und 1945: Weimarer Republik, Drittes Reich, Exil*. Stuttgart: Klett, 1985.

Chandler, Frank W. *Modern Continental Playwrights*. New York & London: Harper, 1931.

Chick, Edson. *Dances of Death: Wedekind, Brecht, Dürrenmatt and the Satiric Tradition*, Studies in German Literature, Linguistics and Culture, 19. Columbia, S.C.: Camden House, 1984.

Cowen, Roy C. *Das deutsche Drama im 19. Jahrhundert*. Stuttgart: Metzler, 1988.

Cowen. *Der Naturalismus: Kommentar zu einer Epoche*, third edition. Munich: Winkler, 1973.

Denkler, Horst. *Drama des Expressionismus: Programm, Spieltext, Theater*, enlarged edition. Munich: Fink, 1979.

Diethe, Carol. *Aspects of Distorted Sexual Attitudes in German Expressionist Drama with Particular Reference to Wedekind, Kokoschka, and Kaiser*. New York: Lang, 1988.

Dittrich, Rainer. *Die literarische Moderne der Jahrhundertwende im Urteil der österreichischen Kritik: Untersuchungen zu Karl Kraus, Hermann Bahr und Hugo von Hofmannsthal*. Frankfurt am Main & New York: Lang, 1988.

Dube, Wolf-Dieter. *Expressionism*. New York: Praeger, 1973.

Durzak, Manfred. *Das expressionistische Drama: Ernst Barlach, Ernst Toller, Fritz von Unruh*. Munich: Nymphenburger, 1979.

Duwe, Wilhelm. *Ausdrucksformen deutscher Dichtung vom Naturalismus bis zur Gegenwart: Eine Stilgeschichte der Moderne*. Berlin: Schmidt, 1965.

Duwe. *Deutsche Dichtung des 20. Jahrhunderts: Vom Naturalismus zum Surrealismus*, 2 volumes. Zurich: Orell-Füssli, 1962.

Edschmid, Kasimir. *Lebendiger Expressionismus: Auseinandersetzungen, Gestalten, Erinnerungen*. Munich: Desch, 1961.

Evans, Richard J., ed. *Society and Politics in Wilhelmine Germany*. London: Croom Helm, 1978; New York: Barnes & Noble, 1978.

Finney, Gail. *Women in Modern Drama: Freud, Feminism, and European Theater at the Turn of the Century*. Ithaca, N.Y.: Cornell University Press, 1989.

Friedmann, Hermann, and Otto Mann, eds. *Expressionismus: Gestalten einer literarischen Bewegung*. Heidelberg: Rothe, 1956.

Garland, H. B. *A Concise Survey of German Literature*. London: Macmillan, 1971.

Garland, Henry and Mary. *The Oxford Companion to German Literature*, second edition. Oxford: Clarendon Press, 1986.

Garten, Hugh F. *Modern German Drama*. London: Methuen, 1959.

Grimm, Reinhold, ed. *Deutsche Dramentheorien: Beiträge zu einer historischen Poetik des Dramas in Deutschland*. Frankfurt am Main: Athenäum, 1971.

Grimm and Jost Hermand, eds. *Die sogenannten Zwanziger Jahre: First Wisconsin Workshop*, Schriften zur Literatur, 13. Bad Homburg: Gehlen, 1970.

Günther, Katharine. *Literarische Gruppenbildung im Berliner Naturalismus*. Bonn: Bouvier, 1972.

Hatfield, Henry. *Modern German Literature: The Major Figures in Context*. Bloomington: Indiana University Press, 1968.

Hinck, Walter. *Handbuch des deutschen Dramas*. Düsseldorf: Bagel, 1980.

Hinck. *Das moderne Drama in Deutschland*. Göttingen: Vandenhoeck & Ruprecht, 1973.

Hoefert, Sigfrid. *Das Drama des Naturalismus*. Stuttgart: Metzler, 1968.

Jaron, Norbert, Renate Möhrmann, and Hedwig Müller. *Berlin—Theater der Jahrhundertwende: Bühnengeschichte der Reichshauptstadt im Spiegel der Kritik (1889-1914)*. Tübingen: Niemeyer, 1986.

Jelavich, Peter. *Munich and Theatrical Modernism: Politics, Playwriting, and Performance 1890-1914*. Cambridge, Mass.: Harvard University Press, 1985.

Jost, Dominik. *Literarischer Jugendstil*, second edition. Stuttgart: Metzler, 1980.

Killy, Walther, ed. *Literaturlexikon: Autoren und Werke deutscher Sprache*, 12 volumes. Gütersloh: Bertelsmann, 1988-1992.

Knapp, Gerhard P. *Die Literatur des deutschen Expressionismus*. Munich: Beck, 1979.

Koebner, Thomas, ed. *Weimars Ende: Prognosen und Diagnosen in der deutschen Literatur und politischen Publizistik 1930-1933*, suhrkamp-taschenbuch, 2018. Frankfurt am Main: Suhrkamp, 1982.

Kohlschmidt, Werner. *Geschichte der deutschen Literatur vom Jungen Deutschland bis zum Naturalismus*, Geschichte der deutschen Literatur von den Anfängen bis zur Gegenwart, 4. Stuttgart: Reclam, 1975.

Kracauer, Siegfried. *From Caligari to Hitler: A Psychological History of the German Film*. Princeton: Princeton University Press, 1947.

Krispyn, Egbert. *Style and Society in German Literary Expressionism*, University of Florida Monographs, 15. Gainesville: University of Florida Press, 1964.

Lehnert, Herbert. *Geschichte der deutschen Literatur vom Jugendstil zum Expressionismus*, Geschichte der deutschen Literatur von den Anfängen bis zur Gegenwart, 5. Stuttgart: Reclam, 1978.

Mann, Otto, and Wolfgang Rothe. *Deutsche Literatur im 20. Jahrhundert*, fifth edition. Munich: Francke, 1967.

McInnes, Edward. *Das deutsche Drama des 19. Jahrhunderts*. Berlin: Schmidt, 1983.

McInnes. *German Social Drama 1840-1900: From Hebbel to Hauptmann*. Stuttgart: Akademischer Verlag Heinz, 1976.

Meixner, Horst, and Silvio Vietta, eds. *Expressionismus—Sozialer Wandel und künstlerische Erfahrung: Mannheimer Kolloquium*. Munich: Fink, 1982.

Müller, Hans-Harald. *Der Krieg und die Schriftsteller: Der Kriegsroman der Weimarer Republik.* Stuttgart: Metzler, 1986.

Müller, Karl Johann. *Das Dekadenzproblem in der österreichischen Literatur um die Jahrhundertwende, dargelegt an Texten von Hermann Bahr, Richard von Schaukal, Hugo von Hofmannsthal und Leopold Andrian.* Stuttgart: Heinz, 1977.

Muschg, Walter. *Von Trakl zu Brecht: Dichter des Expressionismus.* Munich: Piper, 1961.

Nadler, Josef. *Literaturgeschichte Österreichs.* Salzburg: Müller, 1951.

Osborne, John. *The Naturalist Drama in Germany.* Manchester, U.K.: Manchester University Press, 1971; Totowa, N.J.: Rowman & Littlefield, 1971.

Paulsen, Wolfgang. *Deutsche Literatur des Expressionismus.* Bern & New York: Lang, 1983.

Paulsen, ed. *Die deutsche Komödie im 20. Jahrhundert.* Heidelberg: Stiehm, 1976.

Rieckmann, Jens. *Aufbruch in die Moderne: Die Anfänge des Jungen Wien. Österreichische Literatur und Kritik im Fin de Siecle.* Königstein: Athenäum, 1986.

Robertson, J. G. *A History of German Literature*, sixth edition, edited by Dorothy Reich. Edinburgh & London: Blackwood, 1970.

Rothe, Wolfgang, ed. *Expressionismus als Literatur: Gesammelte Studien.* Bern & Munich: Francke, 1969.

Rühle, Günther. *Theater für die Republik 1917-1933: Im Spiegel der Kritik.* Frankfurt am Main: Fischer, 1967.

Scheuer, Helmut, ed. *Naturalismus: Bürgerliche Dichtung und soziales Engagement.* Stuttgart: Kohlhammer, 1974.

Schley, Gernot. *Die freie Bühne in Berlin.* Berlin: Haude & Spener, 1967.

Schrimpf, Hans Joachim, ed. *Literatur und Gesellschaft, vom neunzehnten ins zwanzigste Jahrhundert.* Bonn: Bouvier, 1963.

Shearier, Stephen. *Das junge Deutschland 1917-1920.* Bern & New York: Lang, 1988.

Sloterdijk, Peter. *Literatur und Organisation von Lebenserfahrung: Autobiographien der Zwanziger Jahre.* Munich: Hanser, 1978.

Soergel, Albert, and Curt Hohoff. *Dichtung und Dichter der Zeit*, 2 volumes. Düsseldorf: Bagel, 1961-1963.

Sokel, Walter H. *The Writer in Extremis: Expressionism in Twentieth-Century German Literature.* New York: McGraw-Hill, 1964.

Szondi, Peter. *Theory of the Modern Drama*, translated and edited by Michael Hays. Minneapolis: University of Minnesota Press, 1987.

Trommler, Frank, ed. *Jahrhundertwende: Vom Naturalismus zum Expressionismus (1880-1918)*, Deutsche Literatur: Eine Sozialgeschichte, 8. Reinbek: Rowohlt, 1982.

Ungar, Frederick, ed. *Handbook of Austrian Literature*. New York: Ungar, 1973.

Viviani, Annalisa. *Das Drama des Expressionismus*. Munich: Winkler, 1970.

Vogelsang, Hans. *Österreichische Dramatiker des 20. Jahrhunderts*. Vienna: Braumüller, 1963.

Webb, Benjamin Daniel. *The Demise of the 'New Man': An Analysis of Ten Plays from Late German Expression-ism*. Göppingen: Kümmerle, 1973.

Willett, John. *The Theater of the Weimar Republic*. New York: Holmes & Meier, 1988.

Wilpert, Gero von, and Adolf Gühring. *Erstausgaben deutscher Dichtung: Eine Bibliographie zur deutschen Litera-tur 1600-1960*. Stuttgart: Kröner, 1967.

Contributors

Dieter Wolfgang Adolphs...*Michigan Technological University*
Russell E. Brown...*State University of New York at Stony Brook*
Edson M. Chick ....*Williams College*
Roy C. Cowen ....*University of Michigan*
Richard Critchfield...*Texas A & M University*
Karin Doerr..*Concordia University*
Christopher L. Dolmetsch...*Marshall University*
Steve Dowden...*Yale University*
Christoph Eykman..*Boston College*
Gail Finney ....*University of California, Davis*
John Hibberd...*University of Bristol*
Thomas A. Kamla...*University of Scranton*
Volker M. Langbehn ....*University of California, Los Angeles*
Ward B. Lewis ....*University of Georgia*
Ulrike Rainer ....*Darthmouth College*
Jochen Richter...*Allegheny College*
Jürgen G. Sang..*University of Hawaii*
Pamela S. Saur ....*Lamar University*
H.-J. Schulz ....*Vanderbilt University*
Stephen Shearier ....*Muhlenberg College*
Hans Wagener ....*University of California, Los Angeles*
Raleigh Whitinger ....*University of Alberta*
Michael Winkler ....*Rice University*
Harry Zohn ....*Brandeis University*

312

Cumulative Index

Dictionary of Literary Biography, Volumes 1-118
Dictionary of Literary Biography Yearbook, 1980-1991
Dictionary of Literary Biography Documentary Series, Volumes 1-9

Cumulative Index

DLB before number: *Dictionary of Literary Biography,* Volumes 1-118
Y before number: *Dictionary of Literary Biography Yearbook,* 1980-1991
DS before number: *Dictionary of Literary Biography Documentary Series,* Volumes 1-9

A

C

Cumulative Index

E

G

K

N

O

P

S

Y

Z

(Continued from front endsheets)

80: *Restoration and Eighteenth-Century Dramatists,* First Series, edited by Paula R. Backscheider (1989)

81: *Austrian Fiction Writers, 1875-1913,* edited by James Hardin and Donald G. Daviau (1989)

82: *Chicano Writers,* First Series, edited by Francisco A. Lomelí and Carl R. Shirley (1989)

83: *French Novelists Since 1960,* edited by Catharine Savage Brosman (1989)

84: *Restoration and Eighteenth-Century Dramatists,* Second Series, edited by Paula R. Backscheider (1989)

85: *Austrian Fiction Writers After 1914,* edited by James Hardin and Donald G. Daviau (1989)

86: *American Short-Story Writers, 1910-1945,* First Series, edited by Bobby Ellen Kimbel (1989)

87: *British Mystery and Thriller Writers Since 1940,* First Series, edited by Bernard Benstock and Thomas F. Staley (1989)

88: *Canadian Writers, 1920-1959,* Second Series, edited by W. H. New (1989)

89: *Restoration and Eighteenth-Century Dramatists,* Third Series, edited by Paula R. Backscheider (1989)

90: *German Writers in the Age of Goethe, 1789-1832,* edited by James Hardin and Christoph E. Schweitzer (1989)

91: *American Magazine Journalists, 1900-1960,* First Series, edited by Sam G. Riley (1990)

92: *Canadian Writers, 1890-1920,* edited by W. H. New (1990)

93: *British Romantic Poets, 1789-1832,* First Series, edited by John R. Greenfield (1990)

94: *German Writers in the Age of Goethe: Sturm und Drang to Classicism,* edited by James Hardin and Christoph E. Schweitzer (1990)

95: *Eighteenth-Century British Poets,* First Series, edited by John Sitter (1990)

96: *British Romantic Poets, 1789-1832,* Second Series, edited by John R. Greenfield (1990)

97: *German Writers from the Enlightenment to Sturm und Drang, 1720-1764,* edited by James Hardin and Christoph E. Schweitzer (1990)

98: *Modern British Essayists,* First Series, edited by Robert Beum (1990)

99: *Canadian Writers Before 1890,* edited by W. H. New (1990)

100: *Modern British Essayists,* Second Series, edited by Robert Beum (1990)

101: *British Prose Writers, 1660-1800,* First Series, edited by Donald T. Siebert (1991)

102: *American Short-Story Writers, 1910-1945,* Second Series, edited by Bobby Ellen Kimbel (1991)

103: *American Literary Biographers,* First Series, edited by Steven Serafin (1991)

104: *British Prose Writers, 1660-1800,* Second Series, edited by Donald T. Siebert (1991)

105: *American Poets Since World War II,* Second Series, edited by R. S. Gwynn (1991)

106: *British Literary Publishing Houses, 1820-1880,* edited by Patricia J. Anderson and Jonathan Rose (1991)

107: *British Romantic Prose Writers, 1789-1832,* First Series, edited by John R. Greenfield (1991)

108: *Twentieth-Century Spanish Poets,* First Series, edited by Michael L. Perna (1991)

109: *Eighteenth-Century British Poets,* Second Series, edited by John Sitter (1991)

110: *British Romantic Prose Writers, 1789-1832,* Second Series, edited by John R. Greenfield (1991)

111: *American Literary Biographers,* Second Series, edited by Steven Serafin (1991)

112: *British Literary Publishing Houses, 1881-1965,* edited by Jonathan Rose and Patricia J. Anderson (1991)

113: *Modern Latin-American Fiction Writers,* First Series, edited by William Luis (1992)

114: *Twentieth-Century Italian Poets,* First Series, edited by Giovanna Wedel De Stasio, Glauco Cambon, and Antonio Illiano (1992)

115: *Medieval Philosophers,* edited by Jeremiah Hackett (1992)

116: *British Romantic Novelists, 1789-1832,* edited by Bradford K. Mudge (1992)

117: *Twentieth-Century Caribbean and Black African Writers,* First Series, edited by Bernth Lindfors and Reinhard Sander (1992)